Annotation-Based Semantics for Space and Time in Language

Space and time representation in language is important in linguistics and cognitive science research, as well as artificial intelligence applications like conversational robots and navigation systems. This book is the first for linguists and computer scientists that shows how to do model-theoretic semantics for temporal or spatial information in natural language, based on annotation structures. The book covers the entire cycle of developing a specification for annotation and the implementation of the model over the appropriate corpus for linguistic annotation. Its representation language is a type-theoretic, first-order logic in shallow semantics. Each interpretation model is delimited by a set of definitions of logical predicates used in semantic representations (e.g., past) or measuring expressions (e.g., counts or the counting function k). These definitions, often called *meaning postulates*, then delineate a set of admissible models for interpretation.

KIYONG LEE is Professor Emeritus of Linguistics at Korea University in Seoul. He was President of the Linguistic Society of Korea and the Korean Society for Cognitive Science, and has worked on creating standards for semantic annotation as an ISO working group Convenor and Project Leader. In 1974, he published his University of Texas at Austin dissertation, The Treatment of Some English Constructions in *Montague Grammar*. His published works include *Computational Morphology* and a three-volume book, *Language and the World: Formal Semantics; Tense and Modality: Possible-Worlds Semantics*; and *Situation and Information: Situation Semantics*.

STUDIES IN NATURAL LANGUAGE PROCESSING

Series Editor: Chu-Ren Huang, The Hong Kong Polytechnic University

Series Editor: Qi Su, Peking University

Editorial Board Members:

Nianwen Xue, Brandeis University
Maarten de Rijke, University of Amsterdam
Lori Levin, Carnegie Mellon University
Alessandro Lenci, Universita degli Studi, Pisa
Francis Bond, Nanyang Technological University

Volumes in the SNLP series provide comprehensive surveys of current research topics and applications in the field of natural language processing (NLP) that shed light on language technology, language cognition, language and society, and linguistics. The increased availability of language corpora and digital media, as well as advances in computer technology and data sciences, has led to important new findings in the field. Widespread applications include voice-activated interfaces, translation, search engine optimization, and affective computing. NLP also has applications in areas such as knowledge engineering, language learning, digital humanities, corpus linguistics, and textual analysis. These volumes will be of interest to researchers and graduate students working in NLP and other fields related to the processing of language and knowledge.

Also in the series

"Annotation-based Semantics for Space and Time in Language provides an exhaustive consideration of the syntactic and semantic concerns involved in devising a linguistic annotation scheme. Although focused on spatial and temporal phenomena and presented primarily from the perspective of ISO standardization efforts, Professor Lee's in-depth exposition of the relevant issues will benefit anyone engaged in a linguistic annotation project."

– Nancy Ide, Vassar College

"This book draws on the author's decades of experience working on the standardization of semantic annotation as the convenor of an International Organization for Standardization (ISO) working group to develop a formal model-theoretical semantic interpretation of annotation structures in the domain of space and time. What sets this book apart from most existing work on semantic annotation is its commitment to provide interpretable semantics. This imposes a level of rigor on semantic annotation making it more likely to withstand the test of time. This book is a must-read for researchers interested in the semantics of temporal and spatial structures in language, and semantic annotation in general."

– Nianwen Xue, Brandeis University

"This book investigates spatial and temporal semantic annotations in a principled way. From a natural language processing and downstream applications perspective, the presented knowledge paves the way to integrate the annotation-based semantics in computational models. Most importantly, it provides the means to integrate the symbolic abstractions with the sub-symbolic ones learned by the recent transformer-based deep learning architectures. This book is a comprehensive source of information that formally highlights the basic building blocks of spatial, temporal, and compositional reasoning over natural language."

– Parisa Kordjamshidi, Michigan State University

"Kiyong Lee's monograph is a welcome addition to the field of natural language processing; it nicely sums up his several decades of research written in and focusing on English. In this novel text, Lee proposes annotation-based semantics as part of the construction of spatio-temporal annotation schemes. The beauty of this work is that the proposal is directly applicable to natural language processing and machine learning with little to no modification. This book is a must-read for researchers or students interested in spatial and temporal expressions and their treatments within the context of computational linguistics."

– Chongwon Park, University of Minnesota Duluth

"This important book provides a formal underpinning of the groundbreaking work on the semantic annotation of natural language expressions of time, space, and events in the last 15 years, which has resulted in international annotation standards. The author adopts an approach that has been developed in this context, which distinguishes the abstract syntax of annotations from their concrete encoding, typically using XML, and assigns a compositional semantic interpretation to the annotation structures of the abstract syntax. Using a type-theoretic representation language as an interface between annotation structures and logical forms, a detailed account is given of the interpretation of annotations of spatial and temporal information in model-theoretic terms. Anyone who takes an interest in the computation of meaning should read this book."

– Harry Bunt, Tilburg University

This is a significant contribution to both formal semantics and computational linguistics, providing a situated and small world-based approach.... Readers will find it succinct, timely, and expansive in the topics covered."

– Chu-Ren Huang, Hong Kong Polytechnic University

Annotation-Based Semantics
for Space and Time in Language

KIYONG LEE
Korea University, Seoul

With a Foreword by
JAMES PUSTEJOVSKY
Brandeis University

CAMBRIDGE
UNIVERSITY PRESS

Shaftesbury Road, Cambridge CB2 8EA, United Kingdom

One Liberty Plaza, 20th Floor, New York, NY 10006, USA

477 Williamstown Road, Port Melbourne, VIC 3207, Australia

314–321, 3rd Floor, Plot 3, Splendor Forum, Jasola District Centre, New Delhi – 110025, India

103 Penang Road, #05–06/07, Visioncrest Commercial, Singapore 238467

Cambridge University Press is part of Cambridge University Press & Assessment, a department of the University of Cambridge.

We share the University's mission to contribute to society through the pursuit of education, learning and research at the highest international levels of excellence.

www.cambridge.org
Information on this title: www.cambridge.org/9781108839594

DOI: 10.1017/9781108884532

First published 2023

A catalogue record for this publication is available from the British Library.

Library of Congress Cataloging-in-Publication Data
Names: Lee, Kiyong, author. | Pustejovsky, J. (James), writer of foreword.
Title: Annotation-based semantics for space and time in language / Kiyong Lee, Korea University ; with foreword by James Pustejovsky, Brandeis University.
Description: [New York] : Cambridge University Press, [2023] | Series: SNLP studies in natural language processing | Includes bibliographical references and index.
Identifiers: LCCN 2022053464 (print) | LCCN 2022053465 (ebook) | ISBN 9781108839594 (hardback) | ISBN 9781108884532 (epub)
Subjects: LCSH: Semantics–Data processing. | Space and time in language. | Computational linguistics.
Classification: LCC P325.5.D38 L44 2023 (print) | LCC P325.5.D38 (ebook) | DDC 401/.430285635–dc23/eng/20221122
LC record available at https://lccn.loc.gov/2022053464
LC ebook record available at https://lccn.loc.gov/2022053465

ISBN 978-1-108-83959-4 Hardback

for Ryun Lucy Jungja Ha

Contents

Foreword

James Pustejovsky

The semantic interpretation of natural language utterances remains one of the most challenging problems in computational linguistics. While research in both the identification of syntactic structures as well as the assignment of semantic roles to participants of events have advanced significantly over the past decade, the computational determination of sentence meaning still largely eludes the field, as measured by benchmarked evaluations over even rudimentary semantic tasks. Two of the most difficult dimensions within such semantic analysis are the interpretation of time and space, as expressed in language.

Narratives, dialogues, news articles, and most conversational interactions involve not only the need to locate the events mentioned temporally relative to the speech time, but relative to each other. This temporal pairwise ordering for all events is computationally expensive, but some calculation like it is necessary to be able to reason about event causes and outcomes through time. Similar remarks hold for where events happen, particularly events involving change of location. These are the two important topics addressed in the present volume.

Consider what information is encoded in a semantic labeling or markup of an utterance, according to a particular theory. The conventional way to model the semantics of natural language expressions in theoretical linguistics is to start from a detailed description of the form of linguistic expressions, taking the meaning associated with each to build larger meaningful units, usually assuming a principle of compositionality of meaning of larger expressions from smaller units. The set of types for a general formal semantics must be expressive enough to capture the observed and understood interpretations of the utterances in the language, ranging from individuals, truth-values, measures, events, times, to the needed quantificational and compositional mechanisms to sort them all out appropriately. In such an approach (the conventional theoretical one), every linguistic element in the utterance contributes to the resulting semantic interpretation. If we view the semantic content associated with each expression as an annotation, then we can think of this as providing a lexically complete (or dense) semantic annotation of the utterance. The annotation is the source of the resulting semantic interpretation for the sentence.

Now let us look at a rather different perspective on language annotation, the one adopted by those researchers interested in designing targeted markup as input for other computational linguistic applications. On this view, the annotation of a linguistic expression serves to identify those terms that play a role in some downstream processing, for example, a query, as data storage, or as some other data structure. On this view, rather than modeling the meaning of the entire linguistic utterance, the goal is more modest, where the focus is to identify different kinds of named entities, such as people, companies, countries, cities, and so on. In such a model, the set of types for the terms is defined for the specific domain of interest, along with relations between them, for example, $located\_in(city, country)$. When the annotated expressions are eventually put to use, these terms and relations are then given some interpretation, which may be reference to a database model, grounding to Wikipedia, or something more elaborate. In any case, while there is no intrinsic interpretation, there is always some semantic model associated with an annotation, when it is actually deployed.

While the use of uninterpreted annotation structures is currently the norm, it has become increasingly clear that there are some semantic domains where it is definitely advantageous to provide an interpretation (however shallow) for the annotation structures. Such approaches can be referred to as annotation-based semantic models, where the vocabulary of terms and relations in the syntax are accompanied by explicit semantic interpretations, referencing a data model, and a translation via types into a model. The linguistic phenomena that can benefit most from such models include the semantic domains of time, space, and quantification. Providing an explicit semantics for the annotation structures in each of these domains accomplishes two goals: it clarifies what the expressive capacity of the structure is in an interpreted model, and it creates a syntactically and semantically interoperable structure for evaluating the results from any algorithms using these models.

The present volume by Professor Lee is an elaboration of an annotation-based semantics for how space and time are expressed in natural language. This work develops the approach to semantically interpreting the language of annotation structures themselves, first proposed in Pratt-Hartmann (2005, 2007), Katz (2007), and Bunt (2010). This work is an important development in this tradition, as it outlines the most detailed attempt thus far providing a semantics for the annotation structures associated with temporal and spatial expressions in language. In particular, Lee demonstrates how the annotation structures for linguistic expressions can themselves be semantically represented in a first-order type-theoretic logical language and interpreted with respect to a conventional model, as in Montague Semantics (see Montague (1974), Dowty (1979), and Dowty et al. (1981)).

The language used to mark up a text with a specific linguistic phenomenon, such as temporal or spatial information, is called the annotation scheme (or specification). By identifying a conceptual structure defined by an abstract syntax, specified in set-theoretic terms, Lee separates the associated semantic interpretation from specific annotation structures, and references the interpretation of the abstract syntax itself (Bunt, 2010, 2011). Following these principles, Lee develops a semantic model of ISO-TimeML (ISO, 2012b) and ISO-Space (ISO, 2014b, 2020d) that is true to the original specification, while maintaining compositionality in the interpretation.

Semantic annotation remains a major component of both theoretical and computational linguistics, both for abstracting conceptual information over linguistic data in theoretical modeling, and for providing richly annotated data for training machine learning models. Lee's work is significant in that it bridges these research concerns, by taking the annotation structure at face value and providing a direct semantics for it. This can be used in subsequent computational analysis, as part of the creation of embeddings and vector representations, or can be leveraged in a partial or lightweight semantics of the annotated text, separate from the conventional deep semantic analysis associated with a full type-theoretic compositional analysis.

Preface

Why and What Do I Write?

This book was conceived almost 20 years ago, when I started working as the convenor of the International Organization for Standardization (ISO) working group on representation schemes and semantic annotation, and I have been writing it for over three years. The basic ideas of the book originated from my earlier work on semantic annotation, parts of which were presented at various academic meetings, especially the workshops on Interoperable Semantic Annotation (ISA).[1] As a formal semanticist, I have always wanted to find a way of doing semantics with no or minimal use of complex syntactic analyses and then learned that annotation-based semantics could be an answer. My main purpose in writing this book is to propose such a method of doing semantics with a computationally manageable representation language with shallow semantics.[2]

This book shows how to do model-theoretic semantics for temporal or spatial information in natural language, based on annotation structures. Its representation language is a type-theoretic first-order logic in shallow semantics. Unlike rigidly formulated annotation standards or guidelines, this book covers a flexible range of issues and proposals with formalisms on the annotation of event and motion-associated temporal and spatial information in language.

I propose annotation-based semantics, abbreviated as ABS, as part of the construction of spatio-temporal annotation schemes. There are at least three immediate applications. One use is to validate the adequacy of proposed spatio-

---

[1] Harry Bunt as chair, with Nancy Ide, Kiyong Lee, Volha Petukhova, James Pustejovsky, Laurent Romary, and Ielka van der Sluis, has organized a series of joint workshops of the ACL Special Interest Group on Computational Semantics and ISO/TC 37/SC 4 (Language Resources Management)/WG 2 Semantic Annotation (ISA) since 2005.

[2] In this book, I introduce the two ISO international standards on temporal and spatial annotation, ISO-TimeML (ISO, 2012b) and ISO-Space (ISO, 2014b, 2020d), to support my proposal.

temporal annotation schemes by providing systematic ways of interpreting annotation structures. Another use is to develop compositional semantics with a small but open set of *merge operators* (e.g., conjunctive operator $\oplus$), which frees the representation language of ABS from the need to use recursive λ-operations over deeply embedded λ-structures. The third use is to formulate easily parsable *shallow* semantic forms in an extended *type-theoretic first-order logic* (FOL) à la Neo-Davidsonian Semantics.[3]

For the shallow representation of semantic forms and their interpretation, ABS is enriched with a set of logical predicates, such as tense-aspectual expressions like *past, prog*, and *presPerfect*, semantic role expressions like *agent, patient* and *theme*, and generalized quantifier expressions like *three thousand students* and *twice*. These predicates are to be defined as *logical predicates*, often called *meaning postulates*, possibly in higher-order logic, while delimiting admissible interpretation model structures, as in Montague Semantics.

For the construction of interpretation models, I assume *small-world semantics*. Each semantic form, derived from a set of annotation structures, is interpreted with respect to a small world, often called *situation* or *frame*, instead of referring to all (logically) possible worlds. Such a small world is often constrained by the shared beliefs of ordinary rational agents. People communicate and interact with each other successfully even with partial information, available in a spatio-temporally constrained situation with restricted circumstances and background assumptions. Tellingly, annotation focuses on *agreed-on* common topics and common points of interest by filtering out any irrelevant or syntactically hard-to-process parts in language data to process minimally necessary relevant information.

Prospective Readers: For Whom This Book Is Written

This book is written primarily for formal or computational linguists interested in doing formal computational semantics or for computer scientists who develop semantic annotation schemes for doing natural language semantics. It would also be beneficial to those who work on either spatial or temporal or spatio-temporal annotation of language for natural language processing (NLP) applications. It can be used as a guide (reference) book for computational linguists or language technology professionals who are interested in the construction of annotation schemes. It can also be adopted as a textbook or

---

[3] The representation of semantic forms in ABS matches that of the Discourse Representation Theory (DRT) of Kamp and Reyle (1993) or the Groningen Meaning Bank (GMB), proposed by Bos et al. (2017).

supplementary teaching material for upper-division or graduate courses on computational semantics, natural language understanding, or corpus linguistics that includes semantic annotation.

How Is the Book Organized?

The book is organized into three parts.

- *Part I "Fundamentals"* lays out the theoretical foundation for the book. It consists of six chapters, treating the basics of semantic annotation for computing purposes. Chapter 1 discusses the notion of annotation, seen from the traditional practices to the current computational applications for machine learning. Chapter 2 discusses data segmentation, including ambiguity in word segmentation. Chapter 3 covers modeling a semantic annotation scheme, which is divided into an abstract syntax and an ideally equivalent set of concrete syntaxes for the representation of semantic annotation structures. Chapter 4 treats representation and serialization, reviewing various representation formats in language processing. Chapters 5 and 6 discuss the role of semantics for annotation, while introducing a type-theoretic annotation-based semantics (ABS) with a small but open set of *merge* or *demerge operators* over the semantic (logical) forms of annotation structures.
- *Part II "Time and Events"* consists of four chapters, discussing the annotation of event-linked temporal structures in English. It introduces the basic ontology of temporal objects in Chapter 7 and ways of normalizing TimeML with some modifications in Chapter 8. It then extends the range of temporal annotation to temporal measure expressions, quantified temporal expressions, and adjectival and adverbial modifications in Chapter 9, while showing how temporal relators, often called *signals*, are interpreted in Chapter 10. These semantic forms are interpreted with respect to an admissible model structure of ABS, constrained by a set of the definitions of logical predicates, called *meaning postulates*.
- *Part III "Motion, Space, and Time"* consists of three chapters. Chapter 11 shows how ISO-Space evolved from SpatialML to annotate spatial information that involves motions and trajectories, called *event-paths*. Chapter 12 deals with four types of paths, *static, dynamic, oriented*, and *projected* types, and the dynamic aspect of movers traversing through spatio-temporal domains. Chapter 13 formalizes a spatio-temporal annotation scheme for dynamic information involving motions, time, and space.

Key Features and Benefits

There are at least four features of the book that will benefit the reader.

- The book proposes annotation-based semantics (ABS) without relying on any grammatical theory or syntactic analyses. See, in contrast, Montague Semantics or Discourse Representation Theory (DRT), which depend on Categorial Grammar and Generalized Phrase Structure Grammar (GPSG), respectively, for syntactic analyses. The reader will learn to do semantics without background knowledge of any syntactic theories.
- For the representation of annotation structures, the book adopts a predicate-logic-like representation format (*pFormat*), instead of the conventionally accepted eXtensible Markup Language (XML). The reader will learn an annotation scheme without using XML or learning to use XML schemata.
- The representation language of ABS is a first-order language with quantification, identity, and modification without lambda-operations. Semantic forms can be represented graphically just like Discourse Representation Structures (DRS). The reader will learn how to derive semantic forms from annotation structures without knowing higher-order logic with lambda-calculus, as is used in Montague Semantics.
- Each formalization of an annotation scheme is visualized with a figure of the metamodel and other figures as well as tables. All those figures and tables are fully explicated and illustrated with abundant examples of varying cases. *Formalization* provides the reader with exact and concise knowledge of the proposed annotation scheme, *visualization* helps extend the domain of application of the proposal, and *extended illustrations* help the reader to gain practical knowledge and skills to apply them to the semantic processing and understanding of linguistic information in various communicative situations.

I allocated more space for the basic concepts and mechanisms of annotation while leaving out complicated issues for further study. I have provided many examples and analyzed varying cases to illustrate technical details to help better understand various proposals for the construction of annotation schemes. Note that some of the details are not necessarily requirements, but options open for alternatives.

Acknowledgments

There are three groups of people to whom I owe thanks. The first group consists of those scholars and colleagues who have inspired and interacted with me in conceiving this book. In the late 1990s I got involved in ISO work for the incorporation of over 50,000 Chinese (Hanja) codes, used in East-Asian countries including Korea, into Unicode. That work became the inception of this long and arduous book project. I'd like to thank Hung-Gyu Kim, Younpyo Hong, Joonsuk Lee, and Seungjae Lee for the first stage of my participation in ISO projects. Soon after the inauguration of ISO/TC 37/SC 4 Language resource management in 2002, Las Palmas, Canary Islands, I was nominated as the project leader for the standardization of feature structure representation and several other ensuing projects, working with the TEI's Lou Burnard, Gerald Penn, and ISO's Key-Sun Choi, Laurent Romary, Nancy Ide, Yu Xinli, Changqing Zhou, Maosong Sun, Christian Galinski, Nicoletta Calzolari, Do-sam Hwang, Hyo-Shik Shin, Jason Lee, Hansaem Kim, Sue-Ellen Wright, Jennifer DeCamp, Eric de la Clergerie, Gil Francopoulo, Thierry Declerk, Lee Gillam, Koiti Hasida, Peter Wittenburg, Antonio Pareja Lora, Piotr Banski, Tibor Kiss, Michael Cunningham, Hitoshi Isahara, Kyoko Kanzaki, Andreas Witt, Keith Suderman, Monica Monachini, Tripple Thorsten, Miran Choi, Tianyong Tony Hao, Haitao Wang, Xinyu Cao, and many others.

Since I was made the convenor of the ISO working group on semantic annotation, Harry Bunt and James Pustejovsky deserve my special thanks for being my closest coworkers and editors of the ISO standards on semantic annotation. I also thank Branimir Boguraev for the initial work on ISO-TimeML, Inderjeet Mani for SpatialML, and the Brandeis group of Computer Science and Linguistics on ISO-Space that includes Marc Verhagen, Jessica L. Moszkowicz, Seohyun Im, and Keigh Rim. Besides Harry Bunt, James Pustejovsky, Nancy Ide, and Laurent Romary, I should also thank Hélèn Mazo and Khalid Choukri of ELRA, Volha Petukhova, and Johan Boss for ISA workshops, collocated at LREC and IWCS conferences for almost two decades from their beginnings. I thank Alex Fang and Jonathan Webster, who supported me in visiting and staying at the City University of Hong Kong and working on semantic annotation several times, still owing to them an unfinished book of joint authorship.

The second group directly helped me write this book. I need to mention my two colleagues once again here; James Pustejovsky and Harry Bunt were the primary sources of constant inspiration and driving force for designing the book and writing it. We worked together on semantic annotation for almost 20 years around the ISO community. Chu-Ren Huang invited me to the Hong Kong Polytechnic University for talks and dinners and one time urged me to write a book and to get in contact with Cambridge University Press for its publication. Inderjeet Mani helped to write and revise Chapter 12 with critical but valuable comments, which illustrates how ISO-Space (ISO, 2014b) evolved from SpatialML (MITRE, 2010). Parisa Kordjamshidi helped introduce SpRL (the Spatial Role Labeling scheme). Roland Hausser has been my superb supporter and critical colleague, who has had a significant influence on forming my linguistico-computational mindset, since our Texas days in the early 1970s and through CSLI, Stanford, to Erlangen years till now. Suk-Jin Chang, who is my life-long mentor, proofread the whole manuscript thrice, each chapter almost overnight. Jae-Woong Choi and Aesun Yoon have always responded to my frequent request for consultation and technical questions, and Minhaeng Lee read each of the chapters with detailed comments and suggestions for clarity and improvement. Seungho Nam helped me work on the notion of paths. Keeho Kim and Jongmi Kim helped analyze sound segments, and Chu-Ren Huang, Chinese word segmentation. Chin-Woo Kim and Jong-Bok Kim also read some portions of the manuscript and made valuable comments.

Don Diltz, my life-long friend and colleague from Berkeley, Korea, Hawaii, Stanford, San Francisco, and often out of reach, reviewed and helped edit the whole book. He is responsible for any weird or unintelligible (English) expressions if there are any. However, I drafted, revised, and edited the book and take responsibility for any errors and imperfections in the book. Above all, I owe the most outstanding debt to Chongwon Park and Youngsoon Cho, my former students, who have now become distinguished university professors. For the past two and a half years, they helped revise and edit the manuscript with critical but practical comments, going through every line and paragraph in the manuscript, details in each formulation of the annotation structures, and each of the semantic representations in logical forms that most of the readers would be hesitant to read. Youngsoon Cho, Chongwon Park, and Byong-Rae Ryu reviewed the penultimate version of the book.

The last group concerns my family. I must thank all my family members, especially Ryun Lucy Jungja Ha, my wife, who had to bear with me every hour of every day for the last three years or the duration of our whole marriage: 54 years. I thank my two charming daughters Sue-en, with her husband Jongwon Kim, and her great daughter Sejin and son-in-law Sangsu Jeong, and Jeun-Marie, with her husband David Lovisek and son Taegon Andrew. I then thank my son Ghang with his lovely wife Sungjin and two brilliant daughters, Gio and Gia. I owe special thanks to Ghang for redrawing all the figures in the manuscript for publication.

Finally, I should not forget to thank Kaitlin Leach, editor, Johnathan Fuentes, assistant editor, and Rebecca Grainger, content manager, of Cambridge University Press, for their consultation, encouragement, editorial help, and patience. I also thank Beverley Lawrence for her excellent copy-editing and Shaheer Husanne Anwarali for his magnificent management of typesetting.

PART I

Fundamentals

1

What Is a Semantic Annotation?

1.1 Annotation: Past and Present

1.1.1 Traditional Scholarship

Annotation literally means *adding notes* to text or images. Like commentary work, it is scholarly work with a long historical tradition. It has specific methodological merits for describing or explaining what has been given to scholars or teachers of classical Greek or Latin literature, biblical exegetists of the Hebrew Bible, philosophers of Chinese writings or monks of Buddhist sutras. They have thus produced scholarly books such as *The Aeneid Annotated Virgil*,[1] *Cambridge Annotated Study Bible*,[2] as shown in Figure 1.1, *The New Oxford Annotated Bible*,[3] *A New Translation of Lunyu with Annotations*,[4] or *The Diamond Prajna-Paramita Sutra (The Diamond Sutra): An Annotated Edition with Chinese Text*.[5]

Some people think of annotation as an outdated business or archaic scholarly methodology. You pick up a short list of terms and sometimes make nothing but a lengthy unconnected series of commentaries on those terms, as is sometimes complained. Just as linguists are often understood as polyglots, those who work on annotation would be considered as treating ancient texts or things of antiquities only. Adding notes has, however, been taken as a serious scholarly work through the ages. Figure 1.2 shows that a grammar book was written with *critical notes*.

---

[1] By Virgil. Translated by John Dryden, Kindle Edition.
[2] Edited by Howard Kee, Cambridge University Press, 1993.
[3] Edited by Bruce M. Metzer and Roland E. Murphy, New York: Oxford University Press, 1991,1994.
[4] This is a subtitle for the book *Understanding the Analects of Confucius* by Peimin Ni, Albany, NY: State University of New York Press, March 2017.
[5] Translated and annotated by Ven. Cheng Kuan, 2nd ed., 2017, American Buddhist Temple, USA.

Figure 1.1 Annotated Bible
Reprinted by permission from Cambridge University Press.
Kee, Howard C. (1993) *Cambridge Annotated Study Bible*.

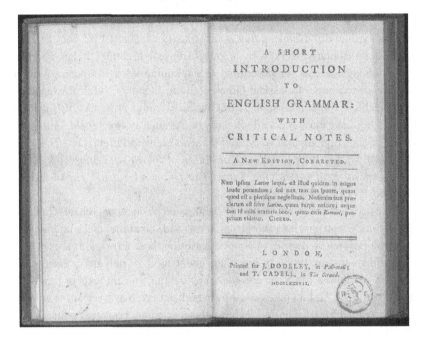

Figure 1.2 Grammar with critical notes
Ghent University Library, BIB.BL.000976.

Annotation is an activity with products that are also called *annotations*. It enriches the main content of a text. It resolves lexical or sentential ambiguities, provides underspecified textual meanings with contextual or background information, and updates described situations that are either diachronically outdated or synchronically outplaced by introducing relevant explanatory information. Formats have thus been developed to represent a variety of information added to the main text.

1.1.2 Formats for Annotation

There are at least four commonly accepted ways of adding notes to the main text: *innotes, footnotes, sidenotes*, and *endnotes*. Innotes are inserted into the main content part of a text with parentheses, especially when notes are brief. Innotes can take up a good portion of the main part of a page, for instance, either by alternating a paragraph with the main content and the following paragraph with commenting notes or by occupying a column within or next to the main part.

Cambridge's annotated Bible contains footnotes at the bottom of a page and two columns of sidenotes on the left and right sides of the page. These notes have different uses, as shown in Figure 1.3.

There are two footnotes at the bottom of the main text in Figure 1.3. They are each linked by an alphabet letter *a* and *b* to the term which is being annotated, as shown by the two arrows. The sidenotes on the left side column are references to citations in the Bible that are related to the verse under discussion, whereas the sidenotes on the right side column contain comments on the verse, or the sequence of verses of the chapter referred to.

Endnotes are listed at the end of a chapter or a book, again being referred to by a number to the annotated term. Whatever format for notes there might have been, all these notes were included by chapter in a volume that carries its main content as a book.

In modern times, the way of providing additional information has become more sophisticated as the technology of printing and photography has developed. The task of adding extra information is carried out by relevant illustrations or photos of varying data to the degree that these visualizations are considered part of the main textual content. *The Cambridge Encyclopedia of the English Language* is a good example (Figure 1.4).The page contains three notes: two notes on the right column of the page and a third one from the previous page linking to a map with several arrows showing the origins of English. The map is a part of the third note.

How to lay out additional information and what to introduce as additional information are issues that are constantly asked. Such questions are seriously taken up when the text turns into electronically manageable files or datasets for the merging, interchange, and evaluation of information in them. A variety

GENESIS

See the Introductions, pp. 2, 30, and 32-33 above.

1.1
Jn 1.1.2; Ps 8.3; Isa 44 24: 42 5; 45.18

1.2
Jer 4.23. Ps 104.30

1.3
Ps 33.6.9, 2 Cor 4.6

1.4
Isa 45.7

1.5
Ps 74.16

1.6
Jer 10.12

1.7
Prov 8.28. Ps 148 4

1.9
Job 26.10. Prov 8.29; Jer 5.22. 2 Pet 3 5

1.10
Ps 33.7

1.11
Lk 6 44

1.14
Ps 74 16, 104 19

1.16
Ps 136.8.9; Job 38 7

1.18
Jer 31 35

1.21
Ps 104.25.26

1.22
Gen 8.17

1.25
Jer 27.5

1.26
Ps 100.3; Acts 17 26; Col 3.10

1.27
1 Cor 11.7; Gen 5.2; Mt 19.4

1.28
Gen 9.1.7; Lev 26.9

Six Days of Creation and the Sabbath

1 In the beginning when God created[a] the heavens and the earth, [2]the earth was a formless void and darkness covered the face of the deep, while a wind from God[b] swept over the face of the waters. [3]Then God said, "Let there be light"; and there was light. [4]And God saw that the light was good; and God separated the light from the darkness. [5]God called the light Day, and the darkness he called Night. And there was evening and there was morning, the first day.

[6] And God said, "Let there be[c] a dome in the midst of the waters, and let it separate the waters from the waters." [7]So God made the dome and separated the waters that were under the dome from the waters that were above the dome. And it was so. [8]God called the dome Sky. And there was evening and there was morning, the second day.

[9] And God said, "Let the waters under the sky be gathered together into one place, and let the dry land appear." And it was so. [10]God called the dry land Earth, and the waters that were gathered together he called Seas. And God saw that it was good. [11]Then God said, "Let the earth put forth vegetation: plants yielding seed, and fruit trees of every kind on earth that bear fruit with the seed in it." And it was so. [12]The earth brought forth vegetation: plants yielding seed of every kind, and trees of every kind bearing fruit with the seed in it. And God saw that it was good. [13]And there was evening and there was morning, the third day.

[14] And God said, "Let there be lights in the dome of the sky to separate the day from the night; and let them be for signs and for seasons and for days and years, [15]and let them be lights in the dome of the sky to give light upon the earth." And it was so. [16]God made the two great lights—the greater light to rule the day and the lesser light to rule the night—and the stars. [17]God set them in the dome of the sky to give light upon the earth, [18]to rule over the day and over the night, and to separate the light from the darkness. And God saw that it was good. [19]And there was evening and

there was morning, the fourth day.

[20] And God said, "Let the waters bring forth swarms of living creatures, and let birds fly above the earth across the dome of the sky." [21]So God created the great sea monsters and every living creature that moves, of every kind, with which the waters swarm, and every winged bird of every kind. And God saw that it was good. [22]God blessed them, saying, "Be fruitful and multiply and fill the waters in the seas, and let birds multiply on the earth." [23]And there was evening and there was morning, the fifth day.

[24] And God said, "Let the earth bring forth living creatures of every kind: cattle and creeping things and wild animals of the earth of every kind." And it was so. [25]God made the wild animals of the earth of every kind, and the cattle of every kind, and everything that creeps upon the ground of every kind. And God saw that it was good.

[26] Then God said, "Let us make humankind[d] in our image, according to our likeness; and let them have dominion over the fish of the sea, and over the birds of the air, and over the cattle, and over all the wild animals of the earth,[e] and over every creeping thing that creeps upon the earth." [27]So God created humankind[d] in his image, in the image of God he created them; male and female he created them. [28]God blessed them, and God said to them, "Be fruitful and multiply, and fill the earth and subdue it; and have dominion over the fish of the sea and over the birds of the air and over every living thing that moves upon the earth." [29]God said, "See, I have given you every plant yielding seed that is upon the face of all the earth, and every tree with seed in its fruit; you shall have them for food. [30]And to every beast of the earth, and to every bird of the air, and to everything that creeps on the earth, everything that has the breath of life, I have given every green plant for food." And it was so. [31]God saw everything that he had made, and indeed, it was very good. And there was evening and there was morning, the sixth day.

1.1-2.4a The Priestly Account of the Creation. The emphasis falls on the sovereignty of God and the orderliness of the process of creation. Throughout this section, God is given the name *elohim* in the Hebrew original.
1.2 *The earth was a formless void.* God forms and orders the world out of existing, chaotic matter. *The deep...the waters.* In the mythology of Canaan and Mesopotamia the waters were the symbols of chaos which the more powerful beneficent deities had to bring under control.
1.3 *God said.* The power of God to achieve his purpose is evident when he speaks his intention and it is accomplished.
1.4 *God separated the light from the darkness.* The ordering of light and darkness establishes the rhythm of time, with evening followed by morning, which is the principle of Israelite days beginning at sundown.
1.6-10 *God...separated the waters...the waters that were gathered together* God's ordering of the world results in the separation of sky and earth, of sea and dry land.
1.14-19 The ordering of day and night is accomplished by the positioning of the sun, moon and stars.
1.26-28 *Let us make humankind in our image.* The Hebrew word for man is *adam,* which serves as the name of the first human being in these creation stories. Essential to the role of humans created in God's image is their exercise of authority over the earth and all living things upon it.

[a] Or when God began to create or In the beginning God created   [b] Or while the spirit of God or while a mighty wind   [c] Heb *adam*   [d] Syr: Heb and over all the earth   [e] Heb him

1

Figure 1.3 Genesis annotated
Reprinted by permission from Cambridge University Press.
Kee, Howard C. (1993) *Cambridge Annotated Study Bible.*

of formats representing annotation have been proposed in the area of computational work, including tabular formats with vertical columns and graphs.

1.1.3 Taking a New Turn

With the advance of the age of information and computation, the status of annotation has changed as it applies to the analysis of human natural language

Figure 1.4 Visual illustration for additional information
Reprinted by permission from Cambridge University Press.
Crystal, D. (2003) *The Cambridge Encylopedia of the English Language.*

rendered in various forms, whether written, spoken, or visualized as static or dynamic images (pictures, photos, or videos). Being subject to computational processing, *text* no longer refers to a simple collection of fragments of written material or printed matter, but a computationally readable file that carries information or messages to convey. Likewise, text messaging or texting refers to the activity of composing and sending electronic messages. The annotation of such text is now an essential part of the field of natural language processing

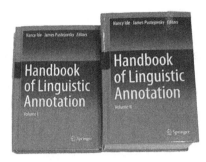

Figure 1.5 *Handbook of Linguistic Annotation*
Reprinted by permission from Springer Nature, Ide, N., and Pustejovsky, J. (eds.)
Handbook of Linguistic Annotation, Volumes 1 and 2, Springer, Berlin, Heidelberg © 2017.

(NLP) with its scientific technology, now called *linguistic annotation*, as witnessed by the appearance of the two-volume *Handbook of Linguistic Annotation* (see Figure 1.5). Linguistic annotation is the basis of NLP.

1.2 Linguistic Annotation

1.2.1 Overview

In the 1960s, linguistic annotation started with the building of large amounts of language data, called *corpus linguistics*. The time of its beginning was not very favorable. First, the research or academic environment for any statistical work was poorly developed. This was especially so because most of the linguists, especially in America, were fascinated with Chomsky's theory of generative grammar that focused on the so-called ideal speaker's intuitive judgments on language facts. This theory may have succeeded in deepening the psychological understanding of how the human faculty works in the use of language, while ignoring the practical limitations of human cognition and linguistic performance. It also underestimated the statistical power of predicting human interactions in communication. Faced with complex issues or even a simple but deeply iterative structure, the performance of human capacity rapidly fails to function reliably. When even well-trained linguistics students are asked to evaluate the well-formedness of strings of words as grammatically correct sentences, they quickly become tired of making a valid and reliable judgment, especially if those strings are repeatedly read out to them or if they are coerced to make a decision.

Second, no materials or tools were easily available. Computer-readable material was almost nil at that time. Personal desktop computers came out around the 1980s. When portable laptops such as Apple or IBM XT were made available, ordinary office workers with no linguistics background were hired to type in text manually to convert it to electronic files. Books and newspapers had not been published electronically. Furthermore, there were no standardized coding systems like the American Standard Code for Information Interchange (ASCII)[6] or Unicode (the Unicode Standard for the Universal Character Set).[7]

Despite all these difficulties, corpus linguistics has now come into the mainstream of linguistics. It has been established not so much as an independent part of general linguistics, but more so as a fundamental methodology applicable to the whole range of linguistics from phonology to morpho-syntax to semantics, pragmatics, and discourse analysis, as well as to the new area of computational linguistics in particular. Here textual annotation forms a basic framework for applying such a methodology to the processing of datasets in language. Tagging, markup, and parsing are kinds of annotation in NLP, each of which applies to the building of so-called *annotated corpora* by providing extratextual information, called *metadata*, to a given dataset.

Large Data From the Internet, we can now quickly obtain a large amount of data from natural language. News items, research articles, maps and pictures, and all other sorts of information in various domains are easily accessible through Wikipedia, Google Maps, Google Search, Research Gate, or ChatGPT. Promotional emails also pour out a lot of information. All of them are now electronically manageable, providing possible data that can be built into a corpus only if some legal barriers such as copyright or privacy laws are resolved.

---

[6] ASCII defines all of the 26 alphabet letters, called Latin characters, in upper or lower case, assigning a unique code point to each of them in the set of 128 character code points represented in 7 bits from 0000000 to 1111111. The capital (upper-case) letter "A", for instance, is represented by 1000001 in binary. The first edition was published in 1963 and the latest edition in 1986, mainly under the American National Standards Institute (ANSI), an active member of the International Organization for Standardization (ISO).

[7] The first draft proposal, called *Unicode*, came out in August 1988 for an international or multilingual text character coding system. The first version of *the Unicode Standard* was published in 1991, and now version 12.0.0 is available by the Unicode Consortium. ASCII was incorporated into Unicode. Lacking a unified coding system, it was impossible to combine various electronic files to build a very large collection of data, which could be genuinely called a *corpus*, in a consistently efficient way. This had been the case with corpora, especially in languages that used non-Latin alphabet characters (Graham, 2000).

1.2.2 Kinds of Tasks

Given some language data, it is segmented into characters or strings of character segments called *tokens*. These tokens are then grouped to form larger strings of characters, called *words*, and each of these words is classified with a morpho-syntactic category such as a noun or a verb. They are also grouped into larger units, called *phrases* or *chunks*, again with appropriate category names. The addition of such category names to a given dataset provides extra information which we have been calling *metadata*. Such segmentation or grouping allows the identification of portions of text or images, called *markables* for annotation. Strictly speaking, such tasks are not part of annotation, but a necessary step of processing primary data before identifying markables for annotation. Annotation, applied to NLP, means not just adding plain notes, but very often adding lexical information with the names of syntactic categories to segmented data. Such work is the most typical sort of corpus annotation, called *part-of-speech (POS) tagging*, contributing to the resolution of lexical or structural ambiguities contained in input phrases or words. Here is a well-known ambiguous sentence, called a *garden path sentence.*

Example 1.1   POS-tagging a garden path sentence
a. The horse raced past the barn fell.
b. The horse raced$_{VVD}$ past the barn fell. (fails to be processed)
c. The horse raced$_{VVN}$ past the barn fell. (succeeds in being processed)

The tagging of a word *raced* as VVD (past-tense verb) fails to process Example 1.1a when the processing step reaches the verb *fell*. In contrast, with the tagging of the word *raced* as VVN (past participle), Example 1.1a is successfully processed, as annotated in 1.2.[8]

Annotation 1.2   Annotating the garden path sentence
The horse [that was raced$_{VVN:past\,participle}$ [past$_{PRP:preposition}$ the barn]] fell$_{VVD:past\,tense}$.

Such a task of tagging words with grammatical categories or class names is a proper part of the annotation. It is, however, treated as a preprocessing step for semantic annotation.

Named entity disambiguation (NED) is, in contrast, considered part of semantic annotation. For example, the string of three words *the White House* refers typically to the official residence and workplace of the US President,

---

[8] The grammatical tags VVD and VVN are taken from the British National Corpus (BNC) Basic (C5) tagset. They stand for the past tense form of lexical verbs (e.g., *forgot, sent, lived, returned*) and the past participle form of lexical verbs (e.g., *forgotten, sent, lived, returned*), respectively.

but sometimes refers to its function as a metonymic expression. Here is a newspaper headline, which illustrates how the words *White House* are used.

Example 1.3   Newspaper headline
WHITE HOUSE ANNOUNCES TRUMP TO VISIT
SOUTHERN BORDER

The annotation of named entities such as one referred to by "WHITE HOUSE" provides different ways of annotating them; for example, as follows.

Annotation 1.4   Named entity disambiguation (NED)
`White House_<facility OR institution>`

The annotation of sentiments or metaphors may also be considered a proper part of annotation and also that of semantic annotation. Such an extension of annotation to language and its analysis requires highly developed technical training of humans and machines (computers) and also computer algorithms that require annotation structures as intermediate data structures for language processing.

1.2.3 Machine Learning

Machine learning theories are applied to natural language annotation to enhance its computational processing.[9] Base segmentation and subsequent tasks of tokenization and categorized chunking (see Chapter 2) as well as text mining for language resources are expected to be carried out by machines (see Figure 1.6).

Machine learning has become an essential topic in computational linguistics. The amount of data keeps increasing in various domains of interactive human languages through social networks or orally conveyed by dynamic human communications through television or communication applications like Skype or Zoom. Linguistic engineers thus find it necessary to be supported by machines or computers, which can run for 24 hours a day without complaining and breaking down, to process such data. Such data processing is ultimately required for the construction of practical systems for various NLP applications as well as various sorts of semantic annotation schemes for information encoding that supports such applications.

Humans train machines to annotate language. Humans form a group of annotation experts to prepare what and how to make machines learn by preparing a set of guidelines or norms, called *gold standards*. In preparing it,

---

[9] See two recent publications on annotation and machine learning: Pustejovsky and Stubbs (2012) and Meteer (2015).

Figure 1.6 Machine learning to annotate language
Reprinted by permission from O'Reilly Media, Inc.
Pustejovsky, J., and Stubbs, A. (2012)
Natural Language Annotation for Machine Learning.

the annotation experts have to reach an agreement, called *interannotator agreement* (IAA), that guarantees the validity and reliability of human judgments on linguistic facts. The validity of IAA, very often measured statistically, supports the correctness of decisions, while the reliability retains the consistency of tasks on differing types of input data for annotation.

Making machines learn is not a simple one-step process. It requires a cycle of repeated but incremental steps of modeling (M) and annotating (A), possibly skipping the four additional steps: train (T), test (T), evaluation (E), and revision (R). The specification of annotation tasks itself needs to be revised continuously. Such a process is called MAMA by Pustejovsky and Stubbs (2012), which is depicted as a part of a longer process, called MATTER, in Figure 1.7.[10]

The process of MATTER consists of six steps in a cycle.

Specification 1.5   The development cycle of MATTER

(1) *Model* a given task to produce an annotation guidelines

(2) *Annotate* sample datasets

(3) *Train* human annotators and machine learners

(4) *Test* annotation results

---

[10] Refer to Pustejovsky and Stubbs (2012, Figure 1-10) for the basic concepts of the MAMA and MATTER cycles. The two inner cycles were added by the author (Kiyong Lee) of this book. MAMA refers to the inner-outer cycle (dotted line) of MATTER, but should also be referring to the innermost cycle, consisting of two steps, Model an algorithm (M) and Annotate (A), as has been pointed out by an anonymous reviewer.

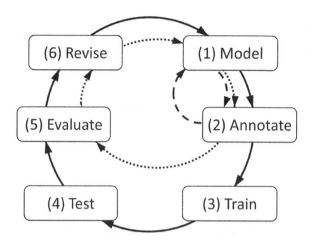

Figure 1.7 Process of training machine to learn
Reprinted by permission from O'Reilly Media, Inc.
Pustejovsky, J., and Stubbs, A. (2012)
Natural Language Annotation for Machine Learning.

(5) *Evaluate* interannotator agreement
(6) *Revise* annotation guidelines or algorithms

These six steps are connected by three cycles: the outermost solid line connecting all of the six steps (1) through (6), and the two inner cycles, one is a dashed line, and the other is a dotted line. The core portion of the figure is MAMA: the repeated cycle (innermost dashed line) of (1) *Model* (M) and (2) *Annotate* (A), supplemented by (5) *Evaluate* (E) and (6) *Revise* (R), as represented by the inner dotted line while bypassing the other two steps (4) *Train* (T) and (5) *Test* (T).[11] Model (M) an annotation task to specify an annotation guideline and then annotate (A). Repeat that process after the evaluation of annotation results and the revision of the annotation guideline. This process is repeated till satisfactory results are obtained.

Finlayson and Erjavec (2017) propose three additional stages, *Idea, Procure,* and *Distribute* for the MATTER and its inner cycle MAMA. The MATTER procedure starts with *Idea* that designs and formulates ideas and concepts for the project proposal, emphasizing the need for solid preparations. The step *Procure* means adopting a good tool for each of the well-defined subtasks of an annotation work with the concomitant belief that the selection of appropriate tools is as important as the designing of a good annotation scheme. The third

---

[11] For further details see Pustejovsky (2006) and Finlayson and Erjavec (2017).

step *Distribute* is added to the end of the MATTER cycle, involving various techniques such as packaging, archiving, and exporting, to make the annotated resources available to the world at large.[12]

1.2.4 Levels of Linguistic Annotation

The traditional classification of linguistic levels was restricted to three areas.

Classification 1.6   Linguistic annotation levels
a. phonology
b. morphology
c. syntax

Phonology deals with patterns of sounds. It describes how sound segments, consonants, and vowels are classed into conceptually or perceptually identifiable *discrete units*, called *phonemes*, in a language, and also how strings of sound segments interact with each other in observationally systematic ways to be formulated as phonological rules of assimilation or ellipsis, etc. *Phonetics* that constructs the system of sounds, either human or physical, used to be treated as a preliminary part of phonology, just as logic was so for the philosophy that consists of metaphysics and epistemology, and so on.

Morphology defines words and their minimal units, called *morphemes*, and classifies words into grammatical categories, often called *parts of speech*, while formulating derivational rules for word formation. Finally, *syntax* formulates the rules of generation to form sentences out of words or sequences of words, called *phrases*, and to define (syntactically) *well-formed* sentences. If a sentence is well-formed with respect to a given set of rules (grammar), then it is said to be grammatical.

At the earlier stage of the history of linguistics, the separation of all these levels was strictly required. For instance, the classification of words in morphology should not depend on syntactic or semantic concepts. During the period of strict Structuralism that was prevalent in the 1930s and 1940s, Nouns and Verbs were thus named *Class 1* and *Class 2*, respectively, so that these class names were introduced as being independent of the semantic types of references expressed by the words that are being classified. Nouns and Verbs are, in contrast, derived from the meaning-bearing Latin words, *nomen* for nominal expressions (Noun) that refer to the names of entities and *verbum* for verbal expressions (Verb) that were the words referring to actions or states. The analysis of sentences should be described only in terms of structural

---

[12] See Figure 1 in Finlayson and Erjavec (2017).

relations without making any reference to the propositional content carried by the sentences being analyzed. The grammatical function of *SubjectOf* is, for instance, defined *structurally* (in terms of structural relations) as a relation between the root of a phrase-structure tree (S) and its daughter node NP or any other category XP that precedes a node called VP (Verb Phrase) or *Predicate*.[13]

Syntax without semantics has now come to be considered useless or even unheard of. Since the 1970s, especially after the introduction of formal semantics like Montague Semantics, as introduced by Dowty et al. (1981), semantics has become an essential part of linguistics and such areas, called *pragmatics* and *analysis of dialogues and discourses*, have also been incorporated into the field of linguistics proper.

In linguistic annotation, the three levels of semantics, pragmatics, and analysis of dialogues and discourses have merged into one area, called *semantic annotation*. The part of morphology that treats word formation and lexical meanings is also incorporated into the semantic annotation. Phonetics is partially related to semantic annotation because some suprasegmental features of sounds such as stress, pitch, or loudness, and intonation patterns affect meaning in general and sentiments and moods in particular. Hence, all levels of linguistics, including multimodal aspects such as *gestures* or *facial expressions* involved in human communication, may be considered as contributing to semantic annotation.

Language is primarily spoken and contextually situated. Before videos were widely available, spoken data was transcribed, and transcribed data was then stored in a corpus. Phonetics and phonology provide scientific means for such transcription. Capturing visual information associated with linguistic data, especially related to human actions and motions of physical objects of intelligent agents, both humans and artificial robots, in time and space, has also become an essential part of linguistic annotation, especially for the contextually situated understanding of interactive human communication or the successful engineering of robotics. The semantic annotation should be contributing to such tasks beyond the treatment of ordinary text and moving towards treating all kinds of data involving multimodal communications that include gestures and facial expressions or the development of human machine interactions.

---

[13] This assumes that there is a phrase structure rule S → XP VP and that the *SubjectOf* relation is a relation [XP, S] according to Chomsky's theory of Generative Syntax. Note that XP is a generalization of NP to accommodate non-NP categories such as *From Seoul to Busan* as subjects in sentences like *From Seoul to Busan is approximately 500 km.*.

1.3 Semantic Annotation

1.3.1 Partial and Situated Information

Semantic annotation is characterized by the partiality and situatedness of information. These two characteristics form a theoretical basis for the modeling of semantic annotation schemes.

Partial Information

The range of markables for semantic annotation is restricted and specialized. It marks up relevant information from text or other media types of data in language that affects human actions only, focusing on some particular aspects of information in a restricted domain. The type and amount of information relevant for semantic annotation are thus very restrictive and partial, for ordinary human actions do not require so much information. Too much or overloaded information rather hinders the proper understanding of a given task, thereby deterring the proper performance of required appropriate actions. In general, semantic annotation works with a small world or a very tiny part of the spatio-temporally constrained world, but very seldom with the limitless universe of all possible worlds. It does not fit into *possible worlds semantics* that talks about the truth-condition or validity of propositions expressed by sentences uttered. Semantic annotation is thus focused on some particular aspects of a situation, viewed from some particular perspectives.

Semantic annotation does not mark up everything in a dataset, but selects a specific list of expressions, called *markables*, from the dataset which refers to certain types of entities. Event-oriented temporal annotation such as TimeML or ISO-TimeML selects those expressions as markables that refer to events and times as well as some time-related expressions such as temporal prepositions or conjunctions. Consider a short passage about the Appalachian Trail that runs from Georgia to Maine along the east coast of the United States. The expressions that are relevant for the question *When to start* are marked in *italics*.

Example 1.7   *When* should you *start* the Appalachian Trail?
The majority of thru-hikers *hikes northbound, beginning* in Georgia *anytime from late March to mid-April. Southbound hikers* generally *begin late May to mid-June.* Some hikers start heading north, then realize that they will not make it to Katahdin before Baxter State Park *closes on Oct. 15.*[14]

---

[14]   Information from https://appalachiantrail.org/explore/hike-the-a-t/thru-hiking/northbound/, dated 2022-12-12.

This passage provides an answer to the question of when to start hiking the Appalachian Trail. There are two possible directions for hiking: one is northbound and the other, southbound. A temporal annotation will focus on its markables, those expressions referring to events and times only, as listed in Annotation 1.8.

Annotation 1.8   Markables
a. hike northbound ... begin ... anytime from late March to mid-April
b. Southbound hikers ... begin late May to mid-June
c. closes on Oct. 15

The last item which contains information about the closing time of Baxter State Park may be left out, for it simply provides background information about the reason why the northbound hike should start sometime in late spring.

Annotation thus focuses only on some relevant parts of the information that is provided by an input dataset without trying to capture all of the available pieces of information. Temporal annotation marks up only those expressions that refer to events and times and those signals that trigger relations over events and times. The annotation scheme will contain two types of markables, *event* and *time*, possibly with an extra type *signal*.[15]

There are, however, several or many different semantic annotation schemes with different foci, perspectives, and points of view, for many different types of information that are needed. The annotation scheme called TimeML, for instance, focuses on time and events, ISO-Space on locations, paths, and motions, or the annotation of semantic roles on participants in events. The integration or merging of all these different sorts of information calls for another task. If all these sorts of information were annotated simultaneously even for a short piece of text, it would take too much time to go through the whole annotation with the resulting annotation being too complicated to process and comprehend. However, if all these annotation schemes are built separately but desigend to be interoperable with each other, then there is no difficulty in merging them as the need arises.

Situated Information

The primary task of semantic annotation is to situate or put into context what has been described or uttered. This context can be a discourse situation in which something has been described or uttered, background information or belief that needs to be shared for successful dialogues, or any other type of situation that puts what needs to be interpreted into the right perspective.

---

[15] Signals have no referential status. They trigger some relations over entities and events.

Suppose a traveler in the Berlin Hauptbahnhof is heading for Frankfurt and looking for a platform where she could hop on her train. She needs help, for the new Berlin Central Train Station is a huge place with 7 platforms and 16 tracks spread out to different destinations. So to be able to help her, one has to know a lot about the station but also where that particular traveler was standing when she asked for directions. The situation becomes more complex if the traveler is calling for someone through a mobile phone. The information provider may be a robot just standing where the traveler was standing or an intelligent phone system for travelers. These artificial agents are then helped by an intelligent interpreter based on some semantic annotation. All these agents need contextually situated information to act appropriately, as framed by Fillmore (1976).

Consider a short dialogue that involves another situation.

Example 1.9 Dialogue between speakers A and B
Speaker A: When did Mia leave for Boston?
Speaker B: At seven o'clock yesterday evening by Korean Airlines.

Speaker B gave the correct answer to A's question, but B's answer needs to be interpreted appropriately.

Ordinary semantics first reconstructs B's answer as a well-formed complete sentence like the following.

Example 1.10 B's answer reconstructed
Mia left for Boston at seven o'clock yesterday evening on Korean Airlines.

Only after some syntactic analysis, for instance, with Categorial Grammar, semantics starts interpreting each of the component phrases in the sentence by providing their meanings or intensions. The temporal expression *yesterday* is, for instance, interpreted as the 24 hours preceding the time of utterance. It is a the lexical meaning of *yesterday* that can be obtained from a lexicon.

Such an interpretation is not adequate for one who is going to wait for Mia's arrival in Boston. For her, the adequate temporal annotation will provide or compute the specific date and hour of Mia's departure by taking in various pieces of information relevant to the situation such as the time of utterance and the time zone difference between the place of Mia's departure and Boston. Annotation thus deals with *situated information* in such a specific way.

1.3.2 Tasks and Applications of Semantic Annotation

Semantic annotation marks up text or other forms of language data with various sorts of information that are necessary or relevant for performing communicative actions with the computer. Given computationally tractable datasets such as base-segmented or, more preferably, morpho-syntactically annotated data, semantic annotation enriches such data with information for high-level NLP applications that include information retrieval (IR), question-answering systems (QAS), machine translation (MT), text summarization, and spoken language understanding.

There are many different types of semantic annotation such as the annotation of word senses (e.g., various parallel corpora with the use of wordNet),[16] semantic roles (e.g., Frame Net, Propbank), time and events (e.g., TimeML, ISO-TimeML), locations and their qualitative spatial or directional relations (e.g., SpatialML), dialogue acts (e.g., DAMSL, DiAML) and discourse relation (e.g., Penn Discourse Treebank), and dynamic motions and transitions (e.g., ISO-Space). Each type of semantic annotation is characterized by its annotation scheme that defines a set of base categories and a set of links over base structures each based on a specific base category.

Illustrations A semantic annotation scheme for semantic role annotation specifies a set of two basic types, for instance, `<event>` and `<participant>`, and a link that relates an event to a participant or a set of participants, while specifying the type of that relation with a semantic role. Semantic annotation may focus on semantic role labeling (SRL). It labels the role of each of the participants in an event referred to by a predicate verb.

Here are two examples, one in German and another in classical Latin.

Example 1.11 German and Latin compared
a. German: Jemand hat Mia einen Ring gegeben.
b. Classical Latin:
  Arma virumque cano, Trojae qui primus ab oris
  Italiam fato profugus Lavinaque venit
  litora ... [17]

If these sentences, especially Example 1.11a in German, are annotated with semantic roles, they can easily be translated to English.

Annotation 1.12 Semantic role labeling of the German fragment
a. Jemand$_{agent}$ hat Mia$_{recipient}$ einen Ring$_{theme}$ gegeben$_{event}$.
b. Someone$_{agent}$ has Mia$_{recipient}$ a ring$_{theme}$ given$_{event}$.
c. Translation: Someone has given Mia a ring.

---

[16] For example, see Shahid and Kazakov (2013) for parallel corpora with word senses related to wordNet synsets.
[17] The first three lines of Virgil's *Aeneid*.

There are three steps to translation: (i) Annotate the source text (German) with semantic roles, (ii) translate each of the words in the source to a corresponding word with the semantic role in the target language (English), and (iii) reorder the word order in it to obtain the translation.

The identical process applies to the Latin text.

Annotation 1.13 Virgil annotated

Arma$_{theme}$ virum$_{theme}$que $\emptyset_{agent:1S}$ cano$_{event1}$,
Trojae qui primus ab oris$_{source}$
Italiam$_{goal1}$ fato profugus Lavinaque $\emptyset_{agent:3S}$ venit$_{event2}$
litora$_{goal2}$ ....[18]

We now go through the step of word-for-word translation and then reorder the words.

Translation 1.14 Virgil translated

a. Annotated translation:
warfare$_{theme}$ and a man$_{theme}$ $I_{agent:1S}$ sing$_{event1}$,
    of Troy who first from the coast$_{source}$
Italy$_{goal1}$ by fate fleeing and Lavinian came$_{event2}$
shore$_{goal2}$ ....

b. Polished translation:
I sing of warfare and a man,
    who, first fleeing from the coast of Troy
to Italy by fate came to the Lavinian
shore ....

Semantic role annotation is also applicable to a question-answering system (QAS). Consider a question like the following.

Example 1.15 Question annotated

a. What did Mia get from Yong?
b. What$_{theme}$ did Mia get from Yong?

To answer this question based on the annotated data, one looks for the expression which carries the semantic role of being a *theme* in that data. It should be the ring in this case.

Issues are more complicated, requiring types of semantic annotation other than semantic role labeling (SRL). Consider one more example.

---

[18] In Latin, every verb carries information about its Subject. Here it is represented by the emptyset symbol Ø. "1S" stands for first person singular and "3S" for third person singular.

Annotation 1.16 Semantic role labeling

Mia$_{agent}$ left$_{pred}$ Seoul$_{initialLoc}$ for Boston$_{goal}$ yesterday$_{time}$.

This is understood to be saying that Mia was the one who departed from Seoul, she was heading for Boston, and the time of her departure was the date referred to by *yesterday*. Seoul was the location where Mia initiated her trip, while Boston was the goal or intended destination of Mia's trip.

The temporal expression *yesterday* is a so-called *indexical* expression with its reference determined contextually. The specification of the date referred to by *yesterday* depends on the utterance time, the time when the dataset was created, and also information on the time zones in Seoul and Boston. The annotation of temporal expressions requires more information than their just being labeled *time*.

Temporal annotation provides exact dates for indexical expressions like *yesterday*, although it is sometimes argued that semantic annotation should give the meaning of *yesterday*.[19]

Annotation 1.17 Temporal annotation

Mia$_{agent}$ left$_{pred}$ Seoul$_{initialLoc}$ for Boston$_{goal}$ yesterday$_{data:2018\text{-}11\text{-}01}$.

This date is calculated on the basis of the time of utterance, the time and date of data creation, and the relevant information about the time zone differences.

Temporal annotation such as TimeML can apply to the evaluation of question-answering situations like the following.

Example 1.18 Question answering

a. Q: When did Mia leave Seoul?
   A: On the first of November.
b. Q: Will she be in Boston today?
   A: She should be if she has taken a direct flight to New York.

1.4 Extended Summary

Annotation provides additional information, called *metadata*, to text or other forms of data in language. As I mentioned, it has a long scholarly tradition, especially working with ancient texts such as the Confucian Analects, the Hebrew Bible, or grammar books to explicate them.

---

[19] This date is not the meaning or intension of *yesterday*, but the date to which the term *yesterday* specifically (extensionally) refers.

A variety of formats have been used to represent annotations: innotes, footnotes, sidenotes, or endnotes. The content of annotation has also varied from simple comments to detailed illustrations to supplement the main content.

Such a scholarly practice was extended to the analysis of language data, called *linguistic annotation*. First, a large amount of textual data is collected and sorted into a machine-readable set of files, called *corpus*. Second, annotation applies to such data collection, involving base segmentation, tokenization, POS-tagging, or syntactic analysis (parsing). Semantic annotation requires data segmentation as a prerequisite, while making use of morpho-syntactic analysis.

This chapter also mentioned machine learning for natural language annotation. The theory and techniques of machine learning have been adopted to train machines as well as humans to learn to work together for annotation. It has become the core of doing linguistic annotation at the current stage.

Linguistics used to be considered as consisting of three levels: phonology, morphology, and syntax. The mixing of linguistic levels was considered unscientific, especially by strict Structural Linguistics in the 1930s and 1940s. Semantics was not accepted into proper linguistics till the mid-1970s. It is now a basis for semantic annotation.

The domain of semantic annotation is much broader than that of formal semantics. Semantic annotation applies to the whole area of language processing from phonetics to pragmatics to the analysis of dialogues and discourses including the multimodal aspects of communication such as gestures and facial expressions that express a variety of sentiments. Semantic annotation works on every type of information that is relevant for communicative actions.

Semantic annotation is characterized by the partiality and situatedness of information. For example, an event-based temporal annotation scheme (e.g., TimeML) annotates those expressions, called *markables*, in a dataset that refers to time or events only. Semantic annotation provides context-specific information only. Given temporal expressions like *yesterday*, annotation specifies its exact date, not just stating that that was a day before today. Suppose someone finds a note, saying *Sorry that I had to spend a day here yesterday. Thanks,* LK. One who reads the note and wonders what date that *yesterday* refers to is not interested in knowing the meaning of the word *yesterday*. Rather than looking up a dictionary, the annotator or message breaker would look for a clue for locating the date for *yesterday* mentioned in the note.

This chapter concludes with a brief illustration of how semantic annotation can apply to some of the NLP applications. Semantic role annotation, for instance, can easily apply to machine translation (MT) and question answering (QA).

2

Data Segmentation

2.1 Overview

2.1.1 Basic Assumptions

Linguistics assumes that natural language, either spoken or written, is *infinite*, meaning that, theoretically speaking, one can produce an infinite number of sentences. At the same time, it also assumes that each phrase or sentence in a particular language like English is a finite sequence of smaller linguistic units such as tokens or words and that any of them can be segmented into a finite sequence of discrete segments. There are several levels of segmentation and grouping: base segmentation and categorized grouping. *Base segmentation* is a segmentation of a string of characters into characters. *Tokenization* is a simple grouping of character segments, *word segmentation* is also a grouping of character segments into units, called *words*, and *chunking* is a grouping of tokens with morpho-syntactic information.

2.1.2 Three Types of Base Segmentation

There are at least three types of basic segmentation, called *base segmentation*, for processing natural language, depending on the three media types of data.

Classification 2.1   Media types of data

a. textual

b. phonemic

c. image segmentation

Textual segmentation cuts a piece of text in language into linguistic units, called *characters*. Phoneme segmentation cuts spoken language data into units, called *phonemes*, each of which represents an abstract class of sound segments

23

(*phones*) in a language that are perceived by native speakers of that language as being identical sounds. Image segmentation cuts digital images into units, called *pixels*, or smaller regions specified with n-dimensional coordinates.

This chapter is mainly concerned with text segmentation. The other two types of segmentation are phoneme segmentation (Section 2.2) and image segmentation (Section 2.3). We discuss them before text segmentation (Section 2.4).

2.2 Phoneme Segmentation

2.2.1 General

Speech sounds are audible, but not visible. Nevertheless, phoneticians have tried for a long time and with much success to analyze speech sounds and visualize them in one way or another. There have been two approaches: one approach (*articulatory phonetics*) is to observe how speech sounds are produced through relevant speech organs, and the other approach (*acoustic phonetics*) is to record and measure some physical features of speech sounds such as their frequencies (vibrations) and intensities (pitch and volume) with the use of experimental laboratory tools such as a sonograph. Both approaches adopt phonetic symbols like the International Phonetic Alphabet (IPA) to identify and represent sound segments both at the level of phones or phonemes.

Convention By convention, phones are braced with a pair of square brackets [ ], whereas phonemes are braced with a pair of slashes / /. For example, [p] represents a phone *p* and /p/, a phoneme. Allophones are phones, so they are also braced with square brackets. For example, the phoneme /p/ of English has three allophones: aspirated, nonaspirated, and unreleased [p]. By using some diacritic marks of IPA such as ^{h} for the phonetic feature *aspirated* and ⌐ for the phonetic feature *unreleased*, the aspirated *p* and the unreleased *p* are represented as [p^{h}] and [p⌐], respectively. The *unaspirated p* is simply represented as [p] without any diacritic mark.

2.2.2 Production of Speech Sounds

In efforts to make speech sounds somewhat visible, articulatory phoneticians usually go through the following three steps.

Proposition 2.2 Three steps

a. Observe and describe the position and manner of articulating each of the speech sounds in various speech organs from the lips to the oral or nasal cavity to the root of the tongue (*dorsum*) to the voice box (*larynx*) that houses the vocal cords with their opening, called *glottis*.
b. Identify and compare each of the phones thus produced with a set of various observations, called *phonetic features*, and make a list of phonemes for each language.
c. Transcribe phones and phonemes into conventionally accepted symbols.

Consider two contrasting phonemes /p/ and /b/ in English. They are *bilabial stops*, which are produced with the closure of the lips followed by a sudden release of air by opening the mouth. These two stop consonants contrast in the feature of *voicing* when an air stream from the lungs goes through the glottis, which is either open wide or closed narrowly at the larynx. If air flows through the open glottis without vibrating the vocal folds, then a *voiceless* sound is produced. In contrast, a *voiced* sound is produced if there is turbulent airflow through the narrow opening of the glottis that vibrates the vocal folds. So /p/ represents the voiceless bilabial stop and /b/ is the voiced bilabial stop.

Phoneme segmentation ignores fine distinctions among a group of similar sounds. Native speakers of English, for example, may not be able to recognize phonetic differences among different occurrences of *p*-sounds in words like *popular* or *speak* or *Pope*, but treat them all as identical sounds. These sounds are thus treated as all belonging to a single phoneme, represented as /p/, in English. On the other hand, the two sound segments [p] and [b] are recognized as two distinct sounds by native speakers of English and thus treated as two different phonemes in English. Their difference in voicing results in differentiating meanings as in /pen/ *pen* in contrast to /ben/ *Ben* or /pæn/ *pan* in contrast to /bæn/ *ban*.

2.2.3 Visualizing Speech Sound Signals

Beyond what articulatory phonetics can provide with its descriptive method, acoustic phonetics offers a more exact way of segmenting and visualizing speech sounds. It used to employ expensive laboratory instruments such as a sonograph in the old days, but now relies simply on a computer program

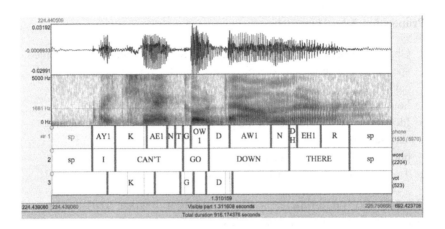

Figure 2.1 Segmentation of speech sounds

or open source tool like Praat[1] or Wavesurfer[2] for sound visualization and manipulation.[3] Receiving a sequence of speech signals, the audio editor displays a digital image like Figure 2.1[4] on its screen.

The image in Figure 2.1 consists of five rows. Row 1 and 2 show a waveform and a spectrogram, respectively, for the input string of sound segments. Row 3 represents the string in ARPAbet, which is a computer-readable set of phonetic symbols replacing the International Phonetic Alphabet (IPA).[5] Row 4 shows an input sentence written in ordinary English. Row 5 shows the Voice Onset Time (VOT) of the three stop consonants [K], [G], and [D]. Each VOT shows an interval of time between the release of a stop and a vocal chord vibration that follows it. The VOT of [K] is shown to be the longest on Row 5 possibly

---

[1] For downloading the latest version of the Windows (7, 8, 9, 10, *etc.*) edition of Praat, refer to https://fon.hum.uva.nl/praat/download_win.html, dated 2022-11-22.

[2] For further information on wavesurfer, see https://wavesufer-js.org, dated 2022-11-22.

[3] Distributed for free by the Centre for Speech Technology (CTT) at the Royal Institute of Technology (KTH) in Stockholm, Sweden.

[4] This image is created at the request of Kiyong Lee for this book with the help of Professor Keeho Kim, Korea University, who uses Praat at his Lab, and with some modification in measuring the VOT segments, marked with the thin vertical line by Professor Jongmi Kim, Gangwon National University, Korea. They gracefully agreed to grant the copyright to the image, if there is any, to Kiyong Lee.

[5] ARPA is an acronym for Advanced Research Projects Agency, an agency of the United States Department of Defense. Besides ARPAbet, Macquarie University (Mannell and Cox, 2015) developed the Australian National Database of Spoken Language (ANDOSL) phonemic symbols representable by ASCII characters.

because the aspiration of [K] has consumed extra time compared to the other two voiced stops [G] and [D].[6]

The waveforms in Row 1 clearly differentiate the vowels from the consonants. The vowels display much more amplitude or vibration than the consonants do. Hence, it is very easy to segment consonants from vowels, either before or after them, unless these segments are liquids or glides. Liquids (e.g., [l] and [r] consonants) and glides (e.g. [y] and [w]) are hard to be differentiated from vowels because their sonority or resonance is almost identical to that of vowels.

The spectrogram in Row 2 is hard for nonprofessionals to interpret. It carries two to four or five thick dark horizontal waves, called *formants*. These formants are associated with vowels, and their tongue positions, as the associated input string is processed by an audio editing program.[7]

As better tools and computer programs rapidly develop, phoneme segmentation requires totally different concepts and techniques of analysis. It is not based on the transcription of spoken data or transcribed text that is presented as spoken data in some of the corpora currently available, but digital data that directly represents individual physical sounds with acoustic features as well as sound sequences with prosodic features such as pitch contours. The segmentation of sound units is necessary to identify them and retrieve (semantic) information from each or all of them either individually or collectively. The identification or recognition of sound segments in spoken data is sometimes accompanied by visual images that represent the multimodal features (gestures and facial expressions) of communication.

Phonetic Alphabet For linguistic annotation, the transcription of spoken data still plays an important role, requiring an appropriate set of visible labeling symbols. Around the early 1890s, a group of linguists in Europe worked together to formulate a list of alphabet-like symbols for the representation of sound segments, phones, or phonemes, in various languages including nonwestern languages. They named it *the International Phonetic Alphabet* (IPA), which could apply to all languages in the world.

IPA was mainly based on the Latin or Greek alphabet letters with their variations for special sound segments and a short list of special marks, called *diacritics*. As an international standard, IPA has been used most widely. Latin

---

[6] The measuring of VOT is done by humans, based on the spectrogram (Row 2). As the two different types of vertical lines, one thick and the other thin, indicate, there are variations in the measurement of the VOT in the current segmentation.

[7] For more technical details, refer to an excellent website run by Mannell and Cox (2015) on acoustics for spoken language.

alphabets like *p, t,* and *k* are used to represent the phonemes /p/, /t/, and /k/ in English. The Greek letter θ is used to represent the phoneme /θ/ (e.g., the initial consonant sound of *think*) in English; IPA still had to introduce symbols like ð to represent the voiced counterpart of θ (e.g., the initial sound of [ðɛɚ] *there*) or ə for the mid-central vowel, called *schwa*, as in [əbawt] *about.*

The use of diacritics in IPA allows a fine-grained representation of speech sounds. For example, the diacritics can represent the rhotacization of [t] or [d] in North American English.[8] The *t* in *water* or *d(d)* in *ladder* is rhotacized, sounding like [r], but more precisely as a flap *r* represented as [ř] or a voiced apical alveolar tap, represented [ɾ].

The IPA symbols are registered in the Unicode code sets so that spoken data in Unicode can be read by the computer. Their code points are not allocated within ASCII, thus creating difficulty in labeling spoken data. The IPA LaTeX codes can type them in, but these codes are not reader-friendly. Hence, alternative phonetic symbol sets like ARPAbet or ANDOSL, as mentioned earlier, were created.[9]

2.3 Image Segmentation

Image segmentation analyzes digital images often to identify the location of a particular image or to describe some features of an object identified. The most common way of segmenting images is first to cut out a small region surrounding them and then to draw up *n*-dimensional coordinates over that region. Geospatial locations are identified with a geographic coordinate system, such as the US government Global Positioning System (GPS) which expresses each of them as a three-dimensional Cartesian vector, consisting of latitude, longitude, and elevation of a location on Earth. Each location is put under a grid, or a map projected to a two-dimensional plane or is given a specific value for each of the dimensions. For illustration, the location of Seoul is given below.

Example 2.3   Seoul is a megacity centrally located in Korea. It is located 37.57 latitude and 126.98 longitude and it is situated at elevation 38 meters above sea level.[10]

---

[8] Rhotacization or rhotacism converts a consonant like [t] to a [r]-related sound. It is typical of North American English, regularly occurring when the alveolar consonant [t] or [d] occurs between two vowels with the first vowel being stressed. The [t] in *atom* is rhotacized because *a* is stressed, but the [t] sound in *atomic* is not because the first vowel *a* is not stressed.

[9] These symbol sets can easily be found on the Internet with the title "ARPABET". Visit https://en.wikipedia.org/wiki/ARPAbet, last edited on August 12, 2022, at 00:38 (UTC).

[10] See "Where is Seoul, South Korea?" on https://worldatlas/com/as/kr/qq/where-is-seoul.html, dated 2022-11-22.

Figure 2.2 Locating a fruit tree and two cats

Image segmentation identifies the location of an object or a sequence of locations associated with the trajectory of a motion. The basic methodology is again to create an n-dimensional coordinate over the object or a group of objects to be identified and to place that object in a small location, which may be called a *pixel*. Consider Figure 2.2 to identify a fruit tree.

In many ordinary cases, the location of an object cannot be identified with an exact location on a coordinate plane. Instead, the object or its location is identified relatively with respect to another object or a location. The frame of seven pictures in Figure 2.2 is divided into three rows, but the columns are not even. It is easy to find a fruit tree. It is found on the second row, left of the house surrounded by trees in the back of a vegetable garden. It may be harder to describe the location of two cats. It is on the first row, between two other pictures. If each of the boxes is numbered or given a specific coordinate, then there is no difference in difficulty between these two objects in locating them.

Dynamic pictures are much harder to segment. Figure 2.3 sketches a scene of two planes in near collision in the air. The analysis of this sketch requires more than cutting the picture into two-dimensional coordinates. Figure 2.3 is a drawing that shows only one single frame of a sequence of many other frames associated with the trajectories of two planes in the air. An air flight tracking radar would provide exact information about those trajectories that are spatio-temporally specified for each of the four dimensions (latitude, longitude, altitude, and calculated distance) measured for each of the time intervals in

Figure 2.3 Potential collision of two planes in the air
Image by Ghang Lee

minutes and seconds and the speed of each of the two flights. The segmentation of such a dynamic image becomes very complex, requiring multidimensional projections.

2.4 Text Segmentation

2.4.1 General

There are four levels of segmenting text to smaller units: (i) *base segmentation*, (ii) *tokenization*, (iii) *morpho-syntactic annotation*, and (iv) *chunking*. Base segmentation cuts a text into characters and identifies each of the characters by their offsets. Then they are grouped into sequences of characters, called *tokens*. This grouping, called *tokenization*, may also be viewed as a way of segmenting a text into tokens. Morpho-syntactic annotation provides a token or a sequence of tokens with morpho-syntactic information. Chunking cuts text into units, called *chunks*, the length of which is larger than or equal to that of tokens while providing each chunk with morpho-syntactic information. Chunks may be tokens, words, or phrases, sometimes consisting of noncontiguous tokens.

The last three levels are not clearly demarcated. Their roles overlap each other significantly, mainly depending on the extent of what tokenization can cover and what kind of applications text segmentation aims at. In this chapter, we view the first two levels, base segmentation and tokenization, as simple processes of segmenting text into characters or sequences of characters without adding any extra information. In contrast, the last two levels, morpho-syntactic annotation and chunking, either assume prior textual segmentation or segment fragments of text into tokens and chunks, respectively and then both annotate them with morpho-syntactic information including so-called

POS-tagging. In theory, the two levels (iii) and (iv) are identical, or one subsumes the other.

2.4.2 Base Segmentation of Text

A fragment of written text can be segmented into sequences of characters. Each character is identified by its position in the text. That position is then delineated with a pair of two integers, starting with the zero 0 in segmenting the given text. These integers represent segment boundaries, called *offsets*. For example, the first segment "M" in the following text fragment is identified with two integers, 0 and 1.

Example 2.4   Raw text: `<text id="t1">Mia's looked me up.</text>`

```
<segments id="st1" target="#t1">
|M|i|a|'|s| |l|o|o|k|e|d| |m|e| |u|p|.|
0 1 2 3 4 5 6 7 8 9 0 1 2 3 4 5 6 7 8 9
                    1
</segments>
```

Each integer or decimal marks a character offset or boundary. Note that whitespace is also considered a character.[11]

Here is another example.

Example 2.5   Raw text: `<text id="t2">Mia won't come.</text>`

```
<segments id="st2" target="#t2">
|M|i|a| |w|o|n|'|t| |c|o|m|e|.|
0 1 2 3 4 5 6 7 8 9 0 1 2 3 4 5
                    1
</segments>
```

Here is an example in French that consists of more than one line.[12]

Example 2.6   French poem

```
<text id="t2-1" lang="fr">
Vienne la nuit sonne l'heure
Les jours s'en vont je demeure
</text>

<segments id="st2-1" target="#t2-1">
  |V|i|e|n|n|e| |l|a| |n|u|i|t| |s|o|n|n|e| |l|'|h|e|u|r|e|
0.0 1 2 3 4 5 6 7 8 9 0 1 2 3 4 5 6 7 8 9 0 1 2 3 4 5 6 7 8
                      1                   2
  |L|e|s| |j|o|u|r|s| |s|'|e|n| |v|o|n|t| |j|e| |d|e|m|e|u|r|e|
1.0 1 2 3 4 5 6 7 8 9 0 1 2 3 4 5 6 7 8 9 0 1 2 3 4 5 6 7 8 9 0
                      1                   2                   3
</segments>
```

---

[11] By convention in TEI P5 (TEI Consortium, 2019), the symbol "#" before an attribute value means that this particular value refers to the piece of data that was processed earlier. The value `#t1` for the attribute `@target` thus refers to the text with `id="t1"`.

[12] The refrain in the poem *Le Pont du Mirabeau* by Guillaume Apollinaire, roughly meaning *Come the night rings the hour. The days go away I remain.*

Each character offset here is marked with a decimal number to mark the lines. The numeral before a decimal point indicates the line on which a character occurs, whereas the numeral after the decimal point identifies a character offset on that line. Each character is then identified with a pair of offsets. The first character "v" in Example 2.6 is anchored to [0.0,0.1]. The first verb "Vienne" in the poem, meaning *Come*, is anchored to [0.0,0.6], while the second verb "sonne", meaning *rings*, is anchored to [0.15,0.20].

Chinese Han Ideographs, Japanese Kana, and Korean Hangul treat syllables as characters[13] each of which has a unique codepoint in Unicode. Base segmentation cuts text in those languages into syllable characters. Here is an example of Korean in Hangul.[14]

Example 2.7   Raw text in Korean

```
<text id="t3" lang="ko">미아가 왔다.</text>
<segments id="st3" target="#t3">
|미||아|가| |왔|다|.|
 0  1  2 3  4  5 6 7
 mi.a.ka  wass.ta
    "Mia came"
</segments>
```

Here are examples for word segmentation in Chinese.[15]

Example 2.8   Word segmentation in Chinese 1

```
a. 日本和服從漢服演變 [original text in traditional characters]
   日本    和服   從    漢服    演變 [segmented]
   riben  hefu  cong hanfu yenbian
   Japan  kimono from Chinese-dress evolve
   "Japanese kimono evolved from Chinese traditional dresses."

b. 榮譽和服從 [original text]
   榮譽    和 服從 [segmented]
   rongyu he fucong
   "honour and obedience"
```

In Example a, 服, fu could meaningfully form a word 和服, hefu (*kimono*) with the morpheme 和, he (*kimono*) to its left or, as in Example b, a word 服從, fucong (*obedience*) with the morpheme 從, cong (*obedience*) to its right. Segmentation ambiguity in these examples arises, depending on how a string of the three characters 和服從, he fu cong is segmented.

---

[13] The term *character* is sometimes replaced by two different terms *letters* and *scripts*, but they all carry the same sense.

[14] If necessary, Hangul syllable characters can be decomposed into smaller units, called *jamo characters*, representing consonant and vowel letters like alphabet letters. See Lee (1994).

[15] Provided for free by Chair Professor Chu-Ren Huang, The Hong Kong Polytechnic University.

Table 2.1 *Tokenization*

`<text id="t1" lang="en">` Mia's looked me up. `</text>`		

id	span	tokens
token1	`from="0" to="3"`	Mia
token2	`from="3" to="5"`	's
token3	`from="6" to="12"`	looked
token4	`from="13" to="15"`	me
token5	`from="16" to="18"`	up
token6	`from="18" to="19"`	.

2.4.3 Tokenization

Beyond base segmentation, a text can also be segmented into linguistic units, called *tokens*. A token is a unit larger than characters. It consists of a sequence of characters that can be defined in terms of character offsets. Here is an example.

Example 2.9   Tokenization

```
<spanGrp xml:id="tokens1" type="token" target="#st1">
  <span xml:id="token1" from="0" to="3"><!-- Mia --></span>
  <span xml:id="token2" from="3" to="5"><!-- 's --></span>
  <span xml:id="token3" from="6" to="12"><!-- looked --></span>
  <span xlm:id="token4" from="13" to="15"><!-- me --></span>
  <span xlm:id="token5" from="16" to="18"><!-- up --></span>
  <span xlm:id="token6" from="18" to="19"><!-- . --></span>
</spanGrp>16
```

The process of tokenization is represented in XML. The attributes @from and @to specify the token boundaries, start and end, respectively, of each token, as in Table 2.1.

In segmented languages such as English, whitespace helps extract tokens. As shown in Example 2.9, there is no blank space between *Mia* and the enclitic *s*, but the latter is treated as a token because it will be submitted later to the process of so-called chunking or parts-of-speech (POS) tagging that annotates it as an abbreviation of a verb *has*. There is no whitespace between *up* and the punctuation ".", but the punctuation is treated as a token.

A token is usually a word, consisting of a sequence of characters. The process of segmenting a text into tokens is called *tokenization*. What should be a token is, however, quite complicated. It depends on the characteristics of languages and their writing systems, and the purposes and methods of

---

[16] Here, `target="#st1"` means that the tokenization refers to the segmented text identified as id=st1.

NLP applications.[17] In nonsegmented languages like Chinese, a sequence of characters can be a token only if it is a meaningful unit. For Chinese, tokenization means *word segmentation*, for each token must be a word, while punctuation is ignored in the process of tokenization or word segmentation.

Consider a third example in Chinese, taken from ISO 24614-1 (ISO, 2010) (see also ISO (2011) 24614-2).

Example 2.10   Raw text

```
<text id="t4" lang="zh">白菜和猪肉</text>
<segments id="st4" target="#t4">
|白|菜|和|猪|肉|
 0  1 2  3 4  5
</segments>
```

The Chinese text consists of five ideographs. There is an ambiguity in the word segmentation of Example 2.10. The base-segmented data is tokenized into three or four words. The two different word segmentations are also represented in XML, as in Examples 2.11 and 2.12.

Example 2.11   Word segmentation 1 in Chinese

```
<spanGrp xml:id="words1" type="word" target="#st4">
  <span xml:id="w1" from="0" to="2">
   <!-- 白菜 "lettuce"--></span>
  <span xml:id="w2" from="2" to="3">
   <!-- 和 "and"--></span>
  <span xml:id="w3" from="3" to="5">
   <!-- 猪肉 "pork" --></span>
</spanGrp>
```

Example 2.12   Word segmentation 2 in Chinese

```
<spanGrp xml:id="words2" type="word" target="#st4">
  <span xml:id="w1" from="0" to="2">
   <!-- 白菜 "lettuce"--></span>
  <span xml:id="w2" from="2" to="3">
   <!-- 和 "and"--></span>
  <span xml:id="w3" from="3" to="4">
   <!-- 猪 "pig" --></span>
  <span xlm:id="w4" from="4" to="5">
   <!-- 肉 "meat" --></span>
</spanGrp>
```

Beesley and Karttunen (2003), Trim (2013), and others point out that *whitespace-based tokenization* has difficulty tokenizing compound words (e.g., *to and fro, take care of*) or named entities (e.g., *Rational Software Architect for WebSphere, The University of Texas at Austin*). As discussed in Trim (2013), there are two approaches to the treatment of these *long* words. One is a naive approach to the tokenization of such expressions, first by routinely running a

---

[17] See Webster and Kit (1992) for details.

Table 2.2 *Naïve whitespace tokenization*

	to and fro	
id	*span*	*tokens*
token1	from="0" to="2"	to
token2	from="3" to="6"	and
token3	from="7" to="10"	fro

whitespace-based tokenizer and then by sending the segmented text to a deep parser like POS-tagger or the process of chunking. Another approach is to tokenize those compound expressions with the aid of a multiword dictionary.

The former approach can be illustrated in Example 2.13.

Example 2.13   Base segmentation

a. Data: `<text id="t5" lang="en">to and fro</text>`
b. Segmentation:

```
<segments id="st5" target="#t5">
|t|o| |a|n|d| |f|r|o|
0 1 2 3 4 5 6 7 8 9 0
                    1
</segments>
```

Based on its base segmentation (Example 2.13), the input sequence is tokenized in a very naive way, as in Example 2.14 and Table 2.2.

Example 2.14   Naïve whitespace tokenization

```
<spanGrp xml:id="tt5" type="character" target="#st5">
  <span xml:id="token1" from="0" to="2"> <!-- to --></span>
  <span xml:id="token2" from="3" to="6"> <!-- and --></span>
  <span xml:id="token3" from="7" to="10"> <!-- fro --></span>
</spanGrp>
```

We then assume some sort of chunking that combines these tokens into a chunk, as in Example 2.15 and Table 2.3.

Example 2.15   Hypothetical chunking

```
<spanGrp xml:id="chunks1" type="chunk" target="#tt5">
  <span xml:id="chunk1" anchors="token1,token2,token3">
  category="AdvP">
    <!-- to and from --></span>
</spanGrp>
```

The *naive whitespace tokenizer* may also work well for the parsing of named entities (e.g., *United States of America*, *Mia Lee*) in segmented languages like

Table 2.3 *Hypothetical chunking*

		to and fro	
id	*anchors*	*chunk*	*annotation*
chunk1	`token1,token2,token3`	to and fro	`cat="advP"`

English. Such tokenization assumes that a list of relevant tokens is combined with anchoring a chunk with morpho-syntactic annotation.[18]

However, *whitespace-based tokenization* fails to perform properly for unsegmented or semisegmented languages like German or Korean. German or Korean text is mostly segmented, but there are some exceptions such as the processing of nouns, names, or compound verbs. For example, compound nouns are mostly nonsegmented in German. Here are some examples.

Example 2.16 Compound nouns in German

a. *Einbahnstraße* "one-way street"

b. *Computerlinguistik* "computational linguistics"

c. *Lebensversicherungsgesellschaftsangestellter* "life insurance company employee"

Just like German, many of the nominal expressions, especially proper names, are not segmented in Korean. Whitespace and punctuations are very recent introductions to Hangul text in Korean. Not being adequately segmented, Korean proper names very often create wrong interpretations. Here is a name, consisting of six syllable characters in Hangul.

Example 2.17 Proper name in Korean
대 학 생 선 교 회
tay.hak.sayng.sen.kyo.hoy

This string of Hangul syllable characters can be segmented in many different ways. As was reported, one segmentation that was erroneously made by a foreign missionary learning Korean in Seoul was the following.

Example 2.18 Wrong segmentation
대학   생선   교회
tay.hak sayng.sen kyo.hoy
college fish   church
"college fish church"

---

[18] Many tokenizers treat multiword expressions like "to and fro" as a token. See Beesley and Karttunen (2003), p. 15.

The missionary himself didn't understand what was meant by that name and was puzzled till he learned that he had made a wrong segmentation of the name. It should have been the following.

Example 2.19   Correct segmentation

```
대학생        선교회
tay.hak.sayng sen.kyo.hoy
college student  mission
"Campus Crusade"
```

The segmentation in Example 2.19 can also be represented with the character offsets marked.

Example 2.20   Segmentation with character offsets

```
|대|학|생|     |선|교|회|
0  1  2  3     4  5  6  7
tay.hak.sayng sen.kyo.hoy
```

More explicitly, we have the following.

Example 2.21   Explicit representation of segmentation

```
a. <text id="t6" lang="ko">대학생선교회</text>
b. <spanGrp xml:id="tokens" type="token" target="#t6">
        <span xml:id="token1" from="0" to="3">
        <!-- 대학생 "college student" -->
        </span>
        <span xml:id="token2" from="4" to="7">
        <!-- 선교회 "mission" -->
        </span>
   </spanGrp>
```

Note that 대학생선교회 (Daehaksaeng Seongyohoe) is a Korean translation of Campus Crusade active in the USA.

Punctuation creates much difficulty and ambiguity in tokenization. The dot "." is, for instance, used either as a sentence ender or for abbreviations.

Example 2.22   Punctuation in tokenization

a. Sentence ender:
   John came. He ate dinner.
b. Abbreviation:
   St. Louis,
      where "St." stands for Saint,
   9th St.,
      where "St." stands for street.
c. Ambiguity:
   234 Queen's Dr. Kim's Clinic

Phrases like *234 Queen's Dr. Kim's Clinic* create difficulty for segmentation because *Dr.* may be understood as an abbreviation of either *Doctor* or *Drive*.

Table 2.4 *Tokens with morpho-syntactic information 1*

	Example 2.23a: *Mia's father lives in Boston.*		
	anchors	*tokens*	*annotation*
token1	[0,3]	Mia	category ="properName"
token2	[3,5]	's	category="nominalSuffix" gFunction="genitive case marking"

2.4.4 Morpho-syntactic Analysis

The success of tokenization very often requires morpho-syntactic information. Consider the two examples in Example 2.23.

Example 2.23   Morpho-syntactic information

```
a. <text id="t7" lang="en">
     Mia's father lives in Boston.
   </text>
b. <text id="t8" lang="en">
     Mia's already left for Boston.
   </text>
```

Here are two occurrences of *Mia's*. They cannot be properly analyzed unless they are associated with some morpho-syntactic information. The first occurrence is a nominal suffix marking a genitive (possessive) case on the preceding noun *Mia*, whereas the second occurrence stands for an abbreviated form of the auxiliary verb *has*. Hence, these two need to be analyzed differently. They both undergo annotated segmentation, called *morpho-syntactic analysis* or *word segmentation*, which does more than what simple segmentation can do.

Annotated segmentation provides morpho-syntactic information while segmenting text into some linguistic units. These units can be morphemes, words, or phrases. Annotations can be represented in feature structures, each consisting of a list of features (attributes) and their values. A sequence of one or more tokens forms a word or chunk each of which has a name for its class, called *category*.

Consider *Mia's* in Example 2.23a to see how it is analyzed morpho-syntactically. Based on the base segmentation given above or through the process of tokenization, *Mia* is identified as a token or word of category `properName`. Then there is another token *'s* which is analyzed as a nominal suffix having a grammatical function (`@gFunction`) of marking a genitive case on the noun preceding it. The result of such a morpho-syntactic analysis is represented in Table 2.4.

Table 2.5 *Tokens with morpho-syntactic information 2*

Example 2.23b: *Mia's left for Boston.*			
id	*anchors*	*tokens*	*annotation*
token1	[0,3]	Mia	category="properNoun" person="3" number ="Sg"
token2	[3,5]	's	category="auxVerb" lemma="have" surfaceForm="has" tense="present" requires="3Sg subject"

Table 2.6 *Tokens with morpho-syntactic information 3*

Example 2.24: Mia's looked me up.			
id	*anchors*	*tokens*	*annotation*
token3	[7,13]	looked	category="verb" tense="past" gForm ="participle"
token4	[14,16]	me	category="pronoun" case="accusative" person="1" number="singular"
token5	[17,19]	up	category="particle"
token6	[19,20]	.	category="punctuation"

The second occurrence of *Mia's* can also be analyzed similarly. In Table 2.5, the token *Mia* is identified as a word of category properNoun. The enclitic (abbreviated) form *'s* of the verb *has* is annotated as a category of auxVerb with its tense being present. Other pieces of relevant morpho-syntactic information are also annotated.

Now consider noncontiguous compound verbs, as in Example 2.24.

Example 2.24   Mia's looked me up.

This can be tokenized with appropriate morpho-syntactic annotation in two alternative ways, as shown in either Table 2.6 or Table 2.7.

In Table 2.7, token 3 and token 5 are jointly anchored to the two noncontiguous spans [7,13] and [17,19], while token 3 subsumes the morpho-syntactic information of token 5.

Table 2.7 *Tokens with morpho-syntactic information 4*

Example 2.24: Mia's looked me up.			
id	*anchors*	*tokens*	*annotation*
token3	[7,13] [17,19]	looked up	category="verb+particle" tense="past" gForm ="participle"
token4	[14,16]	me	category="pronoun" case="accusative" person="1" number="singular"
token6	[19,20]	.	category="punctuation"

Compound verbs (e.g., *look forward to, take off*) or sequences of words, called *multiword expressions* (MWEs), cause difficulty for tokenization. Consider MWEs such as *White House, because of, in terms of, take a walk,* or *by and large*. These examples show that the presence of whitespace is not an absolute criterion for word segmentation. Segmenting these expressions may also be treated adequately with morpho-syntactic annotation, as has been shown.

2.4.5 Chunking with POS-Tagging

Text chunking is a kind of segmenting text or grouping sequences of characters into significant linguistic units, called *chunks*, larger than character segments while providing each of the chunks with a tag that carries appropriate linguistic information. Chunks may refer to anything from tokens to words to phrases and even to sentences. The two tokens *looked* (verb) and *up* (particle) can be combined into a chunk, named verb+particle, while a single token *Mia* is treated as either a one-word chunk, categorized properNoun, or a phrasal chunk, named NP (noun phrase), that can carry a grammatical function like being a subject or object.

In this section, we discuss POS-tagging associated with chunks. POS-tagging is part of chunking linguistic text with the morpho-syntactic annotation that helps resolve many structural or syntactic ambiguities. It is a significant part of corpus linguistics, working on the construction of so-called *tagged corpus*, and that of NLP that uses it for syntactic parsing. Tagged corpus provides grammatical information on morpho-syntactic categories, word classes, and associated lexical features.

Tagsets

For the annotation of word classes, a restricted set of tags, called *tagset*, is set up for an automatic way of naming words or chunks in general. There are two major tagsets for English, one used by the British National Corpus (BNC) and the other by the Open American National Corpus (OANC).

BNC Basic C5 Tagset BNC uses a set of 61 category names or POS-tags, known as the BNC Basic (C5) Tagset.[19] CLAWS5 (C5) is a subset of the CLAWS tagset, where CLAWS stands for the Constituent Likelihood Automatic Word-tagging System. The 100-million-word British National Corpus is tagged with C5. Then there is a two-million-word subset of the BNC, called the Core Corpus, tagged with an enriched tagset known as C7.

Automatic tagging is a very important aspect of managing large corpora. As for BNC, there is an automatic tagger CLAWS4 that has been applied to the tagging of the 100-million-word BNC with approximate rates of error 1.7% of all words, excluding punctuation marks. With an enriched tagger C7 the rates of error was lowered to less than 0.3% with some manual postediting. This was a report made in 1995, more than 20 years ago, so much improvement must have since been made.[20]

Each tag consists of three characters such as NP0 for proper nouns, VDZ the -s form of the verb HAVE such as *has*, *'s*, VVN the past participle form of lexical verbs, PNP for personal pronouns such as *I, you, them*, and AVP for adverb particles such as *up, off, up*. The general separating punctuation marks are tagged PUN. The numeral 0 in the third digit of a tag refers to the most general category. For instance, NN0 is the most general category among common nouns, each of which is tagged NN + *numeral*.

Here is a part of the C5 tags which shows how nouns are tagged.

Example 2.25 From the BNC basic (C5) tagset

a. NN0 Common noun, neutral for number:

e.g., *aircraft, data, committee*

b. NN1 Singular common noun:

e.g., *pencil, goose, time, revlation*

---

[19] See the 1995 edition of the C5 tagset, for it keeps being updated.

[20] See http://ucrel.lancs.ac.uk/claws/, dated 2019-02-28: "CLAWS has consistently achieved 96–97% accuracy (the precise degree of accuracy varying according to the type of text). Judged in terms of major categories, the system has an error-rate of only 1.5%, with c.3.3% ambiguities unresolved, within the BNC. More detailed analysis of the error-rates for the C5 tagset in the BNC can be found within the BNC manual." The reported error rates range from less than 0.3% with manual postediting to 1.5% to 1.7% excluding punctuation marks.

c. NN2 Plural common noun:

   e.g., *pencils, geese, times, revelations*

d. NP0 Proper noun:

   e.g., *London, Michael, Mars, IBM*

Various verbal forms have 25 tags out of the 61 grammatical tags in C5. The tagset explains how the tag names have been formed and also provides detailed notes for some of the tags.

Here is a portion of the tagged corpus in BNC.

Example 2.26   Tagging of BNC dialogue F78.XML

```
<text type="OTHERSP">
  <u who="PS1L6">
    <s n="1">
      <vocal desc="sigh" />
      <w c5="AV0" hw="well" pos="ADV">Well</w>
      <w c5="PNP" hw="we" pos="PRON">we</w>
      <w c5="VBB" hw="be" pos="VERB">'re</w>
      <w c5="AJ0" hw="keen" pos="ADJ">keen</w>
      <w c5="TO0" hw="to" pos="PREP">to</w>
      <w c5="VVI" hw="get" pos="VERB">get</w>
      <w c5="AV0" hw="here" pos="ADV">here</w>
      <w c5="VBB" hw="be" pos="VERB">are</w>
      <w c5="XX0" hw="not" pos="ADV">n't</w>
      <w c5="PNP" hw="we" pos="PRON">we</w>
      <c c5="PUN">?</c>
    </s>
    ....
  </u>
  ....
</text>
```

Each word has two attributes, @c5 and @pos; @c5 follows the C5 tagset, while @pos assigns a more general POS tag, which is much easier to recognize. For example, PNP is a pronoun (PRON), VBB is a verb (VERB), and PRP is a preposition (PREP).

There are many other tagsets. Practically every language has its own, and each national or research group has its own. Besides the BNC Basic (C5) tagset (see Leech (1995)), the Penn TreeBank tagset may be best known and most used in NLP applications. Open American National Corpus (OANC), for instance, adopts the Penn tagset for the tagging of words (tokens).[21]

Penn TreeBank Tagset   The Penn TreeBank tagset contains only 36 tags. It has six tags for verbs, whereas C5 has 25 tags for verbs because C5 has separate

---

[21] The ANC second release, dated December 15, 2005, contained CLAWS part of speech annotations, but they are not available in the current (2022) version of OANC.

Table 2.8 *Penn tagset for verbs*

Example 2.24: *Mia's looked me up.*			
Tags	Description	Examples	C5 Tags
VB	verb, base form	take	VVB
VBD	verb, past tense	took	VVD
VBG	verb, gerund/present participle	taking	VVG
VBN	verb, past participle	taken	VVN
VBP	verb, sing. present, nonthird	take	VVI
VBZ	verb, sing. present, third	takes	VVZ

Table 2.9 *Penn tagset for nouns*

Example 2.24: *Mia's looked me up.*			
Penn Tags	Description	Examples	C5 Tags
NN	noun, mass or neutral for number	data	NN0
	noun, singular collective	committee	NN0
NN	noun, singular	table	NN1
NNS	noun, plural	tables	NN2
	proper noun	London	NP0
NNP	proper noun, singular	John	NP0
NNPS	proper noun, plural	Vikings	rare

tags for the irregular verbs, *be, do,* and *have.* The six Penn Tags for verbs (VB) are listed in Table 2.8.

The *Penn tags* for verbs (VB) are almost identical with the C5 tags for verbs (VV) except that the Penn tags allow two-digit tags like VB, while the C5 tags consistently allow only three-digit tags like VVB. The characters in the third digit are almost the same except for one difference between VBP vs. VVI.

The tags for nouns, as in Table 2.9, also show similarity between the two tagsets:

The *Penn tagset* makes a distinction between nouns and proper nouns, and about their number being either singular or plural. In contrast, the C5 tagset differentiates mass (uncountable) nouns from countable nouns, while ignoring the number difference for proper nouns. A question remains how to harmonize these two tagsets with each other. The design of the American National Corpus

(ANC) aims to harmonize corpora annotated in different ways or make them interoperable by introducing a graph-theoretic representation scheme.[22]

Illustration Here is an illustration showing how the Penn tagset is used for morpho-syntactic annotation in OANC. The data is a tiny portion taken from the face-to-face spoken data `AdamsElissa.txt`:

Example 2.27   Illustration of the use of Penn (hepple) in OANC
a. Data: ... `you've lived in Charlotte for-- Five years.`
b. Annotation:
```
-<struct to="72" from="69" type="tok>
       <feat value="you" name="base"/>
       <feat value="PRP" name="msd"/>
   </struct>
-<struct to="75" from="72" type="tok">
       <feat value="VBP" name="msd"/>
       <feat value="'ve" name="affix"/>
       <feat value="have" name="base"/>
   </struct>
-<struct to="81" tok"="76" type="tok">
       <feat value="VBN" name="msd"'/>
       <feat value="live" name="base"/>
       <feat value="ed" name="affix"/>
   </struct>
-<struct to="84" from="82" type="tok">
       <feat value="in" name="base"/>
       <feat value="IN" name="msd"/>
   </struct>
-<struct to="94" from="85" type="tok">
       <feat value="Charlotte" name="base"/>
       <feat value="NNP" name="msd"/>
   </struct>
```

Each of the values for *msd* conforms to the Penn TreeBank tagset. Then there is a specification of the feature, named *msd* (morpho-syntactic description), for each of the tokens in the data.

2.5 Summary

Semantic annotation should focus on semantic information only. It should not be burdened with the task of segmentation and chunking or of marking up morpho-syntactic information in a text. To free semantic annotation from that burden, I discussed in this chapter three types of segmentation: phoneme (Section 2.2), image (Section 2.3), and text (Section 2.4) segmentations.

---

[22] See ISO 24612 LAF (ISO, 2012a) or Ide and Suderman (2014).

Phoneme segmentation depends on articulatory phonetics and acoustic phonetics. Articulatory phonetics identifies phonemes or allophones as essential speech sound segments by describing the positions and manners of producing speech sounds in the speech organs from the lips of the mouth to the oral or nasal cavity to the larynx which houses the glottis. Acoustic phonetics visually demarcates phoneme boundaries by showing the waveforms or the spectrograms that display the frequencies, intensities, and other physical features of sound segments in a stream of speech sounds. I showed how these approaches complement each other for phoneme segmentation.

I also introduced image segmentation as something new in the area of NLP or computational linguistics. To identify an object situated in a region, I proposed to cover that region with an n-dimensional net of coordinates and then to identify the location of a particular object to be identified for its annotation. When the target for annotation is a dynamic situation like the possible collision of two aircrafts, the task of segmenting it becomes complex.

Since the current state of affairs in NLP has focused on text segmentation, we allocated more time and space for the discussion of textual segmentation. The topic was divided into four subsections: base segmentation (Section 2.4.2), tokenization (Section 2.4.3), morpho-syntactic analysis (Section 2.4.4), and chunking with POS-tagging (Section 2.4.5). POS-tagging is a morpho-syntactic annotation on tokens or chunks in general. I discussed two tagsets: one was the BNC Basic (C5) tagset and the other was the Penn TreeBank tagset, used by the Open American National Corpus (OANC), and briefly compared them, stating that they were almost the same, but that the latter seemed to be preferred because of its brevity (36 tags only) and precise classification of the tags, each designating a more clearly demarcated part of speech.

3

Modeling a Semantic Annotation Scheme

3.1 Overview

The design of a semantic annotation scheme is modeled on a formal grammar of language. Each of the annotation schemes consists of three components: a (nonempty) set of annotation structures, syntax, and semantics. Figure 3.1 thus represents the general design of a semantic annotation scheme.

First, annotation structures carry metadata information on various forms of datasets in language. These structures are like phrasal or dependency structures in a grammar.

Second, the syntax generates or formally defines annotation structures, while the semantics interprets them. Formally defined annotation structures are understood to be *well-formed* syntactically.

By *interpretation*, it is understood that each annotation structure carries some sort of information associated with some object in a given situation, often called *the world*. Such an object can be an individual entity, a set of individuals, an eventuality or a state of affairs in which the mentioned object

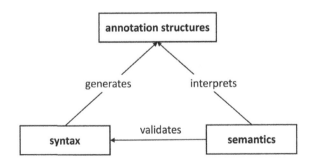

Figure 3.1 Metamodel for semantic annotation scheme

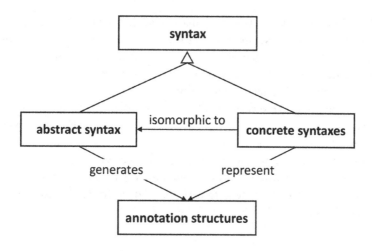

Figure 3.2 Syntax: abstract and concrete

is involved, whether that state of affairs is either being supported by an actual situation or not.

Third, the semantics *validates* or formally supports the formulation of a syntax. Each component of a syntax requires being semantically motivated. It is claimed that, unless it is constrained and supported by semantics, a syntax is of no use, as was rightly claimed by Montague (1974),[1] and that this is especially true for semantic annotation schemes.

3.2 Syntax: Abstract vs. Concrete Syntaxes

Bunt and Schiffrin (2005) and Bunt (2010)[2] proposed that the syntax of a semantic annotation scheme should be divided into two levels: an abstract syntax and an equivalent set of concrete syntaxes. Ideally, each concrete syntax is required to be *isomorphic* to the abstract syntax associated with it. This distinction has been clearly incorporated into the principles of semantic annotation as laid down in ISO 24617-6 SemAF principles (ISO, 2016), as is shown in Figure 3.2.

---

[1] See "Universal Grammar", footnote 2: " ... I fail to see any great interest in syntax except as a preliminary to semantics" in Montague (1974), p. 223.
[2] See also his subsequent works (Bunt, 2011, 2015).

The *abstract syntax* formally defines a set of well-formed annotation structures as tuples in set-theoretic terms. In contrast, each of the concrete syntaxes, isomorphic to the abstract syntax associated with it, provides a representation format for annotation structures. XML, for instance, is such a format for representing annotation structures.

Each of the *concrete syntaxes* is ideally assumed to be structurally isomorphic and semantically equivalent to the other concrete syntaxes. This means that they all carry the same sort and the same amount of information conveyed by the abstract syntax with which they are associated, for the semantics is based on the abstract syntax or, as shown in Figure 3.1, validates it. In practice, however, concrete syntaxes tend to carry more detailed information than the abstract syntax on which they are based.

3.3 Abstract Syntax Proposed

3.3.1 Different Uses of an Abstract Syntax

The term *abstract syntax* is used in various ways. In the Distributed Ontology, Modeling, and Specification Language (DOL) (OMG, 2016), it is used as a parse tree term for a "language for representing documents in a machine-processable way," while the term *concrete syntax* is a "serialization or specific syntactic encoding of such a language." An abstract syntax specifies information on an object language in *abstract* terms, focusing on syntactically or semantically relevant features only. The meta-language that formulates an abstract syntax may vary. It may consist of a conceptual inventory of data types in informal terms, a list of set-theoretic or algebraic definitions, a list of data type declarations or feature specifications represented in the Backus–Naur Form (BNF) or a so-called meta-model with graphic representations using a language like the Unified Modeling Language (UML).

The abstract syntax of Common Logic (ISO/IEC 24707, 2007), for instance, lists abstract syntactic categories and their subcategories and then depicts their allowable structures using UML class diagram notation;[3] OMG (2016) specifies an abstract syntax for DOL in slightly modified ISO/IEC 14977 (eBNF) (ISO/IEC, 1996). Pfenning and Elliott (1988) construct "a higher-order abstract syntax for programs, formulas, rules, and other syntactic objects in program manipulation by using a simply typed λ-calculus enriched with products and polymorphism."

---

[3] All together seven UML diagrams for all the categories (e.g., *text, sentence, module, quantified or Boolean sentence, atom, term, term sequence*) and subcategories listed.

The abstract syntax for the Dialogue Act Markup Language (DiAML) in Bunt et al. (2016) provides a conceptual inventory for DiAML and then characterizes each functional segment (markable) with a 6-tuple $<S, A, H, d, f, Q>$ or 7-tuple $<S, A, H, d, f, Q, \Delta>$ consisting of dialogue act features such as sender S, addressee A, dialogue participants H, dimension d, the communicative function f, qualifier Q, or a set of other dialogue acts Δ, associated with dialogue acts. Bunt and others then formalize a link structure as consisting of a triple $<\eta, E, \rho>$, where η is an entity structure, E a set of entity structures, and ρ is a rhetorical relation that relates the dialogue act in η to one or more entity structures in E. Later in this book, the triple $<\eta, E, \rho>$ is replaced with a quadruple $<\beta, B, \rho, O>$, where β stands for base structures; B, a set of base structures; ρ, a relation between β and B; and O, a set of triggers or other optional items. Entity structures are renamed *base structures* to differentiate them from individual, group, or spatial entity structures.

3.3.2 Structure of the Abstract Syntax

General Structure

Lee (2016) proposes a general abstract syntax $\mathcal{A}Syn$ for semantic annotation schemes. Its formulation follows the principles of its construction that were presented in Bunt (2010, 2011, 2015), ISO 24617-6 SemAF principles (ISO, 2016), and Bunt et al. (2016) in general. The current proposal, however, formulates an abstract syntax in algebraic terms that are often used in defining formal grammars. It also uses ISO/IEC 14977 (eBNF) (ISO/IEC, 1996) as a meta-language to specify various features of data types because the extended BNF is expressively more powerful than simple set-theoretic listing.

Given a collection D of datasets in human communication as primary data for annotation, the *general algebraic structure* of an abstract syntax $\mathcal{A}Syn$ for an annotation language can be formally defined as a tuple.

Specification 3.1 $\mathcal{A}Syn = <M, C, R, @>$, where

(i) M is a set of (possibly null or noncontiguous) strings of communicative segments, called *markables*, in the primary data D, delimited by each category c in the set C of categories of base structures,

(ii) C is a finite set of *categories* of base structures,

(iii) R is a finite set of *categories* of relational (link) structures,

(iv) @ is a finite set of specifications that define or declare a list of attributes and possible value ranges for each category c in C and each relation category r in R.

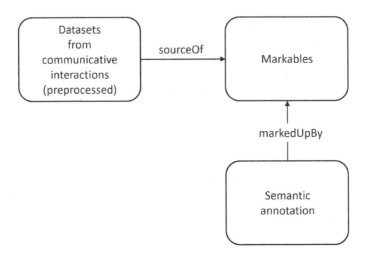

Figure 3.3 Markables for semantic annotation

Categories of base structures are called *base categories*, while categories of relational categories are called *link categories*.

Markables

For semantic annotation, its markables in M are strings of communicative segments in a collection D of datasets, given as its primary data. These segments are typically identified as tokens, words, or phrases in a text while carrying various types of semantico-pragmatic information associated with communicative situations. The content types, size, and representation formats depend on each communicative situation. Datasests D that are collected from human communicative interactions such as dialogues, discourses, or writings thus become sources for linguistic items, called *markable expressions* or briefly *markables*, to be marked up and annotated with semantically relevant information, as shown in Figure 3.3.

It is assumed that these markables, especially textual segments, have been preprocessed by *word-segmentation* or morpho-syntactic analysis, thus being identifiable as strings of linguistic segments. Every markable in M is a string of character segments or a region in one of the datasets in the collection D of language datasets or resources in various forms. The forms of markables are text, images, dynamic pictures, or multimodal communicative gestures.

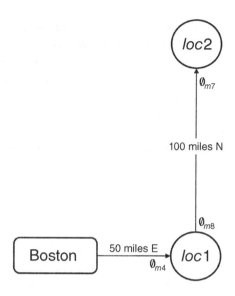

Figure 3.4 Driving from Boston

Nonconsuming Tags Empty strings of textual characters are allowed as markables in M. They represent so-called *nonconsuming tags* with their use licensed in SpatialML (MITRE, 2010).[4]

Example 3.2 Nonconsuming tags
a. Data:
   We drove 50 miles east of Boston. The next day, we drove 100 miles north.
b. Markables:
   We drove (to) $\emptyset_{m4}$ [50 miles]$_{m1}$ east$_{m2}$ of Boston$_{m3}$. The next day, we drove (to) $\emptyset_{m7}$ [100 miles]$_{m5}$ north$_{m6}$ (of) $\emptyset_{m8}$.

Here, $\emptyset_{m4}$, $\emptyset_{m7}$, and $\emptyset_{m8}$ refer to three unmentioned places and the first one $\emptyset_{m4}$ and the third one $\emptyset_{m8}$ are identical: $\emptyset_{m4}$ and $\emptyset_{m8}$ refer to *loc*1 and $\emptyset_{m7}$ to *loc*2 in Figure 3.4. These empty strings of characters are nonconsuming tags.

There are two driving events mentioned in Example 3.2a, but some of the relevant places such as the endpoints, *loc*1 and *loc*2, of the two driving events

---

[4] *Tagging*, labeling, or suffixing tags to markables is one of the simplest ways of representing annotation.

are not mentioned. In Example 3.2b these endpoints as well as the start point of the driving on the second day are annotated as $\emptyset_{m4}$, $\emptyset_{m7}$, and $\emptyset_{m8}$. The driving on the first day covered the distance of 50 miles east of Boston to the unmentioned place $\emptyset_{m4}$ (*loc*1). The second day of driving covered the distance of 100 miles north of the starting point $\emptyset_{m8}$ (*loc*1), which is the endpoint $\emptyset_{m4}$ of the first day's driving, to the unmentioned place $\emptyset_{m7}$ (*loc*2). In annotation, these three unmentioned places are treated as *nonconsuming* tags, for no mentioned character strings are taken up or consumed for the annotation.[5]

Here are two more examples.

Example 3.3   Spatial nonconsuming tags

a. We camped $\emptyset_{loc1}$ near the river.

b. John drove $\emptyset_{ep1}$ to Boston.

These nonconsuming tags refer to spatial objects: a location and an event-path. The tag $\emptyset_{loc1}$ in Example 3.3a refers to a location where the camping took place. It is a nonconsuming tag, again meaning that no nonnull string of characters is taken up for tagging. The tag $\emptyset_{ep1}$ in Example 3.3b refers to an *event-path* with its terminal location being Boston, while the event-path was created by the motion of driving and traversed by John.[6] This event-path is not, however, explicitly mentioned, but only implied.

Categories of Base Structures

C is a very small set of categories of base structures, called *base categories*, that lay the basis of an abstract syntax for semantic annotation. One of the base categories is a category, named *entity*. A referential annotation scheme, for instance, annotates discourse objects and their *objectal relations* such as *coreference*. These objects are often called *discourse entities* or *individual entities*. In the proposed annotation scheme, they are of category *entity*.

In an XML-based concrete syntax, this category is represented by an element, which is tagged ENTITY in uppercase or entity in lowercase. Nominal or pronominal phrases are markables of this category, referring to some discourse entities. By convention they are identified with variable prefixes x, y, z, each with or without a numeric (subscript), while *plurals* are identified with uppercase X, Y, and Z, again with or without a numeric subscript.

---

[5] See SpatialML (MITRE, 2010, section 15 Non-consuming PLACE tags).

[6] Lee (2016, see sections 4 and 5).

Here is an example.

Example 3.4 Category entity
a. Data:
Mia bought apples and baked them into a pie. It was delicious.
b. Markables:
Mia$_{x1}$ bought apples$_{X2}$ and $\emptyset_{x3}$ baked them$_{X4}$ into a pie$_{x5}$. It$_{x6}$ was delicious.

Here every referring expression is marked up. There are six such expressions in the data (Example 3.4a), including the nonconsuming empty tag $\emptyset_{x3}$. Three of them, x_1, X_2, and x_5, each directly refer to a *discourse entity*, while the others, including the pronoun It$_{x6}$, refer to discourse entities by virtue of being linked to the three directly referring expressions. Note that X_2 is in uppercase, referring to a set associated with the plural noun *apples*.

Verbs such as *love, eat*, and *play* are treated of category *eventuality*. In annotation, they are simply represented as `<event/>` or `<EVENT/>` in XML.

SpatialML (MITRE, 2010), an annotation scheme for locations and spatial relations, again introduces a single category referring to locations.

Example 3.5 Category *location*
a. Data: They live in Paris, Texas.
b. Markables: They live in Paris$_{loc1}$, Texas$_{loc2}$.

SpatialML marks up all the names or nominal expressions such as *Paris* and *Texas* that refer to locations.

Categories, Types, and Elements
Categories, types, and *elements* all are inventory names for classification. In the use of the terms *category* and *type*, this book follows Montague (1974): The term *category* is used for doing syntax, while the term *type* is used for semantics. The term *element* is reserved for referring to basic constituents or tags in XML structures. Although it may be a bit confusing, the term *type* is also used very frequently as referring to the name of an attribute for the classification of feature structures or XML elements.

As syntactic categories are mapped to semantic types in Montague Semantics, base or elementary categories in $\mathcal{ASyn}$ are again mapped to types in the corresponding semantic representation scheme. Each of the base categories in C is thus mapped to a semantic type, either base or functional, in a corresponding semantics[7] and to an element in XML, as partially shown in Table 3.1.

---

[7] See Pustejovsky et al. (2019a) for the semantic types listed in Table 3.1.

Table 3.1 *Mapping from marakbles to base categories to XML elements to types*

Markables	Base categories	Elements in XML	Semantic types
Mia	entity	`<entity/>`	e, type of individual objects
stayed	eventuality	`<event/>`	$v \to t$, type of event descriptors
in	spatial relator	`<sRelator/>`	$r \to (r \to t)$, functional type of spatial relations
Jeju	place/region	`<place/>`	$r : p \to t$, functional type of regions
for a month	measure	`<measure/>`	m, type of measures
last year	time	`<time/>`	$I : i \to t$, functional type of time intervals

Pustejovsky et al. (2019a) introduce six basic types.

Specification 3.6   Basic semantic types
a. e, the type of individual objects
b. i, the type of time points
c. p, the type of spatial points
d. v, the type of eventualities
e. m, the type of measures
f. t, the type of truth values

Mia, stayed, and *(for) a month* are treated in Table 3.1 as being associated of the type e of objects, type $v \to t$ of event descriptors, and type m of measures, respectively.

Pustejovsky et al. (2019a) also introduce *type constructors* such as $\to$ to define *functional types*. The place *Jeju*, for instance, can be treated as being of the functional type $p \to t$, a set of spatial points or a *region r*. The spatial relator *in* is treated as being of a complex functional type $r \to (r \to t)$, which is interpreted as a relation between two regions. The time *last year* can be treated as a *time interval I*. It is another functional type $i \to t$, which stands for a set of time points. The type of eventuality descriptors is a functional type $v \to t$, abbreviated as V, while the type of eventuality itself is of type v.

Relational Categories of Link Structures

Relational categories R of link structures, simply called *link categories*, also form a very small set. A referential annotation scheme may just have one single link category that relates one entity to another.

Example 3.7 Link structures

a. Data: Mia bought pork and roasted it. It was delicious.
b. Markables: Mia$_{x1}$ bought pork$_{x2}$ and Ø$_{x3}$ roasted it$_{x4}$. It$_{x5}$ was delicious.
c. Links for referential relations:

```
<link id="rL1" category="referentialLink" object1="x1"
   object2="x3" objectalRelation="coreferential"/>
<link id="rL2" category="referentialLink" object1="x2"
   object2="x4,x5" objectalRelation="coreferential"/>
```

Here there are two chains, rL1 and rL2, of objectal identity, often called *coreference*: rL1 relates the discourse entity x_1 to the empty tag x_3 and the other chain (link) rL2 relates the discourse entity x_2 to the objects, referred to by the two pronominal expressions x_4 and x_5.

The annotation scheme of semantic roles such as ISO 24617-4 SemAF-SR (ISO, 2014a) usually has only one link type which relates each of the participants of an event to that event.

Example 3.8 Link groups

a. Word-segmented data: John$_{w1}$ teaches$_{w2}$ English$_{w3}$.
b. Base structures:

```
<baseStructure id="bs1" category="entity" markable="#w1"/>
<baseStructure id="bs2" category="event" markable="#w2"/>
<baseStructure id="bs3" category="entity" markable="#w3"/>
```

c. Group of link structures for semantic role labeling:

```
<linkGrp category="semanticRoleLabeling">
<link id="rL1" eventID="#bs2" participantsID="#bs1"
   semanticRole="agent"/>
<link id="rL2" eventID="#bs2" participantsID="#bs3"
   semanticRole="theme"/>
</linkGrp>
```

The hash sign #, which is prefixed to an identifier such as w1 or bs1, is an indicator that refers to the markable or some other element in preprocessed data. In Example 3.8c, the links are grouped together: John is annotated as having the role of being an *agent* of the event of teaching, while the role of English is treated as being the *theme* of the same event. The semantic role links each relate the event of teaching to one, named *John*, of its participants as its agent and English as a theme.

Dependency relations can be depicted by a *dependency tree* like that in Figure 3.5.

Assignment for Base Categories

For any base category c in C, every assignment function @$_c$ in @ introduces four required attributes into its domain.

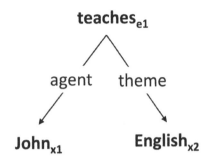

teaches_{e1}

agent   theme

John_{x1}   **English_{x2}**

Figure 3.5 Semantic role annotation

Specification 3.9   Required attributes of $@_c$
@category, @identifier, @target, @aContent.[8]

Their possible value ranges in the codomain are specified as follows.

Specification 3.10   Value ranges
a. the value of @category is c in C, identical to the given base category c,
b. the value of @identifier is any unique identifier,
c. the value of @target is a markable m in M,
d. the value of @aContent refers to annotation content.

Basically, the set C of base categories and the set M of markables constitute the codomain of assignment functions @ that specify a list of attribute-value specifications.

Specifications 3.9 and 3.10 can be formulated in ISO/IEC 14977 (eBNF) (ISO/IEC, 1996) as in Specification 3.11.

Specification 3.11   Attributes and value ranges specified by $@_c$
```
attributes = baseCategory, identifier, target, aContent;
baseCategory = c; (* c in C by default. *)
identifier = unique ID;
target = IDREF; (* refers to the ID of a markable in M. *)
aContent = IDREF; (* refers to the ID of annotation content. *)
```

Such a function $@_c$ may be called an *anchoring function*, forming the substructure $<i, m, a>$, called the *anchoring structure*, of a base structure β_c of base category c,[9] where i is the identifier, m the markable, and a the annotation

---

[8] Strictly speaking, the attribute @identifier is not part of $@_c$, for it has no semantic value other than the function of identifying an object.
[9] An anchoring structure may be called a *referring structure*.

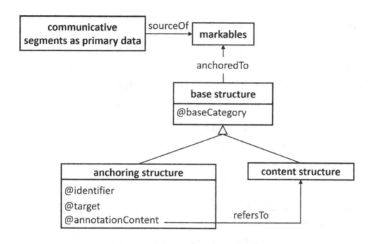

Figure 3.6 Anchoring base structures

information content of the base structure β_c. The markable m is the anchor, to which the base structure of category c is anchored.[10] By an appropriate anchoring function, each base structure is thus categorized, uniquely identified, and anchored to a markable in M, while carrying some information contained on the annotated markable. Anchoring structures themselves have no annotation content, but each of them can refer to an annotation content structure. Such relations are shown by Figure 3.6.

An anchoring structure for category *eventuality* in C can be represented in XML, as illustrated in Example 3.12.

Example 3.12   Anchoring structure of category *eventuality*
a. Data: John visited Seoul in 2010.
b. Word segmentation: John$_{w1}$ visited$_{w2}$ Seoul$_{w3}$ in$_{w4}$ 2010$_{w5}$.
c. Anchoring structure:
```
<anchoring category="event" xml:id="e1" target="#w2" a=""/>
OR <event xml:id="e1" target="#w2" a=""/>
```

The anchoring structure represented in XML, as in Example 3.12c, is understood as anchoring a base structure β_{event} of category event, identified as e1, to the markable *visited* (w2) that refers to an event of visiting. The attribute @a refers to the content structure of a base structure.

---

[10] This markable can be an empty string of characters or images.

There may be more than one markables of the same category in a dataset of D. Here is an example.

Example 3.13   Category *event*

a. Data: Mia flew to Jeju and then took a boat to Busan.

b. Markables: Mia flew$_{event}$ to Jeju and then took$_{event}$ a boat to Busan.

There are two markables, *flew* and *took a boat*, of the same base category *event*. Then there are two anchoring structures, each of which is anchored to a different markable. Each of them can be represented in XML, as shown in Example 3.14.

Example 3.14   Two anchoring structures

a. Word segmentation (id=`"Example3.13"`):
   Mia$_{w1}$ flew$_{w2}$ to Jeju and then {took a boat}$_{[w7,w9]}$ to Busan$_{w11}$.[11]

b. Anchoring structures:
```
<anchorGrp xml:id="anc1" category="event" target="#Example3.13">
  <anchor xml:id="e1" target="#w2" a=""/>
  <anchor xml:id="e2" target="#[w7,w9]" a=""/>
</anchorGrp>
```

Annotation Content   Anchoring structures are each associated with the other part of an annotation structure, called the *content structure*, that carries the information content of annotation. The event of flying mentioned in Example 3.14a is, for instance, understood to have occurred in the past because the markable *flew* is marked with the *past tense*, as is to be shown in Example 3.16.

The assignment function @$_c$ for category c is extended to specify the structure of annotation content. For the base category *eventuality*, the assignment function @$_{event}$ extends its domain as specified next.

Specification 3.15   Extended list of attributes for @$_{event}$
```
attributes = identifier, type, pred, tense, [aspect], [modality], [polarity],
    class]; (* Square-bracketed attributes are optional attributes, which may not
    need to be assigned a value. *)
identifier = "fe" followed by an integer;
type = state | process | transition;
pred = CDATA (character data); (* predicative content *)
tense = CDATA;
    (* closed set of symbols; for English, present|past|future|none *)
aspect = CDATA;
    (* closed set of symbols; for English, perfective|progressive *)
modality = CDATA; (* closed set of symbols *)
polarity = CDATA; (* positive | negative *)
class = CDATA; (* occurrence | state, etc. *)
```

---

[11] Here, [w7,w9] stands for a sequence of words from w7 to w9.

The attributes @identifier, @type, @pred, and @tense are required and the rest are optional.

With this extension, the base structure of a past-tensed verb $flew_{w2:e1, past}$ will be represented as follows.

Example 3.16   Base structure

```
<baseStructure xml:id="bs1" category="event" target="flew_past">
<!-- Anchoring Structure -->
   <anchor xml:id="e1" target="#w2" a="#fs1">
<!-- Content Structure -->
   <fs xml:id="fs1" type="process">
    <f name="pred"><string value="fly"/>
    <f name="tense"><symbol value="past"/>
    <f name="class"><symbol value="occurrence"/>
   </fs>
</baseStructure>
```

The content structure is represented as a typed feature structure `<fs xml:id="fs1" type="process">` with a list of three attribute-value specifications. It is then linked to the anchoring structure for the event `"e1"`.

Collapsing Content Structures to Anchoring Structures As in ISO-TimeML (ISO, 2012b) and ISO-Space (ISO, 2014b), the two substructures of a base structure are collapsed into one. In the process of such a collapse, the tag name `anchor` is replaced by the name of the base category. Example 3.16 can be represented as follows.

Example 3.17   `<event xml:id="e1" target="#w2"`
`type="process" pred="fly" tense="past" class="occurrence"/>`

Assignment for Link Categories

For each relational (link) category r in R, the assignment function $@_r$ forms a link structure λ_r of category r. It specifies how one base structure is related to one or more other base structures while specifying what type of relation it is. Each link structure λ_r of category r in R, formally defined by such an assignment over R and base structures, is thus of the form, as proposed by Bunt et al. (2016).

Specification 3.18   Link structure: $<\beta, B, \rho>$,
```
where β is a base structure,
B is a set of base structures,
and ρ is a relation between β and B.
```

By adding four more attributes, `linkCategory`, @identifier, @type, and @trigger, the general structure of links is formulated in more specific terms (see Figure 3.7).

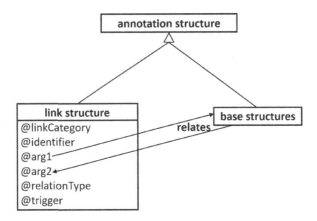

Figure 3.7 Link structure

The link structure, which is depicted by Figure 3.7, is reformulated in Specification 3.19.

Specification 3.19   General structure of links

For any link category r in R, every link structure associated with assignment $@_r$ is of the form, *Link structure* $= <r, i, \beta, B, \rho, O>$, where

r is its link category,

i is its identifier,

β is a base structure,

B is a set of base structures,

ρ is a relation between β and B, and

O is a set of optional attributes such as `@trigger` or `@scopes`.

For a link category r, the assignment function $@_r$ allows a number of optional attributes such as `@trigger` that specifies the type ρ of a relation for a link. The inclusion of these optional attributes in the extended domain of @ makes it a partial function with some of its arguments (attributes) not being provided with a value. The optional attribute `@scopes` determines the scope of quantifiers or logical operators.

Here is a list of attributes licensed by $@_r$, as represented in Extended Backus–Naur Form (eBNF).

Specification 3.20   List of attributes for $@_r$ for every link category r

```
attributes = [identifier], argument₁, argument₂, relation, [trigger];
identifier = "xL" followed by an integer;
    (* x is replaced by a prefix representing the category of each
    link. For example, "sr" is the prefix for the semantic
    role link. *)
```

```
argument₁ = IDREF; (* refers to the ID of a base structure. *)
argument₂ = IDREFS; (* refers to a set of IDs of base structures. *)
relation = CDATA;
  (* type of a relation between argument₁ and argument₂ *)
trigger = CDATA; (* an optional attribute that triggers the link,
  while determining the type of its relation *)
```

The identifier carries no semantic content but is used as a pointer for doing compositional semantics.

In a concrete syntax, this list is made more specific for each link category: $argument_1$ and $argument_2$ are given more specific names, and the values of `relation` are specified more explicitly. A link for semantic role annotation, for instance, the attribute @$argument_1$ may be renamed @event, the attribute @$argument_2$ @participants and the attribute @relation @semRole. The values of @relation are also made explicit, listing semantic role names such as *agent, theme, goal,* and *purpose*. Here is an example of semantic role labeling (srLINK).

Example 3.21 Semantic role labeling
a. Word-segmented data: Mia$_{w1}$ sang$_{w2}$ for$_{w3}$ a musical$_{w5}$.
b. Base structures β:
```
<ENTITY xml:id="x1" target="#w1" type="person" name="Mia"/>¹²
<EVENT xml:id="e1" target="#w2" type="process" pred="sing"
  tense="past"/>
<RELATOR xml:id="r1" target="#w3" type="purpose"/>
<EVENT xml:id="e2" target="#w5" type="process" pred="musical"/>
```
c. Link structures λ_{srL} for semantic role labeling:
```
<srLINK xml:id="srL1" event="#e1" participants="#x1"
  semRole="agent"/>
<srLINK xml:id="srL2" event="#e1" participants="#x2"
  semRole="purpose" trigger="#r1"/>
```

In Example 3.21b, the first semantic role link λ_{srL_1} relates the base structure $\beta_{event:e_1}$, which annotates the event of singing, to the base structure $\beta_{entity:x1}$, which annotates *Mia* as the *agent* of the event. Likewise, the second semantic role link λ_{srL_2} relates the same base structure $\beta_{event:e_1}$ but to the base structure $\beta_{entity:x2}$, which annotates *musical* as the *purpose* of the event.

There can be *plural agents*. Consider Example 3.22, as follows.

Example 3.22 Semantic role labeling of plural agents
a. Word-segmented data:
Mia$_{w1}$ and Kim$_{w3}$ traveled$_{w4}$ to$_{w5}$ Jeju-do$_{w6}$ for$_{w7}$ a workshop$_{w9}$.

---

[12] By the TEI convention, the prefix # to an ID indicates that the ID, which is marked with #, refers to the ID in word-segmented data, as is the case here, or some other annotation structure.

b. Base structures β:

```
<ENTITY xml:id="x1" target="#w1" type="person" name="Mia"/>
<ENTITY xml:id="x2" target="#w3" type="person" name="Kim"/>
<EVENT xml:id="e1" target="#w4" type="transition" pred="travel"
  tense="past"/>
<RELATOR xml:id="r1" target="#w5" type="goal"/>
<PLACE xml:id="pl1" target="#w6" type="island" name="Jeju-do"/>
<RELATOR xml:id="r2" target="#w7" type="purpose"/>
<EVENT xml:id="e2" target="#w9" type="process" pred="workshop"/>
```

c. Link structures λ_{srL} for semantic role labeling:

```
<srLINK xml:id="srL1" event="#e1" participants="#x1,#x2"
  semRole="agent"/>
<srLINK xml:id="srL2" event="#e1" participants="#pl1"
  semRole="goal" trigger="#r1"/>
<srLINK xml:id="srL3" event="#e1" participants="#x2"
  semRole="purpose" trigger="#r2"/>
```

The semantic role link λ_{srL1} marks *Mia and Kim* as the agents of the event of traveling to Jeju-do: They are understood as taking a trip together. Example 3.22 shows three cases of semantic role labeling by the semantic role link λ_{srL}: Each of them is related to the event of *travel*.

3.4 Generation of Annotation Structures

The abstract syntax $\mathcal{A}Syn$ generates annotation structures, just as grammars generate phrasal (parse) trees. By the term *generation* it is meant that the well-formedness of annotation structures is formally defined. The conditions of well-formedness are expressed by eBNF on the set of assignment functions $@_c$ for each base category c in C or assignment functions $@_r$ for each link category r in R. In an XML-based concrete syntax, the statements in eBNF are expressed by DTD (Data Type Declaration) or other means of constraining the generation of annotation structures.

An annotation structure consists of two substructures: *base structures* and *link structures* (see Figure 3.7). Each base structure then consists of an *anchoring structure* and a *content structure* (see Figure 3.6).

3.4.1 Generating Base Structures

Base structures are generated by assignment functions @ over $<M, C>$, a substructure of $\mathcal{A}Syn$, where M is a set of markables, and C a set of categories of base structures. For each base category c in C, an assignment function $@_c$ in @ anchors a base structure to a markable in M and then provides it with annotation content, thereby generating a base structure. The domain of $@_c$ is a set characterized by the tuple $<c, i, m, a>$ and its codomain consists of M and C plus the set of possible values of i for @identifier, while a refers to a content structure. The *content structure* referred to by a is represented by a *typed feature structure* with its attributes listed in the extended domain of $@_c$.

The condition of well-formedness for base structures is declared as follows.

Definition 3.23 Condition of well-formedness
Given a base category c in C, a base structure β_c of category c is well-formed if it conforms to the (extended) specification of $@_c$.

This condition requires every well-formed base structure to be of category c in a well-defined set C of base categories, have a unique identifier (ID), and be anchored to a markable m in M with annotation content provided by the extended attribute-value specification.

For illustration, consider a base structure of base category *place* for spatial annotation for Data, as given in Example 3.24.

Example 3.24 Base category *place*
a. Data: Mia$_{w1}$ flew to Jeju$_{w4}$ and then to Fukuoka$_{w8}$.
b. Markables: {Jeju$_{w4}$, Fukuoka$_{w8}$}
c. Well-formed base structure, represented in XML:
```
<baseStructure category="place">
<anchoring xml:id="pl1" target="#w4" aContent="#fs1"/>
<fs xml:id="fs1" type="place">
    <f name="administrativeType">
      <string value="province"/>
    </f>
    <f name="geographicalType">
      <string value="island"/>
    </f>
    <f name="country">
      <symbol="KOR"/>
    </f>
    <!-- follows ISO 3166-1 Aalpha-3 (3-character) codes
    on country names -->
  </fs>
</baseStructure>
```

To generate the base structure $\beta_{place:pl1}$, the assignment function $@_{place}$ for anchoring and its extended function for annotation content should be properly formulated. The two particular attributes, @administrativeType and @geographicalType, need to be included in the extended domain of $@_{place}$.

Specification 3.25　Extended domain of @ *place*

```
attributes = identifier, type, form, populated,
   [administrativeType], [geographicalType], country;
identifier = "pl" followed by an integer;
type = "place"; (* inherited from the anchoring structure *)
form = "nam" | "nnoml";
populated = "yes | no ";
administrativeType = CDATA (character data) 13;
   (* "province" or "state", "city", "capital", "county",...*)
geographicalType = CDATA;
   (* mountain, mountains, river, harbor, island, lake,...*)
country = CDATA;
   (* follows ISO 3166-1 alpha-3 (3-character) codes on
     country names *)
```

With such an extension, the feature structure fs2 is also treated as a well-formed base structure β_{place}.

Example 3.26　Base structure, represented as a feature structure in XML

```
<baseStructure category="place">
  <anchor xml:id="pl2" target="#w8" a="#fs2"/>
  <fs xml:id="fs2" type="place">
   <f name="form">
    <symbol value="nam"/>
   </f>
   <f name="populated"><boolean value="yes"/>
   </f>
   <f name="administrativeType"><string value="city"/>
   </f>
   <f name="geographicalType"><string value="harbor"/>
   </f>
   <f name="country"><symbol="JPN"/>
   </f>
  </fs>
</baseStructure>
```

The feature structure carries annotation content. Forming its own content structure, it is not embedded in the anchoring structure, although it is part of the base structure, categorized as place, thus being embedded in it.

The *feature structures* are also typed, being constrained by some *type inheritance hierarchy*, the notion of which originates from the constructional view of Sag (2012) on grammar. The attribute @populated, @administrative Type, and @geographicalType, for instance, are all subtypes of place, forming parts of a type hierarchy. The well-formedness of feature structures is also determined by such a type inheritance hierarchy.[14]

---

[13] CDATA means data consisting of strings of characters.
[14] See Sag (2012), section 4 "Well-Formed Feature Structures".

Complex Base Structures

Some base structures refer to other base structures by allowing some of their attributes to take other base structures as values. These structures make the generation of base structures recursively defined. We call such base structures *complex base structure* (see Lee (2016)).

Definition 3.27 Complex base structure

A base structure β_c of base category c is *complex* if at least one of its associated attributes in the annotation (`@aContent`) refers to another base structure $\beta_{c'}$ as value.

Unlike base structures β_{place} of category *place* (e.g., locations referred to by *Busan, Korea* or *city*), base structures β_{path} of category *path* each have a start, an endpoint, and some midpoints, all of which are also base structures of category *place*, although these points may not be explicitly mentioned. The Massachusetts Turnpike, for example, is known to stretch 138 miles from I 90/ Berkshire Connector (West Stockbridge), Canaan, NY, to Route 1A next to Logan International Airport, downtown Boston, with several exits to major cities such as Springfield, Worcester, and Boston. The base structure β_{path} of base category *path* here is treated as a *complex base structure* because its attributes such as endpoints and midpoints refer to all or some of these base structures of category *place* as values.

Consider Example 3.28.

Example 3.28 Word-segmented text

a. `<text id="t1">We drove to Boston.</text>`
b. `<wordSeg id="ws1" target="#t1">`
    We$_{w1}$ drove$_{w2}$ to$_{w3}$ Boston$_{w4}$.
   `</wordSeg>`

Based on the word-segmented text, we can now annotate the input data. Here is a part of the annotation that represents a complex base structure.

Example 3.29 Complex base structure

a. Identifying markables:

We$_{x1}$ drove$_{m1}$ Ø$_{ep1}$ to Boston$_{pl1}$.

b. Event-path as a complex base structure:
```
<baseStructure category="path">
  <anchor xml:id="ep1" target="" a="#fs2"/>
  <fs xml:id="fs2" type="dynamic">
  <f name="trigger"><string value="#m1"/></f>
  <f name="start"><string value="unknown"/></f>
  <f name="end"><string value="#pl1"/></f>
  </fs>
  <baseStructure/>
```

The type `dynamic` of the content structure, as represented by the feature structure (`<fs xml:id="fs2">`), characterizes category *path* of the base structure as being `dynamic`. It is triggered by the motion *drove$_{m1}$*. As a path, this event-path has a start and an end: The start point is unknown, while its endpoint is identified as *Boston$_{pl1}$*. The base structure of category *path* is thus a complex base structure.

3.4.2 Generating Link Structures

Just like base structures, link structures are well-formed if they conform to the general link structure $<r, i, \beta, B, \rho, O>$, as specified earlier in Specification 3.19. Here, r is a link category, i is an identifier, β is a base structure, B is a set of base structures, ρ is a relation type between β and B, and O is a set of optional attributes.

For illustration, consider Example 3.30.

Example 3.30   Link group
a. Mia and Kim traveled to Jeju for a workshop.
b. Base annotation:[15]
   Mia$_{x3}$ and Kim$_{x4}$ traveled$_{e2}$ to Jeju$_{pl1}$ for$_{s2}$ a workshop$_{x5}$.
c. Link group:
```
<linkGrp xml:id="L2" category="semanticRoleLink" target="#3.30b">
  <link xml:id="L21" event="#e2" participants="{#x3,#x4}"
  relType="agent"/>
  <link xml:id="L22" event="#e2" participants="#pl1"
  relType="goal"/>
    <!-- "pl" stands for place. -->
  <link xml:id="L23" event="#e2" participants="#x5"
  relType="purpose" trigger="#s2"/>
</linkGrP>
```

In Example 3.30c, all of the link structures are grouped together under the tag `<linkGrp/>` and each of them conforms to the general link structure. Hence, they are well-formed.

For another illustration, consider the qualitative spatial link λ_{qsLink} in ISO-Space (ISO, 2014b). The following link structure is considered well-formed if *bench, tree*, and *rock* are treated as spatial entities and *between* as a relation type by @$_{qsLink}$.

---

[15] Base annotation annotates each markable with its categorized identifier inline. Each markable may also be identified with its word-segmentation identifier.

Example 3.31 Qualitative spatial link

a. Data: Mia sat on a bench between a tree and a big rock.
b. Word-segmentation:
   Mia_{w1} sat on a $bench_{w5}$ $between_{w6}$ a $tree_{w8}$ and a big $rock_{w12}$.
c. Base annotation:
   $Mia_{x1:w1}$ sat on a $bench_{x2:w5}$ $between_{s1:w6}$ a $tree_{x3:w8}$ and a big $rock_{x4:w12}$.
d. Group annotation:
```
<baseStructureGrp category="spatial" >
<entity xml:id="x1" target="#w1" aContent="#fs1"/>
<entity xml:id="x2" target="#w5" aContent="#fs2"/>
<entity xml:id="x3" target="#w8" aContent="#fs3"/>
<entity xml:id="x4" target="#w12" aContent="#fs4"/>
<signal xml:id="s1" target="#w6"/>
</baseStructureGrp>
```
e. Link:
```
<link xml:id="qsL1" category="qualitativeSpatial"
  figure="#x2" ground="#x3,#x4" relation="between" trigger="#s1"/>
```

Base annotation marks up the categorized identifier of each markable and the segmentation identifier: e.g, $markable_{x1,w1}$. Each of the content structures, identified as `"fs1"`, `"fs2"`, `"fs3"`, and `"fs4"`, inherits the type *spatial* from the embedding element `<baseStructureGrp category= "spatial">`. It should also make the associated link structure λ_{qsLink} in Example 3.31 fully defined. This is done by annotating the three markables, *bench*, *tree*, and *rock*. The link structure example 3.31e conforms to the general link structure and is thus well-formed.

3.5 Summary

This chapter defined an abstract syntax $\mathcal{ASyn}$ for a semantic annotation scheme and related structures in algebraic terms, as summarized next.

Specification 3.32 An abstract syntax $\mathcal{ASyn}$ for a semantic annotation scheme is modeled as a tuple $<M, C, R, @>$, where

- M, a set of markables,
- C, a set of base categories,
- R, a set of link categories,
- $@$, a set of assignment functions for attribute-value specifications for annotation structures.

Specification 3.33 $\mathcal{ASyn}$ formally defines annotation structures, consisting of the following.

- Base structures β_c of category c in C with two substructures:
  (a) anchoring structures and (b) content structures.
- Link structures λ_r of category r in R.

Specification 3.34   Every base structure is of the form $<i, m, a>$ such that each assignment function $@_c$ of base category c maps:

- i to a unique identifier for an anchoring structure,
- m to a markable in M to which an associated entity structure is anchored,
- a to a content structure represented in a feature structure.

The anchoring function $@_c$ that maps a markable to a base structure is extended to specify possible attribute-value mappings for content structures.

Specification 3.35   Every link structure λ_r of category r in R is of the form $<i, \beta, B, \rho, O>$:

- i is an identifier,
- β is a base structure,
- B is a set of base structures,
- ρ is the type of a relation between β and B, and
- O is a set of optional attributes such as @trigger.

The identifier carries no semantic content, but it is necessary for referring to a link structure in the application of merge operators in compositional semantics.

The well-formedness of annotation structures is decided on by the specification of assignment functions @. An annotation structure is well-formed if its base structures and link structures are well-formed, with each of them conforming to the attribute-value assignment of $@_c$ for each base category c in the set C of base categories or for each link category r in the set R of link categories.

4

Representation and Serialization

4.1 Overview

This chapter introduces a concrete syntax. It is ideally isomorphic to an abstract syntax for a semantic annotation scheme while providing a *format* for representing annotation structures. This format can represent them either in a serialized way just like most written ordinary languages from left to right or in graphic images or tabular forms with linking arrows. Human readers may prefer the latter way, especially for illustrations or demonstrations or even for the evaluation of proposed annotation schemes. For the purposes of merging, comparing, or exchanging various types of annotations or different annotations of the same type, graphs are considered useful. ISO 24612 LAF (ISO, 2012a) thus introduces a graphic annotation format, called GrAF (Graphic Annotation Format), for linguistic annotation (see Ide et al. (2012)).

For the construction of larger corpora, however, there are practical computing reasons to prefer a serialization of annotations. One simple reason is that, unlike serialization formats, graphic or tabular formats take up too much space and memory. Another reason is that, unlike drawing graphs or formulating tables, serialization means typing in character data (DATA), thereby producing a text with strings of characters with blank spaces or line breaks which provide the text with some structural shapes and arrangements.

For the serialized representation of annotation structures, this chapter mainly discusses two formats: (i) XML (eXtensible Markup Language) and (ii) pFormat, which is a predicate-logic-like representation format. The main reason for discussing XML first is that it is best accepted by most academic research circles and language technology industries. XML was developed by W3C from an ISO standard on SGML (Standard Generalized Markup

Language) for the representation of data structures. Both the British National Corpus (BNC) and the American National Corpus (ANC) are annotated in XML. The Text Encoding Initiative Consortium (TEI) Guidelines are also based on XML. For instance, most, if not all, of the ISO standards on language resource management that include ISO-TimeML (ISO, 2012b) and ISO-Space (ISO, 2014b) use XML as the primary representation format. GrAF also serializes annotation graphs with XML, while stating annotation structures in terms of graph-theoretic terms such as *node* and *edge*.

In this book, however, I adopt the predicate-logic-like format, or *pFormat* for short, as the primary representation format. Unlike XML, pFormat has no embedded structures. The pFormat is simple with flat linear structures only, easy to read, and light-loaded without carrying any semantically superfluous or irrelevant information or metadata information on datasets.

This chapter first introduces three different ways of annotating text: *inline, standoff*, and *hybrid*, in Section 4.2. Second, it discusses two basic requirements on the representation of annotations in Section 4.3, while introducing *typed feature structures* for the representation of annotation content. Third, it introduces GrAF in Section 4.4. Finally, the pFormat is introduced in detail with illustrations in Section 4.5.

4.2 Representation Formats

4.2.1 Overview

Annotation conveys metadata information such as morpho-syntactic information through POS-tagging. A concrete syntax provides a format representing annotation structures. For the abstract syntax of a semantic annotation scheme, there can be several ideally equivalent concrete syntaxes isomorphic to, or structurally resembling, it. The list of attributes specified by the *at* sign @ remains the same for any concrete syntaxes based on an identical abstract syntax. Nevertheless, their values may be given in a more specific way. A *representation format* provided by one concrete syntax may slightly differ from a representation format provided by another concrete syntax at the level of granularity or descriptive power involving optional attributes. Otherwise, any format can be adopted for the representation of annotation structures. The same sort and amount of information can be conveyed, for instance, in graphic or tabular forms to make annotations easily readable or it can be serialized, or presented linearly, into text for easier processing through the computer. Even among serialized or tabular formats, there are at least three different ways of annotating text: *inline, standoff*, and *mixed* or *hybrid*.

4.2.2 Inline Annotation

Inline annotation is very common and simple. It marks up text directly, adding annotations embedded in the text. Example 4.1 is a simple case.

Example 4.1   Inline annotation

a. Dataset:
```
<data xml:id="d1" mediaType="text" lang="en">
The gangsters were all caught by the police who broke into a bank.
</data>
```
b. Tokenization:
```
<tokens xml:id="td1" type="token" target="#d1">
The_t1 gangsters_t2 were_t3 all_t4 caught_t5 by_t6 the_t7
police_t8 who_t9 broke_t10 into_t11 a_t12 bank_t13._t14
</tokens>
```

Tokenization (Example 4.1b) can be converted to XML and it is still inline.

Example 4.2   Inline in XML
```
<tokens xml:id="td1" type="token" target="#d1">
  <token xml:id="t1"> The </token>
  <token xml:id="t2"> gangsters </token>
  <token xml:id="t3"> were </token>
  <token xml:id="t4"> all </token>
  <token xml:id="t5"> caught </token>
  <token xml:id="t6"> by </token>
  <token xml:id="t7"> the </token>
  <token xml:id="t8"> police </token>
  <token xml:id="t9"> who </token>
  <token xml:id="t10"> broke </token>
  <token xml:id="t11"> into </token>
  <token xml:id="t12"> a </token>
  <token xml:id="t13"> bank </token>
  <token xml:id="t14"> . </token>
</tokens>
```

Here is another example.

Example 4.3   Mia$_{NP0}$'s$_{VDZ}$ looked$_{VVN}$ me$_{PNP}$ up$_{AVP}$.$_{PUN}$

This is equivalent to the following representation in XML.

Example 4.4   Tagging with C5
```
<w C5="NP0">Mia</w>
<w C5="VDZ">'s</w>
<w C5="VVN">looked</w>
<w C5="PNP">me</w>
<w C5="AVP">up</w>
<w C5="PUN">.</w>
```

BNC adopts an inline format, as illustrated below.

Example 4.5 Inline annotation of BNC dialogue F78.XML

```
<stext type="OTHERSP">
  <u who="PS1L6">
    <s n="1">
      <vocal desc="sigh" />
      <w c5="AV0" hw="well" pos="ADV">Well</w>
      <c c5="PUN">,</c>
      <w c5="PNP" hw="we" pos="PRON">we</w>
      <w c5="VBB" hw="be" pos="VERB">'re</w>
      <w c5="AJ0" hw="keen" pos="ADJ">keen</w>
      <w c5="TO0" hw="to" pos="PREP">to</w>
      <w c5="VVI" hw="get" pos="VERB">get</w>
      <w c5="AV0" hw="here" pos="ADV">here</w>
      <c c5="PUN">,</c>
      <w c5="VBB" hw="be" pos="VERB">are</w>
      <w c5="XX0" hw="not" pos="ADV">n't</w>
      <w c5="PNP" hw="we" pos="PRON">we</w>
      <c c5="PUN">?</c>
    </s>
    <s n="2">
      <pause />
      <w c5="PNP" hw="we" pos="PRON">We</w>
      <w c5="VBB" hw="be" pos="VERB">'re</w>
      <w c5="PRP" hw="in" pos="PREP">in</w>
      <w c5="AT0" hw="the" pos="ART">the</w>
      <w c5="AJ0" hw="right" pos="ADJ">right</w>
      <w c5="NN1-VVB" hw="place" pos="SUBST">place</w>
      <c c5="PUN">,</c>
      <w c5="PNP" hw="i" pos="PRON">I</w>
      <w c5="VVB" hw="suppose" pos="VERB">suppose</w>
      <c c5="PUN">.</c>
      <pause />
      <unclear />
    </s>
  </u>
  ....
</stext>
```

Table 4.1 shows how the vertical or column format is used in segmenting word-phrases, called *eojeol*, which is also inline.[1]

This is a sample of the Sejong Corpus, sometimes known as *Korean National Corpus* (KNC). The first column provides an ID for each of the word segments, the second column lists each of the word segments on each row,[2] and the third column marks up each morpheme with a morpho-syntactic tag. Note that, in Korean, words are segmented into morphemes for tagging. The use of the *vertical format* is very common, especially for parallel concordances or occurrences checking.

---

[1] This is a manually formulated table by the author, based on Kim (2006), Figure 4.
[2] Punctuation marks like "." are not separated from the words preceding them. Not separating punctuations marks from the word segments preceding them makes it easier to segment tokens or words by allowing them to be segmented on the basis of the presence of whitespace.

Table 4.1 *Sample of the Sejong corpus in a vertical format*

그가 권하는 대로 나는 그들과 함께 밥을 먹었다. As he advised, I dined with them.		
8BT_051_18516100	그가	그/NP+가/JKS
8BT_051_18516110	권하는	권/NNG + 하/XSV + 는/ETM
8BT_051_18516120	대로	대로 /NNB
8BT_051_18516130	나는	나/NP + 는/JX
8BT_051_18516140	그들과	그/NP + 들/XSN + 과/JKB
8BT_051_18516150	함께	함께/MAG
8BT_051_18516160	밥을	밥/NNG + 을/JKO
8BT_051_18516170	먹었다.	먹/VV +었/EP + 다/EH + ./SF

The Stuttgart vertical format, known as *WPL* (word per line), is also well-known. Here is an example.

Example 4.6 Stuttgart vertical format

a. Data: 20 years ago, I visited Stuttgart.
b. Annotation:
```
20
years
ago
<g/>
,
I
visited
Stuttgart
<g/>
.
```

The *glue* tag <g/> is inserted before each punctuation mark to indicate the absence of whitespace before it.

One advantage of this format is that it is easy to add columns to provide other sorts of information associated with each word such as morpho-syntactic information or even to compare its equivalent expression in a language like Korean, as shown in Table 4.2.

The vertical format may be considered a variation of the tabular format. It is very easy to add rows or columns to add more information. Table 4.2 shows how the two columns are added for the Korean translation.

4.2.3 Standoff Annotation

Standoff annotation keeps raw data intact without changing the original (textual) format. It refers to the base segmentation of datasets, whether textual

Table 4.2 *Translation from English to Korean*

Example 4.6 20 years ago, I visited Stuttgart. 20년 전, 나는 방문하였다 스투트가르트를.

words	Penn Tags	Korean	Comments
20	CD	20	
		\<g/\>	
years	NNS	년	
ago	RB	전	
\<g/\>		\<g/\>	
,	,	,	
I	PRP	나는	나-는_subj
visited	VVD	방문하였다	
Stuttgart	NNP	스투트가르트를	스투트가르트-를_obj
\<g/\>		\<g/\>	
.	.	.	

or not, to identify each markable by specifying the range of its anchor. Consider Example 4.7.

Example 4.7   Standoff annotation

a. ```
<data xml:id="d6" mediaType="text" lang="en">
   20 years ago, I visited Stuttgart.
</data>
```

b. Base segmentation:

```
2 0   y e a r s   a g o ,   I   v i s i t e d   S t u t t g a r t .
0 1 2 3 4 5 6 7 8 9 0 1 2 3 4 5 6 7 8 9 0 1 2 3 4 5 6 7 8 9 0 1 2 3 4
                  1                   2                   3
```

It is assumed that the base segmentation of text is automatically carried out. Then the POS-tagging of the text is represented standoff in XML as follows.

Example 4.8   POS-tagging standoff

```
<spanGrp xml:id="" type="word" annotationScheme="Penn Tags">

</spanGrp>
```
```

While BNC follows the inline format, ANC adopts the standoff format for annotation. Here is an example.[3]

Example 4.9   Standoff annotation of ANC 'AdamsElissa.txt'
All right, this is Elissa Adams and Elissa,
you've lived in Charlotte for–

Noun chunks annotated: 'AdamsEliss-np.xml'
```
<?xml version="1.0" encoding="UTF-8" ?>
<cesAna xmlns="http://www.xces.org/schema/2003"
version="1.0.4">
  <struct type="NounChunk" from="25" to="34" />
  <!-- Elissa? -->
  <struct type="NounChunk" from="36" to="40" />
  <!-- Adams? -->
  <struct type="NounChunk" from="44" to="67" />
  <!-- Elissa? -->
  <struct type="NounChunk" from="69" to="72" />
  <!-- you -->
  <struct type="NounChunk" from="85" to="100" />
  <!-- Charlotte for -->
  ...
</cesAna>
```

VP annotated: 'AdamsElissa-vp.xml'
```
<?xml version="1.0" encoding="UTF-8" ?>
<cesAna xmlns="http://www.xces.org/schema/2003"
version="1.0.4">
  <struct type="VG" from="41" to="43">
    <feat name="voice" value="active" />
    <feat name="tense" value="SimPre" />
    <feat name="type" value="FVG" />
  </struct>
  <struct type="VG" from="72" to="75">
    <feat name="voice" value="active" />
    <feat name="tense" value="SimPre" />
    <feat name="type" value="FVG" />
  </struct>
  ...
</cesAna>
```

4.2.4 Mixed or Hybrid Format

The format, called *vertical*, *column*, or *tabular format*, is a hybrid format, mixed with inline and standoff ways of representing linguistic annotations. The CoNLL-U format[4] offers the most developed or well-defined format

---

[3] The attribute @anchor that specifies the boundary of a markable may be replaced by two attributes @from for the start of a boundary and @to for its end.

[4] CoNLL stands for *Conference on Natural Language Learning*.

Table 4.3 *Illustration 1 of the CoNLL-U format*

lang="es": vámonos al mar. (Let's go to the sea.)			
1-2	vámonos	_	_
1	vamos	ir	VERB
2	nos	nosotros	PRON
3-4	al	_	_
3	a	a	ADP
4	el	el	DET
5	mar	mar	NOUN
6	.	.	PUNCT

Table 4.4 *Illustration 2 of the CoNLL-U format*

ID	FORM	LEMMA	UPOS	FEATs[a]
1	Mia	Mia	PROPN	
2	loves	love	VERB	Tense=Pres | Number=Sing | Person=3
3	bananas	banana	NOUN	Number=Plur
4	and	and	CCONJ	
5	I	I	I	Case=Nom | Number=Sing | Person=1
5.1		love	VERB	Tense=Pres
6	apples	apple	NOUN	Number=Plur
7	.	.	PUNCT	

[a] FEATs is for morphological features.

for a shared task on multilingual parsing or linguistic annotation in general (see Buchholz and Marsi (2006)). It is a hybrid standoff format.[5] Table 4.3 illustrates the hybrid standoff format of CoNLL-U.

The ID (1-2) in Table 4.3 shows how the token *vámonos* is composed of two words *vamos* and *nos*, while the ID (3-4) shows how the token *al* is composed of *a* and *el*. It is hard to specify their parts of speech because they are each composed of two different parts of speech.

With CoNLL-U,[6] one can do all kinds of linguistic annotation from tokenization to syntactic parsing. The first column is for IDs, the second column for FORM, the third column is for LEMMA, the fourth column is for

---

[5] See Ide et al. (2017), section 3.2.4.
[6] See https://universaldependencies.org/format.html, the CoNLL-U Format UD version 2.

UPOS (Universal POS-tags), the fifth column is for XPOS (language-specific POS-tags if there are any), the sixth column is for FEATS (list of morphologic features), and so on. CoNLL-U also allows the marking of empty nodes or tags with the use of decimal points. Table 4.4 presents another illustration of the CoNLL-U format.

Row 5.1 introduces an empty node. Furthermore, Table 4.4 shows how morphological information is added with FEATs. It is also possible to add more columns for syntactic information related to heads and dependency relations.

4.3 Requirements for Representing Annotation Structures

4.3.1 Two Requirements for Linguistic Annotation

There are two basic ISO requirements for the representation of annotation structures.

Specification 4.10 Two requirements
a. Standoff annotation
b. Separation of annotation content from anchoring structures

Standoff vs. Inline Annotation

Standoff annotation is an annotation format required by the ISO standard ISO 24612 LAF (ISO, 2012a). It is adopted by ANC or the Open American National Corpus (OANC) and also by the ISO 24617 series of international standards on semantic annotation. Unlike the original version of TimeML, ISO-TimeML (ISO, 2012b) adopts the standoff annotation format. Likewise, ISO-Space (ISO, 2014b) also follows it in contrast to MITRE's SpatialML (MITRE, 2010) that annotates text inline.

Here is a comparison between the inline annotation of TimeML and the standoff annotation of ISO-TimeML.[7]

Example 4.11 Comparison
a. Data:
Mia lived in Busan last year.
b. TimeML:
```
Mia <EVENT xml:id="e1" tense="PAST"> lived </EVENT> in Busan
<TimeX3 xml:id="tx1" type="DATE" value="2018"> last year </TimeX3>.
```

---

[7] ISO-TimeML requires a preprocessing step of word segmentation as in Example 4.11c (i).

c. ISO-TimeML:

(i) Preprocessing of word segmentation (inline):

```
<seg xml:id="stx2" type="wordSeg" target="#tx2">
Mia lived_{w2} in Busan last_{w5} year_{w6}.
</seg>
```

(ii) Standoff annotation:

```
<isoTimeML xml:id="it1" target="#stx2">
  <event xml:id="e1" target="#w2" pred="live" tense="past"/>
  <TimeX3 xml:id="t1" target="#w5,#w6" type="date" value="2018"/>
</isoTimeML>
```

Below is an example that compares ISO-Space with SpatialML, which adopts the inline format. Given the same data as in Example 4.11, SpatialML has only one markable, as annotated inline, as follows.

Example 4.12 SpatialML

```
Mia lived in <PLACE id="pl" type="PPL" ctv="city"
country="KR"> Busan </PLACE> last year.
```

In contrast, ISO-Space annotates standoff the same markable plus another markable referring to the event of living.

Example 4.13 ISO-Space

a. Word segmentation:

```
Mia lived_{w2} in Busan_{w4} last_{w5} year_{w6}.
```

b. Standoff annotation:

```
<isoSpace xm:id="is1" target="#Example 4.13a">
  <event xml:id="e1" target="#w2" pred="live" tense="past"/>
  <place xml:id="pl1" target="#w4" type="PPL" ctv="city" country="KR"/>
</isoSpace>
```

Justification of Standoff Annotation Here is one particular reason why standoff annotation is preferred to inline annotation. Inline annotation has difficulty marking up some noncontiguous elements as single information units. Consider the following examples.

Example 4.14 Noncontiguous complex words

a.
```
<data xml:id="tx1" mediaType="text">
"Look me up," said John.
</data>
```

b.
```
<data xml:id="tx2" mediaType="text">
Fan bloody tastic.
</data>
```

Suppose we want to treat two tokens *look* and *up* in Example 4.14a as a single compound verb. This then could not be annotated as such by inline annotation. In standoff annotation, on the other hand, these two can be linked together by assigning a sequence of two anchoring values, namely `tok2` and `tok4`, that are not contiguous.

Example 4.15 Annotation of *Look me up*

```
<spanGrp xml:id="tokens2" type="tokens" target="#Example 4.14a">
  <span xml:id="tok1" from="0" to="1"><!-- " --></span>
  <span xml:id="tok2" from="1" to="5"><!-- Look --></span>
  <span xml:id="tok3" from="6" to="8"><!-- me --></span>
  <span xml:id="tok4" from="9" to="11"><!-- up --></span>
  <span xml:id="tok5" from="11" to="12"><!-- , --></span>
  <span xml:id="tok6" from="12" to="13"><!-- " --></span>
  . . .
</spanGrp>
<event xml:id="e3" ref="#tokens2" target="#tok2,#tok4" aContent="#fs1"/>
  <fs xml:id="fs1" type="morpho-syntactic">
    <f name="pos"><symbol value="verb"/></f>
    <f name="tense"><symbol value="present"/></f>
    <f name="eventType"><symbol value="process"/></f>
    <f name="mood"><symbol value="imperative"/></f>
  </fs>
</event>
```

As another example, 4.14b is understood as containing two words *fantastic* and *bloody*, where the second word *bloody* separates the first word into two parts, *fan* and *tastic*. These two, however, cannot be annotated as forming a single word by inline annotation. But again this case can be satisfactorily dealt with by assigning a sequence consisting of two segment sequences, namely [0,3] and [11,17], as value to the attribute @anchor as follows.

Example 4.16 Tokenization of *Fanbloodytastic*

```
<spanGrp xml:id="tokens3" type="token" target="#Example 4.14b">
  <span xml:id="tok1" from="0" to="3"><!-- Fan --></span>
  <span xml:id="tok2" from="4" to="10"><!-- bloody --></span>
  <span xml:id="tok3" from="11" to="17"><!-- tastic --></span>
  <span xml:id="tok4" from="17" to="18"><!-- . --></span>
</spanGrp>
```

Again by the bracket convention, `[0,3]` and `[11,17]` are understood as referring to two sequences of characters.

To avoid such difficulty in inline annotation relating two items in the text as one unit, a markup convention such as the *head only* principle has been introduced, as in the earlier versions of TimeML that had not adopted standoff annotation. This principle may work with cases of complex verbal phrases (e.g., *look up*), just marking up their heads. But it would not work with cases like the one cited above because a word like *fantastic* has no endocentric construction.

Consider an example like the following, where one utterance is again separated by the reporting clause, namely *said John*, into two parts, *Look me up* and *in the morning*.

Example 4.17 "Look me up," said John, "in the morning."

Inline annotation fails to connect these two parts as one utterance. On the other hand, this is not a problem for standoff annotation, for it is easily resolved just by anchoring the two (discontiguous) token values like `<anchor=`
`"[tok1,tok3],[tok10,tok12]">` for the case given above.

Standoff annotation is preferred to inline annotation for several reasons. These reasons can be restated: Standoff annotation is required by computational needs involving the reusability, processability, interoperability, and interchange or merging of different types of annotation structures or by the simple need to treat discontiguous textual segments. Various sorts of annotated datasets become too entangled to be quickly processed or read off if they merge into one big corpus. An extensive collection of linguistic datasets annotated, for instance, with semantic role labeling, annotation of referential relations such as coreference, dialogue acts classification, temporal, spatial, and event markups cannot be quickly processed for its evaluation, updating, and computational applications.

It may, however, be easier to represent low-level annotations such as word segmentation, chunking, or POS-tagging with the inline format. Even semantic roles can easily be annotated inline. Here is an example.

Example 4.18 Semantic role labeling

a. Data:
```
<data xml:id="d1" mediaType="text" lang="en">
The gangsters were all caught by the police who broke into a bank.
</data>
```

b. Inline annotation:
```
<srL xml:id="sr1" target="#d1" as="unspecified">[8]
The gangsters[(theme,e1),(agent,e2)] were all caught[e1] by the
police[(agent,e1)] who broke[e2] into a bank.
</srL>
```

One possible problem is to make all these annotations interpretable in explicit terms. The annotation `gangsters[(theme,e1),(agent,e2)]` should be understood as stating that the gangsters have two roles: One is being the *theme* of the eventuality referred to by `caught[e1]` and the other the *agent* of the eventuality referred to by `broke[e2]`.

---

[8] The attribute @`as` stands for *annotation specification* or *annotation scheme*.

Semantic role labeling may need some morpho-syntactic or syntactic information. Part of that information, especially concerning the segmentation of primary data, may easily be represented inline, while semantic roles are represented standoff. Hybrid standoff annotation or standoff mixed with inline annotation may thus be possible. A simple example is as follows.

Example 4.19 Inline annotation for tokenization

a. Data:
```
<text xml:id="txt1" mediaType="text" lang="en">
The gangsters were all caught by the police
who broke into a bank.
</text>
```

b. Tokenized text:
```
<text xml:id="ttxt1" mediaType="text" lang="en">
The_t1 gangsters_t2 were_t3 all_t4 caught_t5 by_t6 the_t7 police_t8
who_t9 broke_t10 into_t11 a_t12 bank_t13 ._t14
</text>
```

The tokenization of the text (txt1) in Example 4.19 is represented inline in a very simple format, and the segmented text is identified with id="ttxt1". Then, out of 14 tokens, there are only four markables involving semantic role annotation: two markables referring to eventualities of category *event* with their respective identifier and two markables referring to their participants of category *entity*, again with their respective identifier.

Example 4.20 Markables for semantic role annotation

a. Markables referring to eventualities:
```
caught_t5:event1,
broke_t10:event2
```

b. Markables referring to participants:
```
gangster_t2:entity1,
police_t8:entity2
```

Based on the inline representation of tokenization as in Example 4.19b, the four markables are annotated standoff for their semantic roles. The semantic roles associated with the first event (event1) referred to by *caught* in a passive construction and another event (event2), referred to by *broke*, can be annotated according to ISO's annotation scheme ISO 24617-4 SemAF-SR (ISO, 2014a) and also be represented standoff.

The whole process of semantic role annotation is introduced into three steps: representation of (1) the root, (2) the entity structures that involve semantic role annotation, and (3) the semantic role links. First, the root is represented standoff as in Example 4.21.

Example 4.21 Root
```
<annotation xml:id="sr1" type="semantic role labeling"
target="#ttxt1" as="ISO SemAF-SR"/>
```

The root conveys metadata or overall information about the semantic role annotation. The type of annotation is semantic role labeling, applying to the tokenized text identified as `id="ttxt1"` in Example 4.19 with its annotation specification or scheme being the ISO standard SemAF-SR.

Second, the four base structures which are input to the semantic role labeling are listed under the root which is involved in semantic roles either as an event or as participants in that event. There are two event structures, one referred by the markable *caught* and the other by the markable *broke*, and the two participant structures associated with the two event structures. Here are two event structures annotated.

Example 4.22   Event structures annotated
a. `<event xml:id="e1" target="#t5" aContent="#fs1"/>`
b. `<event xml:id="e2" target="#t10" aContent="#fs2"/>`

The two XML-elements listed in Example 4.22 represent how they are linked to the two markables listed in Example 4.20a. As mentioned earlier, each of them forms the anchoring structure of a base structure, which also contains a content structure, either `#fs1` or `#fs2`.

Typed Feature Structures for Annotation Content
Following ISO 24612 LAF (ISO, 2012a), each base structure is separated into two substructures, anchoring and content structures. Content structures are then represented by typed feature structures that conform to the ISO standard (ISO 24610-1 FSR , ISO, 2006) on the representation of feature structures or the TEI P5 (TEI Consortium, 2019) guidelines. Here are examples.

Example 4.23   Annotation content of eventualities
a.
```
<fs xml:id="fs1" type="morphoSyntactic">
    <f name="lemma"> <string value="catch"/></f>
    <f name="pred"> <string value="CATCH"/></f>
    <f name="tense"> <symbol value="past"></f>
</fs>
```
b.
```
<fs xml:id="fs2" type="morphoSyntactic">
    <f name="lemma"> <string value="break"/></f>
    <f name="pred"> <string value="BREAK"/></f>
    <f name="tense"> <symbol value="past"></f>
</fs>
```

The feature structure `<fs xml:id="fs1" type="morphoSyntactic">` represents the morpho-syntactic information of the markable caught_t5, while the feature structure `<fs xml:id="fs2" type="morphoSyntactic">` represents the morpho-syntactic information of the markable broke_t10.

Consider Example 4.24 that was cited earlier (see Example 4.19).

Example 4.24   Inline annotation for tokenization

a. Data:
```
<text xml:id="txt1" mediaType="text" lang="en">
The gangsters were all caught by the police
who broke into a bank.
</text>
```

b. Tokenized data:
```
<text xml:id="ttxt1" mediaType="text" lang="en">
The_t1 gangsters_t2 were_t3 all_t4 caught_t5 by_t6 the_t7 police_t8
who_t9 broke_t10 into_t11 a_t12 bank_t13 ._t14
</text>
```

The anchoring structures of the two participants in these eventualities can be represented in Example 4.25.

Example 4.25   Anchoring structures
```
a. <entity xml:id="x1" target="#t2" aContent="#fs3"/>
b. <entity xml:id="x2" target="#t8" aContent="#fs4"/>
```

The annotation content of these anchoring structures of category *entity* are then represented as in Example 4.26.

Example 4.26   Content structures
```
a. <!-- gansters -->
   <fs xml:id="fs3" type="semantic">
     <f name="pred"> <string value="GANSTER"/></f>
     <f name="quant"> <string value="every"/></f>
   </fs>
b. <!-- police -->
   <fs xml:id="fs4" type="semantic">
     <f name="pred"><string value="POLICE"/></f>
     <f name="definiteness"><symbol value="definite"/></f>
   </fs>
```

Feature values are typed into *string*, *symbol*, and *numeric*. Strings refer to character strings, symbols to a small set of linguistic categories or types, and numerics to integers or other reals to which mathematical operations are applicable.

Finally, the semantic roles are represented by the following link structures.

Example 4.27   Semantic role labeling
```
<LinkGr xml:="srL1" type="semRoles" target="#ttxt1" as="SemAF-SR">
  <link event="#e1" participants="#x1" semRole="theme"/>
  <link event="#e1" participants="#x2" semRole="agent"/>
  <link event="#e2" participants="#x1" semRole="agent"/>
</LinkGr>
```

The attribute-values specification, `<type="semRoles" target="#ttxt1" as="SemAF-SR">`, on `<LinkGr>` in Example 4.27 is inherited from the root (see Example 4.21). The first two links are associated with the eventuality referred to by the markable caught_e1, while the third link is associated with the markable broke_e2.

Simplified Representation of FS The representation of feature structures presented here follows ISO 24610-1 FSR (ISO, 2006) or the *TEI Guidelines P5* (2019). As adopted in the American National Corpus (ANC), the representation of feature values can be simplified without representing their types such as *string*, *symbol* or *numeric*. Then the representation of Example 4.26, for instance, can be replaced by Example 4.28, as follows.

Example 4.28   Simplied representation
a.
```
<!-- gansters -->
<fs xml:id="fs3" type="semantic">
  <f name="pred" value="gangster"/>
  <f name="quant" value="every"/>
</fs>
```
b.
```
<!-- police -->
<fs xml:id="fs3" type="semantic">
  <f name="pred" value="police"/>
  <f name="definiteness" value="definite"/>
</fs>
```

4.3.2 Conventions

Each representation format adopts a certain list of conventions. ISO-Space, for instance, adopts the following conventions.

Specification 4.29   ISO-Space conventions
a. Lower camelCase or medial capitals
b. Naming XML elements and encoding IDs with type information
c. Free choice of lower and upper cases

Use of camelCase

In XML, the names of elements, attributes, or attribute-values may consist of more than one word. Instead of using hyphens or underscores, two words are concatenated into one with the first letter of the second word or the other following words written in uppercase.[9] Such a concatenation is called *camelCase*, *camel caps* or more formally *medial capitals*. If the first word starts in lowercase, then it is called *lower camelCase*. Here are examples.

Example 4.30   *iPhone, eBay, iKiyong, semRoles, myString, lowerCamelCaseConvention*

---

[9] Some programming languages prefer *snake case* by using underscores "_" for the concatenation of words.

ISO-Space adopts the camelCase convention for the representation of its annotation structures. The name ISO-Space does not, however, follow that convention, for ISO and Space are concatenated by the hyphen "-" or else it should have been ISOSpace or ISOspace as was in the first edition of ISO 24617-7 (ISO, 2014b).

Naming Elements and Encoding IDs
The name of an XML element should reflect the type of elements being represented. ISO-Space, for instance, has elements named <place>, <path>, <event>, <motion>, <measure>, or <qsLink>. The tag <place> represents places (locations), <event> several types of eventualities, <motion> motions, <measure> spatial measures such as distances, and <qsLink> a qualitative spatial link that anchors places or some stative eventualities to places. <tLink> in Time-ML stands for a temporal link that anchors places or some stative an eventuality to a time point or interval. These names are also considered as short forms.

Example 4.31   Element names
```
<place> := <location type="place">
<motion> := <event type="motion">
<qsLink> := <link type="qualitative spatial">
<tLink> := <link type="temporal anchoring">
```

The ID of each of these elements is categorized. It is prefixed with a single letter or a short list of letters that stand for the type or name of an element or base structure associated with it. Note that these *categorized ID prefixes* abbreviate the names of categories, called tags in XML. Here are examples.

Example 4.32   Categorized ID prefixes
```
<place> pl
<path> p
<event> e
<motion> m
<measure> me
<qsLink> qsL
```

Then integers follow these prefixes to form IDs. Examples are as follows.

Example 4.33   pl1, p5, e23, m1, me2, qsL4

Use of Lower and Upper Cases
Some annotation schemes have different uses for lower and upper cases. TimeML, for instance, uses upper case for the names of elements or attribute values except for ID values. Here is an example.

Example 4.34
```
<EVENT eid="e1" class="OCCURRENCE" tense="PAST"> walked </EVENT>
```

This book makes no such distinction between lower and upper cases. Everything is represented in lowercase unless uppercase is required, for instance, for representing acronyms XML, DTD, CDATA, or medial characters in camelCase (e.g., *camelCaseConvention*).

4.3.3 Data Type Declaration

The most common format for the representation of annotation structures is machine-readable XML. For XML, the assignment function $@_c$ for a base structure of category c can be stated with a Data Type Declaration (DTD) to guarantee the well-formedness of XML-structures. Here is a DTD for the tag name event for illustration. Unlike its values, the category event is parsed by XML so that it is PCDATA, parsed character data.

Specification 4.35   Attributes for $@_{event}$ for category <event>
```
<!ELEMENT event (#PCDATA ) >
<!ATTLIST event id ID "e"<integer> #REQUIRED >
  <!-- The name of the attribute @id may take a prefix "xml:"
  for XML documents.! -->
<!ATTLIST event target (IDREF | CDATA) #REQUIRED >
<!ATTLIST event type (state | process | transition) #REQUIRED >
<!ATTLIST event pred CDATA #REQUIRED >
  <!-- The attribute @pred refers to the predicative content of an
  event.! -->
<!ATTLIST event tense ( past | present | future | none) #REQUIRED >
<!ATTLIST event aspect ( progressive | perfect | perfectProgressive )
  #IMPLIED >
<!ATTLIST event modality CDATA #IMPLIED >
<!ATTLIST event polarity ( positive | negative ) #IMPLIED >
```

This can be represented equivalently by eBNF.

Specification 4.36   Attributes and their possible values specified by $@_{event}$
```
attributes = id, target, type, pred, tense,[aspect],[modality],[polarity];
id = "e"<integer>;
target = IDREF | CDATA;
type = "state" | "process" | "transition";
pred = CDATA;
tense = "past" | "present" | "future" | "none";
aspect = "progressive" | "perfect" | "perfectProgressive";
modality = CDATA;
polarity = "positive" | "negative";
```

These specifications are not complete, but simply show how they are represented in two different ways, either XML DTD or eBNF, but equivalently.

4.3.4 Variety of Representing Annotation Structures

With an XML-based concrete syntax, there are at least three different, but equivalent ways of representing the entire annotation structure, as illustrated below.

Example 4.37   Content structure in XML

a. Data: Mia moved to Busan.

b. Word segmentation:

Mia_{w1} $moved_{w2}$ to_{w3} $Busan_{w4}$.

c. Base structure of category event with its target $move_{w2}$:

Anchoring structure :=

```
<event xml:id="e1" target="#w2" aContent="#a1"/>
```

Content structure :=

```
<content xml:id="a1" type="transition" pred="move"
tense="past" aspect="none"/>
```

The ISO standard ISO 24612 LAF (ISO, 2012a) requires content structures to be represented in feature structures. To comply with this requirement on annotation, the annotation structure (Example 4.37c) is represented as follows.

Example 4.38   Content structure in feature structure

```
<event xml:id="e1" target="#w2" a="#fs1"/>
  <fs xml:id="fs1" type="aContent">
   <f name="type"><symbol value="transition"/></f>
   <f name="pred"><string value="move"/></f>
   <f name="tense"><symbol value="past"/></f>
   <f name="aspect"><symbol value="none"/></f>
  </fs>
</event>
```

Feature structures can be simplified as in ANC. Values of attributes (features) are not typed into string, symbol, numeric, *etc.* Then the feature structure in Example 4.38 can be represented as simplified, as follows.

Example 4.39   Simplified feature structure

```
<event xml:id="e1" target="#w2" a="#fs1"/>
  <fs xml:id="fs1" type="aContent">
   <f name="type" value="transition"/>
   <f name="pred" value="move"/>
   <f name="tense" value="past"/>
   <f name="aspect" value="none"/>
  </fs>
</event>
```

The third way, which is adopted by ISO-TimeML (ISO, 2012b), is to combine them all into a single XML element.

Example 4.40   Further simplification

```
<event xml:id="e1" target="#w2" type="transition" pred="move"
tense="past" aspect="none"/>
```

This book follows either the first or the second way with the simplified version of feature structure representation, conforming to ISO 24612 LAF (ISO, 2012a).

4.4 Graphic and Serial Representation

4.4.1 Graphic Representation: Trees

Linguistic structures are often represented by graphs. Each *graph* (*G*) consists of a nonempty set of nodes (*N*) and edges or vertices (*V*). Each edge in *V* connects one node to another or more than one node in *N*. In linguistics, metaphoric terms are often used to describe tree-like structures.

Example 4.41   Metaphoric terms

- *tree, branch, root, leaf*
- *parent (mother), child (daughter),*
- *dominate, immediately dominate, command*

These terms are used to describe graphs and their components and the relations over the components. The term *tree*, for instance, refers to a graph as a whole, while the other terms in (Example 4.41) refer to its components: *branch* refers to an edge and *root* and *leaf* refer to particular nodes. A *root* is a node that is not dominated by other nodes or which has no *mother* node. A *leaf* is a terminal node, which does not dominate any other nodes. In contrast, there are non-terminal nodes each of which has a *daughter*.

Graphs are more general than trees. See Figure 4.1.

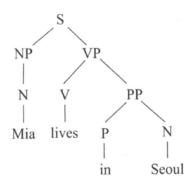

Figure 4.1 Phrase structure tree

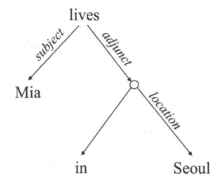

Figure 4.2 Dependency tree

On the tree, represented by Figure 4.1, the node S is the root that dominates all the other nodes, while `Mia, lives, in`, and `Seoul` are terminal nodes.

Trees are single-rooted, while there are graphs that have more than one root. Trees have no siblings connected, but some graphs have siblings or children of the same parent (mother) connected. The relation of domination is acyclic, but some nodes can be cyclic in some graphs. A graph theory can thus be very general. Such a general theory is used in linguistics, doing syntax or semantics.

Nodes and edges may be labeled. In Phrase Structure Grammar (PSG), nonterminal nodes are labeled with the names of grammatical categories such as S, NP, VP, PP, N, V, or P while terminal nodes are then associated with lexical items or words.

In Dependency Grammar, nodes including the root node are labeled with lexical items, whereas edges often represent their grammatical relations such as *subject, adjunct*, and *location*. See Figure 4.2.

4.4.2 GrAF: Graph Annotation Format

Labels for nodes and edges may not be simple atomic categories or other types of names. They can be complex structures. As introduced by Ide and Suderman (2007), *Graph-based Annotation Format* (GrAF) also uses graphs to represent annotation structures. It uses terminal nodes to anchor base structures to markables or segments in primary data, while nonterminal nodes are linked to represent annotation content, as represented by feature structures. Edges represent link structures over base structures, for each of them relates one node to another.

Every graph that conforms to GrAF has four components.

Specification 4.42   Components of GrAF:

a. The *root* provides metadata for annotation, such as information about a dataset to which the annotation applies the type of annotation, or the annotation space or scheme which is to be followed.
b. *Nonterminals* each represent a base structure with its annotation content represented in feature structure.
c. *Terminals* are each linked to a markable in primary data while anchoring a base structure to an extent or sequence of segments in the segmented data.
d. *Edges* are each labeled with the name of a link and its relation type.

Graph Conventions on Nodes and Edges

To guarantee the convertibility of a serialized graph to a graph structure, the following conventions are introduced.

Specification 4.43   Convertibility conventions

a. *Level of a node* (`@level`): The level of a node in a graph is represented by a natural number; 0 refers to a root node and 1 is the daughter of a root.
b. *Precedence relation*: The precedence relation of sister nodes is represented by a decimal; 1.1 refers to the leftmost node of level 1 and 1.2 is a node that is just at the right of node 1.1 on the same level 1.
c. *Range of an edge* (`@range`): The value of @range is a pair of node levels; "0.1,2" refers to a range from level 0.1 to level 2.
d. *Note*: If the element `<edge>` is embedded in an element `<node xml:id="ni">`, then range=`"#ni,#nj"` may be replaced by target=`"#nj"`.[10]

Consider the graph in Example 4.44, which serializes the dependency tree represented by Figure 4.2 in Section 4.4.1.

Example 4.44   Serialized graph

```
<graph xml:id="g1">
  <node xml:id="n1" level="0" label="lives">
    <edge xml:id="e1" target="#n2" label="subject"/>
    <edge xml:id="e2" target="#n3" label="adjunct"/>
  </node>
  <node xml:id="n2" level="1.1" label="Mia"/>
  <node xml:id="n3" level="1.2" label="">
    <edge xml:id="e3" target="#n4" label=""/>
    <edge xml:id="e4" target="#n5" label="location"/>
  <node xml:id="n4" level="2.1" label="in"/>
  <node xml:id="n5" level="2.2" label="Seoul"/>
</graph>
```

---

[10] See ISO 24615-2: 2018, Clause 5, Example 1, ISOTiger graph structure (ISO, 2018).

The serialized graph in Example 4.44 well defines the graph in Figure 4.2.

GrAF as a Graphic Representation of XML Serialization
GrAF can visualize an XML-serialization of annotations that conforms to ISO 24612 LAF (ISO, 2012a). Consider Example 4.45 of an annotation represented in XML.

Example 4.45 Annotation in XML

a. Data: Mia lived in Seoul for 12 years.
b. Markables (id="sd1"): Mia$_{ma1}$ lived$_{ma2}$ in Seoul$_{ma4}$ for 12 years.
c. Spatial annotation:

```
<annotation xml:id="is1" target="#sd1" type="spatial" as="ISO-Space">
  <dEntity xml:id="x1" target="#ma1" type="person" named="Mia"/>
  <event xml:id="e1" target="#ma2" type="state" pred="LIVE"
tense="past"/>
  <place xml:id="pl1" target="#ma4" type="city" named="Seoul"
country="kr"/>
  <qsLink relType="in" figure="#x1", ground="#pl1"/>
  <qsLink relType="in" figure="#e1", ground="#pl1"/>
</annotation>
```

Here, the hash sign # is used to mark an ID that refers to *outside data* or a part of it. The tag dEntity stands for category *discourse entity*. The qualitative spatial link (qsLink), triggered by the spatial relator "in", relates the person named "Mia" and also the stative event "lived" to the city named *Seoul*. Their relation type @relType is characterized by the trigger "in".

The spatial annotation in Example 4.45 in XML is represented graphically as shown in Figure 4.3.

Graph-Theoretic Serialization
Representations in GrAF can be serialized in XML with graph-theoretic terms. First, the root in Figure 4.3 is serialized as follows.

Example 4.46 Serialized root
```
<graph xml:id="GrAF4.3">
  <node xml:id="is1" level="0" target="#sd1" type="spatial"
  as="ISO-Space"/>
</graph>
```

The attribute @level is introduced to represent the level of a node in a graph. This root node dominates the entire tree so that each of the nodes under it inherits the information that the type of annotation is spatial annotation and that the whole annotation follows ISO-Space. The root node may also tell about the domain or data to which the annotation applies.

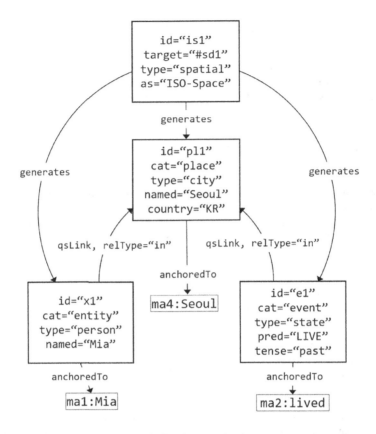

Figure 4.3 Graph annotation format.

Second, there are three nonterminal nodes in Figure 4.3 that are generated (formally defined) by ISO-Space. They are child nodes of the root with each of the three edges (downward arrows) between them labeled with "generates". Each of them represents a base structure with its annotation content. The first child node (id="x1") represents a base structure of category *entity* (discourse entity) that carries information that the discourse entity is a person named *Mia*. The other two nonterminal nodes are also understood as representing the two base structures, one associated with the place named *Seoul* and the other, with the event of living.

Example 4.47 Nodes serialized

```
<node label="entity" id="x1" ref="#n11">
  <fs>
    <f name="type" value="person"/>
    <f name="named" value="Mia"/>
  </fs>
</node>
  <node label="place" id="p11" ref="#n12">
  <fs>
    <f name="type" value="city"/>
    <f name="named" value="Seoul"/>
    <f name="country" value="KR"/>
  </fs>
</node>
  <node label="event" id="e1" ref="#n13">
  <fs>
    <f name="type" value="state"/>
    <f name="pred" value="LIVE"/>
    <f name="tense" value="past"/>
  </fs>
</node>
```

Third, there are two *upward arrows*, v4 and v5, that are *edges* in the graph represented by Figure 4.3. They are the link structures, which are represented in XML as follows.

Example 4.48 Edges (upward arrows) serialized

```
<edge label="qsLink" xml:id="v4" targets="#x1,#p11"
  relType="in"/>

<edge label="qsLink" xml:id="v5" targets="#e1,#p11"
  relType="in"/>
```

These are interpreted as stating that the person named *Mia* is in the city named *Seoul* and that the state of her living was situated in that city.

Finally, all of the base structures are anchored to their respective markables.

Example 4.49 Terminal nodes referencing segments

```
<node xml:id="n21">
  <link targets="#ma1" type="anchoredTo"/>
</node>
<node xml:id="n22">
  <link targets="#ma4" type="anchoredTo"/>
</node>
<node xml:id="n23">
  <link targets="#ma2" type="anchoredTo"/>
</node>
```

These markables are each linked to a token in the segmented primary data.

Example 4.50   Segmented primary data

a. Data:
```
<data xml:id="d1" medium="text" lang="en">
  Mia lived in Seoul.
</data>
```

b. Segmented data:
```
<regions xml:id="sd1" target="#d1"
type="tokens" >
  <region xml:id="token1" anchors="0 3"/>
  <!-- Mia -->
  <region xml:id="token2" anchors="4 9"/>
  <!-- lived -->
  <region xml:id="token3" anchors="10 12"/>
  <!-- in -->
  <region xml:id="token4" anchors="13 18"/>
  <!-- Seoul -->
  <region xml:id="token5" anchors="18 19"/>
  <!-- . -->
</regions>
```

Example 4.51   Markables
```
<markables xml:id="mas1" target="#sd1" type="markables">
  <markable xml:id="ma1" target="#token1" />
  <markable xml:id="ma2" target="#token2" />
  <markable xml:id="ma3" target="#token3" />
  <markable xml:id="ma4" target="#token4" />
</markables>
```

This process of tokenization is not shown in Figure 4.3 except that it demonstrates how each terminal node is linked to a markable, and then to a token in the segmented data.

Consider Example 4.52 to see how spatial and temporal annotations can be merged.

Example 4.52   Merging annotations

a. Data: Mia lived in Seoul for 12 years.
b. Markables (id=sd1): Mia lived$_{ma2}$ in Seoul for [12 years]$_{ma5}$.
c. Temporal measure annotation in ISO-TimeML:
```
<annotation xml:id="it1" target="#sd1" type="temporal" as="ISO-TimeML">
  <event e1 target="#ma2" type="state" pred="LIVE" tense="past"/>
  <measure me1 target="#ma5" type="duration" value="P12Y"/>
  <tLink eventID="#e1" measureID="#me1" relType="DURING"/>
</annotation>
```

The information represented by the temporal measure annotation can be partially represented in GrAF.

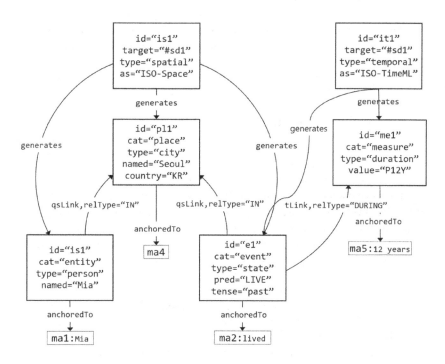

Figure 4.4 Merging of spatial and temporal annotations.

Example 4.53 Temporal measure annotation

```
<graph xml:id="GrAF4.4">
  <node xml:id="it1" level="0" target="#sd1"
   type="temporal" as="ISO-TimeML"/>
  <node xml:id="n11" type="anchoredTo">
   <link targets="#ma2" /> <!-- lived -->
  </node>
  <node xml:id="n12" type="anchoredTo">
   <link targets="#ma5"/> <!-- 12 years -->
  </node>
</graph>
```

The node n11 in Example 4.53, which is anchored to the markable ma2:lived, overlaps the node n13 in Example 4.47. This node constitutes the point of merging the two graphs for spatial and temporal annotations, as shown in Figure 4.4.

Figure 4.4 shows the result of merging the temporal annotation (id="it1") with the spatial annotation (id="is1"). The merged graph shows that the event (id="e1", node="13") of Mia's living is spatially anchored to Seoul `(id="p11", node="n12")` and temporally to the duration of 12 years `(id="t1", node="n14")`, as annotated by ISO-Space and ISO-TimeML, respectively.

4.5 Predicate-Logic-Like Format

4.5.1 Overview

Instead of XML, Pustejovsky (2017b) adopted a predicate-logic-like format to represent annotation structures. I also adopt it as the main representation format for this book, calling it *pFormat*. It is simple and easy to read, carrying adequate and only relevant information for the derivation of logical forms for semantic interpretation. I present some conventions for pFormat in Section 4.5.2 and illustrations in Section 4.5.3.

4.5.2 Conventions for pFormat

Each pFormat follows the basic form $P(x_1, x_2, \ldots, x_n)$ of atomic formulas in ordinary predicate logic, where P is an n-ary predicate and each x_i is its argument. In pFormat, each x_i is represented as a pair of an attribute and its value or simply the value of an attribute, while P stands for the name of the category of a base structure or a link structure. Here are some general conventions for the use of pFormat.

Specification 4.54   Conventions for the use of *pFormat*

a. Concatenation:
   Adopt the *lower camelCase* convention for representing concatenated expressions without using the hyphen "-" or the underscore "_":
   e.g., `eventPath`, instead of `EVENT_PATH`.

b. Structure of representing base structures:
   `categoryName(anchoringStructure, contentStructure)`, where
   `anchoringStructure = valueOfIdentifier, (valueOfTarget)` and
   `conTentStructure = List of attribute-value pairs of the form,`
   $\quad a_i = v_i$ or $a_i = V_i$:
   e.g., `event(e1, w2, type=STATE, pred=live, tense=PAST)`

c. Structure of representing link structures:
   `categoryName(valueOfIdentifier, argStructure)`, where
   `argStructure = relType=VALUE,` $a_0 = ID_0, \ldots, a_k = ID_k$, or
   `argStructure = VALUE,` $ID_0, \ldots, ID_k$:

e.g., `tLink(tL1, relType=BEFORE, eventID=e1, relatedToTimeID=t1)`
or `tLink(tL1, BEFORE, e1, t1)`

d. Options:

   (i) Category names may all or partly be in uppercase:
       e.g., `TLINK`, `tLINK`, `tLink`, or `tlink` are all acceptable.
   (ii) The value of an attribute may be enclosed by a pair of quotation
        marks:
        e.g., `type="STATE"`, instead of `type=STATE`.
   (iii) The value of an attribute may be in lowercase:
         e.g., `type="state"`, instead of `type="STATE"`.
   (iv) An attribute a may be linked to its value v by a colon "`:`", instead of
        the equality symbol "`=`".
        e.g., `type:STATE`, instead of `type=STATE`.

In general, pFormat is a flexible markup language open to many options.

4.5.3 Illustrations

Here is an example that quickly shows how the pFormat represents base and
link structures.

Example 4.55 Representing base and link structures

a. Word-segmented data:
   Mia called$_{w2}$ me yesterday$_{w4}$, but I missed$_{w7}$ it$_{w8}$.

b. Base structures:
```
EVENT(e1, w2, type="PROCESS", pred="CALL", tense="PAST")
TIMEX3(t1, w4, type="DATE", value="2019-08-23")
EVENT(e2, w7, type="PROCESS", pred="MISS", tense="PAST")
EVENT(e3, w8, type="PROCESS", pred="CALL", tense="NONE")
```

c. Link structures:
```
tLink(tL1, DURING, e1, t1)
tLink(tL2, SIMULTANEOUS, e1, e2)
rLink(rL1, IDENTITY, e1, e3),
```
where `rLink` stands for the objectal refer-
   ence link.

Note that pFormat also allows the following representation.

Example 4.56 Alternative pFormat representation

a. Word-segmented data:
   Mia called$_{w2}$ me yesterday$_{w4}$, but I missed$_{w7}$ it$_{w8}$.

b. Base structures:
```
event(e1, w2, type="process", pred="call", tense="past")
timeX3(t1, w4, type="date", value="2019-08-23")
```

```
event(e2, w7, type="process", pred="miss", tense="past")
event(e3, w8, type="process", pred="call", tense="none")
```

c. Link structures:
```
tLink(tL1, during, e1, t1)
tLink(tL2, simultaneous, e1, e2)
rLink(rL1, identity, e1, e3)
```

The sole difference between the two representations in Examples 4.55 and 4.56 is found in the use of uppercase or lowercase letters. The former prefers uppercase for the representation of category names and attribute values, whereas the latter prefers lowercase with the camelCase convention. This book generally follows the alternative pFormat representation presented in Example 4.56.

4.6 Summary

This chapter introduced an XML-based concrete syntax $CSynX$ as providing a representation format for annotation structures. It first discussed three different representation formats: inline, standoff, and hybrid.

- Inline directly marks up datasets.
- Standoff, on the other hand, keeps raw datasets intact, creating new separate files for each type of annotation.
- A hybrid format like CoNLL represents annotation in a tabular format with columns each for a different type of linguistic information.

Two requirements for annotation were discussed. One requires standoff annotation for easier management of linguistic annotation. The other requires the separation of each entity structure into an anchoring structure and an annotation content structure while requiring annotation content to be represented in an XML-serialized feature structure.

GrAF is also introduced as an XML-serialization of graphs that may be used to represent annotations for various purposes of managing, such as merging or comparing, the information conveyed by various types of linguistic annotation.

The chapter ended by proposing the pFormat for representing annotation structures. It replaces the XML-based format to represent annotation structures because of its simplicity, legibility, and adequacy for semantic interpretation. This book will thus follow the newly introduced pFormat for representing annotation structures, especially those related to temporal and spatial annotations, in the following chapters.

5

What Does Semantics Do for Annotation?

5.1 Introduction

The task of semantics for annotation is of two kinds. First, semantics validates the construction of syntax for the generation of well-formed annotation structures. Second, semantics provides a formalism for interpreting those annotation structures that are generated by the syntax.

Specification 5.1 Task of semantics

a. Semantic justification of a proposed annotation syntax

b. Semantic interpretation of annotation structures

This was shown graphically by Figure 3.1 in Chapter 3.

In this chapter, my main concern is to present a general view of what kind of semantics is needed to interpret annotation structures and to lay a general ground for constructing an interpretation scheme for temporal and spatial annotation. This semantics follows the ordinary steps of doing model-theoretic formal semantics such as Montague Semantics (Montague, 1974; Dowty et al., 1981). It goes through an intermediate step of representing semantic content or denotations in logical forms and then interprets them with respect to a model with truth definitions. This chapter consists of three sections. Section 5.2 shows a way of validating a proposed syntax for semantic annotation by justifying each of the attributes that constitute the syntax on the ground of semantic needs. Section 5.3 discusses how the content structures of semantic annotation are represented by a logical language that allows a model-theoretic interpretation. Section 5.4 looks at type-theoretic semantics.

5.2 Validating the Syntax of Semantic Annotation

5.2.1 Overview

To be a meaningful syntax, such a syntax needs to be validated on semantic grounds. Syntax and semantics must work together. To borrow Bertrand Russel's statement (Gellner, 1959), which criticizes linguistic philosophy as not referring to the world, a syntax without semantics is like a clock without a pendulum that runs fast but fails to tell the time. This applies to the case of the relation between syntax and semantics. Montague (1974) also criticized doing syntax without semantics. A syntax for linguistic annotation must also be supported by the semantics that relates linguistic data to the world being referred to.

The work of syntax for semantic annotation is restricted. Its main work is to specify a list of syntactic categories and a list of attributes for each of them, either required or optional. Associated with each of the categories, each bundle of attributes with specific values conveys relevant information about each of the annotation structures that the syntax generates.

For illustration, let's consider a sample syntax, Syn_v, for semantic annotation that specifies the attributes of category *event*, as in Specification 5.2.

Specification 5.2   Tentative list of attributes of category *event* for Syn_v
```
attributes =
    identifier, target, pred, type, pos, tense, number, nationality, age, sex;
```

The validation of Syn_v will consist of justifying each of the attributes for the annotation of actual data in language. It means checking whether each of the listed attributes is required to capture and annotate relevant information contained in the data. By the *validation* of a semantic annotation syntax, I mean the semantic justification of its construction against linguistic data and facts.[1]

5.2.2 Data and Markables

As basic data for the discussion of validating Syn_v, I will use the following fragment of raw data, as presented in Examples 5.3 and 5.4.

Example 5.3   Raw data
Mia called me twice yesterday, but I haven't called her back until now. I have just called her, though. We must have kept talking from ten to twelve, midnight. I had missed her calls because I was sleeping.

---

[1] The notion of *well-formedness* applies to the syntactic or morpho-syntactic characterization of annotation structures. If the specification of an annotation structure conforms according to the rules of syntax, then it is *well-formed* with respect to that syntax.

The raw data in Example 5.3 contains 38 words excluding the punctuation marks.

The application of semantic annotation to linguistic data requires the input data to undergo some morpho-syntactic processing procedures such as *word segmentation* so that markables for annotation can be extracted and identified.

Example 5.4 Words segmented

Mia called$_{w2}$ me twice$_{w4}$ yesterday$_{w5}$, but I haven't called$_{w9}$ her back until now$_{w13}$. I have just$_{w16}$ called$_{w17}$ her, though. We must have kept$_{w23}$ talking$_{w24}$ from ten$_{w26}$ to twelve$_{w28}$ midnight$_{w29}$. I had missed$_{w32}$ her calls$_{w34}$ because I was sleeping$_{w38}$.

A fragment of text is segmented into smaller units, called *words*, according to some principle of word segmentation for each language. The contracted form like *haven't* is, for instance, treated as a single word, although it can be analyzed into an auxiliary verb *have* and a contracted form *n't* of negation. Each of the words is then tagged with a unique identifier so that it can be referred to for doing semantic annotation.

The word-segmented data (Example 5.4) contains eight markables of category *event* each denoting an eventuality of some type. There are also six markables of category *temporal entity* for temporal expressions each of which denotes a time of some sort. Each of them is assigned a unique identifier that is associated with a syntactic category.

Example 5.5 Markables identified

Mia called$_{e1,w2}$ me twice$_{w4}$ yesterday$_{t1,w5}$, but I haven't called$_{e2,w9}$ her back until now$_{t2,w13}$. I have just$_{t3,w16}$ called$_{e3,w17}$ her, though. We must have kept$_{e4,w23}$ talking$_{e5,w24}$ from ten$_{t4,w26}$ to twelve$_{t5,w28}$ midnight$_{t6,w29}$. I had missed$_{e6,w32}$ her calls$_{e7,w34}$ because I was sleeping$_{e8,w38}$.

These markables are the targets of annotation and interpretation to be used for illustration in this chapter. Each of the markables is identified by a subscript pair *markable$_{ci,wj}$*, where *ci* stands for a categorized identifier and *wj*, for a word or token identifier.

Morpho-syntactic Information

Morpho-syntactic annotation is also a prerequired step for semantic annotation. The morpho-syntactic forms of nouns and verbs are, for instance, semantically relevant, thus requiring to be annotated as part of semantic annotation.

There are at least two noun forms.

Example 5.6   Two noun forms
a. Nominals (common nouns): *park, man, building, institution*
b. Names (proper nouns): *John, Winston, Oregon, the White House*

Nominals are generally treated as denoting sets or properties of individuals, whereas names are treated as *rigid designators* of individuals or else like nominals denoting sets of individuals, still referring to individuals rigidly.

The spatial annotation scheme, based on ISO-Space (ISO, 2014b), makes use of the morpho-syntactic information conveyed by these two forms, encoded as nom and nam, that refer to locative expressions and place names, respectively, as in Example 5.6. Such information is needed to differentiate names from nominals semantically or treat them as being of the same semantic type that denotes a set of individuals. Here is an illustration.

Example 5.7   Locative nouns
a. Data: I once visited a safari park$_{nom}$ in Winston$_{nam}$, Oregon$_{nam}$.
b. Base structures:
```
place(pl1, w6, type="park", form="nom")
place(pl2, w8, type="city", form="nam")
place(pl3, w9, type="state", form="nam")
```
c. Link structures:
```
qsLink(qsL1, figure="pl1", ground="pl2", relType="in")²
qsLink(qsL2, figure="pl2", ground="pl3", relType="in")
```

Based on the base and link structures, as represented by Example 5.7, we obtain the semantic forms as in (Example 5.8), where σ is a *semantic function* which maps an annotation structure to its semantic form.

Example 5.8   Deriving semantic forms
a. Base structures interpreted:
$\sigma(park_{nom}) := \{x\}[park(x)]$
$\sigma(Winston_{nam}) := \{y\}[named(y, Winston) \wedge city(y)]$
$\sigma(Oregon_{nam}) := \{z\}[named(z, Oregon) \wedge state(z)]$
b. Link structure interpreted:
$\sigma(qsL1)$
$:= \{x, y\}[[\sigma(park), \sigma(Winston)] \oplus in(x, y)]$

---

² Here, qsLink stands for *qualitative spatial link* that relates one region to another with a spatial relation like *in*.

$$:= \{x, y\}[[park(x) \wedge named(y, Winston) \wedge city(y)] \wedge in(x, y)]^3$$
$$\sigma(\texttt{qsL2})$$
$$:= \{y, z\}[[\sigma(Winston), \sigma(Oregon)] \oplus in(y, z)]$$
$$:= \{y, z\}[[named(y, Winston) \wedge city(y)] \wedge [named(z, Oregon) \wedge$$
$$state(z)]] \wedge in(y, z)]$$

c. Semantic form of the whole annotation structure:

By joining the two occurrences of $\sigma(\texttt{qsL})$ and binding the unbound occurrences of the variables x, y, and z in them with the existential quantifier $\exists$, we obtain:

$$\exists\{x, y, z\}$$
$$[park(x)\wedge$$
$$[named(y, Winston) \wedge city(y)] \wedge in(x, y)\wedge$$
$$[named(z, Oregon) \wedge state(z)] \wedge in(y, z)]$$

Both nominals like *park* and proper names like *Winston* or *Oregon* are treated as one-place predicates, each represented by an open sentence with its unbound variable prelisted, while denoting a set of regions or locations.

Verb Forms The assignment of tense to verbs depends on their verbal forms. *Finite verbs* in English are, for instance, tensed, whereas *nonfinite verbs* that include infinitives, participles, and gerundive forms are not tensed. Quirk et al. (1985, section 3.2) introduce five forms for regular verbs.

Example 5.9 Regular verb forms
- Base form
- *-s* form
- *-ing* participle
- Past form
- *-ed* participle

The *-ing* participles include both participial and gerundive forms. The base form can be either finite or infinite. Both the *-s* form and the past form are finite verbal forms.

Example 5.10 Verb forms based on Quirk et al. (1985)

Mia called$_{w2:pastForm}$ me twice yesterday, but I haven't$_{w8:baseForm}$ called$_{w9:-edParticiple}$ her back until now. I have$_{w15:baseForm}$ just called$_{w17:-edParticiple}$ her, though. We must$_{w21:baseForm}$ have$_{w22:baseForm}$

---

[3] The symbol $\oplus$ is a truth-functional conjunctive operator. It combines all the semantic forms into a conjunctive form with a truth-functional Boolean connective $\wedge$ (*and*), as is formally defined in Chapter 6.

kept$_{w23:\text{-}edParticiple}$ talking$_{w24:\text{-}ingParticiple}$ from ten to twelve, midnight. I had$_{w31:pastForm}$ missed$_{w32:\text{-}edParticiple}$ her calls$_{w34:plural}$ because I was$_{w37:pastForm}$ sleeping$_{w38:\text{-}ingParticiple}$.

Semantic annotation assumes the preprocessing of verb forms, as listed in Example 5.10. On the basis of these verbal forms, tense and aspect are assigned to verbs that denote eventualities. It simply inherits necessary information about @pos (part of speech) or verbal forms from a morpho-syntactic annotation. The semantic annotation schemes, as introduced in this book, however, seldom require complex syntactic analyses, although each of the annotation schemes always assumes some pieces of morpho-syntactic or syntactic information.

Irrelevant Attributes

The attribute specification for category *event* is validated by the adequacy of annotating the given data. Obviously, the attributes @nationality, @age, and @sex, as listed in Specification 5.2, have nothing to do with the semantics of eventualities. They are properties of persons, but not of eventualities. So they should be deleted from the list of attributes of the category, as named *event*, for eventualities.

Attributes for Anchoring Structures

The attributes @*identifier* and @*target* constitute the *anchoring structure* of base structures each of which carries no semantic information by itself. These attributes are listed as required attributes of each of the syntactic categories of semantic annotation for anchoring or referring purposes only. They are not required by any semantic needs. They are, however, kept as required attributes because they are syntactically needed for the construction of base structures and also because the semantic validity of annotation structures presupposes their syntactic well-formedness.

The attribute @*identifier* uniquely identifies each of the base or link structures. Link structures refer to base structures, as shown in Example 5.11. Their identifiers are also used for the derivation of logical forms, as in Example 5.11.

Consider Example 5.11.

Example 5.11 Use of the identifiers

a. Data: Mia called$_{e1,w2}$ me twice yesterday$_{t1,w5}$.

b. Base structures:
```
event(e1, w2, pred="call")
timeX3(t1, w5, type="date", value="yesterday")
```

c. Link structure:

```
tLink(tL1, isIncluded, e1, t1)
```

d. Semantic representation:

$\sigma(\text{e1}) := [call(e_1)]$

$\sigma(\text{t1}) := [date(t_1)]$

$\sigma(\text{tLink}) := [call(e_1) \wedge date(t_1) \wedge occurs(e_1, t_1)]$

The temporal link (tLink) in Example 5.11 refers to the two base structures, event(e1) and timex3(t1), which are identified as e1 or t1, respectively. The logical forms in Example 5.11d refer to each of the base structures by using their identifiers as handles or pointers and also to the link structure that relates the logical forms of the two base structures into a well-formed logical form with its relation type specified as *occurs*.

Complex base structures also refer to other base structures. They are illustrated by Example 5.12.

Example 5.12   Complex base structures

a. Data:

We must have kept talking$_{e4, w24}$ $\emptyset_{t3:tInterval}$ from ten$_{t1, w26}$ to twelve$_{t2, w28}$, midnight$_{t3, w29}$.

b. Simple base structures:

```
event(e4, w24, pred="talk", tense="none")
timeX3(t1, w26, type="date", value="XXXX-XX-XX:T22:00")
timeX3(t2, w28, type="date", value="XXXX-XX-XX:T24:00")
```

c. Complex base structure:

```
timeX3(t3, type="tInterval", start="t1", end="t2")
```

d. Link structure:

```
tLink(tL1, e4, t3, isIncluded)
```

The base structure timex3($\emptyset_{t3}$) in Example 5.12 is a complex base structure, which is represented as a nonconsuming tag (empty markable). It refers to a time interval, which is bounded by the two endpoints, t1 and t2. The time point t1 is the start and the time point t2 is the endpoint. The temporal link (tLink) then relates the event of talking e4 to the time interval t3 bounded by those two time points, t1 and t2, which refer to 10:00 p.m. and to 12:00 p.m., midnight, respectively.

The attribute *@target* is necessary to anchor each of the base structures to a markable in a dataset. Its value can be represented either by a markable itself or with a word identifier (ID), as shown in the base structures in Example 5.11b, especially if the dataset is word-segmented, as shown in Example 5.12.

5.2.3 Attributes for Content Structures

The attribute @*type* determines at least three different internal structures of events each denoted by a predicate, as proposed by Pustejovsky (1991) and Mani and Pustejovsky (2012, p. 38). The *transition* type has two subtypes: *achievement* and *accomplishment*.

Specification 5.13   Types of event structures
- eventuality := state | process | transition
- transition := achievement | accomplishment

Their internal structures are represented by Specification 5.14.

Specification 5.14   Internal structure of achievement and accomplishment
- state → event
- process → $event_1 \ldots event_n$
- $transition_{ach}$ → state state
- $transition_{acc}$ → process state

These event types are illustrated with Example 5.15.

Example 5.15   Illustration
- *States* (e.g., *happy, busy, know, love*) all constitute a single homogeneous event with no changes occurring over a given time interval.
- *Processes* (e.g., *call, walk, study*) are sequences of events, each sequence denoting an activity of indefinite length.
- *Transitions* that undergo changes have two subtypes:

  − *Achievements*: (e.g., *find, die, miss*) change from one state to another with an *instant* culmination.
  − *Accomplishments*: (e.g., *build, create, destroy*) undergo a gradual process of change to a culmination state.

With respect to a temporal reference such as a duration, states are understood to *hold* homogeneously during a given time interval. Processes are, on the other hand, understood to *occur* through a time interval but possibly with some intervening breaks or distractions during that time interval (the convex hull of activity). Transitions are then understood as reaching a *culminating* state that holds at some interval of time. Differences in event types thus affect the interpretation of eventualities in various time frames. The marking of event types is considered necessary for proper semantic annotation, although the implementation of different interpretations of eventualities remains a complex semantic issue.

The attribute *@pred* stands for the term *predicate*, denoting the *predicative content*. It treats eventualities as denoting individuals (first-order objects), as proposed by Reichenbach (1947),[4] Davidson (1967), and others such as Parsons (1990) and Kamp and Reyle (1993) who have developed the *Neo-Davidsonian Semantics*. Such a treatment with Parsons's (1990) modification nicely represents the logical form involving adverbials and semantic roles. Here is an example that was discussed by Davidson (1967).

Example 5.16   Davidson's treatment of events

a. Data:

Jones buttered the toast slowly, deliberately, in the bathroom, with a knife, at midnight.

b. Logical form:

$\exists\{e, x, y, z, w, t\}$

$[butter(e)$

$\wedge\ x{=}Jones \wedge agent(e, x)$

$\wedge\ toast(y) \wedge theme(e, y)$

$\wedge\ slow(e) \wedge deliberate(e)$

$\wedge\ bathroom(z) \wedge place(e, z)$

$\wedge\ knife(w) \wedge instrument(e, w)$

$\wedge\ midnight(t) \wedge time(e, t)]$

The adverbials *slowly* and *deliberately* are treated as predicates, *slow* and *deliberate*, each of which has an eventuality as its argument.[5]

This approach can quickly be adopted for the annotation of eventualities. Here is an example.

Example 5.17   Annotation of eventualities

a. Word-segmented data:

Mia$_{w1}$ took a walk$_{w2}$.

b. Base structures:

```
entity(x1, w1, type="person", form="nam")
event(e1, w2, pred="walk")
srLink(srL1, agent, e1, x1)
```

---

[4] Reichenbach (1947, section 48, chapter 7) mentions individuals of the *event type*, besides spatial and temporal points and individuals of the *thing type*, by adding: *For physics, events are more fundamental units than things.*

[5] What is really meant by these adverbials raises different issues relating to the problem of contextual interpretation or the understanding of intention.

c. Semantic representation:

$\sigma(\text{x1}) := \{x_1\}[named(x_1, Mia) \wedge person(x_1)]$

$\sigma(\text{e1}) := \{e_1\}[walk(e_1) \wedge past(e_1)]$

$\sigma(\text{srL1})$

$:= \{x_1, e_1\}[named(x_1, Mia) \wedge person(x_1) \wedge walk(e_1) \wedge past(e_1) \wedge$

$\qquad agent(e_1, x_1)]$

$:= \exists\{x_1, e_1\}[named(x_1, Mia) \wedge person(x_1) \wedge walk(e_1) \wedge past(e_1) \wedge$

$\qquad agent(e_1, x_1)]$

The verb *took a walk* is treated as a one-place predicate with its sole argument being e_1 referring to the event of taking a walk. By the semantic role link (srLink), the entity x_1 is annotated as participating in the event e_1 as its agent.[6]

The attribute @*tense* creates little controversy at least for English. In most languages, every finite verbal form that refers to an eventuality carries information about its tense. Its values include *past, present,* and *future.* Here is an example.

Example 5.18   Past tense

a. Data:

Mia called$_{w2}$ me twice yesterday$_{w5}$.

b. Annotation:

```
event(e1, w2, type="process", pred="call", tense="past")
timex3(t1, w5, type="date", value="2019-10-27")
tLink(tL1, e1, t1, isIncluded)
```

c. Semantic representation:

$\sigma(\text{e1}) := \{e_1\}[process(e_1) \wedge call(e_1) \wedge past(e_1)]$

$\sigma(\text{t1}) := \{t_1\}[year(t_1, 2019) \wedge month(t_1, October) \wedge day(t_1, 27)]$

$\sigma(\text{tL1}) := \{e_1, t_1\}[call(e_1) \wedge past(e_1) \wedge year(t_1, 2019) \wedge occurs(e_1, t_1)]$

Based on these logical forms, the event of calls is interpreted as stating that it occurred in the past and the date of its occurrence was October 27, 2019. The tense *past* is introduced as a *logical predicate.*[7] The interpretation of the predicate *past* depends on the context of use, as will be discussed later in the chapter.

The attribute @*aspect* needs to be introduced to be able to annotate datasets such as that in Example 5.19.

---

[6] Unlike Davidson (1967), Parsons (1990, p. 147) treats every predicate as a unary predicate with a variable e, as illustrated by: *Agatha sang loudly* $\Rightarrow \exists e[sing(e) \wedge agent(e, Agatha) \wedge loud(e)]$.

[7] The notion of *logical predicates* will be developed in Chapter 7 as meaning postulates that delineate *admissible* models out of *possible* models.

Example 5.19 Attribute @aspect

a. Data:

I haven't called$_{e2,\,w9}$ her back until now$_{t2,\,w13}$.

b. Annotation:

```
event(e2, w9, type="process", pred="call", tense="present",
   aspect="perfect")
```

c. Semantic representation::

$\sigma(\mathrm{e}2) := [call(e_2) \wedge presPerfect(e_2)]$

Here again, *presPerfect* is treated as a logical predicate just like the logical
tense predicate *past*. Such a treatment of the notion of *presPerfect* allows a set
of competing definitions most of which are too complex to be represented as
part of a logical form.[8]

The attribute @*modality* is needed to annotate auxiliary verbs like *must* as
in Example 5.20.

Example 5.20 Modality

a. Data:

We must have kept$_{e4,\,w23}$ talking$_{e5,\,w24}$ from ten$_{t4,\,w26}$ to twelve$_{t5,\,w28}$
midnight$_{t6,\,w29}$.

b. Annotation:

```
event(e4, w23, type="process", pred="keep", tense="present",
    aspect="perfect", modality="must")
event(e5, w24, type="process", pred="talk", tense="none")
aLink(aL1, continues, e4, e5)
```

c. Semantic representation:

$\sigma(\mathrm{e}4) := \{e_4\}[process(e_4) \wedge keep(e_4) \wedge presPerfect(e_4) \wedge must(e_4)]]$

$\sigma(\mathrm{e}5) := \{e_5\}[talk(e_5)]$

$\sigma(\mathrm{aL1})$

$:= \{e_4, e_5\}$

$[continues(e_4, e_5) \oplus [\sigma(e_4), \sigma(e_5)]]$

$:= \exists\{e_4, e_5\}$

$[continues(e_4, e_5) \wedge [process(e_4) \wedge keep(e_4) \wedge presPerfect(e_4) \wedge$

$must(e_4)] \wedge talk(e_5)]$

The aspectual verb $keep(e_4)$ triggers the aspectual link with its relation type
$continues(e_4, e_5)$ such that the event e_5 of talking is interpreted as continuing
to hold and must continue. In the logical form of Example 5.20, *must* is
introduced as a modal operator which is interpreted as denoting the certainty

---

[8] For example, see the definition of the *present perfect* tense by Bennett and Partee (1978): *I have
called her* α is true at the interval of time *I* if and only if *I* is a moment of time, α refers to an
interval of time *I'*, *I* is a member of *I'*, and there exists a subinterval *I''* of *I'* such that either *I*
is a final point for *I''* or *I''* $\prec$ *I* and *call her* is true at *I''*.

or strong possibility of an event or proposition. The aspectual link (aLink), introduced in ISO-TimeML (ISO, 2012b), relates an event of the aspectual type, as denoted by verbs like *keep, start, finish, stop*, to another event (Pustejovsky et al., 2005, pp. 553–554).

The attribute @*polarity* is either positive or negative. The annotation in Example 5.19 fails to capture the negative polarity of *haven't called*$_{w}$9. The attribute specification of category *event* requires the introduction of *polarity*, thus allowing the following annotation structure to be generated.

Example 5.21   Negative polarity
a. Data: I haven't called$_{w}$9 her back till now.
b. Annotation:
```
event(e2, w9, type="process", pred="call", tense="present",
   aspect="perfect", polarity="neg")
```
c. Semantic representation:
$$\sigma(\text{e}_2) := [\neg call(e_2) \wedge presPerfect(e_2)] \text{ OR } \neg[call(e_2) \wedge presPerfect(e_2)]^9$$

The two logical forms in Example 5.21c represent the narrow or the wide scope reading of the negation.

Revised List of Attributes

The list of attributes for the category *event* needs to be revised. Here is a revised list of attributes, either required or optional, that comprises all the markables referring to eventualities.

Specification 5.22   Revised list of attributes of *event*[10]
```
attributes = identifier, target, type, pred, tense, [aspect], [modality],
   [polarity];
```

Square-bracketed attributes are optional attributes. Their possible values are specified as follows.

Specification 5.23   Specification of attribute-values of category *eventuality*[11]
```
identifier = "e" followed by a positive integer;
target = "IDREF"; (* refers to the identifier of a word-segmented markable. *)
type = CDATA;
   (* lists a predicate type by copying a markable with modifications.*)
pred = CDATA; (* predicative content of an event. *)
tense = "past" | "present" | "none";
aspect = "perfect" | "progressive";
modality = CDATA;
polarity = "neg";
   (* Positives are unmarked by default. Only negatives are marked. *)
```

---

[9] For now, I postpone the discussion of the scope involving negation and tense operators.
[10] The format of specifying attributes and its values here follows ISO/IEC 14977 (eBNF) (ISO/IEC, 1996).
[11] This specification is for English only.

Completeness of Specification

There is a question of completeness related to the specification and validation of an annotation scheme. The list of attributes, whether required or not, for the annotation of eventualities is not, nor can be, *complete*. For instance, the proposed list of attributes in Specification 5.23 fails to annotate the mood, which is either indicative or subjunctive, of a verb, the number of occurrences expressed by $twice_{w4}$, and the plurality of events expressed by her $calls_{e6, w36}$ or the referential relation between the event $called_{w2}$ and $calls_{w34}$ in Example 5.10. As stated earlier, I again claim that semantic annotation should be satisfied with *partial information* only, never aiming to achieve *complete annotation*.

5.3 Representing Logical Forms

5.3.1 An Intermediate Step Towards Interpretation

A *model-theoretic interpretation* of annotation structures normally goes through an intermediate step of deriving well-formed formulas in a logical language, called *logical forms*. This intermediate step may be omitted from a theoretical point of view. Then, the process of interpreting annotation structures without logical forms gets complicated especially because many annotation structures carry semantic ambiguity. Linguistic semantics has most commonly accepted the practice of going through that intermediate step of representing the semantic content of annotation structures in a logical form by adopting some logical formalism. Montague Semantics (Dowty et al., 1981), for instance, uses intensional logic as an intermediate representation language. Some semantic systems create their own representation language with a rich vocabulary to represent logical forms. Kamp and Reyle (1993), for instance, have created a visually appealing language with boxes that represents so-called *discourse representation structures* (DRS). This language is equivalent to the first-order quantificational language, but is descriptively more powerful than the ordinary predicate logic to treat natural language phenomena. The intermediate step of deriving logical forms lightens a load of interpretation by sifting only relevant pieces of annotation content into semantically interpretable forms. Here is an example.

Example 5.24   Logical forms for semantic interpretation
a. Markables: $Mia_{x1, w1}$ has $visited_{e1, w3}$ her $aunt_{x2, w5}$.

b. Annotation structures:

```
entity(x1, w1, type="person", nam="Mia")
entity(x2, w5, type="person", pred="aunt")
event(e1, w3, type="process", pred="visit", tense="present",
    aspect="perfect")
```

c. Logical forms:

$\sigma(\text{x1}) := \{x_1\}[person(x_1) \wedge named(x_1, Mia)]$

$\sigma(\text{x2}) := \{x_1, x_2\}[person(x_2) \wedge aunt(x_2, x_1)^{12}]$

$\sigma(\text{e1}) := \{e_1\}[visit(e_1) \wedge presPerfect(e_1)]$

The markables *Mia* and *aunt* are both nouns: one is a proper name and the other, a common noun. Proper names take the attribute @nam, whereas common nouns have the attribute @pred like eventualities. The name is converted to a quantifiable form so that it can be treated as a *rigid designator*[13] of an individual, while the common name like *aunt* is converted to a predicate in the representation language of logical forms that can denote a relation between two persons.

Each logical form is interpreted with respect to a model and a set of truth-definitions. The logical form $\sigma(\text{e1})$ of visiting in Example 5.24c, for instance, requires a truth-definition of *presPerfect* for an eventuality e_1. This logical form is interpretable if the predicate *presPerfect* is defined in explicit terms.

5.3.2 Shallow vs. Deeper Logical Forms

Depending on the way of modeling a semantics, logical forms can be either *shallow* or *deeper*. *Shallow logical forms* structurally resemble annotation structures while letting an interpretation model take up most of the interpretation work with detailed truth definitions.

The logical form in Example 5.25 is represented in a shallow way.

Example 5.25   Shallow representation
a. Word-segmented data: Mia called$_{w2}$ ...
b. Annotation:

```
event(e1, w2, pred="call", tense="past")
```

c. Shallow logical form:

$\sigma(\text{e1}) := \{e_1\}[call(e_1) \wedge past(e_1)]$

The shallow logical form $past(e_1)$ allows a variety of definitions and interpretations. The temporal predicate *past* can be defined as in Definition 5.26.

---

[12] Here, *aunt* is treated as denoting a binary relation.
[13] A meaning postulate can be formulated for the predicate *named* to capture its being of a rigid designator.

Definition 5.26   Definition of *past*

For any eventuality e in E, any time t in T, and a designated time n that denotes the present moment of time in T, a runtime function τ from E to T, and two binary relations, precedence $\prec$ and inclusion $\subseteq$, over $T \times T$, $past(e)$ is true at n if and only if $\tau(e) \subseteq t$ and $t \prec n$.

Depending on the context of use or situation, the inclusion or *anchoring time t* mentioned in the definition may be understood to be an extended duration or as referring to a short interval of time or a definitely designated time interval or point.

Deeper logical forms encode much of the information that is contained in annotation structures by introducing a large number of predicate constants to the representation language of logical forms. Instead of the shallow logical form in Example 5.25, we will have a deeper logical form as in Example 5.27.

Example 5.27   Deeper logical form with an enriched representation language

$$\sigma(\texttt{e1}) := [call(e_1) \wedge \tau(e_1) \subset t \wedge t \prec n]$$

Then this logical form is directly read off as saying that some event e is anchored to a time t which precedes the time n of utterance.

To allow deeper logical forms as in Example 5.27, the representation language ABSr is augmented with a designated time constant n and a predicate *culminates* for transitions, each of which relates or anchors an event to a time in some manner.

Specification 5.28

The representation language ABSr is augmented with:

a. constant n, which refers to a time of utterance;
b. predicates: *anchors* and its subtypes, *holds*, *occurs*, and *culminates* each of which anchors an eventuality of some type to a time.

They form part of the (object) language that represents deeper logical forms for annotation structures.

With the predicate *anchors* properly defined, it is now possible to redefine the logical predicate *past* as in Definition 5.29.

Definition 5.29   Redefinition of the tense *past*

For any eventualities e, any time t in a set of times T, a designated time n in T for the present moment of time, the past tensed event $past(e)$ is true at n if and only if $[anchors(e,t) \wedge t \prec n]$.

Instead of the predicate *anchors*, we may introduce a *temporal anchoring function* $@_t$ such that $@_t(e)$ maps an eventuality e to a time t, as being

understood as equivalent to *anchors(e, t)*. Depending on the aspectual type of
e, the temporal anchoring of an eventuality, $@_t(e)$, means that e holds, occurs,
or culminates at t.

Kamp and Reyle's (1993) DRS in Example 5.30 is a type of deeper logical
form. It spells out the shallow form $past(e_1)$ to a deeper form $t \prec n$, which
requires the definition of the temporal relation $\prec$ and that of the deictic point of
time n.[14] The logical form as in Example 5.27 can be represented in a slightly
different format as follows.

Example 5.30   DRS as a deeper logical form

e_1, t, n
call(e_1)
$t \prec n$
$e_1 \subseteq t$

The only difference between the logical forms in Example 5.27 and Example
5.30 is in the use of a predicate to represent the anchoring relation between the
event of calling and the time of its occurrence: Example 5.27 has introduced the
predicate *anchors* or the temporal anchoring function $@_t$, whereas Example
5.30 has introduced the predicate of *inclusion* $\subseteq$ denoting a relation between an
eventuality and a time interval. Note that ABSr treats $\subseteq$ as a temporal relation
between two time intervals.

Deixis

Shallow logical forms depend on truth-definitions that can easily accommodate
a variety of interpretations. One of the issues related to the interpretation of the
past tense concerns *implicit temporal deixes*. Consider the deictic or situational
use of the past tense.

Example 5.31   Implicit temporal deixes
a. I didn't turn off the stove. [deictic past][15]
b. Did you lock the front door? [situational past][16]

There are explicitly mentioned *deictic* or *indexical* expressions such as *now,*
here, you and *I*. Then there are *implicit deictic expressions* such as the unmentioned times, such as implied by Example 5.31, the specific values of which
are contextually determined. For the deixes of various types, we introduce a
function γ, called *contextual* or *deictic function*. As is contextually determined,
this function assigns *extensionally specific* values to deictic expressions.

---

[14] The tense predicate *past* applies to events, whereas the relation $\prec$ applies to pairs of times.
[15] This is an example cited in Partee (1973, section 3.1 Deictic pronouns and tenses).
[16] Example [5], Quirk et al. (1985, section 4.12 Situational use of the past tense).

Definition 5.32 Contextual function
$$\gamma : D \rightarrow V,$$
where D is a set of deictic expressions of various types (personal, temporal, spatial, etc.) and V, a set of contextually determinable values such as times.

Applied to the shallow approach to the representation of logical forms, the treatment of the so-called *deictic past* tense remains the same as the ordinary use of the past tense. On the other hand, implicit deictic expressions are annotated as nonconsuming tags, while their values are determined by the γ function. This is illustrated in Example 5.33.

Example 5.33 Use of the function γ

a. Annotation structure:

```
event(e1, w3, pred="turn-off", type="process", tense="past")
timex3(t1, Ø, type="time", value="deictic")
tLink(e1, t1, isIncluded)
```

b. Shallow logical forms:

$\sigma(e_1) := [\neg turnOff(e_1) \wedge past(e_1)]$

$\sigma(t_1) := [value(t_1) = \gamma(t_1)]$

$\sigma(\text{tLink}) := [\sigma(e_1) \oplus \sigma(t_1) \oplus anchors(e_1, t_1)]$

$\qquad\qquad := [\neg turnOff(e_1) \wedge past(e_1) \wedge value(t_1) = \gamma(t_1) \wedge$

$\qquad\qquad\qquad anchors(e_1, \gamma(t_1))]$

Here, γ is a function that assigns a specific value to a deictic reference. For temporal deixes, the domain of γ is a set of contextually determinable (unspecified) times, each referring to a specific time. In Example 5.33, the event of not turning off the stove should have occurred *immediately before* leaving the house, but the speaker I failed to do so.

Example 5.31 also involves *temporal deixes* as well as personal deixes, explicitly expressed by *you*. The temporal deictic expression is not mentioned in the text, but the contextual function γ will specify the time of locking the front door as being the time immediately preceding ($\prec_m$) the time of leaving the house.[17] This can be represented as follows.

Example 5.34 Use of the *meet* relation

a. Data: I didn't lock$_{e1, w3}$ the front door before leaving$_{e2, w8}$ the house.

b. Temporal link: `tLink(tL1, iBefore, e1, e2)`

c. Logical form:

$\sigma(\text{tLink}) := [occurs(e_1, \gamma(t_1)) \wedge occurs(e_2, \gamma(t_2)) \wedge \gamma(t_1) \prec_m \gamma(t_2)]$

---

[17] See Pustejovsky and Batiukova (2019, p. 251), for the use of the *meet* relation $\prec_m$.

5.3.3 Enriching the Representation Language

The tripartite treatment of tense and aspect by Reichenbach (1947) introduces three sorts of times: *event time* (E), *reference time* (R), and *utterance time* (U).[18] The past tense is differentiated from the present perfect in English in the manner of how these three points of time interact with each other.

Definition 5.35 Reichenbach's definitions:
Past: $—R,E\longrightarrow U$
Present perfect: $—E—U,R\longrightarrow$

The past event means that the event time (E) precedes the time of utterance (U), while coinciding with the reference time (R). In contrast, the present perfective event means that, as in the case of past events, the event time (E) precedes the time of utterance (U) but the reference time (R) coincides with the utterance time (U).

Cann et al. (2009) adopt the three sorts of times, as introduced by Reichenbach (1947), into the analysis of the present perfect aspect. They then represent it in the form of Kamp and Reyle's (1993) discourse representation structures (DRS) in a fully spelled-out form.

Concerning the representation of the *present perfect aspect*, consider Example 6.100 taken from Cann et al. (2009), p. 200.

Example 5.36 Aspect present perfect

a. Data: The plant has died.
b. Logical form (DRS):

a, e, t, n, r, s, u
$e \subseteq t$
$t \prec n$
$r = n$
$resultFrom'(e, s)$
$s \bigcirc r$
$Die'(e, u)$
$u = a$
$Plant'(u)$
$Dead'(s, u)$

For the construction of DRSs such as Example 5.36b, its representation language has been enriched with the following list of so-called *discourse referents*.

---

[18] Reichenbach (1947, p. 290) calls the time of utterance (U) the time point of speech (S).

Specification 5.37 Types of discourse referents and predicates

a. Discourse referents:

a is an individual entity,

e is an event,

t is an event time,

n is an utterance time,

r is a reference time,

s is a state

u is an individual.

b. Predicates:

$\subseteq$ is an inclusion relation between an event and a time,

$\prec$ is a precedence relation between times,

$=$ is an identity relation between times,

resultFrom is a relation between an event and a state

$\bigcirc$ is an overlap relation between times.

The predicate *resultFrom* needs to be explained as a temporal *abut* relation $\supset\subset$ between a state *s* and a nonstate eventuality *e* which results by a present perfective event. The abut relation $s \supset\subset e$ is understood as meaning that *s* starts the very moment *e* ends.[19] It is equivalent to the immediate precedence or *meet* relation $\prec_m$ of temporal logic, as discussed in Pustejovsky and Batiukova (2019, p. 251). The predicate *Dead* needs to be introduced into the DRS language to represent the resultant state of the event *Die* through a sort of lexical decomposition (see Dowty (1979)).

Shallow semantics represents the present perfect aspect simply, as illustrated.

Example 5.38 Present perfect in shallow semantics

a. Markables: The plant$_{x1}$ has died$_{e1}$.

b. Annotation:

```
entity(x1, w2-3, type="plant")
event(e1, w3-4, pred="call", type="process", tense="present",
    aspect="perfect")
srLink(srL1, theme, e1, x1)
tLink(tL1, holds, e1, γ(t))
```

c. Shallow logical form:

$$\sigma(\text{srL1}) \oplus \sigma(\text{tL1}) := \exists e_1 [call(e_1) \wedge plant(x_1) \wedge theme(e_1, x_1) \wedge$$
$$presentPerfect(e_1) \wedge holds(e_1, \gamma(t))]$$

---

[19] See Kamp and Reyle (1993, p. 573), and Cann et al. (2009, pp.199–200).

The shallow logical form in Example 5.38c is then interpreted by the truth-condition such as the one that properly conveys its meaning. Here is one provided by Bennett and Partee (1978, p. 95).

Definition 5.39   Present perfect tense
The plant has died α is true at the interval of time I if and only if I is a moment of time, α refers to an interval of time I$'$, I is a member of I$'$, and there exists a subinterval of I$'$, I$''$, such that either I is a final point for I$''$ or I$''<$ I and *The plant dies (or is dead)* is true at I$''$.

Types of Anchoring

The anchoring (anchors) is a general relation that relates an eventuality to a time. There are three different ways of anchoring an eventuality to a time. As was mentioned in Section 5.2.3, the aspectual type of each eventuality determines which of the *anchoring predicates* is chosen for its logical form.

Definition 5.40   Basic anchoring predicates
a. The predicate *holds* anchors an eventuality of type *state* to a time interval.
b. The predicate *occurs* anchors an eventuality of type *process* to a time point or interval.
c. The predicate *culminates* anchors an eventuality of type *transition* to a time point or interval.

These relations can be introduced as logical predicates in the representation language of temporal annotation. This is illustrated in Example 5.41.

Example 5.41   Predicates *occurs* vs. *holds*
a. Data: I had missed$_{w15}$ her calls$_{w17}$. I was asleep$_{w20}$.
b. Annotation structures:
    event(e4, w15, pred="miss", type="achievement", tense="past")
c. Shallow logical forms:
    $\sigma(\text{e4}) := [miss(e_4) \wedge achievement(e_4) \wedge past(e_4)]$
    $\sigma(\text{e5}) := [asleep(e_5) \wedge state(e_5) \wedge past(e_5)]$
d. Deeper logical forms:
    $\sigma(\text{e4}) := [miss(e_4) \wedge t \prec n \wedge occurs(e_4, t)]$
    $\sigma(\text{e5}) := [asleep(e_5) \wedge t \prec n \wedge holds(e_5, t)]$

Here is a short description of what is meant by each of these two predicates, *occurs* and *holds*. They are supposed to capture two different interpretations of *states* and nonstate eventualities, which are often called *events*, such as *processes, achievements,* or *accomplishments.* The predicate *holds* is associated with eventualities of the type *state,* implying that a state is held homogeneously throughout the whole interval of time. This means that the state is satisfied in every subinterval of an interval if that state is satisfied in the whole interval. On the other hand, the predicate *occurs* is understood as denoting an eventuality that is satisfied in an interval but not necessarily in every subinterval of it, thus allowing intervening breaks or interruptions, or being satisfied at a portion of an interval.

Parsons (1990) discusses the notion of *culmination,* which is represented as a predicate *Cul,* in contrast to the notion of *holds.* The predicate *culminates* does not apply to states, while the predicate *culminates* can be used to represent the time of a transition that terminates. The notion of culmination also applies to the description of perfective events, as Moens and Steedman (1998) claim that a culmination is predicated of the time referred to, at which the associated consequent state holds.

Here is an example.

Example 5.42 Culmination
a. Data: Harry has reached the top.
b. Logical form:
$[reach(e) \wedge named(x, Harry) \wedge top(l) \wedge culminates(e,t) \wedge t = n \wedge$
$at(x, <l,t>)]$
c. Culmination point:
preparatory process | consequent state

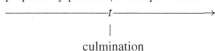

culmination

The event e of reaching the top culminates at the time t, which is *now* (n). The consequent state of Harry being at the top (l) holds at the time t, which is likely to be a time interval.

5.3.4 Constructing a Model Structure for Interpretation

In the shallow approach, discourse referents are treated as part of the interpretation model. Consider how the present perfective aspect is treated. Example 5.43 shows that the shallow approach introduces *presPerfect* as a unary atomic predicate over events just like the tense predicate *past.*

Example 5.43 *presPerfect* as a unary predicate
a. Data: I have just$_{t3, w16}$ called$_{e3, w17}$ her, though.

b. Annotation:

```
event(e3, w17, pred="call", type="process", tense="present",
   aspect="perfect")
timex3(t3, w16, type="time", value="just")
tLink3(tL3, isIncluded, e3, t3)
```

c. Shallow semantic representation:

$\sigma(\text{e3}) := [call(e_3) \wedge presPerfect(e_3)]$

$\sigma(\text{t3}) := [value(t_3) = \gamma(t_3)]$

$\sigma(\text{tL3}) := [occurs(e_3, \gamma(t_3))]$

The shallow logical form $\sigma(\text{e3})$ as in Example 5.43c is then interpreted with a truth-definition as stated in Definition 5.44.

Definition 5.44   Definition of the present perfect
Given times t, r, and n in T and an event e and a state s in E,
$presPerfect(e)$ is true at n iff $[t=r \wedge occurs(e,t) \wedge t \preceq n \wedge holds(s,n)]$

The three types of time t, r and n are understood as referring to the event, reference, and utterance time, respectively, as proposed by Reichenbach's (1947) tripartite treatment of tense. Unlike the past-tensed event, the present perfective event $presPerfect(e)$ clause implies a resultant state as represented by the logical form $holds(s,n)$.

Temporal Model Structure

Specification 5.45   Interpretation model for *tense* and *aspect*
Tense and *aspect* in ordinary language can be proposed as a tuple $<E, V, T, n, N, R, F, v>$ that consists of:

- a set E of individual entities,
- a set V of eventualities,
- a set T of time points,
- a designated time point n in T and its neighborhood N or $\mathcal{N}(n)$,
- a set R of binary relations over T,
- a set F of functions from T or E to T, and
- a valuation v of individual or predicate constants.

Individual entities in E include any objects such as persons or things in general. This modeling also treats eventualities as individuals but in V as in the Neo-Davidsonian Semantics. Consider the following.

Example 5.46   Eventualities as individual entities
a. Data: John sings well.

b. Logical forms:

$\sigma(John) := \{x\}[named(x, John) \wedge person(x)]$

$\sigma(sings) := \{e\}[sing(e)]$

$\sigma(sings\ well) := \{e\}[sing(e) \wedge well(e)]$

$\sigma(John\ sings\ well)$

$:= \{x, e\}[[named(x, John) \wedge person(x)] \wedge [sing(e) \wedge well(e)]]$

   by binding the free occurrences of variables by quantification

$:= \exists\{x, e\}[[named(x, John) \wedge person(x)] \wedge [sing(e) \wedge well(e)]]$

Time intervals are constructed out of the set T that consists of time points. The proposed model licenses an interval temporal logic with a linear order $\prec$ over time intervals T. Every temporal interval $[t_0, t_n]$, which is bounded by the two points t_0 and t_n, the initial and final boundary points, is understood to be a finite sequence $t_0, t_1, \ldots, t_{n-1}, t_n$ of time points such that $t_0 \preceq t_1, \ldots, t_{n-1} \preceq t_n$, while sequences are defined by a function $\mathbf{s}$ in F with its domain being an ordered set W like a set of natural numbers. An interval may also be cut into smaller subintervals.

Definition 5.47 Sequence defined[20]

Let S be a nonempty set and let W be any well-ordered set. An element $\mathbf{s} \in S^W$ is called *a sequence of elements in S indexed by W*.

There are bound, open, and semiopen intervals of time. A fully open interval is represented as (t_0, t_n) that corresponds to a finite sequence $t_1, \ldots, t_{n-1}$.

   There are some *designated times*. One of the designated temporal points in T is n. Associated with n, there is a neighborhood N of n in a topological sense. As for a linearly structured set $<T, \preceq>$, where T is a set of time points, the neighborhood $N(t)$ is defined as follows.

Definition 5.48 Neighborhood of a time point t

Given a linearly structured set $<T, \preceq>$ of time points T and a time point t in T, the neighborhood $N(t)$ is a sequence of times that includes t with an indefinite length greater than zero.

Both n and N, where $N=N(n)$, are specially designated times associated with the *time of utterance*. A designated time point n is understood to be the *present moment of time*, whereas N carries the meaning of *now* or *the present time* in English in an extended sense.

---

[20] Copied from Pierce (1968, p.119).

The set R of binary relations over T is specified by Specification 5.49.

Specification 5.49   Binary relations over T

- $\prec$ is a *precedence* relation,
- $\prec_m$ is an immediate precedence or *meet* relation,
- $=$ is an identity relation, and
- $\leq$ is a precedence or identity relation over times, either points or intervals.

These and other possible relations such as inclusion $\subseteq$ and overlap $\bigcirc$ can apply to time intervals.

The set F of functions maps a time or an event to a time. As introduced by Katz (2007), *the runtime function τ* is a function in F from a set V of eventualities to T or time intervals. This function allows an inclusion condition $e \subseteq t$, as represented in DRS, to be interpreted as denoting a proposition $[\tau(e) \subseteq t]$.

The contextual function γ, which maps a deictic expression to a specific value, can also be introduced into the set of functions F in the model structure. Then the values of deictic expressions remain unspecified at the level of representing logical forms.

5.4 Type-Theoretic Semantics

5.4.1 Overview

For doing semantics in this book, I adopt the *Neo-Davidsonian Semantics* of Parsons (1990), Kamp and Reyle (1993), and many others, that originated from Reichenbach (1947, section 48, chapter 7) and Davidson (1967, 2001). Here both individual entities like John and eventualities like running are treated as first-order objects but not as sets. Eventualities can thus be referred to or *pronominalized* just like individual entities such as John.[21]

Consider Example 5.50.

Example 5.50   Pronominalized events

a. Data: Mia called$_{e1}$ me the day before yesterday and I missed it$_{e1}$.

b. $\exists\{x, e_1, y, e_2\}$
   $[named(x, Mia)$
   $\wedge call(e_1) \wedge agent(e_1, x)$
   $\wedge speaker(y) \wedge theme(e_1, y)$
   $\wedge miss(e_2) \wedge experiencer(e_2, y) \wedge theme(e_2, e_1)]$

---

[21] See Davidson (1967) and Hobbs (1985) for the discussion of pronominalized or nominalized events.

The pronoun *it* in Example 5.50 refers to the event *called*$_{e1}$, which is the call from Mia and it was the call that the speaker missed.

Example 5.51 Number of occurrences
a. Data:
Mia visited$_{e2}$ Berlin, New York, three times last year.
b. Logical form:
$\exists E[|E| = 3 \wedge \forall e[e \in E \rightarrow \exists t[visit(e) \wedge past(e) \wedge agent(e, Mia) \wedge theme(e, Berlin) \wedge occurs(e, t) \wedge year(t, 2018)]]]$

Example 5.51a is understood as stating that there were three instances of Mia's visit to Berlin, New York, in the year 2018. As illustrated by examples like Example 5.51, the *type-theoretic semantics* to be adopted in this book will incorporate eventualities into it as referable individual objects like individual entities.

Both individual entities and eventualities are *first-order objects* but of different *semantic types*. In an extended theory of types to be discussed in Section 5.4.2, individual entities are of type *e*, whereas eventualities are of type *v*. These types systematically constrain the syntactic categorization of base structures that are anchored to markable expressions in language, thereby laying a semantic basis for the construction of semantic annotation schemes.

Montague and Type Theory
Montague (1974) introduced a *type theory* into the construction of natural language semantics. He had only two basic types, *e* for individual entities and *t* for truth-values. From these two, he inductively defined other complex types.[22]

Definition 5.52 Semantic types
a. *e* and *t* are types.
b. If α and β are types, then $<\alpha, \beta>$ are also types.

Intransitive verbs like *walks* or common nouns like *man* refer to objects of type $<e, t>$. Each of them denotes a set of individuals or a function from individuals to truth-values.

Example 5.53 Illustration
a. Sample sentence: John snores.

---

[22] Montague also defined intensional types with an additional clause: If α is a type, then $<s, \alpha>$ is a type. The type of the form $<s, \alpha>$ is an intensional type such as an individual concept $<s, e>$ or a property of an individual $<s, <e, t>>$.

b. Logical forms:

$\sigma(John) := j_e$

$\sigma(sings) := \lambda x[sings'(x)]_{<e,t>}$

$\sigma(John \ sings) := \lambda x[sings'(x)]_{<e,t>}(j_e)$

$\qquad := [snores'(j)]_t$

Here, σ is a semantic function that maps an annotation structure, represented by a markable or its index, to a semantic form represented in formal logic. The semantic form $[sings'(j)]$ is then interpreted with respect to a model as stating that it is true with respect to that model if the individual denoted by the individual j_e is a member of the set of snoring individuals denoted by $snores'_{<e,t>}$.[23]

Type Raising

In Montague Semantics, the basic type e of individuals is raised to the higher type $<<e,t>,t>$ of a set of sets of individuals so that proper names such as *John* and quantified expressions like *every boy* can be treated uniformly or conjoined. Here is an example.

Example 5.54   Quantified expressions

a. Every boy sings.

b. Semantic representation:

$\sigma(every \ boy)_{<<e,t>,t>} := \lambda P\forall x[boy'(x) \rightarrow P(x)]$

$\sigma(sings)_{<e,t>} := sings'$

$\sigma(every \ boy \ sings)_t$

$\qquad := \sigma(every \ boy)_{<<e,t>,t>}(sings'_{<e,t>})$

$\qquad := \lambda P\forall x[boy'(x) \rightarrow P(x)]_{<<e,t>,t>}(sings'_{<e,t>})$

$\qquad := \forall x[boy'(x) \rightarrow sings'(x)]_t$

The type e of $\sigma(John)$ is raised to that of quantifiers $<<e,t>,t>$.

Example 5.55   Type raising of proper names

a. John sings.

b. Type raising:

$\sigma(John) := \lambda PP(j)$

$\sigma(snores)_{<e,t>} := sings'$

$\sigma(John \ snores)_t$

$\qquad := \sigma(John)_{<<e,t>,t>}(sings')$

---

[23] In Montague's (1974) PTQ, the logical form of a name like *John* is raised to a higher type, $\lambda PP(j)_{<<e,t>,t>}$, like that of a quantified expression *every boy*, which is translated into a logical form $\lambda P\forall x[boy'(x) \rightarrow P(x)]_{<<e,t>,t>}$. Note that the s for sense or intensionality is ignored here.

$$:= \lambda PP(j)_{<<e,t>,t>}(sings'_{<e,t>})$$
$$:= sings'(j)_t$$

By raising the type e of $\sigma(John)$ to $<<e,t>,t>$, *John* can easily be coordinated with a quantified phrase *every boy* of the same type $<<e,t>,t>$.

Example 5.56 Coordinated noun phrases John and every boy sing
a. Data: John and every boy sing.
b. Semantic representation:
$\sigma(John \ and \ every \ boy) := \lambda P[P(j) \wedge \forall x[boy'(x) \rightarrow P(x)]]_{<<e,t>,t>}$
$\sigma(sing) := sing'_{<e,t>}$
$\sigma(John \ and \ every \ boy \ sing)$
$:= \lambda P[P(j) \wedge \forall x[boy'(x) \rightarrow P(x)]](sing')$
$:= [sing'(j) \wedge \forall x[boy'(x) \rightarrow sing'(x)]]$

The *type raising* of the denotations of names like $\sigma(Socrates)$ allows names to be represented easily as *rigid designators*, as in Example 5.57.

Example 5.57 Names as rigid designators
$\sigma(Socrates) = \lambda P \exists x[named(x, Socrates) \wedge$
$\forall y[named(y, Socrates) \rightarrow [y{=}x \wedge P(x)]]$

5.4.2 Extension of Basic Types

Following Kracht (2002), Pustejovsky et al. (2019a) extend Montague's (1974) basic set of the two basic semantic types, e and t, to include four more types as basic types.[24]

Definition 5.58 Six basic types
a. e is the type of objects
c. t is the type of truth values
d. i is the type of time points
e. p is the type of spatial points
f. v is the type of events
g. m is the type of measures

The individuals referred to by names such as *Mary* are objects of type e. The type t of truth values typically has two values, *true* and *false*. The present moment n of time may be considered as the basic type i of time points. The boundaries of a spatial interval are spatial points of type p. At the abstract level, measures are of type m.

---

[24] The type of measure m is a new addition in Pustejovsky et al. (2019a).

These basic types may not be associated directly with the denotations of expressions in natural language. Instead, higher types are created from the basic types to be more applicable to the semantics of natural language. These types are derived by binary type constructors such as $\rightarrow$ over types to generate so-called *functional types* that denote sets of the first or higher-order objects or sets.

Functional Types

The binary *type constructor* $\rightarrow$ creates types such as $e \rightarrow t$, denoting a set of individual objects. The type $e \rightarrow t$ is equivalent to the Montagovian type $<e, t>$. Such a type is called a *functional type* because its associated denotation is understood to be a (characteristic) function from a set of entities to the set of truth values. Furthermore, it is syntactically associated with the so-called *functional application* of categorial rules and the λ-conversion of the lambda calculus which is used as an intermediate representation language in Montague Semantics.

Here is an example.

Example 5.59 Functional combination
a. Functional categorial combination:
   John$_{NP}$ walks$_{S/NP}$:= [John walks]$_S$
b. Semantic form for λ-conversion:
   $\sigma(walks)_{<e,t>}(\sigma(John)_e) := \sigma(John \; walks)_t$
   or
   $\lambda x[walk'(x)](j) := walk'(j)_t$

The semantic form of *John walks*, $\sigma(John \; walks)$, is obtained by a λ-conversion, as shown in Example 5.59.

Based on the extended list of basic types (Definition 5.58), the type constructor $\rightarrow$ also allows the derivation of the following functional types.

Definition 5.60 Functional types
a. type of *regions* $r = p \rightarrow t$
b. type of *intervals* $I = i \rightarrow t$
c. type of *event descriptors* $V = v \rightarrow t$

Eventualities are of type v, whereas *eventuality descriptors* like *run* are of type V. Here is an example.

Example 5.61 Eventuality descriptor
a. Data: Fido runs fast.
b. Semantic form:
   $[run(e) \wedge agent(e, fido) \wedge fast(e)]$

The argument *e* of *run* is of type v, while the predicate *run* as an eventuality descriptor is of type $v \rightarrow t$ or V.

The place *Jeju*, for instance, can be treated as the functional type $p \rightarrow t$, a set of spatial points or a *region r*. As a *subtype* of the type of time points *i*, we can also define the type *I* of temporal intervals. Dates such as *November, the year 2020*, or *the first week in December 2019* denote temporal intervals. The neighborhood $N(n)$ of the present time point *n* is also an open time interval.

Example 5.62 Temporal intervals and neighborhood

a. the first week in December 2019:

————[[————-][————-][————-][————-]—]————→

|

first week

December, 2019

b. Neighborhood of the present moment *n*:

————————(————-n————-)————→

|

$N = N(n)$

The event of my visiting Brandeis University occurred more than five times. My visits to Brandeis form a set *V* of events the cardinality of which is greater than 5. Each event instance *e* of my visits to Brandeis is understood to be one of the visits, a member of the set *E*, as represented below.

Example 5.63 Event instances

a. Data: I visited Brandeis University more than five times.
b. Logical form (DRS):

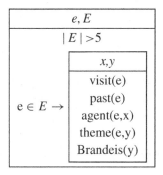

E represents a set of events of my visiting Brandeis, and its cardinality is greater than 5, representing the number of my visits. The *if-then* conditions listed in the embedded DRS box describe what each of the events was.

The whole DRS gives a distributive reading of the more-than-five visits to Brandeis.

Regions

Semantic typing can differentiate spatial points, which are called *positions* in Mani and Pustejovsky (2012), or temporal points, called *instants*, from regions or temporal intervals in a fine-grained way. *Regions* are of functional type r, which is defined to be $p \to t$.

The spatial relator *in* that relates one region to another is treated as of another functional type $r \to (r \to t)$. The denotation of this type is interpreted as a relation between two regions each of which is of type r or $p \to t$. Such a treatment allows the semantic representation of qualitative spatial relations as in Example 5.64.

Example 5.64   Spatial relators

a. Jeju in Korea
b. Annotation:

```
place(pl1, Jeju, ...)
place(pl2, Korea ...)
spatialRelator(sr1, in, ...)
qsLink(pl1, pl2, type:in)
```

c. Semantic representation:

$\sigma(\text{Jeju}) = J_r$

$\sigma(\text{Korea}) = K_r$

$\sigma(in) = \lambda y[\lambda x[in(x, y)]]_{r \to (r \to t)}$

$\sigma(\text{qsLink}) = [[\sigma(in)_{r \to (r \to t)}(\sigma(\text{Jeju})_r)]_{r \to t}(\sigma(\text{Korea})_r)]_t$

$\qquad\qquad = [\lambda y[\lambda x[in(x, y)]]_{r \to (r \to t)}(J_r)](K_r)$

$\qquad\qquad = \lambda x[in(x, K_r)]_{r \to t}(J_r)$

$\qquad\qquad = in(J, K)_t$

The type p of each of the spatial base structures in Example 5.64 is raised to the higher type r or $(p \to t)$ to allow capturing various pieces of information that is annotated to it.

Semantic forms that represent the content of spatial entities and their relations are derived from annotation structures (see Example 5.65).

Example 5.65   Annotation structures

a. Data: Jeju in Korea

b. Annotation structures:

```
place(pl1, Jeju, type="island", form="nam")
place(pl2, Korea, type="country")
spatialRelator(sr1,in, type="qualitativeSpatial")
qsLink(relType="in", figure="pl1", ground="pl2")
```

We then derive semantic forms that represent the content of the annotated base structures and their relations as follows.

Example 5.66   Semantic forms of the base structures
a. $\sigma(\text{Jeju}) = \lambda r_1[named(r_1, \text{Jeju}) \wedge island(r_1)]_{r \to t}$
b. $\sigma(\text{Korea}) = \lambda r_2[named(r_2, \text{Korea}) \wedge country(r_2)]_{r \to t}$
c. $\sigma(\text{in}) = \lambda y \lambda x[in(x, y)]_{r \to (r \to t)}$

All of these base structures are then combined by the qualitative spatial link, as in Example 5.67.

Example 5.67   Semantic form of the qualitative spatial link structure $\sigma(\text{qsLink})$

$$= \lambda R_2[\lambda R_1[R_1(x) \wedge R_2(y) \wedge in(x, y)]]_{(r \to t) \to ((r \to t) \to t)}$$
$$(\sigma(\text{Korea})_{r \to t})$$
$$(\sigma(\text{Jeju})_{r \to t})$$
$$= \lambda R_2[\lambda R_1[R_1(x) \wedge R_2(y) \wedge in(x, y)]]_{(r \to t) \to ((r \to t) \to t)}$$
$$(\lambda r_2[named(r_2, \text{Korea}) \wedge country(r_2)]_{r \to t})$$
$$(\lambda r_1[named(r_1, \text{Jeju}) \wedge island(r_1)]_{r \to t})$$
$$= [[named(x, \text{Jeju}) \wedge island(x)] \wedge [named(y, \text{Korea}) \wedge country(y)]$$
$$\wedge in(x, y)]_t$$

These semantic forms are interpreted with respect to a model in a formal way.

Time Intervals and Event Descriptors

A time interval I is of another functional type $i \to t$, which stands for a set of time points. The time *last year* can be treated as a *time interval* of the type I, denoting the whole extent of time consisting of months, days, and hours.

Time intervals interact with events. An event occurs at a time or holds throughout an interval of time. To treat their relations, the basic type v of events is raised to the type $v \to t$, denoting an event descriptor V, a function from events to truth values.

Consider Example 5.68 involving a temporal interval in which an event occurs.

Example 5.68   Temporal interval
a. Data: Mia visited Boston last year.

b. Annotation:

```
event(e1, w2, type="process", pred="visit", tense="past")
timex3(t1, w4-5, type="date", value="2018-XX-XX")
tLink(tL1, relType="occurs", eventID="e1", timeID="t1")
```

Based on the annotation structures in Example 5.68, we have the following semantic forms for interpretation.

Example 5.69　Semantic forms

a. Base structures:

$$\sigma(\texttt{e1})_{v \to t} := \lambda e_1 [visit(e_1) \wedge past(e_1)]_{v \to t}$$
$$\sigma(\texttt{t1})_{(i \to t) \to t} := \lambda t_1 [year(t_1, 2018)]_{I \to t}$$

b. Link structures:

$$\sigma(\texttt{tLink}) := \lambda T [\lambda E [E(e) \wedge T(t) \wedge occurs(e,t)]]_{(I \to t) \to ((v \to t) \to t)}$$
$$(\lambda t_1 [year(t_1, 2018)]_{I \to t})$$
$$(\lambda e_1 [visit(e_1) \wedge past(e_1)]_{v \to t})$$
$$:= [[visit(e) \wedge past(e)] \wedge year(t, 2018) \wedge occurs(e,t)]_t$$

Temporal Measures

Measures each consist of a pair $<n, u>$ where n is a positive real number in R and u in U, a set of normalized or conventionally accepted units. Temporal measures then represent time amounts or durations (lengths of time intervals) usually in terms of a number of years, months, days, or other calendar times. They are treated as of the basic type m by Pustejovsky et al. (2019a). Consider Example 5.70.

Example 5.70　Measure type

a. Data: Mia slept three hours.

b. Typed:

　Mia$_e$ slept$_v$ three hours$_m$.

The denotations of *Mia, slept,* and *three hours* are of the type e of objects, the type v of events, and the type m of measures, respectively.

　　ISO-Space (ISO, 2020d) introduces a category *measure* (tag) and a measure link (mLink) to annotate measure expressions.

Example 5.71　Annotation of measure expressions

a. Markables: Mia slept$_{e1}$ on a bench for *three hours$_{me1}$*.

b. Annotation:

```
event(e1, w2, type="process", pred="sleep", tense="past")
measure(me1, w7-8, type="timeLength", value="3", unit="hours")
mLink(mL1, relType="duration", figure="e1", ground="me1")
```

The annotation structures in Example 5.71 have the following semantic representation.

Example 5.72 Semantic representation

a. $\sigma(slept) := \lambda e_1[sleep(e_1) \wedge past(e_1)]_{v \to t}$

b. $\sigma(three\,hours) := \lambda v[timeLength(v) \wedge v = (3, hour)]_{m \to t}$

c. $\sigma(\texttt{mLink}) := \lambda E \lambda M[E(e) \wedge M(d) \wedge duration(e,d)]_{(v \to t)((m \to t) \to t)}$
$\qquad\qquad (\sigma(slept)_{v \to t})$
$\qquad\qquad (\sigma(three\,hour)_{(m \to t)})$
$\qquad := [[sleep(e) \wedge past(e)] \wedge [timeLength(v) \wedge v = (3, hour)] \wedge$
$\qquad\qquad duration(e,v)]_t.$

The predicate *duration* is here treated as a predicate that denotes a binary relation between an event and its time amount.[25]

5.4.3 Type Shifting or Coercion

Localization

The *localization* of nonlocational objects into locational objects requires some sort of *type shifting* or *type coercion* as much discussed by Pustejovsky (1995) and many others. A function L can be introduced to convert nonlocational objects like *fly* and *soup*, as in *A fly is in the soup*, to be spatial objects like genuinely locational spatial entities such as places. A qualitative spatial relation like *in* is then treated as a spatial relation over spatial objects that include both genuinely locational objects like places and also localized entities like *fly* or *soup*.

For the coercion of types to type r or $p \to t$, we introduce a *localization function L*.

Definition 5.73 Localization

For any type α and an object X of type α,
$L : X_\alpha \to \lambda x[loc(x, X)]_{p \to t}$

Here, the localization $L(X_\alpha)$ is understood as denoting a set of locations x where an object X of type α is positioned. It can apply to any object of any type, for instance, to the object of an individual type e or an event description of type $v \to t$. Conceptually speaking, localization may be viewed as a spatio-temporal instantiation or realization of an object.

Here is an example from Pustejovsky et al. (2019a) that illustrates how localization coerces type shifting.

[25] Following ISO 8601-1 (ISO, 2019a), *duration* will also be used as a term referring to the quantity (length) of a time interval.

Example 5.74 Type shifting

a. Data: Robin is in Sweden.

b. Annotation:

```
spatialEntity(se1, Robin)
place(pl1, Sweden)
spatialRelator(sR1,in) 26
qsLink(relType="in", figure="se1", ground="pl1")
```

Example 5.75 Semantic representation for interpretation

a. $\sigma(Robin) := R_e$

b. $\sigma(Sweden) := S_r$

c. $L(R_e) := \lambda x[loc(x, R)]_r$

e. $\sigma(in) := \lambda y \lambda x[in(x, y)]_{r \to (r \to t)}$

The denotation of Robin in Example 5.75a is coerced by L with its type being shifted from e to r, as shown in part c. The localized denotation, called *eigenplace* or *eigenspace*, of *Robin* now becomes a semantically appropriate argument for the spatial relation $\sigma(in)$.

Example 5.76 Semantic representation of the `qsLink` structure for interpretation

$$\sigma(\text{qsLink}) := \sigma(in)_{r \to (r \to t)}(\sigma(Sweden)_r)(L(\sigma(Robin))_r)$$
$$:= \lambda y \lambda x[in(x, y)]_{r \to (r \to t)}(S_r)(\lambda x[loc(x, R)]_r)$$
$$:= \lambda x[in(x, S)]_{r \to t}(\lambda x[loc(x, R)]_r)$$
$$:= in(\lambda x[loc(x, R)]_r, S_r)_t$$

The preposition *in* is now treated as denoting a spatial relation over the two regions, one of which is a localized object, *Robin*.

Consider another example.

Example 5.77 A fly$_x$ is in$_{sr1}$ the soup$_y$.

Neither of the markables, fly$_x$ and soup$_y$, is of type *region*. The function L coerces their denotations to be of type $r \to t$, each denoting a set of regions. They are *localized* (L), as represented by the semantic forms in Example 5.78.

Example 5.78 Localization

a. $\lambda x[fly(x)]_{e \to t}$
   $\lambda y[soup(y)]_{e \to t}$

b. $L(\sigma(fly)) := \lambda r_1[loc(r_1, \sigma(fly))]_{r \to t}$
   $L(\sigma(soup)) := \lambda r_2[loc(r_2, \sigma(soup))]_{r \to t}$

---

[26] In ISO-Space (ISO, 2020d), *spatialRelator* is named *spatialRelation* or simply *sRelation*.

Then the type of qsLink (qualitative spatial link) involving the spatial relation *in* is raised to be of type $(r \to t)((r \to t) \to t)$, while showing how the semantic form of *A fly is in the soup* in Example 5.77 is represented.

Example 5.79 Semantic representation

$$\sigma(\text{qsLink}) := \lambda R_2[\lambda R_1[R_1(r_1) \wedge R_2(r_2) \wedge in(r_1,r_2)]]_{(r \to t)((r \to t) \to t)}$$
$$(\lambda r_2[loc(r_2, \lambda y[soup(y)])])_{r \to t})$$
$$(\lambda r_1[loc(r_1, \lambda x[fly(x)])])_{r \to t})$$
$$:= [loc(r_1, \lambda x[fly(x)]) \wedge loc(r_2, \lambda y[soup(y)]) \wedge in(r_1,r_2)]_t$$

5.4.4 Constraining Type Raising

Complexity of Type Raising

Type raising is a powerful mechanism to introduce higher-order types. Especially when dealing with group nouns and predicates and more with generalized quantification over them or predicate modifications, one may find it necessary to define types not only for a set of sets of individuals, $(e \to t) \to t$ but also a set of sets of sets of individuals $((e \to t) \to t) \to t$ or even higher-order types. See Example 5.80.

Example 5.80 Higher-order types

a. A dog is barking.
   $$\lambda P \exists x[dog'(x) \wedge P(x)]_{(e \to t) \to t}(isBarking'_{e \to t})$$
   Or
   $$\lambda P \exists \{X, x\}[|X|=1 \wedge [x \in X \to [dog'(x) \wedge P(x)]]]_{(e \to t) \to t}(isBarking'_{e \to t})$$
b. Dogs bark.
   $$\lambda P \exists \{X, x\}[|X| \geq 2 \wedge [x \in X \to [dog'(x) \wedge P(x)]]]_{(e \to t) \to t}(bark'_{e \to t})$$
c. Every dog barks.
   $$\lambda P \forall x[dog'(x) \to P(x)]_{(e \to t) \to t}(barks'_{e \to t})$$

So far the types remain within the bound of manageable orders, denoting a set of individuals $(e \to t)$ or a set of sets of individuals $((e \to t) \to t)$, as in classical Montague Semantics (Montague, 1974).

Consider, however, examples involving *group nouns* or *group predicates*.

Example 5.81 Group nouns or predicates

a. All dogs gathered in the backyard.
   $$\lambda \mathcal{P} \forall X[^*dog'(X) \to \mathcal{P}(X)]_{((e \to t) \to t)) \to t}(gathered'_{(e \to t) \to t})$$
b. All the subcommittees briefly met this afternoon.
   $$\lambda \mathcal{P} \forall X[subcommittee'(X) \to \mathcal{P}(X)]_{((e \to t) \to t) \to t}(met'_{((e \to t) \to t)})$$

The *group operator* * in Example 5.81 raises the type of the plural common noun *dog* from type $e \rightarrow t$ to the higher type $(e \rightarrow t) \rightarrow t$. The group predicate **dog* now combines with an argument X of a set-type $e \rightarrow t$. Then, as we see in Example 5.81, the type of quantified noun phrases is raised to type $((e \rightarrow t) \rightarrow t) \rightarrow t$, a set of sets of sets of individuals.

Type Raising with Quantifiers

Type raising becomes more complicated with *generalized quantifiers* or transitive verbs, as well argued by Cann et al. (2009, setcion 4.2). Since a quantifier denotes a relation between the two sets of sets, one denoted by the *restrictor* and the other by its scope, its type must be raised accordingly.

Example 5.82   Higher-order type of quantifiers
$((e \rightarrow t) \rightarrow t)(((e \rightarrow t) \rightarrow t) \rightarrow t)$

Higher-order types such as the quantifier type shown in Example 5.82 need to be lowered for doing first-order semantics.

Consider another example such as Example 5.83. For a compositional treatment, the valency and modification of higher-type predicates also require the raising of their types.

Example 5.83   High-order types

a. John$_{(e \rightarrow t) \rightarrow t}$ gave$_{((e \rightarrow t) \rightarrow t)((e \rightarrow t) \rightarrow t) \rightarrow ((e \rightarrow t) \rightarrow t) \rightarrow t}$ Mary$_{(e \rightarrow t) \rightarrow t}$ a beautiful doll$_{(e \rightarrow t) \rightarrow t}$.

b. The crowd of demonstrators gathered$_\tau$ slowly$_{\tau \rightarrow \tau}$ in the square.

The type of denotation of the ditransitive verb *gave* depends on the types of denotations of its two complements. The type of the verb is raised to a higher type as the types of its complements are raised. Likewise, the type of a modifier becomes complex as the type τ of a predicate that it modifies is raised to a higher order.

Structured Sets   Such raising of types has no problem in itself. It is consistent and systematic. Its complexity is, however, found burdensome, counter-intuitive, and against the common-sense understanding of language. This has made Link (1983, 1998) and others go beyond the ordinary notion of sets and adopt a new type of *ontology* that provides a better view of how individuals in a set A are related by the part–whole relation $\leq$. Such a view, called *mereology*, formally constitutes a structured set $<A, \leq>$, based on a lattice theory. This structure is then used to represent singular, plural, group, and mass nouns uniformly all as individuals of type e, the first-order objects.

Individual Sum Consider a small set $A=\{a,b,c\}$ of cardinality 3. The relation $\oplus$ of *summation* or *join* over A defines the following structure, called *individual sums (i-sums)*.

Example 5.84 The i-sum structure of $\{a,b,c\}$
$(a,b,c,a \oplus b, a \oplus c, b \oplus c, a \oplus b \oplus c)$

Each of the i-sums has a *part of relation* $\leq$ or more specifically $\leq_i$, an individual part of relation. The i-sum $a \oplus b$, for instance, has two individual parts (*i-part*): a and b. The single individuals such as a, b, c are called *atomic* because they have no parts other than themselves, although they can also be viewed as the individual sums $a \oplus a$, $b \oplus b$, and $c \oplus c$, respectively.

Group Based on the lattice-theoretic notion of i-structure, *groups* are defined as i-sums, which are of type e like individual entities. By definition, groups comprise both singulars and plurals. Out of a simple predicate P, a *group predicate* $*P$ is formed. If P denotes a set of individuals $\{a,b,c\}$, then the group $*P$, as introduced by Link (1983), denotes the set of i-sums based on the set $\{a,b,c\}$, whereas *plural predicates* $*P$ as denoted by plural nouns like *dogs* denote the set of i-sums other than the atoms.

Definition 5.85 Lattice-theoretic notions
a. *Singulars* (P) denote atomic (i-sum) individuals: e.g., $P := \{a,b,c\}$
b. *Groups*$(*P)$ include both atomic i-sums and those i-sums that are formed by the *join* operation $\oplus$ over atomic individuals:
   e.g., $\{a,b,c,a \oplus b, a \oplus c, b \oplus c, a \oplus b \oplus c\}$
c. *Plurals* $(*P)$ denote the set of nonatomic i-sums:
   e.g., $\{a \oplus b, a \oplus c, b \oplus c, a \oplus b \oplus c\}$

Collective vs. Group Predicates Link (1983) differentiate collective predicates $*P$ from group predicates $*P$. Collective predicates $*P$ are called *proper plural* or *starred* predicates. Unlike group predicates $*P$, collective predicates denote nonatomic i-sums only. Here are examples of *collective verbs* in English.

Example 5.86 Collective verbs in English
agree, date, gather, marry, meet

The verb like *gather* is a *collective* predicate that denotes a nonatomic i-sum. This is why the singular quantifier phrase *every student* cannot be the subject of *gather*, while the plural *all students* are allowed to be its subject (see Cann et al. (2009, p. 131)).

Example 5.87 *every* vs. *all*

a.?* *Every* student has gathered for a party.

b. *All* students have gathered for a party.

Collective verbs such as *meet, marry, date* or verbs modified by an adverb like *together* or *as a group* are also treated as collective predicates.

Example 5.88 Collective modifiers

a. John and Mary sang an aria *together*.

b. One hundred women banded *together* to form a union.

c. Ants *as a group* can build a big mound of mud or sand.

Example 5.89 shows how the collective verb *marry* is annotated and interpreted.

Example 5.89 Collective verb *marry*

a. John and Mary *married* last night.

b. Annotation:

```
entity(x1, w1, type="person", form="name")
entity(x2, w3, type="person", form="name")
event(e1, w4, type="process", pred="marry", qType="collective", tense="past")
srLink(srL1, relType:*agent, event="e1", participants="{x1,x2}")
```

c. Logical form:

$$\sigma(\text{x1}) := \lambda x_1[person(x_1) \wedge named(x_1, John)]$$
$$\sigma(\text{x2}) := \lambda x_2[person(x_2) \wedge named(x_2, Mary)]$$
$$\sigma(\text{e1}) := \lambda e_1[^*marry(e_1) \wedge past(e_1)]$$
$$\sigma(\text{srL1}) := \lambda R \lambda Q \lambda P[R(e) \wedge^* agent(e, [u \oplus v]) \wedge P(u) \wedge$$
$$Q(v)](\sigma(e1))(\sigma(x2))(\sigma(x1))$$
$$:= [^*marry(e) \wedge past(e) \wedge^* agent(e, [u \oplus v])$$
$$\wedge[person(u) \wedge named(u, John)]$$
$$\wedge[person(v) \wedge named(v, Mary)]]$$

The individual sum $u \oplus v$ is then interpreted as $u \leq_i v$ of type e, a *bound single entity* with two individual parts, while satisfying the conditions that u is a person named *John* and v is a person named *Mary*. Here the relation $\oplus$ for individual sums is treated as part of the representation language, while the $\leq_i$ is part of the interpretation model.

Group Nouns There are so-called *collective nouns* such as *army, choir, committee*, and *couple*. Unlike collective verbs, these nouns should be called *group nouns* because each of them may denote any of the i-sums including atomic i-sums in $^*P$. These nouns do not refer to collective predicates, but group predicates.

Example 5.90 Examples of group nouns

a. Our parish *choir*$_{group}$ was disbanded.

b. Napoleon's grand army *staff*$_{group}$ finally met and decided to retreat from Moscow.

c. The whole *army*$_{collective}$ were starving and being frozen to death.

Consider how group nouns are annotated.

Example 5.91 Annotation of group nouns

a. Data: Our parish choir$_e$ Cecilia was disbanded$_{e \to t}$.

b. Annotation:

```
entity(x1, w3, type="choir", qType="group", form="nam")
event(e1, w6, type="process", pred="beDisbanded", qType="collective",
  tense="past")
srLink(srL1, semRole="*theme", event="e1", participant="x1")
```

The annotation of *choir* in Example 5.91 may be interpreted in two different ways. One is to focus on its name *Cecilia* and another on the group noun *choir*. In either case, the link annotates its type as being a group predicate, namely *theme*. Here is the logical form with its focus on the name *Cecilia* of type e.

Example 5.92 Semantic forms focusing on the name *Cecilia*

a. $\sigma(choir)_e := Cecilia$

b. $\sigma(beDisbanded)_{e \to t} := \lambda e_1[beDisbanded(e_1) \wedge past(e_1)]$

c. $\sigma(\texttt{srL1}) := \lambda P[\lambda x[P(e) \wedge^* theme(e,x)]]_{(e \to t) \to (e \to t)}(\sigma(beDisbanded)$
$\qquad {}_{e \to t})(\sigma(choir)_e)$
$\qquad := \lambda x[beDisbanded(e) \wedge past(e) \wedge^* theme(e,x)]_{e \to t}(Cecilia_e)$
$\qquad := [beDisbanded(e) \wedge past(e) \wedge^* theme(e,Cecilia)]_t$

For this, I allow a collective predicate like the verb *beDisbanded* to be combined with the group name *Cecilia* of type e.

In contrast, the semantic representation can focus on the group noun *choir*.

Example 5.93 Semantic representation focusing on the group noun *choir*

a. $\sigma(choir)_e := \lambda x_1[choir(x_1) \wedge named(x_1, Cecilia)]$

b. $\sigma(beDisbanded)_{e \to t} := \lambda e_1[beDisbanded(e_1) \wedge past(e_1)]$

c. $\sigma(\texttt{srLink}) := \lambda Q \lambda P[\lambda x[P(x) \wedge Q(e) \wedge^* theme(e,x)]]_{(e \to t) \to ((e \to t) \to t)}$
$\qquad (\sigma(beDisbanded)_{e \to t})$
$\qquad (\sigma(choir)_{e \to t})$
$\qquad := \lambda P[P(x) \wedge beDisbanded(e) \wedge past(e) \wedge^*$
$\qquad theme(e,x)]_{(e \to t) \to t}(\sigma(choir)_{e \to t})$
$\qquad := [choir(x) \wedge named(x, Cecilia) \wedge beDisbanded(e) \wedge$
$\qquad past(e) \wedge^* theme(e,x)]_t$

Suppose that Cecilia is the name of a girl. Then it cannot be the theme of the predicate *beDisbanded* because *girl* is not a group noun.

Example 5.94 Two different uses of the name *Cecilia*

a. The choir, named *Cecilia*, was disbanded. [well-formed]

   $[beDisbanded(e) \wedge *theme(e,x) \wedge *choir(x)]$

b. The girl, named *Cecilia*, was disbanded. [ill-formed]

   $[beDisbanded(e) \wedge *theme(e,x) \wedge girl(x)]$

Group Operator over Basic Types Kracht (2002) introduces an operator $\bullet$ over types to introduce the type of groups or sets such as $e^{\bullet}$. He identifies $e^{\bullet}$ with the functional type $e \rightarrow t$ that denotes a set of individuals. Landman (1996) also introduces a group operator $\uparrow$ that converts a sum of individuals to a group atom: e.g., from $(a \oplus b)$ to $\uparrow(a \oplus b)$. I do, however, prefer to use the asterisk sign $*$ as a group operator over basic types, just as it is used for the group predicates associated with so-called collective nouns that inherently carry the notion of *group* at the lexical level. I also use the star *, used for proper plural predicates $^{\star}P$, as a proper plural operator over types. Here is a list of such nouns.

Example 5.95 Group events vs. plural events

a. Group entities of type $^{*}e$:

   army, choir, chorus, committee, couple, group,
   school (of fish), team, union

b. Group events of type $^{*}v$:

   agree, date, gather, marry, meet, scatter

c. Plural events of type $^{\star}v$:

   [John and Mary]$_{*e}$ *sang$_{\star v}$ an aria together.

Group nouns of type $^{*}e$ are interpreted as either singulars or plurals, depending on whether their collectivity or individual distributivity is focused on. They can also be pluralized to be genuine plurals: *armies, choirs*, and so on.

Example 5.96 Group entities being either singulars or plurals

a. [The scholarship committee$_{e*}$]$_{(e^* \rightarrow t) \rightarrow t}$ meets$_{e^* \rightarrow t}$ regularly every semester.

b. Annotation:

   ```
   entity(x1, w3, type="committee", qType="group")
   event(e1, w4, type="process", pred="meet", qType="collective")
   srlink(sR1, event="e1", participant="x1", semRole="agent")
   ```

c. Logical form:

   $[*meet(e) \wedge *agent(e,u) \wedge *committee(u)]$

Example 5.97 Collective vs. distributive use

a. The French army$_{e*}$ was defeated in Russia. (collective)

b. The French army$_{e*}$ were starving to death. (distributive)

c. Technical committee 37_{e*} consists of five subcommittees$_{e*}$.

In general, we first introduce the following type of functional application.

Definition 5.98   Extended functional application for groups
For any type α,
$f_{\alpha \to t}, a_\tau \Rightarrow f(a)_t$, where τ is either the type α or the group type $\alpha^\bullet$.

As for the interpretation of $agent(e, C_{e^\bullet})$, C is to be interpreted as denoting a group of individuals. In a lattice-theoretic framework that introduces a partially ordered set $<A, \leq>$ as a basic ontology, groups of individuals are understood as *individual sums (i-sums)*. Given a set $A=\{a,b,c\}$, the oplus binary $\oplus$ over A connects the members of A, to be called *atomic individuals*, to produce an i-sum structure.

The data in Example 5.99 may be annotated in more detail, but still in a shallow way.

Example 5.99   Detailed but shallow semantic representation
a. Data:
   Our parish choir Cecilia sang at this year's Christmas Mass.
b. Annotation:
```
entity(x1, w3, type="group", subtype="choir", name="Cecilia")
event(e1, w5, type="process", tense="past")
srLink(srL1, relTpye="agent", e1, x1)
```
c. Semantic representation:
   (i) $\sigma(choir)_{e^\bullet \to t} := \lambda x_1[group(x_1) \wedge choir(x_1) \wedge named(x_1, Cecilia)]$
   (ii) $\sigma(sang)_{e \to t} := \lambda e_1[sing(e_1) \wedge past(e_1)]$
   (iii) $\sigma(\texttt{srL1})$
   $:= \lambda Q[\lambda P[P(x) \wedge Q(e) \wedge agent(e,x)]](\sigma(sang)_{e \to t})(\sigma(choir)_{e^\bullet \to t})$
   $:= \lambda P[P(x) \wedge sing(e) \wedge past(e) \wedge agent(e,x)]]_{e \to t}(\sigma(choir)_{e^\bullet \to t})$
   $:= [group(x) \wedge choir(x) \wedge named(x, Cecilia) \wedge sing(e) \wedge past(e) \wedge$
   $agent(e,x)]$

The shallow representation here explicitly introduces a particular predicate $group$, thus binding the variable x to an object of group type $e^\bullet$ of individuals. In deeper semantics, the predicate $group$ is represented in lattice-theoretic terms.

The notion of $group$ still allows that bound entity to consist of its parts (Pustejovsky and Batiukova, 2019). These two bring in a mereological ontology into the interpretations of groups which can be formally represented by a lattice theory.

The term *group* is not used here in an algebraic sense, referring to a set constrained by the so-called *group axioms*. It is used in a mereological sense, as discussed in Pustejovsky and Batiukova (2019, section 2.3.3 and elsewhere).

Example 5.100 The committee$_{e\bullet}$ meets$_{v\bullet}$ every Monday.

Nongroup nouns may also form a group noun phrase.

Example 5.101 Group reading
a. [John and Mary]$_{groupNP}$ married$_{groupPredicate}$.
b. {The boys, as a group}, carried the piano upstairs.[27]

The dot $\bullet$ can be used to represent the mereological features [+bound, +internalStructure] for group nouns[28] of type ($e^{\bullet} \rightarrow t$) or group predicates of type $v^{\bullet}$.

Example 5.102 Plural vs. group predicates

a. {John and Mary}$_{*e}$ sang last night.
   Here, the type $*e$ is the same as $e \rightarrow t$.
b. {John and Mary}$_{e\bullet}$ met and dated last night.
   Here, *met* is a group predicate $v^{\bullet}$.

Link's plural predicates $*P$ (presuperstar predicates) can also be differentiated from group predicates $v^{\bullet}$ or $v \rightarrow t$.

5.5 Extended Summary

In this chapter, I have taken up three issues: (i) the validity of a syntax that generates annotation structures, (ii) representation of the logical forms of annotation structures, and (iii) type-theoretic semantics for the sematic representation of annotation structures.

The validity of an annotation syntax requires the semantic justification of the specification of its categories and their attributes and possible values. It simply means that the syntax even for annotation cannot be constructed without semantics supporting it. This chapter focused on the specification of category *event* and its attributes and values. It showed how the proposed specification was justified against various sorts of semantic information associated with

---

[27] The example is taken from Landman (1996, example 6). He introduces a group operator *uparrow* $\uparrow$ that maps a *sum* $\sum$ onto an atomic group individual: for example, $\uparrow (\sigma(*BOY))$, where $*$ is an operator of semantic pluralization that maps singular or atomic individuals to plural individuals which are represented as the sum of individuals.
[28] See Pustejovsky and Batiukova (2019).

eventualities that need to be captured. The listing of the attributes and the range of their values was not complete nor could be complete, but was shown to include attributes like @*type*, @*pred*, @*tense*, @*aspect*, @*modality*, and @*polarity* at least for English.

For the semantic representation of annotation structures, I restricted its language to a *first-order logic*. I left the task of formulating compositional ways of translating annotation structures to logical forms to Chapter 6. I did, however, represent logical forms in a *shallow* way. By *shallow logical forms*, I meant the use of so-called *logical predicates* such as *past* or *presPerfect*, each of which is to be defined as part of an interpretation model like a *meaning postulate* and also to be used as a *constraint* that delimits possible interpretation models to *admissible models*.

For the formulation of type-theoretic semantics, I assumed the Neo-Davidsonian Semantics. I adopted the extended list of seven basic types, as introduced by Kracht (2002) and Pustejovsky et al. (2019a). Functional types are constructed out of the basic types to define such types as temporal intervals, regions, or event descriptors. As part of type-theoretic semantics, I also discussed type raising, shifting, and coercing, as well as the notions of *collectivity*, *distributivity*, and *group*.

6

Annotation-Based Semantics

6.1 Introduction

This chapter introduces a formal semantics, called *annotation-based semantics* (ABS), proposed by Lee (2020). ABS consists of two modules.

Specification 6.1   Two modules of ABS:

a. Representation language ABSr that translates annotation structures to semantic forms.

b. Model-structure M for interpretation, constrained by a set of meaning postulates that define *logical predicates*.

Figure 6.1 shows the general design of ABS.

The representation language ABSr of ABS translates an annotation structure **a**, consisting of base structures and link structures, to a well-defined semantic form $\sigma(\mathbf{a})$ in *type-theoretic first-order logic*. Each semantic form is assigned a semantic type such as t for the truth-valued type or e for the type of individual entities as in Montague Semantics (Montague, 1974), while the composition of semantic forms is constrained by the types of input forms. ABS adopts the extended list of types, introduced by Kracht (2002) and Pustejovsky et al. (2019a), that includes i and p, as basic types of temporal and spatial points, respectively.

Then ABS interprets each semantic form $\sigma(\mathbf{a})$ as denoting a semantic object $[\![\sigma(\mathbf{a})]\!]^{M,D}$, called *denotation*, with respect to a model M and a list D of definitions of *logical predicates*. Logical predicates are defined as meaning postulates that constrain a model. Those logical predicates that occur in semantic forms are then interpreted according to their definitions given in their interpretation model M.

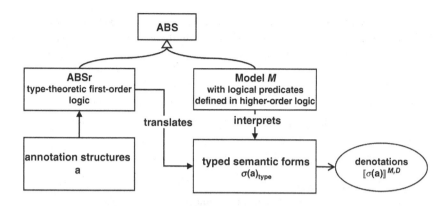

Figure 6.1 General design of ABS
Modified from Figure 1, Lee (2020), which was published within the proceedings of the LREC 2020 [The 16th Joint ACL-SIGSEM – ISO Workshop on Interoperable Semantic Annotation (ISA-16)], ELRA – European Language Resources Association. CC-BY-BC-4.0.

Each $\sigma(\mathbf{a})$ in ABSr is an expression of first-order logic, but each of the logical predicates that occurs in $\sigma(\mathbf{a})$ is defined in terms of possibly higher-order logic as part of the model structure. These logical predicates are used in ABSr, but are defined as part of a model structure like *meaning postulates* (axioms or word meanings) as introduced by Carnap (1947) and Montague (1974) and further developed by Dowty (1979) and Pustejovsky (1995) to enrich interpretation models with lexical meanings.

Structure of the Chapter This chapter grew out of Lee (2020) with extensive revision. It develops as follows. In Section 6.2, I introduce the representation language ABSr as a type-theoretic first-order predicate logic with two types of merge operators, *conjunctive* $\oplus$ and *distributive* $\oslash$, for compositions and their subtypes. These operations are formulated with illustrations in Section 6.3. In Section 6.4, I briefly outline some characteristics of an interpretation model structure for ABS and, in Section 6.5, discuss the *convertibility* of semantic forms of ABS to DRSs or λ-formulas. Section 6.6 summarizes the chapter.

6.2 Representation Language

6.2.1 Motivating ABSr

Annotation-based semantics (ABS) attempts to lighten the burden of automatically generating intermediary interpretations, called *semantic forms* or *logical forms*, of semantic annotation structures. For this purpose, ABS and its representation language ABSr accommodate, in theory, but with some formal modifications, the two well-established and model-theoretically interpretable representation languages.

Example 6.2   Intermediate representation languages for semantics
a. The type-theoretic λ-calculus, used for Montague Semantics (Montague, 1974).
b. Kamp and Reyle's (1993) Discourse Representation Theory (DRT).

The λ-calculus in Montague Semantics is a descriptively powerful language for the semantic analysis of natural language. Its higher-order language is, however, considered too complex to implement the semantics of the ordinary language in a computationally tractable way: ABSr tries not to overuse λ-operations, especially involving higher-order set-theoretic objects, and uses λ-expressions only when needed or more suitable, for instance, to represent properties and propositions, which are objects (complements) of the predicates like *try, intend, want*, or *believe*.

As defined in the following, ABSr subsumes a *type-theoretic first-order logic* (FOL) with the two well-formedness conditions.

Definition 6.3   Well-formedness conditions
a. Every well-formed (semantic) form in ABSr is assigned one of the types, as specified in Section 6.2.2.
b. Every well-formed formula in FOL is a well-formed formula (wff) of type *t* (having a truth-value) in ABSr.

There are two respects in which ABSr differs from Kamp and Reyle's (1993) Discourse Representation Theory (DRT). First, ABSr is based on a type theory just like Montague Semantics. This controls the specification of annotation categories with semantic typing. Second, ABSr introduces a set of logical predicates to represent simple semantic forms while having them defined as meaning postulates in conjunction with a model for interpretation. Thus ABSr is enriched with a practical lexicon for fine-grained interpretation or a *generative lexicon* proposed by Pustejovsky (1995).

6.2.2 Type Theory Revisited

Annotation-based semantics (ABS) adopts the system of semantic types which Kracht (2002) and Pustejovsky et al. (2019a) have developed. To their extended list of basic types, there are two more types added: the type *int* of intervals and the type *vec* of vectors, to define the notions of *static* and *dynamic paths*, as specified in Specification 6.4.

Specification 6.4 Extended list of *basic types*
a. t, the type of truth-values
b. e, the type of individual entities
c. v, the type of eventualities
d. i, the type of time points
e. p, the type of spatial points
f. m, the type of measures
g. int, the type of intervals
h. vec, the type of vectors

Based on the extended list of basic types as specified in Specification 6.4, we now have the definition of functional types.

Definition 6.5 Functional types
If α and β are types, then $\alpha \rightarrow \beta$ is also a type.

Type constructors such as $\rightarrow$, read as *rightarrow*, are introduced to define *functional types*: for example, $e \rightarrow t$, $v \rightarrow t$, $i \rightarrow t$, $p \rightarrow t$ or $e \rightarrow (v \rightarrow t)$. Eventuality descriptors such as *run* or *love* are of type $v \rightarrow t$, which is abbreviated to V (see Pustejovsky (1995)). The functional type $p \rightarrow t$, denoting a set of spatial points, is often represented by a type r of regions.[1] We may call these functional types V and r *pseudo-basic types*, for they are seldom analyzed as functional types.

As introduced by Pustejovsky et al. (2019a), *path types* are defined on the basis of the type of intervals int. Each interval is formally defined as a *bounded interval* $[0, 1]$ in R with the two endpoints 0 and 1, where R is a set of reals. A *path* π will be that function $int \rightarrow p$, which indexes locations on the path to values from the interval $[0,1]$ (see Pustejovsky et al. (2019a)). A *vector path* π_v can also be defined as $int \rightarrow vec$. An event path π_v will be defined as $v \rightarrow \pi_v$ as the function from eventualities to vector paths.

6.2.3 Syntax of ABSr

Like the syntax of an ordinary language, $Syntax_{ABSr}$ consists of a vocabulary and a set of formation rules, as presented in Specification 6.6.

---

[1] See Mani and Pustejovsky (2012) for the discussion of regions as primitive objects vs. as sets of points.

Table 6.1 *IDs, variables, and types*

Categories[a]	IDs	Types	Variables
annotation	a1,...	t	$a_1, \ldots$
entity	x1,...	e	$x, x_1, \ldots$
eventuality	e1,...	v	$s, e, e_1, \ldots$ [b]
event descriptor		$V, v \to t$	$E, \ldots$
time	t1,...	$I, i \to t$	$t, t_1, \ldots$
place	pl1,...	$r, p \to t$	$l, l_0, \ldots$
path	p1,...	$\pi, int \to p$	$p, p_1, \ldots$
event-path	(ep1,...)	$\pi_v, int \to vec$	
measure	me1,...	m	$m, m_1, \ldots$
link		t	

[a] *Note:* Categories are called *tags* or *elements*.
[b] *Note: s* for the eventualities of type *state*, whereas $e, e_1, \ldots$ are for the eventuality of type *process* or *transition*.

Specification 6.6 $Syntax_{ABSr} = <V, R>$ such that

a. V is a vocabulary that consists of

  (i) symbols for predicates,
  (ii) variables of various types, and
  (iii) *merge* operators $\oplus$ and $\oslash$ over the set of semantic forms in ABSr and their subtypes, and

b. R consists of a rule that defines atomic forms and a set of composition rules for merging semantic forms into composed forms.

There are two sorts of *well-formed semantic forms* (wff) in ABSr: basic and composed, each defined by a rule in R, as shown in Specification 6.6.

Variables

There is a list of conventionally used variables for each of the categories or the types in ABSr, as listed in Table 6.1.

The representation of variables is simply conventional. To be precise, for each base structure β that conforms to a recognized annotation scheme such as ISO-TimeML (ISO, 2012b), a variable is defined as a pair $<var, \tau>$ or $<var: \tau>$, where *var* is a variable and τ is a type. Conventionally, any lowercase Latin character such as x, y, e, or s is used as a variable for any one of the basic types, provided that its type is specified: for example, $x: <var, p \to t>$ to use x as a variable ranging over regions of type r, or $p \to t$. Uppercase

Latin characters like V are used for functional types: E is used as a variable for eventuality descriptors such as the denotation of a predicate like *run*. Note that $run(e)$ is of type t, while the eventuality descriptor *run* is of type $v \to t$ and its argument e is a variable of eventuality type v.[2]

Syntactic Rules

Just like any language, either natural or formal, ABSr is a language that consists of a nonempty set of strings of character symbols. Each of such character strings is a well-formed *syntactic logical form* in ABSr, but this syntactic form functions as a *semantic form* or *logical form* of an annotation structure. It serves as an intermediary form that is subject to the model-theoretic interpretation of annotation structures.

Here are some technical remarks that need to be made further to clarify what ABSr is.

Remark 6.7 Semantic function σ

For any **a** that refers to the *abstract specification* of each of the base or link structures, which together constitute an annotation structure, σ maps **a** to a semantic form in ABSr. $\sigma(\mathbf{a})$ is read as the *semantic form* of **a** in ABSr and is a *well-formed form* (wff) of ABSr.

Note that $\sigma(\mathbf{a})$ is considered independent of the format that represents it, but has to check the abstract syntax that validates the abstract specification **a**. Hence, the mapping σ is the same as the interpretation function I that is introduced by Bunt (2020a,b).

Remark 6.8 Model-theoretic interpretation

The symbol $[\![\ ]\!]$ is used to represent a (model-theoretic) interpretation, called *denotation*. Given any semantic form $\sigma(\mathbf{a})$ in ABSr, its denotation or interpretation with respect to a model M and a set D of definitions for *logical predicates* is represented by $[\![\sigma(\mathbf{a})]\!]^{M,D}$.

Remark 6.9 Typing

As ABSr is a type-based language, every well-formed (semantic) form A and any c of its constituents such as variables in ABSr are assigned a type. The type τ of A, c or a variable *var* is represented as a pair: for example, $<A: \tau>$, $<c: \tau>$, $<var: \tau>$, or as a subscript to A or one of its constituents: A_τ, c_τ or x_e.

---

[2] Here, it is a bit confusing to use e as standing for a basic type for individual entities and use it as referring to an eventuality of type v: for example $[run_{v \to t}(e_v) \wedge agent_{e \to (v \to t)}(e_v, x_e)]]$.

Atomic Semantic Forms

Atomic semantic forms are defined by Rule A.

Definition 6.10   Rule A for atomic semantic forms:
For any abstract specification $\mathbf{a}_{\beta:c}$ of a base structure β of category c^3 and a type τ associated with category c, $\sigma(\mathbf{a}_{\beta:c})_\tau$ is a well-formed expression of type τ in ABSr.

In practice, $\mathbf{a}_{\beta:c}$ in $\sigma(\mathbf{a}_{\beta:c})_\tau$ is replaced by the ID of $\beta:c$ or β_c.

Following the Discourse Representation Theory (DRT) (Kamp and Reyle, 1993), the new occurrences of variables in a semantic form are registered.

Specification 6.11   Rule A.1 for variable registry
Any variable that is newly introduced to $\sigma(\mathbf{a}_{\beta:c})$ may be listed in the preamble: i.e., $\Sigma_{var:type}\sigma(\mathbf{a}_{\beta:c})$.

The variables in the preamble $\Sigma_{var:type}$ are treated as *discourse referents*, to which each occurrence of the variables in $\sigma(\mathbf{a}_{\beta:c})$ is bound. Note that these variables may not be registered if they can be recognized contextually.

Consider an example, annotated as in Example 6.12.

Example 6.12   Markables: Fido$_{w1}$ ran$_{w2}$ away$_{w3}$.
a. Annotation(id=a6.12)
```
entity(x1, w1, pred="dog", form="nam")
event(e1, w2-3, pred="runAway", tense="past")
srLink(srL1, agent, e1, x1)
```
b. Semantic representation in ABSr:
$\sigma(\text{x1}:e) := \{x_1:e\}[named(x_1, Fido)]_t,^4$
$\sigma(\text{e1}:v) := \{e_1:v\}[runAway(e_1)_t \wedge past(e_1)_t],$
$\sigma(\text{srL1}:t) := \{x_1:e, e_1:v\}[agent(e_1, x_1)]_t,$
where "$:=$" is a meta-symbol standing for "is".

The second point (Semantic representation in ABSr) in Example 6.12 can be converted to a type-based discourse representation structure (DRS), as in Example 6.13. This semantic representation in ABSr is the same as in DRS. The only possible difference between ABSr and DRS is the type specification of the two discourse referents $x_1:e$ and $e_1:v$ in ABS, as in Bos et al.'s (2017) Groningen Meaning Bank (GMB).

---

[3] In a concrete syntax, this category is often called *tag* or *element*.
[4] As in DRS, names like *Fido* can be treated as unary predicates. Then, $[named(x_1, Fido)]_t$ is simply replaced by the logical form $Fido(x_1)$.

Example 6.13

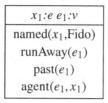

$$
\begin{array}{|c|}
\hline
x_1{:}e\ e_1{:}v \\
\hline
\text{named}(x_1,\text{Fido}) \\
\text{runAway}(e_1) \\
\text{past}(e_1) \\
\text{agent}(e_1,x_1) \\
\hline
\end{array}
$$

Merge Operators for Composed Forms

Two types of *merge* operators, conjunctive $\oplus$ and distributive $\oslash$, and their variants, are introduced in ABSr. Each variant is marked with a different superscript to represent the merging of two or more semantic forms. These operators are non-Boolean connectives. They are needed to be able to merge semantic forms of the type other than the truth-type t. More operators may need to be introduced to treat finer-grained compositions, especially involving the semantics of determiners that include generalized quantifiers, plurals, and the merging of scopes. As suggested by Bunt (personal communication), different symbols will be introduced to represent various subtypes of composition. Bunt (2020a), for instance, introduces the *scope merge operator* $\oplus^s$ and the *possessive scoped merge operator* $\oplus^{ps}$.

For the formulation of composition rules, it is assumed that these rules hold for any well-formed semantic forms A_α, B_β, and C_γ, each of which is typed as α, β, and γ, respectively. Sometimes semantic forms contain some *unbound* occurrences of variables.

Specification 6.14   Unbound occurrences of variables
For any well-formed semantic form A, $A|var{:}\tau$ is also a well-formed semantic form that contains at least one unbound occurrence of a variable of type τ in A.

For these semantic forms, there are two major types of composition: conjunctive $\oplus$ and distributive $\oslash$ each with its subtypes.

Specification 6.15   Types of conjunctive composition (merging) ($\oplus$)
a. *Rule 1^{tr} Truth*-type conjunctive composition ($\oplus^{tr}$) or simply ($\oplus$)
b. *Rule 1^{fa}* Functional conjunctive composition ($\oplus^{fa}$)
c. *Rule 1^{sub}* Substitutive conjunctive composition by substitution ($\oplus^{sub}$)
d. *Rule 1^{eq}* Equative conjunctive composition by equation solving ($\oplus^{eq}$)
e. *Rule 1^{gq}* Conjunctive composition for generalized (cardinal) quantifiers ($\oplus^{gq}$)

Specification 6.16   Types of distributive composition (demerging) ($\oslash$)
a. *Rule 2^{imp}* for material implication $\oslash^{imp}$
b. *Rule 2^{dis}* for disjunction $\oslash^{dis}$

c. *Rule 2^{uq}* for universal quantification with $\oslash^{uq}$

These merge operators may have other subtypes. They are introduced as needs arise. Both of the operators $\oplus$ and $\oslash$ are called *merge operators*. Strictly speaking, conjunctive operators are genuine *merge* operators, whereas distributive operators are *demerging* operators.

6.3 Merge Operations

This section shows how various rules of composition are formulated. It also illustrates the use of each composition rule.

6.3.1 Conjunctive Composition

Conjunctive composition $\oplus$ is the most common merge operation to derive composed forms. There are four types of conjunctive composition for ABSr, but the truth-type conjunctive merge operator is used most.

The *Truth*-Type Conjunctive Composition $\oplus$ or $\oplus^{tr}$

Rule 1^{tr} *truth*-type conjunctive composition $\oplus^{tr}$, or simply $\oplus$, is the most common type of composition that applies to semantic forms of type t, as formulated in the following.

Specification 6.17　Rule 1^{tr} conjunctive composition

a. $[A_t \oplus^{tr} C_t]_\alpha := [A_t \wedge C_t]_t$
b. $[[A_t, B_t]_\alpha \oplus^{tr} C_t] := [[A_t \wedge B_t]_t \wedge C_t]$

Conjunctive composition is *symmetric* so that $[A_t \oplus^{tr} C_t]$ holds if and only if $[C_t \oplus^{tr} A_t]$.

Conjunctive composition *Rule 1^{tr}* applies to most of the annotation structures in ISO-TimeML (ISO, 2012b), ISO-Space (ISO, 2020d), and the ISO standard on semantic role annotation ISO 24617-4 SemAF-SR (ISO, 2014a). For illustration, consider Example 6.18:

Example 6.18　Annotation

a. Markables: Fido is barking.
b. Base structures:
```
entity(x1, w1, type="dog", name="Fido")
event(e1, w2-3, pred="bark", tense="present", aspect="progressive")
```
c. Link structure:
```
srLink(srL1, agent, e1, x1)
```

The annotation of the markables in Example 6.18 consists of two base structures and a link structure over them. Here, srLink specifies the semantic role of the participant x_1 as an *agent* participating in the event e_1 of barking, as illustrated in Semantics 6.19.

Semantics 6.19   Semantic representation

a. Base structures:

$\sigma(\texttt{x1})_t := \{x_1{:}e\}[dog(x_1) \wedge named(x_1, Fido)]_t$

$\sigma(\texttt{e1})_t := \{e_1{:}v\}[bark(e_1) \wedge pres Prog(e_1)]_t$

b. Semantic role link:

$\sigma(\texttt{srL1})_t$

$:= \{x_1{:}e, e_1{:}v\}[[\sigma(\texttt{x1})_t, \sigma(\texttt{e1})_t] \oplus agent(e_1, x_1)_t]$

$:= \{x_1{:}e, e_1{:}v\}[[\sigma(\texttt{x1})_t \wedge \sigma(\texttt{e1})_t] \wedge agent(e_1, x_1)_t]$

$:= \{x_1{:}e, e_1{:}v\}$

$\quad [[dog(x_1) \wedge named(x_1, Fido)] \wedge [bark(e_1) \wedge pres Prog(e_1)] \wedge$

$\quad agent(e_1, x_1)]$

c. Annotation structure:

$\sigma(a_{6.18})$

$:= \sigma(\texttt{srL1})$

$\quad$ by variable renaming and quantifier-binding

$:= \exists\{x{:}e, e{:}v\}$

$\quad [[dog(x) \wedge named(x, Fido)]$

$\quad \wedge [bark(e) \wedge pres Prog(e)$

$\quad \wedge agent(e, x)]]$

The uniform renaming of variables is allowed in ABSr as in predicate logic. Unbound variables are bound by the existential quantifier $\exists$ at the final stage of deriving semantic forms.

ISO-Space (ISO, 2014b) introduces the movement link (moveLink) to annotate motions involving paths. Example 6.20 illustrates how the semantic forms involving motions and paths can be derived through Rule 1^{tr} truth-type conjunctive composition.

Example 6.20   Truth-type conjunctive composition

a. Data: Mia arrived in Boston yesterday.

b. Markables: Mia$_{x1, w1}$ arrived$_{m1, w2}$ $\emptyset_{p1}$ in Boston$_{pl1, w4}$ yesterday.

c. Annotation (base structures):

```
entity(x1,w1, type="person", form="nam")
motion(m1,w2, type="transition", pred="arrive", tense="past")
path(p1,Ø, type="dynamic", start="unspecified", end="pl1",
    trigger="m1")
place(pl1,w4, type="city", name="Boston")
```

d. Annotation (link structure):

```
moveLink(mvL1, relType="traverses", figure="x1", ground="p1")
```

Each markable is identified with an ID associated with its category and anchored to a word. Motions, as denoted by verbs like *arrive*, trigger a *dynamic path*, called *event-path*. This path is marked with a null category or nonconsuming tag Ø because it is not associated with any nonnull string of words. The predicate *traverses* associated with motions is one of the logical predicates that need to be defined in an ABS model structure.

Semantics 6.21   Annotation-based semantic representation

a. Base structures:

$\sigma(\texttt{x1})_t := \{x_1\}[person(x_1) \wedge named(x_1, Mia)]$

$\sigma(\texttt{m1})_t := \{e_1\}[arrive(e_1) \wedge past(e_1)]$

$\sigma(\texttt{p1})_t := \{\pi_1, l_0, l_1, e_1\}$
$\qquad [path(\pi_1) \wedge starts(\pi_1, \gamma(l_0)) \wedge ends(\pi_1, l_1) \wedge triggers(e_1, \pi_1)]$

$\sigma(\texttt{p11})_t := \{l_1\}[named(l_1, Boston) \wedge city(l_1)]$

b. Movement link structure:

$\sigma(\texttt{mvL1})$

$:= [[\sigma(\texttt{x1})_t, \sigma(\pi_1)_t] \oplus traverses(x_1, \pi)_t]$

$:= \{x_1, \pi_1, l_0, l_1, e_1\}$

$\quad [[[person(x_1) \wedge named(x_1, Mia)]$

$\quad \wedge [path(\pi_1) \wedge starts(\pi_1, \gamma(l_0)) \wedge ends(\pi_1, l_1) \wedge triggers(e_1, \pi_1)]$

$\quad \wedge [arrive(e_1) \wedge past(e_1)]$

$\quad \wedge [named(l_1, Boston) \wedge city(l_1)]] \wedge traverses(x_1, \pi_1)]$

c. Semantic representation:

$\sigma(a_{6.20})$

$:= \{x_1, \pi_1, l_0, l_1, e_1\}\sigma(\texttt{mvL1})$

By variable binding by quantification

$=: \exists\{x, \pi_1, l_0, l_1, e\}$

$\quad [[[person(x) \wedge named(x, Mia)]$

$\quad \wedge [path(\pi_1) \wedge starts(\pi_1, \gamma(l_0)) \wedge ends(\pi_1, l_1) \wedge triggers(e, \pi_1)]$

$\quad \wedge [arrive(e_1) \wedge past(e_1)]$

$\quad \wedge [named(l_1, Boston) \wedge city(l_1)]] \wedge traverses(x, \pi_1)]$

Rule 1^{tr} truth-type conjunctive composition is most used, applying to most of the link structures. I have shown how it applies to srLink for semantic role labeling and moveLink for the annotation of motions involving their movers and event-paths. It also applies to tLink for temporal anchoring and qsLink for spatial relations between regions. Semantics 6.22 and Semantics 6.23 illustrate how these two links work.

Semantics 6.22   Temporal relations

a. Data: Mia visited Paris in Texas during the summer of 2005.

b. Base annotation for markables:
   Mia visited$_{e1, w2}$ Paris in Texas during$_{tr1, w6}$ the summer$_{t1, w8}$ of$_{tr2, w10}$
   2005$_{t2, w10}$.

c. Temporal link structures:
   ```
   tLink(tL1, during, e1, t1, trigger:tr1)
   tLink(tL2, isIncluded, t1, t2, trigger:tr2)
   ```

d. Semantic representation (*temporal relations*):
   $\sigma(\texttt{tL1})$
   $:= \{e_1, t_1\}[[\sigma(e_1), \sigma(t_1)] \oplus \tau(e_1) \subseteq t_1)]$
   $:= \{e_1, t_1\}[[visit(e_1) \land past(e1)] \land season(t_1, summer) \land \tau(e_1) \subseteq t_1]$
   $\sigma(\texttt{tL2})$
   $:= \{t_1, t_2\}[[\sigma(t_1), \sigma(t_2)] \oplus t_1 \subseteq t_2]$
   $:= \{t_1, t_2\}[[season(t_1, summer) \land year(t_2, 2005)] \land t_1 \subseteq t_2]$
   $\sigma(\texttt{tL1}) \oplus \sigma(\texttt{tL2})$
   $:= \exists\{e_1, t_1, t_2\}$
   $[[visit(e_1) \land past(e_1)] \land [season(t_1, summer)] \land \tau(e_1) \subseteq$
   $\quad t_1 \land year(t_2, 2005) \land t_1 \subseteq t_2]$

The last logical form represents the two temporal relations, one between the event and its occurrence time and the other between the two times, summer and the year 2005. It is thus correctly understood as stating that the visit was made in the past, occurring in the summer which was part of the year 2005.

Consider now the qualitative spatial link (qsLink) that annotates spatial relations.

Semantics 6.23   Spatial relations

a. Data: Mia visited Paris in Texas during the summer of 2005.

b. Base annotation for markables:
   Mia visited Paris$_{pl1, w3}$ in$_{sr1, w4}$ Texas$_{pl2, w5}$ during the summer of 2005.

c. Qualitative spatial link structure:
   ```
   qsLink(qsL1, pl1, pl2, in)
   ```

d. Semantic representation (*spatial relation*):
   $\sigma(\texttt{qsL1}) := \{l_1, l_2\}[[[\sigma(l_1), \sigma(l_2)] \oplus in(l_1, l_2)]$
   $\qquad\qquad := \exists\{l_1, l_2\}[[named(l_1, Paris) \land town(l_1)] \land$
   $\qquad\qquad [named(l_2, Texas) \land USstate(l_2) \land in(l_1, l_2)]$

The logical form above is understood as stating that the town of Paris is in the US state of Texas. By combining $\sigma(\texttt{tL1})$, $\sigma(\texttt{tL2})$, and $\sigma(\texttt{qsL1})$, the spatio-temporal content of the whole data in Semantics 6.22 is properly captured through the temporal and the spatial annotations.

Functional Conjunctive Composition with $\oplus^{fa}$

Rule 1^{fa} functional conjunctive composition reflects the functional application of a *functor* applying to its argument(s) in Montague Semantics (Montague, 1974). Rule 1^{fa} is formulated in Specification 6.24 with its operator $\oplus^{fa}$.

Specification 6.24   Rule 1^{fa} Functional conjunctive composition

a. $[A_\alpha \oplus^{fa} C_{\alpha \to t)}] := [A_t \wedge C_t]$

     or

b. $[[A_\alpha, B_\beta]] \oplus^{fa} C_{\beta \to (\alpha \to t)}] := [[A_t \wedge B_t] \wedge C_t]$

These relations are again *symmetric*, just like Rule 1^{tr} truth-type conjunctive composition.

     Example 6.18 can be analyzed in terms of a functor-argument analysis by coercing the type of $\sigma(\text{x1})$ and $\sigma(\text{e1})$ to be of a functional type $\alpha \to t$, where α is a type, to the type of each of the annotation structures.

Semantics 6.25   Functor-argument analysis

a. Markables: Fido$_{x1:dog}$ is barking$_{e1:presProg}$.
b. Semantic forms of the base structures:

     $\sigma(\text{x1})_{e \to t} := \{x_1:e\}[dog(x_1) \wedge named(x_1, Fido)]$

     $\sigma(\text{e1})_{v \to t} := \{e_1:v\}[bark(e_1) \wedge presProg(e_1)]$

c. Semantic role link through $\oplus^{fa}$:

     $\sigma(\text{srLink})$

     $:= \{x_1:e, e_1:v\}$

         $[[\sigma(\text{x1})_{e \to t}, \sigma(\text{e1})_{v \to t}] \oplus^{fa} agent(e_1, x_1)_{(v \to t) \to ((e \to t) \to t)}]$

     $:= \{x_1:e, e_1:v\}$

         $[[\sigma(\text{x1})_t \wedge \sigma(\text{e1})_t] \wedge agent(e_1, x_1)_t]$

     $:= \{x_1:e, e_1:v\}$

         $[[dog(x_1) \wedge named(x_1, Fido)]_t \wedge [bark(e_1) \wedge presProg(e_1)]_t \wedge$

         $agent(e_1, x_1)_t]_t$

d. Semantic form of the anotation structure:

     $\sigma(a_{6.18})$

     $:= \sigma(\text{srLink})$

     $:= \{x_1:e, e_1:v\}$

         $[[dog(x_1) \wedge named(x_1, Fido)] \wedge [bark(e_1) \wedge presProg(e_1)] \wedge$

         $agent(e_1, x_1)]$

     With variable renaming and binding

     $:= \exists\{x:e, e:v\}$

         $[[dog(x) \wedge named(x, Fido)] \wedge [bark(e) \wedge presProg(e)] \wedge agent(e, x)]$

Again, the semantic type of $agent(e_1, x_1)$ in Semantics 6.25c is *coerced* to be viewed as of the functional type $(v \rightarrow t) \rightarrow ((e \rightarrow t) \rightarrow t)$.

The functional composition with the operator $\oplus^{fa}$ is equivalent to the *functional application* in λ-calculus, as shown by Semantics 6.26.

Semantics 6.26   Functional application
a. Arguments:
$\sigma(\texttt{x1})_{e \rightarrow t} := \lambda x_1 [dog(x_1) \wedge named(x_1, Fido)]$
$\sigma(\texttt{e1})_{v \rightarrow t} := \lambda e_1 [bark(e_1) \wedge presProg(e_1)]$
b. Functional application for semantic role link applying to the two arguments in (a):
$\sigma(\texttt{srLink})$
$:= \lambda Q \lambda P \exists \{x, e\} [P(x) \wedge Q(e) \wedge agent(e, x)] (\sigma(x_1))(\sigma(e_1))$
$:= \exists \{x, e\} [[dog(x) \wedge named(x, Fido)] \wedge [bark(e) \wedge presProg(e)] \wedge agent(e, x)]$

By applying λ-conversions to $\sigma(\texttt{srLink})$ in Semantics 6.26b, we obtain the same result as Semantics 6.25d. One noticeable problem with the functional application in λ-calculus is the complexity of embedding λ-operations such as $\lambda Q \lambda P \ldots$ as represented in Semantics 6.26b.

Substitutive Conjunctive Composition with $\oplus^{sub}$

The *substitutive conjunctive rule* with the operator $\oplus^{sub}$ applies when one of the inputs to links in an annotation structure is treated as of some basic or pseudo-basic type. Consider Example 6.18 but with a different semantic treatment.[5]

Semantics 6.27   Substitutive conjunction
a. Markables: $Fido_{x1:e}$ is $barking_{e1:v}$.
b. Semantic forms of the base structures:
$\sigma(\texttt{x1})_e := Fido_e$
$\sigma(\texttt{e1})_t := \{e_1:v\} [bark(e_1) \wedge presProg(e_1)]_t$
c. Merging through $\oplus^{sub}$:
$\sigma(\texttt{srLink})$
$:= \{e_1:v\}$
$\quad [[\sigma(\texttt{x1})_e, \sigma(\texttt{e1})_t] \oplus^{sub} agent(e_1, x_1)_t]$
$:= \{e_1:v, x_1:e\}$
$\quad [[Fido_e, [bark(e_1) \wedge presProg(e_1)]_t] \wedge agent(e_1, x_1)_t]$
$:= \{e_1:v\}$
$\quad [[bark(e_1) \wedge presProg(e_1)]_t \wedge agent(e_1, Fido)]$

---

[5] In practice, the semantic treatment of a name is much more complicated than treating it merely for its referential use. Kamp and Reyle (1993) treat names like *John* as a predicate, thus representing it as *John(x)* in a DRS.

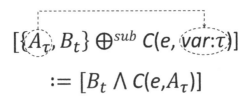

$$[\{A_\tau, B_t\} \oplus^{sub} C(e, var{:}\tau)]$$

$$:= [B_t \wedge C(e, A_\tau)]$$

Figure 6.2 Conjunctive composition $\oplus^{sub}$ by substitution.

The conjunctive composition $\oplus^{sub}$ by substitution replaces all the occurrences of a variable with something like *Fido*, an individual entity of type e, as in Figure 6.2.

The condition for substitution is that there should be type matching between what is being replaced, $var{:}\tau$, and what is replacing A_τ.

Equative Conjunctive Composition with $\oplus^{eq}$

The *equative composition* with ($\oplus^{eq}$) also deals with basic types like names or measures by turning them into an equation form, as formulated in Specification 6.28.

Specification 6.28   Rule 1^{eq} conjunctive composition with equation
$[[A_\tau, B_t] \oplus^{eq} C(var{:}\tau)_t] := [[var{:}\tau{=}A_\tau]_t \wedge B_t \wedge C(var{:}\tau)_t]$,
where $C(var{:}\tau)$ means that at least one of C's arguments is of type $var{:}\tau$ that matches the type of A.

The conjunctive composition $\oplus^{eq}$ with equation coerces A_τ to form an equation, $[var{:}\tau{=}A_\tau]_t$ (see Lee (1983)). This is illustrated by Semantics 6.29.

Semantics 6.29   Equative conjunctive composition
a. Markables: Fido$_{x1:e}$ is barking$_{e1:v}$.
b. Semantic forms of the base structures:
   $\sigma(\mathtt{x1})_e := \{x_1{:}e\}[Fido_e]$
   $\sigma(\mathtt{e1})_t := \{e_1{:}v\}[bark(e_1) \wedge presProg(e_1)]$
c. Semantic forms of a link structure:
   $\sigma(\mathtt{srLink4})$
   $:= \{x_1{:}e, e_1{:}v\}$
   $\quad [[Fido_e, \sigma(\mathtt{e1})_t] \oplus^{eq} agent(e_1{:}v, x_1{:}e)_t]$
   $:= \{x_1{:}e, e_1{:}v\}$
   $\quad [[x_1{=}Fido]_t \wedge [bark(e_1) \wedge presProg(e_1)]_t \wedge agent(e_1, x_1)]$
d. Semantic form of an annotation structure:
   $\sigma(a_{6.18})$
   $:= \sigma(\mathtt{srLink4})$

by renaming and variable binding
$$:= \exists\{x,e\}[x{=}Fido \land [bark(e) \land pres\,Prog(e)]_t \land agent(e,x)]$$
by substitution of identicals
$$:= \exists e[[bark(e) \land pres\,Prog(e)] \land agent(e,Fido)]$$

Unlike the *equation-solving approach* proposed here, Kamp and Reyle (1993) represents names like Fido as $Fido(x)$ of type t in DRSs. This is acceptable but fails to apply the substitution of identicals. Note also that the equation-solving approach can be extended to basic types other than entity type e.

6.3.2 Distributive Composition

Distributive composition $\oslash$ deals with nonconjunctive compositions that involve either implication (conditional) $\to$ or disjunction $\lor$ in Boolean logic, or universal quantification $\forall x$ in predicate logic. Conjunctive composition $\oplus$, in contrast, deals with Boolean composition that combines two or three semantic forms of type t combined with the Boolean connective $\land$ into a semantic form of type t. Distributive composition also applies to a set of semantic forms but *distributively* applying to them with the operator $\oslash$.

Here is a general format for distributive composition.

Specification 6.30 Rule 2 Distributive composition ($\oslash$)
$$[C_{\beta \to (\alpha \to t)} \oslash^o [A_\alpha, B_\beta]] := [A'_t \text{ O } B'_t]_t$$

The connective O in the resultant construction refers to one of the Boolean connectives such as $\to$ for implication and $\lor$ for disjunction dis. There is also a case for universal quantification: $\oslash^{uq}$ but with a more complicated resultant construction.

Here are some subtypes of distributive composition.

Specification 6.31 Subtypes of distributive composition
a. Distributive composition $\oslash^{imp}$ for implication:
   e.g., *If it rains, I'll stay home.*
b. Distributive composition $\oslash^{dis}$ for disjunction:
   e.g., *It will rain or snow tomorrow.*
c. Distributive composition $\oslash^{uq}$ for universal quantification:
   e.g., *Every dog barks.*
      Every dog in the yard is barking.

Distributive Composition $\oslash^{imp}$ for Implication
Annotation 6.32 illustrates how *if*-constructions are annotated and how the distributive composition $\oslash^{imp}$ applies to the annotation of those constructions.

Annotation 6.32 Conditional

a. Markables: If it rains tomorrow, then Mia will stay home.

b. Antecedent annotated (id=$a_{6.32a}$):
```
event(e1, w3, type="process", pred="rain")
timeX3(t1, w4, type="date", value="2020-02-04")
tLink(tL1, e1, t1, isIncluded)
```

c. Consequent annotated (id=$a_{6.32b}$):
```
event(e2, w7, type="state", pred="stay", tense="future")
timeX3(t2, Ø, type="date", value="unspecified")
tLink(tL2, e2, t2, isIncluded)
```

c. Subordination link:
```
sLink(conditional, antecedent="tL1", consequent="tL2")
```

Based on Annotation 6.32, we obtain the semantic form of a conditional, as shown in Semantics 6.33.

Semantics 6.33 Semantic representation

a. Antecedent:

$\sigma(\text{e1})_t := \{e_1\}[rain(e_1)_t]$

$\sigma(\text{t1})_t := \{t_1\}[date(t_1, 2019\text{-}02\text{-}04)]_t$

$\sigma(\text{tL1})$

$:= \{e_1, t_1\}[[\sigma(\text{e1})_t, \sigma(\text{t1})_t] \oplus occurs(e_1, t_1)_t]$

$:= \{e_1, t_1\}[[rain(e_1) \wedge date(t_1, 2019\text{-}02\text{-}04)] \wedge occurs(e_1, t_1)]_t$

b. Consequent:

$\sigma(\text{e2})_t := \{e_2\}[stay(e_2) \wedge future(e_2)]$

$\sigma(\text{t2})_t := \{t_2\}[time(t_2, \gamma(t_2))]^6$

$\sigma(\text{tL2})$

$:= \{e_2, t_2\}[[\sigma(\text{e2})_t, \sigma(\text{t2})_t] \oplus occurs(e_2, \gamma(t_2))_t]$

$:= \{e_2, t_2\}[stay(e_2) \wedge time(t_2, \gamma(t_2)) \wedge occurs(e_2, \gamma(t_2))]$

c. Semantic form of the whole conditional:

$\sigma(\text{sL1})$

$:= [\emptyset \oslash^{imp} [\sigma(\text{tL}_1)_t, \sigma(tL_2)_t]]$

$:= [\sigma(\text{tL}_1) \rightarrow \sigma(\text{tL}_2)]$

$:= \{e_1, t_1\}[rain(e_1) \wedge date(t_1, 2019\text{-}02\text{-}04) \wedge occurs(e_1, t_1)]_t$

$\rightarrow$

$\{e_2, t_2\}[[stay(e_2) \wedge future(e_2)] \wedge time(t_2, \gamma(t_2)) \wedge occurs(e_2, \gamma(t_2))]_t$

d. $\sigma(a_{6.32b})$

$:= \sigma(\text{sL1})$

Variable binding with quantification

$:= \exists\{e_1, t_1\}$

$[rain(e_1) \wedge date(t_1, 2019\text{-}02\text{-}04) \wedge occurs(e_1, t_1)]_t$

$\rightarrow$

$\exists\{e_2, t_2\}[[stay(e_2) \wedge future(e_2)] \wedge time(t_2, \gamma(t_2)) \wedge occurs(e_2, \gamma(t_2))]_t$

---

[6] Here, γ is a function that assigns a time to a deictic temporal expression such as *now, then, at that time*, or a contextually determinable unspecified time.

The *distributive composition* $\oslash^{imp}$ is equivalent to the λ-operation as shown in the following.

Example 6.34   Distribution comparison vs. λ-operation

a. Distributive composition $\oslash^{imp}$:

$[\emptyset_{(t,(t \to t))} \; \oslash^{imp} [A_t, B_t]] := [A_t \to B_t]_t$

b. λ-operation:

$\lambda q \lambda p [p \to q](A_t)(B_t)$, where p and q are variables of type t.

Distributive Composition $\oslash^{dis}$ for Disjunction

Distributive operation $\oslash$ can be extended to the other Boolean operations. Here is an example of distributive composition $\oslash^{dis}$ for disjunction.

Specification 6.35   Rule 2^{dis} Distributive composition for disjunction

$[\emptyset_{(t,(t \vee t))} \; \oslash^{dis} [A_t, B_t]] := [A_t \vee_c B_t]_t$

This then applies to the annotation of disjunctive sentences like Example 6.36b and their semantic representation in ABS.

Example 6.36   Disjunction

a. Markables: It will rain or snow.

b. Annotation, id=a6.36:

```
event(e1, w1-3, type="process", pred="rain", tense="future")
signal(s1, w4, type="boolean", pred="or")
event(e2, w5-6, type="process", pred="snow", tense="future")
timeX3(t1, w7, type="time", value="unspecified")
tLink(tL1, isIncluded, e1, t1)
tLink(tL1, isIncluded, e1, t2)
```

c. Semantic representation with $\oslash^{dis}$:

$\sigma(\text{e1}) := \{e_1\}[rain(e_1) \wedge future(e_1)]$

$\sigma(\text{e2}) := \{e_2\}[snow(e_1) \wedge future(e_1)]$

$\sigma(\text{t}_1) := \{t_1\}[time(t_1) \wedge t_1 = \gamma(t_1)]$

$\sigma(\text{tL1}) := \{e_1, t_1\}[[[\sigma(\text{e1}), \sigma(\text{t1})] \oplus \tau(e_1) \subseteq t_1 \wedge t_1 = \gamma(t_1)]$

$\sigma(\text{tL2}) := \{e_2, t_1\}[[[\sigma(\text{e2}), \sigma(\text{t1})] \oplus \tau(e_2) \subseteq t_1]$

$\sigma(\text{a6.36})$

$:= \{e_1, t_1, e_2\}[\emptyset \oslash^{dis} [\sigma(\text{tL1}), \sigma(\text{tL2})]$

$:= \{e_1, t_1, e_2\}[\sigma(\text{tL1}) \vee \sigma(\text{tL2})]$

$:= \exists\{e_1, t_1, e_2\}$

$\quad [rain(e_1) \wedge future(e_1) \wedge \tau(e_1) \subseteq$

$\quad t_1 \wedge t_1 = \gamma(t_1)] \vee [snow(e_2) \wedge future(e_2) \wedge \tau(e_2) \subseteq t_1]]$

The implicative merge operation $\oslash^{dis}$ applies in a routine way, deriving a disjunctive clause with the Boolean connective $\vee$.

Universal Quantification with $\oslash^{uq}$

Universal quantification may also be treated with the *distributive operator* $\oslash^{uq}$ for universal quantification, formulated as follows.

Specification 6.37 Universal quantification with $\oslash^{uq}$

$[all(var{:}\tau) \oslash^{uq} \{A|var{:}\tau, B|var{:}\tau\}] := \forall var[A|var{:}\tau \to B|var{:}\tau)]$

For illustration, consider a case in which $var{:}\tau$ is a variable x of type e. Then, we have the following.

Specification 6.38 Optional comments

$[all(var{:}x) \oslash^{uq} \{A|x, B|x\}] := \forall x(A|x \to B|x)$, [comment]

As stated in Specification 6.14, $A|var{:}\tau$ means that there is at least one free occurrence of the variable var of type τ in A. Otherwise, it becomes a vacuous quantification. *Optional comments* provide additional information, for instance, about the *scope* relation between quantifiers. Note that the scope relation is treated as metadata information obtainable from some background situation.

For illustration, consider Annotation 6.39.

Annotation 6.39 Universal quantification

a. Data: Every man died in a coal mining accident.
b. Base annotation (markables):

Every$_{q1, w1}$ man$_{x1, w2}$ died$_{e1, w3}$ in a coal mining accident.
c. Annotation:

```
quantifier(q1, w1, type="logical", value="all")
entity(x1, w2, type="man")
event(e1, w3, type="transition", pred="die", tense="past")
srLink(srL1, event="e1", participants="x1", semRole="theme")
qLink(qL1, quantifier="all", restrictor="x1", nuclearScope="srL1(e1)",
    scopes="(e1,x1)")
```

Note that the attribute @scopes is added as an optional attribute for the quantification link (qLink).

Based on Annotation 6.39, we can derive its semantic form with the distributive operation of $\oslash^{uq}$ as in Semantics 6.40.

Semantics 6.40 Semantic representation

a. Base structures:

$\sigma(\mathtt{q1}) := \{x_1\}[every(x_1)]$

$\sigma(\mathtt{x1}) := \{x_1\}[man(x_1)]$

$\sigma(\mathtt{e1}) := \{e_1\}[die(e_1) \wedge past(e_1)]$
b. Link structures:

$\sigma(\mathtt{srL1})$

$:= \{e_1, x_1\}[[\sigma(e_1), \sigma(x_1)] \oplus theme(e_1, x_1)]$

$:= \{e_1, x_1\}[[die(e_1) \wedge past(e_1)] \wedge man(x_1) \wedge theme(e_1, x_1)]$

$\sigma(\mathtt{qL1})$

$:= [all(x_1) \oslash^{uq} [\sigma(\mathtt{x1}), \sigma(\mathtt{srL1})]]$

$$:= \forall x_1[\sigma(\texttt{x1}) \rightarrow \sigma(\texttt{srL1})]$$
$$:= \forall x_1[man(x_1) \rightarrow [[die(e_1) \land past(e_1)] \land man(x_1) \land theme(e_1, x_1)]]$$
(* Refer to `scopes(e1,x1)` in Annotation 6.39c, `qLink(qL1)`. *)

c. Binding the free occurrence of e_1 in wide scope:

$\sigma(\texttt{qL1})$
$$:= \exists e_1 \forall x_1[man(x_1) \rightarrow [[die(e_1) \land past(e_1)] \land man(x_1) \land theme(e_1, x_1)]]$$
(* $man(x_1)$ in the consequent is deleted, for it is superfluous. *)
$$:= \exists e_1 \forall x_1[man(x_1) \rightarrow [die(e_1) \land past(e_1) \land theme(e_1, x_1)]]$$

Semantic representation $\sigma(\texttt{qL1})$ states that there was a (catastrophic) event of all men dying in the accident. The whole sentence takes the following semantic representation.

Semantics 6.41 Semantic representation:
$\exists e_1 \forall x_1[man(x_1) \rightarrow \exists e_2[die(e_1) \land past(e_1) \land theme(e_1, x_1) \land$
$[miningAccident(e_2) \land cause(e_1, e_2)]]]$

The derivation of this semantic representation depended on Semantics 6.40. It is interpreted as stating that the accident e_2 was the cause of the mass death.

6.3.3 Quantificational Composition

Cardinal quantifiers as measure expressions

Cardinal quantifiers can be treated either measure expressions or generalized quantifiers. ABS prefers to annotate them as measure expressions. Cardinal quantifiers are numerals, which are often followed by some units that are not normalized.

Here are examples.

Example 6.42 Cardinal quantifiers

a. Jon ate *six eggs* for breakfast and got sick.
b. Mia drove *80 miles* to a beach.
c. *3000 students* demonstrated.
d. I visited Rome *three times*.
e. Walter Schmidt weighs *85 kg* and is *190 cm* tall.
f. The speed limit is *30 km per hour*.

Example 6.42c, for instance, can be annotated as in Annotation 6.43.

Annotation 6.43 Cardinal quantifier

a. Markables: $3000_{me1,w1}$ students$_{x1,w2}$ demonstrated$_{e1,w3}$.
b. Base structures:
```
measure(me1, w3, type="cardinal", value="3000")
```

```
entity(x1, w2, type="person", pred="student", plurality="yes")
event(e1, w2, type="process", pred="demonstrate", tense="past")
```
c. Link structures:
```
srLink(srL1, e1, x1, agent)
mLink(mL1, x1, me1, counts)
```

Based on Annotation 6.43, it is possible to derive its semantic representation as in Semantics 6.44.

Semantics 6.44   Derivation of semantic forms

a. Base structures:

$\sigma(\text{me1}) := \{v_1\}[v_1=3000]$

$\sigma(\text{x1}) := \{x_1\}[person(x_1) \land student(x_1) \land plural(x_1)]$

$\sigma(\text{e1}) := \{e_1\}[demonstrate(e_1) \land past(e_1)]$

b. Link structures:

$\sigma(\text{srL1})$

$:= \{e_1,x_1\}[[\sigma(e_1),\sigma(x_1)] \oplus agent(e_1,x_1)]$

$:= \{e_1,x_1\}[[demonstrate(e_1) \land past(e_1)] \land [person(x_1) \land student(x_1) \land$
   $plural(x_1)] \land agent(e_1,x_1)]$

$\sigma(\text{mL1})$

$:= \{e_1,x_1,v_1\}[[\sigma(\text{srL1}),\sigma(\text{me1})] \oplus counts(x_1)=v_1)]$

$:= \{e_1,x_1,v_1\}$
   $[[demonstrate(e_1) \land past(e_1)] \land$
   $[person(x_1) \land student(x_1) \land plural(x_1)] \land agent(e_1,x_1) \land$
   $[v_1=3000] \land counts(x_1)=v_1)]$

$:= \exists\{e_1,x_1\}$
   $[[demonstrate(e_1) \land past(e_1)] \land$
   $[person(x_1) \quad \land \quad student(x_1) \quad \land \quad plural(x_1)] \quad \land \quad agent(e_1,x_1) \quad \land$
   $counts(x_1)=3000]$

or

$:= \exists e_1 \exists 3000 x_1$
   $[[demonstrate(e_1) \land past(e_1)] \land$
   $[person(x_1) \land student(x_1) \land plural(x_1)] \land agent(e_1,x_1)]$

Here, *plural* and *counts* are defined as logical predicates in an interpretation model. The logical form $[F(x) \land plural(x)]$, or simply $F^{plural}(x)$, is interpreted as being true if there is a set X such that the cardinality of X is greater than 2 and that, for every x in X, $F(x)$ holds.

Definition 6.45   Logical predicate *plural*

$\exists x[F(x) \land plural(x)] =_{def} \exists X[||X|| \geq 2 \land \forall x[x \in X \to F(x)]]$,
where n is a natural number.

Similarly, $[F(x) \land counts(x)=n]$ is defined as follows.

Definition 6.46 Logical predicate *counts*

$\exists x[F(x) \wedge counts(x)=n]=_{def} \exists X[||X||=n \wedge \forall x[x \in X \to F(x)]]$,
where n is a natural number.

The logical form $[F(x) \wedge counts(x)=n]$ can also be represented as $\exists n x \, F(x)$.

Cardinal Quantifiers as Generalized Quantifiers

Cardinal quantifiers as well as quantifiers such as *several* may be treated as generalized quantifiers. (See Barwise and Cooper (1981) for generalized quantifiers.) Consider Example 6.47.

Example 6.47 Quantification
a. Quantification over events:
   It rained$_e$ *three times* := $\exists 3e[rained(e) \wedge past(e)]$
b. Quantification over individual entities:
   Three Russians$_x$ came$_e$:= $\exists 3x \exists e[Russian(x) \wedge come(e,x) \wedge past(e)]$

The numeral *three* in Example 6.47a modifies the verb *rained*, denoting the number of its occurrences. In Example 6.47b, the number *three* modifies the noun *Russians*, denoting the number of those who came.

Generalized quantifiers, including universal quantifiers, in English refer to noun phrases with determiners like *two, several, some, at least one*, or *all the* as in Example 6.48.

Example 6.48 Generalized quantifiers
a. *Three thousand* students protested.
b. *Some* soldiers ran away.
c. *Several* dogs chased a cat.
d. *All the* soldiers surrendered.

In ABS, I treat all these so-called *generalized quantifiers* as *predicates*, or *operators O*, having two arguments, *restriction R* and *nuclear scope N*, as in the tripartite treatment of quantification. There are, however, two different merge operators introduced: the distributive operator $\oslash^{uq}$ for universal quantification and the conjunctive operator $\oplus^{gq}$ for generalized quantifiers other than the universal quantifier.

The conjunctive merge operator $\oplus^{gq}$ for cardinal quantifiers is then formulated as in Specification 6.49.

Specification 6.49 Merge operator $\oplus^{gq}$ for generalized quantifiers
$[GQ_{var:\tau} \oplus^{gq} \{A|var:\tau, B|var:\tau\}] := GQ_{var:\tau}(A|var:\tau \wedge B|var:\tau)$

Suppose that the *var* in *var*:τ is a variable x of type e. Then we have the following.

Specification 6.50 $[GQx \oplus^{gq} \{A|x, B|x\}] := GQx[A|x \wedge B|x]$

Example 6.48a, for instance, has its semantic form represented as in Example 6.51b.

Example 6.51   Generalized quantifiers
a. Three thousand$_O$ students$_R$ protested$_N$.
b. Semantic representation:
   $\sigma(a) := [3000(x) \oplus^{gq} [student(x), protest(x)]]$
   $:= 3000(x)[student(x) \wedge protest(x)]$ OR
   $\exists 3000x[student(x) \wedge protest(x)]$

Here, the cardinal number 3000 is treated as a quantifier, which may be replaced by the existential quantifier $\exists 3000x$. For cardinal quantifiers in general, we have a meaning postulate as stated in the following.

Definition 6.52   Meaning postulate for cardinal quantifiers
For any natural number $n \in N$,
$\exists nx[P(x) \wedge F(x)]=_{def}\exists\{X\}[|X|=n \wedge \forall[x \in X \rightarrow F(x)]]$

6.3.4 Scope Ambiguity

Scope has been the most studied aspect of quantification in the formal semantics of natural language since Montague (1974). Bunt (2020b) points out that there are two types of scope: One is the relative scope over participants and the other is the relative scope between an event and its participants. Here are examples, as in Classification 6.53.

Classification 6.53   Two types of scopal relations
a. Scopal relation between two sorts of participants:
   Every student$_x$ read five books$_y$.
   $\exists 5y\forall x[student(x) \rightarrow [book(y) \wedge read(x,y)]]$
b. Scopal relation between an event and one of its participants:
   Every student$_x$ danced$_e$.
   $\exists e\forall x[student(x) \rightarrow [dance(e) \wedge past(e) \wedge agent(e,x)]]$

Classification 6.53a represents a scopal relation between the two sorts of participants: student$_x$ and books$_y$. Here, *five books$_y$* has a wide scope over *student$_x$* so that Classification 6.53a is interpreted as saying that there were five books$_y$ that every student$_x$ read. Classification 6.53b, in contrast, represents a scopal relation between the event *dance(e)* and its participant *agent(x)*: the event has a wide scope over its participant $agent(e,x)$. The semantic form in Classification 6.53b is then interpreted as saying that there was an $event_e$ in which every $student_x$ danced.

Thus ABS annotates the example in Classification 6.53a as in Example 6.54 with their semantic forms represented in ABSr, as in Semantics 6.55, where *base annotation* provides each base structure with *anchoring information*.

Annotation 6.54   Scopal relations
a. Data: Every student read five books.
b. Base annotation: Every$_{q1,w1}$ student$_{x1,w2}$ read$_{e1,w3}$ five$_{q2,w4}$ books$_{x2,w5}$.
c. Annotation:
```
quantifier(q1, w1, type="logical", value="(every,x1)")
entity(x1, w2, type="student")
event(e1, w3, type="process", pred="read")
quantifier(q2, w4, type="cardinal", value="(five,x2)")
entity(x2, w5, type="book")
qLink(qL1, quantifier="(everyx1)", restrictor="x1",
   nuclearScope="{e1}")
qLink(qL2, quantifier="(fivex2)", restrictor="x2",
   nuclearScope="{qL1}", scopes="(x2,x1)")
```

Semantics 6.55   Semantic representation
$\sigma(\text{q1}) := every(x_1)$
$\sigma(\text{x1}) := student(x_1)$
$\sigma(\text{e1}) := read(e_1, x_1, x_2)$
$\sigma(\text{q2}) := five(x_2)$
$\sigma(\text{x2}) := book(x_2)$
$\sigma(\text{qL1}) := [every(x_1) \oslash^{uq} [\sigma(\text{x1}), \sigma(\text{e1})]]$
$\qquad\quad := [every(x_1) \oslash^{uq} [student(x_1), read(e_1, x_1, x_2)]]$
$\sigma(\text{qL2}) := [five(x_2) \oplus^{gq} [\sigma(\text{x2}), \sigma(\text{qL1})]]$
$\qquad\quad := [five(x_2) \oplus^{gq} [book(x_2), [every(x_1) \oslash^{uq} [student(x_1),$
$\qquad\qquad read(e_1, x_1, x_2)]]]$
$\qquad\quad := \exists 5 x_2 [book(x_2) \wedge \forall x_1 [student(x_1), \rightarrow \exists e_1 [read(e_1, x_1, x_2)]]]$

The attribute @scopes is introduced into the quantification link (qLink) to annotate a scope relation between two quantificational constructions. Here, the scope of $\exists 5 x_2$ is over the quantifier construction headed by $\forall x_1$. With an appropriate meaning postulate for cardinal and also existential quantifiers for the operator $\oplus^{gq}$, $\sigma(\mathbf{a}_{6.53a})$ is then interpreted as being equivalent to the semantic representation in Semantics 6.56.

Semantics 6.56   Semantic representation
$\exists\{X\}[|X|=5 \wedge \forall x_2 [[x_2 \in X \rightarrow book(x_2)] \wedge \forall x_1 [student(x_1) \rightarrow \exists e_1 [read(e_1, x_1, x_2)]]]]$

The scope of eventualities in Classification 6.53b is, for instance, annotated as in Annotation 6.57.

Annotation 6.57   Scope of eventualities

a. Markables: Every$_{q1,w1}$ student$_{x1,w2}$ sang$_{e1,w3}$.

b. Base structures:
```
quantifier(q1, w1, type="universal", value="(every,x1)")
entity(x1, w2, type="student", number="singular")
event(e1, w3, type="process", pred="sing", tense="past")
```

c. Link structures:
```
qLink(qL1, quantifier="(every,x1)", restrictor="x1",
   nuclearScope="e1", scopes="(e1,x1)")
```

Based on Annotation 6.57b,c, we now have semantic forms as represented in Semantics 6.58.

Semantics 6.58   Semantic forms

a. $\sigma(\text{q1}) := [every(x_1)]$

   $\sigma(\text{x1}) := [student(x_1)]$

   $\sigma(\text{e1}) := [sing(e_1,x_1) \wedge past(e_1)]^7$

   $\sigma(\text{qL1}) := [every(x_1) \oplus^{gq} \{\sigma(\text{x1}),\sigma(\text{e1})\}]$

   $:= every(x_1)[student(x_1) \rightarrow [sing(e_1,x_1) \wedge past(e_1)]]$

b. $\sigma(\text{A}_{6.53b}) := \sigma(\text{qL1})$

   $:= \exists e_1 \forall x_1 [(student(x_1) \rightarrow [sing(e_1,x_1) \wedge past(e_1)]]$

Here, $\sigma(\text{A}_{6.53b})$ is interpreted as denoting an event in which every student sang.

Thus, ABS generalizes the scoping of quantifier binding to objects of any of the semantic types that include the type e of individual entities, the type v of eventualities, the types of time t and spatial points p or the type d of measures referring to distances or lengths of type path π.

Example 6.59 shows how quantified distances are annotated and interpreted.

Example 6.59   Quantification of distances

a. Markables: All the students$_x$ ran *the same distance$_d$*.

b. Semantic representation:

   $\exists d \forall x[[student(x) \wedge plural(x)] \rightarrow [run(e) \wedge agent(e,x) \wedge distance(e,d)]]$

Note here that the quantifier $\exists d$ for the distance of each student running scopes over the quantifier construction $\forall x$.

6.4 Model-Theoretic Interpretation

6.4.1 Model Structure for Interpretation

Semantic forms are subject to a model-theoretic interpretation. Each well-formed semantic form $\sigma(\mathbf{a})$ of an annotation structure $\mathbf{a}$ is interpreted with

---

[7] The semantic role x_1 is ignored here to simplify the illustration.

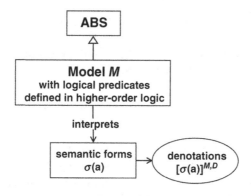

Figure 6.3 Model structure of ABS.

respect to a model M and a set D of definitions, called *meaning postulates*, of logical predicates, and possibly with an assignment g of values to variables. The general model structure represented by Figure 6.3. Then $[\![\sigma(\mathbf{a})]\!]^{M,D}$ is understood as the interpretation or denotation of $\sigma(\mathbf{a})$ with respect to a model M and a set D.

The structure of each model M depends on the kind of semantic annotation. For the interpretation of *temporal annotation*, for instance, a set of times T and a set of temporal relations such as the precedence relation $\prec$ over T become constituting parts of its model structure. Furthermore, the construction of such a model is constrained by some possible uses or definitions of logical predicates.

For general illustration, consider Annotation 6.60.

Annotation 6.60 Quantification of distances

a. Markables: Fido$_{w1}$ ran$_{w2}$ away$_{w3}$.
b. Annotation Structure (id=$"$a$_{6.60}$$"$):
```
entity(x1,w1, name="Fido")
event(e1,w2, type="process", pred="runAway", tense="past")
srLink(srL1, event="e1", participant="x1", semRole="agent")
```

Thus, ABSr translates the annotation structures, represented by Annotation 6.60, into Semantic forms in Semantics 6.61d by combining parts a, b, and c in Semantics 6.61.

Semantics 6.61 *Semantic representation* of semantic role link

a. $\sigma(\texttt{x1}) := \{x_1\}[named(x_1, fido)]$
b. $\sigma(\texttt{e1}) := \{e_1\}[process(e_1) \wedge runAway(e_1) \wedge past(e_1)]$

c. $\sigma(\text{srL1})$

$:= \{e_1, x_1\}[[\sigma(\text{x1}), \sigma(\text{e1})] \oplus^{eq} agent(e_1, x_1)]$

$:= \{e_1, x_1\}[[runAway(e_1) \wedge past(e_1)] \wedge named(x_1, fido) \wedge agent(e_1, x_1)]$

d. Binding the occurrences of variables,

$\sigma(\mathbf{a}_{6.60}) :=$

$\exists\{e_1, x_1\}[[process(e_1) \wedge runAway(e_1) \wedge past(e_1)] \wedge named(x_1, fido) \wedge agent(e_1, x_1)]$

Semantics 6.61d is a well-formed formula in ABSr.

There are two logical predicates in Semantics 6.61d: the tense *past* and the semantic role *agent*. As in Definition 6.62, these logical predicates are defined as meaning postulates (axioms) of a model, while constraining the valuation of predicates such as *past* and *agent*.

Definition 6.62   Logical predicates as meaning postulates

a. MP$_{past}$: For any eventuality e, a time t, the present time n, and a runtime function τ from eventualities to times,

   $past(e)$ is true if and only if $[\tau(e) \subseteq t \wedge t \prec n]$.

b. MP$_{agent}$: For any eventuality e and any participant x,

   $agent(e, x)$ is true if and only if $[\neg state(e) \wedge initiates(x, e) \wedge intends(x, e)]$.[8]

It is now possible to construct a model that satisfies and makes true Semantics 6.61d.

Specification 6.63   Model $M_1 = <A, E, T, n, \prec, \subseteq, \tau, v>$, where

A is a set of individual entities, such that:

   $A = \{a, b, c\}$,

E is a set of eventualities, such that:

   $E = \{e_1, e_2\}$,

T is a set of times, such that:

   $T = \{t_1, t_2, t_3\}$,

n is a designated time, referring to the present moment of time

$\prec$ is a precedence relation over T, such that:

   $R_\prec = \{<t_1, n>, <t_2, n>\}$,

$\subseteq$ is an inclusion relation over T, such that:

   $R_\subseteq = \{<t_1, t_2>\}$

τ is a runtime function from E to T, such that:

   $\tau(e_1) \subseteq t_1$

---

[8] The type of eventuality is a process referring to an activity. It is also assumed that the defining terms $\neg state$, *initiates*, and *intends* are well understood.

v is a valuation that assigns a denotation (semantic value) $[\![c]\!]$ to each of the individual or predicate constants c, such that:

$v(\text{fido})=a$, $v(\text{runAway})=\{e_1\}$.

Now we compute the truth-value or denotation $[\![\sigma(\mathbf{a}_{6.60b})]\!]^{M_1, D}$ for the sentence *Fido ran away* with respect to the model M_1 and the definitions D of the logical predicates *past* and *agent* in Definition 6.62; $[\![\sigma(\mathbf{a}_{6.60b})]\!]^{M_1, D}$ is true, for the individual a denoted by *fido* and named *Fido*. The individual (canine) entity *fido* is involved as an agent in the activity e_1 of running-away which occurred at the time t_1 which preceded the present moment of time n.

6.4.2 Interpretation of Unbound Occurrences of Variables

There may be some unbound occurrences of variables in well-formed semantic forms of ABSr. By Rule A.1 for variable registry, these variables may be either bound to the discourse referents registered before the semantic form of each of the substructures of an annotation structure or bound existentially when their scope is explicitly specified. Or else they can be interpreted with the assignment g as if they were bound existentially.

For illustration, consider the following.

Example 6.64 Binding variables
a. Data: Mia bought some Russian dolls in Moscow.
b. Semantic form:
$[[named(x,mia) \wedge person(x)] \wedge [buy(e) \wedge agent(e,x) \wedge doll(y) \wedge theme(e,y)]]$
c. Existential binding
$\exists\{x,e,y\}[[named(x,mia) \wedge person(x)] \wedge [buy(e) \wedge agent(e,x) \wedge doll(y) \wedge theme(e,y)]]$

The semantic form in Example 6.64b has three variables x, e, and y unbound. These variables are bound existentially as shown in Example 6.64c.

Consider an example of constants.

Example 6.65 Constants
a. Data: Mia left home before it rained.
b. Semantic form:
$[[leave(e_1) \wedge past(e_1) \wedge agent(e_1,m)] \wedge [rain(e_2) \wedge past(e_2)] \wedge \tau(e_1) \prec \tau(e_2)]$,
where τ is a runtime function from events to times at which each of the events occurs.

c. Existential binding:
$\exists\{e_1, e_2\}[[leave(e_1) \wedge past(e_1) \wedge agent(e_1, m)] \wedge [rain(e_2) \wedge past(e_2)] \wedge \tau(e_1) \prec \tau(e_2)]$

In Example 6.65b, Mia is treated as referring to an individual entity m. Since m is a constant, it does not need to be bound.

6.4.3 Meaning Postulates as Constraints

Logical predicates are used in ABS as part of the (object) representation language to simplify the representation of semantic forms or make it flexible to accommodate different interpretations. These predicates in ABSr are defined possibly in terms of higher-order logic as part of the model structure.

Tense and Aspect-Associated Meaning Postulates
The predicate *past* is, for instance, introduced to represent the tense of an event as in Semantics 6.66.

Semantics 6.66   Representing the semantic form of the past in two ways
a. Data: Mia left$_{past}$.
b. Deeper semantic representations:
   DRS: $[leave(e) \wedge e \subseteq t \wedge t \prec n]$
c. Shallow semantic representation:
   ABSr: $[leave(e) \wedge past(e)]$

Discourse representation structure (DRS) (Kamp and Reyle, 1993) represents the denotation of the past as in Semantics 6.66b. In contrast, ABSr represents it as in part c while defining it with a meaning postulate, as in Definition 6.67 and earlier in Definition 6.62a, as part of the meaning postulates.

Definition 6.67   Truth-definition of the predicate *past*
Given an event e, a runtime function τ from events to times, a time t, and the present time n, as specified in a model structure M,
$past(e)$ is true with respect to a model M, or $[[past(e)]]^{M,g}=1$ for any $g(e)$,
   if and only if $\tau(e) \subseteq t$ and $t \prec n$.

The predicate *past* may be defined differently to accommodate its deictic or situational use (see Partee (1973) or Quirk et al. (1985)).

Aspectual features such as *present perfect* and *progressive* are also encoded into annotations just as they are. Consider a case of the present perfect aspect in Example 6.68.

Example 6.68   Aspect *presPerfect*

a. Markable: Mia [has visited]$_{e1}$ Boston.

b. Annotation (id=$a_{6.68}$):

```
event(e1, w2-3, pred="visit", tense="present", aspect="perfect")
```

c. Semantic form: $\sigma(\mathrm{e1}) := [visit(e_1) \wedge presPerfect(e_1)]$

The semantic form in Example 6.68c is then interpreted by the definition of *presPerfect* given as part of a model structure. Otherwise, its representation gets complicated similar to DRS, for instance. Here is an example from Cann et al. (2009).

Example 6.69   DRS: The plant has died.

$$\{a, e, t, n, r, s, u\}$$
$$e \subseteq t, t \leq n, r{=}n$$
$$resultFrom'(e, s)$$
$$s \bigcirc r$$
$$Die'(e, u)$$
$$u{=}a$$
$$Plant'(u)$$
$$Dead'(s, u)$$

In contrast, ABSr yields the following representation.

Example 6.70   ABSr: The plant has died.

a. Annotation:

```
entity(x1, w2, type="plant")
event(e1, w4, pred="die", tense="present", aspect="perfect")
srLink(srL1, theme, e1, x1)
```

b. Semantic representation:

$$\sigma(\mathrm{x}_1) := plant(x_1)$$
$$\sigma(\mathrm{e}_1) := [die(e_1) \wedge presPerfect(e_1)]$$
$$\sigma(\mathrm{srL1}) := [[\sigma(\mathrm{x}_1)_t, \sigma(\mathrm{e}_1)_t] \oplus theme(e_1, x_1)_t]$$
$$\sigma(6.70) := \{e, x\}[plant(x) \wedge die(e) \wedge presPerfect(e) \wedge theme(e, x)]$$

The interpretation of $\sigma(\mathrm{e}_1)$ in Example 6.70b requires the truth definition of *presPerfect(e)* that reflects those notions of the perfective aspect encoded in DRS (Example 6.69) previously.

The progressive aspect has been analyzed in both traditional grammar and a variety of generative grammar. Both of the grammars (see, for instance, Jespersen (1931, 1933), Dowty (1979), and Partee (2004)) have introduced the notions of *duration, expanded tense, time interval,* or *interval semantics* to define the aspect *progressive*. The notion of neighborhood $\mathcal{N}$ of a time, introduced by Lee (2008), is adopted in ABS for the definition of the predicate *presProg* (the present progressive aspect).

Definition 6.71   Definition of *presProg*

For any time interval I and any time point t in I,

presProg(e) is true at t iff $n = t$, $I=\mathcal{N}(n)$, which is *the neighborhood of the present moment n of time*, and e holds in I.

This definition at least captures the notion of *expanded tense* or *time frame*, proposed by Jespersen (1931, 1933).

Semantics 6.72   Interpretation

a. Data: Fido is barking.

b. Semantic form: $[bark(e,x) \wedge named(x, fido) \wedge presProg(e)]$

c. Interpretation: $[\![\exists\{e,x\}[bark(e,x)\wedge named(x, fido)\wedge presProg(e)]]\!]^{M,t,g}=1$
   iff, for some event e, $t = n$, and some assignment $g(x)$, $[\![bark(e,x))]\!]^{M,t,g}=1$,
   and $[\![holds(e)]\!]^{M,\mathcal{N}(t)}=1$.

Furthermore, the proposed way of treating tense, aspect, and other predicates which require complex definitions allows different interpretations or uses of them. Those predicates that constitute part of the representation language of semantic forms in ABSr, however, require truth definitions or *meaning postulates* that constrain and define a set of *admissible model structures* (Carnap, 1947; Montague, 1974; Dowty, 1979).

Meaning Postulates for Plural Events

The semantic representation of plurals often requires the use of *higher-order expressions*. Let us take a look at Example 6.73, involving *plural events* that require the use of *second-order variables*

Example 6.73   Use of second-order variables

a. Markable: Mia fell *three times*.

b. Semantic form: $\exists E[|E|=3 \wedge \forall e[e \in E \rightarrow [fall(e,m) \wedge past(e)]]$

Example 6.73a involves plural events. It is understood as stating that there were three instances of Mia's fall. For this, it is necessary to introduce a second-order variable E standing for a set of different occurrences (instances) of an event of the same type.

In the annotation of the measure link (mLink) in Example 6.74, the markable *three times* is annotated as being of category *measure*, identified with a variable m_1 of type *measure*. The measure link (mLink) then relates the measure (me1) to the event (e1), as in Annotation 6.74b.

Annotation 6.74   Measure link

a. Markables: Mia fell$_{e1}$ three times$_{me1}$.

b. Annotation (id=a$_{6.74a}$):

```
event(e1, w2, pred="fall", tense="past")
measure(me1, w3-4, type="occurrence", value="3")
mLink(mL1, relType="counts", figure="me1", ground="e1")
```

The attribute @figure here refers to the value of the measure and the attribute @ground, the object which is measured.

Based on Annotation 6.74b, the semantic forms are derived for each of the base and link structures, as demonstrated in Semantics 6.75.

Semantics 6.75   Measure link

a. Semantic representation:

$$\sigma(\text{e1}) := \{e_1\}[fall(e_1) \wedge past(e_1)]$$
$$\sigma(\text{me1}) := \{v_1\}[v_1 = (3, occurrence)]$$
$$\sigma(\text{mL1}) := \{(e_1, v_1)[[\sigma(\text{me1}), \sigma(\text{e1})] \oplus counts(e_1) = v_1]$$
$$:= \{(e_1, v_1)[fall(e_1) \wedge past)e_1) \wedge v_1 = (3, occurrence) \wedge$$
$$counts(e_1) = v_1]$$
$$\sigma(\text{a}_{6.74a}) := \sigma(\text{mLink})$$

b. By variable binding by quantification and substitution of identicals

$$:= \exists e_1[fall(e_1) \wedge past(e_1) \wedge counts(e_1) = (3, occurrence)]$$
$$:= \exists e_1[fall(e_1) \wedge past(e_1) \wedge \kappa(e_1) = 3]$$

The last logical form is interpreted as stating that the number of occurrences of the event e_1 of Mia falling was three; κ is a counting function that maps an object to a natural number, representing the number of *instances* or *parts* of that object.

6.5 Comparison

6.5.1 Related Work

There have been several works showing how annotation structures can be interpreted. Hobbs and Pustejovsky (2003) developed a semantics for TimeML (Pustejovsky et al., 2005), based on the OWL-Time ontology. They provided a fine-grained way of annotating and interpreting various temporal relations. ABS is designed to accommodate the OWL-Time ontology in defining its logical predicates related to temporal annotation. Pratt-Hartmann (2005, 2007) proposed a semantics of TimeML, based on Interval Temporal Logic (ITL). Katz (2007) introduced a denotational semantics that directly interprets TimeML annotation structures represented in XML.

Bunt (2007, 2011) introduced a semantics for semantic annotation. Bunt eventually developed a semantics based on the abstract syntax of a semantic annotation scheme. Bunt (2020a,b) also developed QuantML, a markup language for quantification, that can apply to the annotation and interpretation of a full range of features related to quantification such as the definiteness or determinacy, involvement or collectivity (distributivity) of entities, or scope ambiguity involving quantifiers and eventualities.

Lee (2008, 2011) follows the OWL-Time ontology and a compositional approach to work on temporal annotations with extensive use of λ-operations. It shows some degree of complexity in the use of λ-operations when they are recursively embedded, for it is required to raise the order of variables as the embedding gets deeper. One of the reasons for introducing ABSr is to avoid recursive embedding and substitutions (see Hausser (2015)). For now, ABSr has Rule 1^{sub} Substitutive conjunctive composition, but this should be deleted eventually except for the illustration of rudimentary annotations involving names and other basic types. Database Semantics (DBS) (Hausser, 2006) provides a theoretical foundation for the understanding of language analysis and generation without recursions and substitutions, but with the associative linear processing of language. This has motivated the design of ABS to some extent.

Then other types of semantics present different ways of representing meaning in language. Copestake et al. (2005) propose Minimal Recursion Semantics. Banarescu et al. (2013) introduce the Abstract Meaning Representation (AMR) to represent the semantic roles mainly based on PropBank in a logical format, the PENNMAN format, or directed graph structure (see also Flanigan (2018)). He (2018) also introduces a way of annotating semantic roles, which is called *shallow semantics*, without relying on pre-defined syntactic structures but introducing syntax-independent span-based neural models or labeled span-graph networks (LSGNs).

Based on syntax-free annotations, ABSr is also syntax-independent. Its current representation format is strictly linear but needs to move onto a graphic mode for visual purposes. The composition rules of ABSr are constrained by type matching and also syntax-independent, unlike Moens and Steedman's (1998) Categorial Grammar or Kamp and Reyle's (1993) DRSs. Dobnik et al. (2012) and Dobnik and Cooper (2017) introduce a type theory with records to constrain semantic representations and their manipulations in language processing. Their type system, especially related to spatial perception, will adequately orient the spatio-temporal annotation of ISO-Space and meaning representation through ABS. The earlier work of Pustejovsky (2001) on type construction also lays a basis for the type theory of ABS for a finer-grained treatment of entities and eventualities.

For the computational applications of semantic annotations, the Groningen Meaning Bank (GMB, Bos et al. (2017)) is very much related to the primary motivation of ABS in efforts to modify the classical version of DRT by making its syntax based on a (Montagovian) type systems consisting of two types, e and t, and by translating DRSs into a first-order logic only, for instance, while deleting so-called *duplex conditions* in DRSs. The basic design of the Parallel Meaning Bank (PMB) (Abzianidze et al., 2017) also adopts DRT as its formalism for meaning representation while adopting Combinatory Categorial Grammar (CCG) as its syntax. Since it applies to multilingual annotation, ABS can make use of it when the ISO standards on semantic annotation are extended to multilingual annotations, especially for multilingual translations.

Nevertheless, the theoretical framework of ABS and its representation language is conservative in practice, essentially based on the λ-calculus and the graphic representation of Kamp and Reyle's (1993) DRT. This will be shown in Section 6.5.2.

6.5.2 Convertibility

The composition of semantic forms is constrained by their semantic types. These types reflect those in Montague Semantics (Montague, 1974; Dowty et al., 1981) and also the extended type theory by Kracht (2002) and Pustejovsky et al. (2019a), thus making all these semantic forms isomorphic to those λ-constructions in λ-calculus. If such a typing of the semantic forms of annotation structures is ignored or if each of the semantic forms is treated as being of type t, then these semantic forms can easily be converted to DRSs (Kamp and Reyle, 1993).

As shown in Figure 6.4, there is an option to choose a type-theoretic semantics or not: ABS allows both but prefers to choose a type-theoretic semantics to constrain its representation language ABSr, while enriching its interpretation model structure. Unlike ABS or ABSr, DRT and DRSs are not based on a type theory, although the DRT formalism adopted by Bos et al. (2017) is based on a type theory. If a type theory is adopted, then the logical predicates can be defined in terms of type-theoretic higher-order logic.

In ABS, the choice of a theory depends on the treatment of unbound variables and unspecified types; ABS treats logical forms with occurrences of unbound variables as well-formed semantic forms. Individual (or predicate) variables may occur unbound in well-formed semantic forms, as in the interval

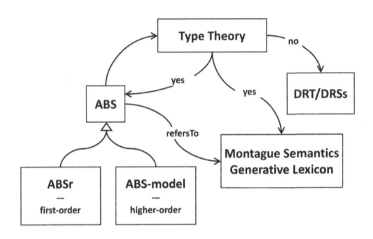

Figure 6.4 Options: type-theoretic or not.
Redrawn from figure 2, Lee (2020), which was published within the proceedings of the LREC 2020 (The 16th Joint ACL-SIGSEM– ISO Workshop on Interoperable Semantic Annotation (ISA-16)), ELRA – European Language Resources Association. CC-BY-BC-4.0.

temporal logic (ITL) of Pratt-Hartmann (2005, 2007).[9] Here is an example with a markable $visited_{e_1}$.

Example 6.76 Markables: Mia$_{x1}$ visited$_{e_1}$ Berlin, NY, [last year]$_{t1}$.
a. Annotation (id=a$_{5.unbound}$):
```
event(e1, m1, pred="visit", tense="past")
timex3(t1, m2, type="gYear", value="2019")
tLink(e1, t1, isIncluded)
```
b. Semantic representation:
$$\sigma(\texttt{e1})_\alpha := \{e_1\}[visit(e_1) \wedge past(e_1)]$$
$$\sigma(\texttt{t1})_\beta := \{t_1\}[gYear=(t_1, 2019)]$$
$$\sigma(\texttt{tLink})_\gamma := \{e_1, t_1\}[\{\sigma(\texttt{e1}), \sigma(\texttt{t1})\} \oplus occurs(e_1, t_1)]$$

Each of the semantic forms in Example 6.76b contains some variables which are registered in its preamble. In ABSr, these variables can be bound in two different ways, either by the existential quantifier or by the λ-operator. The assignment of a type to each semantic form depends on which way these (registered) variables are bound. The type of each semantic form is as follows:

- Case 1: either of type t (truth-value carrying) as if the unbound variables were bound by the existential quantifier ∃: namely,
$\exists\{e\}[visit(e) \wedge past(e)]$ (type t).

---

[9] ABS has no predicate variables.

- Case 2: or of some functional type (predicate) as if the unbound variables were bound by the λ-operator: namely, $\lambda e[visit(e) \wedge past(e)]$ (type $v \to t$).

Depending on which case is chosen, the semantic form of a link like $\sigma(tLink)$ in Example 6.76b undergoes a different rule of composition.

Case 1 allows the conversion of semantic forms in ABSr to DRSs.

Example 6.77 Case 1: Rule 1 Truth-functional conjunctive composition

a. $\sigma(\texttt{tLink}) := [[\sigma(e_1)_t, \sigma(t_1)_t] \oplus occurs(e_1, t_1)_t]$

$\quad := \{e, t\}[[visit(e) \wedge past(e)] \wedge gYear(t, 2019) \wedge occurs(e, t)]$

b. $\sigma(a_{6.76}) = \sigma(\texttt{tLink})$

As shown in Example 6.77, Case 1 (Truth-functional conjunctive composition) ($\oplus^{tr}$) can easily be converted to an equivalent DRS.

Example 6.78 Case 1 in DRS

$e\ t$
visit(e)
past(e)
gYear(t,2019)
occurs(e,t)

Although the application of Rule 1^{tr} (Truth-functional conjunctive composition) is type-constrained, there is no such constraint on the derivation of DRSs.

Case 2 allows the conversion of semantic forms in ABSr to well-formed forms in λ-calculus as in Montague Semantics (Montague, 1974). For the illustration of Case 2, consider Example 6.76, as was just given.

Example 6.79 Case 2 Montague Semantics: Rule 2 Functional conjunctive composition ($\oplus^{fa}$)

a. $\sigma(\texttt{tLink})_t := [[\sigma(e_1)_V, \sigma(t_1)_I] \oplus^{fa} occurs(e_1, t_1)_{I \to (V \to t)}]$

$\quad := [[visit(e_1) \wedge past(e_1)] \wedge gYear(t_1, 2019) \wedge occurs(e_1, t_1)]$

b. $\sigma(a_{6.76}) = \sigma(\texttt{tLink})_t$

The semantic form $\sigma(\texttt{tLink})$ in Example 6.79 is treated as a functional type, $I \to (V \to t)$, where I is $i \to t$ and V is $v \to t$. Then the semantic forms $\sigma(e1)$ and $\sigma(\texttt{t1})$ are treated as arguments of $\sigma(\texttt{tLink})$ such that they are of types V (eventuality descriptor) and I (set of time points), respectively.

In the process of the truth-functional conjunctive composition, the unbound occurrences of the variables are anchored to the discourse referents e and t, as in DRS, or existentially quantified, while adjusting their variable names accordingly.

As for the case of the functional conjunctive composition, the whole process is understood as if all the semantic forms were subject to a series of λ-conversions, as in Example 6.80.

Example 6.80 λ-Operations

a. $\sigma(\mathtt{e_1})_{v \to t} := \lambda e_1 [visit(e_1) \wedge past(e_1)]$

b. $\sigma(\mathtt{t_1})_{i \to t} := \lambda t_1 [gYear(t_1, 2019)]$

c. $\sigma(\mathtt{tLink})_t$

$\quad := \lambda T \lambda E \, \exists \{e, t\} [E(e) \wedge T(t) \wedge occurs(e, t)](\sigma(\mathtt{e_1}))(\sigma(\mathtt{t_1}))$

$\quad := \exists \{e, t\} [\sigma(\mathtt{e1})(e) \wedge \sigma(\mathtt{t1})(t)]$

$\quad := \exists \{e, t\} [visit(e) \wedge past(e) \wedge gYear(t, 2019) \wedge occurs(e, t)]$

It should again be stated that the derivation of semantic forms in ABSr does not undergo such λ-operations. The application of Rule 2 (Functional conjunctive composition) is only implicitly understood to undergo such operations.

Unlike semantic forms that involve λ-operations, the application of the $\oplus^{fa}$ in ABSr does not introduce predicate variables of a higher order, but individual variables of the first order only. This keeps ABSr to remain at the level of first order.

6.6 Extended Summary

This chapter introduced annotation-based semantics (ABS) for the model-theoretic interpretation of linguistic annotation structures; ABS provides a representation language ABSr that represents the semantic forms $\sigma(\mathbf{a})$ of annotation structures $\mathbf{a}$. These semantic forms are represented by first-order predicate logic, each assigned an appropriate semantic type. They do not contain variables of a higher order such as denoting *sets*, *sets of sets*, or *sets of sets* of individual entities.

Not all semantic forms of ABSr are of the truth-valued or sentential type t. Montague Semantics (Montague, 1974) applies λ-operations to expressions of nonsentential types to combine them into a semantic form of truth-type t. Here is an example.

Example 6.81 *Data:* Cato mewed.

a. *Cato$_{np}$* translates to $\lambda P P(c)_{(v \to t) \to t}$.

b. *mewed$_{s/np}$* translates to $\lambda x [past[mew'(x)]]_{v \to t}$[10]

c. By combining (a) and (b), *Cato mewed$_s$* translates to:

---

[10] The tense operator *past* here is treated as a propositional operator of type $t \to t$.

(i) $\lambda PP(c)(\lambda x[past[mew'(x)]])$ [by λ-conversion]

(ii) $\lambda x[past[mew'(x)]](c)$ [by λ-conversion]

(iii) $past[mew'(c)]_t$

In contrast, ABSr avoids using λ-expressions of higher order. Instead, it introduces combinatorial operators such as $\oplus$ and $\oslash$ and their various subtypes for the composition of semantics forms. Each of the two major types is specified as in Specification 6.82.

Specification 6.82 *Merge and demerging operators*

• The merge operator $\oplus$ is a *conjunctive operator* standing like the Boolean conjunctive connective "∧".

• The demerging operator $\oslash^{imp}$ is an *implicative distributive operator* that forms a Boolean implication with the connective "→".

Their subtypes have further specifications as operators for the composition of semantic forms.

Adopting the Neo-Davidsonian Semantics (Davidson, 1967; Parsons, 1990), ABSr treats Example 6.81a as follows in Semantics 6.83.

Semantics 6.83 *Data:* Cato mewed.

a. $\sigma(Cato)_e := c$

b. $\sigma(mewed)_{e\to(v\to t)}$
  $:= [mew(e) \wedge past(e) \wedge agent(e,x)]_{e\to t}$

c. $\sigma(Cato\,mewed)_t$
  $:= [\sigma(Cato)_e \oplus^{fa} \sigma(mewed)_{e\to(v\to t)}]$
  $:= [c_e \oplus^{fa} [mew(e) \wedge past(e) \wedge agent(e,x)]_{e\to(v\to t)}]$

d. Variable binding with existential quantification
  $:= \exists e[mew(e) \wedge past(e) \wedge agent(e,c)]_t$

In ABSr, semantic forms such as in Semantics 6.84, or $\phi|x_n$, in general, containing an n-number of unbound variables, are treated as functional types without binding them with the λ-abstraction.

Semantics 6.84 ABSr vs. Montague Semantics

a. ABSr: $[love(x,y)]_{e\to(e\to t)}$

b. Montague Semantics: $\lambda x\lambda y[love(x,y)]_{e\to(e\to t)}$

In ABSr, free occurrences of variables in semantic forms can also be bound by the existential quantifier $\exists$, thereby converting their functional types, such as $v \to t$ or $e \to (v \to t)$, to type t.

Semantics 6.85 Binding free occurrences of variables

a. $[love(x,y)]_{e \to (e \to t)}$ [functional type]

   $\exists x \exists y[love(x,y)]_t$ [t-type]

b. $[mew(e) \wedge past(e) \wedge agent(e,c)]_{v \to t}$ [functional type]

   $\exists e[mew(e) \wedge past(e) \wedge agent(e,c)]_t$ [t-type]

A limited number of *logical predicates* that simplify the representation of semantic forms are used in ABSr. For the semantic representation of the past verb form *ran*, for instance, ABSr introduces: for example, $[run(e) \wedge past(e)]$ for the past form *ran*, instead of $[run(e) \wedge e \subseteq t \wedge t \prec n]$. These logical predicates are defined by ABS as meaning postulates that constrain the construction of a model M.

We can say that ABS resembles Kamp and Reyle's (1993) DRT by allowing its semantic forms to be represented in DRSs. However, ABS differs from DRT in two respects: first, ABS is based on an extended type theory, and second, ABSr has no embedded structures. From an applicational point of view, ABS rather resembles the Groningen Meaning Bank (GMB), being developed by Bos et al. (2017), which adopts DRT as its working framework with similar modifications.

PART II

Time and Events

7

Temporal Ontology

7.1 Introduction

I understand *ontology* as a science of being. It is comparable to metaphysics in philosophy, called *philosophy of being*. Unlike metaphysics, ontology takes the form of exact science with applications. One such application is in the area of computational semantics. For the semantic annotation of temporal information in text, for instance, *temporal ontology* specifies temporal entities and their relations by treating the subject matter of time formally, or in explicit terms, and, most importantly, with data and facts in natural language, while defining the structure of time as a whole. Temporal ontology is thereby expected to lay a theoretically valid basis for doing temporal annotation in language.

In Aristotelian metaphysics, *time* is one of the accidental properties of physical beings. Type-theoretic semantics, in contrast, *reifies* time as well as events, as proposed by Davidsonian and Neo-Davidsonian Semantics (Davidson, 1967), by treating it like a real thing residing in the world. Temporal ontology like OWL-Time ontology views time as a structured entity, consisting of *points* (*instants*) and *intervals*, and other associated complex temporal entities such as *frequencies* (e.g., every day, weekly) or *durations* and *time amounts* which various types of eventualities are anchored to or predicated of. In Section 7.2, I discuss temporal entities, especially with the view of OWL-Time (World Wide Web Consortium, 2020) ontology, as is treated by Hobbs and Pustejovsky (2003) and Hobbs and Pan (2004).

Temporal entities are related with each other in various ways. The most basic type of temporal relation is *precedence*. Temporal entities are ordered in such a way that one temporal entity *precedes* another temporal entity. Section 7.3 discusses the ordering of temporal entities in a finer-grained way, especially introducing an *interval calculus* with 13 temporal relations that were proposed by Allen (1984) and also treated by Mani and Pustejovsky (2012). Section 7.4

briefly shows how Allen's (1984) base temporal relations are accommodated into the 13 relation types of ISO-TimeML (ISO, 2012b). It also shows how the temporal anchoring of events is expressed in some languages through their tense systems, defined by the basic notion of the present moment and its neighborhood. Section 7.5 summarizes the chapter.

7.2 Temporal Entities

7.2.1 OWL-Time Ontology

Supported by the US Defense Advanced Research Projects Agency (DARPA), DAML-Time was developed as part of the DARPA Agent Markup Language. It was then incorporated into OWL-Time, managed by a working group of the Worldwide Web Consortium (W3C).[1] OWL-Time introduces TemporalEntity as a class that consists of two subclasses, Instant and Interval, as is shown by Figure 7.1.

Instant is defined as an interval with zero length or extent such that the start and end are the same. *Intervals* are understood as containing instants inside.

Definition 7.1   Axiom of interval
$$\forall T[interval(T) \rightarrow \exists t[instant(t) \wedge t \in T]]$$

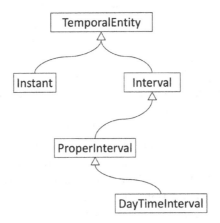

Figure 7.1 OWL-Time core model

---

[1] See www.w3.org/TR/2020/CR-owl-time-20200326/.

As accepted as an axiom, Definition 7.1 presupposes that there is no empty temporal interval. In the extended type theory, which was introduced in Chapters 5 and 6, instants or time points are of basic type i, whereas time intervals are of functional type $i \rightarrow t$, denoting a (nonempty) set of instants.

The *ProperInterval* is a subclass of Interval that excludes the class Instant. Each temporal entity in the class of ProperInterval thus has a nonzero extent with its beginning and end being distinct. Each interval is characterized by a beginning point and an endpoint.

Definition 7.2 Intervals

$$[[begins(t_0, T) \wedge ends(t_i, T)] \rightarrow [instant(t_0) \wedge instant(t_i) \wedge t_0 \prec t_i] \wedge interval(T)]$$

The two boundary points, t_0 and t_i, may or may not be inside the interval T. Thus, T can be either *open* or *closed* intervals. The limit of a day, as represented either as T24:00 or T00:00, can be either the end of a day or the beginning of the next day. If something happened at midnight, it is hard to tell which day it occurred.

The class *DateTimeInterval* is a subclass of ProperInterval. Each of the intervals in DateTimeInterval represents an interval corresponding to a single element in a date–time description (i.e., a specified year, month, week, day, hour, minute, second). Each interval in DataTimeInterval should be aligned with the calendar and timezone indicated. For example, the 24-hour interval beginning at midnight in Seoul can be expressed as a DateTimeInterval, but the 24-hour interval starting at noon cannot. Each DateTimeInterval thus has a beginning conventionally but explicitly specified for each of the calendar dates, while the specification of the end of a month, for instance, varies.

The specification of DateTimeInterval requires the package of *temporal reference systems* (TRS) that determines the position of a date or a time in a temporal axis. ISO 8601-1 (ISO, 2019a) specifies the use and representation of the Gregorian Calendar and clocks telling 24-hour local times or the *Coordinated Universal Time* (UTC) of day for the interchange of temporal information.[2]

7.2.2 Dates and Times

As is adopted by ISO-TimeML (ISO, 2012b) for the annotation of *calendar dates* and *clock times*, ISO 8601-1 (ISO, 2019a) adopts the *Gregorian*

---

[2] UTC provides the basis of standard time, replacing Greenwich Mean Time (GMT). It is exactly based on international atomic time and is generally used by aviation and maritime navigation. See ISO 8601-1 (ISO, 2019a, clause 2.1.12).

calendar, introduced in 1582, to define a calendar year that more closely approximated the tropical or solar year than the Julian calendar. It defines *calendar year* as *cyclic time interval* in the calendar which is required for one revolution of the Earth around the Sun and approximated to an integral number of calendar years. (see ISO 8601-1 (ISO, 2019a, clause 2.2.13).) Then each year refers to the duration of 365 or 366 calendar days; the common years have 365 days, while the leap years have one extra day allocated to the second month, namely February, of the year.

Essential holidays and other memorable days are celebrated according to local calendars. Chinese and Koreans celebrate new year's day according to the *lunar calendar*. In 2020, the lunar day occurred on January 25 and several days surrounding this day were celebrated as holidays in China and Korea. Koreans celebrate Chuseok, the fall festival, on the fifteenth of August according to the lunar calendar, enjoying the full moon and harvest in the autumn, although Korea officially follows the Gregorian calendar in conducting ordinary business. Korean and Japanese farming or fishing people rely on the lunar calendar for seasonal or tidal information for their daily activities, thus checking their Gregorian calendar, which is often decorated with extra information on lunar calendar days naming suitable times for farming and fishing.

Chinese and Koreans used to follow *dynastic* (imperial or royal) *calendars* and Japanese still do. A dynastic or royal calendar opens a new year with the new reign of an emperor or a king. The original version of Hangul, the Korean writing system, with a commentary was promulgated by King Sejong of the Yi Dynasty in Korea in the year of Sejong 28, matching the Gregorian year of 1446 CE. On May 1, 2019, Naruhito ascended the throne as the new Emperor of Japan, opening the *Reiwa* era, meaning *beautiful harmony*. With his enthronement, Akihito's Heisei era closed. The first year of Reiwa lasted till the end of December 2019 and the new year started on the first day of January 2020 according to the Gregorian calendar that has been accepted as an official calendar for Japan since 1873 during the Meiji era.

Islamic countries and Israel have developed their calendars. Their religioso-cultural festivals are celebrated according to their traditional calendars. The Jewish calendar, for instance, determines the day of Passover as the 15th day of the month of Nisan and indirectly Easter for both the Roman Catholic and the Orthodox churches, though assigned to a different date. To annotate all these dates that occur in the text, both ancient and present-day, in that part of the world, one has to study a variety of calendars or rely on automatic date-conversion programs.

ISO weekday	English name	Korean name	Korean and Japanese name in Chinese characters	Chinese name
W1	Monday	월요일	月曜日 (moon)	星期一 (one)
W2	Tuesday	화요일	火曜日 (fire)	星期二 (two)
W3	Wednesday	수요일	水曜日 (water)	星期三 (three)
W4	Thursday	목요일	木曜日 (tree)	星期四 (four)
W5	Friday	금요일	金曜日 (gold)	星期五 (five)
W6	Saturday	토요일	土曜日 (earth)	星期六 (six)
W7	Sunday	일요일	日曜日 (sun)	星期天

Figure 7.2 Naming weekdays

Month and Week The Gregorian calendar divides each year into 12 months from the first month of a year, called *January* in English, to the last month called *December*. Each month has a duration of 28, 29, 30, or 31 calendar days. January has 31 calendar days, while the second month, February, has either 28 days for common years or 29 days for leap years that return every fourth year.

Each week consists of seven days. Monday is the first day of the week according to ISO 8601-1 (ISO, 2019a). Sunday is the last day of the week, although conventional calendars list Sunday on the first or leftmost column of a monthly calendar. The USA and many other countries consider Sunday the first day of a week, but weekends contain both Saturday and Sunday, and even Friday if the weekend is a long weekend with no need to go to work.

The ISO ordering of weekdays matches the naming of weekdays in the Chinese calendar, as in Figure 7.2. The first weekday (W1) is named *star period one* and the sixth weekday (W6), *star period six*, while Sunday, the seventh weekday (W7), named *star period sun (day)* or *star period heaven (sky)*.

The notion of the week has been introduced to daily life in East-Asian countries around the turn of the twentieth century. Till then and even now to some extent, Koreans have, for instance, followed the dividing of a month into three parts, the beginning 10-day period of a month as *cho-swun*, the mid-period centering on the 15th with a full moon, *cwung-swun*, and the last period,

Table 7.1 *UTC offsets for time zones*

Dublin, London	Madrid, Berlin	Seoul, Tokyo	New York[a]
UTC+/-00:00	UTC+01:00	UTC+09:00	UTC-05:00

[a] UTC-04:00 during the period of daylight saving time (DST).

ha-swun. Many Confucian memorial ceremonies for ancestors who passed away and other traditional festivals used to be celebrated according to the tripartite division of a month. New Year's Day is still celebrated on the first day of the first month of a year and the fall festival, named *Chuseok*, is on the 15th of August according to the lunar calendar.

A year does not divide into weeks cleanly. It consists of 52 or 53 weeks. The first day of January is not necessarily the first weekday, Monday, of the first week (W01-1) of a calendar year nor is the last day of December the last weekday, Sunday, of a year. ISO 8601-1 (ISO, 2019a, clause 3.22, note 2) notes: "The first calendar week of a calendar year includes up to three days from the previous calendar year; the last calendar week of a calendar year includes up to three days from the following calendar year." In 2020, for instance, the first day of January was Wednesday. This weekday is treated as the third weekday of the last week belonging to the previous year 2019 (2019-W52-3). In 2021, the first day of January is Friday. Hence, that day will be the 5th day of the first week of the new year (2021-W01-5).

Clock Times Each calendar day is evenly divided into 24 hours, each hour into 60 minutes, and each minute into 60 seconds. According to the Gregorian calendar, a day ends at midnight T24:00, while a day starts at T00:00: both of the clock times refer to the same time position.[3] Hours are, however, different from location to location. Midnight in Seoul is not midnight in New York.

Time-zone designators called UTC *time offsets* are set up by the standard for each of the local times and allow their coordination. Table 7.1 lists some of the UTC offsets.

Most of the UTC time offsets are hour-based, but some countries adopt finer-grained offsets. North Korea used to adopt UTC+09:30 as its official zone designator, showing a 30-minute difference between Pyongyang and Seoul

---

[3] A new day was considered as starting at the sunset of a day in the Israel tradition. This still affects the liturgical practice of Judeo-Christian religious communities. In the Roman Catholic dioceses, for instance, Saturday evening Masses have been accepted recently as a genuine part of the Sunday obligation.

or Tokyo, Japan. New Zealand adopts UTC+12:00 or UTC+13:00 during its DST (daylight saving time or summer period), but UTC+12:45 for its Chatham Islands in the Pacific or UTC+13:45 during the DST.

COVID-19 has forced offsite virtual meetings to be held through the Internet. This requires the feasibility of hours for the meetings by checking the times at various locations. The conversion between two time zones can easily be made by the two equivalent formulas, as listed in Specification 7.3.

Specification 7.3 Conversion of UTC time offsets

For any time t_A in zone A and any time t_B in zone B and any UTC offsets U_A for zone A and U_B for zone B

a. $t_A - U_A = t_B - U_B$
b. $t_A = t_B - U_B + U_A$.

Suppose I want to invite participants from four different time zones, Boston, Tokyo, Beijing, and Tilburg, the Netherlands, to start the meeting at 7:30 a.m. in Boston. A participant from Boston is the keynote speaker and should be given enough time to wake up and prepare for the meeting in the morning, while Asians should not be kept late for their bedtime. Then we have the understandably most suitable meeting time for each location calculated as in Example 7.4.

Example 7.4 Different time zones calculated

a. $t_{Tokyo} = t_{Boston} - (UTC{-}04{:}00) + U_{Tokyo}$
   $t_{Tokyo} = 07{:}30 - (-04{:}00) + 09{:}00 = 20{:}30$
b. $t_{Beijing} = t_{Boston} - (UTC{-}04{:}00) + U_{Beijing}$
   $t_{Beijing} = 07{:}30 - (-04{:}00) + 08{:}00 = 19{:}30$
c. $t_{Tilburg} = t_{Boston} - (UTC{-}04{:}00) + U_{Tilburg}$
   $t_{Tilburg} = 07{:}30 - (-04{:}00) + 01{:}00 = 12{:}30$

7.2.3 Duration and Time Amounts

The OWL-Time ontology also introduces *duration* as a time extent with some time measure or amount. I thus understand it to be a proper time interval, the length of which can be measurable or expressed in terms of a pair of a numeric n and a temporal unit u. ISO 8601-1 (ISO, 2019a) defines it to be a "nonnegative quantity attributed to a time interval, the value of which is equal to the difference between the time points of the final instant and the initial instant of the time interval, when the time points are quantitative marks."

More formally, Hobbs and Pustejovsky (2003) treats *duration* as a function that maps interval and temporal units to reals. This is illustrated in Example 7.5.

Example 7.5 Duration

a. duration([5:14,5:17], minute) = 3

b. duration(T,hour) $= 60\times$ duration(T,minute)

The duration of an interval can be either short or long. Its exact length is given as an amount of time and a unit such as three hours. Two examples in Example 7.6 show how duration differs from an amount of time.

Example 7.6 Duration vs. time amount

a. *How long* did you sleep last night? [duration]

 Six hours from ten to four in the morning.

b. *How many hours* did you teach last week? [amount of time]

 Three class hours.

The quantitative expression *six hours* refers to the duration of the time interval during which a state has held, or an event has occurred continuously. It is also understood as an amount of time. The expression *three class hours* in (b) is an amount of time, denoting the accumulated amount of time consumed by the three occurrences of an event of teaching during the week mentioned.

Period As is noted in ISO 19108, (ISO, 2002) that treats temporal schema in relation to geographic information, there are two types of duration: *period-duration* and *interval length*. While duration is a generic term referring to the length of a time interval, expressed in time-based values such as seconds or nanoseconds, a *period* is an interval of time the length of which is measured and represented in terms of calendar dates (years, months, and days). Like the term *era*, as is used in *before the current (or common) era* (BCE), the term *period* is also used as referring to a time in history or the past such as the Babylonian *period* of the Jewish exile or Antonio Vivaldi as one of the greatest composers in the Baroque *period* of music.

 ISO 8601-1 (ISO, 2019a) represents the prefix "P" to represent a duration: for example, P5DT4H30.7M for five days, four hours, and 30.7 minutes.[4] The prefix "P" really stands for a duration or an amount of time for an interval, delimited by the beginning and endpoints in a temporal axis. It carries no historical connotation, as referring to a particular part of history.

---

[4] This example is taken from ISO 19108, (ISO, 2002, clause 5.2.3.7).

Time amounts also refer to quantities of time intervals. Unlike a duration, an amount of time can be cumulative, summing up several durations. Suppose one teacher taught for three hours, each hour on three different days last week. Then the amount of time she taught last week was three hours. It does not necessarily mean that her teaching last week lasted for three straight hours. ISO-TimeML (ISO, 2012b) treats them differently by introducing a tag <measure> or <amount> and representing its values as a pair $<n, u>$ of a numeric n and a temporal unit u to annotate amounts of time, while following ISO 8601-1 (ISO, 2019a) allows us to annotate the value of duration like P5DT4H30.7M "duration of 5 days 4 hours 30.7 minutes" as a sort of abbreviation.[5]

7.2.4 Representing Dates and Times

The principle of ordering larger temporal units first, as Chinese, Japanese, and Koreans do, is adopted in ISO 8601-1 (ISO, 2019a). Years are thus listed before months, months before days, and days before hours. For example, both *May 15, 2020* and *15 May 2020* are merged into *2020 May 15*. Then there are two representation formats, basic and extended. Dates are represented as in Example 7.7.

Example 7.7 Representing dates
May 15, 2020, 15 May 2020 or *15/05/20*
a. Basic format: YYYYMMDD: i.e., 20200515
b. Extended format: YYYY-MM-DD: i.e., 2020-05-15
c. Reduced formats: YYYY-MM: i.e., 2020-05; or YYYY: i.e., 2020

As in part c, reduced formats are also allowed.
  The solidus "/" is used to indicate an interval of time, not to differentiate dates nor to mark alternation, as shown in Example 7.8b.

Example 7.8 Representing time intervals
a. May 15-18, 2020
b. 2020-05-15/18

Hours, minutes, and seconds are represented as in Example 7.9.

Example 7.9 Representing times
a. *twelve-thirty p.m.*
  Basic format: hhmm: i.e., 1230
  Extended format: hh:mm: i.e., 12:30

---

[5] Instead of the period ".", Europeans use the comma "," to mark a decimal point.

b. *6 seconds after six in the evening*
   Extended format: 18:00:06

The hour *midnight* can be represented in the extended format as 00:00, which refers to the start of the next calendar day. If the represented hours are local time, then the time designator T is placed immediately before the representation of times of day: for example, T18:00:06. The UTC designator Z, sometimes called *Zoolu time of day*, is placed after the representation of hours if they represent the hours, minutes, and seconds of UTC day.

Example 7.10   The UTC designator Z
a. Basic format:
   hhmmssZ: e.g., 103020Z
   hhmmZ: e,g, 1030Z
   hhZ:, e.g., 10Z
b. Extended format:
   hh:mm:ssZ: e.g., 10:30:20Z
   hh:mmZ: e,g, 10:30Z
   hhZ:, e.g., 10Z

Each of the examples in Example 7.11 shows the representation of a local time for Seoul and its difference from the UTC of day.

Example 7.11   Representing a local time for Seoul:
a. 2020-07-29T20:18
b. 2020-07-29T20:18+09:00

From Example 7.11b, we know that T20:18 is the time for Seoul, and also for various locations in Japan as well as both South and North Korea, and the easternmost part of Indonesia (city of Manokwari).

7.2.5 Timeline and History

I view a *history* as a *band* of layers of linearly ordered structures, called *timelines*. Each position on a timeline represents the anchoring of an event to a point in time. The timeline of the Korean War, for instance, consists of a sequence of pairs of a time and an event anchored to it, but the whole story surrounding that war is more complex. Even on a single day, one party was invading, while the other was defending by fighting against the invaders. Three days after the invasion that had started in the early dawn of June 25, 1950, the whole city of Seoul was occupied by the invading North Korean army. As a military strategy to block them from moving further south, a South Korean military commander ordered the sole major bridge that existed over the Han River at that time to be cut off with dynamite, killing hundreds of civilians crossing the bridge without any advanced warning. By then, as has been rumored, President Syngman Rhee of South Korea had left for Daegu, a provincial city 240 kilometers south of Seoul, broadcasting a supposedly prerecorded message exhorting Seoulites to keep staying in Seoul and defend it. The Acheson line had been declared in mid-January 1950, drawn between the peninsula of Korea and Japan, thus excluding South Korea from the US line of defense in the Pacific.

On the international scene, the swift attack of the North Korean forces armed with heavy Russian tanks and artillery was immediately reported to the US Supreme Commanding Head Quarters in Tokyo under General Douglas MacArthur and also to the Korean Embassy and the White House in Washington, DC. The emergency session of the UN Security Council was then invoked to adopt a resolution, reportedly in the absence of the Soviet Union delegation, who could have vetoed, that more than a dozen principal UN members agreed on immediately dispatching their armed forces to aid the Republic of Korea. As part of the UN forces, the first group of the US Army, stationed in Japan, landed in Korea on July 1, a week after the war started. All these events and meetings occurred almost simultaneously to meet the emergency, while the diplomatic hotlines were kept open and busily occupied among Stalin's USSR, Mao's People's Republic of China, and Kim Il Sung's DPRK in Pyongyang, claiming to liberate the fatherland.

To depict such a story as a *meaningful* history requires a broader perspective of recording the entire spectrum of the concurrent events. The two sides tell different stories of the war that was known to have caused the seventh-largest number of war casualties in history. The band of history lines can be represented as a two-dimensional plane, defined by Cartesian $X \times Y$ coordinates, where the X-axis stands for the flow of time and the Y-axis stands for the view or perspective of histories. Consider two or three records of the Second World War, a series of fights in the European frontiers and another series of battles in the Pacific or the Southern part of Asia. All the happenings, even major ones, from the perspective of the united forces, cannot be recorded in a single timeline. Even on the European scene, there were several invading lines, one from Great Britain through Normandy to Paris or the Low Countries, another from northern Africa to Sicily to Rome or Venice, and the attack by Russian forces from the eastern European front through the Nordic countries, Poland, Hungary, or other Balkan countries.

Compared with the European fronts, the Pacific area covers a much larger area involving several time zones from the time zone starting from Indonesia or India to Singapore to the Philippines to China and over various islands in the Pacific to New York and Washington, DC, in the eastern part of the United States. The India Standard Time (IST) is UTC+5:30. Indonesia has three time zones and some areas with DST, ranging from UTC+7 (Jakarta), to UTC+8 (Makassar), to UTC+9 (Manokwari, Japanese standard time, JST, or Korean standard time KST), *etc.* The famous naval Battle of Midway, which took place on June 4–7, 1942, crossed the international date line. The Japanese bombing of the airfields on two of the Midway islands, which were located in the Pacific north-west of Pearl Harbor in Hawaii, began at 4:30 a.m., on the third day of the sixth month in the seventeenth year of Showa, seen from the Japanese side, while the US military history records the battle as lasting for three days from June 4–7, 1942. Every action of dog-fighting and bombing or torpedoing was recorded for hours, minutes, and even seconds on both sides and also made into videos and movies after the war.

7.3 Temporal Relations and Reasoning

7.3.1 Conceptual View of Time

Time can be conceptualized as a structure of temporal points or intervals ordered either partially (possibly branching), linearly, cyclically or even spiral-like, as shown in Figure 7.3.

The *linear view of time* reflects that time continuously flows from the eternal past to the infinite future, independent of how the world changes.

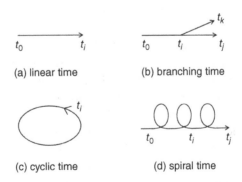

(a) linear time   (b) branching time

(c) cyclic time   (d) spiral time

Figure 7.3 Conceptual view of time

The *branching view* attempts to bring the notion of possible futures or counterfactuals into the temporal development of history in the world. Think of how Iraq and the Middle East would have changed the course of their history if Iraq had not invaded and occupied Kuwait in August 1990, followed by the Gulf War a year later. It would have given a different story of the world in that part of the world.

The *cyclic view of time* describes the return of the four seasons, weekdays, or tidal and celestial cycles. Using the Chinese lunar calendar based on the 10 heavenly bases and the 12 zodiac animals on Earth, Chinese, Korean, and some other East Asian peoples celebrate their sixtieth birthdays as the beginning of the returned new life. The spiral view is a combination of the linear and cyclic views of the time. The Catholic liturgical years starting from Advent through Lent and Easter to the long period of ordinary weeks may better be understood if the time is viewed as running towards the eschatological final days in a spiral manner.

All these views are conceptually possible with some explanatory power of describing natural or philosophico-linguistic phenomena surrounding us. Nevertheless, the linear view is the logically most developed formal view of the temporal structure. Computationally, it is the most straightforward system for treating time. The classical view is thus to accept time as partially ordered, while the ordinary view is to see time as strictly linear, thus defining a *timeline* as being isomorphic to the system of real numbers $\mathcal{R}$ or a one-dimensional temporal axis.

Time can also be viewed as either *continuous, dense,* or *discrete.* For linguistic or logical purposes, time is often described digitally as being discrete, matching dates and hours. Calendar dates and clock hours are developed as representing *discrete-time positions* in the temporal axis or timeline. Classical views are represented by Prior (1967) and Montague (1974). OWL-Time (World Wide Web Consortium, 2020) adopts Allen's (1984) interval calculus with 13 temporal relations.

7.3.2 Interval Calculus

Set-Theoretic Formulation of Time Structure

In set-theoretic terms, the simplest model of temporal ontology $\mathcal{T}$ is a tuple $<T, R>$ which consists of (1) a nonempty set T of points of time and (2) a set R of relations over T. The typical relation in R is an asymmetric, irreflexive, and transitive binary relation $\prec$, called *(strictly) precedes*, over T. This defines the temporal ontology T to be a partially ordered structure. Such an ontology can accommodate both the branching and linear view of time.

This fundamental ontology can be further developed into an interval calculus, modeled as a tuple $<I, R>$, where I is a set of intervals, supported by an interval temporal semantics on a theoretically adequate and consistent algebraic system of intervals. Each *interval* is defined by its *start* and *endpoint*, as in Definition 7.12.

Definition 7.12   Definition of *interval*
Given a nonempty set of reals $\mathcal{R}$ and any reals i, j, and k in $\mathcal{R}$, I is an interval if and only if, for any k in I, $i \preceq k$ or $k \preceq j$.

This means that the interval I is a set of all the reals k between i and j, forming a closed interval $[i, j]$, based on $\mathcal{R}$. The reals i and j are the two limiting or boundary points, the start and the endpoint of I, respectively. Intervals may be of different sorts: it can be a unit interval or a nonempty interval of either an open or a closed type or their combinations. Such a characterization of the notion of *intervals* applies to *temporal interval semantics*.

Base Relations over Time Intervals

Allen (1984) develops an interval calculus with a set of 13 mutually exclusive primitive relations each of which holds between the two intervals I and J of time. He defines what these relations are as they are represented as predicates. Some of them are introduced here in Definition 7.13.

Definition 7.13   Definition of *before*, *starts*, and *finishes*
a. *before*(I, J): time interval I is before time interval J and they do not overlap in any way.
b. *starts*(I, J): time interval I shares the same beginning as J, but ends before J ends.
c. *finishes*(I, J): time interval I shares the same end as J, but begins after J begins.

In Definition 7.13b, c, the interval I can be understood to be a subinterval K of J such that the start of K is the same as that of I and its end is contained in J or that the end of K is the same as that of J and its start is contained in I. The other predicates can be defined in the same manner.

These 13 temporal relations, which include the six inverse relations, are graphically represented in Table 7.2. The time interval I is represented in each row as a string of Xs and the time interval J as that of Ys.

Based on these temporal predicates, Allen (1984) additonally defines the relation of a predicate *in*, as in Definition 7.14.

Definition 7.14   Definition of the logical predicate *in*
$in(I, J) =_{def} [during(I, J) \wedge starts(I, J) \wedge finishes(I, J)]$

Table 7.2 *Interval calculus with base relations*

Relation	Inverse relation	Illustration	Symbol
before(X, Y)	*after*(Y, X)	XXX YYY	< , >
equal(X, Y)		XXX YYY	=
meets(X, Y)	*metBy*(Y, X)	XXXYYY	m, mi
overlaps(X, Y)	*overlappedBy*(Y, X)	XXX YYY	o, oi
during(X, Y)	*contains*(Y, X)	XXX YYYYYY	d, di
starts(X, Y)	*startedBy*(Y, X)	XXX YYYYYY	s, si
finishes(X, Y)	*finishedBy*(Y, X)	XXX YYYYYY	f, fi

Definition 7.14 helps define an essential predicate *holds* that anchors an eventuality e to a time interval T.

Definition 7.15   Definition of the logical predicate *holds*
$holds(e, T) =_{def} \forall t[in(t, T) \rightarrow during(\tau(e), t)]$, where $\tau(e)$ maps an event to a time interval.

Definition 7.15 means that an eventuality holds in an interval if and only if it holds in every subinterval of it. The logical predicate *holds* is then used for the derivation of logical forms of eventualities, especially of type *state* like *know*, *live*, and *love*. Here is an example.

Example 7.16   Temporal relation *holds*
a. Markables: John loved$_{s1}$ Mary a lot when she lived$_{s2}$ with him.
b. Semantic representation:
$\exists\{s_1, s_2, t_1, t_2\}$
$[[love(s_1, j, m) \wedge holds(s_1, t_1)] \wedge [live(s_2, m) \wedge holds(s_2, t_2)] \wedge during(s_1, s_2)]$

The predicate *during* denotes a temporal inclusion relation between two states. Thus, $during(s_1, s_2)$ is understood as stating that the state s_1 holds in the interval during which the state s_2 holds.

7.3.3 Extension of an Interval Calculus

As in OWL-Time (World Wide Web Consortium, 2020), a set of temporal entities is understood to have two subtypes: *interval* and *instant*, thereby extending the domain of various temporal relations over any type of temporal entities, whether they are instants or intervals. Both intervals and instants are primitive objects in the extended interval calculus.

Definition 7.17   Subtypes of temporal entities, *instant* and *interval*
For any interval T, $temporalEntity(T) \rightarrow [instant(T) \vee interval(T)]$

Intuitively, instants are understood to be reals or unit intervals or intervals with zero length such that the two limiting points are identical.

Definition 7.18   Unit interval
$\forall t[instant(t) \rightarrow [interval(t) \wedge length(t)=0]]$

With this extension, it is possible to define the temporal relations $\prec$, $\preceq$, and *before* as a relation over temporal entities, which can be either instants or intervals.

Definition 7.19   Precedence relations
Given an instant t and an interval T,
a. $t \prec T \Leftrightarrow \forall t'[t' \in T \rightarrow [t \prec t']]$
b. $t \preceq T \Leftrightarrow \forall t'[t' \in T \rightarrow [t \preceq t']]$
c. $before(t, T) \Leftrightarrow \forall t'[t' \in T \rightarrow [t \prec t']]$
d. $T \prec t \Leftrightarrow \forall t'[t' \in T \rightarrow [t' \prec t]]$
e. $T \preceq t \Leftrightarrow \forall t'[t' \in T \rightarrow [t' \preceq t]]$
f. $before(T, t) \Leftrightarrow \forall t'[t' \in T \rightarrow [t' \prec t]]$

Such definitions as listed in Definition 7.19 make two assumptions, as stated in Proposition 7.20.

Proposition 7.20   Two assumptions
a. Every interval consists of instants.[6]
$\forall T[interval(T) \rightarrow [T=\{t\,|\,instant(t) \wedge t \in T\}]]$
b. Every interval is non-empty.
$\forall T[interval(T) \rightarrow \exists t[instant(t) \wedge t \in T]]$

Theoretically, an empty interval is possible, but such an interval becomes meaningless from the point of semantics for natural language. Proposition 7.20 implies that Hobbs and Pan (2004) and OWL-Time (World Wide Web Consortium, 2020) treat the two interval-bounding points as instants, but they are silent about Proposition 7.20a without making any commitment.

Instead of the predicates *starts* and *finishes*, which are parts of Allen's (1984) 13 base relations over intervals, it is also possible to define the predicates

---

[6] OWL-Time (World Wide Web Consortium, 2020) does not commit to this assumption. See Hobbs and Pustejovsky (2003).

begins and *ends* as relations between an instant and an interval (see Hobbs and Pustejovsky (2003)).

Definition 7.21 Definition of *begins* and *ends*:
a. $begins(t, T) \rightarrow [instant(t) \land temporalEntity(T) \land t \preceq T]$
b. $ends(t, T) \rightarrow [instant(t) \land temporalEntity(T) \land T \preceq t]$

Definitions 7.21a,b both assume that every temporal entity is either an instant or an interval, as stated in Definition 7.17.

The introduction of the precedence relation $\prec$ with equality $=$ may be sufficient to define other temporal relations. The equality of two temporal intervals, for instance, may be defined as in Definition 7.22.

Definition 7.22 Definition of the predicate *equal*
For any two intervals I_1 and I_2, $equal(I_1, I_2)$ iff $I_1 = I_2$.

The two intervals are identical if and only if they are the same set, preserving the same partial order among the members of the two sets.

7.4 Time and Events

7.4.1 Temporalizing Eventualities

It is also possible to extend the notion of temporal relations as relations between an event and a time or between two events by *temporalizing* eventualities or treating them as intervals (Mani and Pustejovsky, 2012).

Example 7.23 Temporalized eventualities
a. *before* relating an event to a time:
   John left$_e$ Boston before noon$_t$.
   $[leave(e, j, b) \land noon(t) \land before(e, t)]$
b. *before* relating an event to another event:
   John left$_{e1}$ Boston before Mary arrived$_{e2}$ there.
   $[leave(e_1, j, b) \land arrive(e_2, m, b) \land before(e_1, e_2)]$

Otherwise, we should introduce the *run-time function* τ from eventualities to times. For an event e, $\tau(e)$ explicitly represents a time to which the event e is anchored, as illustrated by Example 7.24.

Example 7.24 Run-time function τ
a. John left$_e$ yesterday$_t$.
b. $[leave(e, j) \land yesterday(t) \land \tau(e) \subseteq t]$

Temporal and Event Identities

Related to time and events, there are two types of *identity*: temporal and event identities. The relation of *temporal identity* is represented by the predicate *simultaneous*, whereas that of *event identity* is represented by the predicate *identical*. Each of them is defined as in Definition 7.25.

Definition 7.25　Two types of *identity*
a. Simultaneity: *simultaneous*$(t_1, t_2) \Leftrightarrow t_1 = t_2$
b. Event identity: *identical*$(e_1, e_2) \Leftrightarrow e_1 = e_2$

Here are examples of simultaneous events.

Example 7.26　Simultaneous events
a. The sun was rising$_{e1}$ as we reached$_{e2}$ the top of a mountain.
   simultaneous$(\tau(e_1), \tau(e_2))$
b. A thunder hit$_{e3}$ a tree when I was walking$_{e4}$ by. I was lucky to be alive.
   simultaneous$(\tau(e_3), \tau(e_4))$

An event can also be treated as being simultaneous with a time interval.[7]

Example 7.27　An event being simultaneous with a time interval
John had to work$_e$ [from nine to five]$_{t1}$ last Saturday: *simultaneous*$(\tau(e), t_1)$

The time interval t_1 was an interval [T09:00, T17:00], which was delimited by the two time points, 09:00 and 17:00 (5:00 p.m.). Thus, *simultaneous*$(\tau(e), t_1)$ is interpreted as stating that the time interval of the event e of John working was simultaneous with the time interval from 09:00 to 17:00.
　　Event identity is illustrated by Example 7.28.

Example 7.28　Identical events
a. John dined$_{e1}$ with Mary last night and after the dinner$_{e2}$ he proposed to her:
   identical(e_1, e_2)
b. John drove$_{e1}$ to Boston. During his drive$_{e2}$, he ate a doughnut:
   identical(e_1, e_2)
c. John slept$_{e1}$ well last night. While sleeping$_{e2}$, he snored$_{e3}$, though:
   identical(e_1, e_2), *simultaneous*$(\tau(e_2), \tau(e_3))$

In Example 7.28c, the events e_1 and e_2 are the same events, but the event e_3 is an event different from e_1 or e_2. They did, however, occur at the same time, simultaneously. Simultaneity thus means temporal identity but not the identity of events.

---

[7] See ISO-TimeML (ISO, 2012b, examples 79 and 92, A.3, pp. 56 and 58).

7.4.2 Temporal Relations in ISO-TimeML

Thirteen Relations in TimeML

As presented in Pustejovsky et al. (2005) and ISO-TimeML (ISO, 2012b), TimeML proposes 13 temporal relations. This list includes the two relation types *identity* and *simultaneous* that were just presented.

Specification 7.29 Temporal relations in TimeML:
a. *(event) identity*
b. *simultaneous*
c. *before, after*
d. *includes, isIncluded*
e. *during*
f. *iBefore, iAfter*
g. *begins, begunBy*
h. *ends, endedBy*

The relation *before* and its inverse relation *after* are the two most basic relations, listed among Allen's (1984) list of 13 base relations. The relations *during*, *begins*, *ends*, and their inverses are also in Allen's (1984) list. The relation *includes* and its inverse *isIncluded* are relations between an event and a time interval. The relation *during* in ISO-TimeML relates an event or a series of events to an interval.

Example 7.30 Temporal relations
a. We visited$_{e1}$ New York [last year]$_{t1}$ and went$_{e2}$ to galleries, movies, and some Broadway shows during our stay$_{e3}$ there.
b. Temporal relations:
   $[isIncluded(e_1, t_1) \land during(e_2, e_3) \land identity(e_1, e_3)]$

Note that the event e_2 may refer to not a single event, but a series of various events.

Time Intervals

The relations *begins* and *ends* together specify the two bounding points of a time interval, misleadingly often called *duration*.[8] Example 7.31 shows how

---

[8] The term *duration* needs to be replaced by a term *time interval*, for ISO 8601-1 (ISO, 2019a) defines *duration* as *nonnegative quantity attributed to a time interval* (clause 2.1.6), while the term *time interval* is defined as *part of the time axis limited by two instants* (clause 2.1.3).

the two bounding points, *beginPoint* and *endPoint*, of an interval interact with the occurrence time of an event.

Example 7.31   Bounding points
a. Mia left Kathmandu two hours before the earthquake.
b. Mia left$_{e1,w2}$ Kathmandu [two hours]$_{t1,w4-5}$ before$_{tr1,w6}$ the earthquake$_{e2,w7-8}$.

Based on the time interval of t1, all these positions are calculated by the attribute @temporal Function, which is introduced to ISO-TimeML (ISO, 2012b), as presented in Annotation 7.32.

Annotation 7.32   Annotation with *@temporalFunction*
a. Base structures:
```
event(e1, w2, pred="leave", type="process", tense="past")
tEntity(t1, w4-5, type="interval", value="(2, hours)",
  temporalFunction="true", beginPoint="t11", endPoint="t12")
tRelator(tr1, w6, pred="before")⁹
tEntity(t11, type="instant")
tEntity(t12, type="instant")
event(e2, w7-8, pred="earthquake", type="process")
```
b. Link structures:
```
tLink(t11, t1, relType="begins")
tLink(t12, t1, relType="ends")
tLink(e1, t11, relType="ends")
tLink(e2, t12, relType="begins")
```

As shown in Figure 7.4, the interval t1 of two hours is bounded by the beginning point t11 and the endpoint t12. It is also positioned *before* the occurrence time of the event earthquake(e2).

Annotation 7.32 is now interpreted as follows, by Semantics 7.33.

Semantics 7.33   Semantic form for interpretation
$[[leave(e_1) \wedge past(e_1)] \wedge [interval(t_1) \wedge duration(t_1, <2, h>) \wedge$
$[instant(t_{11}) \wedge begins(t_1, t_{11}) \wedge instant(t_{12}) \wedge ends(t_1, t_{12})] \wedge ends(\tau(e_1), t_{11}) \wedge$
$begins(\tau(e_2), t_{12})]$

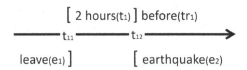

Figure 7.4 Bounding points

---

⁹ *tRelator* stands for the basic entity category *temporal relator* in ISO-TimeML, as modified in this book, and tr is its categorized ID prefix.

Semantics 7.33 represents the interpretation of Annotation 7.32. It says that the process of the departure from Kathmandu *was completed* two hours before the earthquake first *started*, agreeing with the intuitive understanding of what is meant by Example 7.31.

Example 7.34 introduces another type of a time interval.

Example 7.34   Time interval
Mia worked in Oslo *from June to August*.

ISO-TimeML (ISO, 2012b) annotates Example 7.34 as relating the event of Mia's working in Oslo to the interval of time, which is annotated as a nonconsuming tag $\emptyset_{t1:tInterval}$. Its bounding points are specified with the two time points, *June* and *August*. These terms, which refer to months, are understood as denoting temporal instants. Annotation 7.35 shows the details.

Annotation 7.35   Bounding points
a. Word-segmentation:
   Mia worked$_{e1,w2}$ in Oslo $\emptyset_{t1:tInterval}$ from$_{tr1,w5}$ June$_{t11,w6}$ to$_{tr2,w7}$ August$_{t12,w8}$.
b. Base structures:
```
event(e1, w2, pred="work", type="process", tense="past")
tEntity(t1,∅, type="tInterval", value="(3, months)", beginPoint="t11",
   endPoint="t12", temporalFunction="true")
tEntity(t11, w6, type="instant", value="XXXX-06")
tEntity(t12, w8, type="instant', value="XXXX-08")
```
c. Link structures:
```
tLink(e1, t1, relType="simultaneous")
tLink(e1, t11, tr1, relType="begins")
tLink(e1, t12, tr2, relType="ends")
```

Based on Annotation 7.35, we obtain Semantics 7.36 as follows.

Semantics 7.36   Time interval with bounding points
$$[[work(e_1) \wedge past(e_1)] \wedge [interval(t_1) \wedge begins(t_1,t_{11}) \wedge ends(t_1,t_{12})] \wedge$$
$$simultaneous(\tau(e_1),t_1) \wedge begins(\tau(e_1),t_{11}) \wedge ends(\tau(e_1),t_{12})]]$$

The interval like *from June to August* usually means from the beginning of June to the end of August. This interpretation can also be made explicit with the use of the two temporal predicates *begins* and *ends*.[10]

---

[10] The predicate *begins* may be replaced by *starts*.

7.4.3 Tense and Time

Tense is a grammatical feature associated with verbal categories in some languages, whereas *time* is an ontological object that exists in the worlds. Contingent events, which hold or occur in the world, are anchored to times. Such a relation is expressed by tensed verbs in English.

Consider Example 7.37a,b.

Example 7.37   Tense and aspect

a. Mia was sick *yesterday*. [date in the past]
b. Mia has lived in Nepal for *six months*. [duration of time]

In part a, Mia's being sick was anchored to a date in the past, mentioned by *yesterday*. Part b states that the duration of Mia's stay in Nepal has lasted for six months. Each of them has a temporal expression, while the mode of temporal anchoring for each is expressed by the so-called tense or aspectual feature of a verb in languages like European languages or Korean and Japanese. Such a feature is annotated by ISO-TimeML, as in Annotation 7.38.

Annotation 7.38   Tense and aspect annotated

a. Tense annotated: Mia was sick$_{e1,w2-3}$ yesterday$_{t1,w4}$.
```
event(e1, w2-3, pred="beSick", type="state", tense="past")
tEntity(t1, w4, type="date", value="2020-08-13",
  temporalFunction="true")
tLink(e1, t1, relType="isIncluded")
```
b. Aspect annotated: Mia [has lived]$_{e2:w2-3}$ in Nepal for [six months]$_{t2:w7-8}$.
```
event(e2, w2-3, pred="live", type="state", tense="pres",
  aspect="perfect")
tEntity(t2, w4, type="duration", value="P6M")
tLink(e2, t2, relType="simultaneous")
```

Each of the annotation structures is then translated into a logical form for its interpretation.

Semantics 7.39   Logical forms

a. Past tense:
   $[[beSick(e_1) \wedge past(e_1)] \wedge [year(t_1, 2020) \wedge month(t_1, 08) \wedge day(t_1, 13)]$
   $\wedge\, isIncluded(\tau(e_1), t_1)]$
b. Present perfect aspect:
   $[[live(e_2) \wedge presPerfect(e_2)] \wedge [interval(t_2) \wedge duration(t_2){=}{<}6, month{>}]$
   $\wedge\, simultaneous(\tau(e_2), t_2)]$

The logical predicates *isIncluded* and *simultaneous* that occur in these logical forms are defined as follows.

Definition 7.40   Logical predicates *isIncluded* and *simultaneous* defined
For any temporal entities t_1 and t_2,
a. *isIncluded*$(t_1, t_2) \Leftrightarrow [t_1 \subseteq t_2]$
b. *simultaneous*$(t_1, t_2) \Leftrightarrow [t_1 = t_2]$

These definitions allow part a to be interpreted as stating that Mia's sickness
may have lasted all day yesterday or some parts of the day and part b as stating
that Mia lived in Nepal for the whole period of six months.

Expanded Time Frame

Jespersen (1933, p. 263) introduces the term *expanded tense* to refer to the
progressive aspect, as illustrated by Example 7.41.

Example 7.41   Expanded tense
a. Simple tenses:
   e.g., *He works. He worked. He has worked.*
b. Expanded tenses (progressive aspect):
   e.g., *He is working. He was working. He has been working.*

Unlike simple tenses, Jespersen mentions that the expanded tenses require a
larger *temporal frame* to interpret them, encompassing what is referred to by
their related simple tensed statements. Given a time *t* to which a simple tensed
event is anchored, the event with a so-called expanded tense is anchored to a
larger temporal frame that includes the time *t*.

The *expanded frame of time* also applies to the present-tensed eventualities.
The following is an example by Quirk et al. (1985, 4.2).

Example 7.42   Expanded present
e.g., Paris *stands* on the River Seine.

The verb *stands* is marked with the present tense, denoting a situation anchored
to the present moment. Example 7.42 is understood as involving a larger
temporal frame that stretches to the past and also to the future, for Paris has
been standing on the River Seine and will do so in the coming future.

As was discussed earlier in Section 6.4.3, the interpretation of the predicates
past and *presPerfect* or even the present tense requires their definitions based
on the notion of the *present moment n*. The past time interval *past* precedes *n*,
while *n* precedes the future time interval *future*. Thus the present moment *n* is
between them without overlapping with any of them.

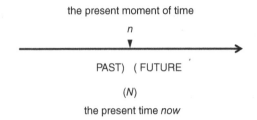

Figure 7.5 The present moment vs. the present time *now* N

Definition 7.43 *Past, future, and between*
a. the tense *past*: *past* ≺ *n*
b. the tense *future*: *n* ≺ *future*
c. the temporal relation *between*: *between*(*n*, *past*, *future*)

As shown in Figure 7.5, the present moment *n* differs from the present time (interval) *N*. Formally speaking, the present time interval is the neighborhood 𝒩(*n*), where the neighborhood 𝒩 is a function that maps an instant *t* to an interval *T*. For the present moment *n* of time, we have its neighborhood 𝒩(*n*) which denotes the *present time interval N*, which is often denoted by the word *now*.

Several propositions on the present time *N* can be made as in Proposition 7.44.

Proposition 7.44 Present-time related propositions
a. The present time *N* is defined: *N* =_{def} 𝒩(*n*),
        where *n* is the present moment.
b. *n* ∈ *N*
c. *overlaps*(*N*, PAST)
d. *overlaps*(*N*, FUTURE)
e. *N* is an open interval.

The time interval *N*, which is the neighborhood 𝒩(*n*) of the present moment *n*, is understood to center around the *present moment n*, while overlapping with the past and the future intervals. It thus provides a larger temporal frame that can interpret cases of the expanded time appropriately.

7.5 Summary

Viewing ontology as a *science of things*, this chapter treats times as real objects in the world. Such a view of the ontology of times, called *temporal ontology*, conforms to Neo-Davidsonian semantics and also to the type-theoretic semantics, which treats time points as one of the basic types that include individual objects, events, and spatial points. It is thus designed to provide a sound basis for the development of semantics for the annotation and interpretation of event-based temporal information in language.

Section 7.2 presents OWL-Time ontology, which classifies temporal entities into instants and intervals. Intervals are considered as consisting of instants. Then intervals are subclassified into proper intervals some of which are date–time intervals. Calendar dates and times of day are treated as denoting date-related intervals. ISO 8601 is introduced, which presents the two normalized formats, basic and extended, for representing calendar dates and times of the day. The notion of *history* is treated as a band of timelines, representable on a Cartesian plane, such that the X-axis represents a line of temporal positions, while the Y-axis represents a set of historical perspectives or interests.

Section 7.3 introduces Allen's (1984) interval calculus with 13 base relations such as *before* or *meet*. Following Mani and Pustejovsky (2012), these temporal relations are shown to apply to the analysis of data in natural language. To make it more applicable to the treatment of natural language data, the interval calculus is extended to points of time, thus making it possible to define temporal relations as relations between time points and time intervals as well.

Section 7.4 discusses how eventualities are *tempolarized* or treated as time intervals to which they are anchored so that temporal relations may apply to them as well as to times. ISO-TimeML is also shown to accommodate Allen's (1984) base relations for the definition of 13 relation types for its temporal link tLink. As a grammatical category, the tense of verbal forms in some languages like most European languages is also discussed. The present or past tense and the aspectual forms of progressive and perfective are defined on the notions of the present moment n and the present time interval N. Formally, the interval N is defined as the neighborhood of n, $N(n)$. As an open interval, N is introduced as containing n, while overlapping the past and the future time intervals. The notion of expanded times is supported by the function of *neighborhood N* from instants to intervals.

8

Normalizing TimeML with Some Modifications

8.1 Initiatives for Event-Based Temporal Annotation

Time and *events* have been, and still are, *hot issues* in logic, grammar, and formal and computational semantics of natural language (see Gabbay and Moravcsik (1980)). They are the main topics of temporal logic, event semantics, or event-focused temporal semantics, of both traditional and formal grammars. *Event-based temporal semantics*, in particular, has made efforts to treat tense, aspects, modality, mood, temporal modifiers, and time intervals with respect to various classes of event-denoting predicates and their types. All of these efforts have aimed at framing a formal or computational system of time and events with their focus of interest ranging or shifting from axiomatic and proof-theoretic syntax to model-theoretic semantics to computational semantics.

For computational semantics, the formulation or adoption of a *semantic representation* language has been a critical issue. Conventionally, semantic analysis has entailed the conversion of natural language expressions to well-formed formulas represented in a semantically specifiable formalized language like higher-order intensional logic, lambda calculus, or a variety of computationally tractable first-order logic such as description logic (DL) or programming languages like Prolog. In recent years, however, the focus of semantic representation has shifted to *semantic annotation*. Instead of trying to analyze the whole text with the maximum degree of granularity, some semantic tasks are now found to be adequate if they can provide necessary and relevant, and yet partial, information, understandably with some underspecification. Annotation or partial tagging, for instance, with referential or temporal information has thus fulfilled such needs.

In the area of *temporal annotation*, especially associated with events,[1] several initiatives were taken up. Central among those were TIMEX2 (Ferro et al., 2005), called TIDES, and TimeML (Pustejovsky et al., 2005) projects. Various technologies, such as those described in Mani et al. (2005) and Mani (2014) have also been developed for annotating temporal and event-denoting expressions in natural language text, particularly very large corpora of English and other languages for computational purposes (see Setzer (2001)). For the semantic Web, Hobbs and Pan (2004) contributed a significant work on temporal ontology, expanding the work initiated by Allen (1984) and his subsequent joint works (Allen and Kautz, 1985; Allen and Ferguson, 1994), particularly for the calculus of interval relations. For the specific purposes of the DARPA Agent Markup Language (DAML) project, Hobbs and Pan (2004) aimed at making information on the semantic Web more accessible to Web users and automatic agents through descriptions of the content of Web resources. Mapping between TimeML and OWL (DAML)-Time was outlined in Hobbs and Pustejovsky (2003).

Backed by all these initiatives and efforts, an ISO working group was formed under ISO's technical subcommittee dealing with language resource management.[2] The subcommittee was established in 2002 to manage and manipulate language resources, approving the working group proposal for the reformulation of TimeML (Lee et al., 2005; Pustejovsky et al., 2005; Schilder et al., 2007) as an ISO standard, named ISO-TimeML. As the first part of ISO international standards on semantic annotation, ISO 24617-1 ISO-TimeML was published in 2012 for the annotation of events and time in text (see Ide et al. (2017), Pustejovsky et al. (2010a), and Pustejovsky (2017a)). It was then applied to languages other than English, producing an Italian version of ISO-TimeML, IT-TimeML (Caselli and Sprugnoli, 2017), and also a Korean version, as introduced in Shin and You (2015). One of the annexes in ISO-TimeML (ISO, 2012b) developed ways of annotating verbs in Korean by accommodating some of the comprehensive works, published in English, on the morpho-syntax or syntax of Korean such as Chang (1996), Lee and Chae (1999), Sohn (1999) and Lee and Ramsey (2000).

As for the model-theoretic interpretation of event-based temporal semantic annotation structures, at least two significant efforts were made. Katz (2007) presented a denotational semantics for the interpretation of event-based temporal annotation structures, which were based on TimeML (Pustejovsky

---

[1] The term *event* is used to cover various types of eventualities including those of type *state*.
[2] ISO/TC 37/SC 4 was first headed by Laurent Romary (chair) and then by Nicoletta Calzolari (chair), and run by Key-Sun Choi (permanent committee manager).

et al., 2005). Around the same time, Pratt-Hartmann (2005, 2007) formulated interval temporal logic for TimeML. Bunt (2007) introduced semantics for semantic annotation, based on the abstract specification of ISO-TimeML. Likewise, following Hobbs and Pan's (2004) OWL-Time ontology, Lee (2008) introduced an OWL-Time-based semantics for ISO-TimeML.

8.2 From TimeML to ISO-TimeML

The formulation of ISO 24617-1 TimeML conforms to the basic annotation principles, laid down by another ISO 24612 international standard, called LAF (linguistic annotation framework).[3] Here are two major modifications made to ISO-TimeML.

Specification 8.1 Two major modifications in ISO-TimeML
a. Abstract specification of an annotation scheme
b. Standoff annotation

Details of the modifications are presented in Section 8.2.1.

In addition to these two modifications, there were two technical modifications introduced to ISO-TimeML.

Specification 8.2 Technical modifications in ISO-TimeML
a. Merging of two tags EVENT and MAKEINSTANCE to EVENT
b. Treatment of duration, such as *two hours*, as involving measurement

These technical modifications are discussed in Section 8.2.2.

8.2.1 Two Major Modifications

Abstract Specification
According to ISO 24612 LAF (ISO, 2012a), it is at the *abstract level* where the specification (design and development) of an *annotation scheme* is normalized and standardized. This requirement for normalized abstract specification has led to an annotation scheme to be reformulated formally. Bunt (2010, 2011) then proposed that each annotation scheme should consist of syntax and semantics with the division of syntax into *abstract syntax* and an equivalent set of *concrete syntaxes* each of which is ideally isomorphic to the abstract syntax proposed.

---

[3] See Ide and Romary (2004), Ide and Suderman (2007), and ISO 24612 LAF (ISO, 2012a) for further details.

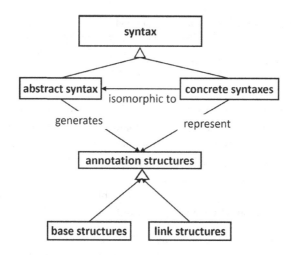

Figure 8.1 Syntax: abstract and concrete

The structure of an annotation scheme, which was presented in Chapter 3 (Figure 3.2), is extended in this chapter by subdividing *annotation structures* into *base structures* and *link structures*, as shown in Figure 8.1.

The *abstract syntax* generates, or formally specifies, in abstract set-theoretic terms, the annotation structures that consist of *base structures*, which are more often called *entity structures*, and *link structures*. Each *concrete syntax*, which is isomorphic to the formulated abstract syntax, provides a format such as an XML-based format for representing base and link structures that constitute each of the annotation structures.

As a sequel to LAF's requirement on the abstract specification of an annotation scheme, it has now become possible to allow a variety of representation formats for linguistic annotation. The adoption of XML for the representation of annotation structures, for instance, is no longer required. Now, one is free to adopt any representation format, as long as it is *interoperable* or *compatible* with other formats in merging and interchanging linguistic information. As proposed in Chapter 4, this book adopts the *predicate-logic-like format (pFormat)* for the representation of annotation structures.

Standoff Annotation

ISO-TimeML (ISO, 2012b) annotates text standoff, while TimeML annotates inline. *Standoff annotation* was shown in Section 4.3 to have some advantages over *inline annotation* in managing language resources. Annotation 8.3 illustrates the use of inline annotation in TimeML.

Annotation 8.3   Inline annotation in TimeML

```
We <EVENT eid="e1" class="OCCURRENCE"> reached </EVENT>
<MAKEINSTANCE eiid="ei1" eventID="e1" tense="PAST"/>
the beach <SIGNAL sid="s1"> near </SIGNAL>
<TIMEX3 tid="t1" type="DATE" value="XXXX-XX:T24:00">
midnight </TIMEX3>.
```

Inline annotation directly inserts annotation tags into a text, cramming the text with a variety of information as annotation progresses and also making it harder to parse the text, besides failing to preserve its original format.

Standoff annotation, however, presupposes that input data should be pre-processed in such a way that each markable is made easily identifiable. Each *base structure* is then anchored to such a markable. Annotation 8.4 shows how ISO-TimeML annotates the same fragment of text standoff.

Annotation 8.4   Standoff annotation in ISO-TimeML

a. Word-segmented data: We reached$_{w2}$ the beach near$_{w5}$ midnight$_{w6}$.

b. Base structures:

```
<EVENT xml:id="e1" target="#w2" pred="reach" type="TRANSITION"
  class="OCCURRENCE" tense="PAST"/>
<SIGNAL xml:id="s1" target="#w5" pred="near" type="spatial"/>
<TIMEX3 xml:id="t1" target="#w6" type="DATE"
  value="XXXX-XX-XX+1D:T00:00"⁴/>
```

Each of the base structures represented in part b is anchored to a word, namely `w2`, `w5`, and `w6`, respectively, as marked up in the word-segmented data in part a.

8.2.2   Two Technical Modifications

Merging MAKEINSTANCE to EVENT

The element MAKEINSTANCE in TimeML is merged into the element EVENT in TimeML, as noticed in two contrasting examples for Annotations 8.3 and 8.4. All the information contained in MAKEINSTANCE is copied into the element EVENT in ISO-TimeML. This change was made because the element MAKEINSTANCE has no denotation in itself except that it carries some pieces of information associated with eventualities. In ISO-TimeML, all such information is encoded into a single element EVENT. Furthermore, each EVENT element is interpreted as denoting not the type of an eventuality, but one of its instances or occurrences. The allowance of a nonconsuming tag in annotation has made it possible to delete an element like MAKEINSTANCE.

Example 8.5   Deleting MAKEINSTANCE

a. Base annotation: John ate$_{e1:w2}$ an apple and Mary $\emptyset_{e2}$ a pear.

b. Annotation in ISO-TimeML:

---

⁴ ISO 8601-1:2019 no longer represents "midnight" as T24:00.

```
<EVENT xml:id="e1" target="w2" pred="EAT" tense="PAST"/>
<EVENT xml:id="e2" target="" pred="EAT" tense="PAST"/>
```

c. Semantics:

$$\exists e_1 \exists x_1 [eat(e_1, j, x_1) \wedge past(e_1) \wedge apple(x_1)] \wedge \exists e_2 \exists x_2 [eat(e_2, m, x_2) \wedge past(e_2) \wedge pear(x_2)]$$

Example 8.5 has two base structures. Both of them are marked with the same tag EVENT, thus being treated as being of the same category *eventuality*. Each of them, however, refers to a different event instance, e_1 and e_2, respectively, in which different objects of different types have participated.

Here is another example.

Example 8.6 Deleting EVENT_INSTANCE

a. Markables: John eats$_{w2}$ an apple on Saturday$_{w6}$ and $\emptyset_{e2}$ on Sunday$_{w9}$.

b. Annotation in ISO-TimeML:
```
<EVENT xml:id="e1" target="#w2" pred="EAT"/>
<TIMEX3 xml:id="t1" target="#w6" type="DATE" value=0000-00-W06/>
<EVENT xml:id="e2" target=" " pred="EAT"/>
<TIMEX3 xml:id="t2" target="#w10" type="DATE" value=0000-00-W07/>
<TLINK eventID="#e1" relatedToTime="#t1" relType="isIncluded"/>
<TLINK eventID="#e2" relatedToTime="#t2" relType="isIncluded"/>
```

c. Semantic form:

$$\exists e_1 \exists t_1 [[eat(e_1) \wedge weekday(t_1, Saturday)] \wedge \tau(e_1) \subseteq t_1] \wedge$$
$$\exists e_2 \exists t_2 [[eat(e_2) \wedge weekday(t_2, Sunday)] \wedge \tau(e_2) \subseteq t_2]$$

The function τ, called *runtime* or *anchoring function*, maps or anchors an eventuality to a time.

The *attribute* @$type$ is introduced into ISO-TimeML. Associated with eventualities, there are three possible values for the attribute @$type$: *state, process,* and *transition*. This attribute is useful in differentiating the types of anchoring an event to a time such as *holds* and *occurs*.

Examples 8.7 and 8.8 illustrate how the specification of @$type$ allows a finer-grained interpretation of an event. The verb *go* in Example 8.7a is a motion verb denoting an event of type *transition*, whereas the adjective *ill* in Example 8.8a denotes a state, an eventuality of type *state*.

Example 8.7 Annotating event types

a. Markables: Mia went$_{w2}$ to New York [last year]$_{6-7}$.

b. Annotation:
```
<EVENT xml:id="e1" target="w2" pred="GO" type="TRANSITION"
  tense="PAST>
<TIMEX3 xml:id="t1" target="w6-7" type="DATE" value="1999"/>
<TLINK eventID="#e1" relatedTOTime="#t1" relType="isINCLUDED"/>
```

c. Semantic representation:

$$\exists e_1 \exists t_1 [go(e_1, m, ny) \wedge past(e_1) \wedge year(t_1, 1999) \wedge \tau(e_1) \subseteq t_1]$$

d. Interpretation:

$past(e_1)$ is interpreted as $[\tau(e_1) \prec n]$ and $[\tau(e_1) \subseteq t_1]$, or $occurs(e_1, t_1)$.

First, the logical predicate *past* is interpreted as $[\tau(e_1) \subseteq t_1 \wedge \tau(e_1) \prec n]$, where n denotes the present moment of time. Second, the anchoring relation between the event e_1 and the time t_1 is interpreted as an occurrence relation, as is defined by Allen (1984), because the event e_1 is of type *transition*. By involving motions in time, events of type *transition* can allow further interpretations about the start or terminating point of a motion involving the transition, as discussed by Mani and Pustejovsky (2012).

Annotation 8.8   Annotating *states*
a. Data: Her aunt [was ill]$_{w3-4}$.
b. Annotation:
```
<EVENT xml:id="e2" target="#w3-4" pred="ill" type="STATE"/>
<TIMEX3 xml:id="t1 target="" type="DATE" value="1999"/>
<TLINK eventID="#e2" relatedToTime="#t1" relType="isINCLUDED"/>
```
c. Semantic representation:
$$\exists e_2 \exists t_1 [ill(e_2, x_1) \wedge aunt(x_1) \wedge past(e_2) \wedge \tau(e_2) \subseteq t_1]$$
d. Interpretation: $[\tau(e_2) \subseteq t_1]$ is replaced by $holds(e_2, t_1)$.

The logical predicate *holds* is defined as in Definition 8.9 (see Allen (1984)).

Definition 8.9   Logical predicate *holds*
$$holds(e, t) \Rightarrow \forall t'[[t' \subseteq t \wedge interval(t)] \rightarrow \tau(e) = t']$$

Definition 8.9 means that an eventuality holding in an interval implies that it also holds in every subinterval of it.

Duration

TimeML annotates durational expressions such as *30 hours* as one of the values of a temporal attribute. So does ISO-TimeML, as in Annotation 8.10b, annotating *30 hours* as the type of duration for TIMEX3, while specifying its value to be `value="P30H"`. Instead of TILINK, ISO-TimeML introduces another link MLINK, called *measure link*, to represent the *measurement* relation between an event and its duration in an explicit way, as in Annotation 8.10c. Note that *duration* is understood as denoting the *quantity* of a time interval.

Annotation 8.10   Durations
a. Word-segmented data: Mia slept$_{w2}$ *for seven$_{w4}$ hours$_{w5}$* last night.
b. Base structures:
```
<EVENT xml:id="e1, target="#w2", type="STATE", pred="SLEEP"
  tense="PAST"/>
<TIMEX3 xml:id="t1" target="#w4-w5", type="DURATION" value="P7H"/>
```
c. Link structure:
```
<MLINK eventID="#e1" relatedToTime="#t1" relType="MEASURES"/>
```

This is interpreted as in Semantics 8.11.

Semantics 8.11   Use of the measure function μ
$$\exists e_1 \exists t_1 \exists v[sleep(e_1) \wedge holds(e_1, t_1) \wedge past(e_1) \wedge \mu(t_1)=(7, hour)]$$

Here, μ is a *measure function* from time intervals to measures, which measures the length of a time interval (Bunt, 1985, pp. 80–81) for a generalized formal definition).

8.3 Modeling ISO-TimeML

ISO-TimeML refers to ISO 24617-1 (ISO, 2012b; *Language resource management – Semantic annotation framework – Part 1: Time and events*). Its conceptual design is depicted by a metamodel.

8.3.1 Metamodel

As in Figure 8.2, as newly designed, the metamodel represents the general conceptual view of ISO-TimeML. It assumes that primary data has been pre-processed through word-segmentation. Markables are (possibly null) strings of words found in the segmented primary data.

Base structures, which form bases of annotation structures, are anchored to these markables, while annotating them with appropriate information.

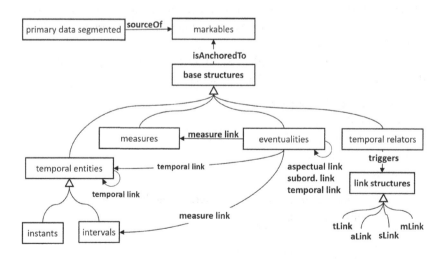

Figure 8.2 Metamodel of ISO-TimeML

Table 8.1 *Base structures of ISO-TimeML illustrated*

Mia visited her aunt for 3 months $\emptyset_{tInterval}$ from June to August last year.

eventuality	temporal/metric relator	measure	tInterval	temporal entity
visited				
	for	3 months		
			$\emptyset_{tInterval}$	
	from			June
	to			August
				last year

8.3.2 Conceptual Design of a Specification Language

ISO-TimeML provides a normalized specification language for the annotation of event-based temporal information in a text. Its syntax consists of four *base categories*.

Classification 8.12   Base categories
a. temporal entity,
   with subcategories: instant and interval
b. eventuality
c. measure (length or amount of time)
d. temporal/measure relator[5]

These categories classify base structures. Table 8.1 illustrates how some markables are annotated into the base structures of these categories in ISO-TimeML.

The syntax of the ISO-TimeML-based specification language also introduces four categories of links over base structures.

Classification 8.13   Link categories
a. temporal link
b. aspectual link
c. subordination link
d. measure link

Each of these links relates one base structure to another, often triggered by a temporal relator, called *signal*.

---

[5] Temporal relators include temporal measure relators such as *for* in *for 30 hours.*

The temporal link relates a base structure of category *temporal entity* or *eventuality* to another base structure of category *temporal entity* or *eventuality*. For example, the temporal link, which is triggered by the temporal relators *from* and *to*, anchors the *interval*, referred to by the markable *from June to August*, to the year 1999, referred by the markable *last year*.

Example 8.14 Temporal link (1)

a. The temporal link relates $\emptyset_{t1:t\,Interval}$ from June to August to last year$_{t2:time}$

b. Logical form:

$\exists\{t_1, t_{11}, t_{12}, t_2\}$

$[[interval(t_1) \wedge month(t_{11}, June) \wedge month(t_{12}, August) \wedge$

$\quad starts(t_1, t_{11}) \wedge ends(t_1, t_{12}) \wedge year(t_2, 1999)] \wedge t_1 \subseteq t_2]$

The logical form $t_1 \subseteq t_2$ is interpreted as the interval t_1 (from June to August) being included in another time interval t_2 (last year or the year 1999).

The temporal link may also hold between an event and a time.

Example 8.15 Temporal link (2)

a. The temporal link relates *visited$_{event}$* to *last year$_{time}$*

b. Semantic form: $\exists e_1 \exists t_2 [visit(e_1) \wedge year(t_2, 1999) \wedge \tau(e_1) \subseteq t_2]$

The time $\tau(e_1)$ of Mia's visiting e_1 is included in the time t_2 (the year 1999).

The measure link is triggered by the temporal measure relator (signal) *for*. It relates (1) either a base structure of category *eventuality* (*visited*) or (2) an interval (*from June to August*) to that of category *measure* (*three months*).

Example 8.16 Measure link (1)

a. The measure link relates *visited$_{event}$* to *3 months$_{measure:t\,Amount}$*

b. Semantic form:

$\exists e_1 \exists t_2 [visit(e_1) \wedge \alpha(\tau(e_1), t_2) = (3, month)]$

Here, $\alpha(\tau(e_1), t_2)$ is the (possibly cumulative) amount of time, which was consumed by the event e_1 of Mia's visit during the time interval t_2 (last year).

Example 8.17 Measure link (2)

a. The measure link also relates $\emptyset_{t_1:t\,Interval}$ *from June to August to 3 months$_{measure:duration}$*

b. Semantic form:

$\exists t_1 [interval(t_1) \wedge \mu(t_1) = (3, month)]$

Here, $\mu(t_1)$ is the measure (length, duration) of the time interval t_1.

The aspectual link relates an event, carrying aspectual information, to another event. It is triggered by aspectual information that refers to various aspects or stages of the process of an event, as listed in Classification 8.18.

Classification 8.18   Various stages or *aspects* of the process of an event
a. Initiation: *start, begin, initiate*
b. Termination: *stop, quit, cancel*
c. Continuation: *continue, keep*
d. Culmination: *finish, complete*
e. Reinitiation: *restart, reinitiate, reignite*

Example 8.19 illustrates how *aspectual verbs* each refer to some stage of an event or events being developed.

Example 8.19   Various stages of the process of an event illustrated
A doctor advised Mia to look after her weight. Mia started$_{initiation}$ to diet immediately. She quit$_{termination}$ drinking, smoking, and eating lunch. She kept$_{continuation}$ walking 10 miles a day. Within a month, she lost 33 pounds. As her doctor agreed, she finished$_{culmination}$ her dieting successfully.

The aspectual link relates all these aspectual events to the other events.

Example 8.20   *Mia started dieting*
a. The aspectual link relates *started$_{event1/initiation}$* to *diet$_{event2}$*
b. Semantic form:
   $\exists e_1 \exists e_2 [start(e_1 : act) \wedge past(e_1) \wedge diet(e_2 : process) \wedge initiates(e_1, e_2)]$

The semantic form (Example 8.20b) is interpreted as stating that there was a starting act e_1 that initiated the process of dieting e_2.

The *subordination link* also relates an event to another. The first event carries (1) modal, (2) factive, (3) counterfactive, (4) evidential, and (5) negative evidential information about the second event. Example 8.21 illustrates how the subordination link works for the case that conveys *modal* information on the event e_2 of John's teaching.

Example 8.21   *John$_{x1}$ wants$_{e1:modal}$ to teach$_{e2}$ on Monday.*
a. Subordination link relates a modal event e_1 to the event e_2 of John's teaching.
b. Semantic form:
   $\exists x_1 \exists e_1 \exists e_2 [[named(x_1, John) \wedge want(e_1) \wedge experiencer(e_1, x_1) \wedge theme(e_1, e_2)]$
   $\rightarrow^{int} [teach(e_2) \wedge agent(e_2, x_1)]]$

The *distributive composition* $\rightarrow^{int}$ is defined as in Definition 8.22 (see Lee (2020 (23))).

Definition 8.22 *Distributive composition* $\rightarrow^{int}$ *for modal interpretation*
Given a model M with a set S of at least two situations s and s' and a rational agent a such that s is an actual situation, caused by a, and s', a situation accessible to the mind (intention) of a:
$[\![\phi \rightarrow^{int} \psi]\!]^{M,s,a}=1$ iff $[\![\psi]\!]^{M,s',a}=1$ provided $[\![\phi]\!]^{M,s,a}=1$.

In *small world semantics*, which I have been proposing, $[\![\phi \rightarrow^{int} \psi]\!]$ can be true even if there is no world in which ψ is true, for some people want to do what is totally or logically impossible.

The modal predicate *want* in Example 8.21b has the event e_2 as its *theme* and that the *agent* of the predicate *teach* in the subordinated complement is John. The implicative operator $\rightarrow^{int}$ combines the logical forms of the two components of the subordination construction in Example 8.21b involving the modal or *intensional* predicate *want*. The distributive composition $\rightarrow^{int}$ is defined as a meaning postulate constraining a model structure, as in Definition 8.22: This means that the event of *teaching (on Monday)* is *realized* only in a situation accessible to the mind of the *wisher John*.

8.4 Abstract Syntax of ISO-TimeML

8.4.1 General

The abstract syntax $\mathcal{ASyn}_{isoTimeML}$ of ISO-TimeML instantiates the general abstract syntax $\mathcal{ASyn}$, presented in Chapter 3. Given a collection D of datasets preprocessed as input data for semantic annotation, the general structure of an abstract syntax $\mathcal{ASyn}$ for an annotation language is formally defined as a tuple.

Specification 8.23 $\mathcal{ASyn} = <M, C, R, @>$, where
  (i) M is a set of (possibly null or noncontiguous) strings of communicative segments, called *markables*, in D, each of which is delimited by E;
 (ii) C is a finite set of *base categories*;
(iii) R is a finite set of *relational (link) categories*;
 (iv) $@_{cat}$ is a finite set of attribute-value *assignments* that define or declare an admissible list of attributes and possible value ranges for each category *cat* in either C or R.

Markables M
Markables include empty strings of characters, sound, or visual segments as *non-consuming tags*. Here is an example.

Example 8.24   Nonconsuming tags
a. Data: John stayed in Amsterdam *from June through August*.
b. Nonconsuming tag:
   John stayed in Amsterdam $\emptyset_{t1:tInterval}$ from June$_{t11}$ through August$_{t12}$.
c. Annotation:
   ```
   <TIMEX3 xml:id="t1" target="" start="t11" end="t12"/>
   ```
d. Semantic representation:
   $\{t_1, t_{11}, t_{t12}\}[tInterval(t_1) \wedge starts(t_1, t_{11}) \wedge ends(t_1, t_{12})]$

The nonconsuming tag in Example 8.24b is interpreted as denoting a time interval starting from the month of June through the month of August.

Categories: Base C and Relational R

For $\mathcal{A}Syn_{isoTimeML}$, each base category c in C and each relational category r in R are instantiated by specifying each category *cat* in $C \cup R$. The specification of C and R just abstractly lists their categories, independent of how these categories are named. As presented in Figure 8.2 and detailed in Section 8.3.2, ISO-TimeML lists four base categories for C and also four link relational categories for R, as in Specification 8.25.

Specification 8.25   Categories
a. Base categories:
   $C=$ {*eventuality, temporal entity, measure, temporal (metric) relator*}
b. Relational (link) categories:
   $R=$ {*temporalLink, aspectualLink, subordinationLink, measureLink*}

Temporal relators include temporal metric relators such as *for* or *in* as in *for three months* or *in two hours*.

Attribute-Value Assignments $@_{cat}$

Annotation structures consist of (i) base structures β_c of category c in C and (ii) link structures λ_r of relational category r in R. The abstract syntax of ISO-TimeML specifies them in abstract (set-theoretic) terms by specifying their attributes and possible value ranges for each of the attributes through the associated assignments $@_{cat}$. The attribute-value assignment $@_{cat}$ is instantiated for each category *cat* in C or R. For each category c in C and each relational link category r in R, the assignments $@_c$ and $@_r$ need to be specified.

Remark 8.26   Two uses of *at*-sign @
TEI P5 (TEI Consortium, 2019) uses the sign @ to mark up the names of attributes: e.g., the attribute @type or @relType. As is used here for the

specification of an annotation scheme, it is used to refer to an *assignment function* from the attributes of each category of these base or link structures to their values: e.g., $@_{event}$.

8.4.2 Abstract Specification of Base Structures

For each base category c in C, $\mathcal{AS}_{isoTimeML}$ specifies a list of attributes, either required or optional, for the generation of base structures β_c. Each list of attributes configures the structure of a base category, called *base structure*, independent of how values are assigned to the attributes. The values, in contrast, provide annotation content for each base structure. Consider Example 8.27.[6]

Annotation 8.27   Base structures
a. Dogs were barking.
```
<EVENT xml:id="e1" target="w2-3" type="PROCESS" pred="BARK"
  tense="PAST" aspect="PRORESSIVE"/>
```
b. Thieves have run away.
```
<EVENT xml:i="e2" target="w2-4" type="PROCESS" pred="RUN-AWAY",
  tense="PRESENT" aspect="PERFECTIVE"/>
```

Here, the two base structures are structurally identical, being characterized by an identical list of attributes. However, their content differs from each other because their attributes are assigned different values, carrying different pieces of information.

The assignment function $@_c$ for each base category c in C thus carries dual roles: the attributes of $@_c$ for each c characterize the structure of a base structure of category c, whereas the values characterize the content of the base structure. Appropriately specified, each assignment $@_c$ is said to formally define or generate the base structure of category c in C.

Base Structures as Set-Theoretic *n*-tuples
As proposed by Bunt (2011), base structures may be specified in abstract terms as set-theoretic tuples. Such a specification makes it possible to define base structures without being forced to decide on the specific names of their associated attributes. Specification 8.28, for instance, specifies the base structure β_{event} of category *eventuality* as a 10-tuple in abstract terms.

Specification 8.28   Base structure β_{event} of category *eventuality*
$\beta_{event} =: <ty, pr, ec, t, a, m, mo, qu, sc, po>$, where
        ty specifies an event type;

---

[6] Base structures should have been represented in more abstract set-theoretic terms, but are represented here in XML for easier illustration.

pr is a predicate form;
ec is an event class;
t is a tense;
a is an aspect;
m is a mood;
mo is a modality;
qu is a quantifier;
sc is a scope relation;
po is a polarity.

The base structure β_{event} of category *eventuality* is a 10-tuple. The other three assignments, $@_{time}$, $@_{measure}$ and $@_{tRelator}$, also generate their abstract base structures as a 10-tuple, a 4-tuple, and a 3-tuple, respectively. The abstract specification of attributes like Specification 8.28 as a set-theoretic tuple frees a base structure from giving a specific name to its attributes.

8.4.3 Attribute-Value Ranges of Base Category Assignments $@_c$

It is not the primary function of the abstract syntax of an annotation scheme to specify the value ranges of the assignment $@_{cat}$ of base or relational categories. It may roughly indicate the general ranges of values for each attribute as specified for each category. This section, however, shows how the syntax $\mathcal{A}Syn_{isoTimeML}$, whether abstract or concrete, defines the *value ranges of the assignment* @ for each of its base categories.

Attribute-Value Ranges of the Assignment $@_{event}$
of Category *eventuality*
The possible values for each of the attributes associated with category *eventuality* are listed in Table 8.2.

Note that a value is assigned automatically to many of the attributes for these categories through morpho-syntactic processing. A value must be assigned to each of the attributes @type, @predicate, @tense, @mood, @modality, and @polarity. The attributes *class*, *tense*, and *aspect* are each assigned a value in advance through morpho-syntactic processing. The default value of @polarity is "true": if it is not marked up, then the value is "true" by default.

Attribute-value ranges of assignment $@_{time}$
for category *temporal entity*
The assignment $@_{time}$ of category **temporal entity** specifies a value range for each of its two required attributes, @type and @value, and each of the other eight attributes, as listed in Table 8.3.

Table 8.2 *Attribute-value ranges for assignment @$_{event}$*

attributes	possible values	sample values
type	specifies the aspectual type of an eventuality	state, process transition
predicate	represents the content of eventuality-denoting expression as a predicate form	run or love as as a predicate form
[*class*]	classifies the semantic features of event-denoting expressions in a subordination construction	occurrence, state, I-state, I-action, perception, reporting
tense	specifies a time position on a timeline	past, present
aspect	specifies the stages of an eventuality	perfect, progressive
[*mood*]	specifies the mode of statements	subjunctive
[*modality*]	indicates the alethic, deontic or epistemic necessity, certainty or possibility of an event	must, should, can
[*quantifier*]	represents a generalized quantifier	every, all, three
[*scopes*]	specifies a quantifier which is scoped over	ID of a time referred to
polarity	indicates the truth-value	false

Table 8.3 *Attribute-value ranges of assignment @$_{time}$*

attributes = type, value, [functionInDocument], [temporalFunction],[anchorTime], [beginPoint], [endPoint],[quantifier], [scopes], [frequency];

attributes	possible values
type	indicates the type of a temporal object such as *day-time, date, duration,* or *set*
value	specific value of the day-time, date, and duration for @type
functionIn-Document	specifies a temporal anchor for other temporal expressions in the document such as *data creation time*
temporal-Function	indicates whether a temporal function is used to calculate a specific time referred to by a temporal expression such as a deitic expression
anchorTime	points to the time to which another time is anchored
beginPoint	points to the start of an interval
endPoint	points to the end of an interval
quantifier	indicates a quantifier
scopes	refers to the quantifier which is scoped over
frequency	specifies temporal frequency

The value range of @type for temporal entities includes *day-time*, *date*, *duration*, and *set*. The type *day-time* refers to clock times or parts of a day. The type *date* refers to the Gregorian calendar years, months, or days. Each of them refers to the temporal reference system (time zones). ISO-TimeML includes the value *duration* as a possible value of @type. ISO-TimeML introduces a category *measure* in its abstract syntax, as in ISO-Space (ISO-Space, ISO, 2014b), to treat the notion of duration that means the length of a time interval. The attribute @duration in ISO-TimeML also annotates temporal expressions that denote or delimit two kinds of intervals, such as *from June to August* or an interval delimited by *two hours before the earthquake*. These intervals are often delimited by their @beginPoint and @endPoint. The value *set* is relevant for the quantification or frequency of events. The value of @anchorTime refers to one of the possible values of @functionInDocument such as a document creation time.

Temporal quantification in ISO-TimeML is treated in its own way with the attribute @scopes. This attribute refers to a scope relation *scopes* between (i) two temporally quantified expressions or (ii) a temporal quantifier and an event quantifier, as in Example 8.29.

Example 8.29   Scopal relation in temporal quantification

a. Markables: John walks [two hours]$_{t1}$ every day$_{t2}$.
b. Scopal relation between two times: t_2 scopes over t_1:
   $\forall t_2 \exists t_1 [day(t_2) \rightarrow \mu(t_1)=(2, hour)]$
c. Scopal relation between a time and an event: t_2 scopes over e_1:
   $\forall t_2 \exists e_1 [day(t_2) \rightarrow [walk(e_1) \wedge \mu(\tau(e_1))=(2, hour)]]$

The attribute @scopes only marks up the quantified base structure, either of type time or of type event in the scope of a quantifier which is annotated with the attribute @scopes.

Attribute-Value Ranges of Assignment @$_{measure}$
for Category *measure*

The value ranges of temporal measures are specified as characterized each by the following and, in more specific terms, in Table 8.4.

Specification 8.30   Value ranges of temporal measures

a. a single value (e.g., *near*)
b. a pair $<n, u>$ of a numeric (real number) n and a unit u (e.g., *6 months*) or a triple $<R_n, n, u>$, where
   R_n is a measure relation (e.g., *more than six months*),

Table 8.4 *Attribute-value ranges for @$_{measure}$*

attributes = value, [unit], [modifier]		
attributes	*possible values*	*sample values*
type	specifies the domain of application	temporal
value	represents the content of measure	2 or near
unit	indicates the unit of a measure	day, hour, minute
modifier	specifies a measure relation	more than, nearly

Table 8.5 *Attribute-value ranges for @$_{t\,Relator}$*

attributes = [type,] pred;		
attributes	*possible values*	*sample values*
type	specifies the domain of application	*temporal*
pred	represents the content of temporal relation	*in, before, during*

n is a numeric (real number), and
u is a unit.

Attribute-Value Ranges of Assignment @$_{t\,Relator}$
for Category *temporal relator*

The value ranges of the attributes for assignment @$_{t\,Relator}$ are specified in Table 8.5. Temporal relators are referred to by markables as listed in Example 8.31.

Example 8.31 *Temporal relators*

a. Prepositions: *at, in, on, after, before, in, on, during, since, etc.*
b. Conjunctions: *after, before, since, when, while, etc.*
c. Special characters: "-", "/" or ".",
   as in "2000-10-20", "2000.10.20." or "8-10 June, 2020"

Temporal relators include temporal measure relators, as listed in Example 8.32.

Example 8.32 Temporal measure relators

a. Prepositions: *for, in*
b. Examples:
   Mia taught *for* 24 hours last month.
   I built a house *in* three months.

The temporal measure relator *for* denotes the (possibly cumulative) amount of time taken by an event, whereas the temporal measure relator *in* denotes the length of a time interval during which an event is completed.

8.4.4 Abstract Specification of Link Structures

$\mathcal{A}Syn_{isoTimeML}$ specifies an assignment $@_r$ for each of the four relational link categories in R.

Specification 8.33   Link attributes $@_r$

a. Temporal link $@_{tLink}$: attributes = tEntity|eventuality, tEntity|eventuality, relation;

b. Aspectual link $@_{aLink}$: attributes = aspectual, eventuality, relation;

c. Subordination link $@_{sLink}$: attributes = eventuality, eventuality, relation;

d. Measure link $@_{mLink}$: attributes = eventuality, measure, relation;

As for the cases of base structures, these link assignments generate well-formed link structures in an abstract form. They generate *abstract link structures* λ_r for each relational link category r in R, as illustrated in Example 8.34.

Example 8.34   Link structures λ_r

a. Temporal link λ_{tLink}: e.g., Mia visited$_{e1}$ her aunt last year$_{t1}$.
   $<event, tEntity, tRelator>$

b. Aspectual link λ_{aLink}: e.g., Mia stopped$_{e1}$ smoking$_{e2}$.
   $<aspectualEvent, event, tRelator>$

c. Subordination link λ_{sLink}: e.g., Mia wants$_{e1}$ to quit drinking$_{e2}$.
   $<modalEvent, event, tRelator>$

d. Measure link λ_{mLink}: e.g., Mia worked$_{e1}$ for three hours$_{t1}$.
   $<event, measure, mRelator>$,
   where *mRelator* refers to a (temporal) measure relator.

8.5 XML-Based Concrete Syntax

The main function of a concrete syntax is to provide a format for representing annotation structures. ISO-TimeML in principle allows any format of representation, but in practice follows the XML format mainly because its predecessors adopted XML as their markup language. Following ISO 24612 LAF (ISO, 2012a), each base structure is represented as consisting of *anchoring* and *content structures*. Each content structure is represented in a typed feature structure, as illustrated by Example 8.35.

Example 8.35   Content structures as feature structures
a. Data: Mia didn't come yesterday$_{w4}$.
b. Representation of a base structure in feature structures:

```
<baseStructure category="tEntity">
  <anchoringStructure xml:id="t1" target="#w4" aContent="#fs1"/>
  <fs xml:id="fs1" type="DATE">
    <f name="DATE"><STRING value="2020-09-01"/></f>
    <f name="temporalFUNCTION"><BOOLEAN value="TRUE"/></f></fs>
</baseStructure>
```

For the representation of base structures, ISO-TimeML collapses the anchoring and the content structures of a base structure into a single XML-element. The first two attributes for identification and anchoring are allocated in the first part of each XML-element, as follows.

Annotation   Representation of a base structure in ISO-TimeML
a. Markable: `yesterday`$_{w4}$
b. Base structure:

```
<TIMEX3 xml:id="t1" target="#w4"
type="DATE" value="2020-09-01" temporalFunction="TRUE"/>
```

8.5.1 Representing Anchoring Structures

For each base structure β_c of base category c, $CSyn_{isoTimeML}$ requires its category c to be part of its *anchoring structure* and the base structure: (i) to be uniquely identified and (ii) to be anchored to a markable.

The identifier of each of the three base categories, *eventuality*, *temporal entity*, and *temporal relator*, is specified as in Table 8.6.

Table 8.6 *Identifiers*

Mia visited$_{e1}$ her aunt for$_{s1}$ 3 months$_{t1}$ [from$_{s2}$ June$_{t21}$ to$_{s3}$ August$_{t22}$]$_{t2}$ last year$_{t3}$.

category	TimeML-tag	ID-prefix	Examples
eventuality	EVENT	e-	Mia visited$_{e1}$ her aunt
temporal relator	SIGNAL	s-	for$_{s1}$
temporal entity	TIMEX3	t-	three months$_{t1}$
temporal entity	TIMEX3	t-	last year$_{t3}$

ISO-TimeML incorporates category *measure* into category *temporal entity* in its concrete syntax and, likewise, incorporates temporal measure expressions such as *3 months* into the annotation of temporal expressions.

The attribute @xml:id is introduced to identify a base structure. Its value is a categorized ID-prefix followed by a positive integer from 1 to *n*.

The attribute @target anchors a base structure to a markable. The value of *@target* is IDREF, meaning that, for its value, *@target* refers to the ID of a string of word segments in word-segmented data. Following the practice of TEI P5 (TEI Consortium, 2019), the # sign is prefixed to the ID to indicate the string being referred to.

An example follows.

Example 8.36   Use of the sign #

a. Data: Mia visited$_{e1:w2}$ her aunt [last year]$_{t1:w5-6}$ $\cdots$
b. Anchoring structures:
```
<EVENT xml:id="e1" target="#w2" .../>
<TIMEX3 xml:id="t1" target="#w5-6" .../>
```

8.5.2 Representing Content Structures

The construction of *content structures* is specified by the assignment @. This section specifies how the attribute-value assignment @ applies to English in order to represent the content structures of base and relational link categories in XML.

Representation of Base Structures

The concrete syntax of ISO-TimeML makes the assignment @ to each of the categories of base structures more specific.

The assignment @$_{event}$ for category *eventuality* (EVENT) is specified for XML as in Table 8.7.

NMTOKEN (name token), CDATA (character data), and IDREF are terms used in XML, which characterizes attribute types for DTDs (document type definitions). Unlike CDATA, NMTOKEN has a strict restriction on the use of characters for naming attributes: for instance, it can contain "-", "_" or ".", but no spaces or whitespace. IDREF refers to the ID of an XML element or an identified segment in text.

Here are some sample annotations for EVENT.

Annotation 8.37

a. Markables:

Mia [has not visited]$_{w2-5}$ Paris in Texas.
b. Base structure:
```
<EVENT xml:id="e1" target="#w2-5" pred="VISIT" type="PROCESS"
class="OCCURRENCE" tense="PRESENT" aspect="PERFECT" polarity="NEG"/>
```

Table 8.7 *Attribute-value ranges for @$_{event}$*

attributes = type, predicate, [class], tense, [aspect], [mood], [modality],
[quantifier], [scopes], polarity;

attributes	*attribute type*	*possible values*
type	NMTOKEN	STATE | PROCESS | TRANSITION
predicate	CDATA	e.g. VISIT | LOVE | WALK | ... as a predicate form
class	NMTOKEN	ASPECUTAL | I-ACTION | I-STATE | OCCURRENCE | PERCEPTION | REPORTING | STATE
tense	NMTOKEN	PAST|PRESENT|FUTURE|NONE
aspect	NMTOKEN	PERFECT | PROGRESSIVE
mood	NMTOKEN	INDICATIVE | SUBJUNCTIVE
modality	CDATA	e.g. CAN| MUST| SHOULD | ...
quantifier	CDATA	EVERY | ALL | SOME | THREE | ...
scopes	IDREF	e.g., #t2 | ...
polarity	NMTOKEN	POS | NEG

Annotation 8.38

a. Markables: Mia [must look]$_{w2-3}$ me up$_{w5}$.

b. Base structure:
```
<EVENT xml:id="e1" target="#w2-3,w5" pred="LOOK_UP" type="PROCESS"
class="OCCURRENCE" tense="PRESENT" modality="MUST" polarity="POS"/>
```

Temporal entity <TIMEX3> has 10 attributes. Their value ranges are specified in Table 8.8.

Here are some sample annotations for TIMEX3.

Annotation 8.39 Temporal base structures

a. Markables: Mia visited her aunt for [three months]$_{w6-7}$ [from June$_{w9}$ to August$_{w11}$]$_{w8-11}$ [last year]$_{w12-13}$.

b. Annotation structures:
```
<TIMEX3 xml:id="t1" target="#w6-7" type="DURATION" value="P3M"/>
<TIMEX3 xml:id="t2" target="#w9" type="DATE" value="XXXX-06"/>
<TIMEX3 xml:id="t3" target="#w11" type="DATE" value="XXXX-08"/>
<TIMEX3 xml:id="t4" target="#w12-13" type="DATE" value="2019"
temporalFunction="TRUE" />
<TIMEX3 xml:id="t5" target="#w8-11" type="DURATION" value="P3M"
beginPoint="#t2" endPoint="#t3" temporalFunction="TRUE"/>
```

Annotation 8.40 Quantified temporal base structures

a.
```
<TIMEX3 xml:id="t1" target="three times a month"
        type="SET" value="P1M" freq="3X"/>
```
b.
```
<TIMEX3 xml:id="t1" target="five days every year"
        type="SET" value="P1Y" quant="EVERY" freq="5D"/>
```
c.
```
<TIMEX3 xml:id="t1" target="every month"
        type="SET" value="P1M" quant="EVERY" />
```

Table 8.8 *Attribute-value ranges for @$_{time}$*

attributes = type, value, [functionInDocument], [anchorTime], [temporalFunction],
[beginPoint], [endPoint], [quant], [freq], [scopes]

attributes	*attribute type*	*possible values*
type	NMTOKEN	TIME | DATE | DURATION | SET
value	CDATA	follows ISO 8601-1 (ISO, 2019a) in representing dayTime, date, and durations,
functionIn-Document	NMTOKEN	CREATION_TIME | EXPIRATION_TIME | MODIFICATION_TIME | PUBLICATION_TIME | RELEASE_TIME | RECEPTION_TIME | NONE
anchorTime	IDREF	refers to one of the FunctionInDocument values
temporal Function	NMTOKEN	FALSE | TRUE
beginPoint	IDREF	refers to the start of an interval
endPoint	IDREF	refers to the end of an interval
quant	CDATA	EVERY | ALL | SOME | THREE | ...
freq	NMTOKEN	e.g., 3 × for 3 times
scopes	IDREF	refers to an event ID within the scope

In ISO-TimeML, *temporal relators* are tagged `<SIGNAL>` with two anchoring attributes: `@identifier` and `@target` only. Temporal relations must be annotated with the content structure, preferably with two additional attributes such as `@pred` and `@type`, as given in Specification 8.41.

Specification 8.41   Assignment @$_{t\,Relator}$ for temporal relations
```
attributes = identifier, target, pred, [type];
pred = CDATA;
(* represents the content of @target. *)
type = pre-defined symbols;
```

The value of `@type` refers to one of the values listed for the `@relType` of TLINK, 13 temporal relations, conforming to Allen's (1984) interval calculus.

With these additional attributes, temporal relations (`SIGNAL`) can be annotated more meaningfully, as illustrated in Annotation 8.42.

Annotation 8.42   Temporal relations annotated

a. Markables: Mia visited her aunt for$_{w5}$ 3 months from$_{w8}$ June to$_{w10}$ August in$_{w12}$ the summer of 2019.

b. Annotation:
```
<SIGNAL xml:id="s1" target="w5" pred="FOR" type="DURING/>
<SIGNAL xml:id="s2" target="w8" pred="FROM" type="BEGINS"/>
<SIGNAL xml:id="s3" target="w10" pred="TO" type="ENDS"/>
<SIGNAL xml:id="s4" target="w12" pred="IN" type="IS_INCLUDED"/>
```

Representation of Link Structures

There are four categories of link structures. ISO-TimeML tags them as in Specification 8.43.

Specification 8.43 Link categories and their respective tag names

a. temporal link: <TLINK>
b. aspectual link: <ALINK>
c. subordination link: <SLINK>
d. measure link: <MLINK>

Their structure is a triple, consisting of two base structures and a relation over them. Their assignments @ are specified as follows.

Specification 8.44 Attribute-value ranges of $@_{tLink}$

```
attributes = relType, [timeID], [eventID], [relatedToTime],
  [relatedToEvent];
relType = BEFORE | AFTER | INCLUDES | IS_INCLUDED | DURING | DURING_INV
        | SIMUTANEOUS | IAFTER | IBEFORE | IDENTITY | BEGINS | ENDS
        | BEGUN_BY | ENDED_BY;
timeID = IDREF;
eventID = IDREF;
relatedToTime = IDREF;
relatedToEvent = IDREF;
```

The assignment $@_{tLink}$ of the temporal link (<TLINK>) relates a time or event to a time or event. The relation types are based on Allen's (1984) interval calculus with some modifications.

Here are some sample annotations for <TLINK>.

Annotation 8.45 TLINK relating an event to a time

a. Markables: Mia climbed$_{w2}$ the Himalayas [the year before last]$_{w5-8}$.
b. Annotation:
```
<EVENT xml:id="e1" target="#w2" pred="CLIMB" tense="PAST"/>
<TIMEX3 xml:id="t1" type="DATE" value="2018"
  temporalFunction="TRUE"/>
<TLINK eventID="#e1" relatedToTime="#t1" relType="DURING"/>
```

Annotation 8.46 Multiple TLINKs

a. Markables: Mia left$_{w2}$ Kathmandu [two hours]$_{w4-5}$ before$_{w6}$ [the earthquake]$_{w7-8}$.
b. Annotation:
```
<EVENT xml:id="e1" target="#w2" pred="LEAVE" tense="PAST"/>
<TIMEX3 xml:id="t1" type="DURATION" value="P2H" beginPoint="t11"
  endPoint="t12" temporalFunction="TRUE"/>
<EVENT xml:id="e2" target="#w7-8" pred="EARTHQUAKE"/>
<TLINK eventID="#e1" relatedToTime="#t11" relType="DURING"/>
<TLINK timeID="#t1" relatedToEvent="#e2" relType="BEFORE"/>
<TLINK eventID="#e1" relatedToEvent="#e2" relType="BEFORE"/>
```

The aspectual link, tagged <ALINK>, relates an aspectual event to its argument event. The value ranges of $@_{aLink}$ for the aspectual link are shown in Specification 8.47.

Specification 8.47   Attribute-value ranges of $@_{aLink}$
```
attributes = relType, eventID, relatedToEvent;
relType = CONTINUES | CULMINATES | INITIATES | REINITIATES |
          TERMINATES |;
eventID = IDREF;
relatedToEvent = IDREF;
```

Here is a sample annotation for <ALINK>.

Annotation 8.48   Aspectual link illustrated

a. Markables: Mia stopped$_{e1}$ smoking$_{e2}$.

b. Annotation:
```
<EVENT xml:id="e1" target="#w2" pred="STOP" tense="PAST"/>
<EVENT xml:id="e2" pred="SMOKE" tense="NONE"/>
<ALINK eventID="#e1" relatedToEvent="#e2" relType="TERMINATES"/>
```

Just like the aspectual link, *the subordination link* relates an event to another. Here is a list of *aspectual verbs* that trigger the subordination (<SLINK>).

Classification 8.49   Aspectual verbs

a. Conditional:

b. Counter_factive: *avoid, cancel, decline, forget (to), prevent, unable (to)*

c. Evidential: Reporting or perception verbs,

d. Factive: *forget (that), manage, regret,*

e. Intentional (Modal): mainly, I-State or I-Action verbs, *want, desire, try, attempt*

f. Neg_evidential: *deny*

The value ranges of the assignment $@_{sLink}$ for the subordination link (<SLINK>) are given in Specification 8.50.

Specification 8.50   Assignment $@_{sLink}$ for the subordination link
```
attributes = relType, eventID, relatedToEvent;
relType = CONDITIONAL | COUNTER_FACTIVE | EVIDENTIAL | FACTIVE |
          INTENSIONAL | NEG_EVIDENTIAL |;
eventID = IDREF;
relatedToEvent = IDREF;
```

Here are two sample annotations for <SLINK>.

Annotation 8.51   Intensional construction

a. Markables: Mia *wanted*$_{e1}$ to go$_{e2}$ to Alaska.

b. Annotation:

```
<EVENT xml:id="e1" target="#w2" pred="WANT" tense="PAST"/>
<EVENT xml:id="e2" pred="GO" tense="NONE"/>
<SLINK eventID="#e1" relatedToEvent="#e2" relType="INTENSIONAL"/>
```

Annotation 8.52 Negative evidential construction
a. Markables: Lee *denied*$_{e1}$ that he went$_{e2}$ to a wine bar.
b. Annotation:
```
<EVENT xml:id="e1" target="#w2" pred="DENY" tense="PAST"/>
<EVENT xml:id="e2" pred="GO" tense="PAST"/>
<SLINK eventID="#e1" relatedToEvent="#e2" relType="NEG_EVIDENTIAL"/>
```

The measure link (<MLINK>) relates an event to a temporal measure. Here is the specification of the assignment @$_{mLink}$ of the measure link.

Specification 8.53 Value ranges of the assignment @$_{mLink}$
for the measure link
```
attributes = relType, eventID, relatedToTime;
relType = MEASURES;
eventID = IDREF;
timeID = IDREF;  (* amount of time *)
```

Here is a sample annotation for the measure link (<MLINK>).

Annotation 8.54 Measure link annotated
a. Markables: Mia visited$_{e1}$ for *three months*$_{t1}$.
b. Annotation:
```
<EVENT xml:id="e1" target="#w2" pred="VISIT" tense="PAST"/>
<MEASURE xml:id="me1" type="tAmount" value="(3,month)"/>
<MLINK eventID="#e1" relatedToMeasure="#me1" relType="MEASURES"/>[7]
```

The value "(3, month)" may refer to a time amount with two possible interpretations. One is to interpret as a duration of three hours (*convex hull* interpretation) or as an accumulated amount of time involving more than one occurrence of Mia's visit (see Bunt and Pustejovsky (2010)).

8.6 Summary

While discussing how ISO-TimeML evolved from its precursors, two major and two technical modifications were mentioned in Sections 8.2.1 and 8.2.2, respectively. Two major modifications were: (i) abstract specification of an annotation scheme and (ii) standoff annotation. Two technical modifications

---

[7] The original version of ISO-TimeML (ISO, 2012b) does not have the base category **measure** (<MEASURE>), as in Figure 8.2. Instead, temporal measures such as *three months* are annotated as of category *time* (<TIMEX3 value="P3M"/>).

were: (i) merging of two tags EVENT and MAKEINSTANCE to EVENT and (ii) treatment of duration, such as *two hours*, as involving measurement.

Section 8.3 discussed the modeling of ISO-TimeML with a metamodel (Figure 8.2) and the conceptual design of its specification language with sufficient semantic support and illustrations. No specific ways of annotation were discussed in this section.

Section 8.4 introduced the abstract syntax of ISO-TimeML as an instantiation of the general abstract syntax $\mathcal{A}Syn=<M, C, R, @>$ of a semantic annotation scheme. Then each of the components was defined and the assignment @ was specified for each of the base categories in C and each of the relational link categories in R in abstract terms but sufficiently in an understandable way.

Section 8.5 specified the XML-based concrete syntax $CSyn_{isoTimeML}$ of ISO-TimeML with detailed illustrations. Following ISO 24612 LAF (ISO, 2012a), $CSyn_{isoTimeML}$ was introduced step by step as in ISO-TimeML (ISO, 2012b) and especially in Pustejovsky (2017a) with sample annotations for each of the base and the link categories.

9

Extending the Range of Temporal Annotation

9.1 Introduction: Extensions

In this chapter, I aim at extending the range of temporal annotation, and introduce an event-based temporal annotation scheme, named eXTimeML. It is an extended variant of ISO-TimeML (ISO, 2012b), as Bunt and Overbeeke (2008) proposed an extensible compositional semantics for temporal annotation. I propose at least three extensions of ISO-TimeML in this chapter.

Proposition 9.1   Extensions of ISO-TimeML

a. Temporal measure expressions are annotated as part of generalized measure:

e.g., *30 hours*.

b. Quantified temporal expressions are annotated as part of generalized quantification:

e.g., *every day*.

c. Adjectives and adverbs are annotated as modifiers of nouns and verbs, respectively:

e.g., *daily, never*.

Despite some differences, both ISO-TimeML and eXTimeML originate from the same source TimeML,[1] as their names indicate.

Temporal measure in eXTimeML is treated as part of *generalized measure*. Temporal measures are of two types: *length* (duration) and *amount*. One type refers to the *length* (duration) of a temporal interval, as denoted by expressions like *from Monday through Friday* or *two weeks from today*. The other type refers to the *amount* of time in a *cumulative sense*. Expressions like *five days* have two interpretations: it can either denote the time length or the time

---

[1] See Pustejovsky et al. (2005) for the introduction of TimeML.

amount, for instance, of *five days*. The length or duration of the temporal interval from Monday through Friday is five days consecutively. Someone may have also worked for five days without respect to the consecutivity or the continuity, for instance, working from Monday through Thursday but then on Saturday, thus working for five days cumulatively. *Frequencies*, as expressed by *twice a day* or *ten times a year*, are also treated as kinds of temporal measure.

Quantified temporal entities, as denoted by temporal expressions like *every Tuesday* or *several weeks*, are introduced as instances of generalized quantification. In eXTimeML, quantification applies to any sort of entities, being categorized as *quantified entity* and represented as a tag qEntity in concrete syntax.

Modification is introduced with temporal adjectives (e.g., *daily, weekly, annual*) and adverbs (e.g., *always, never*) as *modifiers* of nouns, verbs, and times. It also shows how modifiers restrict the *domains of quantification*

The chapter begins by presenting the general conceptual view of eXTimeML with a metamodel, showing how it extends ISO-TimeML (ISO, 2012b).

Each illustration is presented systematically in a fixed format, which consists of three or four levels.

Proposition 9.2   General format for illustration

a. Data

b. Base annotation or markables

c. Temporal annotation

d. Semantic representation

Steps 9.2a and 9.2b may be merged to one step. Data presents raw material. Base annotation marks up each markable *inline* in raw data or text with a pair of two identifiers: a categorized ID and a word-segmentation ID (e.g., *Mia stayed$_{e1,w2}$ in Paris*). Temporal annotation in eXTimeML is represented in pFormat, instead of XML. Semantic representation is formulated in ABSr, the representation language of ABS, which derives semantic (logical) forms $\sigma(\mathbf{a})$ from annotation structures **a**.

9.2 Metamodel and the Abstract Syntax

9.2.1 Metamodel of eXTimeML with Brief Descriptions

A metamodel presents the general conceptual frame of an annotation scheme in a visual form. Figure 9.1 shows that the *base structures*, which are called

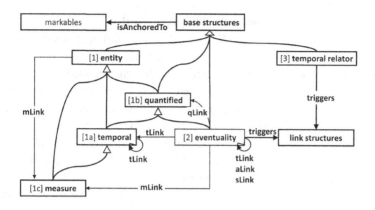

Figure 9.1 Metamodel of eXTimeML

entity structures in ISO-TimeML, are anchored to markables, and it visually shows the basis for a semantic annotation scheme such as eXTimeML. Base structures constitute basic components of each annotation structure on which link structures are constructed.

Categories of Base Structures

As shown by Figure 9.1, eXTimeML classifies *base structures* into three major categories, and the subcategories of [1] entity and those of [1a] temporal, [1b] quantified, and [ic] measure proper.

Classification 9.3   Three major categories

[1] *entity*
[2] *eventuality*
[3] *temporal relator*

Classification 9.4   Subcategories of [1] category entity

[1a] *temporal entity*
[1b] *quantified entity*
[1c] *measure proper*

There are complex subcategorization relations among the subcategories of category *entity*, each of which is marked by a small open triangular arrowhead in Figure 9.1. The category *measure* is a subcategory of *entity* as well as that of subcategory *temporal*. The categories *temporal* and *eventuality* can also be subcategories of *quantified*. Hence, these subcategories are intricately related.

Two Uses of the Term Entity

The term *entity* in ISO-TimeML is used in two different senses. First, it sometimes characterizes *structures* associated with an annotation structure. In this sense, the term *entity* indicates that the said structures are *basic* or *elementary* components of the annotated structure. Second, it is used as the name of a category for the aforementioned structures. In this second sense, it refers to a class of *objects* in general such as individual entities, groups, times, locations, *etc.*, whereas the term *eventuality* denotes a class of *predicates*. In order to clearly differentiate these two different uses, I have proposed that so-called *entity structures* be named *base structures* or *elementary structures* of an annotation structure. The relational term *link structure* then refers to a relation over these base or elementary components of an annotation structure.

Time Interval vs. Duration

The term *time interval* refers to a type of temporal entities of functional type $i \to t$, as opposed to the term *time point* of basic semantic type i. Following ISO 8601-1 (ISO, 2019a), eXTimeML uses the term *duration* as referring to the *quantity* or the *length* of a time interval, contrasted with the term *amount* of time, which allows the *cumulatively additive* interpretation of time amounts. ISO-TimeML (ISO, 2012b), in contrast, uses the term *duration* as referring to one of the types of times such as *time* of the day and *date* of calendar dates. Example 9.5 shows how the two terms, *time interval* and *duration*, are used for temporal annotation and also interpreted.

Example 9.5 Time interval vs. duration
a. Data: Mia stayed in Paris for three months from June through August.
b. Base annotation:

Mia stayed$_{e1, w2}$ in Paris for three months$_{me1, w6-7}$ $\emptyset_{t1, t Interval}$ from June$_{t11, w9}$ through August$_{t12, w11}$.

c. Temporal annotation:

```
event(e1, w2, type="state", pred="stay", tense="past")
measure(me1, w6-7, type="duration/tLength", value="3,month")
timex3(t1, type="tInterval", start="t11", end="t12")
timex3(t11, w9, type="date", value="XXXX-06")
timex3(t12, w11, type="date", value="XXXX-08")
```

d. Semantic representation:

$\sigma(\text{e1}) := \{e_1\}[stay(e_1) \wedge past(e_1)]$
$\sigma(\text{me1}) := \{t_1\}[\mu(t_1)=(3, month)^2]^3$
$\sigma(\text{t1}) := \{t_1, t_{11}, t_{12}\}[tInterval(t_1) \wedge starts(t_1, t_{11}) \wedge ends(t_1, t_{12})]$

---

[2] The value of a measure is given as a pair $<n, u>$ of a real and a unit, which is conventionally represented with a pair of *angled brackets* or with a pair of *parentheses* as here.
[3] Applied to temporal measures, μ is a measure function that maps a time interval to its duration or length.

Each $\sigma(i)$ stands for the semantic form of a base or a link structure, which is identified by its categorized identifier i. Thus, $\sigma(\texttt{e1})$ in Example 9.5d refers to the *semantic form* of the base structure: `EVENT(e1, w2, type="state", pred="stay", tense="past")`.

Relational Link Categories

The proposed eXTimeML inherits four relational categories of link structures from ISO-TimeML.

Classification 9.6   Four relational link categories

a. temporal link (`tLink`)
b. aspectual link (`aLink`)
c. subordination link (`sLink`)
d. measure link (`mLink`)[4]

Triggered either by temporal relators or eventualities, links, in general, generate *link structures* that represent relations over base structures.

Temporal Link As in ISO-TimeML, the temporal link (`tLink`) in eXTimeML generates relations over times and eventualities, while the type of each relation is characterized by a *temporal relator*, denoted by a preposition such as *at, before, in* or a conjunction such as *after, before, when* in English.

Example 9.7   Temporal link illustrated

a. Markables: Mia arrived$_{e1}$ home before$_{tr1}$ midnight$_{t1}$.
b. Temporal link structure:

```
tLink(tL1, figure="e1", ground="t1", relType="before", trigger="tr1")
```

c. Semantic representation:

$$\sigma(\texttt{tL1}) := \exists\{e_1, t_1\}[\tau(e_1) \prec t_1)]$$

The annotation scheme eXTimeML adopts the attribute names *figure* and *ground*, instead of eventID or relatedToTime, in order to follow ISO-Space (ISO, 2020d) in the use of attribute names; $\sigma(\texttt{tL1})$ refers to the semantic form of the *temporal link structure*, which is identified by `tL1`.

The preposition at_{tr1} triggers the temporal relation between the time $\tau(e_1)$ of Mia's arrival$_{e1}$ and the time midnight$_{t1}$ to be the *precedence relation*, which is represented by the logical predicate $\prec$. The runtime function τ maps an event to the time of its occurrence.

Aspectual Link Eventualities, denoted by *aspectual verbs*, trigger the aspectual link (`aLink`).

---

[4] Strictly speaking, the original version of ISO-TimeML (ISO, 2012b) introduced the base category *measure* without the measure link (`mLink`).

Example 9.8   Aspectual link illustrated

a. Markables: Mia stopped$_{e1}$ smoking$_{e2}$.

b. Aspectual link structure:
```
aLink(aL1, figure="e1", ground="e2", relType="terminates",
trigger="e1")
```

c. Semantic representation:

$\sigma(\texttt{aL1}) := \exists\{e_1, e_2\}[terminates(e_1, e_2) \wedge smoke(e_2)]$

The predicate *terminates* needs to be defined as a logical predicate, denoting a binary *temporal relation*, which relates an event e_1 to its *terminal* subevent e_2, as part of an interpretation model.

Subordination Link   The subordination link (sLink) is triggered by *modal, factive, evidential* verbs or their negatives, *counter-factive* and *negative evidential*.

Example 9.9   Subordination link illustrated

a. Markables: Mia$_{x1}$ wants$_{e1}$ to lose$_{e2}$ her weight.

b. Subordination link structure:
```
sLink(sL1, figure="x1", ground="e2", relType="wants",
trigger="e1")
```

c. Semantic representation:

$\sigma(\texttt{sL1}) := \exists\{x_1, e_2\}[named(x_1, Mia) \wedge theme(e_1, x_1) \wedge wants(x_1, e_2)]^5$

The predicates *named, theme,* and *wants* need to be defined properly in an interpretation model for the interpretation of $\sigma(\texttt{sL1})$.

Measure Link   In eXTimeML, the measure link (mLink) relates an eventuality to a measure, which is either the length (duration) of a time interval or the time amount consumed of an event in some time interval. The markable *20 years* in Example 9.10 is annotated and interpreted as a duration, which is the length of a time interval.

Example 9.10   Measure link illustrated

a. Base annotation:

Lee taught$_{e1}$ $\emptyset_{t1}$ for$_{s1}$ over 20 years$_{me1:w4-6}$ at Korea University.

b. Temporal metric annotation:
```
event(e1, w2, type="process", pred="teach", tense="past")
timex3(t1, type="timeInterval", value="#me1")
signal(s1, type="metric", subType="timeLength", pred="for")
measure(me1, w4-5, type="duration", value="P20Y")
tLink(tL1, figure="e1", ground="t1", relType="isIncluded")
mLink(mL1, figure="t1", ground="me1", relType="timeLength",
    trigger="s1")
```

---

^{5} The *want* construction may also be treated as an intensional implicational construction $\rightarrow^{int}$.

c. Semantic representation:

$\sigma(\texttt{tL1}) \oplus \sigma(mL1) :=$

$\exists\{e_1, t_1\}$

$[[teach(e_1) \wedge past(e_1) \wedge \tau(e_1) \subseteq t_1] \wedge$

$[timeInterval(t_1) \wedge \mu(t_1) \geq (20, year)]]$

The semantic content $\sigma(\texttt{tL1})$ merges with that of $\sigma(mL1)$ by the conjunctive operator $\oplus$, while the function μ maps an object like a time to its quantity; $\mu(t_1)$ thus denotes the length (quantity) of the time interval t_1. Note that eXTimeML annotates markables of *temporal metric entities* like *20 years* as a temporal entity as well as a metric entity, thereby capturing both the temporal and the metric nature of such markable expressions.

Extensions As was shown in Figure 9.1, eXTimeML extends the scope of ISO-TimeML by additionally proposing two types of base structures.

Proposition 9.11 Two types of base structures

a. Base structures $\beta_{measure}$ of category *measure* or *temporal metric entity* (e.g., *24 hours*) as substructures of base structures in general, either independent of or partially dependent on temporal entity structures.

b. Base structures $\beta_{qEntity}$ of category *quantified entity* by subsuming *quantified temporal entity* (e.g., *every month*) as its subcategory.

Related to these base structures of category *measure* and *quantified entity* are two links: the *measure link* and the *quantification link* with *scoping*.

Generalized Measure Measures are now of various types, temporal, spatial, physical, or of any possible dimensions. The measure link ($\texttt{mLink}$) is then generalized by relating a base structure β_c of any base category c to a set $B_{measure}$ of base structures of category *measure*. Annotation 9.12, for instance, illustrates how the category *measure* is extended to the type of *weight* and how that measure applies to the person named *John*.

Annotation 9.12 Metric annotation

a. Markables: John$_{x1, w1}$ weighs over 100 kg$_{me1, w3-5}$.

b. Metric annotation:

```
measure(me1, w3-5, type="weight", value="100,kg", modifier="over")
mLink(mL1, figure="x1", ground="me1", relType="measures")
```

Generalized Quantification In eXTimeML, quantification is no longer restricted to temporal entities. Quantified temporal entities like *every month* are now treated as a subtype of quantified entities. Following the tripartite treatment of quantification, the quantifier *every* is treated as ranging over its *domain* restricted to the set of months, while predicating of an event and its object participants as the *nuclear scope*; eXTimeML also introduces *scoping* as part of *quantification link* that applies over quantified entities as well as to logical operators like negation and other truth-functional connectives or modal operators.[6]

9.2.2 Abstract Syntax of eXTimeML

An *abstract syntax* lays a foundation for the formulation of an annotation scheme. The abstract syntax $\mathcal{A}Syn_{eXTimeML}$ of eXTimeML is designed on the basis of the metamodel, which was visually shown by Figure 9.1. It is an instantiation of the general abstract syntax that formally defines a specification language of annotation structures. It specifies the specification language as a set-theoretic tuple as in Specification 9.13.

Specification 9.13 Abstract syntax of eXTimeML

Given a set D of communicative data segments,

$\mathcal{A}Syn_{eXTimeML}$ is a tuple $<M, C, R, @>$, where

a. M is a subset of D that contains (possibly null or noncontiguous) strings of communicative segments, called *markables*, each of which is delimited by the set C of base categories.

b. C is a finite set of base categories:

  [1] *entity*:

  [1a] *temporal*

  [1b] *quantified*

  [1c] *measure*

  [2] *eventuality*

  [3] *temporal relator*

c. R is a finite set of link categories:

  [1] *temporal link* (tLink)

  [2] *aspectual link* (aLink)

  [3] *subordination link* (sLink)

  [4] *measure link* (mLink)

  [5] *quantification link* (qLink) with *scoping*

d. @ is a set of assignments specified for each base structure β_c of category c in C and each link structure λ_r of category r in R.

---

[6] See Bunt et al. (2018, 2022), Pustejovsky et al. (2019b), Bos (2020), and ISO/CD 24617-12 quantification (ISO, 2022a) for the most updated discussions on quantification, scope, and negation. See also Bach et al. (1995).

With each of the attribute-value assignments @ specified in an isomorphic concrete syntax, $\mathcal{A}Syn_{eXTimeML}$ generates, or formally defines, base structures β_c and link structures λ_r. The base structures and the link structures together constitute annotation structures **a**.

Annotation Structures

Each annotation structure **a** consists of (i) base structures β_c and (ii) link structures λ_r. *Base structures β_c of category c in the set of base categories C are specified as follows.*

Specification 9.14   Components of a base structure
Each base structure β_c of base category c is a tuple $<\alpha, \sigma>$, where
a. α is an anchoring structure $<i, m>$,
   where i is a unique *identifier* and m is a markable in M to which each base structure β_c of category c is anchored;
b. σ is a content structure which is defined by the assignment $@_c$ of base category c in C.

In the abstract syntax of an annotation scheme, each base structure is defined with its content structure σ, represented as a set-theoretic tuple that consists of a list of attributes. For example, the base structure $\beta_{measure}$, or strictly speaking, its content structure, can be defined as a 3-tuple $<ty, va, mod>$, where ty is the type of a measure, va is the value of the measure, and mod is a modifier of the value.

Each base structure with an ID i may be instantiated with a specific *value* assigned to each element, called *attribute*. Here is an example.

Example 9.15   Instantiated base structure
$\beta_{measure:i} = $ <i, ty="duration", va="25,hour", modi="greaterThan">

In a concrete syntax, the attributes ty, va, and $modi$ will each have a specific name such as *type*, *value*, and *modifier* as well as the list of possible values and their names.

   Link structures λ_r of category r in R are specified below.

Specification 9.16   Components of a link structure
Each link structure is a triplet $<\beta, B, \rho>$, where:
a. β is a base structure,
b. B is a set of base structures, either basic, complex, or *augmented*, and
c. ρ is a relation from β to B.

Besides the three components of the triplet, there may be some additional attributes such as @trigger of a particular link or @scopes for the quantification link (qLink).

Assignments for Base Structures

An assignment @ is a function from a set A of attributes to a set V of values. Given an attribute a in A for a base structure β_c of category c, $@_c(a)$ is the value of a. In Example 9.17, $@_{event}$(type) is "process", $@_{event}$(pred) is "work" and $@_{event}$(tense), "past".

Example 9.17   Assignment $@_{event}$ for eventualities
a. Markable: John *worked*$_{e1, w2}$ yesterday.
b. Annotation: event(e1, w2, type="process", pred="work", tense="past")

For each c of the three major categories of base structures and the three subcategories of category *entity*, eXTimeML specifies its assignment $@_c$ as a set-theoretic tuple, thus licensing each specified attribute to be named in a free manner.

Assignment $@_{entity}$ for Category *entity* Base structures β_{entity} of category *entity* are defined by assignment $@_{entity}$ as a quintuple as in Specification 9.18.

Specification 9.18   Base structures of category entity
Each base structure β_{entity} of base category *entity* is a 5-tuple $<ty, pr, [fo],$ $[pl], [de]>$, where
a. *ty* is the type of an entity,
b. *pr* is the predicative content of the entity,
c. *fo* is the attribute that determines the form of an entity either as a name or as a nominal,
d. *pl* is the plurality of an entity, and
e. *de* is the determinacy of an entity.

The attributes *ty* and *pr* are each required to be assigned a value. The other square-bracketed attributes do not need to be specified with a value. Here is an example.

Example 9.19   Assignment for category entity
a. Markable: Dogs$_{x1, w1}$ were barking.
b. Annotation:
    entity(x1, w1, type="canine", pred="dog", form="nom",
      plurality="yes")
c. Semantic representation:
    $\sigma(x1) := \exists\{x_1\}[dog(x_1) \wedge plural(x_1)]$

Plurality and Determinacy The logical predicate *plural* is defined in Definition 9.20.

Definition 9.20   Logical predicate *plural*
For any individual entity x of type e and a property P,
$[P(x) \wedge plural(x)]$ is true if and only there is a set X such that $|X| \geq 2$ and
$\forall x[x \in X \rightarrow P(x)]$.

The grammar of most European languages has definite articles, *the* in English and *le, la, les* in French. These definite articles often indicate the *determinacy* of an object, which includes a set or a group, referred to in a communication, meaning the *uniqueness* of the object or that the range of its denotation is restricted by a *resource situation* or background information. Consider an example that illustrates the unique set denoted by a plural determinate.

Example 9.21   Determinate plural objects
a. Markable: Those dogs$_{x1, w1-2}$ are vicious.
b. Annotation:
```
entity(x1, w1-2, type="canine", pred="dog",
  plurality="yes", determinacy="yes")
event(e1, w4, type="state", pred="vicious")
srLink(srL1, relType="theme", figure="e1", ground="x1")
```
c. Semantic representation:
$\sigma(\text{x1}) := \{x_1\}[dog(x_1) \wedge plural(x_1) \wedge determinate(x_1)]$
$\sigma(\text{e1}) := \{e_1\}[state(e_1) \wedge vicious(e_1)]$
$\sigma(\text{srL1})$
$:= \{e_1, x_1\}[\{\sigma(\text{e1}), \sigma(\text{x1})\} \oplus theme(e_1, x_1)]$
$:= \exists\{e_1, x_1\}[state(e_1) \wedge vicious(e_1) \wedge dog(x_1) \wedge plural(x_1) \wedge$
$\quad determinate(x_1) \wedge theme(e_1, x_1)]^7$

The notion of *plural determinacy* involves the notion of a plural object, which is either *group* or *set*, and its *uniqueness*. Sharvy (1980) extends Russell's (1903, 1905) notion of definite descriptions to plurals, as in Definition 9.22.

Definition 9.22   Denotation of a plural determinate object
For a property P,
$[\![the\ P]\!] = \{x : x \in P \wedge \forall y[y \in P \rightarrow y \sqsubseteq x]\}$,
where $\sqsubseteq$ is interpreted as the relation *part of*.

Annotation-based semantics (ABS) admits a variety of interpreting the notion of *determinacy* or *plural determinacy*.

---

^{7} $[P(x) \wedge plural(x) \wedge determinate(x)]$ may be represented as $^{\star}P(x)$ as a proper plural à la Link (1998).

Assignment $@_{tEntity}$ **for Category** *temporal entity*   Base structures $\beta_{tEntity}$ of category *temporal entity* in eXTimeML are defined maximally as an 8-tuple.

Specification 9.23   Base structures of category *temporal entity*
Base structures $\beta_{tEntity}$, defined by $@_{tEntity}$, constitute a tuple $<ty, \{pr, va\},$ $[at], [st], [en], [fu], [tf]>$, where

a. *ty* is the type of a temporal entity structure,
b. *pr* is the base form representing predicative content,
c. *va* is the temporal value depending on the type of a temporal entity,
d. *at* is an anchoring time,
e. *st* is a start point of an interval,
f. *en* is an endpoint of an interval,
g. *fu* is a *function in document* such as the creation time of a document, and
h. *tf* is a temporal function that calculates relevant time points.

Curly-bracketed attributes such as {*pr, va*} above are specified *selectively*: either one of the attributes or all of them are specified. The attribute *ty* is required, while either *pr* or *va* or both of them are specified. The specification of the other attributes is optional.

Example 9.24   Selective value-assignment
a. Markable: Mia went to Paris *last summer.*
b. Attribute-value assignment:

```
timex3(t1, w4-5, type="date", pred="summer", value="2020-SU")
```

The markable `summer` is of type `"date"`, being annotated as a predicate `pred="summer"` or a temporal value `va="XXXX-SU"`. The attributes `@valueFromFunction` and `@comment` in ISO-TimeML are deleted because they can be treated apart from actual annotation.

Assignment $@_{qEntity}$ **of Category** *quantified entity*   The scheme eXTimeML introduces the assignment $@_{qEntity}$ that generates base structures $\beta_{qEntity}$ of category *quantified entity*. Base structures $\beta_{qEntity}$ of category *quantifiedEntity*, or *qEntity* in short, are each specified as a set-theoretic tuple, as in Specification 9.25.

Specification 9.25   Base structures of category *qEntity*
$\beta_{qEntity} = <ty, do, [ind]>$, where
a. *ty* is the type of a quantified entity,
b. *do* is the domain over which the quantified entity ranges, and

c. *ind* is an attribute that determines whether a quantified entity is an individual or a group.

Assignment $@_{event}$ **of Category** *eventuality* Base structures β_{event} of category *eventuality* are each defined by the set-theoretic tuple as specified by Specification 9.26.

Specification 9.26 Base structures defined by $@_{event}$
Each base structure β_{event} constitutes a tuple $<ty, pr, cl, tam, [mo], po>$, where

a. *ty* is an event type,
b. *pr* is the content of an event in a predicate form,
c. *cl* is an event class,
d. *tam* is a tense, aspect, and mood,
e. *mo* is a modality, and
f. *po* is a polarity such as true or false.

The square-bracketed attribute *mo* is optional, whereas the other five attributes are required to be assigned a value. The attribute *tam* may be expanded to *ten, asp, moo*, standing for *tense, aspect* and *mood*, respectively. Events, expressed in a nominal form, such as *workshop* and *war* are *tenseless*, thus being assigned a value "none" for the attribute *tense*.

Assignment $@_{measure}$ **of Category** *measure* This is given as in Specification 9.27 as part of the abstract syntax $\mathcal{ASyn}_{gMeasure}$ of generalized measure in eXTimeML.

Specification 9.27 Base structures of category *measure*, defined by assignment $@_{measure}$
Base structures $\beta_{measure}$ each constitute a tuple $<ty, va, [mod]>$, where

a. *ty* is the type of a measure,
b. *va* is the value of a measure, consisting mostly of a real number *n* and a unit *u*, and
c. *mod* is an optional attribute that modifies the (unitized) value of a measure.

A unit *u* may not be specified if the value of a measure is something like *near* that fails to be expressed in explicitly quantitative terms. Sometimes, measure values have no modifiers such as *greater than* or *about*. A base structure $\beta_{measure}$ will then consist of a $<ty, va>$ assignment, consisting of two attributes only, in a minimal case.

Assignment $@_{tRelator}$ **of Category** *temporal relator* This defines the base structures of category *temporal relator* as in Specification 9.28.

Specification 9.28   Base structures of category *temporal relator*
Base structure β_{tr} of category *tRelator* is defined by assignment $@_{tRelator}$ as a tuple $<ty, [st], pr>$, where
a. ty is the type of a temporal relation,
b. optional st is the subtype of a temporal relation, and
c. pr is the predicative content.

Here is an example of a base structure of category *temporal relator*.

Example 9.29
```
tRelator(tr1, type="bounding", subtype="backward", pred="before")
```

Assignments for Link Structures
Unlike ISO-TimeML, eXTimeML introduces one additional link category *quantification link* besides the four link categories: (i) *temporal link*, (ii) *aspectual link*, (iii) *subordination link*, and (iv) *measure link*. Each of them is defined as a quadruple $<\beta, B, \rho, [O]>$, where β is a base structure, B is a nonempty set of base structures, either basic or augmented, ρ is the type of a relation that relates β to the set B, and O is the set of optional attributes like @trigger that characterizes the type of ρ or @scopes over quantified entities.

Augmented Base Structures
The scheme eXTimeML introduces the notion of *augmented based structures* that the repeated application of links create. The semantic role link, for instance, applies to a list of base structures to derive another base structure that carries additional information. Here is an example.

Annotation 9.30   Augmented base structures
a. Markables: Mary$_{x1, w1}$ swam$_{e1, w2}$ yesterday$_{t1, w3}$.
b. Base structures:
```
entity(x1, w1, type="person", form="name")
event(e1, type="process", pred="swim", tense="past")
timex3(t1, w3, type="date", pred="yesterday")
```
c. Augmented base structure by srLink:
```
srLink(srL1, e1, participants="x1", agent)
:= event(%e1, type="process", pred="swim", tense="past", agent="x1")
```
d. Link structure:
```
tLink(tL1, %e1, t1, isIncludedBy)
```

e. Semantic representation:

$\exists\{x_1, e_1, t_1\}$

$[named(x_1, Mary) \wedge swim(e_1) \wedge past(e_1) \wedge agent(e_1, x_1) \wedge$
$date(t_1) \wedge yesterday(t_1) \wedge \tau(e_{11}) \subseteq \gamma(t_1)]$

The sign %, prefixed to e1, in Example 9.30c, indicates the *augmentation of the base structure* e1 with the additional information agent="x1". The temporal link (tLink) in part d relates the base structure %e1, augmented by srLink (srL1), to the base structure t1. This allows a correct interpretation as represented in part e: Mary$_{x1}$ is represented as the agent of the event $swim_{e1}$.[8]

Consider another example.

Annotation 9.31   Recursively augmented base structures

a. Markables: John$_{x1, w1}$ called$_{e1, w2-3}$ up Mary$_{x2, w4}$.
b. Base structures:

```
entity(x1, w1, type="person", form="nam")
event(e1, w2-3, type="process", pred="call")
entity(x2, w4, type="person", form="nam")
```

c. Augmented base structure by srLink(agent):

```
srLink(srL1, e1, x1, agent)
:= event(%e1, w2-3, type="process", pred="call", agent="x1")
```

d. Augmented base structure by srLink(theme):

```
srLink(srL2, %e1, x2, theme)
:= event(%%e1, w2-3, type="process", pred="call", agent="x1",
   theme="#x2")
```

In Annotation 9.31, event(%e1) is a base structure augmented with the information that its agent is x1. Likewise, event(%%e1) is also a base structure, which is re-augmented with the additional information that x2 is its theme.

Consider a third example, as follows.

Annotation 9.32   Reapplication of links

a. Markables: Jon$_{x1, w1}$ worked$_{e1, w2}$ yesterday$_{t1, w3}$.
b. Base structures:

```
entity(x1, w1, type="person", form="nam")
event(e1, w2, type="process", pred="work", tense="past")
timex3(t1, w3, type="date", value="2022-05-23")
```

---

[8] τ is a *runtime function* from events to times and γ is a *deictic function* from deictic expressions to specific times. $\gamma(t_1)$ provides a specific time referred to by the deictic temporal expression *yesterday*, while $\tau(e_1)$ also provides a specific time for the occurrence of the event e_1.

c. Semantic role link:

```
srLink(srL1, e1, x1, agent)
:= event(%e1, w2, type="process", pred="work", tense="past",
   agent="x1")
```

d. Temporal link:

```
tLink(tL1, %e1, t1, relType="isIncludedBy")
```

e. Semantic representation:

$\exists\{e_1, x_1, t_1\}$

$[named(x_1, Jon) \land person(x) \land$

$process(e_1) \land work(e_1) \land past(e_1) \land agent(e_1, x_1) \land$

$date(t_1) \land year(t_1, 2022) \land month(t_1, May) \land day(t_1, 23) \land$

$\tau(e_1) \subseteq t_1]$

In the derivation of the semantic form in Annotation 9.32e, the semantic form $\sigma(\text{tL1})$ of the temporal link correctly relates or anchors the semantic form $\sigma(\text{\%e1})$ of the augmented base structure of category *event* to the time $\sigma(\text{t1})$.

Complex Base Structures

Intervals form *complex base structures*, which refer to other base structures. Consider Example 9.33.

Example 9.33   *Complex base structures of intervals*

a. Data: Jon took a nap *from two to five* in the afternoon.

b. Base annotation:

Jon took a nap$_{e1:w4}$ $\emptyset_{t1:tInterval}$ from two$_{t10:w6}$ to five$_{t11:w8}$ in the afternoon.

c. Temporal annotation:

```
event(e1, w4, type="process", pred="nap", tense="past")
timex3(t1, type="tInterval", start="#t10", end="#t11")
timex3(t10, type="time", value="T14:00")
timex3(t11, type="time", value="T17:00")
tLink(tL1, e1, t1, isIncluded)
```

d. Semantic representation:

$\exists\{e_1, t_1, t_{10}, t_{11}\}$

$[nap(e_1) \land past(e_1) \land$

$tInterval(t_1) \land starts(t_1, t_{10}) \land ends(t_1, t_{11}) \land$

$clockTime(t_{10}, 14:00) \land clockTime(t_{11}, 17:00) \land$

$\tau(e_1) \subseteq t_1]$

The interval t_1 is a complex base structure, referring to the other two base structures which specify the interval boundary points. In part c, the value of the attribute @start refers to the base structure t_{10} while that of the attribute @end refers to the base structure t_{11}.

Semantic roles can be marked on based structures directly without applying the semantic role link. This is possible if the type of each markable of category *eventuality* is associated with an event structure, called a *frame*, which specifies a list of semantic roles as part of the lexicon. The verb *love*, for instance, is to be associated with a semantic role frame, $<agent, theme>$. Then, for illustration, consider Example 9.34.

Example 9.34 Complex event structures

a. Data: Jon loves Mia.
b. Annotation:
```
entity(x1, w1, type="person", form="nam")
event(%e1, w2, type="state", pred="love", agent="#x1", theme="#x2")
entity(x2, w3, type="person", form="nam")
```

Here, event(e1) is treated as a complex base structure, referring to the other base structures, x1 and x2,

Instead of introducing the *notion of augmented base structures*, I prefer to treat category *eventuality* as a complex base category that refers to semantic role frames in a lexicon. This approach simply adds an optional attribute to the specification of the attribute-value specification $@_{event}$, as in Specification 9.35.

Specification 9.35 Semantic role frame for $@_{event}$
```
attributes = identifier, type, pred, . . . [roleFrame];
roleFrame = LIST; (* List of possible semantic roles *)
```

This approach is less costly than the repeated application of the semantic role link. Here is an example.

Example 9.36 Semantic role frame

a. Data: Jon gave Mia a ring.
b. Markables: Jon$_{x1:w1}$ gave$_{e1:w2}$ Mia$_{x2:w3}$ a ring$_{x3:w5}$.
c. Semantic roleFrame for the verb *give*: (agent, recipient, object)
d. Annotation:
```
event(%e1, w2, type="transition", tense="past",
     agent="#x1", recipient="#x2", object="#x3")
```

9.3 The pFormat-Based Concrete Syntax

The concrete syntax $CSyn_{eXTimeML}$ of eXTimeML (i) specifies the format of representing annotation structures and (ii) defines the specific values or value types for each of the assignments $@_{cat}$ of category cat, of either base or link structures.

9.3.1 Representation Format

Following ISO 24612 LAF (ISO, 2012a), ISO-TimeML makes it explicit that the choice of a representation format is not required. ISO-TimeML thus allows any suitable formats, including tabular or visually easy-to-manage graphic formats, for the representation of annotation structures. Nevertheless, XML is used in ISO-TimeML as if it were part of the standard.

Formulating the pFormat

The scheme eXTimeML adopts a predicate-logic-like format, named *pFormat* in short, as adopted by Pustejovsky (2017b). The pFormat represents annotation structures in a linearized textual form, just as XML does. The new format avoids the use of many non-Latin characters such as the angled brackets (< . . . >), the slash "/" or the underscore sign "_", and uppercase characters for the representation of values for attributes, which occur all over ISO-TimeML documents. It adopts the lowerCamel case conventions that allow representations like "pFormat" or "eXTimeML" instead of "p-format" or "EX-TimeML".

The use of pFormat is outlined by Specification 9.37 (see Section 4.5.2 for more details).

Specification 9.37   Guidelines for the use of pFormat
a. Use the small text typewriter (\small\texttt in LATEX) font in general.
b. Represent only the values without mentioning their attributes, @id and @target, for the anchoring part of each base structure;
c. Provide each link structure with attribute values only, without referring to their attribute names, unless necessary.
d. Do not mark the attribute names for the anchoring part of base structures or link structures to differentiate that part from the content part.

Examples 9.38b and 9.38c compare the representation of XML with that of pFormat.

Example 9.38   Comparison between XML format and pForamt
a. Markables: Fido$_{x1,w1}$ doesn't bark$_{e1,w2-3}$.

b. XML-format:

```
<ENTITY xml:id="x1" target="w1" type="CANINE" form="NAME"/>
<EVENT xml:id="e1" target="w2-3" type="PROCESS" pred="BARK"
  tense="PRESENT" polarity="NEG"/>
<SRLINK xml:id="srL1", eventID="e1" participantID="x1"
  semRole="AGENT"/>
```

c. pFormat:

```
entity(x1, w1, type="canine", form="name")
event(e1, w2-3, type="process", pred="bark",
  tense="present", polarity="neg")
srLink(srL1, event="e1", participants="x1", semRole="agent")
```

Conversion of Elements in XML to pForms

The pFormat language simply consists of nonembedded formulas, called *pForms*. Each pForm corresponds to an atomic formula in predicate logic and also to an element in XML. If necessary, each well-formed element in XML can be converted automatically to each pForm in the pFormat, vice versa, simply by doing the following.

Specification 9.39 Conversion steps

a. Step 1: Change the XML element frame <NAME . . . / > to a predicate form name (. . .).
b. Step 2: Convert the representation (e.g., "CANINE") of attribute values in uppercase to the lowercase characters (e.g., "canine").
c. Step 3: Separate attribute-value specifications with a comma " , ".

As in XML, base structures in pFormat may refer to other base structures for the assignment of values for their attributes. These values may optionally be prefixed with the hash sign # as introduced by TEI P5 (TEI Consortium, 2019). Here is an example.

Example 9.40 Referring to other base structures in Pformat

a. Markables: Interstate I-5$_{p1, w1-2}$ from [Seattle]$_{pl1, w4}$ to [San Diego]$_{pl2, w6}$
b. Annotation;

```
path(p1, w1-2, type="highway", name="I-5", start="#pl1", end="#pl2")
place(pl1, w4, type="city", name="Seattle", state="WA", country="US")
place(pl2, w6, type="city", name="San Diego", state="CA",
  country="US")
```

The values of @start and @end for the attribute path are linked to the pForms pl1 and pl2, respectively. The boundaries defining a (spatial) path or a temporal interval may not be *points*, thus replacing the earlier attribute names @beginPoint and @endPoint with @start and @end, as used in ISO 8601-1 (ISO, 2019a).

9.3.2 Defining Attributes and their Value Ranges

The concrete syntax $CSyn_{eXTimeML}$ defines a set of attributes and their value ranges by instantiating the assignment $@_c$ of category c that defines base structures β_c in the abstract syntax as a set-theoretic tuple. It also provides a specific name for each of the attributes and values or value types. For example, the assignment $@_{event}$ that defines base structures β_{event} of category *eventuality* as a set-theoretic tuple $<ty, pr, cl, tam, [mo], po>$ in the abstract syntax $ASyn_{eXTimeML}$ can be instantiated with a specific name given to each attribute, as in Specification 9.41.

Specification 9.41   Specific assignment $@_{event}$ in $CSyn_{eXTimeML}$
```
category = event, . . . ;
attributes = identifier, target, type, pred, class, tense, aspect,
  mood, [modality], polarity;
    (*Square-bracketed attributes are optional.*)
identifier = categorized ID-prefix;
    (*The ID-prefix "e" followed by a positive integer.*)
target = IDREF; (*Refers to a markable.*)
type = state | process | transition;
pred = base form that represents predicative content;
class = aspectual | i_action | i_state | occurrence |
  perception | reporting | state;
tense = past | present | future | none;
    (*The default value is "present".*)
aspect = progressive | perfect;
mood = indicative | subjunctive; (*The default value is "indicative"*)
modality = necessary | possible | CDATA;
polarity = pos | neg; (*The default value is "pos".*)
```

The attribute `tam` here is expanded to `tense`, `aspect`, and `mood`. In addition, the assignment $@_{event}$ of category *eventuality* in eXTimeML differs from that of ISO-TimeML. The two attributes of ISO-TimeML, @quantifier and @scopes, are incorporated into the specification of quantification in eXTimeML.

9.4 Temporal Measure

9.4.1 Issues

ISO-TimeML annotates *temporal measures* like *twenty and a half years* as part of temporal expressions (<TIMEX3>), as illustrated by Annotation 9.42.

Annotation 9.42   Temporal measures

a. Markables:

Kim taught$_{e1, w2}$ for *twenty and a half years*$_{t1, w4-8}$ at Korea University.

b. Annotation:

```
<isoTimeML>
<EVENT xml:id="e1" target="w2" pred="TEACH"/>
<TIMEX3 xml:id="t1" target="w4-8" type="DURATION" value="P20.5Y"/>
<MLINK eventID="e1" relatedToTime="t1" relType="MEASURES"/>
</isoTimeML>
```

ISO-TimeML annotates *twenty and a half years* as a duration, represented as `"P20.5Y"` and read as *a period (duration) of twenty and a half years*. The interpretation of *twenty and a half years*, however, is ambiguous. It can be interpreted (i) as the *length of a time interval* (period) of 20.5 years, as annotated and represented by `<TIMEX3>` in Annotation 9.42b. It can also be interpreted (ii) as an *amount of time* in a cumulative sense, meaning that the total amount of Kim's teaching was 20.5 years. Annotation 9.42b fails to capture this *cumulative meaning*.

ISO-TimeML has recognized this problem. It thus introduces the *amount (measure) of time* as one of the general base structures in its metamodel and abstract syntax, while treating it as a subtype of temporal objects. The XML-based concrete syntax, however, fails to treat time amounts as forming an *independent category of measure structures*. It is thus necessary to implement the notion of *time amount* in a concrete syntax of ISO-TimeML.

ISO-TimeML also annotates *frequencies* such as *three times a month* as temporal expressions of category `<TIMEX3>`, as in Annotation 9.43.

Annotation 9.43 Frequencies

a. Markable: I go to Seoul *three times a month*$_{t1, w5-7}$.
b. Annotation:

```
<TIMEX3 xml:id="t1" target="#w5-7" type="SET" value="P1M" freq="3X"/>
```

Frequencies involve a time interval as a reference factor for measurement. The frequency, as denoted by *three times a month*, refers to the counting of the occurrences of an event during a month. The expression *three times* itself is not temporal but refers to the number of three occurrences of an event. Thus, eXTimeML interprets *three times a month* as three occurrences of an event in each month and annotates *three times* as of category *measure*, tagged MEASURE in the pFormat-based concrete syntax.

In eXTimeML, a category *measure* is introduced to define base structures $\beta_{measure}$ of category *measure*. The category *measure* applies to measures of all types (e.g., distance, duration, length) or their subtypes or dimensions (e.g., depth, height, breadth). It is then implemented both in its pFormat-based concrete syntax as well as in its abstract syntax. The concrete syntax is, thereby, made ideally isomorphic to the abstract syntax in treating temporal measures as well.

9.4.2 General Specification of Measure

The annotation scheme of eXTimeML for the general specification of measure consists of (i) an abstract syntax $\mathcal{A}Syn_{gMeasure}$, (ii) a pFormat-based concrete syntax $CSyn_{gMeasure}$, and (iii) an ABS-based semantics $Sem_{gMeasure}$ that validates the abstract syntax. $Sem_{gMeasure}$ also interprets each of the annotation structures that are represented in pForms by the concrete syntax.

Abstract Syntax

The abstract syntax $\mathcal{A}Syn_{gMeasure}$ of eXTimeML for general measure is specified below.

Specification 9.44   Abstract syntax of generalized measure
The abstract syntax $\mathcal{A}Syn_{gMeasure}$ constitutes a tuple $<M, C, R, @>$, where

  (i) M is a set of markables, each of which is delimited by E;
 (ii) C is a singleton containing a base category, named *measure*, only;
(iii) R is a singleton containing a link category, named *measureLink*, only;
(iv) @ is a set of assignments for *measure* and *measureLink*.

Assignment @ as a Function from Attributes to Values For each category *cat*, there is an assignment $@_{cat}$, viewed as a function $f: A \rightarrow V$, where A is a set of attributes and V is a set of values. Given an attribute a in A, $@_{cat}(a)$ is understood to be the value v in V for the attribute a in A. In the abstract syntax $\mathcal{A}Syn_{gMeasure}$, $@_{measure}$ is given as in Specification 9.27 to declare the base structure $\beta_{measure}$ of category *measure* as a set-theoretic tuple $<ty, va, [mod]>$, where (i) ty is the type of measure, (ii) va is the value of a measure, consisting mostly of a real number n and a unit u, and (iii) mod is an optional attribute that modifies the (unitized) value of a measure.

Assignment $@_{mLink}$ declares link structures λ_{mLink} of category *measureLink* as a quadruple $<\beta_c, M, \rho, [O]>$, where (i) β_c is a base structure of category c, (ii) M is a set of base structures $\beta_{measure}$ of category *measure*, (iii) ρ is the type of a relation over β_c and M, and (iv) optional element O is a set of optional attributes such as @trigger that determines the type of ρ or @scopes that specifies the scope of a quantifier over another quantifier

pFormat-Based Concrete Syntax

The concrete syntax $CSyn_{gMeasure}$ for general measurement adopts the pFormat of representing annotation structures that consist of base structures and link structures. For the representation of these annotation structures, the concrete syntax specifies in concrete terms for each particular language; for instance, for English, (i) the attribute assignment $@_{measure}$ of each of the

Table 9.1 *Categories, pForm tags, ID for general measurement*

Mia visited her aunt for [three months]$_{me1}$ in the summer of 2019.			
categories in $\mathcal{A}Syn_{gMeasure}$	pForm tags in $\mathcal{C}Syn_{gMeasure}$	ID prefixes	ID examples
measure	measure	me	me1
measureLink	mLink	mL	mL1

attributes for base category *measure*, tagged MEASURE, and (ii) the attribute assignment @$_{measureLink}$ of link category *measureLink*, tagged mLink.

The two categories *measure* and *measureLink* in $\mathcal{A}Syn_{gMeasure}$ are represented by their respective tags measure and mLink in the pForm-based concrete syntax, each with a unique ID prefix, as in Table 9.1.

The categorized ID-prefix for the tag measure is me, and that of mLink is mL. The ID mLN, where N is a natural number, may not be used to refer to a link structure unless it is necessary.

The attribute-value assignment @$_{measure}$ for category *measure* is given in Specification 9.45.

Specification 9.45 Assignment @$_{measure}$ for category *measure*
```
attributes = type, value, [modifier];
(* The square-bracketed attribute @modifier, is an optional attribute. *)
type = amount | count | distance | duration | frequency | height |
   repetition | width | weight | length | radius | angle | CDATA;
(* CDATA allows other possible values. *)
value = (n,u) | CDATA;
(* n is a real number such as 3, 3.5, or 1000 and u is a unit such as
hour, meter, occurrence or box. CDATA is something like near. *)
modifier = moreThan | almost | CDATA;
```

The values of the attribute @value in @$_{measure}$ are not restricted to real numbers. The attribute can have other types of values such as *near* for a distance, which fails to be expressed in exact arithmetic terms. The values of @unit also include nonscientific but conventionally accepted units such as *box* of apples, *head* of cattle, or *group* of boys.

Illustration of Base Structures $\beta_{measure}$
Annotation 9.46 shows how various types of *measure* are annotated.

Annotation 9.46 Various types of measure
a. Markables: John ran [100 meters]$_{me1, w3-4}$ in [less than a minute]$_{me2, w6-9}$ [10 times]$_{me3, w10-11}$.
b. Base structures:

```
measure(me1, w3-4, type="distance", value="100,meter")
measure(me2, w6-9, type="duration", value="1,minute"
  modifier="lessThan")
measure(me3, w10-11, type="repetition", value="10,occurrence")
```

Example 9.47 contains several expressions referring to measures. Each of them needs to be annotated for detailed quantitative measurement information.

Example 9.47   Sample data

[Karl Schmidt]$_{x1}$ will be 88$_{me1}$ soon. He went to Erlangen University Hospital for his general physical checkup. A nurse checked his weight, height, and blood pressure first. He [weighed over 88 kg]$_{me2}$, although he is only [168 cm tall]$_{me3}$. His blood pressure was recorded as [210 systolic (upper)]$_{me4}$ and [115 diastolic (lower)]$_{me5}$. A doctor immediately ordered him to stay at the hospital for [several intensive examinations]$_{me6}$.

The four occurrences of category *measure* in the sample data are given in Annotation 9.48.

Annotation 9.48   Sample data annotated

a. `measure(me1, s1w5-6, type="age", value="88,year")`

b. `measure(me2, s4w2-4, type="weight", value="88,kg", modifier="over")`

c. `measure(me3, s4w9-10, type="height", value="168,cm")`

d. `measure(me4, s5w7-9, type="bloodPressure,systolic", value="210")`

e. `measure(me5, s5w11-13, type="bloodPressure,diastolic", value="115")`

f. `measure(me6, s6w12-14, type="physicalExamination", value="several")`

Attribute-Value Assignment @$_{measureLink}$
for Category measureLink

The measure link, tagged mLink, relates the event of John's running to these measures, as in Annotation 9.49.

Annotation 9.49   Measure link

```
event(e1, w2, type="process", pred="run", tense="past")
mLink(mL1, figure="e1", ground="me1,me2,me3", relType="measures")
```

The measure link mL1 relates the event of John's running e1 to a set of three measures {me1,me2,me3}, as shown in Annotation 9.49.

The measure link (mLink), as generalized, relates not only an event but also any other sorts of entities to a set of measures. This is illustrated by Annotations 9.48 and 9.50 of Example 9.47.

Annotation 9.50   Generalized measure link

```
entity(x1, type="person", pred="Karl Schmidt", form="nam")
mLink(mL1, figure="x1", ground="me1,me2,me3,me4,me5,me6",
relType="measures")
```

The assignment @$_{mLink}$ for category *measureLink* is now specified as follows.

Specification 9.51   Assignment for category measureLink
```
attribute = figure, ground, relType, [trigger];
figure = βc;
  (* βc is a base structure of category c. *)
ground = Bmeasure;
  (* Bmeasure is a nonempty set B of base structures βmeasure of category
    measure.*)
relType = measures, counts, amounts;
trigger = CDATA;
```

The measure link (mLink) relates an object of any type to a measure, not only
a single measure but also a set of measures. It can, for instance, describe all
of the measurement features of a building: its height, width, area, number of
stories, and even the number of rooms.

The value *counts* for @relType applies to cases of counting: for example,
cases of counting boxes of apples, heads of cattle, the number of visiting New
York, or even the number of occurrences (repetitions) of an event (see Lee and
Bunt (2012)). Consider Example 9.52.

Example 9.52   Counting boxes

a. Markables: I ordered [8 boxes]$_{me1, w3-4}$ of [apples]$_{x1, w6}$ for the winter.
b. Annotation:
```
entity(x1, w6, type="count", pred="apple", plurality="yes")
measure(me1, w3-4, type="count", value="8,box")
mLink(mL1, figure="x1", ground="me1", relType="counts")
```

Here is another example of counting.

Example 9.53   Counting event occurrences

a. Markables: John visited Pisa [five times]$_{w4-5}$.
b. Annotation:
```
event(e1, w2, type="transition", pred="visit", tense="past")
measure(me1, w4-5, type="repetition", value="5,occurrence")
mLink(mL1, figure="e1", ground="me1", relType="counts")
```
c. Semantic representation:

$\sigma(e_1) := \{e_1\}[visit(e_1) \wedge past(e_1)]$

$\sigma(me_1) := \{v_1\}[v_1=(5, occurrence)]$

$\sigma(mL1) := \{e_1, v_1\}[\kappa(e_1)=v_1 \oplus [\sigma(e_1), \sigma(me_1)]]$

$\sigma(mL1)$

$:= \exists\{e_1, v_1\}$

$[\kappa(e_1)=v_1 \wedge [visit(e_1) \wedge past(e_1)] \wedge v_1=(5, occurrence)]$

$:= \exists e_1$

$[visit(e_1) \wedge past(e_1) \wedge \kappa(e_1)=(5, occurrence)]$

Here, κ is a counting function that maps the number of objects or the occurrences of an event to a value, which is a pair of a natural number, sometimes

followed by a counting unit. The number of occurrences of an event, for instance, may be represented simply by $\kappa(e_1)=5$ or $\kappa(e_1)=(5,occurrence)$.

Here is an example of measuring time amounts.

Example 9.54 Measuring time amounts

a. Makrable: John ran for *five hours*$_{me1,w4-5}$.

b. Annotation:
```
event(e1, w2, type="process", pred="run", tense="past")
measure(me1, w4-5, type="amount", value="5,hour")
mLink(mL1, figure="e1", ground="me1", relType="amounts")
```

c. Semantic representation:

$\sigma(e_1) := \{e_1\}[run(e_1) \wedge past(e_1)]$

$\sigma(me_1) := \{v_1\}[v_1=(5,hour)]$

$\sigma(mL1) := \{e_1,v_1\}[\alpha(e_1)=v_1 \oplus [\sigma(e_1),\sigma(me_1)]]$

$\sigma(mL1)$

$:= \exists\{e_1,v_1\}$

$\quad [\alpha(e_1)=v_1 \wedge [run(e_1) \wedge past(e_1)] \wedge v_1=(5,hour)]$

$:= \exists e_1$

$\quad [visit(e_1) \wedge past(e_1) \wedge \alpha(e_1)=(5,hour)]$

Here, α is an amount function that maps the quantity of time or some other quantitatively measurable objects to a value, for example, the amount of time consumed by the occurrence of an event.

Semantics of Measure

Semantic Type of Measure According to the extended type theory of ABS, the type of *measure* is defined as follows.

Specification 9.55 Measure as a basic semantic type

a. Measures are of basic semantic type m.

b. Measure descriptors are of functional semantic type $m \to t$.

Measures of basic semantic type m are represented by the variables v, v_1, etc. Measure types such as distance, duration, weight, or various dimensions of length are treated as measure descriptors.

Consider Example 9.56.

Example 9.56 Semantics of measure

a. Markable: Karl Schmidt weighed *more than 85 kg*$_{me1,w4-7}$.

b. Annotation:
```
measure(me1, w4-7, type="weight", value="85,kg", modifier="greaterThan")
```

c. Semantics:

$\exists v[weight(v) \wedge v \geq (85,kg)]$,

where $weight$ is a measure descriptor of semantic type $m \to t$ and v, a variable of type m.

The value $@_{measure:me1}(ty)$ of the attribute ty (type) with respect to the measure structure me1 is "weight". The semantic form $\sigma(@_{measure}(ty))$ is also represented as weight here. It is treated as a *measure descriptor* of functional semantic type $m \to t$, while v is a variable of semantic type m. It is a sort of a predicate having a variable v as its argument just as an event descriptor run of semantic type $v \to t$ has a variable e of type v as its argument: $run_{v \to t}(e_v)$.[9]

Preliminary Conventions for Semantic Rules Some preliminary conventions are listed for the formulation of semantic rules in the representation language of ABSr, as in Specifications 9.57 and 9.59.

Specification 9.57 Convention 1: Semantic form σ of annotation structures
For any well-formed base or link structures s or their instantiations s_i in an abstract syntax $\mathcal{A}Syn$, $\sigma(s)$ and $\sigma(s_i)$ are well-formed semantic forms both of semantic type t, standing for *truth*.

Specification 9.58 Instantiation of well-formed base or link structures
For any s_i, which is a well-formed base or link structure s with an identifier i, s_i is an instantiation of s if all of its attributes are properly assigned a value by an associated assignment $@_i$.

Each semantic representation s_i may adopt a different format of representation while retaining identical semantic content. Different representations of s_i are thus logically or semantically equivalent to each other. For example, the semantic form $\sigma(\beta_{measure})$ of a base structure of category   *measure* or its instantiation $\sigma(\beta_{measure:i})$ are well-formed semantic forms both of semantic type t. The $\beta_{measure}$, specified as a tuple $<ty, va, mod>$, is a well-formed base structure of category *measure* conforming to the abstract syntax $\mathcal{A}Syn_{gMeasure}$; $\sigma(\beta_{measure:i})$ is also a well-formed semantic form if and only if $\beta_{measure:i}$ is a tuple $<i, ty:weight, va:(85, kg), mod:greaterThan>$. This condition conforms to the abstract specification of $\beta_{measure}$ according to $\mathcal{A}Syn_{gMeasure}$.

Specification 9.59 Convention 2: Semantic value of attribute-value pairs
For any assignment $@_c$ of category c that specifies a base structure β_c of category c as a set-theoretic tuple S consisting of possible attributes associated with it, namely β_c, and for any element (attribute) a in S, $\sigma(a)=@_c(a)$.

---

[9] Unfortunately, v is used as the type of eventualities and the variable of measures, just as e is used as the type of individual objects (entities) and also as a variable of eventualities.

For example, for the base structure $\beta_{measure}$ that is specified by $@_{measure}$ as $S=<ty,va,mod>$, $\sigma(@_{measure}(ty))$ is a semantic object denoted by the value of the attribute $@_{measure}$. If such a base structure $\beta_{measure}$ is instantiated as $\beta_{measure:me1}$ such that it is represented with an identifier $me1$ as $<me1,ty:weight,va:(85,kg),mod:moreThan>$, then $\sigma(@_{measure:me1}(ty))=$ "weight" and the semantic value $weight$ is a measure descriptor of semantic type $m \to t$.

Semantic Rules for $\beta_{measure}$ With these conventions of interpretation, $Sem_{gMeasure}$ of general measure, which is based on $\mathcal{A}Syn_{gMeasure}$ of general measure in exTimeML, licenses a set of rules formulated as in Specification 9.60, to apply to the derivation of semantic forms $\sigma(\alpha_i)$ associated with all of the annotation structures generated by $Syn_{gMeasure}$ in general.

Specification 9.60   Semantic rules for measures

a. *Semantic rule 1* for $\beta_{measure}=<ty,va>$:
$\sigma(\beta_{measure}) \Rightarrow \{v\}[\sigma(@_{measure}(ty))(v) \land v=\sigma(@_{measure}(va))]$,
where v is a variable of semantic type m for measure.

b. *Semantic rule 2* for $\beta_{measure}=<ty,va,mod>$:
$\sigma(\beta_{measure}) \Rightarrow \{v\}[\sigma(@_{measure}(ty))(v) \land \sigma(@_{measure}(mod))$
$(v,\sigma(@_{measure}(va)))]$,
where $\sigma\,@_{measure}(mod)$ is a relation between the measure value variable v and a measure value given.

Each base structure $\beta_{measure}$ of category *measure* is maximally a triple $<ty,va,mod>$, where ty is a type, va a value, and mod a modifier of a measure value va, which is often a pair (n,u) of a real number n and a unit u.

Interpretation of Modifiers The attribute $@mod$ stands for *modifier*, which modifies not just measure values such as real numbers but overall measure values. For example, the measure expression *taller than 2 meters* means that the height is some measure v and that the measure v is greater than the measure of 2 meters. Example 9.61 shows the intended interpretation of modified measures.

Example 9.61   Interpretation of modified measures

a. Markables: taller than 2 meters.
b. Base structure:
```
measure(me1, type="height", value="2,meter", modifier="greaterThan")
```
c. Semantic form:
$\sigma(\text{me1}) := \exists v_1[height(v_1) \land v_1 \geq (2,meters)]$

The intended interpretation of modified measures is simply represented as $v \geq (x, unit)$, although it may be represented as $[v=(x, unit) \land v \geq x]$ by applying modifiers to the real numbers x in $\mathcal{R}$.

The third semantic rule for the measure link can be formulated as in Specification 9.62.

Specification 9.62 Semantic rule 3 for measure link

$\lambda_{measureLink} :=$ a tuple $<R_{measures}(\beta_c, B_{measure})>$ such that

$\sigma(\lambda_{measureLink})$

$\Rightarrow [\sigma(R_{measures}) \oplus [\sigma(\beta_c) \oplus \sigma(E_{measure})]]$

$\Rightarrow [measures(var_{ci}, var_{mei}) \oplus [\sigma(\beta_{c:ci}) \oplus \sigma(B_{measure:mei})]]$

(* instantiated case *)

Derivation of Semantic Forms As introduced in Chapter 6, ABS applies to the semantics of measure. It converts each of the base or link structures to a semantic form in order to compositionally derive the overall semantic form of an annotation structure.

For illustration, consider Annotation 9.63b. It represents an instantiated annotation structure of category *general measure*, based on the pFormat-based concrete syntax of eXTimeML.

Annotation 9.63 General measure

a. Markables:

Mia taught$_{e1, w2}$ for [more than 20 hours]$_{me1, w4-7}$ last month$_{t1, w8-9}$.

b. Annotation:

```
event(e1, w2, pred="teach", tense="past")
measure(me1, w4-7, type="tAmount", value="20,hour",
  modifier="moreThan")
timex3(t1, w8-9, type="date", value="XXXX-03")
mLink(figure="e1", ground="me1", relType="amounts")
tLink(figure="e1", ground="t1", relType="isIncluded")
```

In Annotation 9.63b, the measure link (`mLink`) relates the event e1 of Mia's teaching to the measure me1, tagging the type of their relation as `"amounts"`. Based on this link, ABS licenses the derivation of semantic forms, as in Semantics 9.64.

Semantics 9.64 Derivation of semantic forms

a. $\sigma(\text{e1}) := \{e_1\}[teach(e_1) \land past(e_1)]$

b. $\sigma(\text{me1}) := \{v_1\}[tAmount(v_1) \land v_1 \geq (20, hour)]$

c. $\sigma(\text{t1}) := \{t_2\}[month(t_1, \text{March})]$

d. $\sigma(\text{mLink})$

$:= \{e_1, v_1\}[\alpha(e_1) = v_1 \oplus [\sigma(e_1) \oplus \sigma(me_1)]]$

$:= \{e_1, v_1\}[\alpha(e_1) = v_1 \land [teach(e_1) \land past(e_1) \land tAmount(v_1) \land v_1 \geq (20, hour)]]$

e. $\sigma(\text{tLink}) := \{e_1, t_1\}[\tau(e_1) \subseteq t_1]$

f. Semantic form of the whole annotation structure:

$\exists\{e_1, v_1, t_1\}$

$[\alpha(e_1) = v_1 \wedge [teach(e_1) \wedge past(e_1)] \wedge$

$[tAmount(v_1) \wedge v_1 \geq (20, hour)] \wedge$

$month(t_1, March) \wedge \tau(e_1) \subseteq (t_1)]$

The function α maps an event to its time amount, which is the cumulative quantity of intervals in which the event occurs.

Frequencies Frequencies can involve temporal measures, as in Annotation 9.65 and Semantics 9.66.

Annotation 9.65   Frequencies annotated

a. Markables: John runs$_{e1, w2}$ [three times]$_{me1, w3-4}$ a$_{q1, w5}$ week$_{t1, 6}$.

b. Base structures:
```
event(e1, w2, type="process", pred="run")
measure(me1, w3-4, type="counts", value="3,occurrence")
qEntity(q1, w5, type="every", domain="t1")
timex3(t1, w6, type="week", value="P1W")
```

c. Link structures:
```
mLink(mL1, figure="e1", ground="me1", relType="counts")
qLink(qL1, figure="t1", ground="e1", relType="every")
```

Semantics 9.66 is based on Annotation 9.65.

Semantics 9.66   Semantic forms of frequencies

a. $\sigma(\text{e1}) := [process(e_1) \wedge run(e_1)]$

$\sigma(\text{me1}) := [v_1 = (3, occurrence)]$

$\sigma(\text{mL1})$

$:= [\kappa(e_1) = v_1 \oplus [\sigma(\text{e1}), \sigma(\text{me1})]$

$:= [\kappa(e_1) = v_1 \oplus [[process(e_1) \wedge run(e_1)] \wedge [v_1 = (3, occurrence)]]]$

b. $\sigma(\text{q1}) := \forall t_1$

$\sigma(\text{t1}) := \{t_1\}[week(t_1) \wedge duration(t_1) = (1, week)]$

$\sigma(\text{qL1})$

$:= \sigma(\text{q1}) \oslash^{gq} [\sigma(\text{t1}), \sigma(\text{mL1}), scopes(t_1, \{e_1, v_1\})]$

$:= \forall t_1 [[\sigma(\text{t1}) \rightarrow \sigma(\text{mL1})], scopes(t_1, \{e_1, v_1\})]$

$:= \forall t_1 \exists\{e_1, v_1\}$

$[[week(t_1) \wedge duration(t_1) = (1, week)]$

$\rightarrow [process(e_1) \wedge run(e_1) \wedge k(e_1) = v_1 \wedge v_1 = (3, occurrence)]]$

Counting Function κ

The counting function κ differs from the measuring function μ and also from the amount function α. The length of time can be measured, whereas the number of times such as days or hours is counted. For example, you can count with your fingers, but you need a normalized measuring stick to measure the length of your index finger. The number of apples can be counted, but not measured, although their weights can be measured but not counted. So the notion of counting differs from that of measure. In contrast, the quantity (duration) of a time interval is *measured* with the function μ, which maps a time interval to its length. The cumulative amount of time is obtained by the function $\alpha(e)$ that maps an event e to the cumulative amount of time intervals to which the event is anchored. Both κ and α apply to events, but their outputs are different: $\kappa(e)$ yields the number of occurrences of e, whereas α yields the cumulative amount of time intervals to which e is anchored.

Output of Linking

The output of a linking is a base structure, which is augmented with additional information, as discussed in Section 9.2.2. Another linking may apply to this output. Consider Example 9.67.

Example 9.67 Recursive application of links

a. Markables: Mia$_{x1,w1}$ taught$_{e1,w2}$ for [more than 20 hours]$_{me1,w4-7}$ [last month]$_{t1,w8-9}$.

b. Base structures:
```
entity(x1, w1, type="person", pred="Mia", form="name")
event(e1, w2, type="process", pred="teach", tense="past")
measure(me1, w4-7, type="amount", value="20,hours",
    modifier="moreThan")
timex3(t1, w8-9, type="date", value="2020-10")
```

c. Semantic role link:
```
srLink(srL1, event="e1", participants="x1", semRole="agent")
```
Output:
$[\beta_{event:e1} \cup \beta_{entity:x1}] \cup$ agent$=$"#x1"]
```
event(%e1, w2, type="process", pred="teach", tense="past",
    agent="x1")
```

d. Measure link:
```
mLink(mL1, event="%e1", measure="me1", referencePt="t1",
    relType="amount")
event(%%e1, w2, type="process", pred="teach", tense="past",
    agent="x1", measure="me1")
```

e. Temporal link:
```
tLink(tL1, event="%%e1", time="t1", isIncluded)
```

It is now possible to derive the semantic form of the final augmented base structure (e1).

Semantics 9.68 Semantic forms of base structures

a. $\sigma(\text{x1}) := [person(x_1) \wedge named(x_1, Mia)]$

b. $\sigma(\text{e1}) := [process(e_1) \wedge teach(e_1) \wedge past(e_1)]$

c. $\sigma(\text{me1}) := [\alpha(e_1, t_1) \geq (20, hour)]$

d. $\sigma(\text{t1}) := [year(t_1, 2020) \wedge month(t_1, October)]$

The *amount function* α maps an eventuality to the (possibly cumulative) amount of time that the eventuality has taken up in reference to a time interval.

Semantics 9.69   Semantic form of the augmented base structure

$$\exists\{e_1, x_1, t_1\}$$
$$[[[process(e_1) \wedge teach(e_1) \wedge past(e_1)]$$
$$\wedge \, [person(x_1) \wedge named(x_1, Mia)]$$
$$\wedge \, agent(e_1, x_1)]$$
$$\wedge \, [\alpha(e_1, t_1) \geq (20, hour)]$$
$$\wedge \, [[year(t_1, 2020) \wedge month(t_1, October)]$$
$$\wedge \, \tau(e_1) \subseteq t_1]]$$

The semantic form in Semantics 9.69 can also be represented in DRS (Kamp and Reyle, 1993).

Semantics 9.70   DRS

e, x, t
$process(e), teach(e), past(e)$
$person(x), named(x, Mia)$
$agent(e, x)$
$\alpha(e, t) \geq (20, hour)$
$year(t, 2020), month(t, October)$
$\tau(e) \subseteq t$

Semantics 9.69 and Semantics 9.70 DRSs both have exactly the same interpretation: the duration of Mia's teaching in October, 2020, amounted to be more than 20 hours.

9.5 Temporal Quantification

9.5.1 Generalizing Temporal Quantification

ISO-TimeML (ISO, 2012b) annotates quantifier expressions like *every day* or *daily* as part of temporal expressions <TIMEX3>.

Annotation 9.71   Quantification in ISO-TimeML

a. Markables: John walks$_{w2}$ his dog [every day]$_{t1, w5-6}$.

b. Annotation:

```
<isoTimeML>
<EVENT xml:id="e1" target="w2" pred="WALK"/>
<TIMEX3 xml:id="t1" target="w5-6" type="SET" value="1D"
```

```
quant="EVERY" scopes="e1"/>
<TLINK eventID="e1" relatedToTime="t1" relType="isINCLUDED"/>
</isoTimeML>
```

The temporal adverb *daily* is also annotated in the same way.

It is argued that the current treatment of quantified temporal expressions in ISO-TimeML lacks generalization, failing to annotate them as part of general quantification. Following Bunt (2020a,b, 2017, 2018, 2019) and a newly proposed ISO standard on quantification ISO/CD 24617-12 quantification (ISO, 2022a), eXTimeML treats the annotation of *quantified temporal* expressions just like other quantified expressions. This simplifies the specification of annotating temporal expressions, tagged TIMEX3, by removing all of the attributes, such as freq and quant, that are associated with quantification in it from ISO-TimeML to the specification of the domain of general quantification in eXTimeML.

9.5.2 Quantifiers in Natural Language

Tripartite Structure of Quantification

In natural language, quantifiers like *every, all*, or *some* are accompanied by nominal expressions like *dog* and *soldier* or their plural forms *dogs* and *soldiers* even with a determiner like *the* as in *all the soldiers* or *all of the soldiers*.

Example 9.72 *Universal quantifiers*
a. Every dog barks.
b. All the soldiers surrendered.
c. All of the soldiers were starving to death.

In formal semantics, each of these nominal expressions is understood as denoting a set of entities, which is characterized by the property as described. The noun *dog*, for instance, denotes a set of entities that are characterized by the canine property. Over such sets of entities, quantification applies: for example, *every dog* refers to each of the members of the *dog*-set. We call such a set as a *dog*-set a *domain* or *domain restrictor* over which a quantifier like *every* applies. In Montague's higher-order semantics, the denotation of *every dog* is represented as in Semantics 9.73.

Semantics 9.73 Denotation of *every dog*
a. every dog $\Rightarrow \lambda P \forall x [dog(x) \rightarrow P(x)]$
b. barks $\Rightarrow bark(x)$
c. Every dog barks $\Rightarrow \forall x [dog(x) \rightarrow bark(x)]_t$
d. Interpretation:
   $[\![dog]\!] \subseteq [\![bark]\!]$

The quantifier $\forall x$ in Semantics 9.73a,c is functioning like a sentential operator, while binding the free occurrences of the variable x in the formula of semantic type t, namely $[dog(x) \to P(x)]$. The whole form with the λP binding the second-order variable P is interpreted as denoting a set of properties of every individual *dog*. The property of being a *dog* in the antecedent of a conditional is understood to be the *restrictor* of quantification, for it restricts the domain which the universal quantifier $\forall x$ ranges over.

Related to the domain of a quantifier, there is the *nuclear scope*, represented as an open formula like $P(x)$ with free occurrences of a variable, say x, that will be bound by the quantifier. The universally quantified formula is then interpreted as saying that the domain set is a subset of the set denoted by the nuclear scope like $[\![dog]\!] \subseteq [\![bark]\!]$ as in Semantics 9.73d.

Following Partee (1995) and many others (see, for instance, van Benthem (1986) and Cooper (1987)), eXTimeML assumes the tripartite structure of quantification.

Specification 9.74   Quantification
[i] Operator – [ii] Restrictor – [iii] Nuclear scope

Given a quantified sentence like *Every dog barks*, quantifiers like *every* are *operators*, domains like *man* are *restrictors*, and predicates like *barks* are *nuclear scopes*. This tripartite structure is represented in the formulation of universal quantification in ABS, as in Specification 9.75a. The quantifier $every(x)$ of a functional semantic type $t \to t$ is treated as a *binary* sentential operator like conjunction $\wedge$ or implication $\to$ in predicate logic. It thus has a pair of formulas: One of them is a restrictor (domain) and the other is a nuclear scope. The universal quantifier $every(x)_{t \to t}$ applies to the pair as an operator, deriving an implicative ($\to$) form by binding it.

Specification 9.75   Universal quantification in ABS
a. Distributive implicative ($\to$) rule for universal quantification:
   $$every(x)_{t \to t} \ \oslash^{uq} [\sigma(x)_t, \sigma(e,x)_t]$$
   $$\Rightarrow \forall(x)[\sigma(x) \to \sigma(e,x)]_t$$
b. Illustration:
   $$every(x)_{t \to t} \ \oslash^{uq} <[dog(x)_t], [bark(e,x)_t]>$$
   $$:= \forall x[dog(x) \to bark(e,x)]_t$$

Similarly, we can treat existential quantification. Here is an illustration.

Example 9.76   Existential quantification in ABS
a. Two thousand soldiers died.

b. Distributive conjunctive ($\wedge$) rule for existential quantification:
$2000(x)_{t \to t} \quad \oslash^{eq} [\sigma(x)_t, \sigma(e,x)_t]$
$\Rightarrow \exists 2000x[\sigma(x) \wedge \sigma(e,x)]_t$

c. Logical form:
$2000(x)_{t \to t} \quad \oslash^{eq} [[soldier(x)_t \wedge plural(x)_t], die(e,x)_t]$
$:= \exists 2000x[[soldier(x) \wedge plural(x)] \wedge [die(e,x) \wedge past(e)]]_t$

So ABS interprets the logical form in Example 9.76c as being equivalent to Semantics 9.77.

Semantics 9.77
$\exists X[|X|{=}2000 \wedge soldier^{plural}(X) \wedge \forall x[x \in X \to [die(e,x) \wedge past(e)]]]$

How to Annotate Quantified Expressions

Being an annotation-based semantics, ABS requires its input data to be annotated before it is submitted to semantics; eXTimeML provides ways of annotating such data including temporally quantified expressions as well as quantified expressions in general. Partially following Bunt (2020a,b), it specifies how to annotate quantified expressions such as *every day* as well as other quantified expressions in general. For this, eXTimeML introduces a category *quantified entity*, named *qEntity* in short, that also treats quantified temporal entities but as a subcategory of quantified entities.

Specification of Assignment @$_{qEntity}$ for Quantitative Entities For the newly added category, named *qEntity*, of base structures, its attribute-value assignment @$_{qEntity}$ is specified as in Specification 9.78.

Specification 9.78 Assignment @$_{qEntity}$ for quantified entity
```
attributes = type, domain, [individuation];
type = CDATA;
   (* Generalized quantifiers such as every, all, some, two *)
domain = IDREF;
   (* refers to another base structure that represents a set of entities
   over which a quantifier applies *)
individuation = individual | collective;
```

The attribute @type refers to the *involvement* of a quantified entity in its domain. The attribute @domain restricts the range of applications for each quantifier. Given an example *all the soldiers* denoting a quantified entity, the plural noun *soldiers* denotes the domain of the quantifier *all*; *qEntity* is a complex category, referring to a base structure of category *entity*, as specified in Specification 9.79. The attribute @individuation specifies the distributivity of involved objects (i.e., soldiers) either as individuals or a collective group.

Domains of Quantification To annotate nouns, which serve as domains of a quantifier, eXTimeML introduces a category *entity* that consists of all sorts of entities.

Assignment $@_{entity}$ then specifies, as in Specification 9.79, what ranges of values are possible for the attributes associated with the set-theoretic structure of β_{entity}.

Specification 9.79 Assignment $@_{entity}$ for entities in general
```
attributes = [type], pred, [form], [plurality], [determinacy];
type = count | nonCount;
   (* differentiates count nouns from abstract or mass nouns *)
pred = CDATA;
   (* lexical form that represents the predicative content *)
form = nam | nom;
   (*"nam" is for proper names; "nom" is for nominals such as soldiers.*)
plurality = yes | singular | dual ;
   (* differentiates singulars from plurals or duals *)
determinacy = yes;
   (* Default is "no". *)
```

Here are some illustrations.

Example 9.80 Existential quantification

a. Data: *Some dogs* do not bark.
b. Annotation:
```
qEntity(q1, w1, type="some", domain="#x1")
entity(x1, w2, type="count", pred="dog", plurality="yes")
event(e1, w3-5, type="process", pred="bark", tense="present"
  polarity="neg")
```
c. Semantics:
$$\exists x_1[[dog(x_1) \wedge plural(x_1)] \wedge \neg[bark(e_1) \wedge agent(e_1, x_1)]]$$

Example 9.81 Universal quantification

a. Data: *All the soldiers* surrendered.
b. Annotation:
```
qEntity(q1, w1, type="all", domain="x1", individuation="group")
entity(x1, w2-3, type="count", pred="soldier", plurality="yes",
  determinacy="yes")
event(e1, w4, type="process", pred="surrender", tense="past")
```
c. Semantic form:
$$\forall x_1^* \exists e_1[[soldier^{plural}(x_1^*) \wedge determinate(x_1)] \rightarrow [surrender(e_1, x_1^*) \wedge past(e_1)]]$$

The variable x_1^* ranges over objects of group type $e \rightarrow t$. Example 9.81 is interpreted as saying that all the soldiers *as a group* surrendered. Instead of introducing the superscripted variables like x^* and x^{plural}, it may be possible to represent them as $group(x)$ and $plural(x)$. This is then interpreted as stating that x is a variable ranging over groups consisting of more than one entity. The predicate *determinate* is defined as a logical predicate denoting a *unique set* of entities.

Extending the Domain of Quantification
to Temporal Entities

In order to extend the domain of quantification to temporal entities, the abstract syntax $\mathcal{A}Syn_{eXTimeML}$ of eXTimeML introduces a category *temporal entity* as a subcategory of general category *entity*. It then defines base structures $\beta_{tEntity}$ of category *temporalEntity*, or *tEntity* in short, as an 8-tuple $<ty, \{pr, va\}, [at], [st], [en], [fu], [tf]>$, as in Specification 9.23. The pFormat-based concrete syntax then makes the elements of the tuple concrete by naming each of them with a range of possible values for base structures $\beta_{tEntity}$ of category *temporal entity*, tagged TIMEX3.

Specification of Assignment $@_{tEntity}$ The attribute-value assignment for category *tEntity*, tagged TIMEX3 in the concrete syntax, is specified as follows.

Specification 9.82 Assignment $@_{tEntity}$ for temporal entities

```
attributes = type, {pred, value}, [start], [end], [anchorTime],
  [temporalFunction], [functionInDocument];
type = date | time | timeInterval;
pred = CDATA;
  (* predicative content. @pred is specified if @value is not. *)
value = CDATA;
  (*Values of @value are represented according to ISO 8601-1 (2019)
    if @pred is not assigned a value.*)
start = IDREF;
  (* optionally refers to the begin-point or the initial subinterval
    of a time interval *)
end = IDREF;
  (* optionally refers to the endpoint or the final subinterval of
    a time interval *)
anchorTime = IDREF;
  (* optionally specifies the unspecified boundaries of an interval or
    the specific date or time of a deictic time such as last year
    or yesterday *)
temporalFunction = true | false;
  (* optionally used to calculate specific times for deontic (indexical)
    times or anchoring times *)
functionInDocument = creationTime | publicationTime | CDATA;
```

The value *date* for the attribute @type refers to a Gregorian calendar year, months, and/or day. The value *time* refers to a time of the day including parts of a day such as *morning, afternoon, evening*. The representation of calendar dates and clock times follows ISO 8601-1 (ISO, 2019a) and ISO 8601-2 (ISO, 2019b).

Time Interval and Anchor Time The value *timeInterval* of @type refers to a time span, such as one denoted by *from Monday to Friday* or decides on the start and end of a time span. A time interval may consist of (i) its start and end, (ii) a duration and its start, or (iii) a start and its duration. These intervals are represented as in Specification 9.83, according to ISO 8601-1 (ISO, 2019a).

Specification 9.83   Time intervals

a. June through August: `XXXX-06/XXXX-08`
b. two weeks before Christmas: `P2W/XXXX-12-25`
c. two months after the first of January: `XXXX-01-01/P2M`

The attribute @anchorTime refers to a point in a time interval at which an event occurs. The attribute @temporalFunction may be used to decide on the anchorTime. Consider Example 9.84, taken from Pustejovsky et al. (2017, example 18).

Example 9.84   Anchor time, a point in a time interval

a. The course begins *two weeks* from *today*.
b. John *finished* his book *three years* before its *publication*.

The time interval *two weeks* in Example 9.84a is anchored to the time *today*: The start of the interval is the same as the time *today*, while the course begins at the end of that interval. The time interval *three years* in Example 9.84b, in contrast, is anchored to the *publication* time, the time that the book was published: The end of the three-year time interval is identical to the publication time. The start of the interval, on the other hand, is where the event of *finishing* the book took place.

The attribute @functionInDocument provides a metavalue for a document, by specifying its data creation time (`DCT`), release time, or revision time, etc.

Temporal Relators

Temporal relators of category *tRelator*, such as *before*, *after*, or *from*, triggers @temporalFunction as well as the temporal link, named `tLink` in the concrete syntax. Assignment @*tRelator* is given in Specification 9.85.

Specification 9.85   Assignment @*tRelator* for temporal relations:

```
attributes = identifier, type, [subtype], pred;
identifier = "tr" followed by a positive integer;
type = anchoring | ordering | metric | bounding | orienting;
  (* See chapter 10 for further details *);
subtype = amount | length | initial | mid | terminal | forward |
  backward;
pred = CDATA;
  (* lexical form that denotes the relation indicated *)
```

There are five major types of temporal relators: *anchoring, ordering, metric, bounding,* and *orienting.* Then the attribute @subtype specifies their subtypes.

Classification 9.86   Subtypes of the types of temporal relators

a. metric: *amount, length,* or *none*

b. bounding: *initial, mid,* or *terminal*

c. orienting: either *forward* or *backward*

In the pFormat-based concrete syntax of eXTimeML as well as in ISO-TimeML, these relators are tagged *tRelator* with the categorized ID-prefix $\tt tr$. The type of each temporal relator and its subtype may be combined into a single attribute-value specification, as follows.

Specification 9.87   Combined type and subtype specifications
```
type = anchoring | ordering | metric | amount | length | iBounding |
    mBounding | tBounding | fOrienting | bOrienting | CDATA
```

Here is an illustration.

Example 9.88   Subtyping

a. I stayed in Milwaukee in$_{anchoring}$ the summer of 1960$_{date}$.

b. Mia stayed in New York for$_{metric}$ 3 months$_{length}$ from$_{iBounding}$ June$_{date}$ through$_{mBounding}$ July$_{date}$ to$_{tBounding}$ August$_{date}$ in$_{anchoring}$ the summer of 2015$_{date}$.

Here are further illustrations.

Example 9.89   Additional illustrations

a. I woke up at$_{s1}$ [five thirty]$_{t1}$.
```
tRelator(tr1, w4, type="anchoring", pred="at")
timex3(t1, w5-7, type="time", value="T05:30")
```

b. Pope Francis was born on [December 17, 1936]$_{t1}$.
```
tRelator(tr1, w5, type="anchoring", pred="on")
timex3(t1, w6-8, type="date", value="1936-12-17")
```

c. $\emptyset_{t1}$ from$_{s1:w1}$ June$_{t2:w2}$ to$_{s2:w3}$ August$_{t3:w4}$.
```
timex3(t1, type="tInterval", value="P3M", start="t2", end="t3",
    temporalFunction="true")
tRelator(tr1, w1, type="bounding", subtype="initial", pred="from")
timex3(t2, w2, type="date", value="XXXX-06")
tRelator(tr2, w3, type="bounding", subtype="terminal", pred="to")
timex3(t3, w4, type="date", value="XXXX-08")
```

The representation of dates, times, and time intervals follows ISO 8601-1 (ISO, 2019a) and ISO 8601-2 (ISO, 2019b). These ISO standards present normalized ways of representing dates and times for technological applications. The representation of the hour *five thirty in the morning* is, for instance, represented as `XXXX-XX-XXT05:30` and the length (duration) of 3 months is represented as `P3M`, as in Example 9.89.

Representing Complex Temporal Entities

There are different ways of representing complex temporal entities involving time intervals. Consider Annotation 9.90.

Annotation 9.90   Complex temporal entities

a. Markables: Mia visited [New York] $\emptyset_{t1}$ from [[the beginning of June]$_{t2,w5-8}$ to [the end of August]$_{t3,w10-13}]_{t1}$.

b. Simple annotation:
```
timeX3(t1, w5-8,w10-13, type="tInterval",
  value="XXXX-06-01/XXXX-08-31")
```

c. Detailed annotation:
```
timeX3(t1, w5-8,w10-13, type="tInterval", value="P3M",
  start="XXXX-06-01", end="XXXX-08-31", temporalFunction="true")
```

d. Complex annotation:
```
timeX3(t1, type="tInterval", value="me1", start="#t2",
  end="#t3", temporalFunction="true")
timeX3(t2, w5-8, type="date", value="XXXX-06-01")
timeX3(t3, w10-13, type="date", value="XXXX-08-31")
measure(me1, type="tDistance", value="3,month")
```

Annotation 9.90b is the simplest representation of a time interval that conforms to ISO 8601-1 (ISO, 2019a). Annotation 9.90c carries more detailed and explicit information about the start and end of a time interval as well as its length, but carries the same amount of information as Annotation 9.90d. Annotation 9.90d presents a complex representation with the length (duration) of a time interval and the two boundaries of the visit specified. Based on these boundaries, @temporalFunction calculates the length of Mia's visit or the temporal distance from the start of her visit to its end; eXTimeML prefers Annotation 9.90d because it captures the semantic content conveyed by the annotation fragment in Annotation 9.90a.

From Annotation 9.90d, we can derive the forms in Semantics 9.91.

Semantics 9.91   Semantic forms

a. Base annotation:

Mia visited$_{e1,w2}$ [New York] $\emptyset_{t1}$ from [[the beginning of June]$_{t2,w5-8}$ to [the end of August]$_{t3,w10-13}$]

b. Semantic form:

$\exists\{e_1, t_1, t_2, t_3\}$
$[visit(e_1) \wedge agent(e_1, Mia) \wedge theme(e_1, NewYork) \wedge$
$\tau(e_1) \subseteq t_1 \wedge$
$interval(t_1) \wedge \mu(t_1)=(3, month) \wedge$
$starts(t_1, t_2) \wedge month(t_2, June) \wedge day(t_2, 01) \wedge$
$ends(t_1, t_3) \wedge month(t_3, August) \wedge day(t_3, 31)]$

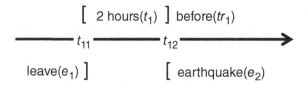

Figure 9.2 Anchored time interval (duration)
(Refer to Figure 8.4 in this book.)

Consider another example.

Annotation 9.92   Anchor point

a. Markables: We $\text{left}_{e1,w2}$ Kathmandu [2 $\text{hours}]_{t1,w4-5}$ $\text{before}_{tr1,w6}$ the $\text{earthquake}_{e2,w7-8}$.

b. Base structures:
```
event(e1, w2, type="transition", pred="leave", tense="past")
timex3(t1, w4-5, type="tInterval", value="P2H", start="#t11",
  end="#12")
timex3(t11, type="time", value="TXX", temporalFunction="true")
timex3(t12, type="time", value="TXX", temporalFunction="true")
tRelator(tr1, w6, type="bOrienting", pred="before")
event(e2, w7-8, type="process", pred="earthquake")
```

c. Link structures:
```
tLink(tL1, t11, t1, starts)
tLink(tL2, t12, t1, ends)
tLink(tL3, t11, e1, simultaneous)
tLink(tL4, t12, e2, simultaneous)
```

The time interval such as one referred to by *2 hours* with a trigger like *before* is called *anchored duration* (Pustejovsky et al., 2017, p. 36), anchored to a time or the occurrence time of an event. The interval of 2 hours mentioned here is anchored to the occurrence time of the *earthquake*. This anchoring relation can be depicted by Figure 9.2.

The end t_{12} of the time interval *2 hours* t_1 is anchored to the occurrence start time of the event of *earthquake*(e_2), while the event *leave*(e_1) is anchored to the start t_{11} of the same interval.

Quantification Link (qLink)

For quantification, eXTimeML introduces a link of category qLink, with its attributes specified as follows.

Specification 9.93   Assignment @$_{qLink}$ for quantification link
```
attributes = qDomain, nScope, qRelator, scopes
```

The attribute @qDomain stands for *a domain of quantification*. It refers to the set of quantified objects, for instance, denoted by a temporal entity *day*, as in *every day*. The attribute @nScope, which stands for *nuclear scope of quantification*, refers to an eventuality that is quantificationally related to the domain. The attribute @qRelator refers to the type of a quantifier such as *every*.

Scope The attribute @scopes represents a scopal relation between two quantifiers, a quantifier specified by the attribute @type and another quantifier occurring in the nuclear scope. *scopes(t,e)*, for instance, is read as "t scopes over e", meaning that Q_e is in the scope of Q_t. In ISO-TimeML, this attribute @scopes is part of quantified *timex3*. In contrast, @scopes is part of qLink in eXTimeML, for it is a relation over quantifiers or logical operators.

Annotation 9.94 illustrates how qLink works.

Annotation 9.94   Working of qLink

a. Markables: John swims$_{e1,w2}$ every$_{q1,w3}$ Sunday$_{t1,w4}$.
b. Base structures:
```
event(e1, w2, pred="swim")
qEntity(q1, w3, type="every", domain="t1")
timex3(t1, w4, type="date", pred="Sunday")
```
c. Link structures:
```
tLink(tL1, t1, e1, includes)
qLink(qL1, t1, e1, every, scopes(t1,e1))
```
d. Semantics:
$$\forall t_1 \exists e_1 [weekDay(t_1, Sunday) \rightarrow [swim(e_1, John) \wedge \tau(e_1) \subseteq t_1]]$$

Note that scopes(t1,e1) in the link structure qLink triggers e$_1$ to be in the scope of t$_1$, as in Annotation 9.94d.

Compositional Semantics of Temporal Quantification

Here again ABS applies. Based on Annotation 9.94, we can go through several steps of composing semantic forms to derive the final semantic form. Each composition is constrained type-theoretically.

Step 1: Semantic forms of base structures
   Here is an example.

Semantics 9.95   Semantic forms of base structures

a. $\sigma(\texttt{e1}) := swim(e_1)_t$
b. $\sigma(\texttt{q1}) := every(t_1)_{t \mapsto t}$
c. $\sigma(\texttt{t1}) := weekDay(t_1, Sunday)_t$

The semantic forms of the base structures are derived straightforwardly. Note, however, that $\sigma(\texttt{e1})$ and $\sigma(\texttt{t1})$ are of semantic type t, whereas $\sigma(\texttt{q1})$ is of a functional semantic type $t \rightarrow t$.

These semantic forms are combined by the temporal link (tLink), as in Step 2.

Step 2: Semantic form of the temporal link structure

Semantics 9.96 Semantic form of a temporal link

a. $\sigma(\text{tL1}) := [<\sigma(\text{e1})_t, \sigma(\text{t1})_t> \oplus isIncluded(e_1, t_1)_t]$

b. $\qquad := [[\sigma(\text{e1}) \wedge \sigma(\text{t1})] \wedge \tau(e_1) \subseteq t_1]$

c. $\qquad := [[swim(e_1) \wedge weekDay(t_1, Sunday)] \wedge \tau(e_1) \subseteq t_1]$

Each of the component semantic forms in Semantics 9.96a is of semantic type t, where the relation *isIncluded* between e_1 and t_1 is translated to $[\tau(e_1) \subseteq t_1]_t$. Hence, these semantic forms are combined through the truth-functional conjunctive operator $\oplus$, yielding logical forms (b) and (c), each of which is composed of truth-functional $\wedge$-conjuncts.

The semantic form of Semantics 9.96 thus derived now undergoes Step 3.

Step 3: Semantic form of the quantification link structure

(1) a. $\sigma(\text{qL1}) := [every(t_1)_{t \mapsto t} \oslash^{uq} <\sigma(\text{t1})_t, \sigma(\text{tL1})_t>]$

  b. $\qquad := every(t_1)_{t \mapsto t}[\sigma(\text{t1})_t \rightarrow \sigma(\text{tL1})_t]_t$

  c. $\qquad := every(t_1)[weekDay(t_1, Sunday) \rightarrow [[swim(e_1) \wedge$
  $\qquad\qquad weekDay(t_1, Sunday)] \wedge \tau(e_1) \subseteq t_1]]$
  $\qquad\qquad$ (* $weekDay(t_1, Sunday)$ occurs in the antecedent and the
  $\qquad\qquad$ consequent. Its occurrence in the consequent is repetitious
  $\qquad\qquad$ and thus deleted.*)

  d. $\qquad := every(t_1)[weekDay(t_1, Sunday) \rightarrow [swim(e_1) \wedge$
  $\qquad\qquad \tau(e_1) \subseteq t_1]]$

The semantic form $\sigma(\text{qL1})$ of *quantificational link* is obtained by applying the quantifier *every*(t_1) of functional semantic type $t \rightarrow t$ *distributively* with the distributive operator $\oslash^{uq}$ for universal quantification over its domain $\sigma(\text{t1})$ and nuclear-scope $\sigma(\text{tL1})$ both of which are of type t. The expected nuclear-scope $\sigma(\text{e1})$ is expanded by $\sigma(\text{tLink})$ to represent the inclusion ($\subseteq$) relation between the event$_{e1}$ and the time$_{t1}$. Otherwise, the quantification *every*(t_1) becomes vacuous.

Step 4: Variable binding and scoping

By convention, first, all of the free occurrences of variables are bound by the existential quantifier $\exists$. Second, the newly introduced existential quantifier is placed properly within the scope of the universal quantifier $\forall t_1$. It is triggered by `scopes(t1,e1)`, which means e1 is in the scope of t1, in `qLink` of Annotation 9.94.

Semantics 9.97 $\forall t_1 \exists e_1 [Sunday(t_1) \rightarrow [swim(e_1) \land \tau(e_1) \subseteq t_1]]$

Temporal Adverbs

Temporal adverbs such as *daily* and *never* can be treated like quantified temporal operators. ISO-TimeML annotates the temporal adverb *daily* just like *every day*, as in Annotation 9.98.

Annotation 9.98   Temporal adverbs:

a. Markables: KAL flies$_{e1,\,w2}$ *daily*$_{t1,\,w3}$ from Seoul to New York.
b. Annotation:
```
<isoTimeML>
<EVENT xml:id="e1" target="w2" pred="FLY"/>
<TIMEX3 xml:id="t1" target="w3" type="SET" value="P1D"
  quant="every"/>
<tLink eventID="#e1" timeID="#t1" relType="isINCLUDED"/>
</isoTimeML>
```

In eXTimeML, quantified temporal expressions such as *every day* are treated as of category *quantified entity*, while its attribute `@type` is annotated as being *every* and its `@domain` as referring to a base structure that annotates *day*. In contrast, temporal adverbs like *daily* and *never* cannot be analyzed morphologically in the same manner. Nevertheless, these adverbs may be forced to be annotated as of category *quantified entity*, tagged `qEntity` in the concrete syntax, as in Annotation 9.99.

Annotation 9.99   Quantified temporal adverbs

a. Base structures:
```
event(e1, w2, pred="fly")
qEntity(q1, w3, type="every", domain="t1")
timex3(t1, w3, type="interval", value="P1D")
```
b. Link structures:
```
tLink(tL1, e1, t1, isIncluded)
event(%e1, w2, pred="fly", anchorTime="t1")
  (* %e1 is an augmented base structure created by tLink(tL1). *)
qLink(qL1, t1,%e1, every, scopes(t1,e1))
```
c. Semantics:

$\sigma(\text{t1}) := \{t_1\}[tInterval(t_1) \land \mu=(1,day)]$

$\sigma(\%\text{e1}) := \{e_1,t_1\}[fly(e_1) \land \tau(e_1) \subseteq t_1]$

$\sigma(\text{qL1}) := [[every(t1) \oslash^{uq} < \sigma(t1), \sigma(\%e1) >], scopes(t1,e1)]$

$\qquad := \forall t_1 \exists e_1 [[tInterval(t_1) \land \mu(t_1)=(1,day)] \rightarrow [fly(e_1) \land \tau(e_1) \subseteq t_1])]$

The semantic form σ(qL1) is interpreted as stating that every day there is at least one flight.

Temporal Adverbs as Modifiers The scheme eXTimeML prefers to treat quantified temporal adverbs like *daily* and *never* as of category *quantified entity* but simply as nonanalyzed *event qualities*, tagged *eQuality*, each of which modifies an event. Then the modifier link (moLink) is introduced to link an event to its modifier, as illustrated by Annotation 9.101. The semantic type of such qualities is defined as a functional type $v \to t$, the same as that of event descriptors as in Specification 9.100.

Specification 9.100 Semantic type of event descriptors and event qualifiers
a. v is the semantic type of eventualities.
b. $v \to t$ is the semantic type of event descriptors and event qualifiers.

Annotation 9.101 Temporal adverb *daily*
a. Markables: KAL flies$_{e1,w2}$ *daily*$_{mo1,w3}$ from Seoul to New York.
b. Annotation:
```
event(e1, w2, type="process", pred="fly")
eQuality(mo1, w3, type="tModifier", pred="daily")
moLink(moL1, figure="e1", ground="mo1", relType="modifiedBy")
```
c. Semantics: σ(moL1) := $\exists e[fly(e) \land daily(e)]$

Temporally modified events such as *daily(e)* are then interpreted with respect to a model constrained by meaning postulates such as Proposition 9.102.

Proposition 9.102 MP_{daily}
$\forall e[event(e) \land daily(e)] \Rightarrow$
$\forall e[event(e) \to \forall t[[tInterval(t) \land \mu(t)=<1,day>] \to \tau(e) \subseteq t]]$

Consider Annotation 9.103.

Annotation 9.103 Temporal modifier *never*
a. Data: I have *never* lived in Nepal.
b. Annotation:
```
event(e1, w2,4, type="state", pred="live", tam="presPerfect")
(* The attribute @tam stands for a 3-tuple tense-aspect-mood. The
default value is the present indicative.*)
eQuality(mo1, w3, type="eModifier", pred="never")
moLink(moL1, figure="e1", ground="mo1", relType="modifiedBy")
```
c. Semantics: $\sigma(moL1) := \exists e_1[visit(e_1) \land never(e_1) \land presPerfect(e_1)]$

The temporal modifier *never(e$_1$)* is then interpreted with respect to a model, constrained by one of the meaning postulates as defined in Proposition 9.104.

Proposition 9.104 *Meaning postulates for temporal adverbs*
For any eventuality of type v,

a. MP$_{\text{daily}}$:

$\forall e[event(e) \wedge daily(e)] =_{df}$

$\forall e[event(e) \rightarrow \forall t[[tInterval(t) \wedge \mu(t)=<1,day>] \rightarrow \tau(e) \subseteq t]]$

b. MP$_{\text{always}}$:

$\forall e[event(e) \wedge always(e)] =_{df} \forall e[event(e) \rightarrow \forall t[time(t) \rightarrow \tau(e) \subseteq t]]$

c. MP$_{\text{never}}$:

$\forall e[event(e) \wedge never(e)] =_{df} \forall e[event(e) \rightarrow \forall t[time(t) \rightarrow \neg[\tau(e) \subseteq t]]]$

Otherwise, these temporal adverbs need to be annotated as quantified temporal expressions, each consisting of a quantifier and a domain.

The current approach of ISO-TimeML just complicates the annotation and representation of the meaning of lexical items like *daily* by analyzing them as quantified temporal expressions at the level of annotation. In contrast, the proposed approach of eXTimeML treats the semantic analysis of temporal adverbs such as *daily* as part of lexical semantics which constrains a set of *admissible interpretation models* with meaning postulates, as in Montague semantics.

9.6 Modification

9.6.1 Issues

Modification is a general linguistic phenomenon that ISO-TimeML needs to be extended to treat. There are several issues involving the annotation and semantics of modification in language.

Grammatical Forms and Semantic Types

Modifiers are either *adjectival* or *adverbial* forms. In Example 9.105a, the adjective *strong* modifies the noun *man*, while the adverb *fast* modifies the verb *runs*.

Example 9.105   Modifiers

a. Data: Joe is a strong$_{adj}$ man$_{noun}$ and runs$_{verb}$ fast$_{adv}$.

b. Semantic form:

$\exists x[[named(x,Joe) \wedge strong(x) \wedge man(x)] \wedge \exists e[run(e) \wedge fast(e) \wedge agent(e,x)]]$

where

the variable x is of individual entity type e and the variable e, of eventuality type v.

Following Neo-Davidsonian semantics (see Davidson (1967) and Parsons (1990)), ABS treats both adjectives and adverbs as predicates, as shown in Example 9.105b. One noticeable difference between adjectival and adverbial modifiers is that their semantic types are different. Just like nouns, the argument of adjectives is of type e of entities, represented by a variable x, whereas the argument of adverbs, like eventualities, is of type v of eventualities, represented by a variable e. The occurrence of the variable x in $agent(e, x)$ is bound by the existential quantifier $\exists x$ in a wider scope, thereby the agent (subject) of the event of *running* is referentially related to Joe the man.

Semantic Types The scheme eXTimeML treats both nouns and adjectives as entity descriptors of type $e \rightarrow t$, while treating verbs and adverbs as event descriptors $v \rightarrow t$. Based on the basic types e and v, their semantic types are defined as functional types as in Specification 9.106.

Specification 9.106 Extended application of semantic types
a. e, the basic semantic type of individual entities;

   $e \rightarrow t$, the functional semantic type of entity descriptors (properties of an entity);
b. v, the basic semantic type of eventualities;

   $v \rightarrow t$, the functional semantic type of event descriptors, including event modifiers.

Temporal adverbs form a different type. Let's consider two examples in Example 9.107.

Example 9.107 Temporal adverbs
a. Joe worked yesterday$_{t\,Adverb}$.

   $\exists\{e, t\}[work(e) \wedge past(e) \wedge yesterday(t) \wedge tInterval(t) \wedge \tau(e) \subseteq t]$
b. Mia visited her aunt in New York [last summer]$_{t\,Adverb}$.

   $\exists\{e, t_1, t_2\}$

   $[visit(e) \wedge season(t_1, summer) \wedge tInterval(t_1) \wedge year(t_2, 1999) \wedge$
   $tInterval(t_2) \wedge t_1 \subseteq t_2]$

The temporal adverb *yesterday* in Example 9.107a is treated as of semantic type $i \rightarrow t$, denoting a time interval. $\tau(e) \subseteq t$ is then interpreted as this: *Joe worked during this time interval*. Likewise, the temporal expression *summer* in Example 9.107b is treated of interval type $i \rightarrow t$ and *last summer* refers to a subinterval of the year 1999. These temporal adverbial expressions may also be called *time descriptors* like entity or event descriptors that function as modifiers.

Specification 9.108 Additional semantic type for temporal modifiers

a. i is the semantic type of time points.
b. $i \rightarrow t$ is the functional semantic type of time intervals or temporal modifiers.

Predicative Use Adjectives have two uses, *attributive* and *predicative*. If an adjective is used predicatively or in a predicative context, it is associated with a *tensed state* of event type v.

Example 9.109 *Predicative use or predicative contextual use*
a. Joe was healthy. [predicative use]
$\exists\{x,s\}[named(x,Joe) \wedge healthy(s) \wedge past(s) \wedge theme(s,x)]$
where s is a variable of event (state) type v.
b. Joe was a healthy person. [predicative context]
$\exists\{x,s\}[named(x,Joe) \wedge person(x) \wedge healthy(s) \wedge past(s) \wedge theme(s,x)]$

The verbal features of adjectives in predicative use such as *tense, aspect*, and *mood* are handled by being incorporated into the eventualities of type *state*, represented by a variable s as in DRS.

9.6.2 Restricting Quantification Domain

Adjectival modifiers restrict the domain of quantification.

Example 9.110 Restricting the domain of quantification
a. The young Persian cats that Kim bought are all pretty and play well with her children.
b. $\forall x_1 \exists\{e_1, e_2, x_2, x_3\}$
$[[[cat(x_1) \wedge young(x_1) \wedge Persian(x_1)] \wedge$
$[buy(e_1, x_2, x_1) \wedge past(e_1) \wedge named(x_2, Kim)]]$
$\rightarrow [pretty(x_1) \wedge play(e_2, x_1, x_3) \wedge well(e_2) \wedge child(x_3) \wedge plural(x_3)]]$

The noun *cats* is the domain of the quantifier *all*, while this domain is restricted by the adjectives *young* and *Persian* and the relative clause *that I bought*.

9.6.3 Annotation and Interpretation

As defined in Specifications 9.106 and 9.108, we can annotate (i) adjectives as each forming a base structure of category *entity* and (ii) adverbs as of category *event*. Annotation 9.111 shows how these modifiers are annotated.

Annotation 9.111 Semantic typing of adjectives and adverbs
a. Markables: Persian$_{x1,w1}$ cats$_{x2,w2}$ are pretty$_{x3,w4}$ and play$_{e1,w6}$ well$_{e2,w7}$.
b. Base structures:
```
entity(x1, w1, pred="Persian", form="adjective")
entity(x2, w2, pred="cat", form="nom", plurality="yes")
entity(x3, w4, pred="pretty", form="adjective")
event(e1, w6, pred="play", form="verb")
event(e2, w7, pred="well", form="adverb")
```

c. Link structures:

```
moLink(moL1, figure="x2", ground="{x1,x3}", relType="modified")
moLink(moL2, figure="e1", ground="e2", relType="modified")
```

To relate an adjective to a noun as its modifier and an adverb to a verb again as its modifier, eXTimeML introduces the modification link, tagged *moLink*.

The extended version eXTimeML of ISO-TimeML specifies the attribute-value assignment @$_{entity}$ as in Specification 9.112, and the assignment @$_{moLink}$ as in Specification 9.113.

Specification 9.112 Assignment @$_{entity}$

```
attributes = identifier, pred, [pos], [plurality];
identifier = moL followed by a positive integer;
pred = CDATA;
(* Base form of a markable *)
pos = noun | verb | adjective | adverb;
plurality = yes;
(* "singular" by default if unspecified. *)
```

Specification 9.113 Assignment @$_{moLink}$

```
attributes = figure, ground, relType;
figure = nom | verb;
ground = adjectives | adverbs;
(* list of modifiers *)
relType = modified;
```

There may be more than one modifier for a single modified noun, verb, or adverb.

Deriving Semantic Forms

Annotation 9.111 allows the derivation of semantic forms as in Semantics 9.114.

Semantics 9.114 *Deriving semantic forms*

a. Semantic forms of the base structures:

$\sigma(\text{x1}) := \{x_1\}[Persian(x_1)]$

$\sigma(\text{x2}) := \{x_2\}[cat(x_2)]$

$\sigma(\text{x3}) := \{x_3\}[pretty(x_3)]$

$\sigma(\text{e1}) := \{e_1, x_2\}[play(e_1) \wedge agent(e_1, x_2)]$

$\sigma(\text{e2}) := \{e_2\}[well(e_2)]$

b. Semantic forms of the link structures:

(i) $\sigma(\text{moL1}) := [<\sigma(\text{x2})_t, \{\sigma(\text{x1})_t, \sigma(\text{x3})_t\}> \oplus modified(x_2)_{t \mapsto t}]$

(* $modified(x_2)$ forces every unbound variable of type e to be bound by $\exists x_2$. *)

$:= \exists x_2[cat(x_2) \wedge Persian(x_1)^{x_1/x_2} \wedge pretty(x_3)^{x_3/x_2}]$

$$:= \exists x_2[cat(x_2) \wedge Persian(x_2) \wedge pretty(x_2)]$$

(ii) $\sigma(\texttt{moL2}) := [<\sigma(\texttt{e1})_t, \sigma(\texttt{e2})_t> \oplus modified(e_1)_{t \mapsto t}]$

```
(* modified(e₁) forces every unbound variable of type υ
to be bound by ∃e₁.*)
```

$$:= \exists\{e_1, x_2\}[play(e_1) \wedge agent(e_1, x_2) \wedge well(e_2)^{e_2/e_1}]$$

$$:= \exists\{e_1, x_2\}[play(e_1) \wedge agent(e_1, x_2) \wedge well(e_1)]$$

(iii) By combining (i) and (ii), we obtain the following.

$$\exists\{x_2, e_1\}$$

$$[[cat(x_2) \wedge Persian(x_2) \wedge pretty(x_2)]\wedge$$

$$[play(e_1) \wedge agent(e_1, x_2) \wedge well(e_1)]]]$$

9.7 Extended Summary

Section 9.1 motivated the introduction of eXTimeML as an extension of ISO-TimeML, especially by generalizing temporal measure and quantification as parts of general measure (Classification 9.4) and temporal quantification (Example 9.5).

Section 9.2 presented the metamodel of eXTimeML as a general conceptual view of its annotation scheme with annotation structures and links over them. This section introduced the abstract syntax $\mathcal{AS}yn_{eXTimeML}$ with (i) two new categories, *measure* and *quantified entity* (qEntity), of base structures $\beta_{measure}$ and $\beta_{qEntity}$, and (ii) a new category of link structures λ_{qLink} of category *quantification link*, abbreviated as qLink, with an additional attribute @scopes.

With appropriately defined assignment $@_c$ of each category c of base structures, the abstract syntax $\mathcal{AS}yn_{eXTimeML}$ of eXTimeML defines well-formed base structures β_c of any syntactic annotation category c as a set-theoretic tuple. For example, base structures $\beta_{measure}$ of category *measure* as a 3-tuple $<ty, va, [mod]>$, where ty is the type of a measure, va its value, and mod, an optional attribute modifying the value v. With an instantiated assignment $@_{c:i}$, the tuple $<i, ty, va, [mod]>$ can also be instantiated with an ID i.

The abstract syntax defines link structures of category r as a triple $<\beta, B, \rho>$, where β is a base structure, B is a nonempty set of base structures, and ρ is the type of a relation between β and each base structure in B. When applied appropriately, each link derives an *augmented base structure* with its ID i, which is represented as %i. For example, the semantic role link srLink:srL1 applies to an event e1 and a participant x1 by augmented information *agent*, meaning that x1 is the agent of e1. Then a new base structure is derived with such added information and is represented as %srL1. Then this new base structure can be subject to another link such as the temporal link tLink.

Section 9.3 discussed the pFormat-based concrete syntax. The concrete syntax $CS_{eXTimeML}$ of eXTimeML adopts the pFormat for the representation of annotation structures. Each pForm that represents an annotation structure, either a base or a link structure, resembles an atomic formula in predicate logic: for example, EVENT(e1, w2, type="process", pred="run"), where the first two arguments form an anchoring structure and the rest, the content structure of a base structure.

The concrete syntax instantiates base or link structures, defined by attribute-value assignments $@_c$ or $@_r$ of category c or r, respectively, as set-theoretic tuples in two ways. First, specific names are given to each of the attributes in set-theoretic tuples. Second, possible value ranges or types are specified for each of the attributes listed in the tuples. For example, given $\beta_{measure}=<ty, va, mod>$ by $@_{measure}$, we have an eBNF.

```
category = measure, ...;
attributes = type, value, [mod];
type = amount | length | CDATA;
value = (n,u) | CDATA;
   (* n is a real number and u is a unit. *)
mo = about | almost | moreThan | CDATA;
```

Section 9.4 incorporated time amounts and other types of temporal measures as part of general measures; eXTimeML differentiates time lengths (durations) (e.g., *a period of 20 and a half years, from June to August*) from time amounts (e.g, *20 years altogether*) and also the type of a measuring relation (e.g., *2 meters tall*) from that of counting (e.g., *20 years old*). Two functions are introduced: μ is a *measuring* function from measurable objects to measure values, whereas κ is a *counting* function that applies to something like boxes of apples or three occurrences of the earthquake. Frequency expressions such as *ten times* are treated as a measure of type *repetition* subject to counting, while being annotated as value="10, count".

Section 9.5 treated quantified temporal expressions such as *every day* as a subcategory of category *qEntity* (quantified entity) like *every man*; eXTimeML adopts the tripartite treatment of quantification that consists of an operator, a domain, and a nuclear scope. Furthermore, eXTimeML treats base structures $\beta_{qEntity}$ as a tuple $<ty, do, [ind]>$, where ty the type of a quantifier like *every*, do its domain that refers to objects of any type including temporal objects as referred by temporal expressions like *Tuesday* of type *date* or *ten o'clock* of type *time*, and *ind* the individuation of a variable that ranges over the domain as either *distributive individuals* or a *collective group*.

Section 9.6 dealt with modification in order to examine how it affects the domain of quantification, especially related to times.

10

Proper Interpretation of Temporal Relators

10.1 Introduction: Issues

Eventualities are related to times or event times by *function words* such as temporal prepositions, conjunctions, and adverbs.

Classification 10.1   Function words

a. Temporal prepositions:

after, around, at, before, by, during, from, in, on, since, through, till, to, towards:[1]

e.g., Jon woke up$_{e:event}$ *at* four o'clock$_{t:time}$.

b. Temporal conjunctions: *after, before, when, since, until*:

e.g., Jon woke up$_{e1:event}$ *before* the cock crowed$_{e2:event}$.

c. Temporal adverbs: *ago, always, never, sometimes*:

e.g., Jon woke up$_{e3:event}$ three hours$_{duration}$ *ago*.

These function words are called *temporal relators*, for they relate eventualities to times.

Temporal Adjuncts   Morphosyntactically, each temporal relator combines with a temporal expression as its object argument to form a *temporal adjunctive construction*, simply called *temporal adjunct*. Each temporal adjunct is then semantically interpreted as denoting a function that maps an eventuality to a proposition (truth value). Here is a simple example that shows how the occurrence time $\tau(e_1)$ of an event e_1 is related to a time t by the relation $\subseteq$ of temporal inclusion.

---

[1] Bennett (1975) lists 38 prepositions, including *in back of*, most of which he claims are used in a spatial or temporal sense, or both senses.

Example 10.2   Temporal adjuncts

a. Data: Mia woke up at four o'clock.

b. Temporal adjunct:

Jon woke up$_{e:event:past}$ [$at_{t\,Relator:isIncluded}$ four o'clock$_{t:time}$]$_{t\,Adjunct}$.

c. Semantic representation:

$\exists\{e_1,t\}[wakeUp(e_1) \wedge past(e_1) \wedge time(t,\text{T4:00}) \wedge \tau(e_1) \subseteq t]$

Here, $\tau(e_1) \subseteq t$ means that the event e_1 occurs at the time t.

Consider another example.

Example 10.3   Temporal relator *before*

a. Jon woke up before the cock crowed.

b. Annotation:

Jon woke up$_{e1:event}$ [$before_{t\,Relator:precedes}$ the cock crowed$_{e2:event}$]$_{t\,Adjunct}$.

c. Semantic representation:

$\exists\{e_1,e_2\}[wakeUp(e_1) \wedge past(e_1) \wedge crow(e_2) \wedge past(e_2) \wedge \tau(e_1) \prec \tau(e_2)]$

The semantic representation (Example 10.3c) is interpreted as stating that the occurrence time $\tau(e_1)$ of the event e_1 of Jon waking up *precedes* the occurrence time $\tau(e_2)$ of the event e_2 of the cock crowing.

Complex Temporal Adjunct Construction   Unlike simple temporal adjunct constructions as in Example 10.2 and Example 10.3, there are complex temporal adjunct constructions each of which requires a complex semantic interpretation. Complex temporal adjunct constructions each introduce a time interval to which other pieces of temporal information are linked for the proper interpretation of temporal relations. In semantic annotation, a nonconsuming tag $\emptyset_{t:tInterval}$ with its categorized identifier t represents the time interval as part of a complex adjunct construction.

Example 10.4   Temporal adjunct

a. Jon played$_{e1}$ tennis from two to five in the afternoon.

b. Annotation of the temporal adjunct:

Jon played$_{e1}$ tennis [$\emptyset_{t:tInterval}$ from two$_{t0}$ to five$_{t1}$ in the afternoon]$_{tAdjunct}$.

c. Semantic representation:

$\exists\{e_1,t,t_0,t_1\}$
$[play(e_1) \wedge process(e_1) \wedge past(e_1)$
$\wedge tInterval(t) \wedge starts(t,t_0) \wedge ends(t,t_1)$
$\wedge time(t_0,\text{T14:00}) \wedge time(t_1,\text{T17:00})$
$\wedge \tau(e_1) \subseteq t]$

In the semantic representation (Example 10.4c), the time interval t, to which the event e_1 of Jon playing tennis is anchored, does not denote a simple time, but a time interval $\emptyset_{t:tInterval}$ bounded with its start and end points, both of which refer to specific times, t_0 and t_1.

Here is another example. The adjunct construction in Example 10.5b contains a nonconsuming tag that represents a time interval $\emptyset_{t:tInterval}$ interacting with the backward orienting temporal relator *ago*. The time interval thus introduced specifies its start point t_0 to be the anchoring point of the event e_1 and its endpoint t_1 as referring to the present time *now*.

Example 10.5   Temporal adjunct construction with ago
a. Data: Jon woke up three hours ago.
b. Annotated:

Jon woke up$_{e1:event}$
[$\emptyset_{t:tInterval}$ three hours$_{me3:timeLength:duration}$ *ago*$_{tRelator:}$ $_{backwardOrienting}$]$_{tAdjunct}$.

c. Semantic representation:

$\exists\{e_1, t, t_0, t_1\}$
$[wakeUp(e_1) \wedge past(e_1)$
$\wedge\, timeInterval(t) \wedge starts(t, t_0) \wedge ends(t, t_1) \wedge now(t_1)$
$\wedge\, \mu(t) = <3, hour> \wedge duration(t_0, t_1) = \mu(t)$
$\wedge\, \tau(e_1) \subseteq t_0]$

In the semantic representation (Example 10.5c), the event e_1 occurred at the time t_0. This occurrence time $\tau(e_1)$ refers to the start t_0 of a time interval that lasted 3 hours; μ is a measure function and $\mu(t)$ is the length of the time interval t.

Figure 10.1 illustrates a case of oriented intervals.

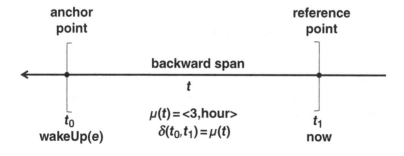

Figure 10.1 Backward span triggered by the temporal relator *ago*

Issues Unlike the cases in Examples 10.2 and 10.3, the case in Example 10.5c as well as the case in Example 10.4c poses challenges for interpretation. The temporal adverb *ago* in Example 10.5a,b is a *backward orienting temporal relator*. It does not simply denote a temporal relation like the first two temporal relators *at* and *before*, which denote the temporal inclusion $\subseteq$ and the temporal precedence $\prec$ relations, respectively. As an orienting temporal relator, *ago* introduces an oriented temporal interval, called *span*, bounded with its start and end points, and often with the specification of a time distance, called *duration* δ (see Quirk et al. (1985)). Unlike other orienting temporal relators (e.g., *after, before*), the temporal adverb *ago* grounds the endpoint t_1 of the span to the present time *now*, while anchoring an event to the start point t_0. Such an interpretation requires a detailed analysis of the role of the temporal relators like *ago*.

Aim To resolve those issues, this chapter further develops my earlier work (Lee, 2017) on temporal relators by classifying them into five types: *anchoring, ordering, metric, bounding*, and *orienting*. I argue that we need such a classification for a proper interpretation of temporal relations over various types of eventualities, times, and temporal measures. I analyze each type of temporal relator with respect to the *temporal tripartite frame* of $<E, T, R>$. E stands for a set of event structures, T for a set of temporal entity structures, and R for a set of temporal relators over E and T.[2] Each temporal relator $r \in R$ combines with a *temporal structure* $t \in T$ as its argument to form a *temporal adjunct*, while relating an eventuality $e \in E$ of various *aspectual types* such as *state, process*, or *transition* to an appropriate temporal structure $t \in T$. This chapter aims to clarify such temporal relations by annotating and interpreting some representative event and temporal entity structures and their relations.

10.2 Basic Ontological Assumptions

For the analysis of temporal relators, I assume there are commonly accepted basic ontologies on event structures,[3] time structures, and temporal measures. These ontologies characterize the tripartite frame $<E, T, R>$ on which each temporal relator is annotated and interpreted.

---

[2] Caselli et al. (2009) also take a similar approach to the analysis of temporal relational structures.
[3] The term *event* is often used interchangeably with the term *eventuality*, coined by Bach (1986).

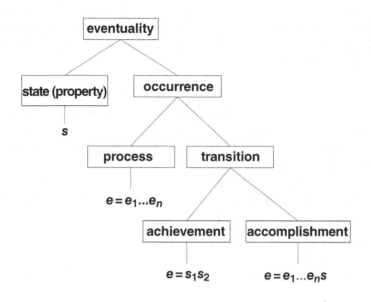

Figure 10.2 Structure of eventuality types

10.2.1 Event Structures

An ontology of eventualities classifies event structures. I assume an ontology of eventualities that amalgamated the theories of event structures by Allen (1984) and Pustejovsky (1991) and then was modified by Pustejovsky et al. (2017, p. 32, example 10). The modified version accommodates Vendler's (1967) aspectual classes of verbs by subclassifying the type of *transition* into *achievement* and *accomplishment* types, as depicted in Figure 10.2.

The types of event structures can be specified more explicitly in extended eBNF (ISO/IEC 14977, eBNF) (ISO/IEC, 1966).

Specification 10.6 Types of event structures

```
eventuality types = state (property) | occurrence;
state (property) = s;
  (* s stands for a single homogeneous eventuality. *)
occurrence = process | transition;
process = e = e_i; (* where 0 ≤ i ≤ 1, where i is a real. *);
  (* A process is defined to be a sequence of more than one
    event instances that may not be homogeneous. *)
transition = transition_ach | transition_acc;
transition_ach = e = s_0 s_1; (* where s_0 and s_1 are states.*);
transition_acc = e = e_i s, where 0 ≤ i ≤ 1, where i is a real;
  (* The sequence e_i is a process and s, a culminating
    state. *)
```

Each *achievement* consists of two states: One state followed by another state. Each *accomplishment* consists of a process, which is a sequence of subevents, and a culminating state.

Event Instances e_i The classification of event structures assumes that each eventuality e of type **occurrence** can be divided into its subparts e_i, called *event instances*, where $0 \preceq i \preceq 1$. We assume that these instances e_i are linearly ordered, possibly bounded by the initial event instance e_0 and the terminal event instance e_1.

We extend the notion of *accomplishment* to include a case in which a state precedes a process as the inverse of an accomplishment. This is represented as follows.

Specification 10.7   Inverse notion of accomplishment

transition$_{iAcc}$ = se_i;

(* where s is an initial state and e_i is a process such that $0 < i \leq 1$. *).

Logical Predicates, Holds and Occurs I also assume the interval temporal logic of Allen (1984) and Allen and Ferguson (1994) with their definitions of two predicates *holds* and *occurs*.

Definition 10.8   Logical predicates *holds* and *occurs*

a. Logical predicate *holds*:

A *state* or *property* is characteristic of a static eventuality that *holds* over an interval of time and every subinterval of it.

b. Logical predicates *occurs*:

An *occurrence* is characteristic of an eventuality that consists of a sequence of subevents that may not be uniform nor contiguous as it develops.

These predicates are *logical predicates* like *meaning postulates* as part of an interpretation model by characterizing the model as an *admissible* model.

Subtypes of Type *transition* There are three subtypes of *transition*.

Classification 10.9   Three types of transition

a. $transition_{ach}$ for achievements:

e.g., *John woke up at seven.*

b. $transition_{acc}$ for accomplishments:[4]

e.g., *Mia wrote a novel.*

---

[4] See Pustejovsky et al. (2017), p. 32, example 10.

c. *transition*$_{iAcc}$ for initiations:

e.g., *Mia left Seoul for Paris yesterday.*

Compare *Mia arrived in Paris yesterday.*

Classification 10.9c implies that Mia was no longer in Seoul.

The event of waking up in Classification 10.9a implies a change of a state from John's being asleep to the state of his being awake. In contrast, John's activity of writing a novel in Classification 10.9b involves a process of writing and then reaches the culminating state of finishing a novel. Mia's leaving for Paris in Classification 10.9c means the initiation of her trip to Paris, whereas Mia's arriving in Paris in Classification 10.9c for comparison means the *culmination* of her trip to Paris.

Logical Predicates, Initiates and Culminates There are two types of *temporal anchoring predicates.*

Classification 10.10   Temporal anchoring predicates

a. Logical predicate *initiates*:

Every eventuality e of type transition *initiates* at the start of t_0 of a time interval t if there is an event instance e_0, which is part of e, that occurs at t_0.

b. Logical predicate *culminates*:

Every eventuality e of type transition *culminates* at the end t_1 of a time interval t if there is an event instance e_1, which is part of e, that holds at t_1.

All of the examples in Classification 10.9 can now be annotated with their respective semantic representations, as in Examples 10.11, 10.12, and 10.13, respectively.

Example 10.11   Transition$_{ach}$ for achievements

a. Base annotation:

John woke$_{s:transition:ach}$ up at seven$_{t1}$.

b. Semantic representation:

$\exists \{s, t_1\}$

$[wake(s) \wedge transition_{ach}(s) \wedge past(s)$

$\wedge \, time(t_1, 07:00)$

$\wedge \, holds(s, t_1)]$

The semantic representation (Example 10.11b) simply states that the state s holds at the time t_1, which was seven o'clock.

Semiclosed Time Intervals The logical predicate *holds* denotes a relation between an eventuality and the whole span of a time interval. In contrast, the logical predicates, *initiates* and *culminates*, each denote a relation between an eventuality and a *semibounded interval*, either start-bounded or end-bounded. In annotation, such intervals are introduced as the *non-consuming tag* $\emptyset_t$, each of which is further specified either as $t : [t_0, t_1)$ for a start-bounded and end-open interval or $t : (t_0, t_1]$ for a start-open and end-bounded time interval. These semibounded intervals are interpreted as stating that the open boundary point of an interval denotes an unspecified point in time. The start-bounded interval $t : [t_0, t_1)$ states that the endpoint of the interval t is not specified.

Consider Example 10.12.

Example 10.12   Transition$_{acc}$ for accomplishment

a. Base annotation:

   John wrote$_{e2:transition:acc}$ a novel $\emptyset_{t=(t_0,t_1]}$.

b. Semantic representation:

   $\exists\{e_2, t, t_1\}$

   $[write(e_2) \wedge transition_{acc}(e_2) \wedge past(e_2)$

   $\wedge\ tInterval(t) \wedge ends(t, t_1)$

   $\wedge\ occurs(e_2, t) \wedge culminates(e_2, t_1)]$

The semantic representation (Example 10.12b) denotes that the event e_2 of writing a book occurred during the interval t and was completed at the end t_1 of that interval.

Consider a case of an event initiating, as in Example 10.13.

Example 10.13   *Transition$_{iAcc}$ for initiations*

a. Base annotation: Mia left$_{e3:transition:iAcc}$ for Paris $\emptyset_{t=[t_0,t_1)}$ yesterday.

b. Semantic representation:

   $\exists\{e_3, t, t_0\}$

   $[leave(e_3) \wedge transition_{iAcc}(e_3) \wedge past(e_3)$

   $\wedge\ tInterval(t) \wedge starts(t, t_0)$

   $\wedge\ occurs(e_3, t) \wedge initiates(e_3, t_0)]$

Example 10.13b represents the *initial* state of Mia's trip to Paris, which involves a start-closed semibounded time interval $\emptyset_{t=[t_0,t_1)}$.

In contrast, consider Example 10.14.

Example 10.14   Culmination

a. Base annotation:

   Mia arrived$_{e4:transition:acc}$ in Paris $\emptyset_{t=(t0,t1]}$ yesterday.

b. Semantic representation:
$\exists\{e_4, t, t_1\}$
$[arrive(e_4) \wedge transition_{acc}(e_4) \wedge past(e_4)$
$\wedge\, tInterval(t) \wedge ends(t, t_1)$
$\wedge\, occurs(e_4, t) \wedge culminates(e_4, t_1)]$

Example 10.14b represents the *culminating* state of Mia's trip to Paris, which involves an end-closed semibounded time interval $\emptyset_{t=(t0, t1]}$. The start-open interval $(0,1]$ represents a semibounded interval with its start 0 as unbounded and unspecified.

10.2.2 Time Structures

I adopt the OWL-time ontology, proposed by Hobbs and Pan (2004), with some modifications. There are, for instance, some logical predicates for temporal relations that I redefine.

Points and Intervals

Points of time are often called *instants*. In a type-theoretic semantics (see Kracht (2002) and Pustejovsky et al. (2019a)), time points are of basic type p but time intervals, of functional type $p \rightarrow t$. In interpreting temporal expressions in natural language, many of these expressions that denote times and dates refer to points as *minimal intervals*, $[0,0]$, such that their bounding points are identical.

Temporal Inclusion $\subset$ or $\subseteq$, Temporalizing Function τ The *inclusion* relation between two time intervals is represented by $\subset$ for proper cases or $\subseteq$ for general cases. Then, the *temporalizing function* τ, called *runtime function* by Katz (2007), maps an eventuality to a time interval. This interval is called *event time*.

Consider Example 10.15.

Example 10.15 Temporal inclusions

a. Jeon died at 8:00 yesterday.
b. Base annotation:
     Jeon died$_e$ at 8:00$_{t1:time}$ yesterday$_{t2:date}$.

c. Semantic representation:

$\exists\{e, t_1, t_2\}$

$[die(e) \wedge past(e)$

$\wedge\, time(t_1, 08{:}00) \wedge yesterday(t_2)$

$\wedge\, \tau(e) \subseteq t_1 \wedge t_1 \subset t_2]$

In the semantic representation (Example 10.15c), the time t_1 is treated as an interval just like the occurrence time $\tau(e)$ of the event die_e and the date $yesterday_{t_2}$. The *temporal inclusion* relations $\subseteq$ and $\subset$ denote relations over intervals by treating temporalized event times as intervals.

Three Types of Bounding Intervals

There are three *types of bounding time intervals*.

Classification 10.16   *Three types of intervals*

a. *open* $(0,1)$
b. *bounded* $[0,1]$
c. *semibounded*

Semibounded intervals are of two subtypes: either *start-bounded* $[0,1)$ or *end-bounded* $(0,1]$, where 0 stands for the start of an interval and 1 for the end of an interval.

Consider examples in Example 10.17, taken from Pustejovsky (2006, p. 34).

Example 10.17   Events anchored to time intervals

a. Mary walked.
b. Mary walked to the store.

Each of the events mentioned is associated with a different type of open or bounded time intervals, as their semantic forms are roughly represented in Semantics 10.18.

Semantics 10.18   Semantic forms

a. Mary walked$_{e1:process}$ $\emptyset_{t1=(0,1)}$:

$\exists\{e_1, t_1\}$

$[walk(e_1) \wedge process(e_1) \wedge past(e_1) \wedge tInterval(t_1) \wedge occurs(e_1, t_1)]$

b. Mary walked $_{e2:transition:accomplishment}$ to the store $\emptyset_{t2=(0,1]}$:

$\exists\{e_2, t_2, t_1\}[walk(e_2) \wedge transition_{acc}(e_2) \wedge past(e_2) \wedge tInterval(t_2) \wedge$
$ends(t_2, t_1) \wedge occurs(e_2, t_2) \wedge culminates(e_2, t_1)]$

Each of the walking events interpreted in Semantics 10.18 is anchored to a time interval but in a different way. As annotated with the nonconsuming tag $\emptyset_{t1=(0,1)}$ with an open interval $(0,1)$, event a is interpreted as denoting a process or activity that occurred during an open interval with its start and endpoints unspecified. Yet, event b is annotated with the nonconsuming tag $\emptyset_{t2=(0,1]}$ with a semibounded interval $(0,1]$. Annotated event b is then interpreted as denoting the accomplishment of the event e_2 that *culminated* at the end t_1 of the time interval t_2.

Logical Predicates, Starts and Ends These two logical predicates relate an interval to its start and end, respectively. They can be used to represent *fully bounded intervals*, $[0,1]$, as in Example 10.19.

Example 10.19 Eventuality anchored to the whole interval
a. Mia took a nap from two to four in the afternoon.
b. Base annotation:
   Mia took a nap_{e1} $\emptyset_{t=[t0,t1]}$ from two_{t0} to $four_{t1}$ for two hours in the afternoon.
c. Semantic representation:
   $\exists\{e_1,t,t_0,t_1\}$
   $[nap(e_1) \wedge state(e_1) \wedge past(e_1)$
   $\wedge tInterval(t) \wedge starts(t,t_0) \wedge ends(t,t_1)$
   $\wedge time(t_1,14\!:\!00) \wedge time(t_2,16\!:\!00)$
   $\wedge holds(e_1,t)]$

The two time points, t_0 and t_1, characterize a fully bounded time interval t as $[t_0,t_1]$. It is also possible to represent two bounding points of an interval I as $start(t_0)$ and $end(t_1)$ such that $I=[t_0, t_1]$.

Time Stamps
Logical Predicates, Time and Date There are at least two kinds of times: clock times and calendar dates. For clock times, *time* is introduced as a logical predicate. For calendar dates, a predicate *date* is introduced, as in Example 10.20.

Example 10.20 Logical predicate *date*
a. We have a meeting at five-thirty in the afternoon, 10 January 2022.
b. Semantic representation:
   $\exists\{e,t\}$
   $[meet(e)$
   $\wedge time(t, 17\!:\!30) \wedge date(t, 2022\text{-}01\text{-}10)$
   $\wedge occurs(e,t)]$

For finer-grained representation, the predicate *date* may be replaced with temporal units such as *day*, *month*, and *year*.

Example 10.21   Logical predicates *day, month*, and *year*
a. Wednesday, 12 January 2022
b. $[weekDay(t,3) \wedge day(t,12), \wedge month(t,01) \wedge year(t,2022)]^5$

Deictic expressions such as *now* and *today* or *yesterday* may also be treated as predicates to represent dates. Or else, the deictic function γ is used to map a deictic expression to a specific value. *yesterday*(t_2) is then replaced by $t_2 = \gamma(t_2)$ and *now*(t_3), by $t_3 = \gamma(now)$.

Example 10.22   Deictic temporal expressions as predicates
a. John left$_{e1}$ on Saturday, Mary left$_{e2}$ yesterday$_{t2}$, and Jim has left$_{e3}$ now$_{t3}$.
b. Semantic representation:
$\exists\{e_1, e_2, e_3, t_1, t_2, t_3\}$
$[leave(e_1) \wedge weekDay(t_1, 6) \wedge occurs(e_1, t_1)$
$\wedge\, leave(e_2) \wedge yesterday(t_2) \wedge occurs(e_2, t_2)$
$\wedge\, leave(e_3) \wedge now(t_3) \wedge occurs(e_3, t_3)]$

Designated Time n and Neighborhood Function $\mathcal{N}$ As discussed in Lee (2008), the designated time n is introduced to denote the present moment of time. Then the neighborhood function $\mathcal{N}$, which maps a time t to an open interval surrounding t, can map n to the interval denoted by the indexical expression *now*. Here is an illustration of their use.

Example 10.23   Interpreting *now*
a. John has left now.
b. $\exists\{e,t\}[leave(e) \wedge now(t) \wedge occurs(e,t)]$

Here, *now* maps a time t either to an instant n or to its neighborhood interval $\mathcal{N}$, which is defined as $\mathcal{N}(n)$.

10.2.3 Temporal Measures

Temporal Measure: Temporal Length, Distance (Duration), and Amount
There are three closely related notions of time measure.

Classification 10.24   Temporal measures
a. time length

---

[5] According to ISO 8601-1 (ISO, 2019a), each week starts not with Sunday, but with Monday. Being the third day of a week, Wednesday is assigned the ordinal number 3 (see clause 2.2.8).

b. temporal distance (duration)

c. time amount

These temporal measures refer to different dimensions of measure but to the same quantity of time. *Duration* is often used as a cover term for all of the three types of temporal measure. I follow ISO 8601-1 (ISO, 2019a) for the use of the term *duration* in a restricted sense, meaning a temporal distance between the two boundary points of an interval.[6]

Example 10.25 Temporal measures

a. Time length:

Jon left Kathmandu three hours$_{t\,Length}$ before the earthquake.

b. Temporal distance:

Jon talked for three hours$_{t\,Amount}$ [from nine in the morning till noon]$_{t\,Distance}$ without a break.

c. Time amount:

Jon spoke for three hours$_{t\,Amount}$ yesterday, two hours$_{t\,Amount}$ in the morning and three hours$_{t\,Amount}$ in the afternoon.

Example 10.25 contains three occurrences of the temporal measure expression *three hours*, one denoting the length of a time span, the second one, the temporal distance (duration) from 09:00 to 12:00, and the last one, the amount of time Jon spent speaking.

Linear Quantity (Length) of a Time Interval

Length is a property of an interval, either spatial or temporal, which constitutes either a path or a time interval. The length of a time interval denotes its linear quantity, normally represented in terms of reals and temporal units. It is formally defined as follows.

Definition 10.26 Time length (linear temporal quantity)

The length of a time interval $t \in T$ is measured by the function:

$$\mu : T \to R \times U,$$

where T is a set of time intervals, R a set of reals, and U a set of temporal units.

The function μ is called *measuring* or *measure function*. This represents the length of a time interval as a pair of a real number and a temporal unit, as in Example 10.27.

---

[6] ISO 8601-1 (ISO, 2019a, clause 3.1.1.8): 3.1.1.8 *duration* nonnegative quantity of time equal to the difference between the final and initial *instants* (clause 3.1.1.3) of a time interval (clause 3.1.1.6).

Example 10.27   Time length
a. *two and a half hour*$_{metric:tLength}$ interval$_t$
b. $\mu(t)=<2.5, hour>$

The SI (International System of Units) base unit for measuring time is *second*. In ordinary modern-day life, we rely on clocks or watches to measure time in terms of the time length units *second, minute, hour, day, week, year* or other larger or smaller temporal units.

Temporal Distance

The notion of *temporal distance (duration)* contrasts with the measure of a path, called *distance*. It is the length of a time interval measured between the two bounding points of a time interval, as defined as follows.

Definition 10.28   Temporal distance (duration)
For any time interval $t \in T$ bounded by its start $t_i \in T$ and its end $t_j \in T$, where T is a set of (possibly minimal) time interval, the temporal distance δ is defined as follows:
$\delta(t_i, t_j)=\mu(t)$,
such that $\mu(t)$ is defined as in Definition 10.26.

Note that the temporal distance from the two endpoints of an interval equals the length of a time interval bounded by those two endpoints.
    Annotation 10.29 shows how temporal distance is annotated.

Annotation 10.29   Temporal distance
a. Mia stayed in Jeju from June to the end of August.
b. Base annotation:
    Mia stayed in Jeju $\emptyset_{t1}$ from June$_{t2}$ to the end of August$_{t3}$.
c. Semantic representation:
    $\delta(t_2, t_3)=\mu(t_1)$
    $\mu(t_1)=<3, month>$
    $\delta(t_2, t_3)=<3, month>$

Both the temporal distance δ and the measure μ have the same value but have different domains; δ maps a pair of two time points to a measure, but μ maps a time interval to a measure, while these two measures are the same.

Time Amount

There is a third measure term *time amount*. We use it in a technical sense to refer to the sum of the time lengths of all of the time intervals to which the *instances* of an event are anchored. As Harry Bunt (personal communication) has proposed, the notion of *event instance* should be introduced into the notion of *time amounts*. The time amount of an event is measured not simply on the kind of an eventuality but on its instances, each of which is anchored to a subinterval of the time associated with that eventuality. In defining the notion of time amount, as in Definition 10.30, I propose to represent *instances* e_i of an eventuality e as its *parts*: $e_i \sqsubseteq e$.

Definition 10.30 Time amount

For any eventuality $e \in E$ and any time interval $t \in T$
such that $T_E(t,e) = \{t_i \,|\, t_i \sqsubseteq t \land \exists e_i [e_i \sqsubseteq e \land \tau(e_i) \subseteq t_i]\}$,
the *time amount* $\alpha(e,t)$ of the eventuality e with respect to the interval t, is
defined as:[7]

$$\alpha(e,t) =_{df} \sum_{t_i \in T_E(t,e)} \mu(t_i)$$

Note that the set T_E is a *restricted set* of the subintervals or parts of the interval t in T, delimited by the occurrences of the event instances e_i of the eventuality $e \in E$. The measure function μ of time lengths is defined as in Definition 10.26, and τ is the *temporalizing or runtime function* from a set E of eventualities to a set T of time intervals.

Consider Example 10.31 to see how the definition of time amount applies.

Example 10.31 Time amount
a. John taught for 20 hours in August.
b. Base annotation:
   John taught$_{e1}$ for 20 hours$_{me1:t\,Amount}$ in August$_{t1}$
c. Semantic representation:
   $\exists\{e_1, t_1\}$
   $[teach(e_1) \land process(e_1) \land past(e_1) \land month(t_1, 8)^8$
   $\land\, \tau(e_1) \subseteq t_1 \land \alpha(e_1, t_1) = <20, hour>]$

The semantic representation in Example 10.31c states that the event e_1 of John's teaching occurred in August and a certain amount of his teaching in that period. This amount was measured in terms of the unit *hour* and was summed up to be 20 hours. It does not, however, tell how many instances the event of his teaching was divided into nor how much time each teaching instance took

---

[7] Harry Bunt (personal communication) helped formulate this definition.
[8] Temporal expressions such as *month* are used either as temporal units or as binary predicates between a time (variable) and its denotation. Or, $month(t_1, 8)$ may also be represented as $[month(t_1) \land named(t_1, August)]$ by treating *month* as a property of times.

up. It simply tells that the total hours of his teaching in August amounted to 20
hours.

Parts of an Eventuality and Time Amount

Each event may consist of several instances or parts. A lecture series, for
instance, refers to more than a single instance of lecturing. Consider Example
10.32, which explicitly mentions instances (parts) of an event and their time
measures, of type either *length* or *amount*.

Example 10.32   Jon's lecture series

a. Jon gave two long lectures on Situation Semantics yesterday. The first
   lecture lasted two hours and the other, three hours. He talked for five hours
   altogether.

b. Word segmentation:
   [Jon gave two long lectures$_{w2-5}$ on Situation Semantics yesterday$_{w9}$.]$_{s1}$
   [The first lecture$_{w1-3}$ lasted two hours$_{w4-5}$ and the other$_{w7-8}$, three
   hours$_{w9-10}$.]$_{s2}$ [He talked$_{e4:w2}$ for five hours$_{me3:w4-5}$ altogether.]$_{s3}$

The event of Jon's two lectures, mentioned first in Example 10.32, is
annotated and interpreted as in Annotation 10.33.

Annotation 10.33   Temporal annotation

a. Sentence 1:
   [Jon gave two long lectures$_{w2-5}$ on Situation Semantics yesterday$_{w9}$.]$_{s1}$

b. Temporal annotation:
   ```
   event(e1, s1w2-5, type="process", pred="lecture", tense="past",
       plurality="yes", cardinality="2")
   timex3(t1, s1w9, type="date", value="1987-05-16",
   functionInDocument="yes")
   tLink(e1, t1, relType="isIncluded")
   ```

c. Semantic representation:
   $\exists 2e_1 \exists t_1$
   $[lecture(e_1) \land process(e_1) \land past(e_1) \land plural(e_1)^9$
   $\land date(t_1) \land year(t_1, 1987) \land month(t_1, 05) \land day(t_1, 16)$
   $\land \tau(e_1) \subseteq t_1]$

---

[9] Note again that $plural(e_1)$ is defined to be $\kappa(e_1) \leq 2$ as a meaning postulate that delimits an
interpretation model, where κ is a counting function that maps an object to its number or the
number of its parts.

The semantic representation in Example 10.33c simply states that there were two lectures on May 16, 1987.

The first e_{11} of the two lectures is annotated and interpreted as an *instance* or *part* of the lecture e_1 as in Annotation 10.34.

Annotation 10.34   The first lecture annotated

a. The first lecture$_{e11:process,w12}$ lasted $\emptyset_{t11:tInterval}$two hours$_{me1:tLength,w15-16}$ and the other one$_{e12:process,w18-20}\emptyset_{t12:tInterval}$three hours$_{me2:tLength,w21-22}$.

b. Temporal metric annotation (* First lecture*):

(* Base structures *)
```
event(e1, s1w2-5, type="process", pred="lecture", tense="past",
     plurality="yes", cardinality="2")
event(e11, w12, type="process", pred="lecture")
timex3(t11, type="tInterval, value="#me1")
measure(me1, w15-16, type="tLength", value="2,hour")
```

(* Link structures *)
```
pLink(e11, e1, relType="partOf")10
tLink(e11, e1, relType="isIncluded")
mLink(t11, me1, relType="measures")
```

c. Semantic representation:

$\exists 2e_1 \exists\{e_{11}, t_1, t_{11}\}$

$[lecture(e_1) \wedge process(e_1) \wedge past(e_1) \wedge plural(e_1)$

$\wedge e_{11} \sqsubseteq e_1$

$\wedge tInterval(t_{11}) \wedge t_{11} \sqsubseteq t_1$

$\wedge \tau(e_{11}) \subseteq t_{11}$

$\wedge \mu(t_{11}) = <2, hour>]$

The semantic representation (Annotation 10.34c) states that the first lecture e_{11} was part of the lecture series e_1 and that its occurrence time $\tau(e_{11})$ is included in the subinterval t_{11} of t_1. The semantic representation was also interpreted as stating that the length $\mu(t_{11})$ of the time interval t_{11} during which the first lecture e_{11} occurred was 2 hours.[11]

The second lecture e_{12} can also be annotated and interpreted in the same way. There are four differences: (1) the lecture e_{12}, as well as the lecture e_{11}, is part of the lecture series e_1, (2) it occurs at another subinterval t_{12} of the whole interval t_1, (3) the lecture e_{12} is preceded by the lecture e_{11}, and (4) the length $\mu(t_3)$ of the second subinterval t_3 is 3 hours, as in the semantic representation of Annotation 10.35:

[10] pLink captures mereological relations over objects like events.
[11] The verb *lasted* implies that the lecture continued contiguously without a break. Otherwise, $\mu(t_{11})=<2,hour>$ can be replaced by the amount statement: $\alpha(e_{11},t_{11})=<2,hour>$.

Annotation 10.35   The second lecture annotated

a. Base annotation:

... and the other one$_{e12:process,:w18-20}$ $\emptyset_{t12:tInterval}$ three hours$_{me2:tLength,w21-22}$.

b. Semantic representation:

$\exists\{e_1, e_{11}, e_{12}, t_1, t_{11}, t_{12}\}$

$[lecture(e_1) \land process(e_1) \land past(e_1) \land plural(e_1)$

$\land e_{12} \sqsubseteq e_1$

$\land \tau(e_{12}) \subseteq t_{12} \land tInterval(t_{12}) \land t_{12} \sqsubseteq t_1$

$\land \tau(e_{11}) \prec \tau(e_{12}) \land t_{11} \prec t_{12}$

$\land \mu(t_{12})=<3, hour>]$

Since the anchoring time $\tau(e_{11})$ is the time interval t_{11} and the anchoring time $\tau(e_{12})$ is the time interval t_{12}, we can also infer that t_{11} precedes t_{12}. The time length of the interval t_{12} is treated as being 3 hours.

Finally, the last sentence in Example 10.32 on Jon's lecture series can be annotated and interpreted similarly.

Annotation 10.36   Summing up the lecture series

a. Base annotation:

Jon gave two long lectures$_{e1,w2-5}$ $\cdots$ yesterday$_{t1,w9}$ $\cdots$ He talked$_{e2:process,w24}$ for five hours$_{me3:tAmount,w26-27}$ altogether.

b. Semantic representation:

$\exists\{e_1, e_2, t_1\}$

$[lecture(e_1) \land process(e_1) \land past(e_1) \land plural(e_1)$

$\land talk(e_2) \land process(e_2) \land past(e_2)$

$\land e_2=e_1$

$\land yesterday(t_1)$

$\land \tau(e_2) \subseteq t_1$

$\land \alpha(e_2,t_1)=<5, hour>]$

Since $e_2=e_1$, we can infer that $\alpha(e_1,t_1)=<5, hour>$. This amount also equals the sum of the two time lengths, *two hours* and *three hours*, of the two time subintervals to which the two lectures were anchored.

Two-Way Classification   Unlike the three-way classification of temporal measures, as proposed in this section, Quirk et al. (1985, 8.57*ff*) introduce only two notions of temporal measures, *span* and *duration*. The term *span* is equivalent to the term *time interval*, while the term *duration* includes the notion of *time amount*. Example 10.37 shows how temporal measures are classified differently.

Example 10.37   Two-way classification of time measures

a. Archie taught at Texas *for more than 40 years$_{t\,Amount/duration}$.*
b. Jim finished a book *in less than three months$_{t\,Interval/span}$.*
c. Jon taught at a high school *six years$_{t\,Interval/span}$* after his military service *for three years$_{t\,Amount/duration}$.*
d. Mia stayed in Paris *from* June *through* August$_{duration}$ *three months$_{t\,Amount/duration}$.*

Example 10.37d clearly shows how the use of the term *duration* differs from that of the term *amount*, while Quirk et al. (1985) do not differentiate the two.

Time Amount and Negation

Katz (2007) introduces a maximizing existential $\exists_{max}$ to treat time amounts and also cases involving negation. Here are some illustrations.

Example 10.38   Maximizing existential quantifier

a. John taught for 20 minutes on Monday.
b. Maximizing existential:
   $\exists_{max} P$
   $[P \sqsubseteq \lambda e[teaching(e)]$
   $\wedge P \sqsubseteq \lambda e[20min(\tau(e))]$
   $\wedge P \sqsubseteq \lambda e[\tau(e) \subseteq Monday)]]$
   $\wedge \exists e[P(e)]$

Here, $\sqsubseteq$ stands for the *part Of* relation between properties.

Example 10.39   Negating maximizing existential

a. John *didn't* teach *for 20 minutes* on Monday.
b. $\exists_{max} P$
   $[P \sqsubseteq \lambda e[teaching(e)]$
   $\wedge P \sqsubseteq \lambda e[20min(\tau(e))]$
   $\wedge P \sqsubseteq \lambda e[\tau(e) \subseteq Monday)]]$
   $\wedge \neg\exists e[P(e)]$

Annotation-based semantics (ABS), proposed in this book, does not require Katz's maximizing existential $\exists_{max}$ to treat the negation of time amount. With Definition 10.30, which defines *time amount*, ABS represents the semantic content of Example 10.38a as follows.

Semantics 10.40   Time amount in ABS

a. Annotation:

John taught$_{e1:process}$ for$_{s1:metric}$ 20 minutes$_{me1:t\,Amount}$ on$_{s2:anchoring}$ Monday$_{t1}$.

b. Semantic representation:

$\exists\{e_1, t_1\}$
$[teach(e_1) \wedge process(e_1) \wedge past(e_1)$
$\wedge\, week(t_1, Monday)$
$\wedge\, \tau(e_1) \subseteq t_1$
$\wedge\, \alpha(e_1, t_1) = <20, minute>]$

Thus, ABS treats the negation of the time amount of an eventuality, as in Semantics 10.41:

Semantics 10.41   Negation and time amount in ABS

a. Base annotation:

John didn't teach$_{e1:process}$ for$_{s1:metric}$ 20 minutes$_{me1:t\,Amount}$ but for$_{s3:metric}$ two hours$_{me2:t\,Amount}$ on$_{s2:anchoring}$ Monday$_{t1}$.

b. Temporal metric annotation:

```
mLink(mL1, figure="e1", ground="me1", relType="negMeasure")
```

c. Semantic representation:

$\exists\{e_1, t_1\}$
$[teach(e_1) \wedge process(e_1) \wedge past(e_1)$
$\wedge\, week(t_1, Monday)$
$\wedge\, \tau(e_1) \subseteq t_1$
$\wedge\, \alpha(e_1, t_1) \neq <20, minute>$
$\wedge\, \alpha(e_1, t_1) = <2, hour>]$

Here is another example.

Example 10.42   Negation in ABS

a. John didn't teach at all on Monday.

b. Base annotation:

John didn't teach$_{e1:process}$ at all on Monday$_{t1}$.

c. Semantic representation:

$\exists\{x_1, e_1, t_1\}$
$[named(x_1, John)$
$\wedge\, teach(e_1) \wedge process(e_1) \wedge past(e_1)$
$\wedge\, agent(e_1, x_1)$
$\wedge\, week(t_1, Monday)$
$\wedge\, \tau(e_1) \nsubseteq t_1]$

Table 10.1 *Temporal relators*

type	tRelators R	tArgStructure	tAdjunct A (example)
1. anchoring	*at, in, on, during*	date, time, eventuality	$A \rightarrow R_{anchoring}T/E$ (*at noon*)
2. ordering	*after, before*	date, time, eventuality	$A \rightarrow R_{ordering}T/E$ (*before noon*)
3. metric	*for, in*	tAmount	$A \rightarrow R_{t\,Amount}M$ (*for two hours*)
		tDistance (duration)	$A \rightarrow \emptyset_{t\,Interval}R_{t\,Distance}M$ ($\emptyset_{t\,Interval}$ *in two years*)
4. bounding	*from – till, since*	date, time, eventuality	$A \rightarrow \emptyset_{t\,Interval}R_{bounding}T/E$ ($\emptyset_{t\,Interval}$ *since 1905*)
5. orienting	*after, before, ago*	date, time, eventuality	$A \rightarrow \emptyset_{t\,Interval}M\,R_{bounding}T/E$ ($\emptyset_{t\,Interval}$ *an hour before the storm*)

The semantic form in Example 10.42c is interpreted as stating that John had no teaching on Monday.

10.3 Temporal Relators and Temporal Adjunct Constructions

10.3.1 Overview

This section focuses on *temporal adjunct constructions*. There are two types: *simple* and *complex*. Each simple temporal adjunct consists of a temporal relator (e.g., *at*) and its grammatical Object argument (e.g., *two o'clock*). Complex temporal adjunct constructions all introduce an interval $\emptyset_{t:interval}$ as a nonconsuming tag in annotation to the core construction that consists of a temporal relator and its object argument.

Table 10.1 shows that temporal argument structures all denote simple entities such as dates, times T, or eventualities E, except for the metric type, which denotes either time amount or time distance M. However, when these temporal structures combine with different types of temporal relators R, they form different types of adjunct constructions, either simple or complex. Simple adjuncts each consist of R and T, E, or M. Anchoring or ordering temporal relators each combine with a date, time, or eventuality-type expression to form a *simple adjunct* (see Section 10.3.2).

There are two metric relators: *for* for time amount and *in* for temporal distance (duration). The time amount relator *for* forms a simple temporal adjunct construction, whereas the duration relator *in* introduces a time interval $\emptyset_{interval}$ as part of its adjunct construction to associate metric information with the time interval thus introduced. Bounding and orienting temporal relators also form *complex temporal adjunct constructions*, each of which introduces a *bounded time interval* as part of its adjunct construction.

10.3.2 Simple Temporal Adjunct Constructions

Anchoring Temporal Relators

The most basic type of temporal relators is the *anchoring type*. Anchoring temporal relators such as *at, during, in*, and *on* form simple temporal adjunct constructions. They simply relate an eventuality to a time. Here is an example.

Example 10.43   Anchoring temporal relator *on*:
a. Mia left for Paris *on* Sunday.
b. Morpho-syntactic analysis (annotation):
   Mia left$_{e1:event}$ for Paris
   [on$_{t\,Relator:anchoring:proper\,Inclusion}$ Sunday$_{t1:time:t\,Argument}$]$_{t\,Adjunct}$
c. Semantic representation:
   $\exists\{e_1, t_1\}$
   $[leave(e_1) \wedge past(e_1)$
   $\wedge sunday(t_1)$
   $\wedge \tau(e_1) \subset t_1]$

In Example 10.43, the temporal relator *on* syntactically governs the temporal expression *Sunday* as its argument (grammatical object). These two together form a *temporal adjunct* that modifies an eventuality temporarily. The *(proper) temporal inclusion relation* $\subset$ in the semantic representation (Example 10.43c) captures the *anchoring* relation, $\tau(e_1) \subset t_1$, between the temporalized event $\tau(e_1)$ of Mia leaving for Paris and the time t_1 Sunday. Both the annotation and the semantic representation here are straightforward.

Here is another example.

Example 10.44   Anchoring temporal relator *during*
a. Mia's parents stayed in Paris *during* the Korean War.
b. Annotation:
   Mia's parents stayed$_{e3:event}$ in Paris
   [during$_{t\,Relator:anchoring:t\,Inclusion}$ the Korean War$_{e4:event:t\,Argument}$]$_{t\,Adjunct}$.
c. Semantic representation:
   $\exists\{e_3, e_4\}$
   $[stay(e_3) \wedge past(e_3)$

$\wedge$ *korean War* (e_4)
$\wedge \tau(e_3) \subseteq \tau(e_4)]$

The temporal adjunct in Example 10.44 also illustrates a structurally simple case of the temporal anchoring of eventualities. The event, which is denoted by *the Korean War* in Example 10.44b, is *temporalized* by the function τ, while referring not to the war itself, but to the time of its occurrence $\tau(e_4)$. The temporal relator *during* combines with the temporalized event, *the Korean War*, to form a temporal adjunct, the configuration of which is still simple. It also denotes a simple semantic relation $\subseteq$ of *temporal inclusion* between the two *temporalized events*, $\tau(e_3) \subseteq \tau(e_4)$.

Ordering Temporal Relators

Temporal ordering $\prec$ is also a simple type. It denotes a binary relation over times in linear order. Here is an example.

Example 10.45   Ordering temporal relator *after*
a. The plane took off *after* midnight.
b. Annotation:
   The plane took off$_{e2:event}$
   [after$_{t\,Relator:ordering}$ midnight$_{t2:time:t\,Argument}$]$_{t\,Adjunct}$.
c. Semantic representation:
   $\exists\{e_2, t_2\}$
   [*take Off*$(e_2) \wedge past(e_2)$
   $\wedge\ time(t_2, 24:00)$
   $\wedge\ t_2 \prec \tau(e_2)]$

The temporal adjunction in Example 10.45b forms a simple configuration, consisting of the temporal relator *after* and the time *midnight* only. The temporal expression *midnight* denotes the last hour of a day. The temporal relator *after* is of the *ordering* type, which denotes the *temporal precedence relation* $\prec$. The semantic relation in Example 10.45c then states that the time t_2, 24:00, precedes the departure time $\tau(e_2)$, meaning that the departure time was after the time t_2, midnight.

Metric Temporal Relator *for*

The metric temporal relator *for* combines with a time measure expression (e.g., *five hours*) to form a simple adjunct construction, [*for*$_{metric:t\,Amount}$ $M_{t\,Measur}$]$_{tAdjunct}$. Here is an example.

Example 10.46   Metric temporal relator *for*

a. Time amount:

Mia played the piano *for*$_{s1:metric:tAmount}$ five hours$_{me1:measure}$ yesterday, two in the morning and three in the afternoon.

b. Annotation:

Mia played$_{e1:process}$ the piano

[for$_{s1:metric:tAmount}$ five hours$_{me1:measure}$]$_{tAdjunct}$ yesterday$_{t1:date}$, two$_{me11}$ in the morning$_{t11:time}$ and three$_{me12}$ in the afternoon$_{t12:time}$.

c. Semantic representation:

$\exists\{e_1, t_1, t_{11}, t_{12}\}$

$[play(e_1) \wedge past(e_1)$

$\wedge\ yesterday(t_1)$

$\wedge\ \tau(e_1) \sqsubseteq t_1$

$\wedge\ \alpha(e_1, t_1) = <5, hour>$

(* total amount of playing the piano yesterday *)

$\wedge\ morning(t_{11}) \wedge t_{11} \sqsubseteq t_1$

$\wedge\ \alpha(e_1, t_{11}) = <2, hour>$

$\wedge\ afternoon(t_{12}) \wedge t_{12} \sqsubseteq t_1$

$\wedge\ \alpha(e_1, t_{12}) = <3, hour>]$

The notation $\sqsubseteq$ here used denotes the *partOf* relation between times as well as between events. There were two event instances of Mia's playing the piano on a day, referred to by *yesterday*. The first one lasted two hours in the morning and the second one, three hours in the afternoon. These two time amounts amounted to five hours.

10.3.3 Complex Temporal Adjunct Constructions

The configurations of temporal adjunction can be complex. There are three types: *metric, bounding,* and *orienting*. They all introduce a *bounded interval* to the configurations of temporal adjunction. Each bounded interval t is represented as a *nonconsuming tag* in annotation. It is also specified with its two bounding points: $starts(t, t_0)$ and $ends(t, t_1)$. These points function either as the *anchoring point* to which an eventuality is anchored or the *reference point* from which an interval is oriented.

Metric Temporal Relator *in*

The metric temporal relator *in* introduces a bounded interval $\emptyset_{t:tInterval}$ into the annotation of their adjunct constructions. Their temporal object arguments (e.g., *three hours*) specify the *quantitative temporal measure* of each bounded interval for the metric temporal relator *in*.

Subtypes of Temporal Measures There are three subtypes of temporal measures.

Classification 10.47   Subtypes of temporal measures
  (i) the measure function μ measures the *length* of a time interval
 (ii) the distance function δ measures a *temporal distance*, often called *duration*, between the two boundary points of a time interval
(iii) the amount function α counts the *time amount* that an eventuality has consumed in a restricted time interval.

The amount function α is a particular case of the counting function κ applied to the counting or summing up of amounts of time.
  Here is an example of the length of a time interval.

Example 10.48   Length of a time interval
a. Markables: Jon wrote a novel in$_{s1:t Length}$ six months$_{me1:measure}$.
b. Annotation:
   Jon wrote$_{e1:process}$ a novel
   $[\emptyset_{t:t Interval}$ in$_{s1:t Length}$ six months$_{me1:measure}]_{t Adjunct}$.
c. Semantic representation:
   $\exists\{e_1, t, t_1\}$
   $[write(e_1) \wedge process(e_1) \wedge past(e_1)$
   $t Interval(t) \wedge ends(t, t_1)$
   $\wedge \mu(t) = <6, month>$
   $\wedge culminates(e_1, t_1)]$

The logical predicate *culminates* indicates its *accomplishment point* of time after a certain time interval involving a process. The process of Jon's writing a novel lasted the length of six months and he completed it at the end of that time interval.

Bounding Temporal Relators
Bounding temporal relators (e.g., *from ... till/through*) and their argument temporal structures form the complex configurations of temporal adjuncts with *bounded intervals*. Bounded intervals have their boundaries, either *start* or *end*, or both. These boundaries are specified in Definition 10.49.

Definition 10.49   Bounded interval

A bounded interval t is a triplet $<t, t_0, t_1>$, or $\lambda t[starts(t, t_0) \wedge ends(t, t_1)]$, such that t_0 is the start and t_1, the end of the interval t, which is the bounded interval $[t_0, t_1]$.

Bounded intervals are annotated as follows.

Annotation 10.50   Bounded interval

a. Annotation:
```
timex3(t, type="tInterval", start="t0", end="t1")
timex3(t0, type="time/date" value="")
timex3(t1, type="time/date" value="")
```
b. Semantic representation:

$\exists\{t, t_0, t_1\}[tInterval(t) \wedge starts(t, t_0) \wedge ends(t, t_1)]$

In natural language, bounded intervals and their boundary points (minimal intervals) are specified by bounding relators (`tRelator(type="bounding")`) such as *from* and *till/through* as a pair.

Consider three examples in Examples 10.52, 10.53, and 10.54 for illustration. These intervals introduce temporal relators as signals of the following types.

Classification 10.51   Types of temporal relators for bounded intervals $[t_0, t_1]$

a. *startBounding*: bounds the *start* of an interval.
b. *endBounding*: bounds the *end* of an interval.
c. *startOpen* $(t_0, t_1]$: the *start* of an interval is open or unspecified.
d. *endOpen* $[t_0, t_1)$: the *end* of an interval is open or unspecified.

Three examples are presented. The first example illustrates a case of a bounded interval $\emptyset_{t:tInterval}$, which is introduced as part of a complex temporal adjunct construction.

Example 10.52   Fully bounded intervals $[t_0, t_1]$

a. Data: Jon talked three straight hours *from* two *to* five in the afternoon.
b. Base annotation:

Jon talked$_{e1:past}$

$[\emptyset_{t:tInterval}$ three straight hours$_{me1:tLength:duration}$

from$_{s1:startBounding}$ two$_{t0:start}$ *to*$_{s2:endBounding}$ five$_{t1:end}$ in the afternoon$]_{tAdjunct}$
c. Semantic representation:

$\exists\{e_1, t, t_0, t_1\}$

$[talk(e_1) \wedge past(e_1)$

$\wedge tInterval(t) \wedge starts(t, t_0) \wedge ends(t, t_1)$

$\wedge \mu(t) =<3, hour>$

$\wedge\, time(t_0, \text{T}14{:}00) \wedge time(t_1, \text{T}17{:}00)$
$\wedge\, \delta(t_0, t_1) = \mu(t)$
$\wedge\, \tau(e_1) \subseteq t]$

The bounded interval t in Example 10.52 is closed with its two endpoints, $time(t_0, \text{T}14{:}00)$ and $time(t_1, \text{T}17{:}00)$. The length $\mu(t)$ of the interval t is 3 hours: $\mu(t) = <3, hour>$. The temporal distance $\delta(t_0, t_1)$ between the two bounding points is the same as the length of the interval: $\delta(t_0, t_1) = \mu(t)$. Then the event time $\tau(e_1)$ of Jon's talk was included in the interval t specified as such: $past(e_1) \wedge \tau(e_1) \subseteq t$.

Here is another example of bounded intervals, which is represented as a nonconsuming tag or an empty set $\emptyset_{t\,Interval}$.

Example 10.53 Bounded intervals annotated as nonconsuming tags
a. Data: Mia slept $\emptyset_{t:t\,Interval}$ from ten till seven.
b. Annotation
   Mia slept$_{e1:state:past}$
   [$\emptyset_{t:t\,Interval}$ from$_{s1:t\,Relator:start\,Bounding}$ ten$_{t0:time}$
   till$_{s2:t\,Relator:end\,Bounding}$ seven$_{t1:time}$]$_{t\,Adjunct}$
c. Semantic representation:
   $\exists\{e_1, t, t_0, t_1\}$
   $[sleep(e_1) \wedge state(e_1) \wedge past(e_1)$
   $\wedge\, tInterval(t) \wedge starts(t, t_0) \wedge ends(t, t_1)$
   $\wedge\, time(t_0, 22{:}00) \wedge time(t_1, 07{:}00 + 1D)$
   $\wedge\, \tau(e_1) \subseteq t]$

The time interval t in the temporal adjunct construction in Example 10.53 specifies a bounded interval $[t_0, t_1]$ with the two explicitly mentioned bounding times, $time(t_0, 22{:}00)$ and $time(t_1, 07{:}00 + 1D)$.

Example 10.54 illustrates the case of a semibounded interval which also functions as part of a temporal adjunct.

Example 10.54 Semibounded intervals $[t_0, t_1)$:
a. Data: Mia will get better *from* now *on*.
b. Annotation:
   Mia will get better$_e$
   [$\emptyset_{t:t\,Interval:[t_0, t_1)}$ from$_{s1:s\,Bounding}$ now$_{t0:time}$ on$_{s2:e\,Open}$]$_{t\,Adjunct}$
c. Semantic representation:
   $\exists\{e, t, t_0\}$
   $[getBetter(e) \wedge future(e)$
   $\wedge\, now(t_0)$

$\wedge\, t Interval(t) \wedge starts(t, t_0)$
$\wedge\, \tau(e) \subseteq t]$

The adverbial particle $on_{s2:e\,Open}$ in Example 10.54 is functioning as part of the temporal adjunct. It indicates that the endpoint of the semibounded time interval t is *open* and unspecified.

Orienting Temporal Relators

As Quirk et al. (1985) suggest, the main function of orienting temporal relators, just like ordering temporal relators, is to locate event times either forward (future-oriented) or backward (past-oriented) with respect to their *reference times*. Here are some examples.

Classification 10.55   Types of temporal relators

a. Forward/posterior/future-orienting temporal relators: *after, since, from*

   (i) Example: Gio left for Paris after Easter.
   (ii) Annotation: Gio left$_{e1}$ for Paris [$after_{s1:forward\,Orienting}$
        Easter$_{t2:reference}$]$_{t\,Adjunct}$
   (iii) Temporal relation: $t_2 \prec \tau(e_1)$

b. Backward/anterior/past-orienting temporal relators: *before, ago*

   (i) Example: Gio returned home *before* Christmas.
   (ii) Annotation: Gio returned$_{e2}$ home [$before_{s2:backward\,Orienting}$
        Christmas$_{t3:reference}$]$_{t\,Adjunct}$
   (iii) Temporal relation: $\tau(e_2) \prec t_3$

Ordering temporal relators such as *after* and *before* are particular cases of orienting temporal relators. The preposition *after* in Classification 10.55a functions as a *forward/posterior/future-orienting* temporal relator. Its object argument t_2 denotes a *reference time*. Together they form a temporal adjunct construction: for example, [after$_{t\,Relator}$ Easter$_{t2:reference}$]$_{tAdjunct}$. The primary function of the orienting temporal relator *after* is to place the anchoring ground of the event e_1 *forward* or *future-oriented* with respect to the reference time Easter$_{t_2}$. In contrast, the preposition *before* is a *backward/anterior/past-orienting* temporal relator. It places the anchoring ground of the event e_2 *backward* or *past-oriented* with respect to the reference time Christmas$_{t3}$.

Span/Oriented Interval   Unlike ordering temporal relators, orienting temporal relators have another important function: they specify the *anchoring ground*

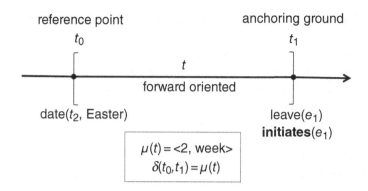

Figure 10.3 Forward (posterior) orientation

of an eventuality with respect to a *reference point* and also to an *oriented interval*. Consider Example 10.56.

Example 10.56 Span/oriented interval

a. Data: Gio left for Paris *two weeks after* Easter.

b. Annotation:

Gio left$_{e1:past}$ for Paris

[$\emptyset_{t:tInterval}$ *two weeks*$_{me1:tLength}$ after$_{s1:forwardOrienting}$ Easter$_{t2:reference}$]
tAdjunct

c. Semantic representation:

$\exists\{e_1, t, t_0, t_1, t_2\}$

$[leave(e_1) \wedge past(e_1)$

$\wedge\ tInterval(t) \wedge starts(t, t_0) \wedge ends(t, t_1)$

$\wedge\ date(t_2, Easter) \wedge t_2 = t_0$

$\wedge\ t_2 \prec \tau(e_1)$

$\wedge\ \mu(t) = <2, week> \wedge \delta(t_0, t_1) = \mu(t)$

$\wedge\ initiates(e_1, t_1)]$

Orienting relators each introduce a time interval t, which is represented as a *nonconsuming* tag $\emptyset_{t:tInterval}$, as part of the configuration of temporal adjunction. The forward-orienting temporal relator *after*$_{s1:forwardOrienting}$ as in Example 10.56b places each oriented time interval $\emptyset_{t:tInterval}$ at a *posterior* position with respect to the reference time *Easter*$_{t2}$. The event e_1 is anchored to one of the boundary points, depending on the directionality of the spatial relator. If a given interval is forward oriented as in Example 10.56b, then the *anchoring ground* is the endpoint t_1 of that interval t, as in Figure 10.3. The event e_1 of Gio leaving for Paris is thus initiated at t_1, as represented in Example 10.56c. All these temporal relations are represented visually in Figure 10.3.

Backward Orientation Consider a case of backward orientation.

Example 10.57 Backward orientation

a. Data: Gio returned home a week *before* Christmas.

b. Temporal adjunct with backward orientation:

Gio returned$_{e2}$ home

$[\emptyset_{t:tInterval}$ a week$_{me2:tLength}$ before$_{s2:backwardOrienting}$
Christmas$_{t2:reference}]_{tAdujunct}$.

c. Semantic representation:

$\exists\{e_2, t, t_0, t_1, t_2\}$

$[return(e_2) \wedge past(e_2)$

$\wedge\, tInterval(t) \wedge starts(t, t_0) \wedge ends(t, t_1)$

$\wedge\, \mu(t) = <1, week> \wedge \delta(t_0, t_1) = \mu(t)$

$\wedge\, date(t_2, Christmas) \wedge t_2 = t_1$

$\wedge\, \tau(e_2) \prec t_1$

$\wedge\, occurs(e_2, t_0)]$

The semantic representation in Example 10.57c states that Mia's return home e_2 occurred before Christmas t_2 and a week earlier.

Forward-Orienting Temporal Relator *since* Here are two typical orienting temporal relators: *since* and *ago*, neither of which is a simple ordering relator. Consider Example 10.58.

Example 10.58 Forward-ordering temporal relators

a. Data: The restaurant has been kept open *since* 1946.

b. Temporal adjunction with forward-oriented interval:

The restaurant has been open$_{e2}$

$[\emptyset_{t:tInterval}$ since$_{s2:forwardOrienting}$ 1946$_{t2}]_{t:tAdjunct}$.

c. Semantic representation:

$\exists\{e_2, t, t_0, t_1, t_2\}$

$[open(e_2) \wedge presPerf(e_2)$

$\wedge\, tInterval(t) \wedge starts(t, t_0) \wedge ends(t, t_1)$

$\wedge\, year(t_2, 1946) \wedge t_2 = t_0 \wedge now(t_1)$

$\wedge\, \delta(t_0, t_1) = \mu(t)$

$\wedge\, holds(e_2, t)]$

The temporal adjunct t as annotated in Example 10.58b consists of a forward-oriented interval t that lasted from the year 1946 up to now. The semantic representation in Example 10.58c then states that the event e_2, which refers to the opening of the restaurant, has held so long.

Backward-Orienting Temporal Relator *ago* Consider Example 10.59.

Example 10.59 Backward-orienting temporal relators
a. Data: There was an earthquake at the southern tip of Jeju Island *a week ago*.
b. Annotation:
There was an earthquake$_{e3}$ at the southern tip of Jeju Island
$[\emptyset_{t:tInterval}$ a week$_{me1:tLengh}$ ago$_{s3:tRelator:backwardOrienting}]_{tAdjunct}$.
c. Semantic representation:
$\exists\{e_3, t, t_0, t_1, t_3\}$
$[earthquake(e_3) \wedge past(e_3)$
$\wedge\, tInterval(t) \wedge starts(t, t_0) \wedge ends(t, t_1)$
$\wedge\, now(t_3) \wedge t_3 = t_1$
$\wedge\, \mu(t) = <1, week> \wedge \delta(t_0, t_1) = \mu(t)$
$\wedge\, occurs(e_3, t_0)]$

The semantic representation in Example 10.59c is interpreted as stating that the event e_3 of the earthquake occurring around Jeju Island occurred one week before today.

10.4 Temporal Relators and Event Structures

10.4.1 Orientation, Reference Point, and Anchoring Ground

Determining the orientation type and the anchoring ground depends on the type of temporal relators as well as the semantic type of eventualities. An orienting relator determines the type of orientation, either *forward* or *backward*, with respect to a *reference point*. The forward orienting relator (e.g., *after*) is *future-orienting* with respect to the *reference point*, whereas the backward orienting relator (e.g., *before*) is *past-orienting* with respect to the *reference point*. The *anchoring ground* is determined by the type of eventuality with respect to an oriented interval. Here is a list of *grounding conditions*.

Specification 10.60 Conditions for anchoring ground
Given an interval t, which is [0,1] with its start point t_0 and endpoint t_1:[12]

---

[12] See Kracht (2002) for the representation of the start $p(0)$ or the end $p(1)$ of an interval [0,1].

a. For an eventuality $e_{transition}$ of a *transition*-type,

    Case 1: if the interval t is *forward oriented*,

                then the endpoint t_1 is the anchoring ground of $e_{transition}$
                with respect to the reference point t_0.

    Case 2: if the interval t is *backward oriented*,

                then the start point t_0 is the anchoring ground of $e_{transition}$
                with respect to the reference point t_1.

b. For an eventuality e_{state} of *state*-type or for an eventuality $e_{process}$ of *process*-type:

    the whole interval t, which is $[0,1]$, is the anchoring ground.

Orienting Temporal Relators with *Transition*-Type Eventualities

Recall that *transition*-type eventualities culminate into a state. There are two subtypes: achievement and accomplishment. Achievements each undergo a change from a state to a state, whereas accomplishments each undergo a process and then culminate into a state (see Mani and Pustejovsky (2012, p. 38)), as in Definition 10.61.

Definition 10.61   Subtypes of transition redefined:

a. Transition$_{ach}$ is a sequence of state state.
b. Transition$_{acc}$ is a sequence of process state.

These culminations occur at a time point, which is a minimal interval.

    Example 10.62 shows how the backward-orienting temporal relator *before* interacts with an event of *transition: achievement*.

Example 10.62   Oriented time interval with temporal distance
a. Data:
Gia got a job at LG *two months before* her graduation.
b. Backward-oriented temporal adjunct:
Gia got a job$_{e1:transition:achievement}$ at LG

[$\emptyset_{t:tInterval}$ two months$_{me1:tLength}$ before$_{s1:backwardOrienting}$ her graduation$_{e2}$]$_{tAdjunct}$

c. Semantic representation:
$\exists\{e_1, t, t_0, t_1, e_2\}$
$[getJob(e_1) \wedge transition^{ach}(e_1) \wedge past(e_1)$
$\wedge tInterval(t) \wedge starts(t, t_0) \wedge ends(t, t_1)$
$\wedge \mu(t) = <2, year> \wedge \delta(t_0, t_1) = \mu(t)$
$\wedge graduation(e_2)$
$\wedge \tau(e_1) \subseteq t_0 \wedge \tau(e_2) \subseteq t_1$

(* t_0 is the anchoring point and t_1, the reference point.*)
$\land \tau(e_1) \prec \tau(e_2)$]

The event e_1 of *Gia getting a job* occurred in the past and *before* her graduation e_2. The event e_1 is, however, a transition type, involving a *backward-oriented* interval. It was thus anchored to the start t_0 of the interval t: the anchoring ground of the event e_1 was the start t_0 of the interval, while the reference point was t_1, the endpoint of the interval t, where the event e_2 of Mia's graduation occurred. There was a temporal distance (duration) $\delta(t_0, t_1)$ between the two bounding points of the interval. The length $\mu(t)$ of the interval t was 2 months, which was the temporal distance length $\delta(t_0, t_1)$.

Temporal Distance (Duration)

In general, orienting relators trigger oriented intervals t each with a *temporal distance* $\delta(t_0, t_1)$, which is the same as $\mu(t)$. This distance is either fully specified or unspecified, as suggested by Gagnon and Lapalme (1996). Consider the following pair of examples.

Example 10.63 Oriented intervals with distances

a. Gia left for Busan $\emptyset_{t:oInterval}$ *two hours*$_{measure:tDistance}$
   after her breakfast$_{referencePoint}$.
b. Gia left for Busan $\emptyset_{t:oInterval}$ *after* her breakfast$_{referencePoint}$.

Example 10.63a is a case in which an oriented interval is specified with *two hours*, its temporal distance from the reference point. Example 10.63b is a case with no specification of the temporal distance of the oriented interval.

An *oriented interval* (span) can thus be characterized as a quadruple $<R, O, T, \delta>$, where R is a set of orienting relators, O is a set of orientations, either *forward* or *backward*, T is a (possibly empty) set of oriented time intervals, and δ is a temporal distance. We then have Definition 10.64.

Definition 10.64 Temporal distance (duration) of an oriented interval (span)

Given a temporal relator r in R with an orientation o in O that delimits a time interval t, [0,1], in T, a temporal distance $\delta(t_0, t_1)$ is either specified or unspecified. If it is specified, then $\delta(t_0, t_1)$ is the measure or linear quantity $\mu(t)$ of the time interval t.

The temporal distance $\delta(t_0, t_1)$, which ranges over the two bounding temporal points, t_0 and t_1, of an interval t, [0,1], is equal to $\mu(t)$, which is the length of the oriented time interval t.

Consider Example 10.65.

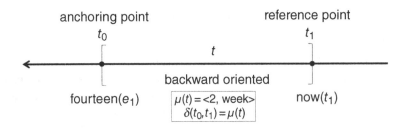

Figure 10.4 Temporal distance of an oriented interval

Example 10.65 Backward orienting temporal relator

a. Data: Jane became fourteen two weeks *ago*.

b. Base annotation: Jane became fourteen$_{e_1:transition^{ach}}$

   [Ø$_t$ two weeks$_{measure:tLength}$ ago$_{tRelator:backwardOrienting}$]$_{tAdjunct}$

Figure 10.4 is a depiction of Example 10.65. It illustrates how a temporal relator, the type of an eventuality, a time interval, and a temporal distance interact with one another.

The adverb *ago* as an orienting temporal relator triggers a backward-oriented interval t with the temporal distance of 2 weeks. The event e_1 occurred at the start t_0 of the backward-oriented interval t. The anchoring ground of Jane's becoming fourteen e_1 is the start t_0 of the backward-oriented interval t because the event e_1 is of type *transition^{ach}*.

These temporal entities together produce Semantics 10.66.

Semantics 10.66 Semantic representation

$\exists\{e_1, t, t_0, t_1\}$

$[getFourteen(e_1) \wedge past(e_1) \wedge transition_{ach}(e_1)$

$\wedge t_0 \prec t_1 \wedge tInterval(t) \wedge starts(t, t_0) \wedge ends(t, t_1)$

$\wedge t_1 = \gamma(n)$

   (* t_1 is the reference point and $\gamma(n)$ is the time point, denoted by *now*. *)

$\wedge \tau(e_1) \prec t_1$

$\wedge \mu(t) = <2, week> \wedge \delta(t_1, t_2) = \mu(t)$

$\wedge \tau(e_1) \subseteq t_0]$

   (* t_0 is the anchoring ground. *)

This representation states that Jane's becoming fourteen occurred in the past and at the start of the period of two weeks from *now* or the present moment n of time, represented by $\gamma(n)$.[13]

---

[13] The function γ maps a deictic expression like *now*, n, to its denotation, a time point.

10.4.2 Bounding Relators with State- or Process-Type Eventualities

Just like orienting relators, *bounding relators* form complex temporal adjuncts by introducing bounded intervals into their configurations. Consider Example 10.67, which shows how a time interval is bounded by its two endpoints.

Example 10.67   Bounding relators

a. Bounding:
   Gio slept *from six* in the evening *till six in the morning* the next day.
b. Annotation:
   Gio slept$_{e1:state}$
   [$\emptyset_t$ from$_{s1:startBounding}$ six$_{t0}$ in the evening till$_{s2:endBounding}$ six$_{t1}$ in the morning the next day]$_{t\,Adjunct}$
c. Semantic representation:
   $\exists\{e_1,t,t_0,t_1\}$
   $[sleep(e_1) \wedge state(e_1) \wedge past(e_1)$
   $\wedge\, tInterval(t) \wedge starts(t,t_0) \wedge ends(t,t_1)]$
   $\wedge\, time(t_0,\text{T18:00}) \wedge time(t_1,\text{T06:00+1D})$
   $\wedge\, holds(e_1,t)]$

The time interval t is explicitly bounded by the two endpoints, t_0 and t_1. The bounding relators (e.g., *from ... to/till*) delimit definite intervals closed with at least one of their boundaries mentioned. The anchoring ground of the *state*-type event e_1 is the entire interval t, bounded by the start t_0 and the endpoint t_1.

10.4.3 Metric Temporal Relators with State- or Process-Type Eventualities

There are at least two types of *metric relators*, *for* and *in*. The trigger *for* works with *state*- or *process*-type eventualities, whereas the trigger *in* marks *transition*-type occurrences. The bounding relator works with an eventuality of any semantic type, either *state*, *process*, or *transition* type. The orienting relators create *oriented intervals (spans)*. States and processes are also interpreted as being anchored to the whole stretch of an oriented interval, but these interpretations are contextually determined.

State- or Process-Type Eventualities with Temporal Measure
State or *process*-type eventualities may each occur with a temporal adjunct that contains a temporal metric relator *for*. Consider Example 10.68.

Example 10.68   Temporal measures

a. State type: Gia has lived in Seoul *for 20 years*.

b. Temporal metric annotation:
   Gia has lived$_{e1:state}$ in Seoul [$\emptyset_{t:tInterval}$ for$_{s1:metric}$ 20 years$_{tAmount}$]$_{tAdjunct}$

c. Semantic representation:
   $\exists\{e_1, t, t_0, t_1\}$
   [$liveInSeoul(e_1) \wedge state(e_1) \wedge presPerfect(e_1)$
   $\wedge tInterval(t) \wedge starts(t, t_0) \wedge ends(t, t_1)$
   $\wedge now(t_1) \wedge \alpha(e_1, t) = <20, year> \wedge holds(e_1, t)$]

The *state*-type eventuality e_1 of Gia having lived in Seoul is interpreted as holding for the time amount (duration) of 20 years up to the present.

Consider Example 10.69, which involves a *process*-type event, an oriented interval, and a time amount.

Example 10.69   *Process*-type event with an oriented interval and a time amount

a. *Process* type:
   Jon taught at a high school *six years after* his military service *for three years*.

b. Base annotation:
   Jon taught$_{e1:process}$ at a high school [$\emptyset_t$ six years$_{me1:tLength:tDistance}$ after$_{s1:forwardOrienting}$ his military service$_{e2}$ $\emptyset_{t2}$ for three years$_{me2:tAmount}$]$_{tAdjunct}$

c. Semantic representation:
   $\exists\{e_1, e_2, t, t_0, t_1, t_2\}$
   [$teach(e_1) \wedge process(e_1) \wedge past(e_1) \wedge militaryService(e_2) \wedge process(e_2) \wedge$
   $\tau(e_2) \prec \tau(e_1)$
   $\wedge tInterval(t) \wedge starts(t, t_0) \wedge ends(t, t_1) \wedge \tau(e_2) \preceq t \wedge t_0 \prec t_1 \wedge$
   $terminates(e_2, t_0) \wedge initiates(e_1, t_1) \wedge \mu(t) = <6, year> \wedge \delta(t_0, t_1) = \mu(t)$
   $\wedge \alpha(e_1, t_2) = <3, year> \wedge \alpha(e_1, t_2) \leq \mu(t_2)$]

Two logical predicates are introduced to the semantic representation in Example 10.69c: *terminates* and *initiates*. The predicate *terminates* relates an event to the termination point (time) of its process, while the predicate *initiates* relates an event to the initiation point (time) of its process. There was an interval of six years between the military service e_2 and Jon's job of teaching at a high school. The start t_0 of that interval t is the termination time of Jon's military service e_2, whereas t_1 is the initial time of Jon's high school teaching. Probably, Jon needed six years to go to college and also to graduate school to become a high school teacher. After that, he taught for three years. The last

Table 10.2 *Annotating temporal relators*

Type	Subtype	Preposition	Tagging
1. anchoring		*at, in, on, during*	tRelator(type="anchoring")
2. ordering		*after, before*	tRelator(type="ordering")
3. metric	tAmount	*for*	tRelator(type="tAmount")
	tLength	*in*	tRelator(type="tLength")
4. bounding	initial	*from, since*	tRelator(type="startBounding")
	mids	*through*	tRelator(type="midBounding")
	terminal	*till, to, through*	tRelator(type="endBounding")
5. orienting	forward	*after, since*	tRelator(type="forwardOrienting")
	backward	*before, ago*	tRelator(type="backwardOrienting")

formula $\alpha(e_1, t_2) \leq \mu(t_2)$ in the semantic representation in Example 10.69c states that there is a time interval t_2, which is not explicitly mentioned in the example, the length of which is greater or equal to the (cumulative) time amount of Jon's teaching.

10.4.4 Implementing Temporal Relators in General

Following ISO-TimeML (ISO, 2012b), eXTimeML represents the annotation of temporal relators with the tag tRelator with its categorized identifier *tr* followed by a positive integer. Various values of the attribute @type is subtyped, as represented in Table 10.2.

The assignment $@_{tRelator}$ for the base structures $\beta_{tRelator}$ of category *temporal relator* is defined as in Specificaiton 10.70.

Specification 10.70 Assignment $@_{tRelator}$:
```
attributes = identifier, target, type, pred, [comment];
identifier = tr + positive integer;
target = IDREF (ID of a markable);
type = anchoring | ordering | tAmount | tLength |
    startBounding | midBounding | endBounding |
    forwardOrienting | backwardOrienting;
pred = CDATA (predicative content);
comment = CDATA (optional);
```

Here is a simple example.

Example 10.71 Temporal relators in general
a. Data: Sejin left Kathmandu before the earthquake.
b. Base annotation:
   Sejin left$_{e1, w2}$ Kathmandu before$_{s1, w4}$ the earthquake$_{e2, w6}$.

c. Temporal annotation in pFormat:
```
tRelator(tr, w4, type="ordering", pred="before")
tLink(tL1, figure="e1", ground="e2", relType="before")
```
d. Semantic representation:

$\exists\{e_1, e_2\}[\tau(e_1) \prec \tau(e_2)]$,

where τ is the *runtime* or *temporalizing function* from eventualities and times.

Both $\tau(e_1)$ and $\tau(e_2)$ refer to the times they are anchored to.

Anchoring Temporal Relators

Anchoring relators such as *at, in, on, during*, and *by* are used in both temporal and spatial senses. These relators all refer to temporal locations, which were also called *time-positions* by Quirk et al. (1985, section 8.51 adjuncts of time). Unlike the prepositions such as *at, in*, and *on*, the preposition *during* is used in a temporal sense only. The preposition *by* is used in both spatial and temporal senses, but these two senses are not related.

The anchoring relators *at* and *in* in Examples 10.72 and 10.73 each anchor an eventuality to an atomic-type time. These anchoring relations can be represented logically with the predicates *culminates*, *occurs*, or *holds*, as shown in the following.

Example 10.72 Anchoring relations *occurs* and *culminates*

a. Data: Jeun-Marie arrived in Boston at nine-fifteen.
b. Base annotation:

Jeun-Marie arrived$_{e1:transition}$ in Boston at$_{s1:anchoring}$ nine-fifteen$_{t1:time}$.
c. Annotation:
```
event(e1, w2, type="transition", class="occurrence",
  pred="arrive", tense="past")
tRelator(tr1, w5, type="anchoring", pred="at")
timex3(t1, w6, type="time", value="XXXX-XX-XXT09:15")
tLink(tL1, figure="#e1", ground="#t1" relType="occurs")
```
d. Semantic representation:

$\exists\{e_1, t_1\}$
$[arrive(e_1) \wedge past(e_1)$
$\wedge time(t_1, T09:15)$
$\wedge [occurs(e_1, t_1) \wedge culminates(e_1, t_1)]]$

Being denoted by the predicate *arrive* of type *transition*, the event of Jeun-Marie's arrival *occurs* and *culminates* at the time of t_1, referred to by the time T09:15.[14]

---

[14] The culmination of the event *arrived*$_{e1:transition}$ here also implies that Jeun-Marie was *in* Boston at the time 09:15. This is treated by ISO-Space (ISO, 2020d).

Here is another illustration.

Example 10.73 Anchoring relation *holds*

a. Data: Mozart lived in the eighteenth century.

b. Base annotation:

Mozart lived$_{e_2:state}$ $in_{s2:anchoring}$ [the eighteenth century]$_{t_2:tInterval}$.

c. Temporal annotation:
```
event(e2, w2, type="state", class="state", pred="live",
  tense="past")
tRelator(tr2, w3, type="anchoring", pred="in")
timex3(t2, w4, type="tInterval", pred="century",
  start="t21", end="t22")
timex3(t21, type="time", value="1701-01-01")
timex3(t22, type="time", value="1800-12-31")
tLink(tL2, relType="holds", figure="e2", ground="t2")
```

d. Semantic representation:

$\exists\{e_2, t, t_2, t_{21}, t_{22}\}$

$[live(e_2) \wedge past(e_2) \wedge holds(e_2, t) \wedge tInterval(t_2) \wedge t \subset t_2 \wedge$

$century(t_2) \wedge starts(t_2, t_{21}) \wedge ends(t_2, t_{22}) \wedge$

$year(t_{21}, 1701) \wedge month(t_{21}, 01) \wedge day(t_{21}, 01) \wedge$

$year(t_{22}, 1800) \wedge month(t_{22}, 12) \wedge day(t_{22}, 31)]$

The predicates *occurs* and *holds*[15] are accompanied by their respective constraints. The predicate *holds* is constrained by an inclusion relation, represented by a subset relation $\subset$, between the two times, t and t_2, as in Example 10.73d. It is a historical fact that Mozart did not live throughout the whole period of the eighteenth century, but for only a portion of it. Following ISO 8601-1 (ISO, 2019a), I have been using the term *time interval* as referring to a time span with its start and end normally specified. As a result, the attribute @type for the element *timex3* has its range of values as specified in Specification 10.74.

Specification 10.74 Assignment @$_{timex3}$(type)
```
type = time | date | tInterval | set;
```

Here are two more examples, given by Example 10.75.[16]

Example 10.75 Anchoring relations and individual part (iPart) relations

---

[15] I follow the interval temporal logic of Allen (1984) and Allen and Ferguson (1994) and their definition of these predicates.

[16] Taken from Quirk et al. (1985, section 9.34): *at, on, in, by*.

a. Anchoring relation *occurs*:

We preferred traveling$_{e3}$ by$_{s3:anchoring}$ night$_{t3}$.[17]

$\exists\{e_3, t, t_3\}[travel(e_3) \wedge occurs(e_3, t) \wedge t=t_3 \wedge iPart(t_3, NI)]$

b. The anchoring relation *holds*: We stayed$_{e4}$ up during$_{s4:anchoring}$ the night$_{t4}$.

$\exists\{e_4, t, t_4\}[stay(e_4) \wedge past(e_4) \wedge holds(e_4, t) \wedge t \subseteq t_4 \wedge iPart(t_4, NI)]$

Here, the *individual part relation (iPart)* refers to a night (NI).[18] The anchoring (locative) prepositions such as *at, on, in*, and *by* are all used with either a clock time, a part of day, a date, or an interval (period) of time. Whether the time was interpreted as punctual or extended depends on the semantic type of each eventuality. Occurrences of the *transition* type are interpreted as taking place at a comparatively more *instantaneous interval* of time, while the states are interpreted as holding at a comparatively more *extended interval* of time.

Conjunctions Conjunctions such as *when* and *while* can also function as temporal relators. Here are examples of conjunctions that function as temporal relators of type *anchoring*.

Example 10.76 Conjunctions as temporal relators

a. All passengers died *when* the plane crashed into the mountain.
   [occurrences, simultaneous]

b. Gia sang *while* dancing. [processes, simultaneous]

c. My wife took a nap *while* I prepared lunch. [processes, simultaneous]

d. Gia was known to be a genius *when* she was young. [states, simultaneous]

Anchoring conjunctions temporarily relate an eventuality to another. These eventualities can be of any of the semantic types. Their run-times or event times are related by either the relation type *simultaneous* ($\bigcirc$) or the relation type *isIncluded* ($\subseteq$).

Metric Relators

Metric temporal relators, denoted by prepositions in English such as *for* and *in*, take temporal measure entities, time amounts, time lengths, or durations (temporal distances), as their arguments. The term *duration* used in ISO 8601-1 (ISO, 2019a) or ISO-TimeML (ISO, 2012b) refers to the *quantity* of a time

---

[17] Again, taken from Quirk et al. (1985, section 9.34): *at, on, in, by*. The temporal adjunct *by night* is an idiom replaceable by *during the night*.

[18] The *iPart* relation can also be represented by $\sqsubseteq$.

interval without specifying whether it refers to the length or the amount of time. In this book, I treat *duration* as a temporal distance in quantity between the two endpoints of an interval, while treating the measure of a time length simply as a linear quantity of an interval.

On the other hand, eXTimeML, the extended version of ISO-TimeML, makes a clear distinction between the length and the amount of time. The length of time is *measured* by the *measure function* μ from intervals to quantities of various temporal units, whereas the amount of time that is consumed by an eventuality is measured by the amount measuring function α *parametrized* with respect to a time interval, as defined in Definition 10.30, that sums up individual counts. The duration function δ maps a temporal distance between the two endpoints of an interval to the measure of the interval.

Here are some examples.

Example 10.77 Temporal metric relators *for* and *in*

a. We worked for$_{t\,Amount}$ 10 hours$_{t\,Amount}$ yesterday.
b. Jeun-Marie waited for$_{t\,Amount}$ more than 2 weeks$_{t\,Amount}$ to get a visa.
c. Gio wrote a book in$_{t\,Length}$ six months$_{t\,Length}$.
d. Breakfast will be ready in$_{t\,Length}$ a few minutes$_{t\,Length}$.
e. Gia slept [from nine to six]$_{duration}$ the next morning.
f. I taught at a university for$_{t\,Amount}$ almost 40 years$_{t\,Amount}$, but have to retire in$_{t\,Length}$ a year$_{t\,Length}$.

As shown in Examples 10.77a–f, the temporal relator *for* may be omitted at times, but the temporal relator *in* may not.

The temporal entities referred to by these measure expressions, however, are of three different types, *time amount, duration*, and *time length*. The time measure associated with the signal *for* is the *time amount* that is consumed by an eventuality. This amount can be a *cumulative quantity*. Example 10.77a, for instance, is thus annotated as follows.

Annotation 10.78 Temporal relator *for*

a. Markables: We worked$_{e1}$ for$_{t\,Amount}$ 10 hours$_{t\,Amount}$ yesterday$_{t1:t\,Interval}$.
b. Temporal metric annotation:

```
event(e1, w2, type="process", pred="work", tense="past")
tRelator(tr1, w3, type="tAmount", pred="for")
measure(me1, w4-5, type="tAmount", value="10,hour")
timex3(t1, w6, type="tInterval", value="yesterday")
mLink(mL1, relType="tAmount", figure="e1", ground="me1")
```

c. Semantic representation:

$\exists\{e_1, t_1\}$

$[work(e_1) \wedge process(e_1) \wedge past(e_1)$

$\wedge\ yesterday(t_1)$

$\wedge\ occurs(e_1, t_1)$

$\wedge\ \alpha(e_1, t_1) = <10, hour>]$

The time amount of 10-hour working is measured by the summing up function α, as defined in Definition 10.30. The signal *in*, in contrast, is simply associated with the length of a time interval at the end of which an associated event comes to a culmination point. Differences in their use have been discussed by Kenny (1963), Vendler (1967), Mourelatos (1978), Croft (2012), and many others in relation to the semantic aspectual types, especially *achievement* and *accomplishment* types, of eventualities that those measure signals are used with.

Time Length (Duration) vs. Time Amount The difference between the notion of *time length (duration)* and that of *time amount* can be shown in a few more use cases. Here is one typical case. The length of a time interval or the duration of the two endpoints of a time interval refers to a single stretch of time applied to a contiguous time span (interval), whereas the amount of time may be a cumulative amount of time taken by an eventuality or a sequence of event instances. Consider Example 10.79.

Example 10.79 Time length vs. time amount

a. Time length with transition:
   Gio woke up $\emptyset_{t1:tInterval/span}$ [two hours]$_{me1:tLength}$ after the sunrise.
b. Time amount with process:
   Gio worked [two hours]$_{me2:tAmount}$ yesterday, one in the morning and another hour in the afternoon.

The temporal measure expression *two hours* in Example 10.79a is used with an *transition*-type occurrence. It is annotated as [two hours]$_{me1:tLength}$, for it refers to a stretch or length of time that delimits an interval of time at the end of which Gio's waking up occurred. Example 10.79a can be annotated and interpreted as in Semantics 10.80.

Semantics 10.80 Temporal measures annotated and interpreted

a. Base annotation:
   Gio woke$_{e1:transition}$ up
   $[\emptyset_{t1:tInterval:span}$ [two hours]$_{me1:tLength}$ after$_{s1:fowardBounding}$
   the sunrise$_{e2}]_{tAdjunct}$.

b. Semantic representation:

$\exists\{e_1, e_2, t_1, t_{11}, t_{12}\}$

$[wakeUp(e_1) \wedge transition(e_1) \wedge past(e_1)$

$\wedge\, tInterval(t_1) \wedge starts(t_1, t_{11}) \wedge ends(t_1, t_{12})$

$\wedge\, \delta(t_{11}, t_{12}) = <2, hour>$

(* temporal distance between t_{11} and t_{12} *)

$\wedge\, occurs(e_1, t_{12})$

(* t_{12}: anchoring ground. *)

$\wedge\, sunRise(e_2) \wedge occurs(e_2, t_{11})$

(* t_{11}: reference point. The sun rose at t_{11}. *)

$\wedge\, \tau(e_2) \prec \tau(e_1)]$

(* The sun rose$_{e2}$ before Gio's waking up$_{e1}$. *)

Example 10.79a does not mention the time interval t_1 and its two endpoints t_{11} and t_{12}. They can, however, be introduced into the semantic representation because the measure (duration) of the temporal distance/span is explicitly mentioned. Following the anchoring ground condition in Specification 10.60 for *transition*-type eventualities, the endpoint t_{12} then becomes the *anchoring ground*, at which the event e_1 of Gio's waking up occurs. If the duration were not mentioned, then one could only say that Gio's waking up occurred after sunrise.

The temporal measure expression *two hours$_{me2:t\,Amount}$* in Example 10.79b is used with the *process*-type eventuality *worked*. It refers to the time amount accumulated with the time length of Gio's working in the morning and also that of her working in the afternoon.

When vs. How Long? Another difference between time length (duration) and time amount shows up in the use of the two temporal expressions. Consider Example 10.81.

Example 10.81 Question when?:

a. Question: *When* did Mia wake up?

b. Answer: She woke up *two hours after* the sunrise.

Example 10.81b is a possible answer to the *when*-type question in Example 10.81a. The answer is made with a transition-type eventuality *woke up* and a complex adjunct construction involving a duration (temporal distance) with an orienting temporal relator *two hours after*.

When a phrase such as *two hours after* as in Example 10.81a, denotes a temporal distance (duration) with a length of time between the two endpoints of a time interval, a sentence associated with such a phrase provides an answer

to a *when*-type question. Example 10.81a, for instance, has an answer like that
in Example 10.81b, as given in Annotation 10.82.

Annotation 10.82   Possible answers

a. Base annotation:

  She [woke up]$_{e1:\,transition:achievement}$

  [$\emptyset_{t1:t\,Interval}$ two hours$_{me1:t\,Length}$ after$_{s1:fOrienting}$ the sunrise$_{e2}$]$_{tAdjunct}$

b. Semantic representation:

  $\exists\{e_1, e_2, t_1, t_{11}, t_{12}\}$

  $[wakeUp(e_1) \land transition^{ach}(e_1) \land past(e_1)$

  $\land sunrise(e_2) \land past(e_2) \land \tau(e_2) \prec \tau(e_1)$

  (* The sun rose$_{e2}$ before Mia woke up$_{e1}$ *)

  $\land tInterval(t_1) \land starts(t_1, t_{11}) \land ends(t_1, t_{12})$

  $\land \delta(t_{11}, t_{12}) = <2, hours>$

  $\land occurs(e_2, t_{11})$

  $\land occurs(e_1, t_{12})]$

The third line in Annotation 10.82b is interpreted as saying that the sunrise
occurred before Mia woke up. The last four lines are interpreted as stating
that there was an interval of two hours between those two events and that the
sunrise occurred at the start of that interval, whereas Mia's waking up occurred
two hours later at the end of the interval.

  Example 10.79b, on the other hand, provides an answer to a *how long*-type
question, as shown in Example 10.83.

Example 10.83   How long?

a. Question: How long did Mia work yesterday?

b. Answer: She worked three and a half yesterday, one hour and a half in the
  morning and two hours in the afternoon.

The answer in Example 10.83b can be annotated as follows.

Annotation 10.84   A possible answer to a how-long question

a. Base annotation:

  Mia worked$_{e1:process}$ *three and a half hours*$_{me1:t\,Amount}$ yesterday$_{t1:time}$,

  $\emptyset_{e11}$ one hour and a half$_{me2:t\,Amount}$ in the morning$_{t11}$ and

  $\emptyset_{e12}$ two hours$_{me3:t\,Amount}$ in the afternoon$_{t12}$.

b. Semantic representation:

  $[work(e_1) \land process(e_1) \land past(e_2)$

  $\land yesterday(t_1)$

  $\land occurs(e_1, t_1)$

  $\land \alpha(e_1, t_1) = <3.5, hour>$

(* 3.5 hour work yesterday *)
$\wedge e_{11} \sqsubseteq e_1 \wedge morning(t_{11}) \wedge t_{11} \sqsubseteq t_1$
$\wedge \alpha(e_{11}, t_{11}) = <1.5, hour>$
(* 1.5 hour in the morning*)
$\wedge e_{12} \sqsubseteq e_1 \wedge afternoon(t_{12}) \wedge t_{12} \sqsubseteq t_1$
$\wedge \alpha(e_{12}, t_{12}) = <2, hour>]$
(* 2 hour in the morning*)]

The first four lines of the semantic representation in Example 10.84b are interpreted as saying that Mia worked yesterday and that the amount of her work yesterday was three hours and a half. The rest of the lines in the semantic representation in Example 10.84b represents how Mia's 3.5-hour work was divided into two halves of the day: the morning's work took 1.5 hours and the afternoon's work took 2 hours.

Bounding Relators

Intervals are often bounded by their boundaries, *start* and *end* points. Here are some examples.

Example 10.85   Bounding temporal relators

a. Gio visited Thailand *from* January 5 *to* 20 this year.
b. Some workmen have to work *from dusk till dawn*.
c. *The lunar New Year holidays lasted from 27 through 30 January this year.*

Bounded intervals may occur with specific measure expressions.

Example 10.86   Bounded intervals

a. Gio slept *the whole morning from early morning till noon*.
b. Kim has been sick *for six straight days from Monday through Saturday*.

The measure expressions supplement the meaning of their respective bounding intervals.

Example 10.86b, for instance, can be annotated and interpreted as follows.

Annotation 10.87   Bounded intervals

a. Base annotation:
   Kim has been sick$_{e1}$ for six straight days$_{me1:t\,Amount}$ $\emptyset_{t1:t\,Interval:span}$ from Monday$_{t11}$ through Saturday$_{t12}$.
b. Semantic representation: $\exists\{e_1, t_1, t_{11}, t_{12}\}$
   $[sick(e_1) \wedge state(e_1) \wedge presPerf(e_1)$
   $\wedge tInterval(t_1) \wedge starts(t_1, t_{11}) \wedge ends(t_1, t_{12})$

$\land\ Monday(t_{11})\ \land\ Saturday(t_{12})$
$\land\ [\alpha(e_1, t_1)=<6, day>\ \land\mu(t_1)=<6, day>]]$

Note here that the time amount of Kim's being sick is equivalent to the duration of Kim's having been sick.

10.5 Extended Summary

Section 10.1 classifies prepositions in English as temporal relators into five types: *anchoring, ordering, metric, bounding*, and *orienting*. Such a classification is required for a proper interpretation of temporal relations over eventualities and times. Each type of temporal relator is then analyzed with respect to the tripartite temporal configuration of $<E, R, T>$, where E is a set of eventualities, R is a set of temporal relators, and T is a set of associated temporal structures while subsuming temporal metric structures $M_{temporal}$.

Section 10.2 makes some basic ontological assumptions on event structures, time structures, and temporal metric structures. Event structures (E) are classified into three types: *state, process*, and *transition* with two subtypes, *achievement* and *accomplishment*. Time structures (T) consist of *instants (points)* and *intervals*. Intervals are then treated as either *open, bounded*, or *semibounded*. Time intervals can be oriented with respect to a linear time structure, either *forward* or *backward*. Temporal metric structures $(M_{temporal})$ are of three types: *temporal measure (length)* of an interval, *temporal distance (duration)*, and *time amount* consumed by an eventuality within a given interval. These classifications become the basis of annotating and interpreting the various types of temporal relators and their relations over event and time structures.

Section 10.3 discusses temporal relators R, with respect to their temporal argument structures T. Each temporal relator and its object argument temporal structure together form various temporal adjunct constructions, either simple or complex. Every *complex temporal adjunct* introduces a bounded temporal interval $\emptyset_{t:t Interval}$ with its bounding endpoints specified and, sometimes with its metric value (length, duration, or time amount) provided quantitatively. These intervals can be oriented with respect to linearized temporal structures, either forward or backward. A forward-oriented interval directs to the future on a time scale, whereas a backward-oriented interval directs to the past.

Section 10.4 discusses each type of temporal relators R with respect to the types of event structures E. The type of *anchoring ground* can either be an *instant* (point of time) or an extended *interval*, depending on either the type of temporal relators R: for example, *at* vs. *during* or the type of event structures E. State- or process-type eventualities are anchored to intervals, while the initiation or the culmination point of transitions is anchored to a time point. The location of anchoring points can be either at the start or the end of an oriented interval, triggered by the forward- or backward-orienting type of temporal relators.

PART III

Motion, Space, and Time

11

ISO-Space Evolving from SpatialML

11.1 Introduction

There are two versions of ISO-Space, both of which provide a specification language for the annotation of spatial information in language. As introduced in Pustejovsky (2017b), the first version was published in 2014 as an ISO international standard on the semantic annotation of spatial information, both static and dynamic, in text. The second version, ISO-Space (ISO, 2020d), has just been published with some revisions, especially for the treatment of dynamic spatial information. Both versions offer ways of annotating both *static* and *dynamic spatial information* in language, but differ in treating dynamic information that involves *motions, movers*, and *event-paths* (trajectories). Need for the revision of ISO-Space (ISO, 2014b) was called for by Pustejovsky and Yocum (2013), Lee et al. (2010, 2011, 2018), and Lee (2016). The revised version focuses on the dynamic aspect of annotating spatial information, while explicitly specifying a (spatio-temporal) relation between motions and movers that traverse various event-paths.

Focusing on the first part of ISO-Space that treats static spatial annotation, this chapter shows how it has evolved from MITRE's SpatialML (MITRE, 2010, version 3.0.1) that also provides a specification language for the annotation of static spatial information in text. Both SpatialML and ISO-Space specify how to annotate mereo-topological, directional, and topo-metric distance information in text.

Section 11.2 presents a formal basis of comparing ISO-Space with SpatialML. It attempts to formalize an annotation scheme for static spatial information in language by articulating its metamodel and then by constructing its abstract syntax, and a concrete syntax in the same manner of developing ISO-Space. The general frame of annotation structures is decided on by an abstract syntax, while a representation scheme of annotation is specified by a concrete syntax. The markup language is also specified in a concrete syntax: for instance, it can be either the conventionally accepted XML or a predicate-logic-like format, called *pFormat*, that is used by Pustejovsky (2017b) and elsewhere.

Section 11.3 outlines some characteristics of SpatialML regarding its intentionally restricted scope and its heavy reliance on preexisting resources for spatial annotation. MITRE's research group was concerned with the practical use of SpatialML and its computational applicability.

Section 11.4 compares ISO-Space with SpatialML to see in concrete terms to what extent they differ from each other. This comparison is particularly important because it lays a basis of bridging ISO-Space to the other annotation schemes that SpatialML aims to make its annotation scheme mappable to or interoperable with.

Section 11.5 briefly introduces the Spatial Role Labeling scheme (SpRL) as a spatial annotation scheme that was developed almost in parallel to ISO-Space (ISO, 2014b). Section 11.6 then concludes the chapter with a summary.[1]

11.2 Formal Basis for Comparison

11.2.1 Overview

MITRE's SpatialML (MITRE, 2010, version 3.0.1) introduces its annotation scheme in a simple non-formal language but with relevant illustrations. This section attempts to formalize a specification language for the annotation of static spatial information in language, in two steps, as proposed by Bunt (2011) and ISO 24617-6 SemAF principles (ISO, 2016): (i) abstract syntax and (ii) a concrete syntax ideally isomorphic to the abstract syntax. This provides a formal basis of comparing ISO-Space with SpatialML (MITRE, 2010), thus showing in clear terms how ISO-Space has evolved from SpatialML.

11.2.2 Metamodel

The metamodel for static spatial annotation, presented in Figure 11.1, is a simplified and modified version of the metamodel for ISO-Space (ISO, 2020d). It is drawn in the manner of Unified Modeling Language (UML), where open triangle-headed arrows are interpreted as each representing the

---

[1] Inderjeet Mani helped me write this chapter with his review and comments. Parisa Kordjamshidi contributed Section 11.5 briefly introducing SpRL, the spatial role labeling scheme.

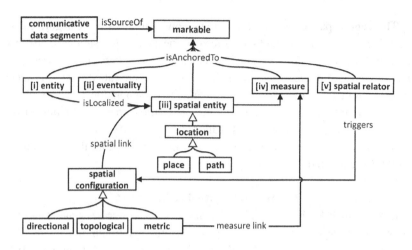

Figure 11.1 Metamodel for static spatial annotation

relation of *subclassification* or *subcategorization*; otherwise, all the arrows are labeled.

The metamodel provides a conceptual basis for formulating a specification language in set-theoretic terms, called *abstract syntax*, for the annotation of static spatial information in language data. Since every abstract syntax of semantic annotation needs to be validated by an associated semantics, the proposed metamodel is assumed to reflect the ontological basis of semantic objects and their relations, compatible with some ontologies such as GUM-space (Hois et al., 2009; Bateman et al., 2010), the *Generalized Upper Model* for spatial language. The metamodel presented by Figure 11.1, however, does not entirely depict spatial ontology in a strict sense but the syntactic structure of spatial annotation centered on the categorization of markable expressions in language.

Figure 11.1 is designed to focus on the part of static spatial annotation that suffices to make ISO-Space comparable to SpatialML. The metamodel consists of three parts. The upper part, consisting of data and markables, forms the core of annotation structures. It shows that communicative data segments are the source from which markables (linguistic expressions for annotation) are selected, while the other parts are *anchored* to those markables. The *markable* may be considered the top node *summum* that dominates linguistic expressions of various syntactic categories of the spatial annotation language.[2]

---

[2] Following Montague (1974), the term *category* is used to refer to a syntactic classification, whereas the term *type* is used as referring to a semantic differentiation.

The central part of Figure 11.1 shows how markables are categorized. It lists five *base categories* and their subcategories: [i] *entity* (simple thing), [ii] *eventuality*, [iii] *spatial entity* and its subcategories or subsubcategories, [iv] *measure* and [v] *spatial relators*. All these categories are called *base categories* because, together with its associated markable or annotation target to which it is anchored, each of them forms the *elementary structure* or *anchoring structure* $<i, m>$ of a constituent, called *base structure*, of each annotation structure, where i indexes the category of a markable and m, the markable to which i is anchored.

Entity and Eventuality Localized

Localization of Entities The category *entity*, which comprises general entities or simple things, participates in spatial relations through the process of *localization* (Klein, 1991, 1994; Kracht, 2002; Mani and Pustejovsky, 2012; Pustejovsky et al., 2019a). Here are some examples.

Example 11.1 Localized entities

a. *Jan* in Amsterdam.

b. *tea* in a *mug*

Neither names like *Jan* nor nominals like *tea* and *mug* denote genuine locations. As localized, they can participate in spatial relations like *in*. The process of localization L of semantic type $e \rightarrow (p \rightarrow t)$ coerces each of them to be mapped to a point, called *eigenplace* (Klein, 1991), in which it is located.[3]

The semantic content of each of the two examples in Example 11.1 can be represented as in Semantics 11.2.

Semantics 11.2 Semantic representations

a. Jan is in Amsterdam: $in(L(Jan), Amsterdam)$

b. Tea is in a mug:
$$\exists\{x_1, x_2\}[tea(x_1) \wedge mug(x_2) \wedge in(\lambda x[loc(x, x_1)], \lambda y[loc(y, x_2)])]$$

The relation *in* is a *mereo-topological relation* between two places, each represented as a set of spatial points by the λ-operator. $L(Jan)$, for instance, is equivalent to $\lambda x[loc(x, Jan)]$ of type $p \rightarrow t$, denoting a set of points, and *loc* is a relation between a spatial point (eigenplace) and an entity or a function from a set of entities to a set of spatial points, called a *region*.

Thus, $\lambda x[loc(x, Jan)]$ is interpreted as denoting a set of spatial points in which Jan is located. The logical form in Semantics 11.2a is then interpreted

---

[3] As cited in Zwarts and Winter (2000), this place is called *eigenspace* by Wunderlich (1991).

as saying that the place in which Jan is located in Amsterdam. Likewise, the logical form in Semantics 11.2b is interpreted as saying that the place where the tea is located is inside the place where the cup is located.

Localization of Eventuality The category *eventuality* of type *existential state* or *locational anchoring* can also be localized, participating in a spatial relation.

Example 11.3 Localization of eventualities

a. Jan *lives* in Amsterdam.
b. I have to *remain* in the country because of COVID-19.
c. John *grew up* in the Bronx, New York.

The event denoted by *lives*, *remain* or *grew up* in Example 11.3a is localized, thus participating in the spatial relation *in*.

Semantics 11.4 Semantic representation

a. Example: Jan lives in Amsterdam.
b. $\exists\{e, x\}[live(e) \land theme(e, Jan) \land in(\lambda x[loc(x, e)], Amsterdam)]$,
   where *loc* is a binary relation meaning that x *locates* the event e.

The domain of the *localization function L* is now extended from a set of entities to that of eventualities that can be anchored to spatial points. Event-motions, in contrast, are not localized to a single spatial point, but each trigger a sequence of spatial points, called *event-path*.

Spatial Entity

The category *spatial entity* provides the most essential markup for spatial annotation. It has a complex structure of subcategorizing markables. First, it contains two sorts of markables: (i) a subcategory *location*, consisting of *genuine locations*, and (ii) a small class of *quasi-locations*, consisting of *localized* entities and eventualities. In ISO-Space, markables of localized *entity* carry the tag SPATIAL_ENTITY, while those of localized *eventuality* retain the tag EVENT.

Second, the genuine *location* has two subcategories, *place* and *path*. At the stage of semantic interpretation, the category *place* may be treated of two different semantic types, *point* and *region*. According to Kracht (2002) and Pustejovsky et al. (2019a), *point* is understood to be of basic type p, while *region* is of functional type $p \to t$, denoting a set r of points. Location names (toponyms) such as *Boston* or names for landmarks such as *the Statue of Liberty* may be viewed as referring to spatial points, whereas nominals such as *capital city* or *swimming pool* each denote a set of spatial points. They are all marked as PLACE in both SpatialML and ISO-Space, but are differentiated by the values of an attribute @form: Names are marked form="NAM" and nominals (common nouns), form="NOM".

The category *path* in ISO-Space is a static type anchored to a markable such as *the Mass Turnpike* or *the Silk Road*. Unlike spatial entities of category *place*, the category *path* involves the ordering relation of *sequentiality*, thus being defined informally as a *sequence of points*. Following Nam (1995),[4] Pustejovsky et al. (2019a) formally defined a *path* as in Definition 11.5.

Definition 11.5   Path

A path is a function π from an interval $[0, k]$ to a set Σ of points, where the interval $[0, k]$ is a *bounded, finite*, and *ordered* subinterval of reals $\mathcal{R}$.

By taking an interval as the domain of the function π, points form a bounded, finite, and ordered sequence. A path π thus defined can be represented as a sequence $<\pi(0), \pi(1), \ldots, \pi(k)>$ such that $\pi(0)$ is the begin point and $\pi(k)$ the endpoint of the path π. For each $0 \leq i \leq k$, $\pi(i)$ is a midpoint. The interval may be understood simply as a bounded finite sequence of reals or some objects like times. If the sequence is understood as a sequence of times, then the path is dynamic.

Generalized Measure

The category *measure* is presented as an independent category in the metamodel. It is not restricted to topo-metric information such as involving distances but covers various dimensions and types of measures such as amount and weight. Here are some examples.

Example 11.6   Various measurement dimensions

a. The newly constructed suspension bridge is *2900 meters* long and sustains *1500-ton weight*.

b. The Empire State Building is a *102-story* skyscraper, located on the west side of Fifth Avenue between West 33rd and 34th Streets and stands a total of *1454 feet (443.2 m)* tall, including its antenna.

Examples 11.6a,b refer to measures of type length, weight, and the number of stories.

---

[4] Nam (1995) does not differentiate points from regions, calling them all *regions r*.

Although it does not appear in the metamodel, *distance measure* is treated as a type, subtyped to qualitative distance measure (e.g., *near, far, very far*) and quantitative distance measure (e.g., *20 km*), as in GUM-Space (Hois et al., 2009).

Spatial Relators and Spatial Configurations

The category *spatial relator* characterizes spatial configurations. There are three associated spatial links each of which is triggered by a spatial relator of various types. Related to spatial information, there are three types of spatial relators.

Classification 11.7   Three types of spatial relators

a. mereo-topological
b. directional or orientational
c. metric

The *mereo-topological link* relates a spatial entity, which includes a set of genuine locations and a set of localized entities and eventualities, to a set of locations, forming a mereo-topological configuration. The *direction link* also relates a location or a localized entity or eventuality to a set of locations but with a frame of reference and a reference point or view point. The *metric link* relates a location to a set of measures. All these configurations and associated links are depicted at the lower part of the metamodel.

The lower part of Figure 11.1 in the metamodel depicts how all these objects are spatially or metrically linked, as triggered by spatial relators. Spatial relators are anchored to functional words in a language, for instance, prepositions in English such as topological or orientational expressions *in, across, behind, left, right* or directional expressions *east, west, south, north, north-west*. Metric configurations are associated with the metric link that relates a spatial entity to a set of measures. Note also that metric information is not restricted to topo-metric information. The metric link, for instance, relates to a highway with a speed limit that carries more than topo-metric information.

11.2.3 Abstract Specification

Referring to the metamodel depicted by Figure 11.1, the abstract syntax $\mathcal{AS}_{staticSpatial}$ formally defines the specification language for the annotation of *static spatial information* in language. Like other semantic annotation schemes, as introduced in earlier chapters, it consists of five components.

Specification 11.8   Abstract syntax for the annotation of static spatial information

Abstract syntax $\mathcal{AS}_{staticSpatial} = <D, M, C, R, @>$, where we have the following.

a. Data D is uniquely identifiable segmented language data.

b. Markables M form a nonempty subset of D, consisting of markable expressions, called *markables*, that are delimited by each of the base categories in C.

c. Categories C constitute a set of base categories, *entity, eventuality, spatial entity, measure*, and *spatial relator*, where the subcategory *location* of *spatial entity* has two subcategories, *place* and *path*.

d. Relational categories R stand for a set of relational link categories each of which relates a base structure β to a set B of base structures,

  (i) either with a mereo-topological type of relation,

  (ii) with a directional or orientational relation,

  (iii) or a metric relation.

e. Assignments: For each base category $c \in C$, $@_c$ is a set of attribute-value assignments $@_c$ over $C \times M$, generating a set B of base structures β_c.[5]

Assignments

Assignment $@_c$ for base category c in C can be viewed as a partial function from a set of attributes to a set of possible values. The domain $Dom(@_c)$, which is a set of attributes for category c, fully determines the *bare structure* of a base structure of category c. This bare structure is referred to when semantic rules are formulated. $Dom(@_c)$ simply lists the attributes of category c without naming them in specific terms.

There are five major base categories: *entity, eventuality, spatial entity, measure*, and *spatial relator*. The category *spatial entity* has a subcategory *location* with its two subsubcategories, *place* and *path*. The semantic distinction between *point* and *region* is not made at the level of annotation, although it may be relevant at the level of type-theoretic semantic interpretation. The domain $Dom(@_c)$ of an assignment for each base category c in C needs to be specified. It is normally represented as a set-theoretic list, consisting of

---

[5] Uses of the *at* sign @: As mentioned earlier in this book, @ has two uses. Following the convention of TEI P5 (TEI Consortium, 2019), @ is prefixed to attributes to make them more visible. It is also used to refer to a set @ of assignment functions from attributes to values or an assignment function $@_c$ for a category such as *place*. These two uses mean the same, for the attribute @place is understood as denoting the function $@_{place}$ of category *place* from its attributes to values.

single- or two-letter codes, to avoid any controversy concerning the naming of attributes. Here are some examples presented.

$Dom(@_{entity})$ consists of three attributes, as in Specification 11.9.

Specification 11.9 Domain of the assignment $@_{entity}$
$Dom(@_{entity})=<ty, pr, pl>$, where
a. ty is the type of an entity: e.g., person for the name *John*;
b. pr is the predicative content of the entity: e.g., named; $named(x, John)$ in semantics;
c. pl is the plurality of the entity: Default is singular.

$Dom(@_{measure})$ is specified as a triplet, as in Specification 11.10.

Specification 11.10 Domain of the assignment $@_{measure}$
$Dom(@_{measure})=<ty, v, u>$, where
a. ty is the type of a measure: e.g., distance;
b. v is the value of the measure: e.g., real number 20;
c. u is the unit, where its value may not be specified: e.g., kilometer.

Since u is an optional attribute, there are two possible base structures: one case consists of ty, v, u for the distance of 20 km or *quantitative distance* in general and the other case consists of ty and v only for the *proximal distance* expressed by a modifier *near* in English. (See Hois et al. (2009) for the classification of distance measure in GUM-Space.)

$Dom(@_{spatialRelator})$ is also a tuple, consisting of two attributes as in Specification 11.11.

Specification 11.11 Domain of the assignment $@_{sRelator}$
$Dom(@_{spatialRelator})=<ty, pr>$, where
a. ty is the type of a spatial relator: e.g., mereo-topological, directional, etc.;
b. pr is the predicative content of the spatial relator: e.g., *in, rightOf*.

$Dom(@_{place})$ has a long list of attributes, as in Specification 11.12.

Specification 11.12 Domain of the assignment $@_{place}$
$Dom(@_{place}) = \{ty, pr, co, cu, su, ga, la, fo, ct, mo, de\}$, where
a. ty is a type;
b. pr is the predicative content of a place: e.g., *town* as in the *town* near Paris in Texas;
c. co is the name or ID of a continent;
d. cu is the name or ID of a country;
e. su is the name or ID of subadministrative division (state or province);
f. ga is a geographic gazetteer reference;

g. *la* is a latitude and longitude;

h. *fo* is a (syntactic) form relevant for semantic interpretation;

i. *ct* is a city, town, or village distinction;

j. *mo* is a modifier, either mereo-topological or directional;

k. *de* is a description for details if necessary.

Being simply a set of attribute-value pairs, base structures of category *place* are simple without any embedded structures. Furthermore, most of the attributes listed in Specification 11.12 are *optional*, meaning they do not need to be assigned a value.

As shown in the metamodel (Figure 11.1), the category *location* has two subcategories *place* and *path*. $Dom(@_{path})$ is the same as $Dom(@_{place})$ except that it carries additional attributes related to the sequentiality of paths, as listed in Specification 11.13.

Specification 11.13   Additional attributes for the domain of the assignment $@_{path}$

$Dom(@_{path}) = Dom(@_{place}) \cup <st, md, en, dr>$, where

a. *st* is the start-point of the path;

b. *md* is the list of midpoints (exits) of the path;

c. *en* is the endpoint of the path;

d. *dr* is the direction of the path.

Attributes *st* (start), *md* (midpoints), and *en* (end) refer to other base structures of category *place*. Static paths have no direction by themselves but can be associated with them, especially when motions are involved.

Assignment $@_r$ for Each Relational Link Category *r* in *R*   In conformance to Bunt (2015) and ISO 24617-6 SemAF principles (ISO, 2016), each category of the spatial links generates, or formally defines, spatial configurations of mereo-topological, directional or metric type structures each as a triplet $<\rho, \beta, B>$ or a quadruple $<\rho, \beta, B, O>$. The quadruple link configuration is specified as by Specification 11.14.

Specification 11.14   Quadruple configuration:

Spatial link configuration := a quadruple $<\rho, \beta, B, O>$, where

a. ρ is the type of relations for the link;

b. β is a base structure being related (*figure*);

c. *B* is a set of base structures in which the base structure β is grounded (*ground*);

d. *O* is a set of optional attributes such as @trigger.

This configuration allows *multiple grounds* to treat topological relations like *between, surroundedBy,* or *multiply connected.*

Optional Attributes Licensed Optional attributes such as *tr* for triggers are licensed into the basic triplet structure. For the directional link (`oLink`), which is named `RLINK` in SpatialML, for instance, optional attributes such as @frame (frameOfReference) and @referencePoint are allowed as part of a link structure.

11.2.4 XML-Based Concrete Syntax

The concrete syntax $XCS_{staticSpatial}$ for the annotation of static spatial information in language decides on four tasks, as specified in Specification 11.15.

Proposition 11.15 Four tasks of a concrete syntax
a. Format of representation and markup language
b. Identification of annotation structures
c. Naming of attributes
d. Specification of value ranges of the attributes

There are several noticeable differences, especially in naming attributes, between SpatialML and ISO-Space, at the level of concrete syntax. These differences are, however, inessential, for they can be made interoperable via a common abstract syntax.

Representation Format and Markup Language
As mentioned earlier in the chapter, SpatialML (MITRE, 2010) adopts XML as a markup language and annotates input data *inline*. As a result, the anchoring structure of a base structure consists of an identifier only, while markables are embedded in an XML element. The three square-bracketed markables in Example 11.16a are annotated inline, where each of the markables is embedded in an XML-element, named `SIGNAL` or `PLACE`.

Example 11.16 Inline annotation in XML:
a. Data: Mia visited [Brownsville] [in] [Texas].
b. Inline annotation in XML:
```
Mia visited
<PLACE id="1">Brownsville</PLACE>
<SIGNAL id="2">in</SIGNAL>
<PLACE id="3">Texas</PLACE>.
<LINK id="4" relType="IN" source="1" target="3" signals="2"/>
```

ISO 24612 LAF (ISO, 2012a) requires standoff annotation, while allowing the adoption of XML or any other markup language. Instead of XML, Pustejovsky (2017b) introduces *pFormat*, a predicate-logic-like format, as a representation language. Example 11.16b can easily be converted to *pForms*, annotation structures in pFormat, as in Annotation 11.17.

Annotation 11.17   Standoff annotation in pFormat

a. Word-segmented data:

Mia visited Brownsville$_{w3}$ in$_{w4}$ Texas$_{w5}$.

b. Standoff annotation in pFormat:
```
PLACE(id="1", target="w3")
SIGNAL(id="2", target="w4")
PLACE(id="3", target="w5")
LINK(id="4", relType="IN", source="1", target="3", signals="2")
```

XML can be used either inline or standoff. In contrast, *pFormat* can be used standoff only because it cannot have markables embedded within one of its pForms. Some attributes in pForms, however, refer to other pForms: for example, the arguments in a link structure refer to base structures, represented in pForms.

Identifiers

Following TimeML (Pustejovsky et al., 2005) and ISO-TimeML (Pustejovsky, 2017a), ISO-Space identifies each of entity or link structures with an ID-prefix followed by a positive integer. Each ID-prefix abbreviates the name of a category either of a base structure or a link structure, as illustrated by Annotation 11.18.

Annotation 11.18   Categorized identifiers

a. Markables: John$_{se1}$ lives$_{e1}$ in$_{s1}$ Boston$_{pl1}$.

b. Base structures:
```
SPATIAL_ENTITY(id="se1", target="w1", type="PERSON")
EVENT(id="e1", target="w2", type="STATE", pred="LIVE",
  tense="PRESENT")
SPATIAL_SIGNAL(id="s1", target="w3", pred="IN")
PLACE(id=pl1, target="w4", type="PPLA", state="US-MA")
```

c. Link structures:
```
QSLINK(id="qsL1", relType="IN", figure="se1", ground="pl1")
QSLINK(id="qsL2", relType="IN", figure="e1", ground="pl1")
```

Each identifier in ISO-Space represents the core $<i, m>$ of a base or link structure, where i is understood as a uniquely categorized identifier and m, a markable in data. In Annotation 11.18c, there are two different instances of qualitative spatial link (QSLINK) for the mereo-topological relation IN. Each is referred to by a different identifying index: qsL1 and qsL2.

Names of Attributes and Attribute-Value Ranges
SpatialML as an XML-based concrete syntax provides a full specification of attributes, and their value ranges by outsourcing to the preexisting geographical references. ISO-Space also follows this practice, importing all of the attribute-value specifications of SpatialML into its concrete annotation scheme.

Optionality The degree of requirement or optionality of attribute value assignments is also dependent on concrete applications. Lighter versions of an annotation scheme may have a smaller or the smallest number of *required* attributes. SpatialML, for instance, has one required attribute, namely @id, the rest of its attributes being *implied* or not being required to be assigned a value.

11.3 Characteristics of SpatialML

This section describes some characteristics of SpatialML (MITRE, 2010, version 3.0.1). Mani et al. (2010) argue that this version has been validly tested for its efficient use. One of the tests obtained a high score on the interannotator agreement with "91.3 F-measure on a corpus of SpatialML-annotated ACE documents released by the Linguistic Data Consortium" (see Linguistic Data Consortium (2005, 2008a,b)). SpatialML is characterized by an intentionally restricted scope and an explicit objective (see Section 11.3.1). It explicitly aims at developing a very simple but rich markup language for spatial locations and their spatial relations. It also aims at making extensive use of existing resources for annotation (see Section 11.3.2).

11.3.1 Restricted Scope

Markables with Tags and Links with Attributes
SpatialML focuses on geography, with geo-topological place names (*toponyms*), and culturally relevant landmarks. It has a single main category with a tag PLACE that marks geographical names and nominals each of which either refers to a spatial location or denotes a spatial property.

Besides the tag PLACE, SpatialML also has a category, with a tag name
SIGNAL, of spatial prepositions. Each of them triggers a *topological* link,
named LINK, that relates two places. For example, it links a city name,
marked <PLACE form="NAM">Saigon</PLACE>, to a country name,
marked <PLACE form="NAM" type="COUNTRY">Vietnam</PLACE>. It
then relates these two places with a mereo-topological relation type IN.

Annotation 11.19   Annotation in SpatialML

a. Data: Saigon in Vietnam
b. Annotation:
```
<PLACE id="1" comment="old name for Ho Chi Minh City">Saigon</PLACE>
<SIGNAL id="2">in</SIGNAL>
<PLACE id="3" type="COUNTRY">Vietnam</PLACE>
<LINK id="4" relType="IN" source="1" target="3" signals="2"/>
```

Besides the topological prepositions such as *in*, SpatialML treats topo-
directional or directional expressions such as *above, below, behind, front* or
cardinal directions like *north, north-west* and distances *20 km* as SIGNAL. They
are annotated with an attribute @type with two possible values: DIRECTION
and DISTANCE, respectively. Then, a new category of link, named RLINK for
relative link, is introduced to relate such two places.

Annotation 11.20   Directional link RLINK

a. Data: Da Nang is 764 km south of Hanoi.
b. Annotation: <PLACE id="1" form="NAM">Da Nang</PLACE> is
```
<SIGNAL id="2" type="DISTANCE">764 km</SIGNAL>
<SIGNAL id="3" type="DIRECTION">south</SIGNAL> of
<PLACE id="4" form="NAM">Hanoi</PLACE>.
<RLINK id="5" distance="763 km" direction="S" source="4" target="1"
   signals="2 3"/>
```

Note Unlike names and nominals, pronominals are not marked in SpatialML,
as in Annotation 11.21.

Annotation 11.21   Pronominals in SpatialML
```
One cannot go up
<PLACE id="1" form="NAM">the Eiffle Tower</PLACE>
<SIGNAL id="2">in</SIGNAL>
<PLACE id="3" form="NAM">Paris</PLACE>.
It is the most popular
<PLACE id="4 form="NOM">landmark</PLACE>
for tourists but is closed temporally because of COVID19.
```

Extent of Annotation

The extent of markables in SpatialML is restricted to the minimum so that the
target of annotation can focus on the head or core of markable expressions. For

example, premodifiers such as adjectives and determiners are not included in the extent unless they are part of a proper name such as *the Netherlands*. For the case of *the foggy river [Thames]*, only *Thames* is marked. The specification allows marking the extent of *eastern* in *[eastern Texas]* but not in *eastern part of [Texas]* because *eastern* is discontiguous with *[Texas]*.

Multiword expressions are each treated as a single word and a single markable. For example, *the White House, the University of Texas at Austin, the United States of America, Wounded Knee*, or *Lake Ontario* are all treated as single words and markables. Example 11.22 illustrates that square bracketed words are the only markables for SpatialML.

Example 11.22 The [city]$_{place}$ [of]$_{signal}$ [Saigon]$_{place}$, officially renamed [Ho Chi Minh City]$_{place}$ in 1975, is the largest, commercially most developed, and most populous [city]$_{place}$ with a population around 9 million [in]$_{signal}$ [Vietnam]$_{place}$.

The preposition *of* is also treated as a markable, marked SIGNAL, for SpatialML, denoting the relation of *equality* (EQ).

Nonconsuming Tags

SpatialML allows annotation structures, called *nonconsuming tags*, that are not anchored to markables from data. There are two kinds of nonconsuming tags: link structures and particular base structures.

Note As discussed earlier in the book, annotation structures consist of two substructures: (i) base structures, which are basic components of annotation, and (ii) link structures that relate one base structure to another structure or possibly more than one base structure to allow one-to-many relations such as *between, externally connects to*, or *surrounded by*.

Both LINK and RLINK are nonconsuming tags. As link structures, they are not anchored to markables, but simply relate base structures by referring to them while specifying their relation type (linkType).

Annotation 11.23 Links as nonconsuming tags in SpatialML
a. Markables: the [city] [of] [Ho Chi Minh City] is located [south]$_{signal}$ of [Hanoi].
b. Inline annotation:
```
The <PLACE id="1">city</PLACE>
<SIGNAL id="2">of</SIGNAL>
<PLACE id="3">Ho Chi Minh City</PLACE> is located
<SIGNAL id="4" type="DIRECTION">south</SIGNAL>of
<PLACE id="5">Hanoi</PLACE>.
<LINK id="6" source="1" target="3" linkType=EQ signals="2"/>
<RLINK id="7" direction="S" source="5" target="3" signals="4"/>
```

The two link structures in Annotation 11.23 are nonconsuming tags, for they are not anchored to any markables. In the case of RLINK that marks the attribute @direction, as in Annotation 11.23b, the attributes @source and @target should be understood as meaning the tail and the head of an arrow, respectively.

Base Structures as Nonconsuming Tags Besides the link structures, there are base structures that function as nonconsuming tags. Annotation 11.24 illustrates such a case.

Annotation 11.24 We camped $\emptyset_{place1}$ near a lake$_{place2}$. It was a gorgeous place$_{place3}$.

Annotation 11.24 says that the campground was near a lake and that it was a gorgeous place, but the place was not mentioned explicitly in the first sentence. This place can be annotated as a nonconsuming tag.

11.3.2 Use of Preexisting Resources for Annotation

In SpatialML, each annotation structure consists of base and link structures. SpatialML has two categories, PLACE and SIGNAL, of base structures and two link structures, LINK and RLINK. Each of the base or link structures is then associated with a list of attributes, either required or implied and their possible values. For the specification of values of these attributes, SpatialML makes extensive use of preexisting external resources. This approach provides a common ground for the *mappability* from SpatialML to other spatial annotation schemes, as in Example 11.25.

Example 11.25 Annotation schemes
a. Automatic Content Extraction (ACE)[6]
b. Toponym Resolution Markup Language (TRML)[7]
c. Geography Markup Language (GML)[8]
d. Keyhole Markup Language (KML) with Google Earth[9]
e. Bremen Generalized Upper Model Ontology (GUM)[10]
f. Suggested Upper Merged Ontology (SUMO) for the future[11]

---

[6] See Doddington et al. (2004), ACE-events, ACE-relations, ACE-entities.
[7] See Schilder et al. (2004); Leidner (2006).
[8] See ISO 19136-1 (ISO, 2020c).
[9] See OGC KML 2.3 (OPen Geospatial Consortium, 2015).
[10] See Hois et al. (2009); Bateman et al. (2010).
[11] See Pease et al. (2002); Huang et al. (2004, 2010); Pease (2011).

Coding of Spatial Coordinates

For the annotation of spatial coordinates, for instance, SpatialML relies on preexisting and readily available gazetteers such as the Integrated Gazetteer Database (IGDB) (Mardis and Burger, 2005) or WordNet Search. The attribute @gazref then copies a value from them by citing the gazetteer name plus a colon followed by an identifier (id); or the attribute @latLong gives a value for spatial coordinates. Here is an example.

Annotation 11.26 Spatial coordinates

```
<PLACE gazref=WordNet:09186888 latLong=21°1'42.6396"N 105°48'17.3412"E>
Hanoi</PLACE>
```

The latitude and longitude coordinates may be given in decimal format: 21.028511, 105.804817 for Hanoi, Vietnam.

Coding of Country and Province Names

SpatialML follows ISO 3166-1 (ISO, 2020a) standard on the two-letter coding of country names and ISO 3166-2 (ISO, 2020b), for the coding of state or province names. Along with the three-letter coding, they are both open for public use and very well accepted at the international level.

Example 11.27 Coding of geographical names (toponyms)

a. Example: Toledo, Spain

b. Annotation:

```
<PLACE id="1" type="PPLA" province="ES-TO" form="NAM">Toledo
</PLACE>
<SIGNAL id="2">,</SIGNAL>
<PLACE id="3" type="COUNTRY" country="ES" form="NAM">Spain</PLACE>
```

ES-TO is the two-letter (alpha-2) code registered by ISO 3166-2 (ISO, 2020b) for the province of Toledo in Spain, while the two-letter code ES is registered by ISO 3166-1 (ISO, 2020a) for the country of Spain. PPLA refers to a state or province-level administrative center or capital. The comma " , " here acts like the preposition *in*, thus being annotated as SIGNAL.

Geographical Types

The implied attribute @type for the element PLACE has a list of values, often presented as part of DTD (Version 3.0) or XML-schema.

Specification 11.28 Attributes of PLACE

```
<! ATTLIST PLACE type (
WATER | CELESTIAL | CIVIL | CONTINENT | COUNTRY |
FAC | GRID | LATLONG | MTN |MTS | PPL | PPLA | PPLC | POSTALCODE|
POSTALBOX | RGN | ROAD | UTM | VEHICLE ) #IMPLIDED >
```

These values are again taken from external resources, the National Geospatial-Intelligence Agency (NGA), the US Geological Survey (USGS), Integrated Gazetteer Database (IGDB), or Alexandria Digital Library (ADL Feature Type Thesaurus) on which the IGDB gazetteer is based.

Mereo-topological or Directional Information

There are at least two kinds of *mereo-topological information*. One kind refers to parts associated with cardinal directions. The other kind refers to the remaining parts. Such information modifying a place is annotated with the attribute @mod. In SpatialML, coded values for @mod, @direction, and @distance are mapped to Ontology: GUM-Space, which stands for the Bremen Generalized Upper Model (GUM) Ontology classes. Here is part of the "MOD codes" for SpatialML (MITRE, 2010, table 3) that includes the cardinal directions (e.g., N, northern) and those directions referred to as the sixteen-point rose in navigation (e.g., NE, northeast, and NNE, north-northeast).

Specification 11.29   Codes for directional modifiers

a. BOTTOM: the *bottom* of the well
b. BORDER: Burmese *border*
c. NEAR: *near* Harvard[12]
d. TOP: the *top* of the mountain
e. CENTRAL: *central* Asia
f. LEFT: the *left* side of the house
g. RIGHT: the *right* side of the car
h. N: *northern* India
i. NE: *northeastern* part of the USA

Directional codes in Example 11.30 illustrate how they are used in annotation.

Example 11.30   Use of directional codes

a. `The peak of <PLACE id=1 type="MTN" mod="TOP">Mt. Halla</PLACE>`
b. `We visited downtown <PLACE id=4 mod="CENTRAL">Boston</PLACE>`
c. `northern <PLACE id=2 mod="N">India</PLACE>`

NEAR as a Distance-Type Signal

NEAR is listed among the @mod values with an example *near Harvard* in SpatialML (see Specification 11.29). The example of *near* in *near Harvard* is not a modifier. In general, the word *near* is not used as a modifier (adjective) but only in a superlative or comparative form.

---

[12] It is not clear how *near* can be a modifier. See the subsequent discussion.

Consider Example 11.31.

Example 11.31 Use of *near* as a comparative form:

a. *We stayed overnight in the *near* hotel.

b. We couldn't find any restaurant *nearer* than a hamburger stand around there.

c. We stayed overnight in the *nearest* hotel.

d. the bookstore *near* Harvard

e. a park *near* my house

As the star * marks, Example 11.31a is considered ill-formed, whereas Examples 11.31b,c are well-formed. Likewise, Example 11.31d,e are well-formed but here the word *near* is not used as an adjectival modifier but as a preposition denoting a spatial relation of proximity between two places.

Directional Expressions These function either as modifiers or as predicates.

Example 11.32 Directional expressions

a. Modification:
Data: Dallas is located in *northern* Texas.
Annotation: <PLACE id="1">Dallas</PLACE>is located
<SIGNAL id="2">in</SIGNAL>northern
<PLACE id="3" mod="north">Texas</PLACE>.
<LINK id="4" source="1" target="3" relType="IN" signals="2"/>

b. Predication:
Data: Dallas is *north of* Houston.
Annotation: <PLACE id="1">Dallas</PLACE>is
<SIGNAL id="2" type="DIRECTION">north</SIGNAL>of
<PLACE id="3">Houston</PLACE>.
<RLINK id="4" direction=N source="3" target="1" signals="2"/>

11.4 SpatialML Compared with ISO-Space

11.4.1 Comparison in General

ISO-Space (ISO, 2014b) has adopted SpatialML (MITRE, 2010) as a basic framework for the development of a full-scale spatial annotation scheme. The initial part of ISO-Space that treats static spatial information involving topological or directional relations is essentially based on SpatialML but with some modifications. As listed in Specification 11.33, these modifications have resulted mainly from the extension and restructuring of base categories of markables in language data but also from the associated spatial configurations and the links that relate the new categories of base structures.

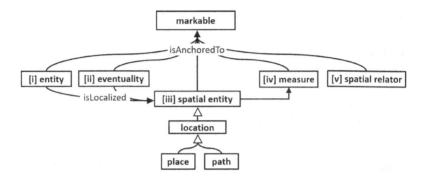

Figure 11.2 Base categories

Specification 11.33   Modifications

a. Extension of the annotation scope by introducing additional base categories:

(a) *entity* as a category of localized spatial entities
(b) *eventuality* as a category of localized events
(c) *path* as a subcategory of *location*
(d) *measure* generalized

b. Fine-grained specification of spatial configurations and links

The second part of ISO-Space is new, treating the annotation of dynamic spatial information. It extends the notion of static *path* to the formulation of dynamic *event-path* (trajectory), triggered by motions and traversed by moving objects. No comparison can, however, be made between SpatialML and ISO-Space with respect to the annotation of dynamic information in language, for this is beyond the scope of SpatialML.

11.4.2 Extension of the Annotation Scope

General: Introducing Additional Base Categories
ISO-Space introduces base categories as shown in Figure 11.2.[13]

The scope of markables in ISO-Space extends from location names (toponyms) and nominals to various linguistic expressions referring to general entities and eventualities through the process of localization (Kracht, 2002; Pustejovsky et al., 2019a). In Figure 11.2, which is part of the metamodel

---

[13] This is part of the metamodel presented by Figure 11.1.

Table 11.1 *Recategorized base structures*

new categories	SpatialML *tags*	ISO-Space *tags*	*examples*
localized entity		SPATIAL_ENTITY	[purse] in a [car]
localized eventuality		EVENT	[lives] in Boston
location path	PLACE	PATH	from [Seattle]
	type="ROAD"	beginPoint="" endPoint="" midPoints="" direction=""	to [Boston] through [northern states] of US [eastward]
measure	SIGNAL type="DISTANCE"	MEASURE type=""	[80 km/h], [200 km], [60 kg]
spatial relation	SIGNAL	sRelation type="" cluster=""	[in] and [out]

presented earlier in Section 11.2, category *entity* and *eventuality* are localized into category *location*, acting as quasi-spatial entities. Besides these two localized categories, basic category *location* has two subcategories: *place* and *path*. The metamodel then introduces two additional categories, *measure* and *spatial relator*. The basic category *measure* accommodates spatial distance, either quantitative or qualitative, as one of its types. The notion of *measure* is extended to other types of measure than topo-metric dimensions. The base category *spatial relator* triggers three kinds of spatial configurations: topological, directional, and metric.

SpatialML and ISO-Space implement these categories differently, as shown in Table 11.1.

ISO-Space differs from SpatialML in specifically implementing recategorized base structures. Table 11.1 shows only partially how the categories and the tag names have changed in ISO-Space with two editions of ISO-Space: ISO-Space (ISO, 2014b) and ISO-Space (ISO, 2020d). The tag SPATIAL_ENTITY in the first edition, for instance, is renamed ENTITY in the second edition.

Category *Entity* as a Category of (Localized) Spatial Entities
SpatialML limits its domain of annotation to geographic names referring to locations and nominals denoting locations. ISO-Space, in contrast, extends its

domain from the set of markables referring to or denoting genuine locations to the set of markables that refer to or denote nonlocational objects that function like locations in general, tagging these markables as SPATIAL_ENTITY.

Consider Example 11.34.

Example 11.34   Jan$_{se1,w1}$ lives in$_{sr1,w3}$ Amsterdam$_{pl1,w4}$.

Jan$_{se1,w1}$ as a figure grounded in some location can be spatially related to Amsterdam$_{pl1,w4}$, a genuine location. The name *Jan* that names a person but is functioning as a location now annotated as SPATIAL_ENTITY in ISO-Space.

Annotation 11.35   Annotation in ISO-Space
```
SPATIAL_ENTITY(id="se1", target="w1", type="PERSON" form="NAM")
SPATIAL_RELATOR(id="sr1", target="w3", type="topological",
  cluster="IN")
PLACE(id="pl1", target="w4", type="PPLC", ctv="CITY", country="NE")
QSLINK(id="qsL1", relType="IN", figure="se1" ground="pl1",
  trigger="sr1")
```

SPATIAL_ENTITY is localized for semantic interpretation. As a localized spatial entity, the individual entity, named *Jan*, is spatially related to the place, named *Amsterdam*.

The localization function *L* can also be extended to objects described by common nouns. Consider Example 11.36.

Example 11.36   Jan always keeps hot *tea*$_{se1}$ [in]$_{s2}$ a big *mug*$_{se2}$.

In Example 11.36, there are two common nouns, *tea* and *mug*, each of which denotes a set of entities of type $e \rightarrow t$ without denoting spatial objects of type $p \rightarrow t$ in a strict sense. They do, however, participate in a spatial relation *in* denoted by a spatial preposition *in*. ISO-Space treats them as markables and annotate them as SPATIAL_ENTITY, as in Annotation 11.37.

Annotation 11.37   Annotation in ISO-Space
```
SPATIAL_ENTITY(id="se1", target="w5", type="BEVERAGE", pred="TEA")
SPATIAL_RELATOR(id="sr2", target="w6", type="topological",
  cluster="IN")
SPATIAL_ENTITY(id="se2", target="w9", type="CONTAINER", pred="MUG",
  form="NOM")
```

The tag SPATIAL_ENTITY triggers the process of localization that turns nonlocational objects into quasi-locational objects so that they can be spatially related.

Category *eventuality* as a Category of Localized Events

Like individual entities, some events also undergo localization when related to a spatial relation. Consider Example 11.38.

Example 11.38 Eventualities localized

a. James *lives*$_{e1}$ in$_{sr1}$ Boston$_{pl1}$.
b. Jim *grew up*$_{e2}$ in$_{sr2}$ Tibet$_{pl2}$.
c. I barely avoided the *earthquake*$_{e3}$ in$_{sr3}$ Nepal$_{pl3}$ in April 2015.

Each of the events mentioned in Example 11.38 is related to a location. Semantic interpretation coerces each of them to be localized so that it can participate in a spatial relation. Example 11.38b, for instance, is annotated as in Annotation 11.39.

Annotation 11.39 Target of anntoation

a. Markables: Jim *grew up*$_{e2}$ in$_{sr2}$ Tibet$_{pl2}$.
b. Annotation:
```
EVENT(id="e2", target="w2-3", type="PROCESS", pred="GROW_UP",
  tense="PAST")
QSLINK(id="qsL1", relType="IN", figure="e2", ground="pl2",
  trigger="sr2")
```
c. Semantic form: $\exists e_2[growUp(e_2) \wedge past(e_2) \wedge in(L(e_2), Tibet)]$

Category *path* as a Subcategory of *location*

As introduced in the metamodel (Figure 11.1), the category *path* is a subcategory of *location* that refers to static paths like the Massachusetts Turnpike or Interstate Highway 90 that carry information about their start, mid, and endpoints. Such information becomes the basis of developing the notion of dynamic paths, called *event-path*, triggered by motions (Pustejovsky and Yocum, 2013; Lee, 2016; Pustejovsky and Lee, 2017; ISO-Space, ISO, 2020d).

With the introduction of a new category *path*, ISO-Space now allows a more enriched annotation, as illustrated by Annotation 11.40.

Annotation 11.40 Annotation of *path* in ISO-Space

a. Markables:
Interstate 90$_{p1}$ runs from Seattle$_{pl1}$, WA$_{pl2}$, to Boston$_{pl3}$, MA, near Logan International Airport eastward$_{sr1}$ through northern states$_{pl6}$ of USA.
b. Annotation:
```
PATH(id="p1", target="w1-2", type="US-interstateHighway",
  country="US", beginPoint="pl1", endPoint="pl3", midPoints="pl6",
  direction="sr1", form="NAM")
```

Annotation 11.41 illustrates how the notion of static paths, tagged PATH, develops to the notion of dynamic paths, tagged EVENT_PATH.

Annotation 11.41   Annotation of *dynamic paths*

a. Markables:

John$_{se1}$ drove$_{m1}$ $\emptyset_{ep1}$ from Seattle$_{pl1}$ to Boston$_{pl2}$ eastward$_{sr1}$ through I-90$_{p1}$. It was a long way$_{p2}$.

b. ISO-Space:

```
MOTION(id="m1", target="w2', type="transition", pred="DRIVE",
    tense="PAST")
EVENT_PATH(id="ep1", target="", trigger="m1", beginPoint="pl1",
    endPoint="pl2", midPoints="p1", direction="sr1")
```

The event-path, represented by a nonconsuming tag $\emptyset_{ep1}$, is triggered by the motion drove$_{m1}$. Event-paths are dynamic paths or trajectories, triggered by motions. ISO-Space annotates them as nonconsuming tags just like static paths, tagged PATH, with attributes @beginPoint, @endPoint, @midPoints, and @direction. Directionality is a required attribute for event-paths, whereas it is an optional attribute for static paths like roads. One could say that the interstate highway I-90 runs from Seattle to Boston, but one may also say it runs from Boston to Seattle. The numbering of its exits, for instance, is ordered but in a conventional way only.

Category *measure* **Generalized**

ISO-Space generalizes category *measure* to annotate types of measure other than temporal or spatio-temporal types (Lee, 2015; Hao et al., 2017, 2018). It thus allows types of spatial metric dimensions other than the linear dimension of distance such as height, depth, and width, or the other metric dimensions of area, volume, and duration.

Example 11.42   Spatio-temporal and metric dimensions

The football (soccer) field$_{x1}$ is about 100 meters$_{measure1}$ *long* and 60 meters$_{measure2}$ *wide*. The time *duration* of the game$_{x2}$ is 90 minutes$_{measure3}$.

ISO-Space then introduces a link, tagged (MLINK), to relate an object to a list of its measures.

The generalized treatment of metric annotation is specified with a base category *measure* (MEASURE) and a link category *measure link* (MLINK), as in Table 11.2.

Table 11.2 *Generalized measure*

category	tag	ID-*prefix*	attributes
measure	MEASURE	me	type, value, [unit], [comment][a]
measure link	MLINK	mel	relType, figure, ground, [trigger]

[a] Square-bracketed attributes are optional attributes. The attribute @unit, for instance, does not need to be specified if the value is a qualitative measure.

Here is an example.

Annotation 11.43 Measures

a. Word-segmented data:

Milwaukee$_{w1}$ is 81.43 miles$_{w3-4}$ north of Chicago$_{w7}._{s1}$ The two cities are one hour thirty-three minutes$_{w5-8}$ apart by car. $_{s2}$

b. Annotation in ISO-Space:

```
MEASURE(id="me1", target="s1w3-4", type="distance",
  value="81.43", unit="mile")
MEASURE(id="me2", target="s2w5-8", type="timeAmount",
  value="93", unit="minute", comment="driving time-amount")
```

The two measures are shown in Annotation 11.43b. Then the two relevant place names, *Milwaukee* and *Chicago*, and the path between them are further annotated. Finally, this path is related to two of its measures, distance and driving time-amount, by the measure link, as follows.

Annotation 11.44 Measure link

```
PLACE(id="p11" target="w1" type="PPL" state="US-WI")
PLACE(id="p12" target="w7" type="PPL" state="US-Il")
PATH(id="p1", beginningPt="p11" endPoint="p12")
MLINK(id="ml1", relType="MEASURE", figure="p1", ground="{me1,me2}")
```

Category *spatial relator* as a Trigger of Links

ISO-Space introduces two attributes @type and @cluster (sense) to enrich *spatial relator* with more relevant information related to spatial configurations (Mani and Pustejovsky, 2012; Pustejovsky, 2017b). Here is an example that contains several prepositions that function as *spatial relators*.

Example 11.45 Prepositions as spatial relators

a. Markables:

John lives [in]$_{sr1,s1w3}$ a cottage [on]$_{sr2,s1w6}$ the top of a hill. There is a driveway [through]$_{sr3,s2w5}$ the woods [up]$_{sr4,s2w8}$ the hill.

Table 11.3 *Spatial relators as triggering spatial links*

SIGNAL @semantic_type	SpatialML	ISO-Space	*Spatial relator*
TOPOLOGICAL	LINK	QSLINK	at, in, around
DIRECTIONAL (ORIENTATIONAL)	RLINK type="DIRECTIONAL"	OLINK	north of, left of up, down
TOPO-DIRECTIONAL	LINK, RLINK, type="TOPO-DIRECTIONAL"	QSLINK, OLINK	above, below, on directly across
METRIC	RLINK type="DISTANCE"	MLINK	by, bewteen, within

b. Annotation:
```
SPATIAL_RELATOR(id="sr1", target="s1w3", type="TOPOLOGICAL"
cluster="IN")
SPATIAL_RELATOR(id="sr2", target="s1w6", type="TOPO-DIRECTIONAL"
cluster="ON")
SPATIAL_RELATOR(id="sr3", target="s2w5", type="DIRECTIONAL"
cluster="THROUGH")
SPATIAL_RELATOR(id="sr4", target="s2w8", type="DIRECTIONAL"
cluster="UP")
```

One may refer to one of the available lexical resources of prepositions (in English) for values of the attribute @cluster.

Spatial relators (SPATIAL_RELATOR) trigger various types of links, as in Table 11.3.

Here are some examples.

Example 11.46   Prepositions as spatial relators

a. We camped *at* the park *near* the temple. [topological, distance]
b. Boston is *north of* New York City. [directional]
c. There is a computer *on* every desk. [topo-directional]
d. Two houses are separated only *by* 1.5 meters. [distance]
e. The enemy was *within* sight. [distance]

General comments

LINK in SpatialML is basically the same as QSLINK in ISO-Space. RLINK differs from OLINK in two respects. First, the annotation of metric information with RLINK in SpatialML is taken up by a generalized measure link, named MLINK, in ISO-Space. Second, the attribute @frame in RLINK is more enriched in OLINK. Details are discussed in the following.

Table 11.4 *Attributes for directo-orientational spatial configurations*

Link tags	SpatialML RLINK	ISO-Space OLINK	Values
attributes			
identifier	id="n"	id="oLn"	"n" is a positive integer
relation type	distance		identifier (*id*) of a measure
	direction	relType	ABOVE, BELOW, FRONT, BEHIND, LEFT OF NEAR, NEXT TO, NORTH, SOUTH, ...
argument 1	source	figure	ID of what is being related (relatum)
argument 2	target	ground	ID of what is being related to (locatum)
trigger	signals	trigger	
frame	frame	frameType	INTRINSIC, ABSOLUTE, (EXTRINSIC),
of reference			RELATIVE (VIEWER)
		referencePt	ground entity, cardinal direction, viewer
projective		projective	TRUE, FALSE

11.4.3 Directional Spatial Configurations

General

SpatialML and ISO-Space are essentially the same in treating mereo-topological spatial configurations. They only differ in naming the link associated with them: LINK in SpatialML vs. QSLINK in ISO-Space. The attributes associated with these links are also named differently. Following Talmy (1975), ISO-Space, for instance, adopts the Gestalt terms like *figure* and *ground*, instead of *source* and *target* in SpatialML. These variations in naming links and attributes are carried over to the renaming RLINK as OLINK and the associated attributes.

The core of the directional spatial link, named RLINK in SpatialML, and that of OLINK in ISO-Space, are almost the same, consisting of (i) relation type, (ii) argument1 (relatum), (iii) argument2 (locatum), and (iv) trigger, although each of the attributes is named differently. Both RLINK and OLINK also treat the notion of *frames of reference* (Levinson, 2003) and (Mani and Pustejovsky, 2012, chapter 3) but in a different degree of implementation, as in Table 11.4.

The attribute @direction in SpatialML is renamed @relType for the orientation link (OLINK) as for the other types of links in ISO-Space but the set of their possible values which includes both orientational expressions such as *above, below, behind*, and *left of* and cardinal expressions is retained as it is specified in the DTD (data type declaration) of SpatialML.

Table 11.5 *Frames of reference related to reference points*

Frame of reference (frameType)	Reference point (referencePt)	Trigger
ABSOLUTE	cardinal direction	*north, east*
INTRINSIC	ground entity	*front, back*
RELATIVE	viewer entity	*next to, left of*

Frames of reference

Both SpatialML and ISO-Space introduce the notion of *frames of reference*, based on the seminal work of Levinson (2003) as an attribute for their respective links. SpatialML (MITRE, 2010) simply names that attribute @frame with three possible values: VIEWER, INTRINSIC, and EXTRINSIC. ISO-Space introduces two related attributes: frameType and referencePt, showing their dependence, as in Table 11.5.

If the frame of reference is absolute, then the value of @referencePt is a cardinal direction referring to the relation type of a link, a bird's eye view of a scene; if the frame is intrinsic, then the value of @referencePt refers to the inherent orientation of a ground entity; if the frame is relative, then the value of @referencePt is a viewer perspective (see Pustejovsky (2017b)).

For illustration, consider Example 11.47. Here are some examples annotated with the attributes @frameType and @referencePt in ISO-Space.

Example 11.47   Sample data annotated

a. Raw data:

Beautiful rice paddies are just in front of my house in the country 50 kilometers northeast of Seoul. An old farmer is sitting on a rock at the right of a stream, taking a break.

b. Base annotation:

Beautiful rice paddies$_{pl1,s1w3}$ are just *in front of*$_{sr1,s1w6-8}$ my house$_{pl2,s1w10}$ in the country 50 kilometers *north-east of*$_{sr2,s1w16-17}$ Seoul$_{pl3,s1w18}$. An old farmer$_{se1,s2w3}$ is siting *on*$_{sr3,s2w6}$ a rock$_{se2,s2w8}$ *at the right of*$_{sr4,s2w9-12}$ an old big tree$_{se3,s2w16}$, taking a break.

This sample data contains four spatial relators.

Classification 11.48   Spatial relators:

a. *in front of*$_{sr1,s1w6-8}$

b. *north-east of*$_{sr2,s1w16-17}$

c. *on*$_{sr3,s2w6}$

d. *at the right of*$_{sr4,s2w9-12}$.

These spatial relators are annotated as each involving a different frame type, as follows.

Annotation 11.49   Frame types differentiated

a. SPATIAL_RELATOR(id="sr2", target="s1:w16-17", type="DIRECTIONAL",
    pred="NORTH-EAST_OF")
    OLINK(id="oL2", relType="NORTH-WEST", figure="pl2", ground="pl3",
    trigger="sr2", frameType="ABSOLUTE", referencePt="pl3")
b. SPATIAL_RELATOR(id="sr3", target="s2:w6", type="TOPO-DIRECTIONAL",
    pred="ON")
    OLINK(id="oL3", relType="ON", figure="se1", ground="se2",
    trigger="sr3", frameType="INTRINSIC", referencePt="se2")
c. SPATIAL_RELATOR(id="sr1", target="s1:w6-8", type="DIRECTIONAL",
    pred="IN_FRONT_OF")
    OLINK(id="oL1", relType="IN_FRONT_OF", figure="pl1", ground="pl2",
    trigger="sr1", frameType="INTRINSIC", referencePt="pl2"
d. SPATIAL_RELATOR(id="sr4", target="s2:w9-12", type="TOPO-DIRECTIONAL",
    pred="AT_THE_RIGHT_OF")
    OLINK(id="oL4", relType="AT_THE_RIGHT_OF", figure="se2", ground="se3",
    trigger="sr4" frameType="RELATIVE", referencePt="VIEWER")

The attribute @projective is another feature that is related to the notion of frames of reference or the sense of an orientational preposition. A preposition such as *over* may mean what it means physically, as in the case of a helicopter hovering *over* the hill. It is used in a *projective* or extended sense if it refers to a village *over* the hill.

Annotation 11.50   Projective frame of reference

a. Data 1: A helicopter is hovering *over* the hill. [projective="FALSE"]
b. Data 2: A village is over the hill. [projective="TRUE"]
c. Data 3: Beautiful rice paddies$_{pl1}$ are just [in front of]$_{sr1}$ my house$_{pl2}$ in the country 50 kilometers *north of*$_{sr2}$ Seoul$_{pl3}$.
d. Annotation of Data 3:
    OLINK(id="oL2", relType="NORTH", figure="pl2", ground="pl3",
    trigger="sr2", frameType="ABSOLUTE", referencePt="pl3",
    projective="TRUE")

Exactly speaking, the country house is located northeast of Seoul. It is north of Seoul only in a projected sense.

11.5 Parallel Work on Spatial Role Labeling

ISO-Space (ISO, 2014b) may be viewed as a direct descendant of SpatialML (MITRE, 2010), as described in this chapter. There are, in contrast, other spatial annotation schemes that have been developed almost in parallel to ISO-Space. One of the noticeable works is the Spatial Role Labeling scheme

(SpRL), introduced in Kordjamshidi et al. (2010). SpRL falls in the middle ground between ISO-Space and SpatialML in terms of generality and granularity of the covered spatial semantics on one side and the practicality for larger-scale annotations and training machine learning models on the other side. It aimed at generalizing SpatialML to cover more generic spatial expressions and concepts beyond geographical locations.

The theory of Holistic Spatial Semantics (Zlatev, 2003) is the basis of this annotation scheme. Moreover, it made an explicit distinction between two representation layers of (i) linguistic semantics and (ii) qualitative spatial reasoning models (Kordjamshidi et al., 2013, 2017a,b). It was designed to train machine learning models to extract spatial information from a text and map it to a formal representation that makes automatic reasoning over spatial language feasible (Kordjamshidi et al., 2010, 2012a,b; Kordjamshidi and Moens, 2015). The conceptualization is based on the two main notions of trajector (i.e., figure) and landmark (i.e., ground). The spatial relations between trajector and landmark or the translocations expressed in the linguistic utterances via prepositions or motion verbs are annotated as spatial-indicators or motion-indicators. The path is represented simply as its beginning, middle, and end. It introduces the frame of reference as a part of the annotation as intrinsic, relative, or absolute.

Given the main focus of SpRL on designing computational models based on machine learning, several evaluation benchmarks and tasks were designed in this line of work and presented in SemEval series of workshops (Kordjamshidi et al., 2012a,b; Kolomiyets et al., 2013; Pustejovsky et al., 2015). The integration of SpRL with Abstract Meaning Representation (AMR) (Banarescu et al., 2013) has been discussed in Dan et al. (2020). Given the high cost of the semantic annotations, in a recent paper, a new dataset is automatically generated and annotated with spatial roles and relations to facilitate training and fine-tuning the modern language models for spatial language understanding (Mirzaee et al., 2021).

11.6 Summary

This chapter has discussed how the first part of ISO-Space that deals with static spatial information in a language evolved from SpatialML. MITRE's SpatialML (MITRE, 2010) and ISO-Space (ISO, 2014b) both offer a specification language for the annotation of spatial information on geographical locations and landmarks. Section 11.2 has laid down a formal basis of comparing ISO-Space and SpatialML with a metamodel and an abstract syntax depicted by the metamodel. The abstract syntax was shown to consist of base categories of markables and their spatial configurations and relations (links) over the categories.

Being compared with SpatialML, ISO-Space was found as its applicational extension with the following modifications.

- The domain of annotation (markables) was extended to general entities (GUM: simple thing) and eventualities as localized spatial entities.
- Category *path* was introduced to lay a basis of dynamic paths with information on the sequentiality of locations.
- Distance measures were extended to measures of other types and dimensions so that spatial annotation can be integrated with other semantic annotation schemes such as temporal annotation.
- The annotation of spatial relators (signals) was enriched to provide a finer-grained specification of spatial configurations, especially related to directional or orientational configurations involving frames of reference.

In general, SpatialML is a very simple and compact annotation scheme. Having only one attribute @identifier required, it can generate very simple annotation structures. By making extensive references to other existing resources and gazetteers on geographical coding, SpatialML is easily mappable to other geospatial annotation schemes. In contrast, ISO-Space is more expressive and complex than SpatialML, meeting the semantic needs of interpreting complex spatial language and computational needs of application envisioned in the coming years.

The chapter has also briefly introduced the Spatial Role Labeling scheme (SpRL) as a spatial annotation scheme that was developed in parallel to ISO-Space (ISO, 2014b).

12

Dynamic Paths, Projection, and Orientation

12.1 Issues: Four Types of Paths

In this chapter, I introduce four types of paths: *static, dynamic, oriented*, and *projected*, and their combined types, and discuss how paths are differentiated. Roads, streets, and highways are kinds of *static paths*, each connecting one location to another by forming a linearly connected sequence of locations. Motions create paths, which are called *event paths* or *trajectories*. Unlike static paths, event paths are *dynamic paths*, each forming a finite directed sequence of spatio-temporally defined locations so that each location is characterized by a pair $<l, t>$ of a place l and a time t. As a finite directed path, each event-path has a start 0 and an endpoint 1, thus being of functional type $int \rightarrow vec$, where int is an interval $[0, 1]$ and vec is a set of vectors (see Nam (1995), Kracht (2002), Pustejovsky et al. (2019a), and SpatialSem (ISO, 2022b)).

Oriented paths are simply paths that are directed to some landmark or location in general. Static paths like mountain routes or walking paths in a park are not directed intrinsically unless some directions are marked. Highways are not oriented, but their lanes are, and so are the entries and the exits. Event-paths are always directed but may fail to reach their final goals. There are event paths with their endpoints unspecified or with their goals failing to be reached. The identification of oriented paths often involves a *frame of reference*, either absolute, relative or intrinsic. I call such paths *oriented paths*. Consider the two mythical figures, one named Daedalus, and the other, his son named Icarus. They made wings of wax and feathers to fly out of prison. Daedalus flew successfully, escaping from a prison in Crete to Naples, but Icarus flew too high and too near to the sun, failing to reach Naples and ending up drowning in the ocean. There were two flights: Daedalus reached the goal, and the path of Icarus's flight must have been oriented to Naples, too, but failed to reach there. These two paths are differentiated by specifying the latter as simply being *oriented*.

Projected paths are associated with either static or dynamic paths. Unlike preexisting static paths or event paths that have been taken, projected paths are *virtual paths* which exist only in the mind of a *rational agent*, who draws them, and one of which is likely to be the shortest direct path from the start to its end. There is no direct route, for instance, from Kyiv, the capital city of Ukraine, to Warsaw, Poland, or any other secure place because of the war. This direct route is a *projected* path if there is any.

To discuss these types of paths in formal terms, I refer to Pustejovsky and Yocum's (2013) two axioms on motions, movers, and event-paths, on which the first edition of ISO-Space was revised and published as ISO-Space (ISO, 2020d). In addition, I propose a *corollary*, inferrable from the two axioms, which validates the *traversal relation* between a mover and the dynamic path, created by a motion. I then describe how these path types, as formally defined, enrich the annotation-based semantics (ABS) for the annotation and interpretation of spatio-temporal information.

Interpreting Motion-Triggered Dynamic Paths

Each motion creates a motion-triggered dynamic path, called *trajectory* or *event-path*, over a spatio-temporally defined domain. Then, there is an object, called a *mover*, that *traverses* that path. Consider Example 12.1 that introduces a motion and a dynamic path created by it.

Example 12.1 Dynamic paths

a. Data: Bob drove to Lake Travis near Austin, Texas, last summer.

b. Markables: Bob$_{x_1:mover}$ drove$_{e_1:motion:past}$ $\emptyset_{p_1:path:motionTriggered}$ to Lake Travis$_{l_1:place:lake}$ near Austin, Texas, last summer$_{t_1:time}$.

c. Link structures:

```
moveLink(mL1, relType="traverses", figure="x1:mover",
   ground="p1:path", trigger="e1:motion")
tLink(tL1, relType="isIncluded", figure="e1", ground="t1")
```

d. Semantic representation in ABSr:

$\exists\{x_1, e_1, p_1, l_1, t_1, e_2\}$
$[named(x_1, Bob)$
$\wedge drive(e_1) \wedge past(e_1)$
$\wedge triggers(e_1, p_1)$
$\wedge path(p_1) \wedge ends(p_1, l_1)$
$\wedge place(l_1) \wedge named(l_1, Lake Travis) \wedge lake(l_1)$
$\wedge time(t_1) \wedge season(t_1, summer) \wedge year(t_1, 2021)$

$\wedge\, traverses(e_2) \wedge mover(e_2, x_1) \wedge theme(e_2, p_1) \wedge isCausedBy(e_2, e_1)$
$\wedge\, \tau(e_1) \subseteq t_1 \wedge \tau(e_2) \subseteq t_1]$

Example 12.1b assumes an integrated semantic annotation scheme that makes two annotation schemes, ISO-TimeML (ISO, 2012b) and ISO-Space (ISO, 2020d), interoperable. The semantic representation language ABSr of the proposed annotation-based semantics ABS then translates all of the base structures into appropriate semantic forms and links them all into a single interpretable quantified semantic form.

The semantic representation (Example 12.1d), which forms a single existentially quantified logical form, carries the spatio-temporal information conveyed by the data (Example 12.1a), as annotated by the two steps of annotation (Example 12.1b,c). The motion-event of Bob driving to Lake Travis not only creates a dynamic path $_{p_1:path:dynamic}$, but also causes the mover Bob x_1 to follow through that path p_1 and reach Lake Travis l_1. This motion-event $_{e_1}$ of Bob driving occurs during the summer t_1 of 2021 and so does the motion-event $_{e_2}$ of his traversing the path p_1. They are one identical event.

Movers may not be agents. Consider Example 12.2.

Example 12.2   Movers

a. Data: Jon threw a stone over the fence to scare away wild cats.
b. Markables: Jon threw $_{e_2:motion}$ a stone $_{x2:mover}$ over $\emptyset_{p2:path:dynamic}$ the fence $_{x3}$ to scare away wild cats.
c. Link structure:

```
moveLink(mL2, relType="traverses", figure="x2:mover",
ground="p2:path:dynamic", trigger="e2:motion")
```

d. Semantic representation:
$\exists\{e_2, p_2, x_2, e_3\}$
$[throw(e_2) \wedge past(e_2)$
$\wedge\, path(p_2) \wedge mids(p_2, x_3)$
$\wedge\, stone(x_2) \wedge fence(x_3)$
$\wedge\, triggers(e_2, p_2)$
$\wedge\, traverses(e_3) \wedge mover(e_3, x_2) \wedge theme(e_3, p_2) \wedge isCausedBy(e_3, e_2)]$

In Example 12.2c, the mover was not Jon, but the stone that was thrown over the fence. The path, represented by $\emptyset_{p2:path:dynamic}$, was the trajectory of a stone $_{x2}$ moving over the fence $_{x3}$. This trajectory was created by Jon's action e_2 of throwing the stone over the fence, and this action also caused the stone to traverse e_3 the path p_2.

To describe these relations among motions, movers, and dynamic paths, called *event-paths*, in explicit terms, Section 12.2 introduces two motion-related axioms and a corollary. They together lay a theoretical basis for the annotation and interpretation of event-paths and related spatio-temporal dynamic information.

Interpreting Projected Paths

Event-paths are paths triggered by motions. Some paths are related to motions but differ from event-paths. Unlike event-paths, these paths are *virtual*, which I call *projected paths*. Consider Example 12.3.

Example 12.3   Projected path
Mike Kalton drove *north-west*, first *north* from Chicago to Milwaukee and then *west* toward Madison.

This example mentions three directional expressions: *north-west, north*, and *west*. Unlike north and west, north-west is not an actual direction that was taken by Mike Kalton. Instead, it is the combinatorial outcome of the two sequential movements: the first movement was toward the north, and the other one was toward the west. Such a direction is then annotated as an attribute of the category *path* and also marked type="projected", as in Annotation 12.4b.

Annotation 12.4   Path annotated
a. Markables:
  Mike Kalton$_{x1}$ drove$_{e1:motion:past}$ $\emptyset_{p1:projectedPath}$ north-west$_{d1:projectedDirection}$, first north$_{d2}$ from Chicago to Milwaukee and then east$_{d3}$ toward Madison$_{projectedGoal}$.
b. Annotation:
```
path(p1, type="projected", trigger="x1", direction="north-west",
   start="Chicago", goal="Madison")
```

Unlike even-paths, the projected path, mentioned in Annotation 12.4, is triggered not by the motion of driving. It was instead triggered by Mike Kalton$_{x1}$, the driver, for Madison was his *intended goal*.

The rest of the chapter develops as follows. Section 12.2 discusses the two axioms on motions, which were proposed by Pustejovsky and Yocum (2013), and a corollary based on them. Section 12.3 presents ISO-Space (ISO, 2014b, 2020d) modified with restored event-paths and enriched spatial relators with the newly introduced notions of *projection* and *projected paths*. Section 12.4 discusses orientations with respect to *frames of reference*. Section 12.5 summarizes the chapter.

12.2 Two Axioms and a Corollary

There are two axioms on the mover of a motion and an event-path triggered by the motion. There is also a corollary, derived from the two axioms, that relates the mover to the event-path. This section explicates the basic terms that constitute the axioms: *motion, mover, event-path*, and the relation *loc* between an event-path and a motion.

12.2.1 Two Axioms

Related to motions, Pustejovsky and Yocum (2013) propose two axioms.

Axiom 12.5   Every motion involves a *mover*.[1]
$$\forall e \exists x [motion(e) \rightarrow mover(e, x)]$$

Axiom 12.6   Every motion involves an *event-path*.[2]
$$\forall e \exists p [motion(e) \rightarrow [path(p) \wedge triggers(e, p) \wedge loc(e, p)]]$$

These two axioms lay a theoretical basis of conceptualizing an annotation scheme for dynamic spatial information in language. There are four key predicates in the axioms: *motion, mover, event-path*, and *loc*. The predicate *loc* denotes a relation of *localization* between an object, like an event-motion or an individual entity and a location like a path p here. These are theory-internal terms that need to be explicated for their application to the specification of an annotation scheme for dynamic information in language.

12.2.2 Axiom-Based Basic Concepts

Motion

The term *motion* is used as a subcategory of category *eventuality* for the dynamic spatial annotation specification language ISO-Space (ISO, 2020d). It denotes a *translocational* change of an object through a four-dimensional spatio-temporal domain. Each location, either a point or a set of points, called *region*, that involves a change is characterized not only by its spatial dimension but also by its temporal dimension. The dynamic property of motions is characterized by the *dynamicity*, metaphorically called *flow*, of time, conceived as a dimension of the world that continues to move from the past to the future.

Motions are understood primarily as physical occurrences. Not all motion verbs refer to genuinely physical events, but they may be used in a figurative sense. Here are some examples.

---

[1] A mover is an object that moves.
[2] An event-path is a path triggered by a motion.

Example 12.7 Jim was *driving* through western Texas. The temperature *reached* 105 degrees. Jim got upset and his blood pressure *rose* to 185.

There are three motion verbs mentioned in Example 12.7: *driving, reached,* and *rose.* The first verb is used in a physical sense, whereas the other two are used in a figurative sense. The flows of thinking or emotional movements are also understood as motions but only refer to epistemic or emotive phenomena, as illustrated by Example 12.8a,b.

Example 12.8 Epistemic or emotive movements

a. Epistemic: Your argument *runs* reasonably well.
b. Emotive: His anger *burst out* and became *devastating.*

Mover

Understood in a physical sense, each motion denotes a finite, bounded, and directed movement of an object. This object is called a *mover.* The term *mover* is a technical word easy to be misunderstood. It is used here to refer to an object that moves from one location to another, meaning it undergoes a translocational change. A mover is not necessarily an agent. Consider Example 12.9.

Example 12.9 Movers

a. John *emptied* a bottle of wine.
b. Mia was *disturbed* by her new neighbor.
c. Mary *pushed* a big rock weighing a ton over the hill.
d. John and Mary *drove* a car to a beach.
e. Don't *move*; there's a snake.

Emptying wine from a bottle involves a change, but it does not change location. There was no mover. Mia was disturbed, so something was moving in her mind or brain. But there was no locational change in her. If Mary pushed a rock over the hill, then she was the pusher (agent), but she may have avoided moving an inch, herself, by using a machine, instead. The mover was only the rock. If John and Mary drove a car to a beach, then both John and Mary as well as the car were movers, for all of them underwent a translocational change, reaching a sea or lakeside. Referring to a mover, the verb *move* is used as an intransitive verb, as in Example 12.9e.

Dynamic Notion of Event-Path

The term *event-path* is also a technical term. It refers to a dynamic route or *trajectory* triggered by a motion. Consider Example 12.10.

Example 12.10   Event-paths

a. Mary threw a stone over the lake.
b. The arrow hit the target.
c. Jim drove on a highway from Frankfurt to Milan.
d. Mike drove west from Milwaukee toward Rapid City.
e. KAL flew over Siberia.

If someone throws a stone over a lake, then the stone flies over the lake, making a parabolic trajectory in the air. If an arrow is released from a bow, it moves toward the target, flying through the air. Jim followed a highway through the Alps while driving from Frankfurt, Germany, to Milan, Italy. It must have been a long drive, requiring the driver to go off the road occasionally to some resting places. The actual course of his driving, which was the event-path of Jim's driving, must not have always stayed on the specified route of the highway. If Mike drove west toward Rapid City, he was simply heading in that direction with no guarantee that he reached that city. If KAL flies over Siberia, the pilot should be aware of navigating through the designated aviation route and avoiding any deviations. All these movements create certain paths, called *event-paths*. These paths are called such because they are created by event-motions.

Event-paths are *dynamic* routes or trajectories, triggered by event-motions. They differ from *static* paths or roads. Consider another set of examples in Example 12.11.

Example 12.11   Dynamic vs. static paths

a. A truck sped$_{motion1}$ $\emptyset_{eventPath1}$ off a winding road$_{path1}$ going$_{motion2:figurative}$ down a hill and crashed into a long and deep valley$_{path2}$.
b. John took California State Highway 1_{path1}, the most beautiful scenic road$_{path2}$ in the USA, to drive$_{motion1}$ $\emptyset_{eventPath1}$ south from San Francisco to Los Angeles through historic Carmel and Big Sur.
c. Interstate 5_{path1} is the main north–south Interstate Highway$_{path2}$, running$_{motion1:figurative}$ largely parallel to the Pacific Coast Byway$_{path3}$.

The actual course$_{eventPath}$ of the truck speeding off the winding road and of its crashing into the valley differs from the road$_{path1}$ itself. There was no road leading to the crash point in the valley. John's driving$_{motion1}$ south to Los Angeles did not exactly match the entire course of the mountain road$_{path1}$ or that of the California highway$_{path2}$. There must have been many sideways to stop to look at the scenery and take some breaks. I-5$_{path1}$ runs almost parallel to the Pacific Coast Scenic Byway$_{path3}$. There occur two motion verbs *going down* and *running* in Example 12.11a,c, used in a figurative sense each without triggering any event-paths.

Event-paths are *dynamic paths*, differing from roads or routes that are *static paths*. They can be defined in a few different ways, either intuitively or formally. A static path is informally defined as a spatial entity that consists of a sequence of locations (ISO-Space (ISO, 2020d, clause 3.13)). The winding road mentioned in Example (12.11a) is a static path that can be defined by its start, mid, and end points. Nam (1995, section 3.3.1) formally defines a path as in Definition 12.12.

Definition 12.12 Path defined
A *path* is a *function* π from the interval $[0, k]$ of natural numbers to a set Σ of spatial points.

This path can also be represented as a sequence $<\pi(0), \ldots, \pi(i), \ldots, \pi(k)>$ such that $\pi(0)$ is the begin point of the path and $\pi(k)$, its endpoint. Its midpoints are $\pi(i)$ such that i is between 0 and k. By limiting the domain of the function π to an interval $[0, k]$, each path is defined to be a *bounded finite linearly ordered object*.

Defining Motion-Triggered Dynamic Paths
The actual course of the truck speeding off the mountain road and crashing into a valley was a dynamic path. Each of the subpaths, associated with each of the turning points, sometimes called *anchor points*, on the path, was both temporally and spatially specifiable. Static paths are there, independent of time factors whether taken or not, whereas dynamic paths are created only by some *translocational motion ordered by time*. Event-paths can thus be viewed either from a functional point or from a formal point but defined in simple descriptive terms.

Definition 12.13 Event-path
a. Functional definition:
   A motion-triggered path, called *event-path*, is functionally defined as a *dynamic route*, triggered by a motion-event.
   Remark: Each dynamic route traces the locational (physically necessary spatio-temporal) transition or trajectory of some object, called *mover*, of a motion-event.
b. Formal definition:
   An event-path is formally defined as a *finite, bounded* or *semibounded*, and *directed* nonnull sequence of spatio-temporal locations.

Remark Each of the spatio-temporal locations can be represented as a pair $<l,t>$ or $l@t$, read l at t, where l stands for a (possibly multidimensionally definable) spatial location, either region or point, and t refers to a temporal point.

The functional definition is a reiteration of the two axioms proposed by Pustejovsky and Yocum (2013).[3]

The start of an event-path is characterized with $<l_0, t_0>$, but its end is characterized with $<l_1, t_1>$ with a denumerable number of intervals $<l_i, t_i>$ between them such that each event-path itself is represented as a finite and directed line, called a *vector*. The directionality of an event-path is assumed by the linearity of a temporal structure. The domain of an event-path as a function can be either a *bounded interval* $[0, 1]$ or a *semibounded interval* $[0, 1)$ of reals. The semibounded interval allows directional paths such as Example 12.14b.

Example 12.14   Bounded intervals

a. Mike drove north *from* Chicago *to* Milwaukee. [bounded interval]
b. Mike drove *west*. [semibounded interval]
c. Mike drove *west from* Milwaukee *toward* Rapid City. [semibounded interval]

Following Zwarts (1997), Zwarts and Winter (2000), and Pustejovsky (2020), event-paths can be formally defined each as a function π_v, based on the notion of *vector space*.

Definition 12.15   Event-path as a function

An *event path* is a *function* $\pi_v : int \rightarrow vec$,
where int is a bounded interval $[0, 1]$ or a semibounded interval $[0, 1)$ of reals and vec is a set of vectors.

The reals in int may represent an interval of linearly ordered times. Vectors are characterized by two properties: direction and magnitude. Each vector $\vec{a}$ is defined by its direction and quantity $||a||$ (distance) between its start (*head*) and end (*tail*).

Vectors can be either straight or curved, including a third type, *closed* or *circular*. The direction of a straight vector and its magnitude can easily be measured. But, if it is a curved vector or a vector representing a curved path, then its direction, as well as its magnitude, requires an extra measure based on the notions of *projection* and *sum*.

Consider Example 12.16.

---

[3] Also refer to Mani and Pustejovsky (2012) and Lee (2016).

Example 12.16 Event path as a vector

a. Data:

Mike Kalton *left* Chicago early at *five in the morning* heading *north*. He drove about *10 miles* and ran into a traffic jam. He made a detour till he got back to the main road toward Milwaukee. He *drove 102 miles*, 9 miles more than the normal driving distance of 93 miles, from Chicago to Milwaukee in *two hours*.

b. Annotation:

```
vector(type="curved", direction="north", distance="102mi",
start="Chicago@05:00", end="Milwaukee@07:00")
```

Figure 12.1 shows how the direction and magnitude (distance) of the event-path, mentioned in Example 12.16, is measured.

The actual path of Mike's driving from Chicago to Milwaukee is represented as one curved series of vectors with eight *anchor points* (boxes), which include the endpoint arrow. The anchor points segment the curved vector into a sequence of seven subvectors, allowing the measuring of the driving distance as a *sum* of the length of each of the subvectors. The direction of the driving event-path is that of the *straight vector*, projected from Chicago to Milwaukee. It is represented by a dotted straight line, called the *projected path*.

Consider Figure 12.2. The actual path of driving from Milwaukee toward Rapid City consists of one curved vector from Milwaukee to Rochester and a straight vector from Rochester to Rapid City. The direction of the *projected path* from Milwaukee to Rapid City is marked *west* in the figure. The direction of the other projected path from Milwaukee to Rochester should be marked *north-west*. The *projected direction* from Milwaukee to Rapid City is then

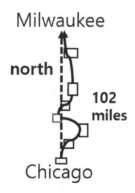

Figure 12.1 Driving north from Chicago to Milwaukee

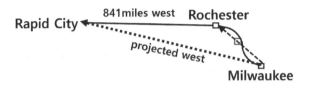

Figure 12.2 Projected direction from Milwaukee to Rapid City

marked *west*. The distance between Milwaukee and Rochester is measured by summing up the distances of actually two *curved series of vectors* (arcs), one of which is marked with anchor points, between the two cities. This measure is then added to the distance between Rochester and Rapid City as being 841 miles.

The narration in Example 12.17 corresponds to the content of Figure 12.2.

Example 12.17   Narration of driving towards Rapid City

a. Narration: Mike kept driving west from Milwaukee towards Rapid City, South Dakota, mostly following I-90W through Rochester, Minnesota. The estimated driving distance between Milwaukee and Rapid City was 841 miles (11 hours and 50 minutes).

b. Event-path:
$\vec{b}$ = [type:curved, direction:north-west, start:Milwaukee, end:Rochester],
$\vec{c}$ = [type:straight, direction:west, start:Rochester, end:RapidCity]
$\vec{d} = \vec{b} \oplus \vec{c}$
= [type:projected, direction:west, start:Milwaukee, end:RapidCity]

Localization

Motions themselves do not move. As asserted by Axiom 12.6, every motion is related to an event-path through *localization*. This does not, however, mean that the motion *e* moves along the path *p*. What moves is not the motion itself, but the object triggered to move by that motion, as asserted by Axiom 12.5. Assuming that each eventuality including motions is decomposed into substructures, each substructure of a motion can be associated with a part of the event-path it creates.

The formula *loc*(*e*, *p*) in Axiom 12.6 is interpreted as asserting that the path *p* is the *location of* a motion *e*. It means that each of the substructures of a motion matches a part of the path to which the event is localized. The predicate *loc* denotes a binary relation *locationOf* between a location and an object that is situated in that location. Axiom 12.6 extends the location from points or regions to paths. For some object x, $loc(x)$ can also be understood as a function such that $loc(x)(y)$ is of truth (propositional) type t, represented as $loc(x)=y$ or $loc(y,x)$. Following Zwarts and Winter (2000) and Kracht (2002), the predicate loc is thus treated as denoting a function that *locates* an object to a location. The object can be either an individual entity or an eventuality that includes motions, while the location is a spatial point, region, or path as in Axiom 12.6. Such a location is called *eigenspace* by Wunderlich (1991) or *eigenplace* by Kracht (2002), while the predicate loc defines a localization function L that maps an object to its eigenspace or eigenplace.

Definition 12.18 Notion of localization L
For any object c of type τ, which is either e (individual entity) or $v \rightarrow t$ (eventuality descriptor):
$$L(c) =_{df} \lambda x[loc(x,c)],$$
where x is a spatial point or a path such that $\lambda x[loc(x,c)]$ is of functional type $(p \rightarrow t) \rightarrow t$ and x is of functional type $p \rightarrow t$.

This definition of localization applies to the interpretation σ of a spatial relation between an individual entity and a region by localizing the entity. Consider Example 12.19.

Example 12.19 Localization
a. Data: Mia in Boston
b. Semantic representation:
  i. $\sigma(Mia) = M_e$
  ii. $\sigma(Boston) = B_r$, where $r = p \rightarrow t$
  iii. $L(M) = \lambda x(x,M)_{p \rightarrow t}$, where x is of type p
  iv. $\sigma(in) = \lambda y \lambda x[in(x,y)]$, where in is of type $r \rightarrow (r \rightarrow t)$
  v. $in(\lambda x(x,M)_{p \rightarrow t}, B_r)_t$, where the type $p \rightarrow t$ that denotes a set of points is the type r, denoting a region, by definition.

The semantic representation in Example 12.19 shows how the spatial relation $\sigma(in)$ of type $r \rightarrow (r \rightarrow t)$ relates $L(M)$ of type r, or $p \rightarrow t$, to Boston of type r through a type-constrained composition.

12.2.3 Corollary

From the two respective Axioms 12.5 and 12.6 on movers and event-paths, a corollary can be proposed.

Corollary 12.20   A mover traversing an event-path

If there occurs a motion e,

then there is a mover x which traverses a path p, triggered by the motion e.

$\forall e \exists \{x, p, e'\}$

$[motion(e) \rightarrow [mover(e, x) \wedge path(e, p) \wedge traverses(e') \wedge mover(e', x) \wedge path(e', p)]]]$

Axiom 12.5 states that there is a mover associated with a motion, while Axiom 12.6 states that there is a path triggered by a motion. Corollary 12.20 states that, if there is a motion e, then there is an associated motion *traverses e'* such that the mover x of e is also the mover of e', which follows through the path p.

Just as entities are localized to regions, motions are localized to event-paths. Each motion is thus characterized by an event-path. Motions themselves do not, however, move. Instead, movers do, each traversing the event-path to which each of their associated motions is localized. Consider Example 12.21.

Example 12.21   Jim drove from Frankfurt to Munich.

The event-path of Jim's driving to Munich starts from Frankfurt and so does his driving. But what moves is the vehicle and Jim also moves by sitting in the vehicle.

Definition of the Predicate *traverses*

Associated with paths, Nam (1995) introduces a predicate TRAV, standing for *traverses*, as denoting a ternary relation among x, π, T, where x is an object, π is a path, and T is a time interval. The relType *traverses* of ISO-Space (ISO, 2020d) in its movement link (moveLink) is also treated as a predicate but denoting a binary relation between an object x and an event-path π with respect to a motion m. Here, the event-path π denotes a function from an interval $[0, 1]$ of reals, which are understood to be linearly ordered time points, to a set of spatial points. The predicate *traverses* can thus be defined as in Definition 12.22:

Definition 12.22   Logical predicate *traverses*

$[[\mathbf{traverses}(x, \pi)]]^m = 1$ iff, for each real (time point) $i \in [0, 1]$, $[[in(L(x), \pi(i))]]^m = 1$,

where L is a localization operator that, for any entity x, returns the spatial point (eigenplace) where it is located.

Consider Example 12.23:

Example 12.23   Motions *leave* and *arrive*:

a. Data: Kalton left$_{m1}$ Chicago at five in the morning and arrived$_{m2}$ in Milwaukee at seven.

b. Interpretation:

$[\![traverses(Kalton, p_1)]\!]^{m_1, m_2} = 1$ if

$[\![in(L(Kalton), Chicago@05 : 00)]\!]^{m_1} = 1,$

$[\![in(L(Kalton), Milwauke@07 : 00)]\!]^{m_2} = 1,$ and,

for each location l between Milwaukee and Chicago and
for each time point i between 5:00 a.m. and 7:00 a.m.

$[\![in(L(Kalton), l@i)]\!]^{m_1, m_2} = 1.$

The preposition *in* here is a relation between the place $L(Kalton)$, where Kalton is located, and a temporally defined location, $l@i$.

12.3 Enriching ISO-Space with Event-Paths

Following Lee (2016) and Pustejovsky and Lee (2017), the two axioms of Pustejovsky and Yocum (2013) on motions and event-paths were implemented in the formulation of the annotation scheme of ISO-Space (ISO, 2020d). This has required spatial relators to be specified as triggers of various types of spatial configurations.

Proposition 12.24   Two proposals

a. Restoration of event-path as a base category
b. Respecification of spatial relators as triggers of various spatial configurations

I focus on these two proposals in this section.

12.3.1 Event-Paths Restored

Why not event-paths?

The preliminary versions of ISO-Space such as Pustejovsky et al. (2010b) and Pustejovsky and Moszkowicz (2012) originally had event-paths as part of their spatial annotation scheme. There were, however, two simple arguments against the introduction of event-paths as a base category: one argument was syntactic and the other, semantic. The syntactic argument was that, unlike other basic entity categories, event-paths could not be anchored to any overt markables, only being annotated as *nonconsuming tags*. The semantic argument was that event-paths could be inferred axiomatically from their associated event-motions that trigger them, thus allowing adequate semantic interpretations without their being annotated. Despite these arguments, ISO-Space (ISO, 2020d) adopts *event-path* as a genuine base category.

Annotation of Event-Paths as Nonconsuming Tags

Event-paths are not mentioned in text but are sometimes referred to. Instances of category *event-path* have no associated textual segments to which they can be anchored. Each of them is annotated as a nonconsuming tag with a unique ID: $\emptyset_{epN}$, where N is a positive integer, as in Example 12.25.

Annotation 12.25   Annotating event-paths as nonconsuming tags

a. Data: John drove from Chattanooga, Tennessee, to Tucson, Arizona, via Dallas, Texas, going on different highways. It was a long way to drive.

b. Base annotation:

John *drove* $\emptyset_{ep1:eventPath}$ from Chattanooga, Tennessee, to Tucson, Arizona, via Dallas, Texas, going on different highways$_{p1:path}$. $It_{pro1:ep1:eventPath}$ was a long *way*$_{p2:path}$ to drive.

John's driving to Tucson was a single event, creating a single event-path starting from Chattanooga and ending in Tucson, although several paths (highways) were taken each of which had different entrance points, different exit points, and different intersections. These highways or other types of roads may also have had slightly different directions. The whole event-path going through several US states was not mentioned in Example 12.25a, but was referred to by the pronoun *It* in Example 12.25.

Attributes of Category Event-Path   Unlike category *path*, category *event-path*, which is tagged as eventPath in annotation, has a null string $\emptyset$ as its @target value: target="". As a dynamic path, category *event-path* must be triggered by a motion so that the value of its attribute @trigger is specified with the identifier of a triggering motion: trigger="motionID". It must also be directed so that its two endpoints are specified with two distinct attributes @start and @end and possibly with a list of @mids for places between the two endpoints. Here is an example of annotation.

Annotation 12.26   Event-paths with two endpoints

a. Data: John drove from Chattanooga to Tuscon via Dallas and Santa Fe.

b. Base annotation:

John drove$_{m1,w2}$ $\emptyset_{ep1}$ from Chattanooga$_{pl1,w4}$ to Tucson$_{pl2,w6}$ via Dallas$_{pl3,w8}$ and Santa Fe$_{pl4,w10}$.

c. Spatial annotation, represented in XML:

```
<eventPath xml:id="ep1" target="" trigger="#m1" start="#pl1"
end="#pl2" mids="{#pl3,#pl4}"/>
<place xml:id="pl1" target="w4" type="city" form="nam"/>
<place xml:id="pl2" target="w6" type="city" form="nam"/>
```

```
<place xml:id="pl3" target="w8" type="city" form="nam"/>
<place xml:id="pl4" target="w10" type="city" form="nam"/>
```

d. Semantic representation:

$\sigma(ep1) := \{p_1, l_1, l_2, l_3, l_4\}$

$[path(p_1) \land [starts(p_1, l_1) \land city(l_1) \land named(l_1, Chatanooga)]$

$\land [ends(p_1, l_2) \land city(l_2) \land named(l_2, Tucson)]$

$\land [mids(p_1, \{l_3, l_4\}) \land city(l_3) \land named(l_3, Dallas) \land city(l_4) \land named(l_4, SantaFe)]$

The values of @start, @end, and @mids can each be specified with a pair of a location and a time: for example, start="placeID,timeID".

Annotation 12.27 Spatio-temporal locations

a. Data: John left Chatanooga at four in the morning and arrived in Tucson 10 minutes before midnight.
b. Base annotation:
John left$_{m1}$ Chatanooga$_{pl1}$ at [four in the morning]$_{t1}$ and arrived$_{m2}$ in Tucson$_{pl2}$ [10 minutes before midnight]$_{t2}$.
c. Annotation of eventPath:
```
<eventPath xml:id="ep1" target="" trigger="#m1,#me2"
start="#pl1,T04:00" end="#pl2,T23:50"/>
```

Each location on a dynamic path consists of a spatial-temporal point, represented as a pair of a place and a time.

Identifying Motions as Triggers and Event-Paths as Dynamic Paths
Event-paths are *dynamic paths* that are directed and temporally delimited. Roads and highways are *static paths*, which are *atemporal* with no direction involved, unless they are activated by a motion and referenced to an event-path, created by that motion. If someone drives on I-5 from San Francisco towards San Diego, then the highway is considered to be directed to San Diego and stretched approximately 502 miles south.

Subevents and Subpaths Events and event-paths are easily divisible. An event-path or motion may consist of several *subpaths* or *subevents*, triggered by them. Consider Example 12.28 to identify the subpaths of an event-path against ordinary paths or roads.

Example 12.28 Climbing Mt. Halla in Jeju, Korea, 2015
Covering the whole island of Jeju with its 368 extinct satellite volcanic eruptions, called *oreum*, Mt. Halla stands out as the highest mountain

in South Korea. It is 1950 meters high above sea level, facing south toward the north-eastern part of the Pacific Ocean. In late spring, 2015, I *climbed*$_{motion1}$ $\emptyset_{eventPath1}$ part of Mt. Halla by taking the easiest and most scenic *route*$_{path1}$ up to Witse-oreum through the *Yeongsil valley*$_{path2}$. I had rented a car and *driven*$_{motion2}$ $\emptyset_{eventPath2}$ up to the *parking lot*$_{place1}$ in *Yeongsil*$_{place2}$ at the elevation 1280 meters. From *there*$_{place1}$, I started my *hiking*$_{motion3}$ $\emptyset_{eventPath3}$ at 10 a.m., *walking*$_{motion4}$ $\emptyset_{eventPath4}$ up the stone steps through the 1.5 km steep *valley*$_{path3}$, *reaching*$_{motion5}$ $\emptyset_{eventPath5}$ the midpoint, called *Byeongpung Bawi "the Rock"*$_{place3}$. It took 50 minutes to *get*$_{motion6}$ $\emptyset_{eventPath6}$ there but I needed a 10-minute break. Then there stretched a long wooden *path*$_{path4}$ *reaching*$_{motion7:figurative}$ *Witse-oreum*$_{place4}$ with little slope. It was an easy *walk*$_{motion8}$ $\emptyset_{eventPath7}$ taking only 40 minutes for the distance of 2.2 kilometers, covered with shrubs, azaleas, and wild flowers. Witse-oreum was a group of three oreums, providing a wind-protected resting place at its sunken plateau. It was known as the most beautiful vista point on the island with a panoramic view of the whole ocean, while the peak of Mt. Halla looked almost touchable.

All of the key places and the sequence of the subevents of the whole climbing event are marked up appropriately. The event-paths are each marked with the nonconsuming tag, represented by $\emptyset_{eventPath}$ with a numeric ID.

The sequence of the *subevents* of climbing to Witse-oreum can be visualized with the two paths and their three *anchor points* (stopping places) as in Figure 12.3.

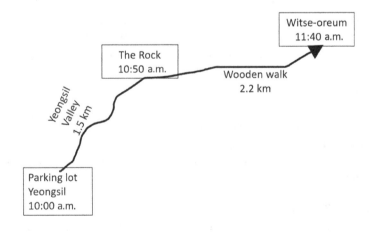

Figure 12.3 Subevents of the event of climbing to Witse-oreum

Eight markables are referring to motions found in the passage in Example 12.28. Except for the figuratively used verb *reaching* (motion7:figurative) that predicates the long wooden walk$_{path4}$, all of the other motions trigger event-paths. There are seven *subpaths* of the event of climbing Mt. Halla identified *in toto*, but some of them are found identical with all reducing to three subpaths: ep2, ep3, and ep6. The identification of the markables that refer to motions and their associated event-paths makes it possible to analyze the entire course of an event into its subevents. The event-path $\emptyset_{eventPath1}$, triggered by *climbed$_{motion1}$* first mentioned, refers to the whole event of climbing from the parking lot to Witse-oreum.

The subevents are annotated with more detail than Figure 12.3 with three associated event-paths as in Annotation 12.29.

Annotation 12.29   Climbing to Witse-oreum
a. Climbing to Witse-oreum:
```
eventPath(ep1, trigger="m1", start="", end="Witse-oreum",
  mids="YoungsilValley")
```
b. Getting to the parking lot:
```
eventPath(ep2, trigger="motion2", start=" ",
  end="parkingLot(pl1)", manner="driving")
place(pl1, type="parkingLot", location="Yeongsil(pl2)",
  elevation="1280m")
```
c. Leaving the parking lot and getting to the rock, midpoint:
```
eventPath(ep3, trigger="hike(motion3)",
  start="parkingLot(pl1),T10:00", mids="valley(p3)",
  end="Rock(pl3)", manner="walking",
  comment="ep3 is the same as ep4")
place(pl3, type="rock", name="Rock")
path(p3, type="valley", length="1.5km")
eventPath(id="ep5", trigger="reach(motion5)", start="",
  end="Rock", duration="50min",
  comment="ep5 is the terminal of ep3 or ep4")
```
d. Walking through the wooden walk to Witse-oreum:
```
eventPath(ep6, trigger="walk(motion8)", distance="2.2km",
  duration="40min", start="Rock(pl3),11am",
  mids="woodenPath(p4)", end="Witse-oreum(pl4)",
  manner="walking")
path(p4, type="wooden path", start="pl2",
  end="Witse-oreum(pl4)")
place(pl4, type="volcanicEruption", name="Witse-oreum")
```

```
pathLink(pL1, relType="partOf", figure="ep1", ground="{ep2,ep3,ep4,
  ep5,ep6}")
```

Note that event-paths are annotated as nonconsuming tags that carry null marakbles and also that identifiers are just specified with their values only in pFormat to differentiate the anchoring parts of base structures.

Interpreting Motion-Related Information

Category *event-path* as a genuine basic entity category provides an elegant way of interpreting motion-related information. Consider two interpretations of Example 12.30a.

Example 12.30 Two interpretations, *metric* vs. *temporal*

a. Data: Jim drove *1734 miles* for *25 hours*. It was a long drive and also a long way from Chattanooga, Tennessee, to Tucson, Arizona.

b. Base annotation:
   Jim_{x1} drove_{m1} $\emptyset_{ep1}$ 1734 miles_{me1} for 25 hours_{me2}. It was a long drive_{m1} and also a long way_{ep1} from Chattanooga_{pl1}, Tennessee, to Tucson_{pl2}, Arizona.

c. Annotation of `event-path` and `moveLINK`:
   ```
   eventPath(ep1, trigger="m1", start="pl1", end="pl2",
     distance="1734,mi", timeAmount="25,hour")
   moveLink(mvL1, relType="traverses", figure="x1", ground="ep1")
   ```

d. Semantic representation:
   $\exists\{e, l_1, l_2, p, t, x\}$
   $[drive(e) \wedge past(e)$
   $\wedge\, named(l_1, Chatanooga) \wedge named(l_2, Tucson)$
   $\wedge\, path(p) \wedge triggers(e, p) \wedge starts(p, l_1) \wedge ends(p, l_2)$
   $\wedge\, \delta(l_1, l_2) = (1734, mi) \wedge \alpha(e, t) = (25, hour)$
   $\wedge\, named(x, Jim)$
   $\wedge\, traverses(x, p)]$

The distance function δ maps a pair of locations to a distance, while the amount function α maps a pair of an event e and a limiting time t to the amount of time taken by the event e during the unmentioned indefinite time t. Since p is a dynamic path, triggered by the motion of Jim driving to Tucson, its start l_1 and end l_2 can be specified as pairs of a place and a time such that $l_1 = (Chatanooga, t)$ and $l_2 = (Tucson, t + 25h)$, respectively.

There are two interpretations of measuring Jim's driving to Tucson, Arizona. Interpretation (i) represents the measuring of the driving time (duration or time amount), whereas interpretation (ii) represents the measuring of the distance of the actual path (event-path) *p* taken for the driving. This is not the distance between the two cities, but the length of the event-path traversed by Jim while driving to Tucson. To measure such a length thus requires introducing paths triggered by motions, called *event-path*.

Returning to the discussion of Example 12.28 about climbing Mt. Halla, the distances and times associated with each of the three places, the parking lot, the Rock, and the volcanic eruption Witse-oreum refer to those of the event-paths either inferred from the length of the valley that the mover *I* followed or measured by the mover walking through the wooden path, as in Example 12.31.

Example 12.31   Event-paths measured

a. Distance inferred:

```
eventPath(ep3, trigger="hike(motion3)",
  start="parkingLot(pl1),T10:00", mids="valley(p3)",
  end="Byeongpung Bawi(pl3)", manner="walking")
path(p3, type="valley", length="1.5 km")
```

b. Measured:

```
eventPath(ep6, trigger="walk(motion8)", distance="2.2km",
  duration="40min", start="Byeongpung Bawi(pl3),T11:00",
  mids="woodenPath(p4)", end="Witse-oreum(pl4)", manner="walking")
path(p4, type="wooden path", start="pl3",
  end="Witse-oreum(pl4)")
```

The length of each of the two event-paths, one inferred from the length of the associated path (p3) and the other measured, can be represented as in Example 12.32.

Example 12.32   Two kinds of measure

a. Inferred length:
$$\sigma(ep3) := [path(\pi_3) \wedge triggers(m_3, \pi_3) \wedge valley(p_3) \wedge$$
$$length(p_3)$$
$$=<1.5, km> \wedge length(\pi_3) \geq length(p_3)]$$

b. Measured length:
$$\sigma(ep6) := [path(\pi_6) \wedge triggers(m_8, \pi_6) \wedge length(\pi_6)=<2.2, km>]$$

The inferred length states that the length of the event path π_3 is greater or equal to the length of the valley p_3. These examples have shown that category *event-path* needs to be introduced to discuss the measures of event-paths.

12.3.2 Spatial Relators as Triggers of Spatial Configurations

Spatial relators are either static or dynamic. Static spatial relators trigger qualitative spatial configurations, as discussed in Chapter 11. Dynamic spatial relators, in contrast, characterize motions and associated event-paths. Directional spatial relators can be either static or dynamic.

Static Spatial Relators

In Chapter 11, three types of spatial relators, mostly denoted by prepositions in English, were introduced as triggering static spatial configurations, mereo-topological, orientational, or metric. Here is a list of spatial prepositions from Pustejovsky (2017b, p. 993) with some additions (see also O'Keefe (1996)).

Classification 12.33   Three types of spatial relators

a. Mereo-topological: *at, in, on, inside, outside, part of, touching, not touching, between*
b. Orientational: *above, below, under, behind, in front of, to the left of, north of*
c. Metric: *near, far, close by*

Zwarts (2005) calls these spatial relators *(static) locative prepositions*.

Dynamic Spatial Relators

In contrast to these locative or static prepositions, Zwarts (2005, p. 741) introduces a list of prepositions, called *(dynamic) directional prepositions*.[4]

Classification 12.34   Dynamic directional prepositions
across, along, around, away from, down, from, into, off, onto, out of, over, past, through, to, towards, up, via

These dynamic directional prepositions then constitute five different types of path-related prepositions (see also Zwarts (2005, p. 759)).

Classification 12.35   Five types of path-related prepositions

a. Start-defining type: *from, out of, off*
b. End-defining type: *to, into, onto*
c. Path-defining type: *through, across, over, past, via*
d. Direction-defining type: *along, against, up, down*
e. Projective or goal-defining type: *toward(s), away from, across*

---

[4] Since the term *direction* can be used in either a static sense or a dynamic sense, it may be better to call Zwarts's directional prepositions *dynamic directional* prepositions.

12.3.3 Projection and Projected Paths

The goal-defining or projective type such as *toward* is *multityped*. It is a goal-defining type as well as a direction-defining type (see Jackendoff (1983, 1990, 2002), Mani and Pustejovsky (2012)). It is a goal-defining function with its path *unbound*, carrying only the sense of direction. It is a dynamic directional spatial relator being used with motion verbs but also a *static directional* or *orientational* spatial relator. Consider Example 12.36.

Example 12.36 Directions involving a projection

a. The Buddha had deep compassion and respect *toward* all living beings.
b. My house faces *toward* a big mountain.
c. A tall and long diving board on a lake stretched out *toward* the deep water.
d. Our talks made very little progress *toward* agreement.
e. We sat *toward* the sun to see it rise early in the dawn.
f. We walked *toward* the sea to see whales swimming.
g. We had to make a very long detour to drive *toward* Madison, going up through Fond du Lac from Milwaukee.

None of the examples in Example 12.36 except for the last two (f and g) involves any sort of motion, for there is no object that has moved. Nevertheless, they all carry a sense of direction involving a projection from one object to another. The preposition *toward* is a spatial relator simply denoting a direction.

Static Projection

Jackendoff (2002, p. 362) cites two cases of projection, involving the path-defining spatial relator *across*: (i) nontemporal extension (EXT) and (ii) orientation (ORIENT) (see Chapter 11).

Example 12.37 Static projections

a. EXT(x,Path):
   Nontemporal extension: e.g., *The road goes across the river.*
b. ORIENT(x,Path):
   Orientation: e.g., *The sign points across the river.*

In both cases, an object is related to a (static) path without involving any time. In the first case, the road is also a path. Hence, the spatial relator *across* denotes a relation between two paths such that the road crosses the river. In the second case of orientation, the sign retains the relation of pointing to every point on the projection almost to its endpoint reaching the bank of the river on the other side.

Static cases used with the spatial relator *toward* can be annotated in ISO-Space (ISO, 2020d) with its orientation link (oLink).

Annotation 12.38   Spatial relator *toward*

a. Data: The house faces toward a big mountain.
b. Base annotation: The house$_{x1,\,w2}$ faces$_{e1,\,w3}$ toward$_{sr1,\,w4}$ a big mountain$_{x2,\,w7}$.
c. Annotation:

```
sRelator(sr1, w4, type="projective", pred="toward")

path(p1, type="projective", start="x1", end="x2", trigger="e1,sr1")

oLink(oL1, relType="projectivetoward", figure="x1", ground="p1",

  trigger="sr1")
```

In Annotation 12.38, oLink(oL1) relates the house (x) to the path p1, triggered by the spatial relator sr1, that denotes a static path p_{toward}. The relation of the house facing a big mountain continues to hold at every point on the entire path p_{toward}, the endpoint of which *approaches* the location of the big mountain.

Dynamic Projection

Event-paths are triggered by motions but are also characterized by the type of spatial relators associated with them. This requires the enrichment of annotating spatial relators, for instance, expressed by prepositions in English.

Annotation 12.39   Event-paths characterized by spatial relators

a. Data: Mike drove 93 miles north from Chicago to Milwaukee.
b. Base annotation:
   Mike$_{x1,\,w1}$ drove$_{m1,\,w2}$ $\emptyset_{p1}$ 93 miles$_{me1,\,w3-4}$ north$_{sr1,\,w5}$ from$_{sr2,\,w6}$ Chicago$_{pl1,\,w7}$ to$_{sr3,\,w8}$ Milwaukee$_{pl2:w9}$.
c. Spatial relators annotated:

```
sRelator(sr1, w5, type="direction", pred="north")
sRelator(sr2, w6, type="start-defining", pred="from")
sRelator(sr3, w8, type="end-defining", pred="to")
path(p1, type="dynamic", mover="x1", distance="93mime1",
  direction="northsr1", start="Chicagopl1", end="Milwaukeepl2",
  trigger="m1,sr1,sr2,sr3")
```

Marked as in Annotation 12.39b, *base annotation* categorizes word-segmented markables into basic entity categories of the spatial annotation scheme. There are three occurrences of spatial relators among the categorized markables: The first one is type *direction*, the second one is type *start-defining*, and the third one is type *end-defining*. They specify the direction, start, and end of an event-path, created by the motion *drive*.

Consider Annotation 12.40 to see how the preposition *toward(s)* is annotated as a spatial relator.

Annotation 12.40 Annotating the preposition *toward*

a. Data: Mike drove . . . *west from* Milwaukee *toward* Madison.

b. Base annotation: Mike$_{x1,w1}$ drove$_{m1,w2}$ . . . $\emptyset_{p2}$ *west*$_{sr1,w3}$ *from*$_{sr2,w4}$ Milwaukee$_{pl1,w5}$ *toward*$_{sr3,w6}$ Madison$_{pl2,w7}$.

c. Annotation:

```
path(p2, type="dynamic", distance="", direction="westsr1",

  start="Milwaukeepl1", goal="Madisonpl2", trigger="m1,sr4,sr5,sr6")

sRelator(sr1, w3, type="direction", pred="west")

sRelator(sr2, w4, type="start-defining", pred="from")

sRelator(sr3, w6, type="projective, goal-defining", pred="toward")
```

The preposition *toward* as a projective spatial relator has two roles: It marks not only the *direction* of a dynamic path p1, triggered by the motion m1 of Mike driving, but also its *goal* to which the path is directed. Note that the goal of a path is a point to which the path *approaches*.

Consider a third case.

Annotation 12.41 Dynamic projection

a. Data: Mike headed for Madison but ended up in Green Bay.

b. Base annotation: Mike$_{x1,w1}$ headed$_{m1,w2}$ $\emptyset_{p1}$ for Madison$_{pl1,w4}$ but ended up$_{m2,w6-7}$ $\emptyset_{p2}$ in Green Bay$_{pl2,w9}$.

c. Spatial annotation:

```
path(p1, type="projected", trigger="m1", goal="pl1")

path(p2, type="projected", trigger="m2", end="pl2")
```

d. Semantic representation:

$\exists\{x_1,e_1,l_1,e_2,l_2,p_1,p_2\}$
$[named(x_1,Mike) \wedge head(e_1) \wedge past(e_1)$
$\wedge named(l_1,Madison) \wedge city(l_1)$
$\wedge endUp(e_2) \wedge past(e_2)$
$\wedge named(l_2,Green\ Bay) \wedge city(l_2)$
$\wedge path(p_1) \wedge projected(p_1) \wedge goal(p_1,l_1)^5 \wedge path(p_2) \wedge ends(p_2,l_2)$
$\wedge traverses(x_1,p_2)]$

---

[5] The predicate *goal* also needs to be defined. If the mover reaches the goal, then the endpoint of the path is the same as the goal.

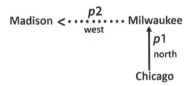

Figure 12.4 Projected dynamic path

There are two dynamic paths annotated in Anntoation 12.41. The first one is, however, annotated as a *projective* path. It is an intended path, but is not a path actually taken. Here, the predicate *projective* is interpreted as being equivalent to the meaning of *intended*.

Interpretation of *toward* as a Projective Dynamic Spatial Relator
In Annotation 12.40, there is a path *p2* as a projected dynamic path. It is a projected dynamic path (event-path) because it is triggered by a projective spatial relator *toward* and the motion of type MOVE.

Figure 12.4 shows two directed paths, *p1* and *p2*: one is represented as a solid arrow and the other, as a dotted arrow. The first one is simply called a *dynamic path* (event-path) and the second one, *projected dynamic path*. Both of them are dynamic, for they were triggered by the motion of Mike's driving from Chicago. An ordinary projected path may not be a physical path, but something abstract like a directed line that a surveyor draws in his perspective to measure the height of a mountain or the boundaries of a piece of land. In contrast, a *projected-dynamic path* is a physical path, for it is a path, triggered by a motion and *projected* to be traversed by the mover of that motion.

Compared with the interpretation of the preposition *to*, the preposition *toward(s)* is often claimed to carry the sense of proximity between the goal and the projected goal only if it involves a motion. Based on the notion of *relative nearness* (Nam, 1995), for instance, the *projected goal* is defined as in Definition 12.42:

Definition 12.42   Projected goal
Let a path p denote a function from the interval $[0,1]$ of reals to a set of vectors. If p is triggered by a motion and the spatial relator *toward x*, where x refers to a region, then its goal $p(1)$ is *nearer to* the target region x than its start $p(0)$ but *neither through x nor equal to x*.

Consider Example 12.43, as depicted by Figure 12.5.

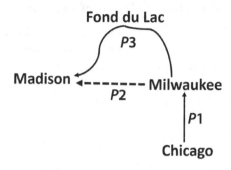

Figure 12.5 Projected path with a detour

Example 12.43 Mike had to make a long detour to drive *toward* Madison, going up through Fond du Lac from Milwaukee.

As in Example 12.43, there may be a projected path that is not straight but curved with detours, making it difficult to think of the notion of proximity at some points of a motion.

Zwarts (2005) argues that Nam's (1995) definition, simply based on the notion of relative nearness, is very weak because it includes the denotations of the goal *to*, while overlapping the denotation of a route preposition *through*. The additional clause *neither through x nor equal to x* in Definition 12.42 excludes the unwanted cases mentioned in Zwarts (2005).

12.4 Orientation and Frame of Reference

The notion of projection is closely related to *orientation* and *frame of reference*. Consider two mappings involving the orientation link in ISO-Space (ISO, 2020d). Just like the qualitative spatial link (qsLink), the orientation link (oLink) anchors an object, called *figure*, to a location, called *ground*. But, unlike cases of the qualitative spatial link, this location (ground) needs to be identified for oLink against a frame of reference triggered by a spatial relator (sRelator). In analyzing various languages, Levinson (2003) identified three types of *frames of reference*: (i) absolute, (ii) relative, and (iii) inherent. Mani and Pustejovsky (2012) then applied such an analysis of frames of reference to the formulation of spatial ontology and region calculus. This section shows how a frame of reference affects the annotation and interpretation of spatial orientation and projection in language.

12.4.1 Absolute Frame of Reference

Cardinal directions such as north (N), south (S), west (W), and east (E) and their subdirections such as north-west (NW) are typical examples of the *absolute type of frame of reference*. English complex prepositions *north of, south of* or *north-west of* that refer to cardinal directions are annotated as spatial relators (sRelator) in ISO-Space (ISO, 2020d), triggering the orientational link (oLink) with the absolute type of reference frame. I claim in this chapter that spatial relators each project a *grounded oriented linear path $\vec{p}$*, called *vector* or *projection*, pointing to a cardinal point and that this path is made as a frame of reference for identifying the location of the figure in the orientation link. This claim can be stated in the form of propositions, as formulated in Propositions 12.44 and 12.45.

Proposition 12.44 Cardinal directions as spatial relators
Every spatial relator R_{dr} in a language that denotes a cardinal direction *dr* projects a vector $\overrightarrow{p(l_0)}$ grounded on some bounded region $\Omega(l_0)$ that contains a point l_0 of location as its start point, where l_0 is of type p of spatial point.

Proposition 12.45 Identifying the location of a place
The location of a place is identified as a bounded region $\Omega(l_1)$ with the endpoint e of a vector $\overrightarrow{p([l_0,l_1])}$, grounded on a bounded region $\Omega(l_0)$ and also delimited by that point l_1 as its endpoint with a finite length specified.

Proposition 12.44 simply states that there is a *grounded projection* towards a cardinal direction which may be of nonfinite length. Proposition 12.45, in contrast, states that a grounded projection can be terminated at some point if its length is specified.

Consider how these propositions apply to the annotation and interpretation of text such as Example 12.46 that contains a spatial relator *north-west of*.

Example 12.46 Waltham, Massachusetts
Waltham, MA, is located ... about 11 miles (18 km) *north-west of* downtown Boston.[6]

Figure 12.6 captures what is conveyed by the fragment of Example 12.46 and annotated as in Annotation 12.47. Waltham (F=p11:$\Omega(l_1)$) is annotated as being *north-west* of downtown Boston (G=p12:$\Omega(l_0)$). The projection from Boston to Waltham is annotated as a subtype of category *path*: path(p1,

---

[6] Refer to https://en.wikipedia.org/Waltham,_Massachusetts #Geography. The city of Waltham in Massachusetts is exactly located at $42°22'50''$N , $71°14'6''$W.

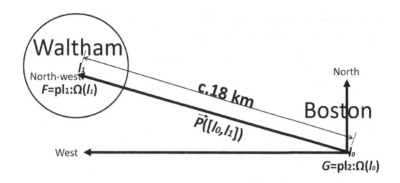

Figure 12.6 Locating Waltham, MA

`type="oriented"`). Its start $p12:\Omega(l_0)$ identifies the location of the figure (F=p11) to be a bounded region $\Omega(l_1)$ of its endpoint l_1. This end region $\Omega(l_1)$ could have been one of the midpoints of the projection if its distance *18 kilometers* were not specified as its length, for the projection associated with a cardinal direction can stretch out infinitely. Note that the figure F=p11 is a complex base structure, triggered by β_{sr1}, that refers to the other base structures, β_{pl2}, β_{pl1}, and β_{me1} as marked by the hash symbol # in `path(p1)`.

Annotation 12.47 Locating Waltham, Massachusetts

a. Base annotation: Waltham$_{pl1,w1}$, MA, is located ... about 11 miles (18 km)$_{w5-9}$ north-west of$_{sr1,w10-11}$ downtown Boston$_{pl2,w12-13}$.

b. Base structures:

```
place(pl1, w1, type="city", named="Waltham", state="MA")
sRelator(sr1, w10-11, type="orientation", pred="north-west",
  referenceFrame="absolute")
path(p1, type="oriented", start="pl2", end="pl1",
  direction="NW", distance="me1", shape="straight",
  trigger="sr1")
measure(me1, w5-9, type="length", value="(18,km)", mod="about")
place(pl2, w12-13, type="city-center", pred="downTown",
  city="Boston", state="MA")
```

c. Link structures:

```
meLink(meL1, relType="measure", object="p1", value="me1")
oLink(oL1, relType="north-west", figure="<pl1,p1>", ground="pl2")
```

Based on the semantics in Annotation 12.47b,c, we can now derive Semantics 12.48.

Semantics 12.48   Semantic representation

a. Semantic representation of base structures:

$\sigma(\text{pl1}) := [city(r_1) \wedge named(r_1, Waltham) \wedge state(r_1, \text{MA})]$

$\sigma(\text{sr1}) := [oriented(s) \wedge direction(s, \text{NW})]$

$\sigma(\text{pl2}) := [cityCenter(r_2) \wedge city(r_2, Boston) \wedge state(r_2, \text{MA})]$

$\sigma(\text{p1}) := [path(p_1) \wedge oriented(p_1)$
$\qquad \wedge starts(p_1, l_0) \wedge ends(p_1, l_1)$
$\qquad \wedge direction(p_1, \text{NW}) \wedge distance(l_0, l_1) = \mu(d_1)$
$\qquad \wedge straight(p_1)$
$\qquad \wedge in(r_1, \Omega(l_1)) \wedge in(r_2, \Omega(l_0))]$

$\sigma(\text{me1}) := [\mu(d_1) \approx 18\_km]$

b. Semantic representation of oLink structure:

$\sigma(\text{oL1}) :=$
$\exists\{r_l, r_2, p_1, l_0, l_1, d_1\}$
$[northWest(r_1, r_2) \oplus <\sigma(\text{pl1}), \sigma(\text{p1})>]$

c. Full representation:

$\exists\{r_l, r_2, p_1, l_0, l_1, d_1\}$
$[northWest(r_1, r_2)$
$\quad \wedge [city(r_1) \wedge named(r_1, Waltham) \wedge state(r_1, \text{MA})]$
$\quad \wedge [cityCenter(r_2) \wedge city(r_2, Boston) \wedge state(r_2, \text{MA})]$
$\quad \wedge [path(p_1) \wedge starts(p_1, l_0) \wedge ends(p_1, l_1)$
$\quad \wedge direction(p_1, \text{NW}) \wedge distance(l_0, l_1) = \mu(d_1)$
$\quad \wedge [\mu(d_1) \approx 18km]$
$\quad \wedge straight(p_1)$
$\quad \wedge in(r_1, \Omega(l_1)) \wedge in(r_2, \Omega(l_0))]]$

Semantics 12.48 adequately represents a case of the orientational link (oLink), involving the absolute frame of reference related to cardinal directions. It is understood as stating that Waltham r_1 is north-west of downtown Boston r_2 and that the city of Waltham is located in the bounded region $\Omega(l_1)$ of the end point l_1 of the NW-directed projection p_1 from its start point l_0 in downtown Boston r_2 with the distance between the two points l_0 and l_1 being approximately 18 km.

12.4.2 Relative Frame of Reference

The notion of *projection* also applies to the annotation and interpretation of the relative type of frames of reference, as expressed by prepositional phrases such as *on the right of*. A projection to some point from the perspective of a viewer divides a coordinate plane into two halves, one half is called *right*, and the other, *left*, as stated in Example 12.49.

Example 12.49 Witse-oreum

The most easily accessible and popular vista point, named *Witse-oreum*, is [on the right side of]$_{sr1:relative}$ Mt. Halla just below its peak if you look at it from Jeju International Airport.

Figure 12.7 depicts how the relative frame of reference is understood in interpreting Example 12.49.

In Figure 12.7, the viewer $V:r_4$, who is located (i) at some place in Jeju International Airport r_4, sees (ii) the peak r_3 of Mt. Halla r_2. She wants to climb (iii) Witse-oreum r_1 and finds it near the peak $R:r_3$ and (iv) within the projected range θ accessible from $R:r_3$, which is formed by the two vertical projections $\overrightarrow{p_1}$ and $\overrightarrow{p_2}$.

To identify the location of Witse-oreum, one of over 350 volcanic eruptions on Jeju Island, South Korea, one has to understand what is meant by the spatial relator *on the right ... of*, as mentioned in Example 12.49. For a fuller understanding, one has to know of the whole frame of relative reference or viewer's perspective that includes (i) the position $V:r_4$ of *viewing*, (ii) the points $R:r_2$ and $R:r_3$ of reference, called *reference points*, (iii) the position of the object $F:r_1$ being talked about, called *figure*, and (iv) the vertical projections p_i that include the two, $\overrightarrow{p_1}$ and $\overrightarrow{p_2}$ from the point of viewing to the three relevant objects, Mt. Halla $R:r_2$, its peak $R:r_3$, and Witse-oreum $F:r_1$.

In the case of relative frames of reference, the *ground G* of identifying objects includes both the viewing position V and the reference point R. In this case, $V:r_4$, $R:r_2$, and R_3 are the three relevant objects for the ground G of the figure $F:r_1$. Witse-oreum $F:r_1$ is rightly claimed to be on the right of Mt. Halla

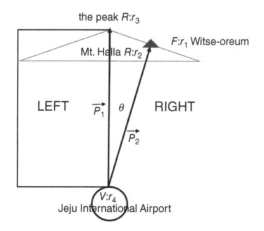

Figure 12.7 Relative frame of reference locating Wits-oreum

$R{:}r_2$ or its peak $R{:}r_3$ because it is located on the projection path $\overrightarrow{p_2}$ on the right of the projection path $\overrightarrow{p_1}$ in the range θ accessible from the view position $V{:}r_4$ or projected from the reference point $R{:}r_3$, the peak of Mt. Halla $R{:}r_2$.

Example 12.49 can be annotated accordingly as in Annotation 12.50 and Annotation 12.51.

Annotation 12.50   Base annotation (markables)

a. Data: The most easily accessible popular vista point, named *Witse-oreum*, is on the right side of Mt. Halla just below its peak if you look at it from Jeju International Airport.

b. Base annotation (markables):

The most easily accessible popular vista point, named *Witse-oreum*$_{pl1,\,w9}$, is [on the right side of]$_{sr1:relative,\,w11-15}$ Mt. Halla$_{pl2,\,w16}$ just below its peak$_{pl3,\,w20}$ if you look$_{v1,\,w23}$ look at it from Jeju International Airport$_{pl4,\,w27}$.

Annotation 12.51   Semantic annotation (annotation structures)

a. Base structures annotated:

```
place(pl1,w9,
    type="volcanicEruption",
    name="Witse-oreum",
    province="Jeju",
    country="KOR")
sRelator(sr1,w11-15,
    type=orientational,
    pred="rightSide",
    referenceFrame="relative")
place(pl2,w16,
    type="mountain",
    name="Mt.Halla",
    province="Jeju",
    country="KOR")
place(pl3,w20,
    type="mountain",
    pred="peak",
    province="Jeju",
    country="KOR")
place(pl4,w27,type="airport",
    name="Jeju International Airport",
    province="Jeju",
    country="KOR")
```

```
view(v1,w23,type="process",
  pred="view",
  viewPosition="pl4",
  viewReference="pl3",
  inView="{pl1,pl2,pl3}",
  focus="pl1",trigger="sr1")
```

b. Link structures:

```
qsLink(qsL1,relType="partOf",
  figure="pl1",
  ground="pl2")
oLink(oL1,relType="rightSide",
  figure="pl1",
  ground="{pl3,v1}")
qsLink(qsL2,relType="partOf",
  figure="pl3",
  ground="pl2")
```

The relation type *part of* is introduced here as a more refined notion of the relation *in*.

Based on Annotation 12.51, we can now derive the semantic forms, represented in the DRS format, which together identify the relative location of Witse-oreum in Jeju, Korea.

Semantics 12.52 DRS

r_1, r_2, r_3, r_4, v_1
volcanicEruption(r_1), named(r_1,WitseOreum) province(r_1,Jeju), country(r_1, KOR)
mountain(r_2), named(r_2, Mt. Halla) province(r_2,Jeju), country(r_2,KOR) peak(r_3) airport(r_4) named(r_4,Jeju International Airport) province(r_4,Jeju), country(r_4,KOR)
viewPosition(v_1, r_4), viewReference(v_1, r_2, r_3) inView(v_1, r_1, r_2, r_3), focus(v_1, r_1)
part(r_1, r_2) rightSide(r_1, r_3) part(r_3, r_2)

Unlike the DRS forms in Semantics 12.52, Semantics 12.53 shows how each of the base and link structures in Annotations 12.50 and 12.51 is converted to a semantic form σ.

Semantics 12.53   Semantic representation

a. Semantic forms of the base structures:

$\sigma(\text{pl1}) := [volcanicEruption(r_1) \wedge named(r_1, WitseOreum) \wedge$
$\qquad\qquad province(r_1, Jeju) \wedge country(r_1, \text{KOR})]$

$\sigma(\text{pl2}) := [mountain(r_2) \wedge named(r_2, Mt. Halla) \wedge province(r_2, Jeju)$
$\qquad\qquad \wedge country(r_2, \text{KOR})]$

$\sigma(\text{pl3}) := [mountain(r_3) \wedge peak(r_2, r_3)]$

$\sigma(\text{pl4}) := [airport(r_4) \wedge named(r_4, Jeju\ International\ Airport) \wedge$
$\qquad\qquad province(r_4, Jeju) \wedge country(r_4, \text{KOR})]$

$\sigma(\text{v1}) := [viewPosition(v_1, r_4) \wedge viewReference(v_1, r_2, r_3) \wedge inView$
$\qquad\qquad (v_1, \{r_1, r_2, r_3\}) \wedge focus(v_1, r_1)]$

b. Semantic forms of the link structures:

$\sigma(\text{qsL1}) := \exists\{r_1, r_2\}[part(r_1, r_2)]$

$\sigma(\text{oL1}) := \exists\{r_1, r_2, r_3, r_4, v_1\}[rightSide(r_1, r_3) \oplus <\sigma(pl1), \sigma(v1)>]$

$\sigma(\text{qsL2}) := \exists\{r_3, r_2\}[part(r_3, r_2)]$

The semantic form of the whole annotation structure may refer to Semantics 12.52, represented in the DRS format.

12.4.3 Intrinsic Frame of Reference

Words like *head, tail,* or *face* refer to parts of living bodies,[7] while words like *front, back, side, bottom,* or *top* refer to parts of all physical objects or artifacts including vehicles like cars and trucks, TV sets, big buildings, and small houses. Combined with some prepositions such as *in* or *of* like *in front of, side of* or *back of*, these words form complex spatial prepositions to refer to some coordinates in space. A basic example takes a viewer herself as a frame of reference, called *self-reference*, to partitioned four directional spatial coordinates, when restricted to a two-dimensional plane, as shown in Figure 12.8.

The space that she faces is the front and the opposite space, the back. The right-hand side is the right and the left-hand side, the left.

Consider how the notion of *intrinsic self-reference* applies to the annotation of text such as Annotation 12.54.

---

[7] Don Diltz (personal communication) has suggested that the anatomical positioning terms be used to refer to parts of the body: *superior (cranial), inferior (caudal), anterior, posterior, medial, distal, lateral, proximal, superficial, deep.*

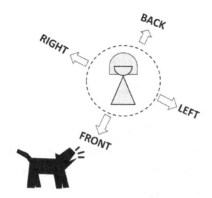

Figure 12.8 Viewer herself as a frame of reference
Image by Ghang Lee

Annotation 12.54 Intrinsic self-reference

a. Markables: A dog$_{x1,w2}$ in front of$_{s1,w3-5}$ me$_{x2,w6}$ is barking$_{e1,w8}$ at me$_{x2,w10}$.

b. Annotation:

```
entity(x1, w2, type="animate", pred="dog")
sRelator(sr1, w3-5, type="topDir", pred="inFrontOf")
entity(x2, w6, type="human", pred="ego")
event(e1, w8, type="process", pred="bark",
  tense="pres", aspect="progressive", agent="x1", theme="x2")
view(e2, type="process", pred="view", agent="x2", theme="x1",
  viewPosition="x2", viewReference="x2", focus="x1", trigger="sr1")
oLink(oL1, inFrontOf, figure="x1", ground="x2", referencePt="e2")
oLink(oL1, inFrontOf, figure="e1", ground="x2", referencePt="e2")
```

There is an event$_{e2}$ of viewing a dog$_{x1}$ and its barking$_{e1}$ in front of the viewer x_2, the speaker herself, and she herself or her position becomes a reference point for the spatial relation *in front of*. She sees a dog and it is in front of her or where she views$_{e2}$ the dog barking$_{e1}$. Both the viewer x_1 and the event e_2 of her viewing are *localized* to one and the same location, functioning as a ground and a reference point.

Here is another example that illustrates how the spatial relator *in front of* is annotated and interpreted. See Annotation 12.55.

Annotation 12.55 The spatial relator *in front of*

a. Base annotation: I$_{x1,w1}$ planted a big pine-tree$_{x2,w5-6}$ in front of$_{s1,w7-9}$ a new house$_{x3,w12}$.

b. Semantic annotation:

```
entity(x1, type="human", pred="ego")
```

```
entity(x2, W5-6, type="plant", pred="pine-tree")

sRelator(sr1, w7-9, type="topDir", pred="inFrontOf")

entity(x3, w12, type="facility", pred="house")

view(e1, type="process", pred="view", agent="x1", theme="x2,x3",

  focus="x2", viewPosition="unspecified", viewReference="x3",

  trigger="sr1")

oLink(oL1, inFrontOf, x2, {x3,e1})
```

We can derive the semantic form (Semantics 12.56) in DRS from Annotation 12.55b, where oLink locates x2 to the front of x3 and the view position of e1.

Semantics 12.56 ABSr vs. DRS

a. ABSr: $\sigma(\text{oL1}) := [inFrontOf(x_2, x_3) \oplus [\sigma(\text{x2}) \oplus \sigma(\text{e1})]]$

b. DRS:

x_1, x_2, x_3, e_1
inFrontOf($L(x_2), L(x_3)$)
human(x_1), ego(x_1)
plant(x_2), pineTree(x_2)
facility(x_3), house(x_3)
process(e_1), view(e_1)
agent(e_1, x_1), theme($e_1, \{x_2, x_3\}$), focus(e_1, x_2)
viewReference($e_1, L(x_3)$)

The conjunctive list of the semantics forms in Semantics 12.56b is interpreted as stating that, as the viewer x_1 sees, the location $L(x_2)$, where a pine-tree x_2 is planted, is in front of $L(x_3)$ where a house x_3 is located. The viewer sees the tree and the house but focuses on the tree. The location of the tree is said to be in front of the house, independent of the viewer's point of view, for the frontal part of the house has been designed as such, thus being said to be *intrinsic*.

Houses are normally designed as having a front, a back, and sides. Consider my house in Korea as Example 12.57.

Example 12.57 My house

I have a farmhouse near Seoul. I had built it *facing* the main entrance gate but later had to move the *front* door around to *face* the inner court and add a staircase with lower and less slippery wooden steps than the earlier stone steps. The *front door* or main entrance door is now in the *back* of my house.

Mail or parcel deliverers still get confused about where to leave their items, despite the large sign posted on the old front door pointing to the new main entrance.

Example 12.58 Sign post
> Go around
> to the *inner$_{sr1, s1:w5}$* court.
> Leave delivery items
> at the new *front$_{sr2, s2:w7}$* door.
> Thanks.

The main question here is how to envision the whole situation and locate the inner court and the new front door of a house. One possibility is to assume that one approaches the house from its old front, goes around it to the back of the house, and faces it, finding a door. This door could be the new front door.

Mountains are considered each having a front and a back, although the part facing the viewers is said to be its front and the other side, the back. Two cities on opposite sides often argue about which side of the mountain separates them, the front or the back. Natural objects like mountains may not have directional characteristics such as the front or the back inherently, although each of their sides is oriented towards a cardinal direction.

Motions involve directionality. Consider Example 12.59.

Example 12.59 Near collision on a Welsh road
a. A little story:
A truck was driving away from a big rock sitting in front of it, but then another vehicle came down the road heading towards it. An old man was crossing the road. These two vehicles could have had a head-on collision besides hitting the man on the road. It is not easy to drive on a country road, especially in a foreign land like Wales or the Scottish highlands.
b. Partially annotated:
A truck$_{x1}$ was driving$_{e1:motion}$ away from a big rock$_{x2}$ sitting$_{e2:state}$ *in front of it* but then another vehicle$_{x3}$ came$_{e3:motion}$ down the road heading$_{sr1:direction}$ towards it. There was an old man$_{x4}$ crossing$_{e4:motion}$ the road. These two vehicles could have had a *head-on* collision besides hitting the man on the road. It is not easy to drive on a country road, especially in a foreign land like Wales or the Scottish highlands.

The situation described here involves four objects, located on a Welsh or Scottish road where you drive on the left lane: a truck$_{x1}$, a big rock$_{x2}$, another vehicle$_{x3}$, and an old man$_{x4}$. Then there are three motions and one state described. It is very unusual, but there is a big rock blocking the road while there are three moving objects, two vehicles moving in two different directions, and a man crossing the road illegally. In describing or annotating such a situation, *paths* and their *directionality* are the key factors in the motions

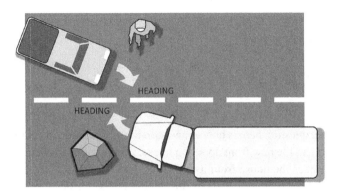

Figure 12.9 Near-collision on a Welsh road
Image by Ghang Lee

involved. Several keywords refer to the directionality of a motion like *driving*. The expressions like *came*, *heading*, and *head-on* in this example refer to the reference point or position of the narrator or the inherent properties of vehicles.

The task of annotating all these pieces of information in a serial form such as XML or pFormat can be quite complex. Instead, depicting them in a visual form can be easily understandable. Figure 12.9 depicts the situation, which is described by the story in Example 12.59.

This example and all other verbal descriptions that carry complex dynamic information call for a simpler way of organizing and representing such information. Visualizing information can be an answer (see Lee (2013)).

12.5 Summary

In this chapter, I classified category *path* into four types: *static, dynamic, oriented*, and *projected* paths and analyzed their characterizing features for the proper interpretation of path-related information in language. Roads are typical static paths, understood to be sequences of landmarks or places in general, whereas dynamic paths are trajectories caused by event motions. Intrinsically, static paths are not directed. They are finite paths with two endpoints, but one cannot tell which is the start and which is the endpoint. Nevertheless, highways with their entries, exits, and lanes are specified with directions. Motion-events trigger dynamic paths, but some of them are simply directed to some goals. This chapter treats them as *oriented paths*. Projected paths are *virtual* or *intended* paths that are not traversed but devised in the mind of a human or rational agent.

To discuss their characteristic features in formal terms, I introduced Pustejovsky and Yocum's (2013) two motion-related axioms, one for the mover and another for the event-path, both caused by a translocational motion. Based on the two axioms, I proposed a corollary that relates a mover to an event-path. I then showed how this corollary provided an axiomatic basis for the re-formulation of the movement link (moveLINK), which links a mover to a motion-triggered event-path with the relation *traverses*. Similarly, the notions of orientation and projection were analyzed with respect to Levinson's (2003) frames of reference, either absolute, relative or intrinsic, and applied to the annotation and interpretation of oriented or projected paths. While closing the chapter, I pointed out the need to visualize complex information, instead of serialized annotation.

13

Toward a Dynamic Annotation Scheme

13.1 Overview

This chapter focuses on the formal aspects of an extended version of ISO-Space (ISO, 2020d) as a dynamic spatio-temporal annotation scheme. I call this extended version *dSpace*, for the range of its annotation is extended, covering the *dynamic spatio-temporal domains* of three-dimensional space and time over motions. The temporal dimension characterizes various types of base structures β_{time} of category *time* in the annotation and interpretation of dynamic paths and motions anchored to each location on the paths. Various types of temporal relations also interact with spatial relations (see Lee (2012)). As a spatio-temporal semantic annotation scheme; *dSpace* amalgamates the two standardized annotation schemes, ISO-TimeML (ISO, 2012b) and ISO-Space (ISO, 2020d), into a single integrated annotation scheme or a combined system of two interoperable annotation schemes; *dSpace* also generalizes the notion of paths by subtyping them into five types: *static, dynamic, projected, bounded,* and *oriented*, while introducing a new link, called *path link* (pathLink), over paths with various relation types such as *meet* and *deviate*.

Consider Example (13.1).

Example 13.1 *Phil Gough flying from Seoul to Bogota*

a. Data: Five years ago, Phil Gough flew from Seoul to Bogota, Colombia, via New York. He left for New York at six in the morning and arrived in Bogota at six in the evening the next day. It took a day and a half to get to Bogota. Originally he wanted to fly through Los Angeles, but the tickets were all sold out.

b. Markables: Five years$_{me1:timeLength}$ ago, Phil Gough flew$_{m1:transition}$ $\emptyset_{p1:dynamicPath}$ from Seoul to Bogota, Colombia, via New York. He left$_{m2}$

$\emptyset_{p2:dynamicPath}$ for New York at six$_{t1:time}$ in the morning and arrived$_{m3}$ $\emptyset_{p3:dynamicPath}$ in Bogota at six$_{t2:time}$ in the evening the next day. It took a day and a half$_{me2:timeAmount}$ to get$_{m4}$ $\emptyset_{p4:dynamicPath}$ to Bogota. Originally he wanted to fly$_{m5}$ $\emptyset_{p5:projectedPath}$ through Los Angeles, but the tickets were all sold out.

The story is simple but gets complex as it is annotated and interpreted. As annotated in Example 13.1b, the little story contains five verbs referring to motions that involve five spatio-temporally defined paths: *flew, left, arrived, get,* and *fly.* It also contains two occurrences of a clock-hour expression *six,* each of which refers to a different hour on a different day, and two temporal measure expressions, one denoting the length of *five years* of a time interval and the other, the quantity of time amounting to a day and a half. The temporal measure expression *a day and a half* refers to the total amount of time taken by Phil's flying from Seoul to Bogota, but not to the time amount of the two actual flights, one from Seoul to New York and another from New York to Bogota.

None of the place names, the spatial relators (e.g., *from, to, via, in, through*), or the temporal relators (e.g., *ago, at, in*), which occur in the data, is annotated in base annotation of Example 13.1b. If they are annotated, then practically every word in the data will be marked up as a markable expression. The dynamic spatio-temporal annotation scheme *dSpace* aims at presenting ways of annotating all these markables and systematically interpreting them.

The rest of Chapter 13 develops as follows: Section 13.2 discusses the annotation structures of *dSpace* in informal terms, whereas Section 13.3 formally specifies it with illustrations. Section 13.4 makes a summary.

13.2 Annotation Structures

In accordance with the formulation of syntaxes of other annotation schemes, the syntax Syn_{dSpace} of *dSpace* is formally specified as generating well-formed annotation structures as consisting of (i) base structures β_c of each base category c in the set C_β of base categories and (ii) link structures λ_c of the quintuple $<c, \rho, \beta, B, \gamma>$, as depicted by Figure 13.1.[1]

---

[1] I coined the name *dSpace* to avoid any pretension of presenting any of the officially sanctioned versions, either preliminary or published, of ISO-Space (ISO, 2014b) or ISO-Space (ISO, 2020d) and also the use of the prefix ISO, the copyright of which belongs to ISO, the International Organization for Standardization.

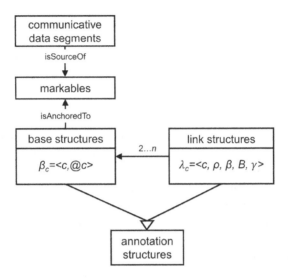

Figure 13.1 Annotation structures: base and link structures

The set of markables is a subset M of the set D of communicative data segments, which are delimited by the set C_β of base categories. To these markables, base structures are anchored. The quintuple structure of $<c, \rho, \beta, B, \gamma>$ of link structures λ_c consists of a relational link category c, ρ a relation type of the link, β a base structure, B a set of base structures, and γ a set of optional attributes such as @trigger or @scopes for quantification.

Preliminary Segmentation of Data For semantic annotation, language data, collected from a variety of human communications either in a textual form or visual images, is first *segmented* into linguistic units such as tokens, words, or even pixels. Some (possibly null) sequences of segments in presegmented communicative data are selected as *markables* for some specific type of a semantic annotation scheme. A temporal annotation scheme, for instance, selects linguistic segments such as *six o'clock in the morning* denoting a clock hour as a *markable expression*, simply called *markable*. Sometimes, null sequences of linguistic segments are treated as markables. *Dynamic paths*, often called *event-paths*, illustrate such a case.

Annotation 13.2 Dynamic paths

a. Data: We often walked to Brandeis University from downtown Waltham.

b. Markables: We often walked$_{m1,w3}$ Ø$_{p1}$ to Brandeis University from downtown Waltham.

c. Annotation of motions:

```
motion(m1, w3, type="transition", class="MOVE_to", tense="past")
path(p1, type="dynamic", start="downtown Waltham", end="BrandeisU")
```

The base structure β_{motion} of category *motion* is anchored to the word *walked*$_{w3}$. In contrast, the base structure $\beta_{path:dynamic}$ is not anchored to any overt markable, while it carries some spatial information referring to its start and end locations. The empty string $\emptyset_{p1}$, which is called a *nonconsuming tag*, represents an event-path created by the moving of us walking to Brandeis University. It is not anchored to any sequence of overt segments in data. Each base structure is thus *anchored* to a markable while allowing an exception for so-called *nonconsuming tags* for the phenomena of gapping, deletion, or *pro-drop* in natural language.

13.2.1 Base Structures

Overview

The syntax Syn_{dSpace} of the dynamic spatio-temporal annotation scheme *dSpace* as a specification language formally defines *well-formed* annotation structures. The *abstract syntax* specifies in set-theoretic abstract terms how well-formed base and link structures are generated. A *concrete syntax*, which is ideally isomorphic to the abstract syntax, provides a representation format for each of the annotation structures and their two substructures which are base structures and link structures. Instead of the most commonly accepted markup language XML, *dSpace* adopts the predicate-logic-like format, named *pFormat*, with the lowerCamelCase convention, to represent annotation structures (see Pustejovsky (2017b)).

Base Annotation

Each base structure β_c of category c is a triple $<i, m, a>$, where i is the identifier, m is a markable, and a is the annotation of the markable. The annotation a of a markable is a pair $<c, @_c>$, where c is the category of the markable m, and $@_c$ is an assignment function, associated with category c, from a set of attributes to a set of their possible values. *Base annotation* provides a basis for semantic annotation by marking each markable with a pair c_i, w_j, where c_i a *categorized identifier* and w_j is a *word identifier*. To this pair, each base structure is anchored. Here is an example of base annotation.

Example 13.3 Base annotation

a. Data: John left for Miami at two in the morning.

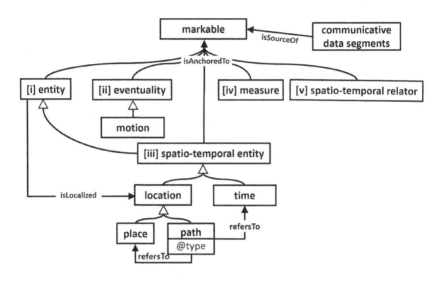

Figure 13.2 Base categories

b. Base annotation:

John$_{x1,w1}$ left$_{m1,w2}$ for$_{sr1,w3}$ Miami$_{pl1,w4}$ at$_{tr1,w5}$ [two   in   the morning]$_{t1,w6-9}$.

Base Categories

The base structures of *dSpace* are of five major categories with their subcategories, as depicted in Figure 13.2.

The five base categories and their subcategories, as shown in Figure 13.2, are listed as follows:

Specification 13.4   Base categories and subcategories
  (i) entity
 (ii) eventuality: motion
(iii) spatio-temporal entity:[2]
            location: place, path[@type]
            time
 (iv) measure
  (v) spatio-temporal relator.

These categories are classifiers of markables, which are linguistic expressions to be marked up. Their classification is based on domain-restricted (*small-*

---

[2] Spatio-temporal entity may be treated as a subcategory of *entity*.

world) semantics, but may not fully represent the spatio-temporal ontology. Categories such as *measure* and *eventuality* may be treated as subcategories of category *entity*, but treated in *dSpace* as independent categories. Category *spatio-temporal entity* is a subcategory of category *entity* because many of the spatial entity expressions are of category *entity*.

Anchoring

Figure 13.2 not only lists these categories, but also visually represents how they are related to each other. Each of the base categories and their subcategories is anchored to a markable in linguistic data. There are, however, some annotation schemes such as SpatialML (MITRE, 2010) and ISO-Space (ISO, 2020d) that allow the introduction of so-called *nonconsuming tags*. They are not anchored to any markables, but represented by the empty string Ø of characters. *Markables* are thus defined as strings (possibly null) of characters or other forms of communicative segments in language.

Category *entity*

Base category *entity* includes individual entities such as persons, institutions, or any other objects that include location-denoting objects. Example 13.5a contains eight markables of category *entity*: *Joe Biden, USA, Government, Republic of Korea*, two occurrences of *president*, and two occurrences of *White House*. Example 13.5b represents the base annotation of the data in Example 13.5a, where each markable of category *entity* is identified with the categorized identifier prefix x.

Example 13.5 Base annotation

a. Data: Joe Biden is the current president of the USA running the Government at the White House. Today, the White House has announced the state visit of the president of the Republic of Korea.

b. Base annotation:
   [Joe Biden]$_{x1,s1w1}$ is the current president$_{x2,s1w5}$ of the USA$_{x3,s2w8}$, running the Government$_{x4,s1w11}$ at the [White House]$_{x5,s1w14}$.
   Today, the [White House]$_{x6,s2w3}$ has announced the state visit of the president$_{x7,s2w11}$ of the [Republic of Korea]$_{x8,s2w14}$.

All of the eight occurrences of markables in Example 13.5 are marked as of category *entity*. There are two occurrences of *White House*, one of which denotes a location. Such occurrences as *White House*$_{x5,s1w14}$ are marked as *spatial entity* in ISO-Space, but *dSpace* does not differentiate them at the level of annotation. Hence, in *dSpace*, both *White House*$_{s1w14}$ and *White House*$_{s2w3}$

are annotated as of category *entity*, while location-denoting entities are differentiated from other general entities at the level of semantic interpretation only.

Categories *eventuality* **and** *motion*

Base category *motion* is a subcategory of category *eventuality*. Motion semantics as well as the semantic annotation of motion verbs focuses on the *translocational* type of motions involving paths, although there are other types of physical motions such as *rotation, oscillation* and *deformation* types. By referring to Talmy (1985, 2000), Mani and Pustejovsky (2012, p. 49) present a revised frame of motions for a qualitative model for the translocational type of motions.

Specification 13.6   Frame of motions
a. The *event* or situation involved in the change of location
b. The object that is undergoing movement (*Figure*)
c. The region or *path* traversed through the motion
d. A distinguished point or region of the path (*Ground*)
e. The *medium* through which the motion takes place[3]

Motions denoted by verbs like *leave, arrive, drive* or *walk, swim*, and *fly* undergo the change of locations. In such motions, there is at least one object that undergoes movement. Such an object is seen as a figure. One may either drive through a park (*region*) or drive through a highway (*path*). There is a dynamic process, called *event-path*, triggered by a motion. This path is characterized by its start, end, and midpoint(s) that together lay a *ground* for the figure traversing the path. The medium refers to something like air, water, and solid that differentiates where the motions of *fly, swim*, and *walk* are activated. Without air, one cannot fly; one needs water to swim, and one cannot walk in the air or the water, requiring solid ground to walk except for miraculous or ultra-scientific cases such as Jesus walking on the Sea of Galilee.

This frame of motion also applies to the semantic annotation of dynamic spatial information. Consider Example 13.7, where the subscript letters a, b, c, etc., refer to those in Specification 13.6.

Example 13.7   Frame of motions exemplified
a. Data: Liz left New York for Bali via Seoul by KAL.
b. Frame of motion:

   Liz$_{b:mover}$ left$_{a:motion}$ $\emptyset_{c:path}$ New York$_{d:ground}$ for Bali$_{d:ground}$ via Seoul$_{d:ground}$ by KAL$_{e:medium}$.

---

[3] The term *means* such as cars or boats refers to a specific type of medium.

The name *Liz* refers to (*b*) the *mover* and the motion verb *left* is (*a*) the *motion* that underwent movement. The *places* (*d*) were mentioned by *New York, Bali,* and *Seoul*, together constituting (*c*) the *path* traversed. The *medium* (*e*) is flying through the *air*.

Mani and Pustejovsky (2012) also make a survey of the concept of *motion* by introducing Jackendoff (1983, 1990), Talmy (1983, 1991, 2000), Langacker (1987, 1992, 2008), Baker et al. (1998, 2003), and others on motion verbs, while viewing motions as either *action-based* or *path-based predicates*. This distinction requires the classification of motion verbs into *manner-of-motion* verbs (e.g, *walk, run, drive, fly,* and *bike*) and *path* verbs (e.g., *arrive, leave,* and *land*). Mani and Pustejovsky (2012, section 2.3.4), however, mention the possibility of treating manner verbs as subtypes of an atomic predicate MOVE, which constitutes one of the 11 basic semantic classes of motion verbs. Based on Muller (1998), Pustejovsky and Moszkowicz (2008) present a modified classification of motion verbs, as listed in Classification 13.8 (see also Levin (1993) and Mani and Pustejovsky (2012, Table 1.1)).

Classification 13.8   Motion verbs

a. MOVE: *drive, fly, run, walk, swim*

b. MOVE_EXTERNAL: *drive around, pass*

c. MOVE_INTERNAL: *walk around the hospital*

d. LEAVE: *desert, leave*

e. REACH: *arrive, enter, reach*

f. ATTACH: *approach*

g. DETACH: *disconnect, pull away, take off*

h. HIT: *hit, land*

i. FOLLOW: *chase, follow*

j. DEVIATE: *flee, run from*

k. STAY: *remain, stay*

This type of classification of motion verbs allows them to be mapped to FrameNet (Baker et al., 1998, 2003; Ruppenhofer et al., 2016) and VerbNet (Kipper-Schuler, 2005; Kipper et al., 2006). Mani and Pustejovsky (2012, Table 1.1) show that the 11 verb classes except for DETACH match those of FrameNet. This difference is insignificant, for DETACH (*pull away*) is the inverse of ATTACH: (*approach*). By adopting Mani and Pustejovsky's (2012) motion classes to annotate motions, ISO-Space (ISO, 2020d) can also accommodate *FrameNet* into the annotation of semantic roles of motion participants. This classification can specify the relation type of the movement link (moveLink) in *dSpace*.

Example 13.9 illustrates how *FrameNet* annotates transportation-type motion verbs.

Example 13.9   *FrameNet*

a. Example: Jim drove a new TESLA Model S Plaid from Chicago to Milwaukee and then from Milwaukee along I-43 toward Green Bay.

b. Annotation: Jim$_{driver\,(mover)}$ drove$_{target}$ [a new TESLA Model S Plaid]$_{vehicle\,(means)}$ from Chicago$_{source}$ to Milwaukee$_{goal}$ and then from Milwaukee$_{source}$ along I-43$_{path}$ toward Green Bay$_{path}$.[4]

The FrameNet annotation of motion verbs generally accords the motion frame proposed by Mani and Pustejovsky (2012). It can also be accommodated into *dSpace*, as in Annotation 13.10.

Annotation 13.10   FrameNet motion frame

a. Base structures:[5]

Jim$_{x1:driver\,(mover)}$ drove $_{m1:drive\,(motion)}$ a new TESLA Model S Plaid$_{x2:vehicle\,(means)}$ [from Chicago$_{pl1:source}$ to Milwaukee$_{pl2:goal}$]$_{p1:path}$ and then [from Milwaukee$_{pl2:source}$ along I-43$_{p2:path}$ toward Green Bay$_{pl3:goal}$]$_{p3:path}$.]

b. Path structures:[6]

```
path(p1, type="dynamic", start="pl1", end="pl2", means="x2")
path(p2, type="dynamic", direction="pl3", start="pl2", end="")
```

The classification of motion verbs also allows such motion classes to be formally interpreted, for instance, by the dynamic interval temporal logic (DITL) as shown by Mani and Pustejovsky (2012, section 2.3.4) or some dynamic logic simpler to use.

Semantics 13.11   Semantic representation:

a. Example: Jim drove a new TESLA Model S Plaid from Chicago to Milwaukee and then from Milwaukee along I-43 toward Green Bay.

b. Base annotation:

Jim$_{x1:person:mover}$ drove$_{e1:transition}$ [a new TESLA Model S Plaid]$_{x2:vehicle:means}$

---

[4] In FrameNet, the attribute "target" is defined as *the lemma under consideration and in respect to which annotation is provided.* Therefore, in Example 13.9b the verb *drove* is annotated as the value of the attribute target see http://framenet.icsi.berkeley.edu.

[5] The colon : is used to provide additional information: for example, $x1$:*entity* means that the identifier $x1$ is of category *entity*.

[6] *I-43* is a static path, but its annotation is omitted to simplify the discussion.

$\emptyset_{p1:dynamic}$ from$_{start}$ Chicago$_{pl1:city}$ to$_{end}$ Milwaukee$_{pl2:city}$ and then $\emptyset_{e2:drive:transition}$ $\emptyset_{p2:dynamic}$ from$_{start}$ Milwaukee$_{pl2:city}$ along I-43 toward$_{direction}$ Green Bay$_{pl3}$.

c. Semantic representation:

$\exists\{x_1, e_1, x_2, p_1, l_1, l_2, e_2, p_2, l_3\}$

$[named(x_1, Jim) \wedge person(x_1) \wedge mover(e_1, x_1)$

$\wedge\, drive(e_1) \wedge transition(e_1) \wedge past(e_1)$

$\wedge\, named(x_2, TESLA) \wedge vehicle(x_2) \wedge means(e_1, x_2)$

$\wedge\, path(p_1) \wedge dynamic(p_1) \wedge triggered(e_1, p_1)$

$\wedge\, starts(p_1, l_1) \wedge ends(p_1, l_2)$

$\wedge\, named(l_1, Chicago) \wedge city(l_1)$

$\wedge\, named(l_2, Milwaukee) \wedge city(l_2)$

$\wedge\, drive(e_2) \wedge transition(e_2)$

$\wedge\, path(p_2) \wedge dynamic(p_2) \wedge triggered(e_2, p_2)$

$\wedge\, starts(p_2, l_2) \wedge directed(p_2, l_3)$

$\wedge\, named(l_3, Green Bay)$

$\wedge\, traverses(x_1, \{p_1, p_2\})]$

The representation in Semantics 13.11c is then interpreted model-theoretically with respect to a model, while the predicate $traverses(x, \pi)$ is defined as a logical predicate.

Category *spatio-temporal entity*

Base category *spatio-temporal entity* includes those markables that denote (i) locations and (ii) time points and intervals of category *time*. Locations are then subcategorized to *place* and *path*. Each place may be a point or region.

Example 13.12 Place and static path

a. Data: Our new apartment will be located at the One Bailey Complex on Sinbanporo in Seoul.

b. Annotation: Our new apartment$_{entity}$ will be located at the One Bailey Complex$_{entity}$ on Sinbanporo$_{path:street}$ in Seoul$_{place}$.

The nouns *apartment* and *the One Bailey Complex* denote a localized entity. They are no longer annotated as category *spatial entity*. The street name *Sinbanporo* is of category *path*, while *Seoul* is of category *place*.

There are three subcategories of category *spatio-temporal entity*: *place*, *path*, and *time*. These are introduced subsequently.

Subcategory *place*

There are two forms, which are names and nominals (common nouns), of markables referring to places. If the form of a markable is nam, then the predicate *named* is introduced for its semantic representation, as in Example 13.13c.

Example 13.13   Nominals vs. names

a. Data: New York is the largest city in the USA

b. Annotation:

New York$_{pl1:nam:city}$ is   the   largest   city$_{pl2:nom}$ in$_{sr1:anchoring}$ the USA$_{pl3:nam:country}$.

c. Semantic representation:

$\exists\{l_1, l_2, l_3\}$

$[named(l_1, New\ York) \wedge city(l_1)$

$\wedge\ city(l_2) \wedge l_1 = l_2$

$\wedge\ named(l_3, USA) \wedge country(l_3)$

$\wedge\ in(l_1, l_3)]$

As in Example 13.13, there are three markables of category *place*: two of them, *New York* and USA, are names, whereas the markable *city* is a common name (nominal). In semantics, nominals are treated as predicates, as in Montague Semantics. As for names, ABS introduces the predicate *named* so that an individual entity may have different names. The planet *Venus* may be validly named *the Morning Star* or *the Evening Star*.

Subcategory *path*

Unlike ISO-Space, *dSpace* merges two categories *path* and *event-path* to a single category, named *path*, but by subtyping them. There are five types of path: *static, dynamic, projected, bounded,* and *oriented*, and some of their combinations, *projectedStatic* and *projectedDynamic*. An *oriented* path is also a projected path but depends on a frame of reference.

Dynamic path refers to event-paths triggered by motions. There is a *projected static path*, triggered by a directional spatial relator (e.g., *toward*), and also a *projected dynamic path*, triggered by both a directional spatial relator and a motion. Example 13.14 shows different types of category *path*.

Example 13.14   Different types of paths

a. Data: Mike drove from Chicago to Milwaukee and then took I-43 from Milwaukee toward Green Bay. He stopped in Sheboygan. There he owned a cottage on a hill facing toward Lake Michigan.

b. Annotation: Mike drove Ø$_{dynamic}$ from Chicago to Milwaukee and then took I-43$_{static}$ from Milwaukee Ø$_{projectedDynamic}$ toward$_{sr:direction}$ Green Bay. He stopped in Sheboygan. There he owned a cottage on a hill facing Ø$_{projectedStatic}$ toward$_{sr:direction}$ Lake Michigan.

Just like dynamic paths (event-paths), projected paths have no overt markables to which they are anchored. They are annotated as nonconsuming (empty) tags.

Static Paths The highway *I-43* in Example 13.14 is a static path.

Subcategory *time*

Subcategory *time* comprises all of the temporal entities in ISO-TimeML (ISO, 2012b), which are tagged as TIMEX3. Combined with a time t, each location l may be represented as a pair (l, t) or $l@t$, where a location l is either a spatial point or a region, and a time t is either a point or an interval. Example 13.15 illustrates how each place is associated with a time or a duration (time amount).

Example 13.15 Place temporally associated

a. Data: Jim left Chicago at six in the morning and arrived in Milwaukee in an hour and a half.
b. Base annotation:
   Jim left$_{e1:motion}$ Chicago$_{pl1}$ at [six in the morning]$_{t1}$ and arrived$_{e2:motion}$ in Milwaukee$_{pl2}$ $\emptyset_{t2}$ in [an hour and a half]$_{timeLength}$.
c. Semantic representation:
   $\exists\{e_1, l_1, t_1, e_2, l_2\}$
   $[[leave(e_1) \wedge past(e_1)$
   $\wedge\ named(l_1, Chicago) \wedge city(l_1)$
   $\wedge\ time(t_1, \text{T06:00})$
   $\wedge\ \tau(e_1) \subseteq <l_1, t_1>] \wedge$
   $[arrive(e_2) \wedge past(e_2)$
   $\wedge\ named(l_2, Milwaukee) \wedge city(l_2)$
   $\wedge\ \tau(e_2) \subseteq <l_2, t_2>$
   $\wedge\ \delta(t_1, t_2) = 1.5h]]$

The departure point is marked with a pair $<l_1, t_1>$ and the arrival point is marked with a pair $<l_2, t_2>$, where the time point t_1 refers to the time T06:00 and the value of the time point t_2 can be calculated to be 07:30 based on the time length $\delta(t_1, t_2) = 1.5h$.

Two Relations over Spatio-temporal Base Structures

Figure 13.2, given earlier in this chapter, depicts two types of relations, *isLocalized* and *refersTo*. These relations link a spatio-temporal base structure to another base structure.

The relation *isLocalized* maps an entity to a *location* where the entity is located. The markable denoting such an entity was tagged spatialEntity in the first version of ISO-Space, but is now tagged ENTITY in uppercase or entity in lowercase and then undergoes the process of *localization* at the level of semantic representation.

Consider Example (13.16).

Example 13.16   Spatial entity
a. Data: John lost a purse while buying a new car. He left it in his old car.
b. Annotation in ISO-Space (ISO, 2014b):
   John lost a purse$_{x1:entity}$ while buying a new car$_{x2:entity}$.
   He left it$_{se1:spatialEntity}$ in$_{s1:signal}$ his old car$_{x3:spatialEntity}$.
c. Annotation in ISO-Space (ISO, 2020d) and *dSpace*:
   John lost a purse$_{x1:entity}$ while buying a new car$_{x2:entity}$.
   He left it$_{x3:entity}$ in$_{sr1:in}$ his old car$_{x4:entity}$.
d. Semantic representation for *a purse in a car*:
   $$\exists\{x_3, x_4\}$$
   $$[purse(x_3) \land car(x_4)$$
   $$\land\, in(\lambda yloc(y, x_3), \lambda zloc(z, x_4))]^7$$

Both of the common nouns *purse* and *car* refer to entities as in Example 13.16a,b. In Example 13.16c, they are localized, being spatially related by the spatial preposition like *in* and tagged `spatialEntity` by ISO-Space (ISO, 2014b). In ISO-Space (ISO, 2020d) and *dSpace*, localized entities are no longer annotated as `spatialEntity`, but as `entity` like other general entities.

The Relation *refersTo* in Figure 13.2 relates some attributes of a base structure of category *path* to another base structure, thus forming a complex base structure. Example 13.17 illustrates such a case.

Example 13.17   Complex base structures
a. Markbles: I-90$_{path:p1, w1}$ is a US west–east$_{spatialRelator:sr1, w5}$ transcontinental highway$_{path:p2, w7}$ from Seattle$_{place:pl1, w9}$ to Boston$_{place:pl2, w11}$.
b. Annotation:

```
path(p2,w7, type="static", subtype="highway", direction="#sr1",
  start="#pl1", end="#pl2")
```

The base structure `path(p2)` that annotates *highway*$_{path:p2, w7}$ refers to *west–east*$_{sRelator:sr1, w5}$ for its direction, *Seattle*$_{pl1, w9}$ for its start, and *Boston*$_{pl2, w11}$ for its endpoint. The base structure like `path(p2)` that refers to other base structures is called a *complex base structure*. In general, base structures of category *path*, whether static or dynamic, are complex base structures.

---

[7] The predicate *in* is defined by Randell et al.'s (1992) Region Connection Calculus (RCC-8). For details, see Mani and Pustejovsky (2012, chapter 3).

Category *measure*

There are two types of temporal measures: *time lengths (durations)* and *time amounts*. In ISO-TimeML (ISO, 2012b), lengths of time or time intervals are extended to spatial measures such as distances or areas. By treating a distance and a duration (length of a time interval) as measures, one can easily calculate other measures such as *speed*. Example 13.18 shows how measures are annotated.

Example 13.18   Distance and duration
a. Data: Jim drove around 90 miles from Chicago to Milwaukee in an hour and a half.
b. Annotation: Jim drove [around 90 miles]$_{me1:distance}$ from Chicago to Milwaukee in [an hour and a half]$_{me2:duration}$.

There are two markables of category *measure*: one for the driving distance and another for the length of time taken. On the basis of these two measures, Jim's driving speed is calculated to be around 60 miles per hour. The maximum speed limit in Illinois and Wisconsin is 65 miles per hour. So Jim had a safe drive through these two states.

Category *spatial relator*

In English, there are a lot of prepositions that function as spatial relators. Associated with motions, prepositions like *from, to, toward(s)* or *through* not only indicate their start, end or midpoints, but also characterize different types of motions. The motion $move_{toward}$, modified with the *toward* prepositional phrase, is defined differently from the motion $move_{to}$. The former does not guarantee the reaching of the goal, but the latter does. Mani and Pustejovsky (2012, p.107, example 65), for instance, define $move_{toward}$ in terms of *dynamic interval temporal logic* (DITL) as in Definition 13.19.

Definition 13.19   Motion verb $move_{toward}$
a. Example: The car (x) *approached (move toward)* the intersection (w).
b. $move_{toward}(x, w) =_{df} loc(x) := y, b := w; (y := z, d(b, z) < d(b, y))^{+}$[8]

Assume that y was the original point where the car was located and that b was the boundary endpoint where the intersection w was. Then, as the location of the car moved to z, the distance d between the boundary endpoint b and the new location z of the car becomes shorter than the distance between the boundary endpoint b and the original location y of the car. In contrast, $move_{to}$

---

[8] The symbol $^{+}$ refers to the Kleene iteration, referring to an incremental increase of the distance between b and y.

Table 13.1 *Categorized identifiers*

	John$_{x1}$ drove$_{m1}$ $\emptyset_{p1}$ to$_{sr1}$ Monterey$_{pl1}$ in$_{tr1}$ [two hours]$_{me1}$ along$_{sr2}$ I-5$_{p2}$ and [had lunch]$_{e1}$ ...			
categories	ISO-Space (ISO, 2014b) tags	ISO-Space (ISO, 2020d) modified (*dSpace*)	ID prefixes	TAGGED markables
entity	SPATIAL_ENTITY	entity	x	John$_{x1}$
place	PLACE	place	pl	Monterey$_{pl1}$
path	PATH	path: static	p	I-5$_{p2:static}$
event-path	EVENT_PATH	path: dynamic	p	$\emptyset_{p1:dynamic}$
eventuality	EVENT	event	e	had lunch$_{e1}$
motion	MOTION	motion	m	drove$_{m1}$
measure	MEASURE	measure	me	two hours$_{me1}$
spatial relator	SIGNAL	sRelator	sr	to$_{sr1}$, through$_{sr2}$

can be defined by stating that the final location of the mover is the same as the endpoint of an interval traversed.

Assignments for Base Categories

Corresponding to each base category *cat*, there is an assignment @$_{cat}$. The abstract syntax of *dSpace* specifies each of the assignments.

Identifiers Each of the annotation structures and their substructures, base and link structures, is uniquely identified. In both ISO-TimeML (ISO, 2012b) and ISO-Space (ISO, 2014b, 2020d), these structures are identified each with a *categorized numeric* identifier, as in Table 13.1.

In *dSpace*, both entities and localized entities are tagged *entity* without being differentiated at the stage of annotation. As shown in Example 13.20b, the spatial relation *in* coerces its two arguments to be spatial entities, thus requiring the denotations of *purse* and *car* to be localized.

Example 13.20   Coercing entities to spatial entities
a. Base annotation:
   Mia$_{x1}$ left her purse$_{x2}$ in a car$_{x3}$.
b. Semantic representation:
   $\exists\{x_1, x_2, x_3\}$
   [$named(x_1, Mia) \wedge purse(x_2) \wedge car(x_3)$

$$\wedge\, leave(e_1) \wedge past(e_1)$$
$$\wedge\, agent(e_1, x_1) \wedge theme(e_1, x_2)$$
$$\wedge\, in(\lambda x loc(x, x_2), \lambda y loc(y, x_3))]$$

Two categories, *path* and *event_path* are merged into one category *path*, for they share attributes such as *distance (length), direction, start, mids, end*, etc. They are differentiated by the attribute @type with a list of possible values *static, dynamic, projected, oriented*, and their combinations. The attribute @subtype may also be introduced to provide more specific information, as in Example 13.21.

Example 13.21   Subtypes of paths
a. Jim drove $\emptyset_{p1}$ along I-43$_{p2,\,w4}$ north from Milwaukee towards Green Bay.
b. Annotation:

```
path(p1, type="projectedDynamic", direction="north, Green Bay",
   start="Milwaukee")
path(p2, w4, type="static", subtype="highway", direction="north")
```

Specification of the Assignments for Base Categories

A concrete syntax specifies the general format of representing annotation structures each with a unique identifier and the specific tag names of (i) categories, (ii) their attributes, and (iii) the range of their possible values. For the modified version of ISO-Space (ISO, 2020d) presented in this chapter, Table 13.1 provides the names of the tags. Their attributes and possible values may be specified in ISO/IEC 14977 (eBNF) (ISO/IEC, 1996).

The Assignment @$_{entity}$ for Base Category *entity* This is given by Specification 13.22.

Specification 13.22   Assignment @$_{entity}$ of category entity

```
Attributes = identifier, type, pred | name, [plurality],
   [definiteness], [individuation];
   (* The square-bracketed attributes are optional: They
   do not need to be assigned a value.*)⁹
identifier = x, which may be followed by a natural number including 0;
type = ontological type;
   (* e.g., facility, institution, person, vehicle, ...*)
pred = predicative content if the form is a nominal;
   (* pred="president" *)
name= name if the form is a proper name;
   (* name="Joe Biden" *)
plurality = singular | plural | dual;
```

---

[9] In extended BNF (eBNF), optional attributes are bracketed, each comment begins with " (* " and ends with " *) ", while each clause ends with a semicolon " ; ".

```
definiteness = def | indef;
individuation = distributive | collective;
```

Example 13.23 illustrates how markables of category *entity* are annotated as each forming a base structure.

Example 13.23   Entities annotated

a. Data: Joe Biden is the US president.

b. Base annotation: Joe Biden$_{x1,w1}$ is the US$_{x2,w4}$ president$_{x3,w5}$.

c. Base structures:

```
entity(x1, w1, type="person", name="Joe Biden")

entity(x2, w4, type="country", name="US")

entity(x3, w5, type="person", pred="president")
```

d. Semantic forms:

$\sigma(\text{x1}) := [person(x_1) \wedge named(x_1, \text{Joe Biden})]$

$\sigma(\text{x2}) := [country(x_2) \wedge named(x_2, \text{US})]$

$\sigma(\text{x3}) := [x_1 = x_3 \wedge person(x_3) \wedge president(x_3, x_2)]$

$\sigma(\text{x1}) \oplus \sigma(\text{x2}) \oplus \sigma(\text{x3}) :=$

$\exists\{x_1, x_2, x_3\}$

$[person(x_1) \wedge named(x_1, \text{Joe Biden})$

$\wedge country(x_2) \wedge named(x_2, \text{US})$

$\wedge x_1 = x_3$

$\wedge president(x_3, x_2)]$

The conjunctive operation over $\sigma(\text{x1})$ and $\sigma(\text{x3})$ requires a link such as the referential link (rLink) that annotates them as being *identical* referentially.

Assignment @$_{path}$ of Base Category *path* The annotation scheme *dSpace* merges category *path* and *event-path* into a single category by specifying the possible values of category *path* as in Specification 13.24.

Specification 13.24   Assignment @$_{path}$ of category *path*

```
Attributes = identifier, type, form, [start], [end], [mids], [direction],
   [distance], [duration], [referenceType], [gazref], [latLong], [elevation],
   [modifier];
identifier = p, which may be followed by a natural number including 0;
type = static | dynamic | projected | oriented | CDATA;
   (* CDATA includes combinations of the values listed above *)
form = nam | nom;
   (* If the value is nom, then an attribute nam may be introduced
      additionally to spell out the name *)
start = IDREFS;
   (* refers to locations or pairs of a location and a time *)
end = IDREFS;
   (* refers to locations or pairs of a location and a time *)
mids = IDREFS ;
   (* refers to locations or pairs of a location and a time *)
```

```
direction = CDATA;
distance = IDREF; (*refers to distance measure *)
duration = IDREF; (* refers to the measure of a time interval *)
referenceType = absolute | relative | intrinsic;
 (* required if the value of the attribute type is oriented *)
gazref = IDREF;
 (* refers to a gazatteer name plus a colon plus an identifier *)
latLong = IDREF; (* refers to geographic information *)
elevation = IDREF; (* refers to geographic information *)
modifier = CDATA; (* spatially or temporally relevant modifier *)
```

Think of annotating the two long sentences in Example 13.25

Example 13.25   Enjoying Leffe at a cafe in the Latin Quarter
a. Data:
   Harry and I once had Leffe beer at a cafe to the left of Shakespeare and
   Company in the Latin Quarter, facing Notre Dame Cathedral across from
   the Seine River in Paris. There was a narrow path for pedestrians running
   parallel to the river, both separating us sitting at the cafe about 400 meters,
   from the cathedral.
b. Base annotation:
   Harry$_{x1,s1w1}$ and I$_{x2,s1w3}$ once had Leffe beer$_{e1,s1w5-7}$ at$_{sr1,s1w8}$ a cafe
   $_{pl1,s1w10}$ [to the left of]$_{sr2,s1w11-14}$[Shakespeare and Company]$_{pl2,s1w15-17}$
   in$_{sr3,s1w18}$ [the Latin Quarter]$_{pl3,s1w19-21}$, facing$_{sr4,s1w22}$ [Notre
   Dame Cathedral]$_{pl4,s1w23-25}$ [across from]$_{sr5,s1w26-27}$ [the Seine
   River]$_{pl5,s1w28-30}$ in$_{sr6,s1w31}$ Paris$_{pl6,s1w32}$. There was a narrow
   path$_{p1,s2w5}$ for pedestrians running [parallel to]$_{sr7,s2w9-10}$the river$_{p2,s2w12}$,
   both$_{\{p1,p2\},s2w13}$ separating$_{sr8,s2w13}$ us$_{\{x1,x2\},s2w14}$ sitting at$_{sr8}$ the
   cafe$_{pl1,s2w10}$ [about 400 meters]$_{me1,s2w12-14}$ from$_{sr9,s2w15}$ the
   cathedral$_{pl7,s2w17}$.

To locate the cafe, where Harry and I were enjoying beer, one may have to
visualize a map surrounding it. The first sentence alone contains at least six
spatial relations to be annotated with various link relations. *dSpace* is supposed
to perform that task by identifying some of the sites and positioning them with
respect to the location of the cafe and by annotating them with appropriate base
structures or link structures.

13.2.2 Link Structures

Two Categories of Links

The *movement link* and the *path link* are two prominent link categories in
dSpace. They are triggered by motions. In addition to the well-defined *qualitative spatial link* (qsLink), the *orientation link* (oLink), and the *measure link*

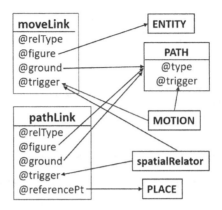

Figure 13.3 Depiction of moveLink and pathLink

(mLink) as in ISO-Space (ISO, 2020d), *dSpace* introduces two categories of link structures, the *movement link* (moveLink) and the *path link* (pathLink) for the annotation of dynamic information in language.

The movement link (moveLink) relates an entity to a dynamic path (event-path), triggered by a motion and a spatial relator. These two triggers determine the type of link relation. The attributes of these links are related to each other, as depicted in Figure 13.3.

The path link (pathLink) relates a path to another path, triggered by a spatial relator such as *parallel to*, as illustrated by Annotation 13.26.

Annotation 13.26   Path link

a. Markables: California Highway One from Monterrey to Los Angeles runs almost [*parallel to*]$_{spatialRelator}$ Interstate 5.

b. Base annotation:
California Highway One$_{p1:static:highway, w1}$ $\emptyset_{p2}$ from Monterrey$_{pl1, w3}$ to Los Angeles$_{pl2, w5}$ runs almost [*parallel to*]$_{sr1:spatialRelator}$ Interstate 5$_{p3:static:highway, w10}$.

c. Annotation structures:
```
path(p1, w1, type="static", subtype="highway", name="California
     Highway One")
path(p2, type="static", subtype="highway", start="pl1", end="pl2")
path(p3, type="static", subtype="highway", name="Interstate 5")
pathLink(pL1, relType="partOf", figure="p2", ground="p1")
pathLink(pL2, relType="parallel", figure="p2", ground="p3")
```

Note that these two highways are parallel to each other in a restricted interval, possibly in the portion from Monterrey to Los Angeles only.

The Movement Link Reformulated

Based on Corollary 12.20, the movement link that relates a mover to an event-path can be formulated as in Specification 13.27.

Specification 13.27   Assignment $@_{moveLink}$ for the movement link

```
attributes = identifier, relType, figure, ground, [trigger], [manner],
  [goalReached];
identifier = mvL + natural number;
relType = traverses or a motion class;
  (*refer to Classification 13.8 for the classification of motion verbs*)
figure = ID of an entity that moves;
ground = IDs of event-paths that the mover traverses;
trigger = IDs of spatial relators and motions that have created each
  of the dynamic paths (event-paths);
manner = character string;
goalReached = true | false.
```

The movement link (`moveLink`) relates a mover to a dynamic path, created by a motion. It deals with *translocational motions*. The default value of its attribute `@relType` is *traverses*. It can, however, be made more specific by the types of motion and the spatial relators that together characterize their associated dynamic path. The spatial relator *to*, for instance, yields the value "true" for the attribute `@goalReached`. The value "false" refers to negative cases as well as to *unknown* cases. Consider Annotation 13.28.

Annotation 13.28   Spatial relators for motions

a. Data: Mike drove *west from* Milwaukee *toward* Madison.

b. Base annotation:

Mike$_{x1,w1}$ drove$_{m1,w2}$ $\emptyset_{p1}$ west$_{sr1,w3}$ from$_{sr2,w4}$ Milwaukee$_{pl1,w5}$ toward$_{sr3,w6}$ Madison$_{pl2,w7}$.

c. Annotation:

```
entity(x1, w1, type="person", name="Mike")
motion(m1, w2, type="move", pred="drive", tense="past")
path(p1, type="projectedDynamic", direction="westsr1, Madisonpl2",
  start="Milwaukeepl1", trigger="m1,sr1,sr2,sr3")
sRelator(sr1, w3, type="direction", pred="west")
sRelator(sr2, w4, type="start-defining", pred="from")
sRelator(sr3, w6, type="direction", pred="toward")
```

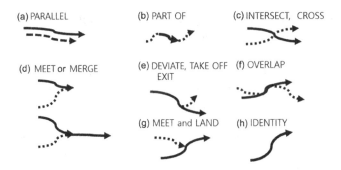

(a) PARALLEL

(b) PART OF

(c) INTERSECT, CROSS

(d) MEET or MERGE

(e) DEVIATE, TAKE OFF EXIT

(f) OVERLAP

(g) MEET and LAND

(h) IDENTITY

Figure 13.4 Relations of paths

```
moveLink(mvl1, relType="move_toward", figure="x1", ground="p1",
    trigger="m1,sr3", manner="driving", goalReached="false")
```

Base annotation marks each markable with (i) a categorized symbol and (ii) the numeric identifier of a markable to which the identified base structure is anchored. The identifier of each markable generally refers to a segmented word. The predicate *move_toward* can be interpreted as referring to an incremental translocational movement or approach to the target point without guaranteeing the mover's reaching that target.

Path Link Introduced

The *path link* (pathLink) is newly introduced in *dSpace* to annotate various relations between paths, either static or dynamic. This link captures various relations of paths, as presented in Figure 13.4.

Relations of Paths Figure 13.4 presents eight cases of paths being related at random. The relation *parallel* (a) can be defined with respect to the relation *intersection* (c) as being *non-intersecting*: parallel paths (at least in the Euclidean plane) never intersect or meet. The relation *part-of* (b) is a case of *partial overlap*, while the relation *identity* (h) is a case of *total overlap*; see also the relation *overlap* (f). The relation *intersect* or *cross* (c) can also be defined in terms of the relations *meet* (g) and *deviate* (e), which are the inverses of each other. The motions *take off* and *land* create three-dimensional event-paths that can be compared to two-dimensional runways. By referring to a theory of *geometrical relations*, these *path relations* can be defined systematically with some basic relations.

Here are some examples.

Example 13.29 Path relations

a. Massachusetts Turnpike is a *part of* I-90, extending from West Stockbridge to East Boston. Interstate 90 travels 138.15 miles across Massachusetts from the Berkshire Section of the New York Thruway to Route 1A at Logan International Airport in Boston. The entire route of I-90 stretches over 3099 miles from Seattle, WA, to Boston, MA, and then further toward New York.

b. Interstate 90 *is* an east–west transcontinental freeway connecting the Pacific Ocean with the Atlantic Ocean in the East.

c. We *crossed* the Han River by rowing a tiny fishing boat.

d. I-90 *intersects* I-5 in Seattle, WA, and I-82 in Ellensburg, WA.

e. Mike drove north along I-94 from Chicago and *switched* to I-43 in Milwaukee to keep heading north towards Green Bay.

f. I-94 *merges* with I-90 in Madison, heading north-west. They *run together* quite a distance until they *separate* around Oakdale before reaching Tomah in Monroe County. I-90 keeps heading north-west toward Eau Claire and then turns west toward La Cross.

Annotations 13.30 and 13.31 show how path relations are annotated.

Annotation 13.30   Path relations annotated

a. Data: I-94 *merges* with I-90 in Madison, heading north-west.

b. Base annotation: I-94$_{p1}$ *merges* with I-90$_{p2}$ in Madison$_{pl1}$, heading north-west.

c. Path relation annotated:

```
pathLink(pL1, relType="merge", figure="p1", ground="p2",
  referencePt="pl1")
```

The *reference point* Madison refers to the point of the two highways, I-94 and I-90, meeting and overlapping.

Annotation 13.31   Path relations

a. Data: Mike drove north from Chicago to Milwaukee along I-94 and switched to I-43 in Milwaukee, heading north toward Green Bay.

b. Base annotation: Mike drove $\emptyset_{p1}$ north from Chicago$_{pl1}$ to Milwaukee$_{pl2}$ along I-94$_{p2}$ and switched to I-43$_{p3}$ in Milwaukee, heading $\emptyset_{p4}$ north toward Green Bay$_{pl3}$.

c. Link structures:

```
pathLink(pL1, relType="overlap", figure="p1", ground="p2",
  referencePt="pl1,pl2")
pathLink(pL2, relType="intersect", figure="p2", ground="p3",
  referencePt="pl2")
pathLink(pL3, relType="overlap", figure="p4", ground="p3",
  referencePt="pl2,pl3")
```

Event-paths (dynamic paths) are also related to static paths (roads). The event-path of Mike's driving from Chicago to Milwaukee partially overlaps the interstate highway I-94. The relation *overlap* refers to the two points, Chicago and Milwaukee.

Assignment $@_{pathLink}$ for the path link (pathLink) is given in Specification 13.32.

Specification 13.32 Assignment $@_{pathLink}$ for the path link

```
attributes = identifier, figure, ground, referencePt;
identifier = pL + natural number;
figure = refers to a path ID;
ground = refers to one or more path IDs;
referencePt = refers to one or more place IDs.
```

Here is an example.

Example 13.33 Paths and motions
a. Data: Mia walked along the river.
b. Base annotation: Mia$_{x1}$ walked$_{m1}$ $\emptyset_{p1}$ along$_{sr1}$ the river$_{p2}$.
c. Link structures:

```
pathLink(pL1, relType="parallel", figure="p1", ground="p2",
  trigger="sr1")
moveLink(mvL1, relType="move_along", figure="x1", ground="p1",
  trigger="sr1,m1")
```

The path link (pL1) relates the path of Mia's walking to the river, viewed as a path, along which Mia walked. These two paths are annotated as being *parallel*. The movement link (mvL1), in contrast, relates Mia, who is the mover, to the event-path of her walking and is interpreted as Mia moving through the event-path. Here, the preposition *along* is interpreted as being *parallel, beside*, or *through*.

Two Types of Triggers

As introduced in Figure 13.3, there are two types of triggers: spatial relators and motions.

Spatial Relators as Triggers Spatial relators, such as spatial prepositions in English and other European languages, trigger spatial or temporal configurations to be generated by their associated links. As in Example 13.34, the spatial relator *in* triggers a qualitative spatial relation (qsLink) between two spatial objects, *fish* and *pond*, where *fish* is localized.

Example 13.34   Spatial relator *in*

a. Data: Fish in the pond
b. Markables: Fish$_{x1,w1}$ in$_{sr1,w2}$ the pond$_{pl1,w4}$
c. Annotation:

```
entity(x1, w1, type="fish", pred="fish")
sRelator(sr1, w2, type="anchoring", pred="in")
place(pl1, w4, type="water", pred="pond")
qsLink(qsL1, relType="in", figure="x1", ground="pl1", trigger="sr1")
```

d. Semantic representation:
$$\exists\{x_1,l_1\}[fish(x_1) \wedge pond(l_1) \wedge in(\lambda yloc(y,x_1),l_1)]$$

The predicate *in* anchors the localized fish in the pond.

Motions as Triggers   Motions trigger dynamic paths (event-paths) or move-ment link configurations (moveLink). Here is an example.

Example 13.35   Motions as triggers

a. Data: Jim walked to a drugstore.
b. Markables: Jim$_{x1,w1}$ walked$_{m1,w2}$ $\emptyset_{p1}$ to$_{sr1,w3}$ a drugstore$_{pl1,w5}$.
c. Annotation:

```
entity(x1, type="person", name="Jim")
motion(m1, w2, type="move", pred="walk", tense="past")
path(p1, type="dynamic", start=" ", end="pl1", trigger="m1,sr1")
sRelator(sr1,w3, type="end-defining", pred="to")
moveLink(mvL1, relType="MOVE_to", figure="x1", ground="p1",
   trigger="m1,sr1", goalReached="yes")
entity(x2, type="drugstore", pred="drugstore")
```

d. Semantic representation:
$$\exists\{x_1,e_1,p_1,x_2,e_2\}$$
$$[person(x_1) \wedge named(x_1,Jim)$$
$$\wedge\, walk(e_1) \wedge move_{to}(e_1) \wedge past(e_1)$$
$$\wedge\, path(p_1) \wedge triggered(e_1,p_1) \wedge ends(p_1,l_1)$$
$$\wedge\, drugstore(x_2) \wedge l_1 = \lambda yloc(y,x_2)$$
$$\wedge\, traverses(e_2) \wedge agent(e_2,x_1) \wedge theme(e_2,p_1)]$$

The motion *walked* triggers both the dynamic path p1 and the movement link mvL1. For the movement link, the motion *walked* and the spatial relator *to* together specify its relation type to be *move_to* or, more generally, *move_dir* or *traverses*.

13.3 Formal Specification

13.3.1 General

The overall structure of a semantic annotation scheme is graphically represented by Figure 13.5.

Semantic annotation presupposes that its input primary data has undergone the process of base segmentation such as tokenization or word segmentation. Markable expressions, briefly named *markables*, to which base structures are anchored refer to these tokens or words, or their (possibly noncontiguous or null) sequences. Annotation structures are generated by an annotation scheme modeled by its abstract syntax and represented by one of many possible concrete syntaxes, isomorphic to the abstract syntax.

The abstract syntax models an annotation scheme in general terms, defining the overall frame of annotation structures in some semantic domain. Based on the abstract syntax thus formulated, there can be a series of concrete syntaxes isomorphic to that abstract syntax, being semantically equivalent

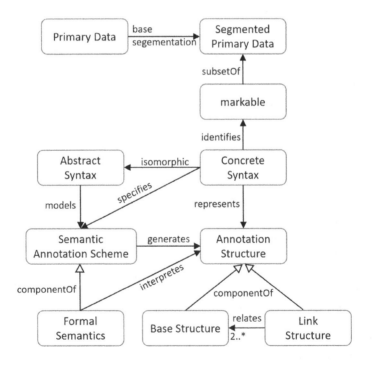

Figure 13.5 Semantic annotation scheme
Redrawn from Figure 1, Lee (2018)

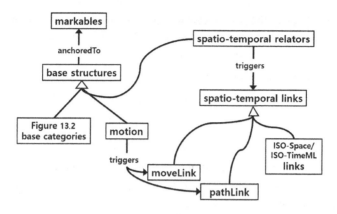

Figure 13.6 Metamodel of *dSpace*

to each other. Concrete syntaxes implement the abstract syntax in more specific terms, particularly specifying how each of the annotation structures is generated and also how it is represented in some markup language like XML or a predicate-logic-like format, called *pFormat*, as used in Pustejovsky (2017b) and this book. ISO-TimeML, for instance, is an XML-based concrete syntax conforming to the abstract syntax of SemAF-Time, introduced in the ISO 24617-1 standard on event-related temporal annotation (ISO, 2012b).

Annotation structures consist of *base structures* and *link structures*. These structures are then interpreted by formal semantics such as Kamp and Reyle's (1993) DRT or annotation-based semantics (ABS) proposed in this book, based on the abstract syntax of an annotation scheme. To interpret dynamic information involving translocational motions, these semantics need to be implemented with the *dynamic interval temporal logic* (DITL), as introduced by Mani and Pustejovsky (2012).

13.3.2 Metamodel

The metamodel, as depicted by Figure 13.6, visualizes the conceptual view of *dSpace*, a modified version of ISO-Space (ISO, 2020d) with its focus on the annotation of motion-related spatio-temporal information.

Figure 13.6 depicts the metamodel of *dSpace* with its focus on moveLink and pathLink both of which are triggered by motions. Spatio-temporal relators also play an important role in *dSpace*, as in ISO-TimeML and ISO-Space. They trigger the various spatio-temporal links as specified again in

ISO-TimeML and ISO-Space; *dSpace* thus integrates these two annotation schemes with its focus on the movement link (moveLink) and the path link (pathLink).

13.3.3 Annotation Syntax

As proposed by Lee (2016) but with some modifications in this chapter, the abstract syntax of *dSpace* is specified as a set-theoretic tuple.

Specification 13.36   Abstract syntax $\mathcal{AS}yn_{dSpace}$ of dSpace =
$<D, M, C, @, R>$, where
D is a primary data,
M is a nonempty set of (possibly null or noncontiguous) strings of character segments or pixels, called *markables*, constituting a subset of D delimited by C,
C is a set of base categories:
   (i) *entity* that includes *localized entities*;
   (ii) *spatio-temporal entity* with its subcategories: *location* and *time*, where *location* is again subcategorized to *place* and *typed path*;
   (iii) *eventuality* with its subcategory, *motion*;
   (iv) *measure*;
   (v) *spatio-temporal relator*,[10]

$@$ is a set of assignments $@_c$ for each base category $c \in C$, and
R is a set of link relations that include:
   (i) *movement link*
   (ii) *path link*
   (iii) *qualitative spatial link*,
   (iv) *orientational link*,
   (v) *measure link*,
   (vi) *temporal link*, and the other links in ISO-TimeML.

The abstract syntax of *dSpace* is a modified version of the abstract syntax of ISO-Space (ISO, 2020d). The dynamic spatio-temporal annotation scheme *dSpace* merges two separate categories *path* and *event-path* in ISO-Space into a single category *path*, but subtypes it into five different sorts, and an additional link, called *path link*.

Here are two remarks.

---

[10] This category replaces various signals such as spatial or motion signals in ISO-Space.

Remark 13.37 We say that $@_c$ is a set of attribute-value assignments $@_c$ over $C \times M$, deriving a set B of *base structures* β_c such that each $\beta_c \in B$ is a set-theoretic tuple defined by $@_c$.

Remark 13.38 Each link λ_r of type r in R is formally specified as a function
$\lambda_r : (B \times \mathcal{P}(B) \times R) \to B_\rho$
such that $<\beta_i, \{\beta_{j1}, \ldots, \beta_{jn}\}, r(i, \{j_1, \ldots, j_n\})>$ is a base structure in B_ρ iff
a. β_i is a base structure with its identifier i in B,
b. $\{\beta_{j1}, \ldots, \beta_{jn}\}$ is a subset of $\mathcal{P}(B)$ with identifiers $j_1, \ldots, j_n$, and
c. r is a relation type in R.

Attribute-Value Assignments

Assignment $@_c$ maps a pair $<c, m>$ to a base structure β_c such that β_c is a set-theoretic tuple well-defined for category c, as in Specification 13.40. The pair $<c, m>$ constitutes the anchoring structure of a base structure, where c is a *categorized identifier* and m is a markable. Here is an example.

Example 13.39 Base structure β_{motion} of category *motion*
a. Data: Mike drove to Milwaukee.
b. Markables:
   Mike$_{x1, w1}$ drove$_{m1, w2}$ Ø$_{p1}$ to$_{sr1}$ Milwaukee$_{pl1}$.
c. Assignment $@_{motion}$: (m1,w2) $\mapsto$ β_{motion}
   such that β_{motion} is a tuple $<ty, pr, tam, [mo]>$,
   where ty is the type (motion class), pr the predicative content, *tam* the tense, aspect, and mood, *mo* the optional modality of a motion verb.
c. Annotation in pFormat:

```
motion(m1, w2, type="move", pred="drive", tense="past")
```

Base Structures as Set-Theoretic Tuples Assignment $@_c$ for each category c formally specifies in abstract terms each β_c of the base structures of category c as a set-theoretic tuple as in Specification 13.40.

Specification 13.40 Base structures
Categories = *entity, place, path, eventuality, motion, measure, sRelator*

(i) $\beta_{entity} = <ty, pr, [pl], [de], [ind]>$, where
   ty is the type,
   pr is the predicative content or the name,
   optional pl is the plurality,
   optional de is the determinacy, and
   optional ind is the individuation for distributivity or collectivity
      of an entity referred to or denoted by a markable of category *entity*.

(ii) $\beta_{place} = <ty, pr, [lo]>$, where
    ty is the type,
    pr is the predicative content or the name, and
    optional lo is the location
        (village, town, city, county, state or province, country, elevation, etc.)
    of a place
    referred to or denoted by a markable of category *place*.

(iii) $\beta_{path} = <ty, [sb], pr, [dr], [ds], [st], [en], [mi], [lo]>$, where
    ty is the type,
    optional $[sb]$ is the subtype,
    pr is the predicative content or name,
    optional dr is the direction,
    optional ds is the distance,
    optional st is the start,
    optional en is the end,
    optional mi is the midpoints,
    optional lo is for the location
        (village, town, city, county, state or province, country, elevation, etc.)
    of a path
    referred to or denoted by a markable of category *path*.

(iv) $\beta_{event} = <ty, pr, tam, [mo], [roleFrame]>$, where
    ty is the type,
    pr is the predicative content,
    tam is the tense, aspect, and mood,
    optional mo is the modality, and
    optional $roleFrame$ is the attribute, which lists possible semantic roles,
        of an eventuality referred to or denoted by a markable of category
        eventuality.

(v) $\beta_{motion} = <ty, pr, tam, [mo]>$, where
    ty is the type (motion class),
    pr is the predicative content,
    tam is the tense, aspect, and mood,
    optional mo is the modality,
        of a motion denoted by a markable of category *motion*.

(vi) $\beta_{measure} = <ty, va, [un], [mod]>$, where
    ty is the type or dimension,
    va is the value,
    optional un is the unit, and

optional *mod* is the modifier
of a measure denoted by a markable of category *measure*.
(vii) $\beta_{sRelator} = <ty, pr, [fr]>$, where
ty is the type,
pr is the predicative content, and
optional fr is the frame of reference of a spatial relation denoted by a
markable of category *spatial relator*.

The abstract specification of attributes for each of the basic entity categories
gives freedom for their naming in a concrete syntax that provides a representation format.

Link Structures as Set-Theoretic Tuples

In addition to the four links (Classification 13.41a–d), which were inherited
from ISO-Space (ISO, 2020d), *dSpace* introduces a new link category *path
link*, for the annotation of dynamic information.

Classification 13.41 Link categories
a. qualitative spatial link
b. orientation link
c. measure link
d. movement link
e. path link

Each link structure λ_r of relational link category r in R specifies a minimal
configuration of the form $<\rho, \beta, B>$, where ρ is a relation type, β is a base
structure, and B is a nonempty set of base structures. This is a minimal
structure, for it may have one or more optional attributes, such as `@trigger`,
which refers to spatial relators or motions, and the attribute `@scopes`, which
applies to a list of quantifiers or logical operators.

The two links, *movement link* and *path link*, apply to the annotation of
dynamic information in language. Here is the specification of their attribute-value assignments.

The attribute-value assignment for the movement link is specified as in Table
13.2.

Example 13.42 illustrates how the abstract specification of the movement
link is instantiated for a concrete annotation case.

Example 13.42 Movement link (`moveLink`)
a. Data: Mike drove to Milwaukee.
b. Markables: $\text{Mike}_{x1,w1}$ $\text{drove}_{m1,w2}$ $\emptyset_{p1}$ $\text{to}_{sr1,w3}$ $\text{Milwaukee}_{pl1,w4}$.

Table 13.2 *Movement link* (moveLink)

Abstract specification: $\lambda_{movement}=<\rho, \beta_{entity}, \beta_{dPath}, [tr]>$		
attribute	*name*	*possible value*
ρ	relType	*traverses* or a motion class
β_{entity}	figure	refers to β_{entity} as a mover
β_{dPath}	ground	refers to $\beta_{path(dynamic)}$
tr optional	triggers	refers to $\beta_{sRelator}$ or β_{motion}

Table 13.3 *Path link (pathLink)*

Abstract specification: $\lambda_{path}=<\rho, \beta_{path}, B_{path}, [tr], [re]>$		
attribute	*name*	*possible value*
ρ	relType	one of the path relations
β_{path}	figure	refers to B_{path}
B_{path}	ground	refers to B_{path}
tr optional	triggers	refers to $\beta_{sRelator}$ or β_{motion}
re optional	referencePt	refers to reference points

c. Movement link:

```
moveLink(mvL1, relType="move_to", figure="x1", ground="p1",
trigger="sr1,m1")
```

The value move_to of @relType is determined by the two triggers sr1 and m1. This link is interpreted as stating that the mover Mike$_{x1}$ moved to the place Milwaukee by traversing through the dynamic path (event-path$_{p1}$).

The attribute-value assignment λ_{path} for the path link is specified in Table 13.3.

The abstract specification of the path link as in Table 13.3 can be instantiated and represented in pFormat, as in Example 13.43.

Example 13.43   Path link (pathLink)

a. Data: In California, US highway 101 runs north–south *parallel* to Interstate 5 but they *merge* in Los Angeles.

b. Markables:
In California$_{pl1, w2}$, [US highway 101]$_{p1, w3}$ runs north–south parallel to [Interstate 5]$_{p2, w8}$ but they$_{p1-p2, w10}$ merge in [Los Angeles]$_{pl2, w13}$.

c. Path links:

```
pathLink(pL1, relType="parellel", figure="p1", ground="p2",
 referencePt="pl1")
```

```
pathLink(pL2, relType="merge", figure="p1", ground="p2",
  referencePt="pl2")
```

13.4 Summary

In this chapter, I first discussed in informal terms base structures and link structures that constitute annotation structures for dynamic spatial information centered on motions and dynamic paths. I then formally specified the dynamic spatial annotation scheme, named *dSpace*, which was based on ISO-Space (ISO, 2020d) but with some substantial modifications. As in ISO-Space (ISO, 2014b), *dSpace* merged paths that denote roads and event-paths that are triggered by motions into a single category *path* but introduced them as being of two different types. The paths that denote roads are assigned the type *static*, whereas event-paths are assigned the type *dynamic*. This allowed the two additional types, *projected* and *oriented*.

As depicted in the metamodel of *dSpace*, category *time* became a genuine part of category *spatio-temporal entity*. Instead, *dSpace* could be linked to the temporal annotation scheme ISO-TimeML (ISO, 2012b). The temporal link (tLink) is part of *spatio-temporal link*, but is linked to ISO-TimeML. Likewise, category *time* is tagged "timex3" in *dSpace*, inheriting the specification of its attributes and values from TimeML or ISO-TimeML.

The abstract specification of base and link structures was introduced to show how they are represented in pFormat, independent of naming tags or attribute names and defining their possible values. The latter was specified in a concrete syntax, ideally isomorphic to the abstract syntax of an annotation scheme but independent of it at the level of implementing the annotation scheme in concrete terms. Directly relating to the annotation of dynamic spatial information, I focused on the specification of the two links, *movement link* (moveLink) and *path link* (pathLink).

References

Abzianidze, Lasha, Bjerva, Johannes, Evang, Kilian, Haagsma, Hessel, Noord, Rik van, Ludmann, Pierre, Nguyen, Duc-Duy, and Bos, Johan 2017. The Parallel Meaning Bank: Towards a multilingual corpus of translation annotated with compositional meaning representations. *Proceedings of the 15th Conference of the European Chapter of the Association for Computational Linguistics*, pp. 242–247. Valencia, Spain: Association for Computational Linguistics.

Allen, James F. 1984. Towards a general theory of action and time. *Artificial Intelligence* **23**, 123–154. Reprinted in Mani et al. (eds.) (2005), pp. 251–276.

Allen, James F. and Ferguson, George 1994. Actions and events in interval temporal logic. *Technical Report* 521 (July 1994), The University of Rochester Computer Science Department, Rochester, New York; and also in Oliviero Stock (ed.), *Spatial and Temporal Reasoning*, pp. 205–245. Dordrecht: Kluwer Academic Publishers, 1997.

Allen, James F. and Kautz, Henry A. 1985. A model of naive temporal reasoning. In Jerry R. Hobbs and Robert C. Moore (eds.), *Formal Theories of Common Sense World*, 251–268. New York: Ablex Publishing Co.

Bach, Emmon 1986. The algebra of events. *Linguistics and Philosophy* **9**, 5–16. Reprinted in Mani et al. (eds.) (2005), pp. 61–69.

Bach, Emmon, Jelinet, Eloise, Kratzer, Angelika, and Partee, Barbara H. (eds.) 1995. *Quantification in Natural Languages*. Dodrecht: Kluwer Academic Publishers.

Banarescu, Laura, Bonial, Claire, Cai, Shu, Georgescu, Madalina, Griffitt, Kira, Hermjakob, Ulf, Knight, Kevin, Koehn, Phillip, Palmer, Martha, and Schneider, Nathan 2013. Abstract meaning representation or Sembanking. *Proceedings of the 7th Linguistic Annotation Workshop and Interoperability with Discourse*, pp. 178–186, August 8–9, 2013, Sofia, Bulgaria.

Baker, Collin F., Fillmore, Charles J., and Lowe, John B. 1998. The Berkeley FrameNet project. In *ACL '98/COLING '98: Proceedings of the 36th Annual Meeting of the Association for Computational Linguistics and 17th International Conference on Computational Linguistics*, vol. 1, August 1998, pp. 86–90. www.aclweb.org/anthology/P98-113.pdf

Baker, Collin F., Fillmore, Charles J., and Cronin, Beau 2003. The structure of the FrameNet database. *International Journal of Lexicography* **16**(3), 281–296.

Barwise, Jon, and Cooper, Robin 1981. Generalized quantifiers and natural language. *Linguistics and Philosophy* **4**, 159–219.

Bateman, John A., Hois, Joana, Ross, Robert, and Tenbrink, Thora 2010. A linguistic ontology of space for natural language processing. *Artificial Intelligence* **174** (2010), 1027–1071.

Beesley, Kenneth, and Karttunen, Lauri 2003. *Finite State Morphology*, CSLI Studies in Computational Linguistics. Stanford: CSLI Publications.

Bennett, David C. 1975. *Spatial and Temporal Uses of English Prepositions: An Essay in Stratificational Semantics*. London: Longman.

Bennett, Michael, and Partee, Barbara H. 1978. Toward the logic of tense and aspect in English. Indianapolis: The Indiana University Linguistics Club. Reprinted in Partee (2004), pp. 59–109.

Bos, Johan 2020. Separating argument structure from logical structure in AMR. In *Proceedings of the 2nd International Workshop on Designing Meaning Representations*, pp. 13–20. Barcelona, Spain (Online), December 13, 2020.

Bos, Johan, Basile, Valerio, Evang, Kilian, Venhuizen Noortje J., and Bjerva, Johannes 2017. The Groningen Meaning Bank. In Nancy Ide and James Pustejovsky (eds.), *Handbook of Linguistic Annotation*, pp. 463–496. Berlin: Springer.

Buchholz, Sabine, and Marsi, Erwin 2006. CoNLL-X shared task on multilingual dependency parsing. In *Proceedings of the 10th Conference on Computational Natural Language Learning (CoNLL-X)*, pp. 149–164, June 2006, New York City. © Association for Computational Linguistics.

Bunt, Harry 1985. *Mass Terms and Model-theoretic Semantics*. Cambridge: Cambridge University Press.

Bunt, Harry 2007. The semantics of semantic annotations. *Proceedings of the 21st Pacific Asia Conference on Language, Information and Computation*, pp. 13–28. Seoul: The Korean Society for Language and Information.

Bunt, Harry 2010. A methodology for designing semantic annotation languages exploiting syntactic-semantic iso-morphisms. In Alex Fang, Nancy Ide, and Jonathan Webster (eds.), *Proceedings of ICGL 2010, the Second International Conference on Global Interoperability for Language Resources*, pp. 29–45, City University of Hong Kong.

Bunt, Harry 2011. Abstract syntax and semantics in semantic annotation, applied to time and events. Revised version of "Introducing abstract syntax + semantics in semantic annotation, and its consequences for the annotation of time and events." In Eunryoung Lee and Aesun Yoon (eds.), *Recent Trends in Language and Knowledge Processing*, pp. 157–204, Seoul: Hankukmunhwasa.

Bunt, Harry 2015. On the principles of interoperable semantic annotation. In Harry Bunt (ed.), *Proceedings of the 11th Joint ACL–ISO Workshop on Interoperable Semantic Annotation (ISA-11)*, pp. 1–13, April 14, 2015, Queen Mary University of London, UK.

Bunt, Harry 2017. Towards interoperable annotation of quantification. In Harry Bunt (ed.), *Proceedings of the 13th Joint ACL–ISO Workshop on Interoperable Semantic Annotation (ISA-13)*, pp. 1–13. Workshop at the 12th International Conference on Computational Semantics (IWCS 2017), September 19, 2017, Montpellier, France.

Bunt, Harry 2018. Semantic annotation of quantification in natural language. TiCC TR 2018-15, Tilburg Center for Creative Computing, Tilburg University.

Bunt, Harry 2019. A semantic annotation scheme for quantification. In *Proceedings of the 13th International Conference on Computational Semantics*, pp. 31–42, May 23–27, 2019, IWCS 2019 (International Workshop on Computational Linguistics), Gothenburg, Sweden. www.aclweb.org/anthology/W19-0403.

Bunt, Harry 2020a. Semantic annotation of quantification in natural language. Tiburg: TiCC/Department of Cognitive Science and Artificial Intelligence, Tilburg University.

Bunt, Harry 2020b. Annotation of quantification: the current state of ISO 24617–12. In Harry Bunt (ed.), *Proceedings of the 16th Joint ISO–ACL/SIGSEM Workshop on Interoperable Semantic Annotation*, pp. 1–13. Marseille, France: A satellite workshop at LREC 2020, May 11–15, 2020.

Bunt, Harry, and Overbeeke, Chwhynny 2008. An extensible compositional semantics for temporal annotation. In Nancy Ide et al. (eds.), *Proceedings of LAW II, the Second Annotation Workshop*, a satellite workshop at LREC2008, Marakech, Morocco. Paris: ELRA.

Bunt, Harry, and Schiffrin, Amanda 2005. Methodological aspects of semantic annotation and representation. *LIRICS Report: Deliverable*, D4.1, unpublished report.

Bunt, Harry and Pustejovsky, James 2010. Annotating temporal and event quantification. In Harry Bunt (ed.), *Proceedings of the Fifth Joint ISO–ACL/SIGSEM Workshop on Interoperable Semantic Annotation*, pp. 15–17, January 15–22, 2010. Hong Kong: Department of Chinese, Translation and Linguistics, City University of Hong Kong.

Bunt, Harry, Petukhova, Volah, Malchanau, Andrei, Fang, Alex, and Wijnhoven, Kars 2016. The DialogBank corpus. *Proceedings of the 10th Edition of the Language Resources and Evaluation Conference (LREC 2016)*. Portorož, Slovenia. https://aclanthology.org/L16-1503.pdf.

Bunt, Harry, Pustejovsky, James, and Lee, Kiyong 2018. Towards an ISO standard for the annotation of quantification. In *Proceedings of the 11th International Conference on Language Resources and Evaluation (LREC2018)*, Phoenix Seagaia Resort, Miyazaki, Japan, May 7–12, 2018. https://aclanthology.org/L18-1282.

Bunt, Harry, Amblard, Maxime, Bos, Johan, Fort, Karën, de Groote, Philippe, Guillaume, Bruno, Le, Chuyuan, Ludmann, Pierre, Musiol, Michel, Pavlova, Siyana, Perrier, Guy, and Pogadalla, Sylvain 2022. Quantification annotation in ISO 24617-12, second draft. In *Proceedings of the 13th Conference on Language Resources and Evaluation (LREC 2022)*, pp. 3407–3416, June 20–25, 2022. Marseille, France. ELRA. Licensed under CC-BY-NC-4.0.

Cann, Ronnie, Kempson, Ruth, and Gregoromichelaki, Eleni 2009. *Semantics: An Introduction to Meaning in Language*. Cambridge: Cambridge University Press.

Carnap, Rudolf 1947. *Meaning and Necessity: A Study in Semantics and Modal Logic*. Chicago: The University of Chicago Press, (2nd ed. 1956).

Caselli, Tommaso, and Sprugnoli, Rachele 2017. IT-TimeML and the ITA-TimeBank: Language specific adaptations for temporal annotation. In Nancy Ide and James

Pustejovsky (eds.), *Handbook of Linguistic Annotation* vol. II, pp. 969–988. Dordrecht: Springer.

Caselli, Tommaso, Dell'Orletta, Felice, and Proclanof, Irina 2009. Temporal relations with signals: the case of Italian temporal prespositions. In *16th International Symposium on Temporal Representation and Reasoning*, pp. 125–132. IEEE Xplore Digital Library, doi: 10.1109/TIME.2009.23.

Chang, Suk-Jin 1996. *Korean*. Amsterdam/Philadelphia: John Benjamins Publishing Co.

Cooper, Robin 1987. Preliminaries to the analysis of generalized quantifiers in situation semantics. In P. Gärdenfors (ed.), *Generalized Quantifiers: Linguistic and Logical Approaches*. Dordrecht: D. Reidel.

Copestake, Ann, Flickinger, Dan, Sag, Ivan, and Pollard, Carl 2005. Minimal recursion semantics: an introduction. *Research on Language and Computation* **3**(2–3), 281–332.

Croft, William 2012. *Verbs: Aspects and Clausal Structure*. Oxford: Oxford University Press.

Dan, Soham, Kordjamshidi, Parisa, Bonn, Julia, Bhatia, Archna, Cai, Zheng, Palmer, Martha, and Roth, Dan 2020. From spatial relations to spatial configurations. In *Proceedings of the 12th Language Resources and Evaluation Conference (LREC2020)*, pp. 5855–5864, May 2020, Marseille, France. ELRA. https://aclanthology.org/2020.lrec-1.717.

Davidson, Donald 1967. The logical form of action sentences. In N. Rescher (ed.), *The Logic of Decision and Action*, pp. 81–120. Pittsburgh: University of Pittsburgh Press.

Davidson, Donald 2001. *Essays on Actions and Events*, 2nd ed. Oxford: Oxford University Press.

Dobnik, Simon, and Cooper, Robin 2017. Interfacing language, spatial perception and cognition in type theory with records. *Journal of Language Modelling* **5**(2), 273–301.

Dobnik, Simon, Cooper, Robin, and Larsson, Staffan 2012. Modelling language, action, and perception in type theory with records. In D. Duchier and F. Parmentier (eds.), *Constraint Solving and Language Processing – 7th International Workshop on Constraint Solving and Language Processing, CSLP 2012*, Orleans, France, September 13–14, 2012. Revised selected papers, no. 8114 in *Publications on Logic, Language and Information (FoLLI)*, Berlin: Springer, 2013.

Doddington, George, Mitchell, Alexis, Przybocki, Mark, Ramshaw, Lance, Strassel, Stephanie, and Weischedel, Ralph 2004. The automatic content extraction (ACE) program – tasks, data, and evaluation. In *Proceedings of of the Fourth International Conference on Language Resources and Evaluation 2004*, pp. 837–840. Lisbon, Portugal.

Dowty, David R. 1979. *Word Meaning and Montague Grammar: The Semantics of Verbs and Times and Generative Semantics and Montague's PTQ*. Dordrecht: Reidel.

Dowty, David R., Wall, Robert, and Peters, Stanley 1981. *Introduction to Montague Semantics*. Dordrecht: Reidel.

Ferro, Lisa, Gerber, Laurie, Mani, Inderjeet, Sundheim, Neth, and Wilson, George 2005. *TIDES: 2005 Standard for the Annotation of Temporal Expressions.* Approved for release, MITRE.

Fillmore, Charles J. 1976. Frame semantics and the nature of language. In *Annals of the New York Academy of Sciences: Conference on the Origin and Development of Language and Speech* **280**, 20–32.

Finlayson, Mark A., and Erjavec, Tomaž 2017. Overview of annotation creation: process and tools. In Nancy Ide and James Pustejovsky (eds.), *Handbook of Linguistic Annotation*, pp. 167–192. Dordrecht: Springer.

Flanigan, Jeffrey 2018. *Parsing and Generation for the Abstract Meaning Representation.* Ph.D. dissertation in Language and Information Technologies. Language Technologies Institute, School of Computer Science, Carnegie Mellon University.

Gabbay, Dov, and Moravcsik, Julius 1980. Verbs, events, and the flow of time. In Christian Rohrrer (ed.), *Time, Tense, and Quantifiers: Proceedings of the Stuttgart Conference on the Logic of Tense and Quantification*, pp. 59–83. Tübingen: Max Niemyer Verlag.

Gagnon, Michel, and Lapalme, Guy 1996. From conceptual time to linguistic time. *Computational Linguistics* **22**(1), 91–127.

Gellner, Ernest 1959. *Words and Things with an Introduction by Bertrand Russell.* Middlesex, UK: Penguin Books.

Graham, Tony 2000. *Unicode: A Primer.* Foster City, CA: M & T Books.

Hao, Tiyanong, Wei, Yunyan, Qiang, Jiaqi, Wang, Haitao, and Lee, Kiyong 2017. The representation and extraction of quantitative information. In Harry Bunt (ed.), *Proceedings of the 13th Joint ACL–ISO Workshop on Interoperable Semantic Annotation (ISA-13)*, pp. 74–83. Workshop of IWCS 2017, September 19, 2017, Montpellier, France.

Hao, Tiyanong, Wang, Haotai, Cao, Xinyu, and Lee, Kiyong 2018. Annotating measurable quantitative information for an ISO standard. In Harry Bunt (ed.), *Proceedings of the 14th Joint ACL–ISO Workshop on Interoperable Semantic Annotation (ISA-14)*, pp. 69–75. Workshop of COLING 2018, August 25, 2018, Santa Fe, NM, USA.

Hausser, Roland 2006. *A Computational Model of Natural Language Communication: Interpretation, Inference, and Production in Database Semantics.* Berlin: Springer.

Hausser, Roland 2015. From Montague grammar to database semantics. *Language and Information* **19**(2), 1–16. Available at lagrammar.net

He, Luhengn 2018. *Annotating and Modeling Shallow Semantics Directly from Text.* Ph.D. dissertation in Computer Science and Engineering. University of Washington.

Hobbs, Jerry R. 1985. Ontological promiscuity. In *Proceedings of the 23rd Annual Meeting of the Association for Computational Linguistics*, pages 61–69. July 8–12, 1985, University of Chicago. https://aclanthology.org/P85-1008.pdf

Hobbs, Jerry R., and Pan, Feng 2004. An ontology of time for the semantic Web. *ACM Transactions on Asian Language Information Processing (TAKIP)*, **3.1**, 66–85.

Hobbs, Jerry, and Pustejovsky, James 2003. Annotating and reasoning about time and events. In *Proceedings of AAAI Spring Symposium on Logical Formalization of*

Common Sense Reasoning. Stanford, CA: Reprinted in Mani et al. (eds.), 2005, pp. 301–315.

Hois, Joana, Tenebrin, Thora, Ross, Robert J., and Bateman, John A. 2009. *GUM-Space. The Generalized Upper Model spatial extension: a linguistically motivated ontology for the semantics of spatial language*. Bremen: Technical Report, University of Bremen, SFB/TR8 Spatial Cognition.

Huang, Chu-Ren, Chang, Ru-Yng, and Lee, Shiang-Bin 2004. Sinica BOW (Bilingual Ontological Wordnet): Integration of Bilingual Wordnet and SUMO. In *Proceedings of 4th International Conference on Language Resources and Evaluation (LREC2004)*. Lisbon. Portugal, May 26–28, 2004.

Huang, Chu-Ren, Calzolari, Nicoletta, Gangemi, Aldo, Lenci, Alessandro, Oltramari, Alessandro, and Prévot, Laurent (eds.) *Ontology and the Lexicon: A Natural Language Processing Perspective*. Cambridge University Press and Peking University, Press reprint 2014.

Ide, Nancy, and Pustejovsky, James (eds.) 2017. *Handbook of Linguistic Annotation*. Dordrecht: Springer.

Ide, Nancy, and Romary, Laurent 2004. International standard for a linguistic annotation framework. *Natural Language Engineering* 10(3–4), 211–225.

Ide, Nancy, and Suderman, Keith 2007. GrAF: a graph-based format for linguistic annotations. In *Proceedings of the Linguistic Annotation Workshop (LAW)*, pp. 1–8, Prague.

Ide, Nancy, and Suderman, Keith 2014. The linguistic annotation framework: a standard for annotation interchange and merging. *Language Resources and Evaluation* **48**(3), 395–418.

Ide, Nancy, Chiarcos, Christian, Stede, Manfred, and Cassidy, Steve 2012. Designing annotation schemes: From model to representation. In Nancy Ide and James Pustejovsky (eds.), *Handbook of Linguistic Annotation*, pp. 73–111. Dordrecht: Springer.

Ide, Nancy, Calzolari, Nicoletta, Eckle-Kohler, Judith, Gibbon, Dafydd, Hellmann, Sebastian, Lee, Kiyong, Nivre, Joakim, and Romary, Laurent 2017. Community standards for linguistically-annotated resources. In Nancy Ide and James Pustejovsky (eds.), *Handbook of Linguistic Annotation*, pp. 113–165. Dordrecht: Springer.

ISO 2002. *ISO 19108 Geographic information – Temporal schema*. Geneva: The International Organization for Standardization.

ISO 2006. *ISO 24610-1 Language resource management – Feature structures – Part 1: Feature structure representation (FSR)*. A joint work with the TEI Consortium. See *TEI Guidelines P5*. Project leader: Kiyong Lee, Convenor: Nancy Ide. Geneva: The International Organization for Standardization.

ISO 2010. *ISO 24614-1 Language resource management – Word segmentation of written texts – Part 1: Basic concepts and general principles*. The International Organization for Standardization, Geneva. Project leader: Maosong Sun, Convenor: Kiyong Lee. Geneva: The International Organization for Standardization.

ISO 2011. *ISO 24614-2 Language resource management – Word segmentation of written texts – Part 2: Word segmentation for Chinese, Japanese and Korean*.

Project leaders: Maosong Sun, Key-Sun Choi, and Hitoshi Isahara, Convenor: Kiyong Lee. Geneva: The International Organization for Standardization.

ISO 2012a. *ISO 24612 Language resource management – Linguistic annotation framework (LAF).* Project leaders: Nancy Ide and Laurent Romary, Convenor: Nancy Ide. Geneva: The International Organization for Standardization.

ISO 2012b. *ISO 24617-1 Language resource management – Semantic annotation framework – Part 1: Time and events (SemAF-time, ISO-TimeML).* Project leaders: James Pustejvosky and Kiyong Lee, Convenor: Kiyong Lee. Geneva: The International Organization for Standardization.

ISO 2014a. *ISO 24617-4:2014(E) Language resource management – Semantic annotation framework – Part 4: Semantic roles (SemAF-SR).* Project leaders: Martha Palmer and Harry Bunt, Convenor: Kiyong Lee. Geneva: The International Organization for Standardization.

ISO 2014b. *ISO 24617-7:2014(E) Language resource management – Semantic annotation framework – Part 7: Spatial information (ISO-Space),* 1st ed. Project leaders: James Pustejovsky and Kiyong Lee, Convenor: Kiyong Lee, Geneva: The International Organization for Standardization.

ISO 2016. *ISO 24617-6 Language resource management – Semantic annotation framework – Part 6: Principles of semantic annotation (SemAM Principles).* Project leader: Harry Bunt, Convenor: Kiyong Lee. Geneva: The International Organization for Standardization.

ISO 2019a. *ISO 8601-1:2019(E) Date and time – Representations for information interchange – Part 1: Basic rules).* Geneva: The International Organization for Standardization.

ISO 2019b. *ISO 8601-2:2019(E) Data and time – Representations for information interchange – Part 2: Extensions).* Geneva: The International Organization for Standardization.

ISO 2020a. *ISO 3166-1:2020 Codes for the representation of names of countries and their subdivisions – Part 2: Country subdivision code.* Geneva: The International Organization for Standardization. Note: The first edition, 2013.

ISO 2020b. *ISO 3166-2:2020 Codes for the representation of names of countries and their subdivisions –Part 1: Country codes.* Geneva: The International Organization for Standardization. Note: the first edition, 2013.

ISO 2020c. *ISO 19136-1:2020 Geography Markup Language (GML) – Part 1: Fundamentals.* Geneva: The International Organization for Standardization. Note: ISO 19136:2007 withdrawn.

ISO 2020d. *ISO 24617-7 Language resource management – Semantic annotation framework – Part 7: Spatial information (ISO-Space),* 2nd ed. Project leaders: James Pustejovsky and Kiyong Lee, Convenor: Kiyong Lee. Geneva: The International Organization for Standardization.

ISO 2022a. *ISO/CD 24617-12 Language resource management – Semantic annotation framework – Part 12: Quantification.* Project leader: Harry Bunt, Convenor: Kiyong Lee. Geneva: The International Organization for Standardization.

ISO 2022b. *ISO/DIS 24617-14 Language resource management – Semantic annotation framework – Part 14: Spatial semantics.* Project leaders: James Pustejovsky and Kiyong Lee, Convenor: Kiyong Lee. Geneva: The International Organization for Standardization.

ISO/IEC 1996. *ISO/IEC 14977:1996 Information technology – Syntactic metalanguage – Extended BNF*. Geneva: The International Organization for Standardization and International Electrotechnical Commission.

ISO/IEC 2007. *ISO/IEC 24707:2007 Information technology – Common Logic (CL): a framework for a family of logic-based languages*. Geneva: The International Organization for Standardization and the International Electrotechnical Commission.

Jackendoff, Ray 1983. *Semantics and Cognition*. Cambridge, MA: The MIT Press.

Jackendoff, Ray 1990. *Semantic Structures*. Cambridge, MA: The MIT Press.

Jackendoff, Ray 2002. *Foundations of Language: Brain, Meaning, Grammar, Evolution*. Cambridge, MA: The MIT Press.

Jespersen, Otto 1931. *A Modern English Grammar on Historical Principles*, Part IV. London: George Allen & Unwin. (Reprinted 1961 and 1965.)

Jespersen, Otto 1933. *Essentials of English Grammar*. London: George Allen & Unwin.

Kamp, Hans, and Reyle, Uwe 1993. *From Discourse to Logic: Introduction to Model-theoretic Semantics of Natural Language, Formal Logic and Discourse Representation Theory (Studies in Linguistics and Philosophy)*. Dordrecht: Kluwer.

Katz, Graham 2007. Towards a denotational semantics for TimeML. In Frank Schilder, Graham Katz, and James Pustejovsky (eds.), *Annotating, Extracting and Reasoning about Time and Events*, pp. 88–106. Berlin: Springer.

Kenny, Anthony 1963. *Action, Emotion, and Will*. New York: Routledge.

Kim, Hansaem 2006. Korean National Corpus in the 21st century Sejong project. *Proceedings of the 13th NIJL International Symposium*, pp. 49–54, National Institute for Japanese Language, Tokyo.

Kipper, Karin, Korhonen, Anna, Ryant, Neville, and Palmer, Martha 2006. Extending VerbNet with novel verb classes. In *Proceedings of the Fifth International Conference on Language Resources and Evaluation (LREC 2006)*, Genoa, Italy.

Kipper Schuler, Karin 2005. *VerbNet: A broad-coverage, comprehensive verb lexicon*. Ph.D. dissertation, Department of Computer and Information Science, University of Pennsylvania.

Klein, Wolfgang 1991.Raumausdrücke. *Linguistische Berichte* **132** (1991), 77–114. Westdeatscher Verlag.

Klein, Wolfgang 1994. *Time in Language*. London: Routledge.

Kolomiyets, Oleksandr, Kordjamshidi, Parisa, Moens, Marie-Francine, and Bethard, Steven 2013. SemEval-2013 task 3: Spatial role labeling. In *Proceedings of the Seventh International Workshop on Semantic Evaluation (SemEval 2013)*, vol. 2, pp. 255–262. Collocated with the Second Joint Conference on Lexical and Computational Semantics, June 2013, Atlanta, GA, USA.

Kordjamshidi, Parisa, Moens, Marie-Francine, and van Otterlo, Martijn 2010. Spatial role labeling: task annotation and annotation scheme. In Nicoletta Calzolari, Choukri Khalid, and Maegaard Bente (eds.), *Proceedings of the Seventh Edition of the International Conference on Language Resources and Evaluation (LREC2010)*, pp. 413–420, May 17–23, 2010, Malta.

Kordjamshidi, Parisa, Bethard, Steven, and Moens, Marie-Francine 2012a. SemEval-2012 Task 3: Spatial Role Labeling. *Proceedings of the First Joint Conference on Lexical and Computational Semantics: Proceedings of the Sixth International*

Workshop on Semantic Evaluation (SemEval), vol. 2, pp. 365–373. SIGLEX/ACL, the Association of Computational Lingistics.

Kordjamshidi, Parisa, Frasconi, Paolo, van Otterlo, Martijn, Moens, Marie-Francine, and De Raedt, Luc 2012b. Relational learning for spatial relation extraction from natural language. In *The Proceedings of the 21st International Conference on Inductive Logic Programming* (Windsor Great Park, UK, July 31–August 3, 2011) (ILP 2011). *Lecture Notes in Computer Science*, vol. 7207, pp. 204–220. Berlin: Springer Nature.

Kordjamshidi, Parisa, Hois, Joana, van Otterlo, Martijn, and Moens, Marie-Francine 2013. Learning to interpret spatial natural language in terms of qualitative spatial relations, In Thora Tenbrink, Jan M. Wiener, and Christophe Claramunt (eds.), *Representing Space in Cognition: Interrelations of Behavior, Language, and Formal Models, Series Explorations in Language and Space*, pp. 115–146. Oxford: Oxford University Press.

Kordjamshidi, Parisa, and Moens, Marie-Franchine 2015. Global machine learning for spatial ontology population. *Journal of Web Semantics* **30C**, 3–21. doi: https://doi.org/10.1016/j.websem.2014.06.001. Amsterdam: Elsevier Science Publishers B.V.

Kordjamshidi, Parisa, van Otterlo, Martijn, and Moens, Marie-Francine 2017a. Spatial role labeling: towards extraction of spatial relations from natural language. *ACM – Transactions on Speech and Language Processing* **3**(4), 1–36.

Kordjamshidi, Parisa, van Otterlo, Martijn, and Moens, Marie-Franchine 2017b. Spatial role labeling annotation. In Nancy Ide and James Pustejovsky (eds.), *Handbook of Linguistic Annotation*, pp. 1025–1052. Dordrecht: Springer.

Kracht, Marcus 2002. On the semantics of locatives. *Linguistics and Philosophy* **25**, 157–232. Dordrecht: Kluwer.

Langacker, Ronald W. 1987. *Foundations of Cognitive Grammar, Volume 1: Theoretical Prerequisites*. Stanford: Stanford University Press.

Langacker, Ronald W. 1992. Transitivity, case, and grammatical relations (handouts). In *Proceedings of SICOL '92: 1992 Seoul International Conference on Linguistics*, pp. 149–154. Oragnized by the Linguistic Society of Korea, Seoul.

Langacker, Ronald W. 2008. *Cognitive Grammar: A Basic Introduction*. Oxford: Oxford University Press.

Landman, Fred 1996. Plurality. In Lappin (ed.), pp. 425–457.

Lappin, Shalom (ed.) 1996. *The Handbook of Contemporary Semantic Theory*. Oxford: Blackwell.

Lee, Kiyong 1974. *The Treatment of Some English Constructions in Montague Grammar*, Ph.D. dissertation in Linguistics, University of Texas, Austin. Published as main part of *On Montague Grammar*, Seoul: Han Shin Publishing Company, 1985.

Lee, Kiyong 1994. Hangul, the Korean writing system, and its computational treatment. *LDV-Forum: Forum der Gesellschaft für Linguistische Datenverarbeitung (GLDV)*, **11** (2), pp. 26–43.

Lee, Kiyong 1983. Equation solving. In Chungmin Lee and Beom-mo Kang (eds.), *Language, Information and Computation*, pp. 14–26. Seoul: Taehaksa.

Lee, Kiyong 2008. Formal semantics for interpreting temporal annotation. In Piet van Sterkenburg, (ed.), *Unity and Diversity of Languages*, pp. 97–108. Invited talk at the 18th Congress of Linguists, held in Seoul on July 21–26, 2008. Amsterdam: John Benjamins Publishing Co.

Lee, Kiyong 2011. A compositional interval semantics for temporal annotation. In Eunryoung Lee and Aesun Yoon (eds.), *Recent Trends in Language an Knowledge Processing*, pp. 122–156. Seoul: Hankookmunhwasa.

Lee, Kiyong 2012. Towards interoperable spatial and temporal annotation schemes. In Harry Bunt (ed.), *Proceedings of The Joint ISA-7, SRSL-3 and I2MRT Workshop on Interoperable Semantic Annotation*, pp. 61–68. Workshop of The Eighth Edition of Language Resources and Evaluation Conference (LREC 2012), Istanbul.

Lee, Kiyong 2013. Multi-layered annotation of non-textual data for spatial information. In Harry Bunt (ed.), *Proceedings of the 9th Joint ACL-SIGSEM–ISO Workshop on Interoperable Semantic Annotation (ISA-9)*, pp. 15–24. Workshop of the 10th International Conference of Computational Semantics (IWCS 2014), March 2013, Potsdam, Germany.

Lee, Kiyong 2015. The semantic annotation of measure expressions in ISO standards. In Harry Bunt (ed.), *Proceedings of the Eleventh Joint ALC–ISO Workshop on Interoperable Semantic Annotation (ISA-11)*, pp. 55–66. Workshop of the 11th International Conference on Computational Semantics (IWCS 2015) April 14, 2015, Queen Mary University of London.

Lee, Kiyong 2016. An abstract syntax for ISOspace with its <moveLink> reformulated. In Harry Bunt (ed.), *Proceedings of the 12th Joint ACL–ISO Workshop on Interoperable Semantic Annotation (ISA-12)*, pp. 28–37. Workshop at LREC2016, May 28, 2016, Portorož, Slovenia.

Lee, Kiyong 2017. Four types of temporal signals. In Harry Bunt (ed.), *Proceedings of the 13th Joint ACL–ISO Workshop on Interoperable Semantic Annotation (ISA-13)*, pp. 107–118. Workshop at the 12th International Conference on Computational Semantics (IWCS 2017), September 19, 2017, Montpellier, France.

Lee, Kiyong 2018. Revising ISO-Space for the semantic annotation of dynamic spatial information in language. *Language and Information* **22**(1), 221–245. Seoul: The Korean Society for Language and Information.

Lee, Kiyong 2020. Annotation-based Semantics. In Harry Bunt (ed.), *Proceedings of the 16th Joint ISO–ACL SIGSEM Workshop on Interoperable Semantic Annotation (ISA-16)*, pages 37–49. An LREC2020 workshop, May 22, 2020, Marseille, France.

Lee, Kiyong, Pustejovsky, James, and Boguraev, Branimir 2005. Towards an international standard for annotating temporal information. In Yuli Wang, Yu Wang, and Ye Tian (eds.), *Proceedings of the International Conference on Terminology, Standardization and Technology Transfer*, pp. 25–35. Beijing: Encyclopedia of China Publishing House.

Lee, Kiyong, and Bunt, Harry 2012. Counting time and events. In Harry Bunt (ed.), *Proceedings of the Eighth Joint ISO–ACL SIGSEM Workshop on Interoperable Semantic Annotation (ISA-8)*, pp. 34–41, January 3–5, 2012, University of Pisa, Faculty of Foreign Languages and Literatures and Istituto di Linguistica Computazionale Antonio Zampolli.

Lee, Kiyong, Webster, Jonathan and Fang, Alex Chengyu 2010. eSpaceML: an event-driven spatial annotation framework, *Proceedings of the 24th Pacific Asia*

Conference on Language, Information and Computation (PACLIC 24), pp. 223–232. November 4–7, 2010, Tohoku University, Sendai.

Lee, Kiyong, Fang, Alex and Pustejvosky, James 2011. Multilingual verification of the annotation scheme ISO-Space. *Proceedings of The First Workshop on Semantic Annotation for Computational Linguistic Resources (SACL-1), the 5th IEEE International Conference on Semantic Computing.* Stanford University, Palo Alto, CA.

Lee, Kiyong, Pustejovsky, James and Bunt, Harry 2018. Revising ISO-Space and the role of the movement link. In Harry Bunt (ed.), *Proceedings of the 14th Joint ACL–ISO Workshop on Interoperable Semantic Annotation (ISA-14)*, pp. 35–44, August 25, 2018, at COLING 2018, Santa Fe, NM, USA.

Lee, Ik-Seop and Chae, Wan 1999. *Lecture on Korean Grammar* [written in Korean]. Seoul: Hakyeon-sa.

Lee, Ik-Seop and Ramsey, S. Robert 2000. *The Korean Language.* Albany: State University of New York Press.

Leech, Geoffrey 1995. *A Brief User's Guide to the Grammatical Tagging of the British National Corpus.* Oxford: Oxford University. www.natcorp.ox.ac.uk/docs/gramtag.html.

Leidner, Jochen L. 2006. Toponym resolution: a first large-scale comparative evaluation. *Institute for Communicating and Collaborative Systems.* School of Informatics, University of Edinburgh.

Levin, B. 1993. *English Verb Classes and Alternations: A Preliminary Investigation.* Chicago: University of Chicago Press.

Levinson, Stephen C. 2003. *Space in Language and Cognition: Explorations in Cognitive Diversity.* Cambridge: Cambridge University Press.

Linguistic Data Consortium 2005. *ACE (Automatic Content Extraction) English Annotation Guidelines for Events* Version 5.4.3 2005.07.01. `http://ldc.upenn.edu/Projects/ACE/`

Linguistic Data Consortium 2008a. *ACE (Automatic Content Extraction) English Guidelines for Relations* Version 6.2 2008.04.28. `http://ldc.upenn.edu/Projects/ACE/`

Linguistic Data Consortium, 2008b. *ACE (Automatic Content Extraction) English Guidelines for Entities* Version 6.6 2008.06.13. `http://projects.ldc.upenn.edu/ace/`

Link, Godehard 1983. The logical analysis of plurals and mass terms: a lattice-theoretical approach. In Rainer Bauerle, Christoph Schwarze, and Arnim von Stechow (eds.), Meaning, Use, and Interpretation of Language, pp. 302–323. Berlin: De Gruyter. Reprinted as chapter 1 in Link (1998).

Link, Godehard 1998. *Algebraic Semantics in Language and Philosophy.* Stanford: CSLI Publications.

Mannell, Robert, and Cox, Felicity 2015. Speech resource pages. Department of Linguistics, Macquarie University, Sydney. http://clas.mq.edu.au/speech/resources.html

Mani, Inderjeet 2014. Temporal processing. *The Oxford Handbook of Computational Linguistics*, ed. by Ruslan Mitkov, 2nd ed. Oxford: Oxford University Press.

Mani, Inderjeet, Pustejovsky, James, and Gaizauskas, Robert (eds.) 2005. *The Language of Time: A Reader*. Oxford: Oxford University Press.

Mani, Inderjeet and Pustejovsky, James 2012. *Interpreting Motion: Grounded Representations for Spatial Language*. Oxford: Oxford University Press.

Mani, Inderjeet, Doran, Christy, Harris, Dave, Hitzeman, Janet, Quimby, Rob, Richer, Justin, Wellner, Ben, Mardis, Scott, and Clancy, Seamus 2010. SpatialML: Annotation scheme, resources and evaluation. *Language Resources and Evaluation* **44**, 263–280.

Mardis, Scott and Burger, John 2005. Design for an Integrated Gazetteer Database technical description and user guide for a gazetteer to support natural language processing applicaitons. *MITRE Technical Report*, MTR 05B0000085, November 2005.

Meteer, Marie 2015. *Developing Language Annotation for Machine Learning Algorithms*. Sebastopol, CA: O'Reilly Media, Inc.

Mirzaee, Roshanak, Rajaby Faghihi, Hossein, Ning, Qiang, and Kordjamshidi, Parisa 2021. SPARTQA: A textual question answering benchmark for spatial reasoning. In *Proceedings of the 2021 Conference of the North American Chapter of the Association for Computational Linguistics: Human Language Technologies*, pp. 4582–4598, June 2021. Association for Computational Linguistics. https://aclanthology.org/2021.naacl-main.364. doi: https://doi.org/10.18653/v1/2021.naacl-main.364.

MITRE 2010. *SpatialML: Annotation Scheme for Marking Spatial Expressions in Natural Language*, June 28, 2010. Version 3.0.1. Bedford, MA: The MITRE Corporation.

Moens, Marc, and Steedman, Mark 1998. Temporal ontology and temporal reference. *Computational Linguistics* **14**(2), 15–28. (Association of Computational Linguistics). Reprinted in Inderjeet Mani, James Pustejovsky, and Rob Gaizausakas (eds.) (2005), pp. 93–114.

Montague, Richard 1974. *Formal Philosophy: Selected Papers of Richard Montague*, ed. Richmond H. Thomason. New Haven and London: Yale University Press.

Mourelatos, Alexander P. D. 1978. Events, processes, and states. *Linguistics and Philosophy* **2**, 415–434.

Muller, Philippe 1998. A qualitative theory of motion based on spatio-temporal primitives In A. G. Cohn L. K. Schubert, and S. C. Shapiro (eds.), *Principles of Knowledge Representation and Reasoning: Proceedings of the Sixth International Conference (KR'98)*, pp. 131–141. San Mateo, CA: Morgan Kaufmann.

Nam, Seungho 1995. *The Semantics of Locative Prepositional Phrases in English*. Doctoral dissertation, University of California, Los Angeles.

Open Geospatial Consortium 2015. *Open Geospatial Consortium KML*, version 2.3, edited by David Burggraf. Copyright ©2015 Open Geospatial Consortium. To obtain additional rights of use, visit www.opengeospatial.org/legal/.

O'Keefe, John 1996. The spatial prepositions in English, vector grammar, and the cognitive map theory. In Paul Bloom, Mary A. Peterson, Lynn Nadel, and Merril G. Garrett (eds.), *Language and Space*, pp. 277–316. Cambridge, MA: The MIT Press.

OMG 2016. *The Distributed Ontology, Modeling, and Specification Language (DOL)*, Version 1.0. Object Management Group.

Parsons, Terence 1990. *Events in the Semantics of English: A Study in Subatomic Semantics*. Cambridge, MA: The MIT Press.

Partee, Barbara H. 1973. Some structural analogies between tenses and pronouns in English. *The Journal of Philosophy* **LXXX**(18), 601–609. Reprinted in Partee (2004), pp. 50–58.

Partee, Barbara H. 1995. Quantification structures and compositionality. In Emmon Bach, Eloise Jelinek, Angelika Kratzer, and Barbara H. Partee (eds.), *Quantification in Natural Languages*, pp. 541–601. Dordrecht: Kluwer Academic Publishers.

Partee, Barbara H. 2004. *Compositionality in Formal Semantics: Selected Papers by Barbara H. Partee*. Malden, MA: Blackwell.

Pease, Adam, Niles, Ian, and Li, John 2002. The Suggested Upper Merged Ontology: A large ontology for the semantic Web and its applications. In *Working Notes of the AAAI-2002 Workshop on Ontologies and the Semantic Web*, July 28–August 1, 2002, Edmonton, Canada.

Pease, Adam 2011. *Ontology: A Practical Guide*. San Jose, CA: Articulate Software Press.

Pierce, Richard S. 1968. *Introduction to the Theory of Abstract Algebras*. New York: Holt, Rinehart and Winston.

Pfenning, Frank, and Elliott, Conal 1988. Higher-order abstract syntax. *Proceedings of the ACM–SIGPLAN Notices, '88 Symposium on Programming Language Design and Implementation*, vol. 23, pp.199–208. doi: https://doi.org/10.1145/960116.54010

Pratt-Hartmann, Ian 2005. From TimeML to TPL. http://drops.dagstuhl.de/opus/votexte/2005/318 (date of citation: 2006-12-01).

Pratt-Hartmann, Ian 2007. From TimeML to interval temporal logic. *Proceedings of the Seventh International Workshop on Computational Semantics*, pp. 166–180. Tilburg University.

Prior, Arthur 1967. *Past, Present, Future*. Oxford: Oxford University Press.

Pustejovsky, James 1991. The syntax of event structure. *Cognition* **41**, 47–81. Reprinted in Mani et al. (eds.) (2005), pp. 33–60.

Pustejovsky, James 1995. *The Generative Lexicon*. Cambridge, MA: The MIT Press.

Pustejovsky, James 2001. Type construction and the logic of concepts. In Pierrette Bouillon and Federica Busa (eds.), *The Language of Word Meaning*, pp. 91–135. Cambridge: Cambridge University Press.

Pustejovsky, James 2006. Unifying linguistic annotations: A TimeML case study. In *Proceedings of the Ninth International Conference on Text, Speech, and Dialogue (TSD 2006), Text, Speech, and Dialogue Conference*, September 11–15, 2006, Brno, Czech Republic.

Pustejovsky, James 2017a. ISO-TimeML and the annotation of temporal information. In Nancy Ide and James Pustejovsky (eds.), pp. 941–968.

Pustejovsky, James 2017b. ISO-Space: Annotating static and dynamic spatial information. In Nancy Ide and James Pustejovsky (eds.), *Handbook of Linguistic Annotation*, pp. 941–968. Berlin: Springer.

Pustejovsky, James 2020. Tutorial: representation, learning, and reasoning on spatial language for downstream NLP tasks (Part 2). *The 2020 Conference on Empirical Methods in Natural Language Processing*, November 20, 2020. Unpublished.

Pustejovsky, James, and Batiukova, Olga 2019. *The Lexicon*. Cambridge: Cambridge University Press.

Pustejovsky, James and Lee, Kiyong 2017. Enriching the notion of path in ISO-Space. In Harry Bunt (ed.), *Proceedings of the 13th Joint ACL–ISO Workshop on Interoperable Semantic Annotation (ISA-13)*, pp. 134–139. Collocated at IWCS2017, September 19, 2017, Montpellier, France.

Pustejovsky, James and Moszkowicz, Jessica L. 2008. Integrating motion predicate classes with spatial and temporal annotations. In *Proceedings of the 22nd International Conference on Computational Linguistics*, pp. 95–98, Manchester, UK.

Pustejovsky, James and Moszkowicz, Jessica 2012. ISO-Space Specifications: Version 4.1. Unpublished.

Pustejovsky, James, and Stubbs, Amber 2012. *Natural Language Annotation for Machine Learning*. Sebastopol, CA: O'Reilly Media, Inc.

Pustejovsky, James and Yocum, Zachary 2013. Capturing motion in ISO-Space Bank. In Harry Bunt (ed.), *Proceedings of the 9th Joint ACL–ISO Workshop on Interoperable Semantic Annotation (ISA-9)*, pp. 25–34. Collocated at IWCS2013, Potsdam, Germany

Pustejovsky, James, Ingria, Robert, Saurí, Roser, Castaño, José, Littman, Jessica, Gaizauskas, Rob, Setzer, Andreas, Katz, Graham and Mani, Inderjeet 2005. The specification language TimeML. In Inderjett Mani, James Pustejovsky, and Rob Gaizauskas (eds.), *The Language of Time: A Reader*, pp. 545–557. Oxford: Oxford University Press.

Pustejovsky, James, Lee, Kiyong and Bunt, Harry 2010a. ISO-TimeML: An international standard for semantic annotation. In *Proceedings of LREC 2010, the Seventh Edition of the International Conference on Language Resources and Evaluation*, pp. 394–397, Valletta, Malta.

Pustejovsky, James, Moszkowicz, Jessica L., and Verhagen, Marc 2010b. ISO-Space Specification: Version 1.3 (October 5, 2010) with discussion notes from the Workshop on Spatial Language Annotation, the Airlie Retreat Center, VA, September 26–29, 2010.

Pustejovsky, James, Kordjamshidi, Parisa, Moens, Marie-Francine, Levine, Aaron, Dworman, Seth, and Yocum, Zachary 2015. SemEval-2015 task 8: Spaceeval. In *Proceedings of the 9th International Workshop on Semantic Evaluation (SemEval 2015)* pp. 884–894, June 4–5, 2015, Denver, CO. https://lirias.kuleuven.be/handle/123456789/500427.

Pustejovsky, James, Bunt, Harry, and Zaenen, Annie 2017. Designing annotation schemes: from theory to model. In Nancy Ide and James Pustejovsky (eds.), pp. 21–72.

Pustejovsky, James, Lee, Kiyong, and Bunt, Harry 2019a. The semantics of ISO-Space. In Harry Bunt (ed.), *Proceedings of the 15th Joint ACL–ISO Workshop on Interoperable Semantic Annotation (ISA-15)*, pp. 46–53, May 23, 2019, at IWCS 2019, Gothenburg, Sweden.

Pustejovsky, James, Xue, Nianwen, and Lai, Kenneth 2019b. Modeling quantification and scope in Abstract Meaning Representation. In *Proceedings of the First International Workshop on Designing Meaning Representations*, pp. 28–33, August 1, 2019, Florence, Italy. ©2019 Association for Computational Linguistics.

Quirk, Randolph, Greenbaum, Sidney, Leech, Geoffrey, and Svartvik, Jan 1985. *A Comprehensive Grammar of the English Language*. London and New York: Longman.

Randell, David A. Cui, Zhan, and Cohn, Anthony G. 1992. A spatial logic based on regions and connection. In *Proceedings of the Third International Conference on Knowledge Representation and Reasoning*, pp. 165–176. San Mateo, CA: Morgan Kaufmann.

Reichenbach, Hans 1947. *Elements of Symbolic Logic*, New York: The Free Press, Collier-Macmillan.

Ruppenhofer, Josef, Ellsworth, Michael, Schwarzer-Petruck, Miriam R. L., Johnson, Christopher R., Baker, Collin F., and Scheffczyk, Jan 2016. *FrameNet II: Extended Theory and Practice*, revised November 1, 2016. Available on the website as an eBook.

Russell, Bertrand 1903. *Principles of Mathematics*, New York: W. W. Norton & Company, Inc.

Russell, Bertrand 1905. On denoting, *Mind* **14**, 479–493.

Sag, Ivan A. 2012. Sign-based construction grammar: An informal synopsis. In Hans C. Boas and Ivan A. Sag (eds.), *Sign-Based Construction Grammar*, pp. 61–188. Stanford, CA: Center for the Study of Language and Information.

Schilder, Frank, Versley, Yannick, and Habel, Christopher 2004. Extracting spatial information: Grounding, classifying, and linking spatial expressions. In *Proceedings of the Workshop on Geographic Information Retrieval*, workshop of the 27th ACM SIGGIR Conference, Sheffield, UK.

Schilder, Frank, Katz, Graham, and Pustejovsky, James (eds.) 2007. *Annotating, Extracting and Reasoning about Time and Events*, International Seminar Dagstuhl Castle, Germany, April 2005, revised papers. Berlin: Springer.

Setzer, Andrea 2001. *Temporal Information in Newswire Articles: an Annotation Scheme and Corpus Study*. Ph.D. dissertation, University of Sheffield.

Shahid, Ahmad R., and Kazakov, Dimitar 2013. Using parallel corpora for word sense disambiguation. *Proceedings of Recent Advances in Natural Language Processing*, pp. 336–341. September 7–13, 2013, Hissar, Bulgaria.

Sharvey, Richard 1980. A more general theory of definite description, *The Philosophical Review* **89**, 607–623.

Shin, Hyopil, and You, Hyun-Jo 2015. *Events and Temporal Expressions in Korean*. Seoul: Seoul National University Press. (Note: written in Korean).

Sohn, Homin 1999. *The Korean Language*. Cambridge: Cambridge University Press.

Talmy, Leonard 1975. Figure and ground in complex sentences. *Proceedings of the First Annual Meeting of the Berkeley Linguistics Society*, pp. 419–430. Organized by UC Berkley Linguistics Department.

Talmy, Leonard 1983. How language structures space. In Herbert Pick and Linda Acredolo (eds.), *Spatial Orientation: Theory, Research, and Application*. Plenum Press. Reprinted in *Toward a Cognitive Semantics*, vol.1, chapter 3. Cambridge, MA: The MIT Press.

Talmy, Leonard 1985. Lexicalization patterns: Semantic structure in lexical forms. In T. Shopen (ed.), *Language Typology and Syntactic Description: Vol. 3, Grammatical Categories and the Lexicon*, pp. 36–149. Cambridge: Cambridge University Press.

Talmy, Leonard 1991. Path to realization: A typology of event conflation. Berkley Working Papers in Linguistics, pp. 480–519.

Talmy, Leonard 2000. *Toward a Cognitive Semantics, vol. 1: Concept Structuring Systems*. Cambridge, MA: The MIT Press.

TEI Consortium 2019. *TEI P5: Guidelines for Electronic Text Encoding and Interchange*. Text Encoding Initiative Consortium.

Trim, Craig 2013. The art of tokenization (language processing), *IBM Community Blogs: Language Processing*, January 24, 2013. www.ibm.com/ developerworks/community/blogs/nlp/entry/tokenization

van Benthem, Johan 1986. *Essays in Logical Semantics*. Dordrecht: D. Reidel.

Vendler, Zeno 1967. Verbs and times. *Linguistics in Philosophy*, chapter 4. Ithaca, NY: Cornell University Press. Reprinted in Mani et al. (eds.) (2005), pp. 21–32.

Webster, Jonathan J., and Kit, Chunyu 1992. Tokenization as the initial phase in NLP. In *Proceedings of COLING-92*, pp. 1106–1110. August 23–28, 1992, Nantes, France.

World Wide Web Consortium 2020. *Time Ontology in OWL*. www.w3org/TR/owl-time.

Wunderlich, Dieter 1991. How do prepositional phrases fit into compositional syntax and semantics. *Linguistics*, **29**, 591–621.

Zlatev, Jordan 2003. Holistic spatial semantics of Thai. In *Cognitive Linguistics and Non-Indo-European Languages*, pp. 305–336. Berlin: De Gruyter.

Zwarts, Joost 1997. Vectors as relative positions: a compositional semantics of modified PPs. *Journal of Semantics*, 14:57–86.

Zwarts, Joost, and Winter, Yoad 2000. Vector space semantics: a model-theoretic analysis of locative prepositions. *Journal of Logic, Language and Information*, **9**(2):171–213.

Zwarts, Joost 2005. Prepositional aspect and the algebra of paths. *Linguistics and Philosophy* **28**, 739–779.

Index

454

Printed in the United States
by Baker & Taylor Publisher Services